OTHER BOOKS BY THE AUTHOR

Inflation, Saving and Growth in Developing Economies
Regional Growth and Unemployment in the United Kingdom (*with R. Dixon*)
Financing Economic Development
Balance-of-Payments Theory and the United Kingdom Experience (Fourth Edition *with H. Gibson*)
Nicholas Kaldor
UK Industrialisation and Deindustrialisation (Third Edition *with S. Bazen*)
The Performance and Prospects of the Pacific Island Economies in the World Economy
Economic Growth and the Balance-of-Payments Constraint (*with J. McCombie*)
The Economics of Growth and Development: Selected Essays, Vol. 1
Macroeconomic Issues from a Keynesian Perspective: Selected Essays, Vol. 2
The Euro and 'Regional' Divergence in Europe
The Nature of Economic Growth: A
    Performance of Nations
Trade, the Balance of Payments an
Essays on Balance of Payments Cor
    McCombie)

EDITED WORKS

Keynes and International Monetary
Keynes and Laissez-Faire
Keynes and the Bloomsbury Group
Keynes as a Policy Adviser
Keynes and Economic Development
Keynes and the Role of the State (
European Factor Mobility: Trends ar
The Essential Kaldor (*with F. Target*
Further Essays in Economic Theory
    Papers of N. Kaldor (*with F. Targ*
Causes of Growth and Stagnation in
    N. Kaldor *with F. Targetti*)
Economic Dynamics, Trade and Grow
    Rampa and L. Stella)

ONE WEEK LOAN

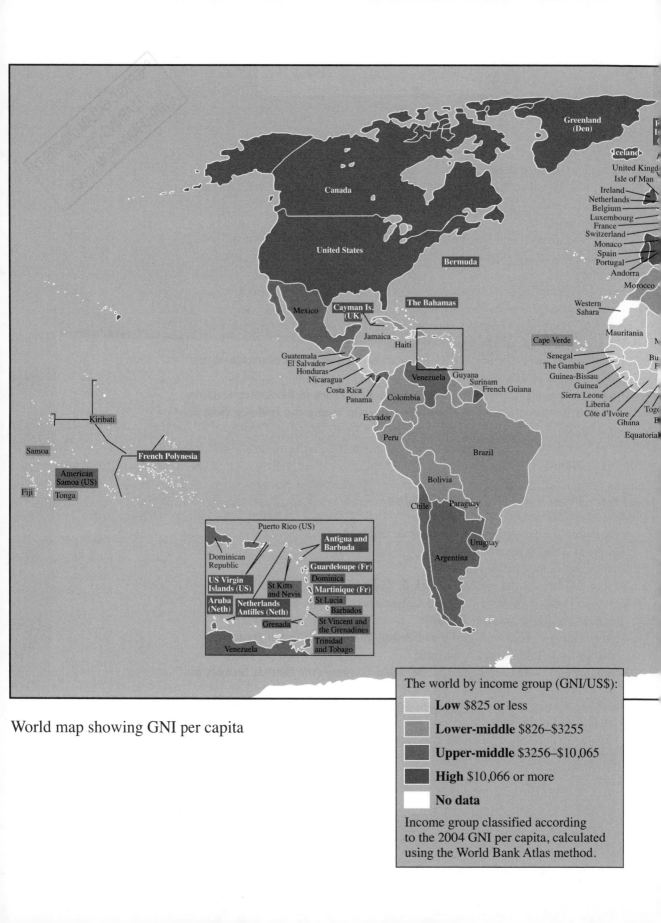

World map showing GNI per capita

The world by income group (GNI/US$):

Low $825 or less

Lower-middle $826–$3255

Upper-middle $3256–$10,065

High $10,066 or more

No data

Income group classified according to the 2004 GNI per capita, calculated using the World Bank Atlas method.

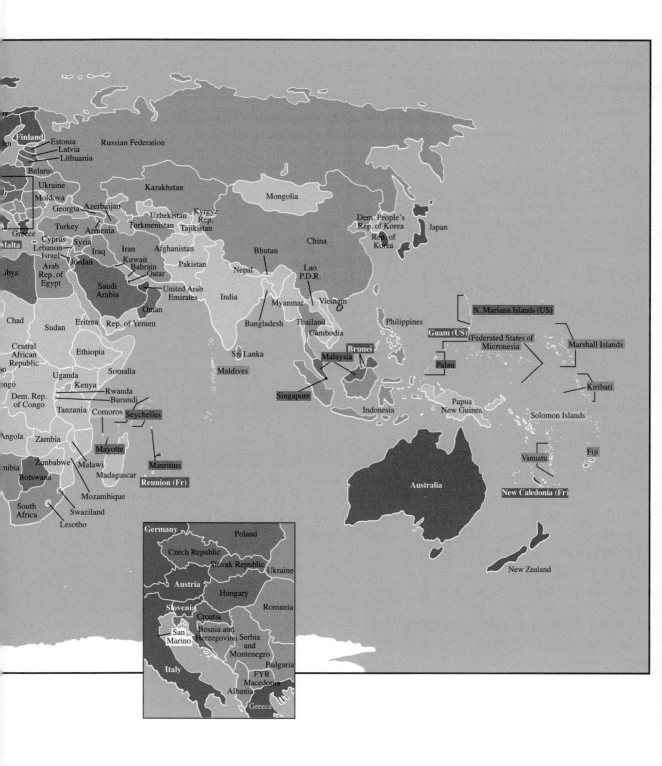

Finland
Estonia
Latvia
Lithuania
Belarus
Ukraine
Moldova
Georgia
Azerbaijan
Armenia
Turkey
Greece
Malta
Cyprus
Lebanon
Israel
Jordan
Syria
Iraq
Kuwait
Bahrain
Qatar
Arab Rep. of Egypt
Libya
Saudi Arabia
United Arab Emirates
Oman
Rep. of Yemen
Russian Federation
Kazakhstan
Uzbekistan
Turkmenistan
Kyrgyz Rep.
Tajikistan
Iran
Afghanistan
Pakistan
Mongolia
China
Nepal
Bhutan
India
Bangladesh
Myanmar
Lao P.D.R.
Vietnam
Thailand
Cambodia
Dem. People's Rep. of Korea
Rep. of Korea
Japan
Philippines
N. Mariana Islands (US)
Guam (US)
Palau
(Federated States of Micronesia)
Marshall Islands
Kiribati
Brunei
Malaysia
Singapore
Indonesia
Papua New Guinea
Solomon Islands
Fiji
Vanuatu
Australia
New Caledonia (Fr)
New Zealand

Chad
Sudan
Eritrea
Central African Republic
Ethiopia
Uganda
Kenya
Somalia
ongo
Dem. Rep. of Congo
Rwanda
Burundi
Tanzania
Comoros
Seychelles
Mayotte
Mauritius
Reunion (Fr)
Angola
Zambia
Zimbabwe
Malawi
Madagascar
Mozambique
nibia
Botswana
South Africa
Swaziland
Lesotho
Sri Lanka
Maldives

Germany
Poland
Czech Republic
Slovak Republic
Ukraine
Austria
Hungary
Slovenia
Romania
Croatia
San Marino
Bosnia and Herzegovina
Serbia and Montenegro
Italy
Bulgaria
FYR Macedonia
Albania
Greece

Growth & Development

With Special Reference to Developing Economies

A. P. Thirlwall

Professor of Applied Economics
University of Kent

Eighth Edition

palgrave
macmillan

First edition 1972
Second edition 1978
Third edition 1983
Fourth edition 1989
Fifth edition 1994
Sixth edition 1999
Seventh edition 2003
Eighth edition 2006

Published by
PALGRAVE MACMILLAN
Houndmills, Basingstoke, Hampshire RG21 6XS and
175 Fifth Avenue, New York, N.Y. 10010
Companies and representatives throughout the world

PALGRAVE MACMILLAN is the global academic imprint of the Palgrave Macmillan division of St. Martin's Press, LLC and of Palgrave Macmillan Ltd. Macmillan® is a registered trademark in the United States, United Kingdom and other countries. Palgrave is a registered trademark in the European Union and other countries.

ISBN-13s: 978-1-4039-9600-8 hardback
ISBN-10: 1-4039-9600-8 hardback
ISBN-13s: 978-1-4039-9601-5 paperback
ISBN-10: 1-4039-9601-6 paperback

This book is printed on paper suitable for recycling and made from fully managed and sustained forest sources. Logging, pulping and manufacturing processes are expected to conform to the environmental regulations of the country of origin.

A catalogue record for this book is available from the British Library.

Library of Congress Cataloging-in-Publication Data

Thirlwall, A. P.
   Growth and development, with special reference to developing economies / A. P. Thirlwall.—8th ed.
      p. cm.
   Includes bibliographical references and index.
   ISBN 1-4039-9600-8 (cloth)—ISBN 1-4039-9601-6 (paper)
   1. Economic development. 2. Development countries—Economic condition. I. Title.
   HD82.T48 2006
   338.9'009172'4—dc22   2005047559

14   13   12   11   10   9   8   7   6   5
17   16   15   14   13   12   11   10   09   08

Printed and bound by Cromwell Press, Trowbridge, Wiltshire

To Penélope P-L

For love and friendship

Brief contents

Contents

PART VI

International trade, the balance of payments and development 511

16 Trade and development 513

List of figures

List of tables

List of case examples

Preface to the eighth edition

Since *Growth and Development* was first published in 1972 it has been widely used as a text for courses in economic growth and development in both developed and developing countries. In 1978, 1983, 1989, 1994, 1999 and 2003 new editions were published. In this eighth edition, further extensive revisions have been made to add to and update statistics, to include new theoretical ideas and institutional material, and to improve on the exposition to aid students and teachers alike.

The purpose of the book remains the same: to introduce students to the exciting and challenging subject of development economics, which draws on several branches of economics in order to elucidate and understand the development difficulties facing the economies of the world's poor countries. This does not mean that the book provides a recipe or blueprint for development: far from it. There can be no general recipes of this nature, and even if there were there would have to be more than economic ingredients.

The book combines description and analysis, with an emphasis on the elaboration of simple and useful theoretical economic models for an understanding of the issues that comprise the subject matter of development economics. I make no apology for the use of conventional economic theory. I concur with Theodore Schultz, the Nobel-Prize-winning economist, who has said of development economics:

> This branch of economics has suffered from several intellectual mistakes. The major mistake has been the presumption that standard economic theory is inadequate for understanding low-income countries and that a separate economic theory is needed. Models for this purpose were widely acclaimed until it became evident that they were at best intellectual curiosities. The reaction of some economists was to turn to cultural and social explanations for the alleged poor economic performance of low income countries. Quite understandably, cultural and behavioural scholars are uneasy about this use of their studies. Fortunately the intellectual tide has begun to turn. Increasing numbers of economists have come to realise that standard economic theory is just as applicable to scarcity problems that confront low income countries as to the corresponding problems of high income countries. (T. W. Schultz, 'The Economics of Being Poor', *Journal of Political Economy*, August 1980)

This is not to say, of course, that *all* standard theory is useful and relevant for an understanding of the development process. The relevance of static equilibrium theory may be particularly questioned. Nor is it possible to ignore non-economic factors in the growth and development process. The fact is, however, that the desire for material improvement in developing countries is very strong, and economics does have something positive to offer by way of analysis unadulterated by political, sociological and other non-economic variables. In the final analysis, growth and development must be considered an economic process in the important practical sense that it is unlikely to proceed very far in the absence of an increase in the quantity and quality of the resources available for production. The book lays particular emphasis on the economic obstacles to development and the economic means by which developing countries may raise their rate of growth of output and living standards.

For those new to the book, or for those now using the seventh edition, I outline below the main contents of each chapter and the changes introduced in the eighth edition.

The material in Part I of the book, 'Development and underdevelopment', consists of four major chapters which provide a basis for an understanding of the nature of poverty and underdevelopment in low-income countries, and therefore constitutes an important background for the rest of the book.

Chapter 1 addresses the subject matter of development economics, the meaning of development and the challenge of development economics. The globalization and interdependence of the world economy is emphasized, and there is a discussion of the call for a new international order, including a statement of the Millennium Development Goals.

Chapter 2 portrays the magnitude of the development gap between rich and poor countries in the world economy and discusses the measurement of poverty, including the attempt by the United Nations Development Programme (UNDP) to construct a Human Poverty Index and Human Development Index. There is discussion of the World Bank's approach to tackling poverty based on the ideas of empowering the poor and extending their capabilities as discussed in the *World Development Report*, 2000/2001. Research is also reviewed on whether the global and international distribution of income is widening or narrowing.

Chapter 3 outlines the characteristics of underdevelopment and gives quantitative evidence of various dimensions of the development gap with respect to employment and unemployment, education, health, nutrition and income distribution. The major characteristics of underdevelopment identified include the dominance of low-productivity agriculture and lack of industrialization, low levels of capital accumulation, rapid population growth, an export trade dominated by primary products, the 'curse of natural resources' and weak governance and institutions. These topics are discussed more fully in later chapters. The process of structural change is also addressed, as is the role of industrialization in this process.

Chapter 4 introduces students to various theories of economic growth. There are sections on classical growth theory (Adam Smith, Malthus, Ricardo and Marx), the Harrod–Domar growth model, neoclassical growth theory, and the 'new' endogenous growth theory, which now dominates the literature on the applied economics of growth, with its stress on the importance of physical and human capital formation and research and development effort as the prime determinants of growth. Many empirical studies are surveyed, with regard both to the production function approach to understanding the growth process and to the macro-determinants of growth approach, using 'new' growth theory. If you find the technical details too difficult, you should proceed straight to Chapter 5 – but you will be missing a lot!

Chapter 5 deals with the role of agriculture and surplus labour in the development process. Particular attention is paid to the influential Lewis model of economic development with unlimited supplies of labour. There is explicit treatment, following on from Lewis, of the interaction and complementarity between agriculture and industry, with a number of interesting insights into the importance of demand expansion from agriculture as a stimulus to industrial growth and of achieving an equilibrium terms of trade between the two sectors. There is also a discussion of barriers to agricultural development.

Chapter 6 is on the role of capital accumulation and technical progress in the development process and contains sections on the importance of infrastructure investment and empirical evidence on the rates of return to investment in human capital.

Chapter 7 is on dualism and Myrdal's concept of the process of circular and cumulative causation. This chapter describes the various mechanisms by which economic divisions between regions and countries tend to be perpetuated and widened. The chapter includes the early centre–periphery models of Prebisch and Seers, together with discussion of the new economic geography pioneered by Krugman. The views of Marxist writers, including Emmanuel's model of unequal exchange, are also presented.

Chapter 8 is on population and development and attempts to evaluate the debate on whether population expansion is a growth-inducing or growth-retarding force. Particular attention is devoted to the early work of Enke and to the recent work of Simon. The facts on population growth are clearly outlined with a discussion of the determinants of fertility.

Chapter 9 is on resource allocation in developing countries and considers the market mechanism versus the role of the state. Market imperfections, market failures and corruption are highlighted, as are the limited capabilities of the state, drawing on the extensive analysis contained in the World Bank's *World Development Report, 1997*. Some of the broader issues of development strategy are also considered, including the case for planning.

Chapter 10 is devoted exclusively to social cost-benefit analysis, highlighting the distinction between the financial, economic and social appraisal of projects. The main emphasis is on comparing and contrasting the approaches of Little and Mirrlees (using world prices) on the one hand and the United Nations (using domestic prices and shadow exchange rates) on the other. Attention is given to the relation between the shadow exchange rate and the standard conversion factor used by Little and Mirrlees for the repricing of non-traded goods. The chapter contains a lengthy discussion of the determination of the shadow wage rate, and how to take account of the distributional effects of project choice.

Chapter 11, written by my colleague Dr John Peirson, discusses how environmental issues may be incorporated into social cost-benefit analysis, and the new and important concept of sustainable development.

Chapter 12 is concerned with the choice of techniques and with the potential conflicts involved in moving towards the use of more labour-intensive techniques: between employment and output on the one hand, and between employment and saving on the other. The role played by multinational corporations in dictating technological choice is also examined.

Chapter 13 introduces the student to the technique of input–output analysis and its role in planning and forecasting. It is shown how input–output analysis can be used to forecast output, import requirements and labour and capital requirements.

Chapter 14 turns to the financing of development from domestic sources. There is a full discussion of the theory of financial liberalization, together with critiques and empirical evidence of the relationship between real interest rates, saving, investment and growth. There is new material on the financial system in developing countries and the relationship between financial development and economic development. Fiscal policy and taxation are also discussed, together with the topic of forced saving through inflation. New research is reported on the relation between inflation and growth.

Chapter 15 looks at the financing of development from external sources. All the statistics relating to foreign resource inflows have been updated. The whole aid debate is reviewed, and the impact of aid on development. Structural adjustment lending by the World Bank, and the role of foreign direct investment in the development process are both examined. The debt-servicing problems created by foreign borrowing are thoroughly surveyed, and there is extensive discussion of the debt crisis of the 1980s, which still lingers today, together with the schemes designed to reduce the debt burden of highly indebted countries.

Chapter 16 is devoted to the topic of trade and development. The gains from trade are thoroughly explored, as are the ways in which the present pattern of trade works to the relative disadvantage of developing countries. The tendency for the terms of trade to deteriorate, and for balance-of-payments difficulties to arise, is stressed. The case for protection, and the relative merits of import substitution and export promotion, are examined. There are new sections on the theory of customs unions and free trade areas, and the most recent research is reported on the impact of trade liberalization on export performance, economic growth and poverty reduction.

Chapter 17 is on the balance of payments and development, and discusses the important concept of balance-of-payments-constrained growth and the various policy responses to this constraint at the national and international level. The latter involves a consideration of the extensive facilities afforded by the International Monetary Fund (IMF) for balance-of-payments support. Some of the criticisms levelled at the IMF are also considered. There is an analysis of the different types of exchange rate systems that developing countries can adopt, and lessons to be drawn from the financial crisis in East Asia in 1997. The chapter ends with a discussion of Special Drawing Rights (SDRs) as a potential form of international assistance to developing countries.

A new feature of this edition is the addresses of **web-sites**, chapter by chapter, to guide students to relevant information and data on the Internet. By the time the ninth edition of this book becomes due in 2009, the facts pertaining to developing countries will again be out of date, and no doubt there will have been new institutional changes and new innovations in thinking about development strategy. To keep abreast with what is going on, students are encouraged to consult such publications as the World Bank's *World Development Report*, the IMF's *Finance and Development* (published quarterly in several different languages), *The Human Development Report* published by the United Nations Development Programme (UNDP) and *The Least Developed Countries Report* published by UNCTAD, and journals such as *World Development, Journal of Development Studies, Journal of Development Economics, Journal of International Development, Economic Development and Cultural Change, Oxford Development Studies* and the *World Bank Economic Review*.

I am deeply grateful to Carol Wilmshurst for preparing the typescript for this new edition; to Penélope Pacheco-López for technical assistance; to Antice Hughes and Keith Povey for copy-editing; and Anthony Horton for the indexing. Visit the author's web-pages: *www.kent.ac.uk/economics/staff/at4/*

Universal Declaration of Human Rights

Everyone has the right to a standard of living adequate for the health and well-being of himself and of his family, including food, clothing, housing and medical care and the necessary social services and the right to security in the event of unemployment, sickness, disability, widowhood, old age or other lack of livelihood in circumstances beyond his control.

(Article 25 adopted by the UN General Assembly 10th December 1948)

Acknowledgements

The author and publishers wish to thank the following organizations for permission to use material previously contained in their publications: *The Times* Newspaper Group; *The Financial Times*; Institute of Development Studies, University of Sussex; the American Economic Association and Pergamon Press.

Development and underdevelopment

The study of economic development

DEVELOPMENT ECONOMICS AS A SUBJECT

The study of development economics as a separate subject is a relatively recent phenomenon. For the student today it will be difficult to appreciate that as recently as fifty years ago a course in development economics was a rare feature of an undergraduate programme in economics, and that textbooks on economic development were few and far between. Today no respectable department of economics is without a course in economic development; there are scores of texts and thousands of case studies and articles on the subject. And as in medicine, the perceived ills seem to multiply as the diagnosis deepens.

The political and public concern with the poorer nations of the world is of equally recent origin. The majority of the national and international bodies to promote development that exist today, such as national development banks, the World Bank and its affiliates, and agencies of the United Nations, have all been established since the Second World War. Before the war, when most of today's poor countries were still colonies, there was very little preoccupation with the economic and social problems of the developing (dependent) economies that we are concerned with today. Perhaps the facts were not so well known, or perhaps it was that the attention of most people was focused on depression and underemployment in the developed countries. Whatever the reason for this neglect, the situation today is very different. The development of the Third World (the collective name for the developing countries), meaning above all the eradication of primary poverty, is now regarded as one of the greatest social and economic challenges facing mankind. As the Pearson Report (1969) remarked over 30 years ago 'the widening gap between the developed and the developing countries has become the central problem of our times'.

What accounts for this change in attitude and upsurge of interest in the economics of development and the economies of poor countries? A number of factors can be pinpointed, which interrelate with each other.

- First, in the wake of the great depression and in the aftermath of war there was a renewed academic interest among professional economists in the growth and development process and in the theory and practice of planning.
- Second, the poor countries themselves have become increasingly aware of their own backwardness, which has led to a natural desire for more rapid economic progress.
- Third, the absolute numbers of poor people are considerably greater now than in the past, and greater awareness has struck a humanitarian chord.
- Fourth, there has been a growing recognition by all concerned of the interdependence between countries in the world economy. The political and military ramifications and dangers of a world divided into rich and poor countries are far more serious now than they were in the past; at the same time the old Cold War between the capitalist West and the communist East led the major developed countries to show a growing economic and political interest in poor and ideologically uncommitted nations. The recognition of interdependence has been heightened in recent years by the process of globalization making all countries more vulnerable to shocks and financial crises.

ACADEMIC INTEREST IN DEVELOPMENT

Academic interest in the mechanics of growth and development is a *renewed* interest rather than a new preoccupation of economists. The progress and material well-being of people and nations have traditionally been at the centre of economic writing and enquiry. It constituted one of the major areas of interest of the classical economists. Adam Smith, David Ricardo, Thomas Malthus, John Stuart Mill and Karl Marx all dealt at some length (with divergent opinions on many issues) with the causes and consequences of economic advance (see Chapter 4). It is entirely natural that thinkers of the day should comment on the contemporary scene, and there is perhaps an analogy here between the preoccupation of the classical economists at the time of Britain's industrial revolution and the concern of many economists today with the economics of development and world poverty, the nature of which has been brought to the attention of the world so dramatically in recent decades. The list of modern-day economists who have turned their fertile minds to the study of economic development reads like a *Who's Who* of economics. Distinguished economists that immediately come to mind are Pranab Bardhan, Jagdish Bhagwati, Hollis Chenery, Partha Dasgupta, Albert Hirschman, Harry

Johnson, Nicholas Kaldor, Michal Kalecki, Paul Krugman, Simon Kuznets, Harvey Leibenstein, Arthur Lewis, James Mirrlees, Gunnar Myrdal, Raúl Prebisch, Joan Robinson, Paul Rosenstein-Rodan, Walt Rostow, Theodore Schultz, Amartya Sen, Hans Singer, Joseph Stiglitz and Jan Tinbergen (my apologies to those I have left out!).

Development also represents a challenge equivalent to that of depression and mass unemployment in the 1930s, which attracted so many brilliant minds to economics, Keynes among them. But the nature of the challenge is of course very different. In the case of unemployment in the 1930s, there was an orthodox theory with which to grapple; the task was to formulate a theory to fit the facts and to offer policy prescriptions. As it turned out, the solution to the problem was to be costless: expand demand by creating credit and bring idle resources into play. Fancy, an economic problem solved costlessly!

The challenge of development is very different. There is no divorce between theory and the observed facts. The mainsprings of growth and development are well known: increases in the quantity and quality of resources of all kinds. Countries are poor because they lack resources or the willingness and ability to bring them into use. The problems posed by underdevelopment cannot be solved costlessly. It would be reassuring to think, however, that advances in growth theory, coupled with more detailed understanding of the sources of growth and the refinement of techniques for resource allocation, have all increased the possibility of more rapid economic progress than hitherto. Certainly, particular theoretical models and techniques have been used extensively in some countries, presumably in this belief. For example, models for calculating investment requirements to achieve a target rate of growth invariably form an integral part of a development plan; and now the so-called 'new' growth theory (see Chapter 4) provides the rationale and impetus for improving the quality of investment through education, research and development, and infrastructure investment. Good governance must also play a vital role.

The question is often posed as to what lessons, if any, the present developing countries can draw from the first-hand observations of the classical writers, or more directly from the development experience of the present advanced nations. One obvious lesson is that while development can be regarded as a natural phenomenon, it is also a lengthy process, at least left to itself. It is easy to forget that it took Europe the best part of three centuries to progress from a subsistence state to economic maturity. Much of development economics is concerned with the time scale of development, and how to speed up the process of development consistent with freedom and democracy. In the present millennium, when primary poverty in most countries will, it is hoped, have been eradicated, courses in development economics will undoubtedly take a different form. The emphasis will be on intercountry comparisons, rather than on the process of development as such and the growth pains accompanying the transition from a primarily agrarian to an industrial or service economy.

As far as classical theory is concerned, the gloomy prognostication of Ricardo, Malthus and Mill that progress will ultimately end in stagnation would seem to be unfounded. It has certainly been confounded by experience. Population growth and diminishing returns have not been uniformly depressive to the extent that Ricardo and Malthus supposed. Rising productivity and per capita incomes appear quite compatible with the growth of population and the extension of agriculture. Classical development economics greatly underestimated the beneficial role of technical progress and international trade in the development process. It is these two factors above all which seem to have confounded the pessimism of much of classical theory. With access to superior technology there is hope, and some evidence, that material progress in today's developing countries will be much more rapid than in countries at a similar stage of development one hundred years ago. The pool of technology on which to draw, and the scope for its assimilation, is enormous. Used with discretion, it must be considered as the main means of increasing welfare.

The role of trade, however, is more problematic. A lot will depend on how rapidly the developing countries can alter their industrial structure, and on movements in the terms of trade. Currently the developing countries are probably in an inferior position compared with the present advanced countries at a comparable stage of their economic history. The dynamic gains from trade are present but the static efficiency gains are less and the terms of trade in most commodities are worse. The gains from trade accrue mainly to the rich industrialized countries, notwithstanding the rapid increase that periodically takes place in some commodity prices. The fact that the gains from trade are unequally distributed does not, of course, destroy the potential link between trade and growth, or constitute an argument against trade. Rather, it represents a challenge for altering the structure of trade and the terms on which it takes place.

Then there is the question of planning. Classical economists were generally antithetical to interference with the market mechanism, believing that the free play of market forces would maximize the social good. But fashions change in economics, and after the Second World War there was a much greater acceptance of interference with the market mechanism, and planning in developing countries was seen by many as one of the main means by which development could be accelerated. The experience of planning in many countries, however, has not been favourable and planning has come into disrepute, not least because of the economic disarray of the rigidly planned economies of the old Soviet Union and Eastern Europe. It should never be forgotten, however, that no country in the world ever made such a swift economic advance in such a short space of time as the Soviet Union did after 1918, through a planned allocation of resources that favoured investment at the expense of consumption. The fact that planning may be operated too rigidly, or for too long and go wrong, should not be allowed to obscure the fact that it also has merits, and that unfettered free enterprise can also lead to economic disaster and social deprivation. There can be market failure as well as government failure. What is required in most developing countries is a judicious mix of public and private enterprise, of the use of markets combined with different types of government involvement, for the maximization of social welfare (see Chapter 7).

Planning requires a certain amount of model building, and this too has been inspired by economists. The most common type of model, which forms the basis of much of the model building that developing countries indulge in, is to calculate the investment requirements necessary to achieve a target rate of growth of per capita income – commonly referred to as a Harrod–Domar model (see Chapter 4). Neither the models of Harrod (1939) or Domar (1947) were designed for the purpose to which they are now put in developing countries, but their growth equations have proved to be an indispensable component of macroeconomic planning. We shall consider in Chapter 9 the strengths and weaknesses of using this type of aggregate model in development planning, and the pros and cons of planning in general.

As a result of the apparent failure of development planning and the slow progress made by many developing countries in the 1970s, the status of the discipline of development economics began to be called into question in the 1980s and several obituaries were written (see, for example, Hirschman, 1981; Little, 1982; Lal, 1983). I will concentrate here on the worries expressed by Hirschman, the practitioner who first rang the alarm bells most vigorously. Hirschman argues that development economics was originally born out of a rejection of monoeconomics (that is, the universality of neoclassical economics) on the one hand and of neo-Marxism on the other. Neo-Marxism asserted that economic relations between developed and less developed countries could only lead to the development of underdevelopment. The two themes at the forefront of the rejection of monoeconomics were (1) the existence of a massive amount of surplus labour in agriculture in developing countries and (2) late industrialization – the latter demanding active state intervention. In terms of policy, the major strategic themes emphasized and pursued by developing countries were the mobilization of underemployed manpower, rapid capital accumulation and industrialization, for all of which planning was thought to be necessary.

Hirschman's first explanation of the alleged demise of development economics is the resurgence of neoclassical orthodoxy and rejection of the view that there is a separate economics applicable to poor countries, as distinct from the developed ones. The defence of monoeconomics has been buttressed by the observed success of some ostensibly free-market developing countries, such as South Korea, Hong Kong, Taiwan and Singapore (the so-called 'East Asian miracle' countries), and the failure of planning in others.

Early development economics not only asserted the need for a separate economics applicable to developing countries, but also believed that the integration of developing countries into the world economy would bring material benefits to both rich and poor alike. Hirschman's second explanation of the alleged demise of development economics is that the subject has not only been attacked by the neoclassical school, but also by neo-Marxists who reject the claim of mutual benefit. Thus development economics has been squeezed, as if in a vice, from both ends of the politico-economic spectrum.

What can be said in response? It is not difficult to defend the traditional preoccupations of development theory and development policy. Amartya Sen (1983) and Syed Naqvi (1996) show that the focus on **mobilizing surplus labour, capital accumulation and industrialization** has not been misplaced. It can be seen from the international evidence that many high-growth countries (and this is particularly true of South-East Asian countries today) have drawn extensively on surplus labour from the rural sector; that investment and growth are highly correlated across countries; and that the best growth performers are those countries where the share of industrial output in gross domestic product (GDP) is rising most rapidly. Those defending the rejection of mono-economics have not retreated into their shells, and very few economists would disagree that there is mutual benefit to be had from country interaction. It is not conceivable that the majority of developing countries would be absolutely better off if they were isolated and autarchic, although this is not to say that some 'delinking' may not be desirable and that the gains from globalization and interdependence could not be more equitably distributed.

But is there a separate development economics? Most observers would still argue that poor countries differ from the rich in such a way that different concepts, models and theories are required to understand their functioning in many respects. While it might be argued that the basic microeconomic assumptions about how people behave are similar for all countries, developing countries still differ *structurally* from rich ones and therefore require different models. The differences between the two sets of countries are large, particularly in relation to resource allocation and matters relating to long-term growth. It is not accidental that social cost-benefit analysis has been largely developed and refined within the context of developing countries, nor that developing countries have been the breeding ground for theories of tendencies towards disequilibrium in economic and social systems – models of virtuous and vicious circles and centre–periphery models of growth and development. But as Arthur Lewis, one of the fathers of development economics, once said in his presidential lecture to the American Economic Association, the central task of development economics is to provide a general framework for an understanding of the pace and rhythm of growth and development. As he put it: 'the economists' dream would be to have a single theory of growth that took an economy from the lowest level . . . past the dividing line . . . up to the level of Western Europe and beyond . . . or to have at least one good theory for the developing economy . . . to the dividing line' (Lewis, 1984). That is what development economics is all about. Development economics is the only branch of economics that attempts to offer an adequate explanation of the nature of the development process (Naqvi, 1996).

But even if the need for a separate development economics could not be established, would this jeopardize the status of the subject? It might be argued that in the interests of scientific respectability there is a strong case for thinking of economics as a unified body of theory and doctrine, and not a subject of compartments. But what leads to compartmentalization is the wide diversity of subject areas, which then leads to the descriptive labels of monetary economics, labour economics, regional economics and so on, but all these subdisciplines employ a large measure of theory that is common to economics as a whole.

What distinguishes the subdiscipline is first and foremost the area of application and only secondarily the distinctive theory. A favourite definition of economics is that 'economics is what economists do'. By analogy, 'development economics is what development economists do'. The development literature indicates that they do a number of things that other economists do not do, and in the process they both invent new models, and adapt and modify existing theory in the light of circumstances. Any contribution that a subdiscipline makes by way of theoretical development enriches economics as a whole, and may well have application elsewhere. New models, concepts and ideas invented by development economists include the following:

- The concept of the low-level equilibrium trap
- The theory of the 'big push'
- Dynamic externalities
- Models of dualism
- The theory of circular and cumulative causation
- The concept of dependency
- Growth pole analysis
- Models of population and growth
- Models of rural–urban migration

- Refinements to social cost–benefit analysis
- The notion of immiserizing growth
- Models of structural inflation
- The concept of dual-gap analysis
- The theory of missing markets
- The study of rent-seeking; and so on.

None of these innovations has been borrowed from other branches of economics, but other branches of economics have borrowed liberally from the expanding tool kit forged by development economists. International economics is no longer taught within the straitjacket of equilibrium economics. Labour economics has taken on board the concepts of dualism and dual labour markets, while structural inflation and dual-gap analysis are part of the language of macroeconomics. As Bardhan (1993) concludes:

> While the problems of the world's poor remain as overwhelming as ever, studying them has generated enough analytical ideas and thrown up enough challenges to the dominant paradigm to make all of us in the profession somewhat wiser, and at least somewhat more conscious of the possibilities and limitations of our existing methods of analysis.

Finally, how should one respond to the charge that development economics has not produced the results expected of it? As Hirschman (1981) puts it, the developing countries were 'expected to perform like wind-up toys and "lumber through" the various stages of development single-mindedly . . . these countries were perceived to have only *interests* and no passions'. If the expectations have not materialized, this probably has more to do with the expectations being unrealistic than deficiencies in the theory and practice of development economics. This in turn may have something to do with economists in general losing their historical sense and perspective. The process of development is a long, protracted process. It took over two hundred years for the present developed countries to progress from Rostow's traditional stage of economic development to economic maturity and high mass consumption. Arthur Lewis (1984) bemoans the loss of historical perspective, which he attributes to the poor training of economists: 'If our subject is lowering its sights, this may be because the demise of economic history in economics departments has brought us a generation of economists with no historical background. This is in marked contrast with the development economists of the 1950s, practically all of whom had some historical training, and guided by Gerschenkron and Rostow, looked to history for enlightenment on the processes of development.' Students beware: Learn your history!

Where do we stand today? At the present time there is a resurgence of academic interest in the growth and development process, inspired by the 'new' endogenous growth theory and the increased availability of large data sets that facilitate interesting and rigorous econometric work on the major determinants of intercountry growth performance. Paul Krugman (1992) has described the 1950s and 1960s as the years of 'high development theory', when many important models of development were formulated but were lost sight of because they were not formulated rigorously enough. Now the ideas are being brought back into play by more skilled theoreticians. The central core of ideas that emerged in the 1950s and 1960s, which were largely swept away during the neoclassical counter-revolution but which Krugman believes still remain valid, were **external economies, increasing returns, complementarity between sectors** and **linkages**. It is these ideas that have been recaptured by the 'new' endogenous growth theory (and which remained alive outside the mainstream in the works of such economists as Nicholas Kaldor and Kenneth Arrow – see Chapter 4).

New growth theory provides an answer to the question of why per capita income differences in the world economy seem to be as persistent as ever when conventional neoclassical growth theory predicts convergence. The answer is that there are many externalities that prevent the marginal product of capital from falling as countries get richer, so that the level of investment matters for growth, and growth is endogenous in this sense – not simply determined by an exogenously given rate of technical progress, common to all countries. Indeed technical progress is also largely endogenous, determined by research and development (R&D) and education. This theory tells us what sustains growth, but it does not address the question of what it is that gets growth started. To answer this we need to go to the roots of economic development, which initially lie in the performance of the rural economy and agriculture (see Chapter 5).

THE NEW INTERNATIONAL ECONOMIC ORDER

Another major factor accounting for the upsurge of interest in the growth and development process has been the poor nations' own increased awareness of their inferior economic and political status in the world, and their desire for material improvement and greater political recognition through economic strength. This was precipitated by decolonization and increased contact with the developed nations, and has been strengthened from within by rising expectations as development has proceeded. Development is wanted to provide people with the basic necessities of life, for their own sake, and to provide a degree of self-esteem and freedom for people, which is precluded by poverty. Wealth and material possessions may not provide greater happiness but they widen the choice of individuals, which is an important aspect of freedom and welfare. The developing countries have also called for a fairer deal from the functioning of the world economy, which they view, with some justification, as biased in favour of countries that are already rich.

The official call for a **new international economic order** was made during the Sixth Special Session of the United Nations General Assembly in 1974. The United Nations pledged itself

> to work urgently for the establishment of a new international economic order based on equity, sovereign equality, common interest and cooperation among all States, irrespective of their economic and social systems, which shall correct inequalities and redress existing injustices, make it possible to eliminate the widening gap between the developed and the developing countries and ensure steadily accelerating economic and social development and peace and justice for present and future generations.

The programme of action called for such things as:

- Improved terms of trade for the exports of poor countries
- Greater access to the markets of developed countries for manufactured goods
- Greater financial assistance and the alleviation of past debt
- Reform of the International Monetary Fund and a greater say in decision-making on international bodies concerned with trade and development issues

■   An international food programme
■   Greater technical cooperation.

The call for a new international economic order has been reiterated several times by various UN agencies. In 1975 the United Nations Industrial Development Organization (UNIDO) produced the **Lima Declaration**, which set a target for the developing countries to secure a 25 per cent share of world manufacturing production by the year 2000 compared with the share then of 10 per cent. The 2005 share is only 15 per cent and the target has not been met. On the monetary front, in 1980 the **Arusha Declaration** demanded a UN Conference on International Money and Finance to create a new international monetary order 'capable of achieving monetary stability, restoring acceptable levels of employment and sustainable growth' and 'supportive of a process of global development'.

In 1995 a UN World Development Summit was held in Copenhagen, focusing on social development and employment issues. The **Copenhagen Declaration** made several commitments:

■   Full employment, equality between men and women, and universal access to education and health care should be basic priorities.
■   Overall development aid should be increased for spending in areas of social policy.
■   Developed countries should allocate 20 per cent of their aid to basic social projects and in return developing countries should spend at least 20 per cent of their budgets on social needs.
■   The IMF and the World Bank should pay more attention to social factors when designing programmes.

The United Nations Conference on Trade and Development (UNCTAD) regularly calls for new policy initiatives in the four major areas of debt relief, international aid, commodity policy and trade promotion for developing countries.

MILLENNIUM DEVELOPMENT GOALS

The latest commitment endorsed by the World Bank and the United Nations (UN) is for the percentage of the world's population living in absolute poverty to be halved by the year 2015, compared to the level in 1990. This means a reduction from 30 per cent to 15 per cent. In 2005 the level is just over 20 per cent, although it is much higher than this in particular countries. In addition several other development goals and targets have been set, outlined fully in Case example 1.1. They relate to:

■   Enrolling all children in primary school by 2015
■   Making progress towards gender equality, particularly in education
■   Reducing child mortality
■   Reducing maternal mortality
■   Providing universal access to reproductive health services
■   Implementing national strategies for sustainable development and to reverse the loss of environmental resources.

Each of the goals addresses an aspect of poverty, and all are mutually reinforcing. For example, higher school enrolment, especially for girls, reduces poverty and mortality. Better basic health care will increase school enrolment and reduce poverty. Many poor people earn their living from the environment, so a better environment will help poor people.

To achieve the major goal of halving the poverty rate by the year 2015 will require a sustained growth of per capita income in the countries affected, at rates much higher than experienced in the recent past, particularly in Africa. On average, the poverty rate tends to fall by about one per cent for every one per cent increase in per capita income, so a 50 per cent increase in per capita income would be required to reduce the poverty rate from, say, 40 per cent to 20 per cent. This is the challenge facing Africa over the next ten years if the Millennium targets are to be met (see Chapter 2 p. 41 for more detailed calculations).

Case example **1.1**

Millennium Development Goals and Targets

Goal 1: Eradicate extreme poverty and hunger
Target 1: Halve, between 1990 and 2015, the proportion of people whose income is less than $1 a day.
Target 2: Halve, between 1990 and 2015, the proportion of people who suffer from hunger.

Goal 2: Achieve universal primary education
Target 3: Ensure that, by 2015, children everywhere, boys and girls alike, will be able to complete a full course of primary schooling.

Goal 3: Promote gender equality and empower women
Target 4: Eliminate gender disparity in primary and secondary education, preferably by 2005 and in all levels of education no later than 2015.

Goal 4: Reduce child mortality
Target 5: Reduce by two-thirds, between 1990 and 2015, the under-five mortality rate.

Goal 5: Improve maternal health
Target 6: Reduce by three-quarters, between 1990 and 2015, the maternal mortality ratio.

Goal 6: Combat HIV/AIDS, malaria and other diseases
Target 7: Have halted by 2015 and begun to reverse the spread of HIV/AIDS.
Target 8: Have halted by 2015 and begun to reverse the incidence of malaria and other major diseases.

Goal 7: Ensure environmental sustainability
Target 9: Integrate the principles of sustainable development into country policies and programmes and reverse the loss of environmental resources.

▶

Target 10: Halve by 2015 the proportion of people without sustainable access to safe drinking water.

Target 11: Have achieved by 2020 a significant improvement in the lives of at least 100 million slum dwellers.

Goal 8: Develop a global partnership for development

Target 12: Develop further an open, rule-based, predictable, non-discriminatory trading and financial system (includes a commitment to good governance, development, and poverty reduction – both nationally and internationally).

Target 13: Address the special needs of the least developed countries (includes tariff- and quotafree access for exports, enhanced programme of debt relief for and cancellation of official bilateral debt, and more generous official development assistance for countries committed to poverty reduction).

Target 14: Address the special needs of landlocked countries and small island developing states (through the Programme of Action for the Sustainable Development of Small Island Developing States and 22nd General Assembly provisions).

Target 15: Deal comprehensively with the debt problems of developing countries through national and international measures in order to make debt sustainable in the long term.

Target 16: In cooperation with developing countries, develop and implement strategies for decent and productive work for youth.

Target 17: In cooperation with pharmaceutical companies, provide access to affordable essential drugs in developing countries.

Target 18: In cooperation with the private sector, make available the benefits of new technologies, especially information and communications technologies.

Source: UNDP, *Human Development Report 2002* (New York: Oxford University Press, 2002).

GLOBALIZATION AND INTERDEPENDENCE OF THE WORLD ECONOMY

A third major factor responsible for the growing interest and concern with Third World development is the increased **globalization** of the world economy leading to a greater interdependence between countries of the world. There have been three major eras of globalization in the last 150 years. The first was from 1870 to the First World War (1914) which witnessed large scale capital flows and labour migration from Europe to the American continent and the colonies. The second started after the Second World War with the freeing of trade. The third phase started in the 1980s based on technological advances in communications and transport. Fischer (2003) has given a useful, succinct definition of globalization:

> the ongoing process of greater economic interdependence among countries reflected in the increasing amount of cross-border trade in goods and services, the increasing volume of international financial flows and increasing flows of labour.

As far as the interdependence between developed and developing countries is concerned, developing countries depend on developed countries for resource flows and technology, while developed countries depend heavily on developing countries for raw materials, food and oil, and as markets for industrial goods. The term globalization refers to all those forces operating in the world economy that increase interdependence and at the same time make countries more and more dependent on forces outside of their control, as time, space and borders diminish in importance. Foremost among these forces are:

- The widening and freeing of trade. Over 20 per cent of the world's output of goods and services is now traded.
- The growth of global capital markets and the greater flow of short-term speculative capital: over 2 trillion dollars are exchanged on the world's currency markets every day.
- More foreign direct investment (FDI) by giant multinational corporations with more power and assets than many national governments.
- The growth of global value chains with firms sourcing inputs from the cheapest international markets.
- The greater movement of people than ever before, breaking down cultural barriers – but also leading to the spread of disease (e.g. AIDS) and international crime in drugs, prostitution and arms.
- The spread of information technology (IT) which can exacerbate contagion in financial markets (e.g. the 1997 financial crisis in South-East Asia).
- New institutions, such as the World Trade Organization (WTO), with authority over national governments, and new multilateral agreements on trade, services, intellectual property, etc., which reduce national autonomy.

All these aspects of globalization and interdependence make countries more vulnerable to shocks such as: world recessions and downturns in world trade; financial crises, such as the Asian crisis of 1997 which became contagious and spread like a disease affecting not only the region of South-East Asia, but other parts of the world too; and decisions by big multinational companies to withdraw investment or relocate. In recent years there have been major protests at meetings of the WTO and the World Economic Forum in Davos (Switzerland) by groups concerned with the damage done by globalization, particularly to the poorer countries in the world economy which tend to be most exposed to, and suffer most from, the forces of competition and global capital movements. Competitive markets may be the best guarantee of efficiency, but not necessarily of equity. As the *Human Development Report* of the United Nations Development Programme (UNDP) (1999) put it:

> The challenge of globalisation in the new century is not to stop the expansion of global markets. The challenge is to find the rules and institutions for stronger governance – local, national, regional and global – to preserve the advantages of global markets and competition, but also to provide enough space for human, community and environmental resources to ensure that globalisation works for people – not just for profits.

So far, more progress has been made in promoting the institutions of globalization than in protecting people against the consequences of globalization. The UNDP calls for globalization tempered by:

- **Ethics** – less violation of human rights
- **Equity** – less disparity within and between nations
- **Inclusion** – less marginalization of people and countries
- **Human security** – less instability of countries and less vulnerability of people
- **Sustainability** – less environmental destruction
- **Development** – less poverty and deprivation.

When the actions of any one country, or group of countries, result in consequences for others (good or bad), the effects become a type of **public good** or **externality**. The task of the international community in these circumstances is to maximize the spread of public goods which confer positive externalities (e.g. technology, information, health care) and to minimize the spread of public 'bads' (e.g. disease, pollution, financial contagion). It is in the self-interest of the international community to particularly assist developing countries not only because they are poor but also to enable them to make their contribution to the provision of essential global public goods (and to minimize the production of public 'bads', e.g. AIDS in Africa).

Globalization and interdependence particularly means that the malfunctioning of one set of economies impairs the functioning of others. This was never more evident than in the world economy in the 1980s, when owing to the rising price of energy and the debt crisis, there was mounting economic chaos. The 1980 Brandt Report, entitled *North–South: A Programme for Survival* (1980), and its sequel *Common Crisis: North–South Co-operation for World Recovery* (Brandt Commission, 1983), stressed the mutual benefit to all countries of a sustained programme of development in the Third World, and documented the prevailing adverse trends in the world economy, which pointed to a sombre future if not tackled cooperatively:

- Growing poverty and hunger in the Third World
- Rising unemployment with inflation
- International monetary disorder
- Chronic balance of payments deficits and mounting debts in most Third World countries
- Protectionism, and tensions between countries competing for energy, food and raw materials.

Development economics addresses itself to many of the issues contributing to disarray in the world economy.

There is not only a moral case for greater efforts to raise living standards in Third World countries, but a purely practical case that it is in the interests of the developed countries themselves. The ability of poor countries to sustain their growth and development means a greater demand for the goods and services of developed countries, which generates output and employment directly and also helps to maintain the balance-of-payments stability of these countries, which is so crucial if there is to be a reciprocal demand for the goods of developing countries. Any constraint on demand in the system arising from, say, poor agricultural performance in poor countries, or a balance-of-payments constraint on demand in developed countries, will impair the functioning of the whole system and reduce the rate of progress below potential. Herein lies the importance of the transfer of resources to poor countries to maintain their momentum of development (global Keynesianism), and of international monetary reform to smooth the burden of balance-of-payments adjustment and to shift more of the burden of adjustment from the deficit to the surplus countries.

The Brandt Report called for a short-term emergency programme as a prelude to longer-term action, consisting of four major elements:

- A large-scale transfer of resources to developing countries
- An international energy strategy to minimize the dislocation caused by sudden and rapid increases in the price of oil
- A global food programme
- A start on some major reforms in the international monetary system.

To date, very little has been done.

In the longer term the Brandt Report called for:

- A twenty-year programme to meet the basic needs of poor countries, involving additional resource transfers of $4 billion a year.
- A major effort to improve agricultural productivity to end mass hunger and malnutrition.
- Commodity schemes to stabilize the terms of trade for primary commodities.
- Easier access to world markets for the exports of developing countries.
- Programmes for energy conservation.
- The development of more appropriate technologies for poor countries.
- An international progressive income tax, and levies on trade and arms production, to be used by a new World Development Fund (to fund development programmes rather than projects).
- A link between the creation of new international money and aid to developing countries.
- Policies to recycle balance-of-payments surpluses (as accumulated by the Arab oil exporting countries since 1973, for example) to deficit countries to remove balance-of-payments constraints on demand and remove the risk of a slide into international protectionism.

We could add to this list new forms of global governance to cope with the consequences of globalization, and which at the same time also represent the interests of those countries that suffer most from the effects of globalization: the poor and marginalized.

We shall discuss many of these issues in the course of this book. Such a programme of action would be of mutual benefit to all parties, rich and poor. It would create investment confidence, which is the crucial ingredient maintaining the dynamics of any economic system; it would stimulate trade and investment, and help the prospects of sustained growth in the world economy.

It would be wrong to give the impression, however, that the developed countries' concern with world poverty is motivated exclusively by the selfish realization that their own survival depends on economic and political harmony, which cannot thrive in a world perpetually divided into rich and poor. There has also been an affirmation by many developed countries of a moral obligation towards poorer nations. Not all aid and development assistance is politically inspired. Particularly over the last three decades, the developed countries have shown a genuine humanitarian concern over the plight of

Third World countries, which has resulted in the establishment and support of several institutions to assist developing countries, and which led the period 1960–70 to be named the 'First Development Decade'.

We are now in the Fifth Development Decade, and the pledge to assist developing countries out of humanitarian concern has been reaffirmed. The goal of a greater degree of income equality between the citizens of a nation seems to be gaining support, albeit slowly, as an objective among nations. Moreover the propagation of this ideal is not confined to the supranational institutions that have been especially established to further it. Recent years have witnessed the spontaneous creation of several national pressure groups in different parts of the world, whose platform is the abolition of world poverty; and the Church, which remained silent and inactive for so long, periodically makes its voice heard. Aid from voluntary agencies to developing countries now amounts to over $5 billion annually. But whatever the motive for concern, the reality of world poverty and underdevelopment cannot be ignored. Furthermore, primary poverty in developing countries is likely to persist for many years to come. The economist has a special responsibility to contribute to an understanding of the economic difficulties that poor countries face and to point to possible solutions. This is a textbook devoted to that end.

We start by considering the meaning of development and the perpetuation of underdevelopment. Then in Chapters 2 and 3 we consider the measurement of poverty, the magnitude of the development gap in the world economy, and the major characteristics of underdevelopment, particularly the employment situation, the income distribution, the level of nutrition and other basic needs such as education and health care.

THE MEANING OF DEVELOPMENT AND THE CHALLENGE OF DEVELOPMENT ECONOMICS

Development implies change, and this is one sense in which the term development is used, that is, to describe the process of economic and social transformation within countries. This process often follows a well-ordered sequence and exhibits common characteristics across countries, which we shall discuss later in the chapter. But if development becomes an objective of policy, the important question arises of: development for what? Not so long ago the concept of development, defined in the sense of an objective or a desired state of affairs, was conceived of almost exclusively in terms of growth targets, with very little regard to the beneficiaries of growth or the composition of output. Societies are not indifferent, however, to the distributional consequences of economic policy, to the type of output that is produced, or to the economic environment in which it is produced. A concept of development is required that embraces the major economic and social objectives and values that societies strive for. This is not easy. One attempt is by Goulet (1971), who distinguishes three basic components or core values in this wider meaning of development, which he calls **life-sustenance, self-esteem** and **freedom**.

Life-sustenance is concerned with the provision of basic needs, which we shall discuss in Chapter 3. The basic needs approach to development was initiated by the World Bank in the 1970s. No country may be regarded as fully developed if it cannot provide all its people with such basic needs as housing, clothing, food and minimal education. A major objective of development must be to raise people out of primary poverty and to provide basic needs simultaneously.

Self-esteem is concerned with the feeling of self-respect and independence. No country can be regarded as fully developed if it is exploited by others and does not have the power and influence to conduct relations on equal terms. Developing countries seek development for self-esteem; to eradicate the feeling of dominance and dependence that is associated with inferior economic status.

Freedom refers to freedom from the three evils of 'want, ignorance and squalor' so that people are more able to determine their own destiny. No person is free if they cannot choose; if they are imprisoned by living on the margin of subsistence with no education and no skills. The advantage of material development is that it expands the range of human choice open to individuals and societies at large.

All three of these core components are interrelated. Lack of self-esteem and freedom result from low levels of life sustenance, and both lack of self-esteem and economic imprisonment become links in a circular, self-perpetuating chain of poverty by producing a sense of fatalism and acceptance of the established order – the 'accommodation to poverty' as Galbraith (1980) once called it.

Goulet's three core components of development are also related to Amartya Sen's vision of development (Sen, 1983, 1984, 1999), defined in terms of the expansion of **entitlements** and **capabilities,** the former giving life sustenance and self-esteem; the latter giving **freedom**. Sen defines entitlements as 'the set of alternative commodity bundles that a person can command in a society using the totality of rights and obligations that he or she faces', and entitlements generate the capability to do certain things. Economic development should be thought of in terms of the expansion of entitlements and capabilities, which are not well captured by aggregate measures of output growth. For most people, entitlements depend on their ability to sell their labour and on the price of commodities. It is not only the market mechanism that determines entitlements, however, but also such factors as power relations in society, the spatial distribution of resources in society, such as schools and health care, and what individuals can extract from the state.

In the final analysis, it is **freedom** that Sen views as the primary objective of development, as well as the principal means of achieving development. Development consists of the removal of various types of 'unfreedoms' that leave people with little choice and opportunity. Major categories of 'unfreedom' include famine and undernourishment, poor health and lack of basic needs; lack of political liberty and basic civil rights, and economic insecurity. Development should be regarded as a process of expanding the real freedoms that people enjoy. The growth of per capita income is only a means to that end. The ideas and views of Amartya Sen, who won the Nobel Prize for Economics in 1998 for his work on the interface between welfare and development economics, have been enormously influential within the international community and can be most recently seen in the World Bank's *World Development Report 2000/2001* which is devoted to the topic of how to expand the entitlements, capabilities and freedom of poor people (see Chapter 2).

The focus and stress on expanding entitlements and capabilities for *all* people is a natural extension of the earlier switch in development thinking away from growth maximization to concern with the structure of production and consumption and the distribution of income. Sen's dissent is that income is often a very inadequate measure of entitlement, which he tries to illustrate with reference to the incidence of famines across the world. He finds that most famines have been associated with a lack of entitlements, not with a lack of food.

Using Goulet's and Sen's concept of development, therefore, and in answer to the question 'development for what?', we can say that development has occurred when there has been an improvement in basic needs, when economic progress has contributed to a greater sense of self-esteem for the country and individuals within it, and when material advancement has expanded people's entitlements, capabilities and freedoms. The fact that many of these ingredients of development are not measurable does not detract from their importance: the condition of being developed is as much a state of mind as a physical condition measurable by economic indices alone.

The challenge of development economics lies in the formulation of economic theory, and in the application of policy, in order to understand better and to meet these core components of development. Clearly the range of issues that development economics is concerned with is quite distinctive and because of this the subject has developed its own *modus vivendi* (way of doing things), although drawing liberally on economic theory, as do other branches of economics.

If it is to be useful, however, a great deal of conventional economic theory must be adapted to suit the conditions prevailing in developing countries, and many of the assumptions that underlie conventional economic models have to be abandoned if they are to yield fruitful insights into the development process. Static equilibrium theory, for example, is ill-suited to the analysis of growth and change and of growing inequalities in the distribution of income between individuals and countries. It is probably also true, as Todaro and Smith (2003) strongly argue, that economics needs to be viewed in the much broader perspective of the overall social system of a country (which includes values, beliefs, attitudes towards effort and risk taking, religion and the class system) if development mistakes are to be avoided that stem from implementing policy based on economic theory alone.

THE PERPETUATION OF UNDERDEVELOPMENT

The study of economic development helps us to understand the nature and causes of poverty in low-income countries, and the transformation of societies from primarily rural to primarily industrial, with the vast bulk of resources utilized in industrial activities and in service activities that serve the industrial sector. But why have some countries hardly participated in this process or have been left behind? The first industrial revolution gave the present developed countries an initial advantage, which they then sustained through the existence of various cumulative forces against those left behind. In the last fifty years there has been a second industrial revolution, which has propelled another bloc of countries (the so-called 'newly industrialized countries' of South-East Asia and Latin America) into a virtually industrialized state, and many others into a semi-industrialized state. But many countries are still left behind in a semi-feudal state, including the very poorest, which have now become the prime focus of concern of the World Bank and other development agencies.

There are many theories of the perpetuation of underdevelopment but none seems to have universal validity. The state of agriculture is of foremost importance. It was, first of all, settled agriculture that laid the basis for the great civilizations of the past, and it was the increase in agricultural productivity in England in the eighteenth century that laid the basis for, and sustained, the first industrial revolution. If there is one overriding factor that explains why some countries developed before others, and why some countries are still backward without a significant industrial sector, it lies in the condition of agriculture, which in the early stages of development is the sector that must provide the purchasing power over industrial goods.

The condition of agriculture depends on many factors, institutional as well as economic, and physical conditions are also of key importance. Climate particularly affects the conditions of production. Heat debilitates individuals. Extremes of heat and humidity also reduce the quality of the soil and contribute to the low productivity of certain crops. It cannot be coincidence that almost all developing countries are situated in tropical or subtropical climatic regions and that development 'took off' in the temperate zones.

The condition of agriculture has not been helped by what Lipton (1977) called **urban bias**, which in many countries has starved agriculture of resources. This has happened because ruling elites generally originate from, or identify with, the non-rural environment, and because policy-makers have been led astray both by empirical evidence that shows a high correlation between levels of development and industrialization, and by early development models that stressed investment in industry.

Many other internal conditions have acted as barriers to progress in poor countries, barriers that interacted in a vicious circle. In some countries population size presents a problem, combined with low levels of human capital formation. The latter in turn perpetuates poverty, which is associated with high birth rates and large family size. This is a form of 'accommodation to poverty' (Galbraith, 1980), which then perpetuates low living standards in a circular process. Other countries may lack the psychological conditions required for modernization, built on individualism and the competitive spirit, coupled with a strong work ethic, rationalism and scientific thought, which characterized the industrial revolutions of eighteenth- and nineteenth-century Europe, and which played a large part in the emergence of the newly industrialized South-East Asian countries in the latter half of the twentieth century.

External relations between countries also play a part in the poverty perpetuation process, and this has given rise to **structuralist** and **dependency** theories of under-development. It seems to be the general lesson of history that once one set of countries gains an economic advantage, the advantage will be sustained through a process of what Myrdal (1957) has called 'circular and cumulative causation', working through the media of factor mobility and trade. (For a full discussion, see Chapter 7.) Favoured regions denude the backward regions of capital and skilled labour, and they trade in commodities whose characteristics guarantee that the gains from trade accrue to them. **Colonialism** was an extreme form of dependency, and many of the countries so exploited are still poor today. On the other hand a number of countries that were never colonized, such as Ethiopia and Thailand, are equally backward.

Dependence can take more subtle forms, however, based on the international division of labour, for example, which leads to unequal exchange relations between rich and poor, with the poor dependent on the rich for capital and technology to equip their industrial sectors. The current indebtedness of the less developed countries, the 'increasing price' that poor countries have to pay for development inputs relative to the price they receive for their exports, and the growing number of poor people are manifestations of this dependency. There are exceptions to the thesis of 'circular and cumulative causation', but in most cases it requires a strong exogenous shock to break out of a vicious circle of poverty and dependency.

We shall take up some of these issues in Part III of this book, but in Chapter 2 we turn our attention to the magnitude of poverty in developing countries and the world distribution of income.

DISCUSSION QUESTIONS

1 What constitutes the study of development economics?

2 Do you think there is a case for a separate subject of development economics, and what are the arguments against it?

3 What accounts for the political and academic interest in Third World development?

4 Why was the status of the discipline of development economics called into question in the 1970s?

5 How would you define the process of economic development?

6 What do the developing countries want from a 'new international economic order'?

7 Do you think that the Millennium Development Goals are achievable?

8 What forces perpetuate underdevelopment?

9 What lessons, if any, can poor countries learn from the development experience of today's industrialized countries?

10 What is meant by 'globalization' and the mutual dependence between rich and poor countries?

11 What do you see as the major challenges confronting development economics and the developing countries?

WEBSITES

The study of development economics requires a good deal of reading and familiarity with case-study material, as well as access to statistical sources. Below is a list of general Internet sites that can be accessed with links to topics, countries, regions and international organizations. Other sites on specific topics will be given at the end of other chapters.

Institutes of Development Studies

Canadian International Development Agency (Virtual Library on International Development) http://w3.acdi-cida.gc.ca/virtual.nsf

Institute of Development Studies, University of Sussex (British Library for Development Studies) www.ids.ac.uk/blds/index.html

School of Development Studies, University of East Anglia www.uea.ac.uk/dev/

International organizations

World Bank   www.worldbank.org

International Monetary Fund   www.imf.org

United Nations Conference on Trade and Development (UNCTAD)   www.unctad.org

United Nations Development Programme (UNDP)   www.undp.org

Food and Agricultural Organization (FAO)   www.fao.org

World Trade Organization (WTO)   www.wto.org

World Health Organization (WHO)   www.who.int

United Nations Industrial Development Organization (UNIDO)   www.unido.org

International Labour Organization (ILO)   www.ilo.org

African Development Bank   http://afdb.org

Asian Development Bank   www.adb.org

Inter-American Development Bank   www.iadb.org

World Development Movement   www.wdm.org.uk

Centre for Global Development (Washington)   www.cgdev.org

Non-Governmental Organizations Global Network   www.ngo.org

Heritage Foundation   www.heritage.org

Databases

Penn World Tables (accessed through the National Bureau of Economic Research)   www.nber.org/pub/pwt56.html

Economic Growth Resources (Jon Temple, Bristol University)   www.bris.ac.uk/Depts/Economics/Growth

World Bank   http://econ.worldbank.org/prr/globalisation

IMF/World Bank Library Network   http://jotis

Globalization

Department for International Development, UK   www.globalisation.gov.uk

Centre for Research on Globalization   http://www.globalresearch.ca

The Globalization Website   http://www.emory.edu/soc/globalization/

Institute for International Economics   http://www.iie.com/research/globalization.htm

New Economics Foundation   www.neweconomics.org/gen

The development gap and the measurement of poverty

THE DEVELOPMENT GAP AND INCOME DISTRIBUTION IN THE WORLD ECONOMY

By any standard one cares to take, the evidence is unequivocal that the world's income is distributed extremely unequally between nations and people, and that there exists in the world a broad north–south division into rich and poor countries. The World Bank classifies the countries of the world into three broad categories: low-income countries, middle-income countries, and high-income countries. Table 2.1 gives the level of per capita income in 2002 for all countries in the world with populations greater than 1 million; and at the bottom of the table the average levels of per capita income are given for the low-, middle- and high-income countries. Ignoring for the moment measurement difficulties (see later) we see that for the low-income countries, the average level of income per head is only US$430 per annum, compared to US$26,490 for the high-income countries (measured at current exchange rates). This gives some idea of the range of income differences, but it is an understatement of the degree of income inequality in the world economy because it compares only *average* income for poor and rich

Table 2.1 Size of the economy, 2002

	Population	Gross national income per capita		PPP gross national income per capita	
	millions	$	rank	$	rank
Afghanistan	28	–	–	–	–
Albania	3	1 450	120	4 960	112
Algeria	31	1 720	114	5 530	103
Angola	13	710	146	1 840	163
Argentina	36	4 220	74	10 190	72
Armenia	3	790	144	3 230	139
Australia	20	19 530	29	27 440	19
Austria	8	23 860	18	28 910	12
Azerbaijan	8	710	146	3 010	142
Bangladesh	136	380	171	1 770	165
Belarus	10	1 360	124	5 500	105
Belgium	10	22 940	21	28 130	16
Benin	7	380	171	1 060	185
Bolivia	9	900	140	2 390	149
Bosnia and Herzegovina	4	1 310	125	–	–
Botswana	2	3 010	88	7 740	84
Brazil	174	2 830	91	7 450	86
Bulgaria	8	1 770	111	7 030	87
Burkina Faso	12	250	187	1 090	184
Burundi	7	100	206	630	204
Cambodia	12	300	178	1 970	159
Cameroon	16	550	156	1 910	162
Canada	31	22 390	23	28 930	11
Central African Republic	4	250	187	1 170	183
Chad	8	210	194	1 010	187
Chile	16	4 250	73	9 420	76
China	1 280	960	136	4 520	125
Hong Kong, China	7	24 690	16	27 490	18
Colombia	44	1 820	109	6 150	98
Congo, Dem. Rep.	52	100	206	630	204
Congo, Rep.	4	610	153	710	202
Costa Rica	4	4 070	77	8 560	81
Côte d'Ivoire	17	620	152	1 450	177
Croatia	4	4 540	71	10 000	74
Czech Republic	10	5 480	68	14 920	55
Denmark	5	30 260	9	30 600	8
Dominican Republic	9	–	–	6 270	97
Ecuador	13	1 490	118	3 340	138
Egypt, Arab Rep.	66	1 470	119	3 810	132
El Salvador	6	2 110	101	4 790	120
Eritrea	4	190	196	1 040	186
Estonia	1	4 190	75	11 630	63
Ethiopia	67	100	206	780	200
Finland	5	23 890	17	26 160	25
France	59	22 240	24	27 040	21
Gabon	1	3 060	87	5 530	103
Gambia, The	1	270	184	1 660	169
Georgia	5	650	151	2 270	152
Germany	82	22 740	22	26 980	22
Ghana	20	270	184	2 080	156
Greece	11	11 660	48	18 770	43
Guatemala	12	1 760	112	4 030	129

▶

Table 2.1 continued

	Population	Gross national income per capita		PPP gross national income per capita	
	millions	$	rank	$	rank
Guinea	8	410	169	2 060	157
Guinea-Bissau	1	130	205	680	203
Haiti	8	440	165	1 610	172
Honduras	7	930	138	2 540	147
Hungary	10	5 290	69	13 070	58
India	1 049	470	161	2 650	146
Indonesia	212	710	146	3 070	141
Iran, Islamic Rep.	66	1 720	114	6 690	91
Ireland	4	23 030	20	29 570	9
Israel	7	16 020	37	19 000	41
Italy	58	19 080	30	26 170	24
Jamaica	3	2 690	93	3 680	134
Japan	127	34 010	7	27 380	20
Jordan	5	1 760	112	4 180	127
Kazakhstan	15	1 520	117	5 630	101
Kenya	31	360	174	1 010	187
Korea, Rep.	48	9 930	53	16 960	51
Kuwait	2	16 340	36	17 780	47
Kyrgyz Republic	5	290	181	1 560	175
Lao PDR	6	310	176	1 660	169
Latvia	2	3 480	86	9 190	77
Lebanon	4	3 990	79	4 600	123
Lesotho	2	550	156	2 970	143
Liberia	3	140	201	–	–
Lithuania	3	3 670	83	10 190	72
Macedonia, FYR	2	1 710	116	6 420	95
Madagascar	16	230	191	730	201
Malawi	11	160	200	570	207
Malaysia	24	3 540	84	8 500	82
Mali	11	240	189	860	192
Mauritania	3	280	183	1 790	164
Mauritius	1	3 860	81	10 820	67
Mexico	101	5 920	66	8 800	80
Moldova	4	460	164	1 600	173
Mongolia	2	430	166	1 710	167
Morocco	30	1 170	128	3 730	133
Mozambique	18	200	195	990	189
Namibia	2	1 790	110	6 880	89
Nepal	24	230	191	1 370	179
Netherlands	16	23 390	19	28 250	15
New Zealand	4	13 260	44	20 550	39
Nicaragua	5	710	146	2 350	150
Niger	11	180	197	800	195
Nigeria	133	300	178	800	195
Norway	5	38 730	3	36 690	3
Oman	3	7 830	59	13 000	59
Pakistan	145	420	168	1 960	160
Panama	3	4 020	78	6 060	99

Table 2.1 continued

	Population millions	Gross national income per capita $	rank	PPP gross national income per capita $	rank
Papua New Guinea	5	530	158	2 180	153
Paraguay	6	1 170	128	4 590	124
Peru	27	2 020	103	4 880	117
Philippines	80	1 030	134	4 450	126
Poland	39	4 570	70	10 450	70
Portugal	10	10 720	50	17 820	46
Romania	22	1 870	108	6 490	93
Russian Federation	144	2 130	99	8 080	83
Rwanda	8	230	191	1 260	182
Saudi Arabia	22	8 530	57	12 660	60
Senegal	10	470	161	1 540	176
Serbia and Montenegro	8	1 400	123	–	–
Sierra Leone	5	140	201	500	208
Singapore	4	20 690	27	23 730	31
Slovak Republic	5	3 970	80	12 590	61
Slovenia	2	10 370	52	18 480	45
South Africa	45	2 500	94	9 810	75
Spain	41	14 580	40	21 210	36
Sri Lanka	19	850	142	3 510	135
Sudan	33	370	173	1 740	166
Swaziland	1	1 240	127	4 730	122
Sweden	9	25 970	12	25 820	26
Switzerland	7	36 170	4	31 840	7
Syrian Arab Republic	17	1 130	130	3 470	136
Tajikistan	6	180	197	930	191
Tanzania	35	290	181	580	206
Thailand	62	2 000	104	6 890	88
Togo	5	270	184	1 450	177
Trinidad and Tobago	1	6 750	63	9 000	79
Tunisia	10	1 990	105	6 440	94
Turkey	70	2 490	95	6 300	96
Turkmenistan	5	–	–	4 780	121
Uganda	25	240	189	1 360	180
Ukraine	49	780	145	4 800	119
United Arab Emirates	3	–	–	24 030	30
United Kingdom	59	25 510	13	26 580	23
United States	288	35 400	6	36 110	4
Uruguay	3	4 340	72	7 710	85
Uzbekistan	25	310	176	1 640	171
Venezuela, RB	25	4 080	76	5 220	110
Vietnam	80	430	166	2 300	151
West Bank and Gaza	3	1 110	131	–	–
Yemen, Rep.	19	490	160	800	195
Zambia	10	340	175	800	195
Zimbabwe	13	–	–	2 180	153

Table 2.1 continued

	Population	Gross national income per capita	PPP gross national income per capita
	millions	$	$
World	**6 199**	**5 120**	**7 820**
Low income	2 495	430	2 110
Middle income	2 738	1 850	5 800
Lower middle income	2 408	1 400	5 290
Upper middle income	329	5 110	9 550
Low & middle income	5 282	1 170	4 030
East Asia & Pacific	1 838	960	4 280
Europe & Central Asia	473	2 160	6 900
Latin America & Carib.	525	3 280	6 950
Middle East & N. Africa	306	2 240	5 670
South Asia	1 401	460	2 460
Sub-Saharan Africa	689	450	1 700
High Income	966	26 490	28 480

Source: World Bank, *World Development Indicators, 2004* (Washington, DC: World Bank).

countries. If the income per head of the poorest countries of Burundi, the Democratic Republic of Congo and Ethiopia are compared with the richest listed country (Norway), the gap is clearly wider: $100 and $38,730, respectively. Furthermore if the income per capita of the poorest people in poor countries is compared with the income per head of the richest people in rich countries, the gap becomes colossal. For example, the ratio of the average income of the richest 5 per cent of the world's population to the average income of the poorest 5 per cent of the world's population is roughly 120:1. The richest 1 per cent of people in the world receive as much income as the bottom 60 per cent. Or, to put it another way, the 60 million richest people receive as much income as 2.7 billion poor. The total income of the richest 25 million Americans is equal to the total income of 2 billion of the world's poorest people. The assets of the world's 400 billionaires (mostly in rich countries) exceed the total amount of income of nearly one-half of the world's total population. It is no wonder that the United Nations Development Programme (UNDP) has described the world as 'gargantuan in its excesses and grotesque in its human and economic inequalities'.[1]

We can illustrate this inequality with a simple picture (Figure 2.1) which divides the world's population up into equal 20 per cent shares (quintiles) from poorest to richest, and then shows the percentage of income that each share receives. Interestingly, and ironically, the picture resembles a champagne glass with a very narrow stem in the hands of the poor and a wide open bowl (containing the champagne) in the hands of the rich (Wade, 2001).

The above discussion indicates that there are two aspects to the measurement of income inequality across the world. The first is the inequality between nations, which may be termed **international inequality**. The other is the inequality between people across the world, which also takes account of the distribution of income *within* countries, which may be termed **global inequality**. Both may be portrayed using a **Lorenz curve** diagram, and measured by the **Gini ratio**, which uses information on how income is

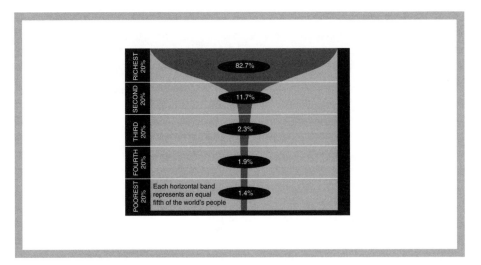

Figure 2.1 Distribution of world income, 1989 (percent of total, with quintiles of population ranked by income)

distributed across the whole population, not just between the extremes of rich and poor (as dramatized above).

Let us first consider **international inequality** and what the Gini ratio shows. If for simplicity of exposition we use the World Bank's threefold classification of low-, middle- and high-income countries, we find that the low-income countries contain approximately 40 per cent of the world's population and receive only 3 per cent of the world's income; the middle-income countries contain 45 per cent of the world's population and receive 16 per cent of world income; and the rich industrialized countries contain 15 per cent of the world's population yet receive 81 per cent of world income. Income distribution data of this type can be represented graphically on a so-called **Lorenz curve diagram**, as shown in Figure 2.2.

The 45° line in Figure 2.2 represents a perfectly equal distribution of income across the population of countries. The bowed curve is the Lorenz curve, showing graphically the degree of inequality. To draw the curve, first rank countries, or groups of countries, in ascending order according to the ratio between the percentage of income they receive and the percentage population they contain; then cumulate the observations and plot on the diagram. Taking the data given above, our ranking is obviously low-income, middle-income and high-income. The *cumulative* distribution of income is 3/40, then 19/85 when the middle-income country figures are added to the first observation figures for the low-income countries, and 100/100 when the high-income country figures are added. Plotting these distributions gives the Lorenz curve shown in Figure 2.2. If historical data are available, changes in the distribution of income through time can be shown. It is possible, however, that two (or more) Lorenz curves may cross, precluding a definite conclusion as to whether the distribution has narrowed or widened from a visual inspection of the curves alone. In this case a more precise measure of distribution is required. One measure is to express the area enclosed between the Lorenz curve and the 45° line as a ratio of the total area under the 45° line. This is the **Gini ratio**, which varies from 0 (complete equality) to 1 (complete inequality).

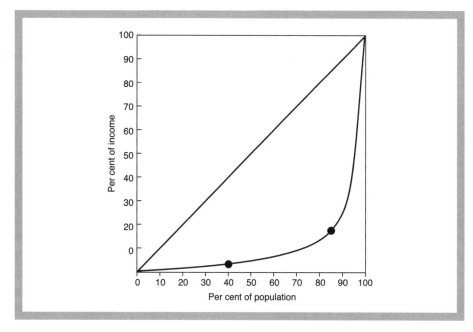

Figure 2.2 Lorenz curve diagram

The question now is: what has been happening to the international distribution of income over time? Is inequality increasing or decreasing? The answer depends on the measure of inequality taken; and also seems to depend on whether the per capita income of countries is measured in US dollars at the official rate of exchange, or in terms of purchasing power parity (PPP) (i.e. what a dollar will buy in the individual country concerned). There is no doubt that the **range** or absolute gap between the very richest and the very poorest countries has been increasing over time and also the **relative** income gap. According to Easterlin (2000), in 1820 the income ratio between the richest and poorest countries was approximately 3:1. For example, average per capita income in Great Britain in 1820 was roughly $1765 (measured at 1990 prices) compared to $523 in China. Now the ratio of average income in the richest and poorest country is 380! But while some countries have fallen behind the richest, others have caught up, which is why the Gini ratio is a more appropriate measure of distribution because it exploits the information for all countries.

There has been a mass of recent studies measuring and summarizing what has been happening to international inequality since the 1950s, e.g. Norwegian Institute of International Affairs (2000), Maddison (2003), Ghose (2004), Wade (2004), Sutcliffe (2004), Svedberg (2004), which reach the following conclusions:

■ International inequality measured by the Gini ratio, giving equal weight to each country, has stayed the same or increased slightly, but certainly hasn't fallen (the Gini ratio is about 0.55).

■ International inequality measured by the Gini ratio, with each country weighted by the size of its population, has decreased since 1980 because of the fast growth of China (which contains one-fifth of the world's population), but without China in the sample the weighted distribution of income is also more unequal.

■ Measuring living standards using PPP estimates of per capita income, the gap between the richest and poorest countries has increased, but the overall Gini ratio has declined slightly largely because of the fast growth of China. If China is removed from the sample, international inequality has stayed roughly the same as in 1965 (Norwegian Institute of International Affairs, 2000).

■ Taking a large sample of developing countries, only 20 per cent of countries have converged on the per capita incomes of developed countries, and that is why international inequality has increased (Ghose, 2004).

■ The ratio of the income of the top decile of the world's population to the bottom decile has increased, and the ratio of the average income per head of the 10 richest countries to the 10 poorest countries has increased from 36 in 1950 to 47 in 2001 (Sutcliffe, 2004).

Turning now to **global inequality**, what does the evidence show? Since global inequality also takes account of the distribution of income within countries (as well as the country's average per capita income), global inequality can be expected to be higher than international inequality, but by how much? The most comprehensive study is by Milanovic (2002). He derives measures of income distribution for 1988 and 1993 based on household survey data for 91 countries, covering 84 per cent of the world's population and 93 per cent of world GDP, measuring income at PPP rates of exchange. The Gini ratio was calculated as 0.63 in 1988 and 0.66 in 1993.[2] The ratio is higher than for international inequality, but not by much. Most of the global inequality (88 per cent) is the result of between-country inequality rather than within-country inequality. And the slight increase in global inequality between 1988 and 1993 was largely the result of increasing differences between countries rather than rising inequality within countries. In some countries inequality increased, but in others it decreased. Four major factors are cited as the cause of increased global inequality within this limited period: (1) the faster growth of Organization for Economic Cooperation and Development (OECD) countries than developing countries; (2) faster population growth in developing countries than in OECD countries; (3) slow growth of output in rural China, India and Africa, and (4) the widening gap between rural and urban China.

The general conclusion must be that however the distribution of income is measured, there is a huge development gap in the world economy between rich and poor countries and between rich and poor people. This development gap naturally extends into other aspects of human welfare such as health; nutrition; life expectancy; education; employment opportunities etc., as we shall come to see later in this chapter and in Chapter 3. Before this, however, we must discuss some technical problems concerning the measurement and comparability of per capita income across countries, and the measurement of poverty itself.

THE MEASUREMENT AND COMPARABILITY OF PER CAPITA INCOME

When using per capita income (PCY) figures to measure poverty, to classify countries into rich and poor and to compare the rate of development in different countries over time, the difficulties of measuring real per capita income and real living standards between countries must be continually borne in mind. There are two issues to discuss. The first concerns the problems associated with national income accounting, particularly in developing countries. The second is the problem of converting each country's per capita income in *domestic* currency into a common unit of account (that is, the US dollar) so as to be able to make meaningful international comparisons of living standards. This leads to the topic of **purchasing-power parity** (**PPP**) estimates of PCY.

Turning first to national income accounting, the first point to bear in mind is that only goods that are produced and then sold in the market are included in the value of national income, measured by either the output or the expenditure method. Much output in developing countries never reaches the market, particularly in the rural sector where production is for subsistence purposes. If no allowance is made for the subsistence sector, this will bias downwards the calculation of national income, and therefore PCY. This point also implies that any long-term growth estimates will have an upward bias as a result of the extension of the money economy and the shift of economic activities from the household and subsistence sector to the market place. Furthermore, if no allowance is made for the subsistence sector in some countries, it may be misleading to compare periods in these countries' history and to compare growth rates between countries. Part of the observed trend of faster GDP growth in developing countries over the last 50 years may be partly a statistical illusion arising from the changing balance between the informal subsistence sector and the modern exchange sector.

Growth rates may also be biased upwards by using prices as weights when compiling national income totals from the output statistics of different sectors of the economy (unless the weights are revised frequently), since goods with high prices, which subsequently fall, are usually the fastest growing. This is more of a danger in developing countries than in developed countries because of their less sophisticated accounting techniques, the greater difficulty in revising price weights, and the more widespread introduction of new goods with high initial prices.

A consideration of prices is also necessary when deciding what price index to use as a deflator of money national income in order to obtain an index of *real* income. The task of converting money income statistics into real income raises all the difficulties, not peculiar to developing countries, connected with the use of index numbers, such as which base year to take, how to take account of changes in the quality of products, which weighting system to employ, and so on. These are conceptual issues to be sorted out by the national income statistician rather than by the development economist, but it is important for the economist to know how figures for real national income, or per capita income, have been arrived at prior to analysis.

But apart from the problems of bias and choice of price deflator, there is the sheer practical difficulty of measuring money national income in a rural economy where communications are bad, illiteracy rife, and many of the goods produced and consumed are not exchanged for money. Differences in the extent of the subsistence economy between developing countries, and differences in the ease and difficulty of collecting data, may markedly influence estimates of national income, and therefore of per capita income differences, between these countries and the rest of the world. Attempts are now being made in developing countries to make some allowances for production that never reaches the market place, but the estimates are likely to be subject to a wide margin of error.

Some testimony to the role that the subsistence sector must play in the economies of most developing countries is provided by the inconceivability that 60 per cent of the world's population could remain alive on the equivalent of $1,000 per annum. But this is not the whole story.

PURCHASING POWER PARITY (PPP)

The other part of the story, and probably the major part, concerns the understatement of living standards in developing countries when their national incomes measured in local currencies are converted into US dollars (as the common unit of account) at the official rate of exchange. If the US dollar is used as the unit of account, the national per capita income of country X in US dollars is given by

$$\frac{\text{GNP}_X}{\text{Population}} \div \text{Exchange rate}$$

For example, if the GNP of country X is 100 billion rupees, its population is 5 million, and there are 10 rupees to the dollar, then the per capita income of country X in dollars is

$$\frac{100 \text{ billion}}{5 \text{ million}} \div 10 = \$2,000$$

But if the living standards of the two countries are to be compared by this method, it must be assumed that 10 rupees in country X buys the same living standard as $1 in the United States. It is well known, however, that official exchange rates between two countries' currencies are not good measures of the PPP between countries, especially between countries at different levels of development. The reason is this: exchange rates are largely determined by the supply of and demand for currencies based on goods and assets that are traded, the prices of which tend to be equalized internationally. PPP, however, depends not only on the prices of traded goods, but also on the prices of non-traded goods, which are largely determined by unit labour costs, and these tend to be lower the poorer the country. As a general rule, it can be said that the lower the level of development and the poorer the country, the lower the ratio of the price of non-traded goods to traded goods and the more the use of the official exchange rate will *understate* the living standards of the developing country measured in US dollars.

Let us give a simple example. The motor car is an internationally traded good. Suppose that the dollar price of a particular model of car is $10,000 and there are 10 rupees to the dollar. Ignoring transport costs, tariffs and so on, the price of the car in India will be $10,000 × 10 = 100,000 rupees, otherwise a profit will be made by dealers buying in the cheapest market and selling in the most expensive. The forces of demand and supply (and arbitrage) will equalize the price of traded goods. But let us now consider a non-traded good such as a haircut. Suppose a haircut in the United States costs $10. At the official exchange rate of 10 rupees to the dollar, a haircut in India should be 100 rupees. But suppose that in fact it is only 25 rupees. This would mean that as far as haircuts are concerned, the value of the rupee is underestimated by a factor of four.

The PPP rate of exchange for haircuts alone is $10 \div 25$ rupees, or $1 = 2.5$ rupees. If the national income of country X measured in rupees was divided by 2.5 instead of 10, the national income of country X in dollars, and therefore PCY in dollars, would now be four times higher: $8,000 per head instead of $2,000 per head as in the example above.

As development proceeds the ratio of the price of non-traded goods to traded goods tends to rise as wage levels in the non-traded goods sector rise but productivity growth is slow – slower than in the traded goods sector. **To make meaningful international comparisons of income and living standards, therefore, what is required is a measure of PPP, or a *real* exchange rate, between countries.**

There are several methods of constructing PPP ratios in order to make binary comparisons (one country with another) or 'multilateral' comparisons in which the currency of any one of a group of countries can act as the unit of account without altering the ratios of living standards between countries.

The most common way of constructing a PPP ratio between two countries is to revalue the national incomes of the two countries by selecting a comparable basket of goods and services in each country and estimating the purchasing-power equivalent of each item in country A relative to country B. Thus if P_{ia} is the price of item i in country A and P_{ib} is the price of item i in country B, the purchasing-power equivalent of item i in country A relative to country B is P_{ia}/P_{ib}. By extending this calculation to all goods and applying the price ratios to the average quantities consumed of each item in the two countries, we obtain a formula for the overall purchasing-power equivalent in country A relative to country B:

$$\frac{\sum_i Q_i P_{ia}}{\sum_i Q_i P_{ib}}$$

where Q_i is the geometric mean of the quantities of each good consumed in the two countries. The purchasing-power-equivalent ratio can then be used to convert one country's national income measured in local currency into another country's currency as the unit of account (for example the US dollar). To use our earlier example, suppose that the official exchange rate between the Indian rupee and the US dollar is 10:1, while the purchasing-power-equivalent ratio is 2.5:1. This means that converting the Indian national income into US dollars at the PPP rate will quadruple the amount received at the official exchange rate.

Irving Kravis and his associates (1975, 1978) have developed a method of making **multilateral** comparisons of real per capita incomes across countries by constructing world price ratios based on price and quantity data for over 100 commodity categories in over 100 countries. The international prices are then used to value quantities in each of the countries. The international prices and product values are expressed in international dollars (I$). An international dollar has the same overall purchasing power as a US dollar for national income as a whole, but relative prices for each country are relative to average world prices rather than US prices. This multilateral approach allows a direct comparison between any two countries using any country's currency as the unit of account.

In this method, the **purchasing-power parity rate of exchange (PPPR)** is equal to the official exchange rate divided by the extent to which conversion of PCY at the official exchange rate understates the true level of PCY when measured at international prices. Suppose, for example, there are 7 Kenyan shillings to 1 US dollar, and that the official exchange rate conversion understates the Kenyan PCY by 50 per cent when Kenyan national income is measured in international dollars. The PPPR of Kenyan shillings to US dollars is therefore PPPR = 7/1.5 = 4.66. That is, to compare living standards between Kenya and the United States, the real exchange rate of 4.66 ought to be used, not the official exchange rate of 7 shillings to one dollar.

The pioneering work of Kravis is now regularly extended and updated by his collaborators, Summers and Heston, who have produced international comparisons of price levels and real per capita incomes at international prices for all the major countries in the world since 1950, which can be compared with the World Bank estimates of per capita incomes based on official rates of exchange with the US dollar (see, for example, Summers and Heston, 1988, 1991).

The difference between estimates of PCY measured at the official exchange rate and PPP estimates of PCY is shown in Table 2.1 (p. 24). By comparing the figures and ranks in columns 2 and 3, it can be seen that the difference is quite dramatic, and in general the difference is greater the poorer the country. In India, for example, the PPP estimate of PCY is $2650 compared with an estimated $470 at the official exchange rate. In Kenya the figure is $1010 compared with $360.

In the high-income countries, however, there is hardly any difference between the two estimates. Norway enjoys the highest standard of living in the world, with the US a close second using the PPP method.

PER CAPITA INCOME AS AN INDEX OF DEVELOPMENT

Now let us turn to the question of the use of per capita income figures as an index of development and for making a distinction between developed and developing countries, as well as between rich and poor. While there may be an association between poverty and underdevelopment and riches and development, there are a number of reasons why some care must be taken when using per capita income figures alone as a criterion of development (unless underdevelopment is *defined* as poverty and development as riches). Apart from the difficulty of measuring income in many countries and the difficulty of making intercountry comparisons, using a single per capita income figure to separate developed from developing countries is inevitably somewhat arbitrary, as it ignores such factors as the distribution of income within countries, differences in development potential and other physical indicators of the quality of life. It is not so much a question of whether or not low-income countries should be labelled 'underdeveloped' or 'developing', but what income level should be used as the criterion for separating the developed from the developing countries, and whether all high-income countries should be labelled 'developed'. In many ways it should be the *nature* and *characteristics* of the countries that determine which income level should be used as the dividing line. It also makes sense to categorize separately the oil-rich countries, which have high per capita incomes but cannot be regarded as developed by the criteria discussed in Chapter 1.

Within the countries outside the industrialized bloc, the per capita income level dividing the low- and middle-income countries is arbitrary, but none is fully industrialized and all are 'developing' in this sense. Acronyms abound to describe the different stages of development. Perhaps the most amusing set is attributable to the Brazilian economist Roberto Campos, who distinguishes five categories of countries: the HICs, PICs, NICs, MICs and DICs. These stand for hardly industrialized countries, partly industrialized countries, newly industrialized countries, mature industrialized countries and decadent industrialized countries! The HICs and the PICs would certainly cover all the low-income countries and at least the lower half of the middle-income countries. The NICs cover most of the upper half of the middle-income countries – Brazil, Mexico, Hong Kong and Singapore being prime examples. The MICs and DICs cover most of those countries classified as 'industrial market economies', with the exception of Ireland, New Zealand and Australia, which have become rich through agriculture.

But bearing in mind the arbitrariness of per capita income, it is still very convenient to have a readily available and easily understandable criterion for classifying countries, and perhaps per capita income is the best single index we have. It also has one positive advantage, namely that it focuses on the *raison d'être* of development: raising living standards and eradicating poverty. And in the last resort per capita income is not a bad proxy for the social and economic structure of societies. If developing countries are defined on the basis of a per capita income level so as to include most of the countries of Asia, Africa and Latin America, striking similarities are found between the characteristics and development obstacles of many of the countries in these continents. These include:

- A high proportion of the labour force engaged in agriculture but low agricultural productivity
- A high proportion of domestic expenditure on food and necessities
- An export trade dominated by primary products and an import trade dominated by manufactured goods
- A low level of technology
- A high birth rate coupled with a falling death rate
- Savings undertaken by a small percentage of the population.

There are, of course, some countries that on a per capita income basis are classified as developed and possess most of the above-mentioned characteristics (e.g. some oil-producing countries), but the exceptions are few, and the reverse of this situation is almost inconceivable. Also these countries have many social problems in common, such as growing unemployment in urban areas, inegalitarian income distributions, and poor health and standards of education – about which we shall say more later.

In general, therefore, we conclude that per capita income may be used as a starting point for classifying *levels* of development, and can certainly be used to identify the *need* for development. The only major reservation that we shall have to consider later concerns the case of geographically dual economies, where an aggregate per capita income figure can disguise as great a need for the development of a sizeable region within the country as the need for the development of the country itself.

There is a difference, however, between using per capita income as a guideline for classifying countries into developed or underdeveloped at a point *in time* and using the growth of per capita income as an index of development *over time*. The difficulty of using per capita income for the latter purpose is the obvious one that if, in a particular period, per capita income did not grow because population growth matched the growth of a country's total income, one would be forced into the odd position of denying that a country had developed even though its national product had increased. This is an inherent weakness of linking the concept of development to a measure of living standards.

This leads on to the distinction between **growth** and **development**. Development without growth is hardly conceivable, but growth is possible without development. The upswing of the trade cycle is the most obvious example of the possibility of growth without development; and examples of abortive 'take-offs' are not hard to find where countries have grown rapidly for a short time and then reverted to relative stagnation. Historically, Argentina is a case in point. On the other hand development is hardly possible without growth; but development is possible, as we have suggested, without a rise in per capita income. It would be a strange, rather purposeless, type of development, however, that left per capita income unchanged, unless the stationary per capita income was only temporary and a strong foundation was being laid for progress in the future. For the ultimate rationale of development must be to improve living standards and welfare, and while an increase in measured per capita income may not be a sufficient condition for an increase in individual welfare, it is a necessary condition in the absence of radical institutional innovations, such as an increase in public goods.

An increase in income is not a sufficient condition for an increase in welfare, because an increase in income can involve costs as well as benefits. It may have been generated at the expense of leisure or by the production of goods not immediately consumable. **If development is looked upon as a means of improving the welfare of present generations, probably the best index to take would be consumption per man-hour worked**. This index, in contrast to an index of per capita income, focuses directly on the immediate utility derivable from consumption goods in relation to the disutility of the work effort involved in their production.

MEASURING POVERTY

The World Bank defines poverty as the inability of people to attain a minimum standard of living.[3] This definition gives rise to three questions. How do we measure the standard of living? What is meant by a *minimum* standard of living? How can we express the overall extent of poverty in a single measure?

The most obvious measure of living standards is an individual's (or household's) real income or expenditure (with an allowance made for output produced for own consumption). The same level of real income and expenditure in different countries, however, may be associated with different levels of nutrition, life expectancy, infant mortality, schooling and so on, which must be considered as an integral part of 'the standard of living'. Measures of living standards based on per capita income, therefore, may need to be supplemented by further measures that include these other variables. We discuss later the attempt by the United Nations Development Programme (UNDP) to construct a **Human Poverty Index** and a **Human Development Index**, which take some of these factors into account.

To separate the poor from the not so poor, an arbitrary per capita income figure has to be taken that is sufficient to provide a minimum acceptable level of consumption. There are two main ways of setting a consumption poverty line in order to measure poverty and make comparison across countries: the **PPP method** and the **food energy method**. As we saw above, a country's PPP is defined as the number of units of the country's currency required to buy the same amount of goods and services in the domestic market as a dollar in the United States. The World Bank publishes the PPP levels of per capita income for all countries (see Table 2.1). For the measurement of poverty, to give an example, the PPP poverty line could be set at, say, $30 per month or $360 per annum. By definition, people on this PPP poverty line in any country have the purchasing power to obtain the same level of consumption of any person on the poverty line in any other country. But the composition of the consumption bundle is very likely to differ. The PPP poverty line is not explicitly linked to nutritional intakes derived from different consumption bundles, so there are likely to be intercountry differences in nutrition on the PPP poverty line.

The **food energy method** of setting a consumption poverty line is one way of dealing with this problem by defining a minimum internationally agreed calorie intake line, and converting consumption bundles into calorie intakes using the nutritional values of consumption goods (with non-food goods having a zero value). The problem here, however, is that consumers in different countries may choose different combinations of food and other goods which then require different incomes to meet nutritional requirements. Indeed the nature of the society and the stage of development reached may *require* different combinations. What are regarded as optional extras in some countries may be necessities in others. The United Nation's Food and Agriculture Organisation (FAO) defines undernourishment as 'food intake that is continuously insufficient to meet dietary energy requirements.'

A consumption-based poverty line can therefore be thought of as comprising two elements: an objective measure of the expenditure necessary to buy a minimum level of nutrition; and a subjective additional amount that varies from country to country, reflecting the cost to individuals of participating in the everyday life of society.

All this is in theory. In practice, to measure the extent of absolute poverty in the Third World, the World Bank takes the figure of $1 a day. For details on how this poverty line is calculated, and its historical antecedents, see Case example 2.1. Once the poverty line has been decided, the simplest way to measure the amount of poverty is by the **head count index** which simply adds up the number of people who fall below the poverty line (sometimes expressed as a proportion of the total population). By this measure, the World Bank has calculated that the number of poor people in the developing countries is nearly 1.2 billion. The trend in numbers, and the distribution of the poor across regions, is shown in Table 2.2. It can be seen that, since 1987, the trend in numbers has been fairly static. Poverty in South Asia and Africa has been increasing, but this increase has been offset by falls in East Asia and Pacific. Poverty is also most concentrated in South Asia and Africa where more than 40 per cent of the population are living on less than $1 per day.

Measuring Income Poverty, 1899 and 1998

In a classic study first published in 1901, Seebohm Rowntree calculated that 10 per cent of the population of the English city of York in 1899 was living in poverty (below minimum needed expenditures). The World Bank calculates that a quarter of the population of the developing world – about 1.2 billion people – is now living in poverty (below $1 a day). These two calculations of income poverty are separated by a century and have very different coverage. Nevertheless, the basic concepts and methods they embody have strong similarities.

Rowntree's approach

Rowntree's method was to conduct a survey covering nearly every working-class family in York to collect information on earnings and expenditures. He then defined poverty as a level of total earnings insufficient to obtain the minimum necessities for the maintenance of 'merely physical efficiency', including food, rent, and other items. He calculated that for a family of five – a father, mother, and three children – the minimum weekly expenditure to maintain physical efficiency was 21 shillings, 8 pence; he proposed other amounts for families of different size and composition. Comparing these poverty lines with family earnings, he arrived at his poverty estimate.

The World Bank's approach

The World Bank has been estimating global income poverty figures since 1990. The latest round of estimation, in October 1999, used new sample survey data and price information to obtain comparable figures for 1987, 1990, 1993, 1996, and 1998 (the figures for 1998 are preliminary estimates).

Consumption   Poverty estimates are based on consumption or income data collected through household surveys. Data for 96 countries, from a total of 265 nationally representative surveys, corresponding to 88 per cent of the developing world's people, are now available.

   Consumption is conventionally viewed as the preferred welfare indicator, for practical reasons of reliability and because consumption is thought better to capture long-run welfare levels than current income. Where survey data were available on incomes but not on consumption, consumption was estimated by multiplying all incomes by the share of aggregate private consumption in national income based on national accounts data. This procedure, unchanged from past exercises, scales back income to obtain consumption but leaves the distribution unchanged.

Prices   To compare consumption levels across countries, estimates of price levels are needed, and the World Bank's purchasing power parity (PPP) estimates for 1993 were used. These estimates are based on new price data generated by the International

▶

Comparison Programme (ICP), which now covers 110 countries, up from 64 in 1985, and a more comprehensive set of commodities.

Poverty lines   The 1990 calculations of the international poverty lines had to be updated using 1993 price data and the 1993 PPP estimates. That line is equal to $1.08 a day in 1993 PPP terms (referred to as '$1 a day'). This line has a similar purchasing power to the $1 a day line in 1985 PPP prices, in terms of the command over domestic goods.

Country-specific poverty lines   The $1 a day poverty estimates described here are useful only as indicators of global progress, not to assess progress at the country level or to guide country policy and programme formulation. Country-specific poverty lines, reflecting what it means to be poor in each country's situation and not affected by international price comparisons, are used in country-level analysis.

Source: Based on *World Development Report 2000/2001: Attacking Poverty* (New York: Oxford University Press, 2000).

One weakness of the head count index, however, is that it ignores the *extent* to which the poor fall below the poverty line, so that crude comparisons between countries, or over time, may be misleading. To overcome this weakness, the concept of the **poverty gap** may be used. This measures the transfer of income required to bring the income of every poor person up to the poverty line, or the aggregate income shortfall of the poor as a percentage of aggregate consumption. It is interesting to note that despite the massive number of people in absolute poverty, the transfer needed to leave everybody above the poverty line is relatively small – only about 3 per cent of total consumption in the developing countries as a whole. The World Bank calculated for Latin America that 'raising all the poor of the continent to just above the poverty line would cost only 0.7 per cent of regional GDP – the approximate equivalent of a 2 per cent income tax on the wealthiest fifth of the population'.[4]

The focus of the World Bank is now very much on poverty eradication. When Robert McNamara was President of the World Bank in the 1970s, he defined absolute poverty as 'a condition of life so degraded by disease, illiteracy, and malnutrition and squalor, as to deny its victims basic human necessities – [a condition] so limited as to prevent the realisation of the potential of the genes with which one was born'. In May 1992 the then President of the World Bank, Lewis Preston, declared that poverty reduction will be 'the benchmark by which our performance as a development institution will be measured'. And in the *World Development Report 2000/2001*, the President, James Wolfensohn, wrote: 'poverty amidst plenty is the world's greatest challenge. We at the Bank have made it our mission to fight poverty with passion and professionalism, putting it at the centre of all the work that we do.'

Table 2.2 Income poverty, by region, selected years, 1987–98

Region	People living on less than $1 a day (million)				
	1987	1990	1993	1996	1998
East Asia and Pacific	417.5	452.4	431.9	265.1	278.3
Excluding China	114.1	92.0	83.5	55.1	65.1
Europe and Central Asia	1.1	7.1	18.3	23.8	24.0
Latin America and the Caribbean	63.7	73.8	70.8	76.0	78.2
Middle East and North Africa	9.3	5.7	5.0	5.0	5.5
South Asia	474.4	495.1	505.1	531.7	522.0
Sub-Saharan Africa	217.2	242.3	273.3	289.0	290.9
Total	1,183.2	1,276.4	1,304.3	1,190.6	1,198.9
Excluding China	879.8	915.9	955.9	980.5	985.7

Region	Share of population living on less than $1 a day (per cent)				
	1987	1990	1993	1996	1998
East Asia and Pacific	26.6	27.6	25.2	14.9	15.3
Excluding China	23.9	18.5	15.9	10.0	11.3
Europe and Central Asia	0.2	1.6	4.0	5.1	5.1
Latin America and the Caribbean	15.3	16.8	15.3	15.6	15.6
Middle East and North Africa	4.3	2.4	1.9	1.8	1.9
South Asia	44.9	44.0	42.4	42.3	40.0
Sub-Saharan Africa	46.6	47.7	49.7	48.5	46.3
Total	28.3	29.0	28.1	24.5	24.0
Excluding China	28.5	28.1	27.7	27.0	26.2

Source: *World Development Report 2000/2001* (New York: Oxford University Press, 2000)

MEETING THE MILLENNIUM POVERTY REDUCTION TARGET

To meet the Millennium Goal of halving the proportion of people living in absolute poverty by 2015 compared to the level in 1990 requires a sustained growth in the level of per capita income. To calculate the growth required, the elasticity of the poverty rate with respect to the level of per capita income needs to be known. This can be estimated using the equation below:

$$\log P_i = a + b \log PCY_i \tag{2.1}$$

Where P_i is the headcount poverty rate for country i, PCY_i is the level of per capita income, and b is the elasticity of the poverty rate. Besley and Burgess (2003) calculate this elasticity for developing countries as a whole and for different continents. The results are shown in Table 2.3. The elasticity for the whole sample of countries is 0.73 which means that the poverty rate declines by 0.73 per cent for every one per cent increase in per capita income (given the distribution of income). To reduce the poverty rate by 50 percent (say from 50 per cent to 25 per cent) would therefore require income growth of approximately 70 per cent. The annual growth of per capita income can then be calculated. The rate calculated for developing countries as a whole is 3.8 per cent per annum compared

Table 2.3 Growth and poverty across the globe, 1990–2015

	Whole Sample	East Asia and Pacific	Eastern Europe & Central Asia	Latin America and Caribbean	Middle East and North Africa	South Asia	Sub-Saharan Africa
Elasticity of poverty with respect to income per capita	−0.73	−1.00	−1.14	−0.73	−0.72	−0.59	−0.49
Annual growth rate needed to halve world poverty by 2015 (%)	3.8	2.7	2.4	3.8	3.8	4.7	5.6
Historical growth 1960–1990 (%)	1.7	3.3	2.0	1.3	4.3	1.9	0.2

Source: T. Besley and R. Burgess, 'Halving Global Poverty', *Journal of Economic Perspectives*, Summer 2003.

to the historical growth of only 1.7 per cent per annum 1960–90. In South Asia and Africa, the required growth rates are much higher, and even further out of line with historical experience. The depressing conclusion to be reached is that it is unlikely that most countries will achieve the millennium poverty reduction target – the required growth rates are too high – unless poverty is also tackled at the 'grass-roots' by income and wealth redistribution and institutional change. This is the World Bank's new approach to tackling poverty.

TACKLING POVERTY FROM THE 'GRASS ROOTS'

Poverty not only means low income and consumption, and low levels of human development in terms of education and health care, but also feelings of powerlessness, vulnerability and fear because poor people are not free, and are exposed to greater risk, living on the margin of subsistence.

What it means to be poor is well illustrated from the World Bank's study *The Voices of the Poor*, which asked 60,000 poor people in 60 countries to articulate their feelings about their physical and mental state. The answers are contained in Case example 2.2, which are both moving and revealing. Feelings of helplessness, humiliation and lack of self-esteem are paramount.

The World Bank proposes a three-pronged strategy for poverty reduction: **promoting opportunity**; **facilitating empowerment** and **enhancing security**.

Promoting opportunity is partly about expanding economic opportunities for poor people through the process of economic growth, and partly about expanding the asset base of poor people and increasing the return on those assets. The major causes of individual poverty can be linked to a lack of assets and/or a low return on assets. Important assets to enable people to grow out of poverty include (1) natural assets, such as land; (2) human assets, such as education and health; (3) financial assets, including access to credit, and (4) social assets, such as networks of contacts. The return on assets once acquired depends on the institutional framework of a country, the performance of the economy, and what is happening in the world economy. The state has a role to play in expanding poor people's assets because markets do not work well for poor people owing to lack of access, power and collateral. The state can help in three major ways: first by using its power to redistribute resources; secondly through institutional reforms to deliver services more effectively, particularly in the fields of health and education; and thirdly by facilitating the engagement of poor people in programmes which help them to acquire assets, such as land and credit.

Case example 2.2

The Voices of the Poor

Poor people in 60 countries were asked to analyse and share their ideas of well-being (a good experience of life) and 'ill-being' (a bad experience of life).

Well-being was variously described as happiness, harmony, peace, freedom from anxiety, and peace of mind. In Russia people say, 'Well-being is a life free from daily worries about lack of money.' In Bangladesh, 'to have a life free from anxiety'. In Brazil, 'not having to go through so many rough spots.'

People describe ill-being as lack of material things, as bad experiences, and as bad feelings about oneself. A group of young men in Jamaica ranks lack of self-confidence as the second biggest impact of poverty: 'Poverty means we don't believe in self, we hardly travel out of the community – so frustrated, just locked up in a house all day.'

Although the nature of ill-being and poverty varies among locations and people – something that policy responses must take into account – there is a striking commonality across countries. Not surprisingly, material well-being turns out to be very important. Lack of food, shelter, and clothing is mentioned everywhere as critical. In Kenya a man says: 'Don't ask me what poverty is because you have met it outside my house. Look at the house and count the number of holes. Look at my utensils and the clothes I am wearing. Look at everything and write what you see. What you see is poverty.'

Alongside the material, physical well-being features prominently in the characterizations of poverty. And the two meld together when lack of food leads to ill health – or when ill health leads to an inability to earn income. People speak about the importance of looking well fed. In Ethiopia poor people say, 'We are skinny', 'We are deprived and pale', and speak of life that 'makes you older than your age'.

Security of income is also closely tied to health. But insecurity extends beyond ill health. Crime and violence are often mentioned by poor people. In Ethiopia women say, 'We live hour to hour,' worrying about whether it will rain. An Argentine says, 'You have work, and you are fine. If not, you starve. That's how it is.'

Two social aspects of ill-being and poverty also emerged. For many poor people, well-being means the freedom of choice and action and the power to control one's life. A young woman in Jamaica says that poverty is 'like living in jail, living in bondage, waiting to be free'.

▶

Linked to these feelings are definitions of well-being as social well-being and comments on the stigma of poverty. As an old woman in Bulgaria says, 'To be well means to see your grandchildren happy and well dressed and to know that your children have settled down; to be able to give them food and money whenever they come to see you, and not to ask them for help and money.' A Somali proverb captures the other side: 'Prolonged sickness and persistent poverty cause people to hate you.'

The following quotations are an illustration of what living in poverty means:

Certainly our farming is little; all the products, things bought from stores, are expensive; it is hard to live, we work and earn little money, buy few things or products; products are scarce, there is no money and we feel poor. (From a discussion group of poor men and women, Ecuador)

We face a calamity when my husband falls ill. Our life comes to a halt until he recovers and goes back to work. (Poor woman, Zawyet Sultan, Egypt)

Poverty is humiliation, the sense of being dependent on them, and of being forced to accept rudeness, insults, and indifference when we seek help. (Poor woman, Latvia)

Source: World Bank, *World Development Report 2000/2001: Attacking Poverty* (New York: Oxford University Press, 2000).

A growing economy is absolutely crucial for poverty reduction. Poverty cannot be reduced in a stagnant economy. There is a strong negative association across countries between the average growth of income and consumption and the *share* of people living on less than $1 per day. A 1 percentage point growth of income above the average is associated with a 2 percentage point reduction in the share of people living in poverty.

On the other hand, similar rates of growth of countries are associated with different rates of poverty reduction. This is the result of existing inequalities in the distribution of income, assets and access to opportunities. Growth is much more effective in reducing poverty where the income distribution is more equal than where there are big inequalities. The World Bank estimates that when inequality is low, growth reduces poverty by nearly twice as much as when inequality is high. If income inequality remains unchanged in Latin America and sub-Saharan Africa, the Bank's poverty targets will not be met even if per capita income grows at 4 per cent per annum to the year 2015 (which itself is optimistic).

Research at the World Bank by Dollar and Kraay (2000) taking 80 countries over the last 40 years shows that growth benefits the poor as much as the rich. On average, incomes of the poor rise one-for-one with incomes overall. This means that growth itself is not a cause of income inequality. Nor is there evidence that inequality promotes growth because some rich people are able to save and invest more. If anything, unequal societies impair growth through inefficiency and political instability.

Facilitating empowerment is a new departure in the thinking of the World Bank compared to its 1990 *Report*. Empowering poor people means strengthening the participation of poor people in decision-making; eliminating various forms of discrimination – ethnic, religious, sexual – and making state institutions more accountable and responsive to poor people. The great challenge here is to tackle the institutional structures of poor countries that continue to marginalize, discriminate against, and disenfranchise vulnerable sections of society. The law, the church, bureaucrats and local elites, and customs and traditions, all play a part. The state has a role to play in helping to empower people by (1) curbing corruption and harassment, and using the power of the state to redistribute resources for actions benefiting the poor; (2) ensuring that the legal system is fair and accessible to the poor; (3) making sure that the delivery of local services is not captured by local elites; (4) encouraging the participation of poor people in the political process; and (5) galvanizing political support for public action against poverty.

Enhancing security means reducing poor people's vulnerability to the various forms of insecurity that affect people's lives such as economic shocks; natural disasters; crop failures; ill health; violence; wars, etc. and helping people to cope with these adverse shocks when they occur. The wide range of risks that poor people are exposed to is highlighted in Case example 2.3. This vulnerability to risk requires a range of insurance mechanisms for managing risk such as: health and old-age insurance; unemployment insurance and workforce programmes; social funds and cash transfers; microfinance programmes; insurance against crop failures and price instability, and so on.

The World Bank points out, however, that promoting opportunities, facilitating empowerment, and enhancing security are *necessary* conditions for tackling poverty, but not *sufficient* conditions in an interdependent, global economy. International action is also required to help poor people in at least five ways:

- Promoting global financial stability and reducing the risks of economic crisis
- Opening up markets (particularly in developed countries) to the goods of poor countries
- Encouraging the production of international public goods that benefit poor people; for example, the control of disease; agricultural research; the dissemination of knowledge
- More foreign aid and debt relief
- Giving a greater voice to poor countries and peoples in the global forums and multilateral institutions of the world such as the World Bank, IMF and WTO.

Case example **2.3**

Poor People's Exposure to Risk

Poor people are exposed to a wide range of risks.

Illness and injury

Poor people often live and work in environments that expose them to greater risk of illness or injury, and they have less access to health care. Their health risks are strongly connected to the availability of food, which is affected by almost all the risks the poor face (natural disasters, wars, harvest failures, and food price

▶

fluctuations). Communicable diseases are concentrated among the poor, with respiratory infections the leading cause of death. A recent study of poverty in India found that the poor are 4.5 times as likely to contract tuberculosis as the rich and twice as likely to lose a child before the age of two.

Illness and injury in the household have both direct costs (for prevention, care and cure) and opportunity costs (lost income or schooling while ill). The timing, duration and frequency of illness also affect its impact. A study of South India found that households can compensate for an illness during the slack agricultural season, but illness during the peak season leads to a heavy loss of income, especially on small farms, usually necessitating costly informal borrowing.

Old age

Many risks are associated with ageing: illness, social isolation, inability to continue working and uncertainty about whether transfers will provide an adequate living. The incidence of poverty among the elderly varies significantly. In most Latin American countries the proportion of people in poverty is lower for the elderly than for the population at large. In contrast, in many countries of the former Soviet Union the incidence of poverty is above average among the elderly, particularly among people 75 and older. Women, because of their longer life expectancy, constitute the majority of the elderly, and they tend to be more prone to poverty in old age than men. The number of elderly people in the developing world will increase significantly in coming decades with the rapid demographic transition.

Consultations with poor people show that income security is a prime concern of the elderly, followed closely by access to health services, suitable housing, and the quality of family and community life. Isolation, loneliness, and fear all too often mark old people's lives.

Crime and domestic violence

Crime and domestic violence reduce earnings and make it harder to escape poverty. While the rich can hire private security guards and fortify their homes, the poor have few means to protect themselves against crime. In São Paulo, Brazil, in 1992 the murder rate for adolescent males in poor neighbourhoods was 11 times that in wealthier ones. Poor people frequently voice their fear of violence and the resulting powerlessness. 'I do not know whom to trust, the police or the criminals.'

Crime also hurts poor people indirectly. Children exposed to violence may perform worse in school. A study of urban communities in Ecuador, Hungary, the Philippines and Zambia showed that difficult economic conditions lead to destruction of social capital as involvement in community organizations declines, informal ties among residents weaken, and gang violence, vandalism and crime increase. Violence and crime may thus deprive poor people of two of their best means of reducing vulnerability: human and social capital.

▶

Unemployment and other labour market risks

Labour market risks include unemployment, falling wages, and having to take up precarious and low-quality jobs in the informal sector as a result of macroeconomic crises or policy reform. The first workers to be laid off during cutbacks in public sector jobs are usually those with low skills, who then join the ranks of the urban poor, a pattern observed in Africa and Latin America during the structural adjustment reforms of the 1980s and early 1990s. The East Asian crisis also had pronounced effects on labour markets, with real wages and non-agricultural employment falling in all affected countries. As state enterprises in Eastern Europe and the countries of the former Soviet Union were privatized, poverty increased among displaced workers with low education and obsolete skills, not qualified to work in emerging industries.

Fluctuations in demand for labour often disproportionately affect women and young workers. Most public sector retrenchment programmes have affected women's employment more than men's, and women are more likely than men to work for small firms, which tend to be more sensitive to demand fluctuations. As incomes fall, poor households try to increase their labour market participation, especially for women and children.

Harvest failure and food price fluctuations

Weather-related uncertainties (mainly rainfall), plant disease and pests create harvest risk for all farmers, but technologies for reducing such risks (irrigation, pesticides, disease-resistant varieties) are less available in poor areas. In 1994–6 less than 20 per cent of all cropland was irrigated in low- and middle-income countries (only 4 per cent in Sub-Saharan Africa).

Fluctuations in food prices are a related risk. Since poor households spend a large part of their income on food, even small price increases can severely affect food intake. Households that meet their food needs through a subsistence agriculture are less vulnerable than households that have to buy all their food.

Liberalization of markets often boosts the price of staples – a benefit to small farmers if they are net sellers of food. Hurt are the urban poor and the landless rural poor, as net food buyers, and farmers who engage in seasonal switching, selling food after the harvest when food is plentiful and cheap and buying it when it is scarce and expensive. Where transport facilities are good, traders can step in and equalize prices over the year through arbitrage, but such infrastructure is lacking in many areas.

Source: World Bank, *World Development Report 2000/2001: Attacking Poverty* (Oxford: Oxford University Press, 2000).

HUMAN POVERTY INDEX AND HUMAN DEVELOPMENT INDEX

To overcome the limitation of taking a single measure of PCY as an index of development and the problem of using PCY as a measure of living standards, the United Nations Development Programme (UNDP) has developed two alternative indices by which to compare the level of development and the progress of countries: **the Human Development Index (HDI)** and the **Human Poverty Index (HPI)**. These indices give alternative measures of the economic well-being of nations that do not necessarily accord with the usual measure: the level of per capita income. As the UNDP says in its *Human Development Report* (2004) 'although GNP growth is absolutely necessary to meet all essential human objectives, countries differ in the way that they translate growth into human development'. The UNDP defines human development as 'a process of enlarging people's choices'. This depends not only on income but also on other social indicators such as life expectancy, education, literacy and health provision.

We consider first the Human Development Index because the UNDP uses this index to rank countries. The **Human Development Index** is based on three variables:

- Life expectancy at birth
- Educational attainment, measured by a combination of adult literacy (two-thirds weight) and combined primary, secondary and tertiary school enrolment ratios (one-third weight)
- Standard of living measured by real PCY at PPP.

These variables are shown in the first four columns of Table 2.4. To construct the index, fixed minimum and maximum values are taken for each of the variables. For life expectancy at birth the range is 25–85 years. For adult literacy the range is 0–100 per cent. For real per capita GDP the range is $100–40,000. For any component of the HDI, the individual indices can be computed according to the general formula:

$$\text{Index} = \frac{\text{Actual value} - \text{Minimum value}}{\text{Maximum value} - \text{Minimum value}} \tag{2.2}$$

The index thus ranges from 0 to 1. If the actual value of the variable is the minimum, the index is zero. If the actual value is equal to the maximum value, the index is one. Let us take the example of life expectancy in India (country 127). The life expectancy is 63.7 years, and if we put this value into (2.2) we get $(63.7 - 25)/(85 - 25) = 38.7/60 = 0.64$.[5]

The three indices are shown in columns (5), (6) and (7) of Table 2.4. The HDI is an average of the three indices and is given in column (8), with countries ranked from highest to lowest. The ranking of countries by HDI is then compared with the ranking by PCY in column (9). Among the developing countries, some are shown to have much higher HDIs than PCY, and vice versa. In the former category are countries such as Cuba, Jamaica, Philippines, and many countries of the former Soviet Union, while in the latter category are many of the oil-producing countries, such as Qatar, Saudi Arabia and Oman, and South Africa and Botswana.

Table 2.4 Human Development Index, 2002

High human development

HDI rank	Life expectancy at birth (years) 2002	Adult literacy rate (% ages 15 and above) 2002	Combined gross enrolment ratio for primary, secondary and tertiary schools (%) 2001/02	GDP per capita (PPP US$) 2002	Life expectancy index	Education index	GDP index	Human development index (HDI) value 2002	GDP per capita (PPP US$) rank minus HDI rank*
1 Norway	78.9		98	36,600	0.90	0.99	0.99	0.956	1
2 Sweden	80.0		114	26,050	0.92	0.99	0.93	0.946	19
3 Australia	79.1		113	28,260	0.90	0.99	0.94	0.946	9
4 Canada	79.3		95	29,480	0.90	0.98	0.95	0.943	5
5 Netherlands	78.3		99	29,100	0.89	0.99	0.95	0.942	6
6 Belgium	78.7		111	27,570	0.90	0.99	0.94	0.942	7
7 Iceland	79.7		90	29,750	0.91	0.96	0.95	0.941	1
8 United States	77.0		92	35,750	0.87	0.97	0.98	0.939	-4
9 Japan	81.5		84	26,940	0.94	0.94	0.93	0.938	6
10 Ireland	76.9		90	36,360	0.86	0.96	0.98	0.936	-7
11 Switzerland	79.1		88	30,010	0.90	0.95	0.95	0.936	-4
12 United Kingdom	78.1		113	26,150	0.88	0.99	0.93	0.936	8
13 Finland	77.9		106	26,190	0.88	0.99	0.93	0.935	6
14 Austria	78.5		91	29,220	0.89	0.96	0.95	0.934	-4
15 Luxembourg	78.3		75	61,190	0.89	0.91	1.00	0.933	-14
16 France	78.9		91	26,920	0.90	0.96	0.93	0.932	0
17 Denmark	76.6		96	30,940	0.86	0.98	0.96	0.932	-12
18 New Zealand	78.2		101	21,740	0.89	0.99	0.90	0.926	6
19 Germany	78.2		88	27,100	0.89	0.95	0.94	0.925	-5
20 Spain	79.2	97.7	92	21,460	0.90	0.97	0.90	0.922	5
21 Italy	78.7	98.5	82	26,430	0.89	0.93	0.93	0.920	-3
22 Israel	79.1	95.3	92	19,530	0.90	0.94	0.88	0.908	5
23 Hong Kong, China (SAR)	79.9	93.5	72	26,910	0.91	0.86	0.93	0.903	-6
24 Greece	78.2	97.3	86	18,720	0.89	0.95	0.87	0.902	5
25 Singapore	78.0	92.5	87	24,040	0.88	0.91	0.92	0.902	-3
26 Portugal	76.1	92.5	93	18,280	0.85	0.97	0.87	0.897	6
27 Slovenia	76.2	99.7	90	18,540	0.85	0.96	0.87	0.895	3
28 Korea, Rep. of	75.4	97.9	92	16,950	0.84	0.97	0.86	0.888	9
29 Barbados	77.1	99.7	88	15,290	0.87	0.95	0.84	0.888	11
30 Cyprus	78.2	96.8	74	18,360	0.89	0.89	0.87	0.883	1
31 Malta	78.3	92.6	77	17,640	0.89	0.87	0.86	0.875	3

#	Country									
32	Czech Republic	75.3	—	78	15,780	0.84	0.92	0.84	0.868	7
33	Negera Brunei Darussalam	76.2	93.9	73	19,210	0.85	0.87	0.88	0.867	−5
34	Argentina	74.1	97.0	94	10,880	0.82	0.96	0.78	0.853	14
35	Seychelles	72.7	91.9	85	18,232	0.80	0.90	0.87	0.853	−2
36	Estonia	71.6	99.8	96	12,260	0.78	0.98	0.80	0.853	10
37	Poland	73.8	99.7	90	10,560	0.81	0.96	0.78	0.850	13
38	Hungary	71.7	99.3	86	13,400	0.78	0.95	0.82	0.848	3
39	Saint Kitts and Nevis	70.0	97.8	97	12,420	0.75	0.98	0.80	0.844	6
40	Bahrain	73.9	88.5	79	17,170	0.81	0.85	0.86	0.843	−4
41	Lithuania	72.5	99.6	90	10,320	0.79	0.96	0.77	0.842	10
42	Slovakia	73.6	99.7	74	12,840	0.81	0.91	0.81	0.842	1
43	Chile	76.0	95.7	79	9,820	0.85	0.90	0.77	0.839	11
44	Kuwait	76.5	82.9	76	16,240	0.86	0.81	0.85	0.838	−6
45	Costa Rica	78.0	95.8	69	8,840	0.88	0.87	0.75	0.834	14
46	Uruguay	75.2	97.7	85	7,830	0.84	0.94	0.73	0.833	16
47	Qatar	72.0	84.2	82	19,844	0.78	0.83	0.88	0.833	−21
48	Croatia	74.1	98.1	73	10,240	0.82	0.90	0.77	0.830	4
49	United Arab Emirates	74.6	77.3	68	22,420	0.83	0.74	0.90	0.824	−26
50	Latvia	70.9	99.7	87	9,210	0.76	0.95	0.75	0.823	6
51	Bahamas	67.1	95.5	74	17,280	0.70	0.88	0.86	0.815	−16
52	Cuba	76.7	96.9	78	5,259	0.86	0.91	0.66	0.809	39
53	Mexico	73.3	90.5	74	8,970	0.81	0.85	0.75	0.802	5
54	Trinidad and Tobago	71.4	98.5	64	9,430	0.77	0.87	0.76	0.801	1
55	Antigua and Barbuda	73.9	85.8	69	10,920	0.82	0.80	0.78	0.800	−8

Medium human development

#	Country									
56	Bulgaria	70.9	98.6	76	7,130	0.77	0.91	0.71	0.796	10
57	Russian Federation	66.7	99.6	88	8,230	0.69	0.95	0.74	0.795	3
58	Libyan Arab Jamahiriya	72.6	81.7	97	7,570	0.79	0.87	0.72	0.794	6
59	Malaysia	73.0	88.7	70	9,120	0.80	0.83	0.75	0.793	−2
60	Macedonia, TFYR	73.5	96.0	70	6,470	0.81	0.87	0.70	0.793	15
61	Panama	74.6	92.3	73	6,170	0.83	0.86	0.69	0.791	18
62	Belarus	69.9	99.7	88	5,520	0.75	0.95	0.67	0.790	24
63	Tonga	68.4	98.8	82	6,850	0.72	0.93	0.71	0.787	5
64	Mauritius	71.9	84.3	69	10,810	0.78	0.79	0.78	0.785	−15
65	Albania	73.6	98.7	69	4,830	0.81	0.89	0.65	0.781	31
66	Bosnia and Herzegovina	74.0	94.6	64	5,970	0.82	0.84	0.68	0.781	15
67	Suriname	71.0	94.0	74	6,590	0.77	0.87	0.70	0.780	6
68	Venezuela	73.6	93.1	71	5,380	0.81	0.86	0.67	0.778	21
69	Romania	70.5	97.3	68	6,560	0.76	0.88	0.70	0.778	5
70	Ukraine	69.5	99.6	84	4,870	0.74	0.94	0.65	0.777	25
71	Saint Lucia	72.4	94.8	74	5,300	0.79	0.88	0.66	0.777	19
72	Brazil	68.0	86.4	92	7,770	0.72	0.88	0.73	0.775	−9

Table 2.4 continued

HDI rank	Life expectancy at birth (years) 2002	Adult literacy rate (% ages 15 and above) 2002	Combined gross enrolment ratio for primary, secondary and tertiary schools (%) 2001/02	GDP per capita (PPP US$) 2002	Life expectancy index	Education index	GDP index	Human development index (HDI) value 2002	GDP per capita (PPP US$) rank minus HDI rank*
73 Colombia	72.1	92.1	68	6,370	0.78	0.84	0.69	0.773	4
74 Oman	72.3	74.4	63	13,340	0.79	0.71	0.82	0.770	-32
75 Samoa (Western)	69.8	98.7	69	5,600	0.75	0.89	0.67	0.769	10
76 Thailand	69.1	92.6	73	7,010	0.74	0.86	0.71	0.768	-9
77 Saudi Arabia	72.1	77.9	57	12,650	0.79	0.71	0.81	0.768	-33
78 Kazakhstan	66.2	99.4	81	5,870	0.69	0.93	0.68	0.766	4
79 Jamaica	75.6	87.6	75	3,980	0.84	0.83	0.61	0.764	28
80 Lebanon	73.5	86.5	78	4,360	0.81	0.84	0.63	0.758	21
81 Fiji	69.6	92.9	73	5,440	0.74	0.86	0.67	0.758	7
82 Armenia	72.3	99.4	72	3,120	0.79	0.90	0.57	0.754	33
83 Philippines	69.8	92.6	81	4,170	0.75	0.89	0.62	0.753	22
84 Maldives	67.2	97.2	78	4,798	0.70	0.91	0.65	0.752	13
85 Peru	69.7	85.0	88	5,010	0.74	0.86	0.65	0.752	7
86 Turkmenistan	66.9	98.8	81	4,300	0.70	0.93	0.63	0.752	16
87 Saint Vincent & the Grenadines	74.0	83.1	64	5,460	0.82	0.77	0.67	0.751	0
88 Turkey	70.4	86.5	68	6,390	0.76	0.80	0.69	0.751	-12
89 Paraguay	70.7	91.6	72	4,610	0.76	0.85	0.64	0.751	9
90 Jordan	70.9	90.9	77	4,220	0.76	0.86	0.62	0.750	14
91 Azerbaijan	72.1	97.0	69	3,210	0.78	0.88	0.58	0.746	23
92 Tunisia	72.9	73.2	75	6,760	0.79	0.74	0.70	0.745	-23
93 Grenada	65.3	94.4	65	7,280	0.67	0.85	0.72	0.745	-28
94 China	70.9	90.9	68	4,580	0.76	0.83	0.64	0.745	5
95 Dominica	73.1	76.4	74	5,640	0.80	0.76	0.67	0.743	-11
96 Sri Lanka	72.5	92.1	65	3,570	0.79	0.83	0.60	0.740	16
97 Georgia	73.5	100.0	69	2,260	0.81	0.89	0.52	0.739	29
98 Dominican Republic	66.7	84.4	77	6,640	0.70	0.82	0.70	0.738	-27
99 Belize	71.5	76.9	71	6,080	0.78	0.75	0.69	0.737	-19
100 Ecuador	70.7	91.0	72	3,580	0.76	0.85	0.60	0.735	11
101 Iran, Islamic Rep. of	70.1	77.1	69	6,690	0.75	0.74	0.70	0.732	-31
102 Occupied Palestinian Territories	72.3	90.2	79	–	0.79	0.86	0.52	0.726	21
103 El Salvador	70.6	79.7	66	4,890	0.76	0.75	0.65	0.720	-9

104 Guyana	63.2	96.5	75	4,260	0.64	0.89	0.63	0.719	-1
105 Cape Verde	70.0	75.7	73	5,000	0.75	0.75	0.65	0.717	-12
106 Syrian Arab Republic	71.7	82.9	59	3,620	0.78	0.75	0.60	0.710	4
107 Uzbekistan	69.5	99.3	76	1,670	0.74	0.91	0.47	0.709	35
108 Algeria	69.5	68.9	70	5,760	0.74	0.69	0.68	0.704	-25
109 Equatorial Guinea	49.1	84.2	58	30,130	0.40	0.76	0.95	0.703	-103
110 Kyrgyzstan	68.4	97.0	81	1,620	0.72	0.92	0.46	0.701	33
111 Indonesia	66.6	87.9	65	3,230	0.69	0.80	0.58	0.692	2
112 Viet Nam	69.0	90.3	64	2,300	0.73	0.82	0.52	0.691	12
113 Moldova, Rep. of	68.8	99.0	62	1,470	0.73	0.87	0.45	0.681	36
114 Bolivia	63.7	86.7	86	2,460	0.64	0.86	0.53	0.681	6
115 Honduras	68.8	80.0	62	2,600	0.73	0.74	0.54	0.672	3
116 Tajikistan	68.6	99.5	73	980	0.73	0.90	0.38	0.671	45
117 Mongolia	63.7	97.8	70	1,710	0.64	0.89	0.47	0.668	21
118 Nicaragua	69.4	76.7	65	2,470	0.74	0.73	0.54	0.667	1
119 South Africa	48.8	86.0	77	10,070	0.40	0.83	0.77	0.666	-66
120 Egypt	68.6	55.6	76	3,810	0.73	0.62	0.61	0.653	-12
121 Guatemala	65.7	69.9	56	4,080	0.68	0.65	0.62	0.649	-15
122 Gabon	56.6	71.0	74	6,590	0.53	0.72	0.70	0.648	-50
123 São Tomé and Príncipe	69.7	83.1	62	1,317	0.75	0.76	0.43	0.645	29
124 Solomon Islands	69.0	76.6	50	1,590	0.73	0.68	0.46	0.624	21
125 Morocco	68.5	50.7	57	3,810	0.72	0.53	0.61	0.620	-17
126 Namibia	45.3	83.3	71	6,210	0.34	0.79	0.69	0.607	-48
127 India	63.7	61.3	55	2,670	0.64	0.59	0.55	0.595	-10
128 Botswana	41.4	78.9	70	8,170	0.27	0.76	0.73	0.589	-67
129 Vanuatu	68.6	34.0	59	2,890	0.73	0.42	0.56	0.570	-13
130 Cambodia	57.4	69.4	59	2,060	0.54	0.66	0.50	0.568	1
131 Ghana	57.8	73.8	46	2,130	0.55	0.65	0.51	0.568	-3
132 Myanmar	57.2	85.3	48	1,027	0.54	0.73	0.39	0.551	26
133 Papua New Guinea	57.4	64.6	41	2,270	0.54	0.57	0.52	0.542	-8
134 Bhutan	63.0	47.0	–	1,969	0.63	0.48	0.50	0.536	0
135 Lao People's Dem. Rep.	54.3	66.4	59	1,720	0.49	0.64	0.47	0.534	2
136 Comoros	60.6	56.2	45	1,690	0.59	0.53	0.47	0.530	4
137 Swaziland	35.7	80.9	61	4,550	0.18	0.74	0.64	0.519	-37
138 Bangladesh	61.1	41.1	54	1,700	0.60	0.45	0.47	0.509	1
139 Sudan	55.5	59.9	36	1,820	0.51	0.52	0.48	0.505	-3
140 Nepal	59.6	44.0	61	1,370	0.58	0.50	0.44	0.504	11
141 Cameroon	46.8	67.9	56	2,000	0.36	0.64	0.50	0.501	-9

Low human development

142 Pakistan	60.8	41.5	37	1,940	0.60	0.40	0.49	0.497	-7
143 Togo	49.9	59.6	67	1,480	0.41	0.62	0.45	0.495	5
144 Republic of Congo-Brazzaville	48.3	82.8	48	980	0.39	0.71	0.38	0.494	17

Table 2.4 continued

HDI rank	Life expectancy at birth (years) 2002	Adult literacy rate (% ages 15 and above) 2002	Combined gross enrolment ratio for primary, secondary and tertiary schools (%) 2001/02	GDP per capita (PPP US$) 2002	Life expectancy index	Education index	GDP index	Human development index (HDI) value 2002	GDP per capita (PPP US$) rank minus HDI rank*
145 Lesotho	36.3	81.4	65	2,420	0.19	0.76	0.53	0.493	-24
146 Uganda	45.7	68.9	71	1,390	0.34	0.70	0.44	0.493	4
147 Zimbabwe	33.9	90.0	58	2,400	0.15	0.79	0.53	0.491	-25
148 Kenya	45.2	84.3	53	1,020	0.34	0.74	0.39	0.488	11
149 Yemen	59.8	49.0	53	870	0.58	0.50	0.36	0.482	16
150 Madagascar	53.4	67.3	45	740	0.47	0.60	0.33	0.469	20
151 Nigeria	51.6	66.8	45	860	0.44	0.59	0.36	0.466	15
152 Mauritania	52.3	41.2	44	2,220	0.45	0.42	0.52	0.465	-25
153 Haiti	49.4	51.9	52	1,610	0.41	0.52	0.46	0.463	-9
154 Djibouti	45.8	65.5	24	1,990	0.35	0.52	0.50	0.454	-21
155 Gambia	53.9	37.8	45	1,690	0.48	0.40	0.47	0.452	-15
156 Eritrea	52.7	56.7	33	890	0.46	0.49	0.36	0.439	8
157 Senegal	52.7	39.3	38	1,580	0.46	0.39	0.46	0.437	-11
158 Timor-Leste	49.3	58.6	75	—	0.41	0.64	0.26	0.436	19
159 Rwanda	38.9	69.2	53	1,270	0.23	0.64	0.42	0.431	-6
160 Guinea	48.9	41.0	29	2,100	0.40	0.37	0.51	0.425	-30
161 Benin	50.7	39.8	52	1,070	0.43	0.44	0.40	0.421	-5
162 Tanzania, U. Rep. of	43.5	77.1	31	580	0.31	0.62	0.29	0.407	12
163 Côte d'Ivoire	41.2	49.7	42	1,520	0.27	0.47	0.45	0.399	-16
164 Zambia	32.7	79.9	45	840	0.13	0.68	0.36	0.389	3
165 Malawi	37.8	61.8	74	580	0.21	0.66	0.29	0.388	9
166 Angola	40.1	42.0	30	2,130	0.25	0.38	0.51	0.381	-38
167 Chad	44.7	45.8	35	1,020	0.33	0.42	0.39	0.379	-8
168 Congo, Dem. Rep. of the	41.4	62.7	27	650	0.27	0.51	0.31	0.365	4
169 Central African Rep.	39.8	48.6	31	1,170	0.25	0.43	0.41	0.361	-15
170 Ethiopia	45.5	41.5	34	780	0.34	0.39	0.34	0.359	-1
171 Mozambique	38.5	46.5	41	1,050	0.22	0.45	0.39	0.354	-14
172 Guinea-Bissau	45.2	39.6	37	710	0.34	0.39	0.33	0.350	-1
173 Burundi	40.8	50.4	33	630	0.26	0.45	0.31	0.339	0
174 Mali	48.5	19.0	26	930	0.39	0.21	0.37	0.326	-11
175 Burkina Faso	45.8	12.8	22	1,100	0.35	0.16	0.40	0.302	-20
176 Niger	46.0	17.1	19	800	0.35	0.18	0.35	0.292	-8
177 Sierra Leone	34.3	36.0	45	520	0.16	0.39	0.28	0.273	-1

Developing countries	64.6	76.7	60	4,054	0.66	0.71	0.62	0.663	–
Least developed countries	50.6	52.5	43	1,307	0.43	0.49	0.42	0.446	–
Arab States	66.3	63.3	60	5,069	0.69	0.61	0.65	0.651	–
East Asia and the Pacific	69.8	90.3	65	4,768	0.75	0.83	0.64	0.740	–
Lat. Amer. and the Carib.	70.5	88.6	81	7,223	0.76	0.86	0.72	0.777	–
South Asia	63.2	57.6	54	2,658	0.64	0.57	0.55	0.584	–
Sub-Saharan Africa	46.3	63.2	44	1,790	0.35	0.56	0.48	0.465	–
Central & Eastern Europe & CIS	69.5	99.3	79	7,192	0.74	0.93	0.72	0.796	–
OECD	77.1	–	87	24,904	0.87	0.94	0.92	0.911	–
High-income OECD	78.3	–	93	29,000	0.89	0.97	0.95	0.935	–
High human development	77.4	–	89	24,806	0.87	0.95	0.92	0.915	–
Medium human development	67.2	80.4	64	4,269	0.70	0.75	0.63	0.695	–
Low human development	49.1	54.3	40	1,184	0.40	0.50	0.41	0.438	–
High income	78.3	–	92	28,741	0.89	0.97	0.94	0.933	–
Middle income	70.0	89.7	71	5,908	0.75	0.84	0.68	0.756	–
Low income	59.1	63.6	51	2,149	0.57	0.59	0.51	0.557	–
World	66.9	–	64	7,804	0.70	0.76	0.73	0.729	–

Note: * A positive figure indicates that the HDI is higher than the PCY rank, and vice versa for a negative figure.
Source: UNDP, *Human Development Report 2004* (New York: Oxford University Press, 2004).

The **Human Poverty Index** is based on three main indices:

- The percentage of the population not expected to survive to the age of 40 (P_1)
- The adult illiteracy rate (P_2)
- A deprivation index based on an average of two variables: the percentage of the population without access to safe water and the percentage of underweight children under five years old (P_3).

The formula for the HPI is given by:

$$\text{HPI} = [1/3(P_1^3 + P_2^3 + P_3^3) - 3]^{1/3} \tag{2.3}$$

The data and the results for 177 developing countries are shown in Table 2.5.

The total number of those suffering deprivation and various aspects of human poverty is shown in Table 2.6 (by continent and area of the world). At the start of the third millennium, over 1 billion people still lack access to safe water, nearly 1 billion are illiterate, and half a billion will die before the age of 40. The UNDP calculates, however, that the cost of eradicating poverty across the globe is relatively small compared with global income, and that 'political commitment, not financial resources, is the real obstacle to poverty eradication'. Basic social services could be made available to all people in developing countries at the cost of $40 billion over 10 years. A further $40 billion over 20 years could eradicate income poverty across the world. A cost of $80 billion is less than 0.3 per cent of the global world income of $32,000 billion.

CAN THE POOR COUNTRIES EVER CATCH UP?

If living standards are largely determined by the level and growth of productivity, the interesting question is whether the developing countries will ever catch up with the performance of the rich industrialized countries. There are at least three possible mechanisms by which **catch-up** may occur.

First, it is sometimes argued that the larger the gap between a country's technology, productivity and per capita income on the one hand and the level of productivity in the advanced countries on the other, the greater the scope for a poor country to absorb existing technology and to catch up with richer countries. Technology is thought of as a public good, so for a given amount of technological investment a poor country can reap high returns because it has paid none of the development costs. Clearly, there also has to be the willingness and ability to invest. A productivity gap is a necessary but not a sufficient condition for catch-up by this means.

Second, the process of development is characterized by a shift of resources from low-productivity agriculture to higher-productivity industrial and service activities. Other things being equal, this should also produce a move towards convergence to the extent that the resource shifts are greater in poor countries than in rich countries.

Third, mainstream neoclassical growth theory predicts convergence (see Chapter 4) because of the assumption of diminishing returns to capital. Rich countries with a lot of capital per head will have a lower productivity of capital than poor countries. Thus if tastes and preferences are the same, the same amount of saving and investment in poor countries should lead to faster growth than in rich countries.

Table 2.5 Human Poverty Index

HDI rank	Human poverty index Value (%)	Probability at birth of not surviving to age 40 (% of cohort) 2000–05	Adult illiteracy rate (% ages 15 and above) 2002	Population without sustainable access to an improved water source (%) 2000	Children under weight for age (% under age 5) 1995–2002
High human development					
23 Hong Kong, China (SAR)	–	1.8	6.5	–	–
25 Singapore	6.3	1.9	7.5	0	14
28 Korea, Rep. of	–	3.4	2.1	8	–
29 Barbados	2.5	2.6	0.3	0	6
30 Cyprus	–	2.9	3.2	0	–
33 Brunei Darussalam	–	2.8	6.1	–	–
34 Argentina	–	5.1	3.0	–	5
35 Seychelles	–	–	8.1	–	6
39 Saint Kitts and Nevis	–	–	–	2	–
40 Bahrain	–	4.0	11.5	–	9
43 Chile	4.1	4.1	4.3	7	1
44 Kuwait	–	2.6	17.1	–	10
45 Costa Rica	4.4	3.7	4.2	5	5
46 Uruguay	3.6	4.4	2.3	2	5
47 Qatar	–	5.1	15.8	–	6
49 United Arab Emirates	–	3.4	22.7	–	14
51 Bahamas	–	16.0	4.5	3	–
52 Cuba	5.0	4.1	3.1	9	4
53 Mexico	9.1	7.6	9.5	12	8
54 Trinidad and Tobago	7.7	9.1	1.5	10	7
55 Antigua and Barbuda	–	–	–	9	10
Medium human development					
58 Libyan Arab Jamahiriya	15.3	4.5	18.3	28	5
59 Malaysia	–	4.2	11.3	–	12
61 Panama	7.7	6.8	7.7	10	7
63 Tonga	–	8.9	1.2	0	–
64 Mauritius	11.3	4.6	15.7	0	15
67 Suriname	–	6.5	–	18	13
68 Venezuela	8.5	5.9	6.9	17	5
71 Saint Lucia	–	5.7	–	2	14
72 Brazil	11.8	11.5	13.6	13	6
73 Colombia	8.1	8.4	7.9	9	7
74 Oman	31.5	5.0	25.6	61	24
75 Samoa (Western)	–	6.6	1.3	1	–
76 Thailand	13.1	10.2	7.4	16	19
77 Saudi Arabia	15.8	5.2	22.1	5	14
79 Jamaica	9.2	4.9	12.4	8	6
80 Lebanon	9.5	4.3	13.5	0	3
81 Fiji	21.3	5.4	7.1	53	8
83 Philippines	15.0	7.4	7.4	14	28
84 Maldives	11.4	10.2	2.8	0	30
85 Peru	13.2	10.2	15.0	20	7
87 St. Vincent & the Grenadines	–	3.9	–	7	–

▶

Table 2.5 continued

HDI rank	Human poverty index Value (%)	Probability at birth of not surviving to age 40 (% of cohort) 2000–05	Adult illiteracy rate (% ages 15 and above) 2002	Population without sustainable access to an improved water source (%) 2000	Children under weight for age (% under age 5) 1995–2002
88 Turkey	12.0	8.0	13.5	18	8
89 Paraguay	10.6	8.0	8.4	22	5
90 Jordan	7.2	6.6	9.1	4	5
92 Tunisia	19.2	4.9	26.8	20	4
93 Grenada	–	–	–	5	–
94 China	13.2	7.1	9.1	25	11
95 Dominica	–	–	–	3	5
96 Sri Lanka	18.2	5.1	7.9	23	29
98 Dominican Republic	13.7	14.6	15.6	14	5
99 Belize	16.7	11.3	23.1	8	6
100 Ecuador	12.0	10.3	9.0	15	15
101 Iran, Islamic Rep. of	16.4	7.0	22.9	8	11
102 Occupied Palestinian Territories	–	5.2	–	14	4
103 El Salvador	17.0	9.9	20.3	23	12
104 Guyana	12.9	17.6	1.4	6	14
105 Cape Verde	19.7	7.6	24.3	26	14
106 Syrian Arab Republic	13.7	5.7	17.1	20	7
108 Algeria	21.9	9.3	31.1	11	6
119 Equatorial Guinea	32.7	36.4	15.8	56	19
111 Indonesia	17.8	10.8	12.1	22	26
112 Viet Nam	20.0	10.7	9.7	23	33
114 Bolivia	14.4	16.0	13.3	17	10
115 Honduras	16.6	13.8	20.0	12	17
117 Mongolia	19.1	13.0	2.2	40	13
118 Nicaragua	18.3	10.3	23.3	23	10
119 South Africa	31.7	44.9	14.0	14	12
120 Egypt	30.9	8.6	44.4	3	11
121 Guatemala	22.5	14.1	30.1	8	24
122 Gabon	–	28.1	–	14	12
123 São Tomé and Príncipe	–	10.0	–	–	13
124 Solomon Islands	–	6.8	–	29	21
125 Morocco	34.5	9.4	49.3	20	9
126 Namibia	37.7	52.3	16.7	23	24
127 India	31.4	15.3	38.7	16	47
128 Botswana	43.5	61.9	21.1	5	13
129 Vanuatu	–	7.3	–	12	20
130 Cambodia	42.6	24.0	30.6	70	45
131 Ghana	26.0	25.8	26.2	27	25
132 Myanmar	25.4	24.6	14.7	28	35
133 Papua New Guinea	37.0	19.0	35.4	58	35
134 Bhutan	–	17.3	–	38	19
135 Lao People's Dem. Rep.	40.3	27.9	33.6	63	40
136 Comoros	31.4	18.1	43.8	4	25
137 Swaziland	–	70.5	19.1	–	10
138 Bangladesh	42.2	17.3	58.9	3	48

▶

Table 2.5 continued

HDI rank	Human poverty index Value (%)	Probability at birth of not surviving to age 40 (% of cohort) 2000–05	Adult illiteracy rate (% ages 15 and above) 2002	Population without sustainable access to an improved water source (%) 2000	Children under weight for age (% under age 5) 1995–2002
139 Sudan	31.6	27.6	40.1	25	17
140 Nepal	41.2	19.3	56.0	12	48
141 Cameroon	36.9	44.2	32.1	42	21
Low human development					
142 Pakistan	41.9	17.8	58.5	10	38
143 Togo	38.0	37.9	40.4	46	25
144 Congo	31.9	39.3	17.2	49	14
145 Lesotho	47.9	68.1	18.6	22	18
146 Uganda	36.4	41.1	31.1	48	23
147 Zimbabwe	52.0	74.8	10.0	17	13
148 Kenya	37.5	49.5	15.7	43	21
149 Yemen	40.3	19.1	51.0	31	46
150 Madagascar	35.9	29.0	32.7	53	33
151 Nigeria	35.1	34.9	33.2	38	36
152 Mauritania	48.3	30.5	58.8	63	32
153 Haiti	41.1	37.3	48.1	54	17
154 Djibouti	34.3	42.9	34.5	0	18
155 Gambia	45.8	29.6	62.2	38	17
156 Eritrea	41.8	27.5	43.3	54	44
157 Senegal	44.1	27.7	60.7	22	23
158 Timor-Leste	–	33.0	–	–	43
159 Rwanda	44.7	54.3	30.8	59	27
160 Guinea	–	35.9	–	52	23
161 Benin	45.7	34.6	60.2	37	23
162 Tanzania, U. Rep. of	36.0	46.4	22.9	32	29
163 Côte d'Ivoire	45.0	51.7	50.3	19	21
164 Zambia	50.4	70.1	20.1	36	28
165 Malawi	46.8	59.6	38.2	43	25
166 Angola	–	49.2	–	62	31
167 Chad	49.6	42.9	54.2	73	28
168 Congo, Dem. Rep. of the	42.9	47.2	37.3	55	31
169 Central African Rep.	47.7	55.3	51.4	30	24
170 Ethiopia	55.5	43.3	58.5	76	47
171 Mozambique	49.8	56.0	53.5	43	26
172 Guinea-Bissau	48.0	41.3	60.4	44	25
173 Burundi	45.8	50.5	49.6	22	45
174 Mali	58.9	35.3	81.0	35	33
175 Burkina Faso	65.5	43.4	87.2	58	34
176 Niger	61.4	38.7	82.9	41	40
177 Sierra Leone	–	57.5	–	43	27

Source: UNDP, *Human Development Report 2004* (New York: Oxford University Press, 2004).

Table 2.6 Human poverty in developing countries, 1990s (million)

Region or country group	Illiterate adults (1995)	People lacking access to health services (1990–5)	People lacking access to safe water (1990–6)	Malnourished children under 5 (1990–6)	People not expected to survive to age 40 (1990s)
All developing countries	842	766	1213	158	507
Least developed countries	143	241	218	34	123
Arab States	59	29	54	5	26
East Asia	167	144	398	17	81
Latin America and the Caribbean	42	55	109	5	36
South Asia	407	264	230	82	184
South-East Asia and the Pacific	38	69	162	20	52
Sub-Saharan Africa	122	205	249	28	124

Source: UNDP, *Human Development Report 2004* (New York: Oxford University Press, 2004).

The standard procedure for testing the convergence hypothesis is to do a simple correlation across countries between the rate of growth of per capita income (y) as the dependent variable and the initial level of per capita income (or productivity) as the independent variable, and to see whether the relation is significantly negative. If it is, this means that per capita income is growing faster in poor countries than in rich countries, which is a necessary condition for convergence to take place (often called **beta convergence** in the literature). One of the earliest studies of this type (Baumol, 1986) showed a strong inverse correlation between a country's productivity level and its average productivity growth among industrial countries and those at an intermediate stage of development, but no evidence of convergence as far as the poorer countries are concerned.

Zind (1991) focused on 89 developing countries and regressed the rate of growth of per capita income on the level of per capita income in 1960. He could find no evidence of overall convergence, but there was some evidence of convergence taking place between countries with per capita incomes in excess of $800 per annum. One reason appears to be that in these latter countries there was a positive relation between per capita income and the rate of growth of investment per capita.

Another study by Dowrick (1992) across 113 countries shows that while there is some evidence of catch-up in the last 30 years in the sense that growth rates have been negatively related to initial levels of productivity, other factors have caused per capita income growth to be faster the higher level of per capita income, producing a *divergence* of living standards across the world.

Similarly, Pritchett (1997) takes 117 countries over the period of 1960–86 and regresses the rate of growth of per capita income on the initial level of per capita income relative to the leading country and finds no evidence of unconditional convergence, as shown in Table 2.7, because the coefficient of 0.4 is positive. It is interesting to note, however, that when differences in investment and schooling between countries are allowed for the coefficient becomes negative (-0.32), indicating conditional convergence. The problem is, however, that rich countries are able to save and invest more, and do devote more

Table 2.7 Explaining growth of per capita GDP, 1960–88

Effect of	Unconditional divergence	Conditional convergence	The richer accumulate faster	
	Average growth of GDP per capita (1)	Average growth of GDP per capita (2)	Investment level (3)	Primary school enrolment (4)
Initial level of GDP per capita relative to leader	0.40	−0.32	4.43	14.57
Average level of investment	–	0.07	–	–
Average enrolment in primary school	–	0.03	–	–

Source: L. Pritchett, 'Divergence, Big Time', *Journal of Economic Perspectives*, 11, 1997.

resources to education, which perpetuates their growth advantage. Columns (3) and (4) in Table 2.7 show a strong positive relation between the initial level of per capita income and the investment level on the one hand, and primary school enrolment on the other. Poor countries tend to grow more slowly than rich ones in spite of the potential advantages conferred by backwardness. When conditional convergence is found, however, it is not possible to distinguish between the various sources of catch-up, that is, easy access to technology as a public good, resource shifts, or diminishing returns to capital. A negative sign on the initial per capita income variable could be picking up any one of these effects, or all three.

All this confirms what we found earlier that there is no tendency for the international distribution of income to narrow, as measured by the Gini ratio. A necessary condition for the Gini ratio to fall is that poor countries grow faster than the rich, but this has not been happening overall. Some poor countries are narrowing the gap with the rich, but others are falling behind, leaving the overall distribution of income unchanged.

The interesting question then arises of how fast would the average developing country have to grow in order to narrow and eventually eliminate the 'development gap' by a specific date? The following analysis and calculations attempt to answer these questions. We shall take as a target the average per capita income of the industrialized countries and attempt to answer four specific questions as reliably as the data will allow:

- Given the recent growth experience of the poor countries, how long would it take for them to reach the *current* average level of per capita income in the industrialized countries?
- Given the recent growth experience of the poor countries relative to the industrialized countries, how many years would it take for the per capita income gap to be *eliminated*?
- Given the rate of growth of the industrialized countries from now until the year 2020 (say), how *fast* would the poor countries have to grow for per capita incomes to be equalized by that date?
- Given the rate of growth of the industrialized countries, how fast would the poor countries have to grow merely to prevent the absolute per capita income gap between rich and poor countries from being *wider* in the year 2020 than now?

By asking the first two questions, some idea can be obtained of the time scale of the catching up process by the poor countries given their recent growth performance. The answers to the latter two questions give some idea of the growth task facing the poor countries in their struggle not only for parity of living standards, but also in simply preventing the absolute gap from widening.

Given the basic data, the answers to the questions posed involve little more than simple manipulation of the formula for compound interest:

$$S = P(1 + r)^n$$

where P is the principal sum and S is the sum to which the principal grows at an annual rate of growth, r, over n years. For illustration:

Let Y_{Dt} be the current level of per capita income in the industrialized countries, say, $25,000

Y_{DCt} be the current level of per capita income in the poor countries, say, $1,200

r_D be the per capita income growth rate in the industrialized countries from the year 2000 to 2020, say, 3 per cent per annum

r_{DC} be the actual per capita income growth rate in the poor countries, say, 2 per cent per annum

Y_D^* be the assumed level of per capita income in the industrialized countries in the year 2020, say, $45,000 at today's prices (assuming 3 per cent growth)

and r_{DC}^* be the required per capita growth rate of the poor countries.

The solution to the first question is then obtained from the formula:

$$Y_{Dt} = Y_{DCt} (1 + r_{DC})^n$$

from which

$$n = \frac{\log \dfrac{Y_{Dt}}{Y_{DCt}}}{\log (1 + r_{DC})}$$

Applying the assumed values above gives

$$n = \frac{\log \dfrac{25,000}{1,200}}{\log (1.02)} \simeq 153 \text{ years}$$

In other words, at a growth rate of 2 per cent it would take the average poor country, with a per capita income of $1,200, 153 years to reach the *current* living standards enjoyed in the industrialized countries.

The solution to the second question is obtained from the expression

$$Y_{Dt} (1 + r_D)^n = Y_{DCt} (1 + r_{DC})^n$$

from which we can find how long it would take (n) for the per capita income gap to be eliminated between rich and poor countries, as long as the rate of per capita income growth in poor countries is greater than in the industrialized countries – otherwise, of course, the absolute gap would widen for ever.

$$n = \frac{\log \dfrac{Y_{Dt}}{Y_{DCt}}}{\log(1 + r_{DC}) - \log(1 + r_D)}$$

A calculation can be made for any individual country whose average per capita income growth is in excess of that of the industrialized countries. Malaysia, for example, has a per capita income of approximately \$4,000 and per capita income has been growing at approximately 6 per cent per annum. At this rate, how long would it take Malaysia to catch up with the present industrialized countries growing at 3 per cent? The answer is

$$n = \frac{\log \dfrac{25,000}{4,000}}{\log(1.06) - \log(1.03)} = 64 \text{ years}$$

The lower the initial level of per capita income and the smaller the excess of growth above 3 per cent, the longer it would take to catch up. For a country starting with an average level of per capita income of \$1000 and growing at 4 per cent, it would take over 300 years!

The solution to the third question is obtained from the expression:

$$Y_D^* = Y_{DCt}(1 + r_{DC})^n$$

where Y_D^* is the assumed level of per capita income in the industrialized countries in the year 2020. We can then solve for the required growth rate of the poor countries between the base period (2000) and the year 2020 ($n = 20$) to equalize per capita incomes

$$r_{DC}^* = \sqrt[n]{(Y_D^*/Y_{DCt})} - 1$$

Applying the assumed magnitudes of the variables gives

$$r_{DC}^* = \sqrt[20]{45,000/1,200} - 1$$
$$\simeq 20 \text{ per cent}$$

The required growth rate is 20 per cent per annum and hardly feasible. The magnitude of the development task is clearly colossal if defined in terms of achieving roughly comparable living standards throughout the world within the next two decades. For most of the poor countries, per capita income growth would have to increase sixfold, necessitating a ratio of investment to national income of 50 per cent or more. Investment ratios of this order are simply not feasible, and in any case the countries themselves could not absorb such investment.

The solution to the fourth question is obtained from the expression

$$Y_{Dt} - Y_{DCt} = Y_D^* - Y_{DCt}(1 + r_{DC})^n$$

where the left-hand side represents the base level per capita income gap and n is 20 years. Solving for the growth rate that would have to be achieved to prevent the *present* gap from widening gives:

$$r_{DC} = n\sqrt{[Y_D^* - (Y_{Dt} - Y_{DCt})]/Y_{DCt}} - 1$$

Applying the assumed magnitudes of the variables gives:

$$r_{DC} = 20\sqrt{[45,000 - (25,000 - 1,200)]/1,200} - 1 \simeq 12 \text{ per cent}$$

Again, this growth rate is not feasible, the implication being that the absolute per capita income gap between rich and poor countries will almost certainly be wider in the year 2020 than now, given the assumed 3 per cent average growth rate of the industrialized countries.

All the above calculations are sensitive to the assumed future growth rate of the industrialized countries, the choice of the target year in the future and the base-year level of per capita income taken for the poor countries. No one can possibly know with precision what the future rate of advance of the industrialized countries will be, and 3 per cent per capita income growth – the historical average from 1950 to 2000 – would seem to be as reasonable an assumption as any. But the lower the growth rate, the less formidable the growth effort the poor countries need to achieve parity of living standards. No special significance should be attached to the year 2020 as the choice of target year. A year has to be taken to make these 'catching-up' calculations – not too close to the present to give no hope and not too far away for the goal to be lost sight of. As far as the base-year level of per capita income in the poor countries is concerned, if the income statistics understate the value of production in poor countries, the calculations of the catching-up time and the growth rate required for parity of living standards will be exaggerated. The degree of overestimation, however, is not likely to be so great as to invalidate the conclusion that the growth rates required for parity of living standards by the year 2020 are not feasible, and that on current growth performance some countries will never catch up.

It can be argued, of course, that world income equality is an impracticable ideal, and that the primary aim is not equality of living standards throughout the world but 'tolerable' living standards in all countries, which is a very different matter. This seems to be the attitude of the World Bank which argued in its *World Development Report* (2000) that rising income inequality 'should not be seen as a negative' provided that incomes at the bottom do not fall, and the number of people in poverty falls or does not rise. The problem is to define 'tolerable' living standards, and to specify an acceptable income distribution at that average level of real income. The time scale involved to reach 'tolerable' living standards is clearly less than that required to eliminate the income gap entirely, but even so, if the average level of per capita income now enjoyed in the industrial countries is regarded as the tolerable level, we estimate it will take over a century for the average poor country on current performance to attain it. Can these countries wait that long?

On the other hand, it is easily forgotten that the rich–poor country divide is a relatively recent phenomenon. All countries were once at subsistence level, and as recently as 200 years ago, at the advent of the British industrial revolution, the absolute differences in living standards between countries cannot have been great. The average per capita income of the developing countries today is approximately $1400 per annum, and this is not far below the average level of real per capita income in Western Europe in the mid-nineteenth century, measured at current prices. If we regard $1400 as only barely above subsistence, the major part of the present income disparities between developed and developing countries must have arisen over the twentieth century. Some countries, through a combination of fortune and design, have managed to grow much faster than others. The overriding influence has been industrialization and the technological progress associated with it. The close association between industrialization and living standards spells out the clear policy message that to base a development policy on agricultural activities *alone* would be misguided, however attractive such aphorisms as 'back to the land' and 'small is beautiful' may sound to those disillusioned with the industrialization experience of the developing countries. Sutcliffe (1971) is right when he argues:

> It is understandable that vague memories of the oppression of the working class in 19th century Britain, the contemporary horrors of American machine-age society, and the Stalinist attack on the Russian peasantry, should arouse feelings which are hostile to industrialisation. Yet to oppose machines altogether, like Gandhi, or to argue that a long run rise in the standard of living is possible without industrialization, are no more than forms of sentimentalism, especially when the condition of most of the population of the non-industrialized world is now both terrible and worsening. It is not sentimentalism to demand that the process of industrialisation should be made as humane and as painless as possible and that the long term aims of equality at a higher standard of living should be constantly borne in mind as the process goes on.

The concentrated impact of industrialization on living standards in the Western world is dramatically emphasized by the observation that if 6,000 years of 'civilized' human existence prior to 1850 is viewed as a day, the last century or so represents little more than half an hour; yet in this 'half-hour' more real output has been produced in the developed countries than in the preceding period. It is true that living standards in most developing countries have risen faster since 1950 than at any time in the past; but so too have the living standards in the developed countries, and the gap between rich and poor countries continues to widen. Although development consists of more than a rise in per capita incomes, income disparities are the essence of the so-called 'development gap'.

DISCUSSION QUESTIONS

1 How would you measure the development gap in the world economy?

2 How would you construct a Lorenz curve and calculate the Gini ratio for the measurement of income inequality?

3 What has been happening to the international and global distribution of income over time?

4 What difficulties arise in measuring and comparing the per capita incomes of poor countries using the US$ as the unit of account?

5 What do you understand by the concept of purchasing power parity (PPP), and how would you make PPP calculations of per capita income across countries?

6 What difficulties are encountered in the measurement of poverty?

7 How would you calculate the growth required in order to meet the Millennium Goal of halving the proportion of people living in poverty by 2015 (compared to the 1990 level)?

8 What is the World Bank's new thinking concerning the attack on world poverty?

9 What is the rationale for the UNDP to construct a Human Poverty Index (HPI) and Human Development Index (HDI)?

10 Are there any theoretical reasons for supposing that poor countries might catch up with the rich countries?

11 How would you analyse whether poor countries are catching up with the rich countries?

NOTES

1. UNDP (1997).
2. Using per capita incomes measured at current exchange rates, the Gini ratio was calculated at 0.8 in 1993.
3. The 1990 and 2000/2001 *World Development Reports*, published by the World Bank, were devoted to a consideration of the measurement, magnitude and nature of poverty in the Third World, and how to tackle it.
4. *World Development Report 1990* (World Bank, 1990).
5. The construction of the income index is slightly more complex. See UNDP (2001), technical note, p. 240.
6. See UNDP (2001), technical note, p. 241.

WEBSITES ON POVERTY AND INCOME DISTRIBUTION

World Bank (Poverty Reduction Learning Network)　www.prln.org

www.worldbank.org/poverty

UNCTAD/UNDP　www.unctad-undp.org

UNDP (Human Development Report)　http://hdr.undp.org

Inter-American Development Bank　http://www.iadb.org/sds/pov/index-pov-e.htm

Oxfam　www.oxfam.org.uk

War on Want　www.waronwant.org

The characteristics of underdevelopment and structural change

THE CHARACTERISTICS OF UNDERDEVELOPMENT

There cannot be an increase in living standards and the eradication of poverty without an increase in output per head of the working population, or an increase in labour productivity. This is the *sine qua non* of development. Rich developed countries have high levels of labour productivity; poor developing countries have low levels of labour productivity. The questions that naturally arise are: what are the major causes of low productivity, and what are the primary sources of productivity growth? In this chapter we first of all briefly outline some of the distinguishing characteristics of developing countries that contribute to low levels of labour productivity and poor economic performance. We then go on to consider in more detail some of the other dimensions of the 'development' gap between rich and poor countries that low productivity is associated with. Some of the characteristics of underdevelopment are both symptoms *and* causes of poverty, for example low levels of education, poor nutrition, an excess supply of labour, low rates of saving and so on. Lastly, we consider the process of structural change and the role played by industrialization in raising productivity and living standards.

THE DOMINANCE OF AGRICULTURE AND PETTY SERVICES

One of the major distinguishing characteristics of poor developing countries is the fact that their economies are dominated by agriculture and petty service activities. There is very little by way of manufacturing industry. Table 3.1 shows the distribution of employment by sectors of the economy in the low-income, middle-income and high-income countries. It can be seen that in the low-income countries, 65 per cent of the labour force still relies on agriculture to make a living. This compares with just under 30 per cent in the middle-income countries and 5 per cent in the high-income countries.

Most of those working on the land in poor countries are either subsistence farmers (producing only for themselves), tenant farmers (with no land rights and no incentive to increase output) or landless labourers (selling their labour in a daily labour market). Some high-productivity commercial agriculture does exist, but it is a small proportion of total agricultural activity. The dominance of agriculture has a number of implications and poses a number of problems for developing countries. First of all, agriculture is a **diminishing returns** activity because land is ultimately a fixed factor of production. There are only a few incontrovertible laws in economics, but one is that if a variable factor is added to a fixed factor its marginal product will eventually fall: **the law of diminishing returns**. This principle is illustrated in Figure 3.1.

Table 3.1 Distribution of employment, by sector

Countries	Agriculture	Industry	Services
Low-income	65	18	17
Middle-income	28	32	40
High-income	5	28	67

Source: International Labour Organization, *Labour Force Statistics* (Geneva: ILO, 2002).

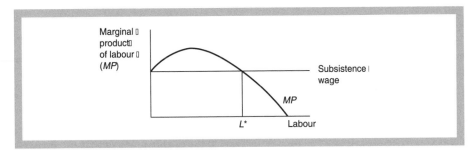

Figure 3.1 The law of diminishing returns

As labour is added to the land, the marginal product of labour first of all rises because it requires a certain amount of labour for each unit of labour to work with maximum efficiency, but then the marginal product declines and could become zero (or even negative in extreme cases where there is so much labour on a fixed piece of land that everyone gets in each other's way, reducing total output!)

If the marginal product of labour falls below the subsistence wage, the unit of labour will not be able to survive unless total output is shared. This may characterize family farms. If labour is hired, however, or works on commercial farms, no (profit-maximizing) employer will pay a wage above the marginal product of labour. We reach the conclusion that in a diminishing returns activity, such as agriculture, there is always a limit to employment set by the minimum subsistence wage. This can lead to unemployment, open or disguised (see Chapter 5), particularly in a society where the population is growing rapidly and there are limited alternative employment opportunities.

Secondly, on the demand side, the demand for most agricultural products (and other primary products derived from the land) is **income inelastic**. This means that the rise in demand is proportionately less than the rise in income, and the growth of demand for agricultural output is less than the growth of supply potential determined by the growth of the labour force plus the growth of labour productivity. For example, suppose that the agricultural labour force is growing at 2 per cent and labour productivity is growing at 1 per cent, so that the growth of productive potential is 3 per cent. Now suppose that income growth is 3 per cent but the income elasticity of demand for agricultural products is only one-half (0.5). The demand for output therefore grows by only 1.5 per cent. The gap between the growth of supply and demand is 1.5 per cent, which will manifest itself in unemployment.

There are thus two major causes of surplus labour in agriculture: one arises from the low income elasticity of demand for agricultural output; the other arises from the fact that agriculture is a diminishing returns activity so that there is a limit to the employment of (paid) labour set by the minimum subsistence wage. What happens to this surplus labour? First, it may stay in the rural sector and work is spread, with each unit of labour working a suboptimal day. This is described as **disguised unemployment** (see Chapter 5). This, of course, depresses labour productivity and therefore per capita income. Second, the surplus agricultural labour may migrate to the towns to find alternative work. If work cannot be found in the formal sector of the economy, the labour attempts to make a living in the informal sector by providing petty services of various kinds: street trading, haircutting, shoe-shining, transport and so on. These are also very low-productivity activities.

Industry has very different characteristics from agriculture. It is not a diminishing returns activity. If anything, it is an increasing returns activity. All factors of production are variable, and no limit to employment is set by the marginal product of labour falling below the minimum (subsistence) wage. Secondly, the demand for most industrial goods is income elastic so that the demand for labour may rise faster than labour productivity, leading to increases in employment – at least in the early stages of industrialization. Also, there is greater scope for capital accumulation in industry, which enhances labour productivity. Overall, the productivity of labour in industry is much higher. As we shall see later, there is a strong association across countries between per capita income, output growth and the share of resources devoted to industrial activities.

LOW LEVEL OF CAPITAL ACCUMULATION

A second major distinguishing characteristic of developing countries is their low level of capital accumulation – both physical and human. Physical capital refers to the plant, machinery and equipment used in the production of output. Human capital refers to the skills and expertise embodied in the labour force through education and training. (The role of education in the development process will be discussed later in the chapter.) Low levels of capital accumulation are a cause of low productivity and poverty, but are also a *function* of poverty, because capital accumulation requires investment and saving and it is not easy for poor societies to save. The process of development can be described as a generalized process of capital accumulation, but the levels and rates of capital accumulation in poor countries are low. The amount of physical capital that labour has to work with in a typical developing country is no more than one-twentieth of the level in Europe and North America. This reflects the cumulative effect over time of much higher savings and investment ratios in the rich countries. The savings and investment ratios for low-income, middle-income and high-income countries are shown in Table 3.2.

Domestic investment can differ from domestic saving owing to investment from abroad. The figures for low-income countries are distorted by China, which in 2002 saved over 40 per cent of its national income. If we exclude China the savings ratio of the low-income countries is less than half that of the middle- and high-income countries, although their investment ratio is still relatively high because of capital inflows from abroad. These are not always stable, however.

The distinguished development economist, Sir Arthur Lewis, once described development as the process of transforming a country from a net 5 per cent saver and investor to a 12 per cent saver and investor.[1] Rostow, in his famous book *The Stages of Economic Growth* (1960), defines the **take-off** stage of self-sustaining growth in terms of a critical ratio of savings and investment to national income of 10–12 per cent (see p. 107 for a discussion of Rostow's model). What is the significance of this ratio? It has to do with a very simple growth formula, which originally came from the growth model of the famous British economist (Sir) Roy Harrod (see Chapter 4). The formula is

$$g = s/c \hspace{4cm} (3.1)$$

Table 3.2 Savings and investment as a percentage of GDP, 2002

Countries	Gross domestic investment	Gross domestic savings
Low-income[a]	20	19
Middle-income	23	27
High-income	19	19

Note:
[a] Including China which saved 43 per cent and invested 40 per cent of GDP.
Source: World Bank, *World Development Indicators, 2004* (Washington, DC: World Bank, 2004).

where g is the growth of output ($\Delta Y/Y$), s is the savings ratio (S/Y) and c is the incremental capital–output ratio – that is, how much investment needs to take place in order to increase the flow of output by one unit ($I/\Delta Y$). Substituting these definitions of s and c into (3.1) shows that in an accounting sense the formula is an identity since in the national accounts $S = I$

$$\Delta Y/Y = (S/Y)/(I/\Delta Y) \tag{3.2}$$

That is, if $S = I$, then $g = s/c$.

Now, for the level of per capita income to rise, output growth must exceed population growth. If population growth is 2 per cent per annum, output growth must exceed 2 per cent per annum. It can be seen from (3.1) that how much saving and investment as a proportion of national income is required for growth depends on the value of the incremental capital–output ratio (c). If 4 units of capital investment are required to produce a 1 unit flow of output year by year over the life of the investment, then $c = 4$, so s must be at least 8 per cent for the growth of output to exceed 2 per cent. A net rate of saving and investment to national income of at least 8 per cent or more is therefore necessary if there is to be sustained growth of per capita income. In most developing countries, the net savings and investment ratio is above this critical magnitude, but the fact remains that a major cause of low productivity and poverty in developing countries is the low level of capital that labour has to work with. In Case example 3.1 the difference in the savings and investment climate between India and China is highlighted and discussed.

RAPID POPULATION GROWTH

A third distinguishing feature of most developing countries is that they have a much faster rate of population growth than developed countries, and faster than at any time in the world's history (see Chapter 8 for a full discussion). This can confer advantages, but it also imposes acute problems. Population growth in the low-income countries as a whole averages 1.8 per cent per annum, resulting from a birth rate of 29 per 1,000 population (or 2.9 per cent) and a death rate of 11 per 1,000 population (or 1.1 per cent). The rapid acceleration of population growth compared with its historical trend is the result of a dramatic fall in the death rate without a commensurate fall in the birth

Savings and Investment in India and China: A Comparison

In 2000, India's population was 1016 billion (bn) second largest in the world after China's 1275bn. These two countries contained 38 per cent of the world's population. By 2050, India is forecast to have the bigger population. By then, according to the United Nations population division, its population may be about 1500bn.

Comparisons between these two giants are irresistible. Both are performing well, by historical standards, but China is doing better on most measures of economic performance.

In 1980, real incomes per head were much the same in the two countries. By 2000, however, according to the World Bank, China's gross national income per head at purchasing power parity was close to 70 per cent higher than India's at $3,920. China' real gross domestic product per head rose 9 per cent a year in the 1990s, according to the World Bank, while India' rose 4.1 per cent. This is the difference between an increase of some 140 per cent and one of 50 per cent in incomes per head over a decade.

Behind China's superior growth lies a higher national savings rate. This reached 40 per cent of gross national product in 2000 against India's 24 per cent. The incremental capital–output ratio (which is the ratio of the investment rate to the growth rate) is much the same in both countries. This suggests that the efficiency with which capital is deployed is much the same in the two countries.

Nevertheless, China's superior growth and increasing outward orientation has made it far more significant to the world economy. In 2001, China was the world's sixth largest merchandise exporter, ahead of Canada and Italy. India was 30th, behind Denmark.

Experience with inward direct investment has been even more lopsided. By the end of 2001, according to the World Investment Report of the United Nations, the total stock of foreign direct investment in China was £395bn, against a mere $22bn in India.

A World Bank study of the Indian investment climate, made in collaboration with the Confederation of Indian Industries, analyses the obstacles to the country's economic dynamism at the level of individual businesses. It helps explain China's relative attraction for foreign investors and its superior trade performance.

It takes 10 permits to start a business in India against six in China, while the median time it takes is 90 days in India against 30 days in China. A typical foreign power project requires 43 clearances at central government level and another 57 at state level. These obstacles are far smaller in China.

In restrictions on the hiring and firing of workers, India ranked 73rd out of 75 countries in the Global Competitiveness Report for 2001. China ranked 23rd. Bankruptcy is almost impossible for large businesses. Sixty per cent of liquidation

▶

processes before the Indian High Court have continued for more than 10 years. Public administration is also poor. It takes an average of 10.6 days to clear goods at customs into India, against 7.8 into China.

As important as regulatory barriers to competition is India's poor infrastructure. Paved roads are only 56 per cent of the total, against over 80 per cent in China. Shipping a container of textiles to the US costs 35 per cent more than from China. Because of power shortages, 69 per cent of Indian companies have their own generator, compared with just 30 per cent in China.

These comparisons are bad news for India in one way, but good news in another. If India can sustain growth of 6 per cent a year when so much does not work very well, imagine what could be achieved if it did.

Source: *Financial Times*, 4 April 2003.

rate. Population growth in developed countries averages no more than 0.7 per cent per annum. The population growth rate in low-income, middle-income and high-income countries is shown in Table 3.3.

Table 3.3 Population growth, 1980–2002 (per cent per annum)

Low-income	2.1
Middle-income	1.3
High-income	0.7

Source: World Bank, *World Development Indicators 2004* (Washington, DC: World Bank, 2003).

Rapid population growth, like low capital accumulation, may be considered as both a cause of poverty and a consequence. High birth rates are themselves a function of poverty because child mortality is high in poor societies and parents wish to have large families to provide insurance in old age. High birth rates also go hand in hand with poor education, a lack of employment opportunities for women and ignorance of birth control techniques. Population growth in turn helps to perpetuate poverty if it reduces saving, dilutes capital per head and reduces the marginal product of labour in agriculture. The pressure of numbers may also put a strain on government expenditure, lead to congestion and overcrowding, impair the environment and put pressure on food supplies – all of which retard the development process, at least in the short run. In the longer run, population growth may stimulate investment and technical progress, and may not pose such a problem if there are complementary resources and factors of production available, but the short-run costs may outweigh the advantages for a considerable time.

EXPORTS DOMINATED BY PRIMARY COMMODITIES

A fourth distinguishing characteristic of developing countries is that their trade tends to be dominated by the export of primary commodities and the import of manufactured goods. This has consequences for the terms of trade of developing countries, the distribution of

Table 3.4 Primary commodities as a percentage of exports

East Asia and Pacific	16
South Asia	22
Latin America and Caribbean	50
Middle East and North Africa	79
Sub-Saharan Africa	62

Source: World Bank, *World Development Report 2002* (Washington, DC: World Bank, 2001).

the gains from trade between developed and developing countries, and the balance of payments situation – all of which may adversely affect real income per head. Table 3.4 shows primary commodities as a percentage of the total exports of different continents. The trade of Africa, the Middle East, Latin America and the Caribbean is still dominated by primary commodities. Only Asia and the Pacific have made headway in reducing dependence on commodity exports.

The **barter terms of trade** measures the ratio of export prices to import prices. There has been a historical tendency for the terms of trade of primary goods relative to manufactured goods to deteriorate over the last 100 years or so – by about 0.5 per cent per annum on average. This tendency is known in the literature as the **Prebisch–Singer thesis** (see Chapter 16). The falling price of exports relative to imports reduces the real income of a country because more exports have to be exchanged to obtain a given quantity of imports.

A second point to note is that the income elasticity of demand for primary commodities in world trade is less than unity, while the income elasticity of demand for manufactured goods is greater than unity. This means that as world income grows, the demand for primary commodities grows at a slower rate, but if developing countries grow at the same rate as the world economy their demand for manufactured imports grows at a faster rate. As a consequence, developing countries specializing in the production of primary commodities suffer acute balance-of-payments difficulties. Often, the only means available to developing countries to adjust the balance of payments is to slow down their economies in order to reduce the growth of imports.

The prices of primary commodities are also more cyclically volatile than the prices of manufactured goods. This can also cause havoc to a country's balance of payments and its government's tax revenue if it relies heavily on trade taxes. The resulting instability makes planning difficult and may deter private domestic investment and investment from overseas.

For all these reasons, the structure of trade poses severe problems for many developing countries and may keep countries poorer than they would be if they were able to produce and export more industrial goods. It is not possible to understand the growth and development process – and the perpetuation of divisions in the world economy – without reference to the unequal trading relations between rich and poor countries and the balance-of-payments consequences of specializing in primary commodities.

THE CURSE OF NATURAL RESOURCES

In general, it seems to be the case that the more natural resources a country has, the poorer it performs. This phenomenon is referred to in the literature as the 'curse of natural resources' (Sachs and Warner, 2001; Gylfason, 2001). This is illustrated in Figure 3.2 which shows a scatter diagram for 105 countries of the relationship between the growth of per capita income over the period 1965–1998, and the share of the labour force employed in the primary sector. There is a very strong negative relationship ($R^2 = 0.7218$), and the regression coefficient of –0.0871 indicates that a country with a primary sector share 11 percentage points above the average has experienced a growth of per capita income of one percentage point below the average (controlling for the initial level of per capita income). This represents a substantial loss of welfare.

The same negative pattern emerges when the growth of per capita income is regressed against the export of natural resources as a share of GDP; and the negative relation persists even when controlling for other variables such as differences in the level of investment between countries, and for climate and geography (Sachs and Warner, 2001). Most countries that have grown rapidly in recent decades started as resource poor, not resource rich. There are exceptions to this general rule – countries such as Malaysia, Thailand, Indonesia, Botswana, for example – but most of these exceptional countries have grown fast not through the exploitation of natural resources but through diversification into manufacturing industry.

What lies behind this 'curse of natural resources'? A number of factors can be mentioned, which interrelate with each other, that seem to affect adversely many of the important determinants of development. Gylfason shows a negative relation across countries between

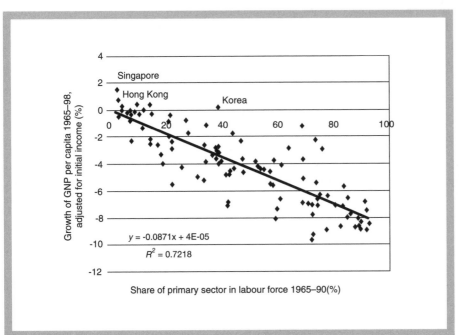

Source: J. Gylfason, 'Nature, Power and Growth', Scottish Journal of Political Economy, November 2001.

Figure 3.2 Natural resources and economic growth

the share of the primary sector in the labour force and export performance, domestic and foreign investment and education, and a positive relation with the size of external debt, the level of protection, corruption and income inequality. We have already seen why primary production can lead to poor export performance because many natural resources are income inelastic and suffer terms of trade deterioration, but why should natural resource abundant countries neglect investment and education, and be more corrupt? There are two major explanations.

Firstly, natural resource abundance may 'crowd-out' other activities through two mechanisms: (1) higher wages or earnings in the natural resources sector impairing entrepreneurial activity and innovation in other sectors, and (2) revenues from natural resource exports keeping the exchange rate artificially high which makes the rest of the economy uncompetitive. This is known as the **Dutch Disease** – so named because of the effect that the discovery of natural gas in Holland in the 1960s had on the exchange rate and other sectors of the economy. Sachs and Warner (2001) test this 'crowding out' hypothesis across 99 countries and find a positive correlation between natural resource abundance and the domestic price level. The higher relative price level is then found to impede the export growth of manufactured goods. It could also be that a country rich in natural resources simply neglects to develop other sectors of the economy.

A second major explanation why natural resource abundance may lead to poor performance is that the **rents** from natural resources may be misused by politicians and bureaucrats. Democracy and the rule of law seem to be inversely related to natural resource abundance, and Gylfason (2001) shows corruption to be more widespread in natural resource abundant countries. This is not surprising since limiting access to a resource provides a rent, and where the state owns the resource, bureaucrats will take bribes in return for exploitation rights. Rent earners may not be interested in schooling and education, having lined their own pockets, and those of their children, without acquiring an education. Thus, rent seeking leads to low levels of expenditure on education and school enrolment. It is also the case that the primary sector of an economy does not have the same educational needs as a more diversified economy.

WEAK INSTITUTIONAL STRUCTURES

Economies cannot function in an institutional vacuum, otherwise there is economic (and political) chaos. At the very minimum there has to be the rule of law; the protection of property rights, and constraints on power and corruption if private individuals are to be entrepreneurial, to take risks and invest. In many developing countries, the rule of law and the protection of property rights is still rudimentary, and politicians (and bureaucrats) abuse their powers. Many economists (e.g. Acemoglu, 2003) have recently argued that it is weak institutional structures that are the fundamental cause of underdevelopment because the character of institutions is the determinant of all the proximate causes of progress such as investment, education, trade and so on. Some of the measures of institutional quality that economists focus on are outlined and described in Case example 3.2. Three main ones are highlighted: the extent of legal protection of private property; the quality of governance (including the strength of the rule of law), and the limits placed on political leaders. Attempts have been made to distinguish econometrically the relative

Defining and Measuring Institutions

What do we mean by institutions?

The term institutions has been defined in different ways. Douglass North (1990) describes institutions very broadly, as the formal and informal rules governing human interactions. There are also narrow (and easier to grasp) definitions of institutions that focus on specific organizational entities, procedural devices and regulatory frameworks. At a more intermediate level, institutions are defined in terms of the degree of property rights protection, the degree to which laws and regulations are fairly applied, and the extent of corruption. It is narrower than North's definition, which includes all of the norms governing human interactions. Much of the recent research into determinants of economic development has adopted the intermediate definition.

How is institutional quality measured?

Recent empirical analyses have typically considered three relatively broad measures of institutions – **the quality of governance**, including the degree of corruption, political rights, public sector effiiency, and regulatory burdens; **the extent of legal protection of private property** and how well such laws are enforced; and **the limits placed on political leaders**. The measures themselves are not objective but, rather, the subjective perceptions and assessments of country experts or the assessments made by residents responding to surveys carried out by international organizations and nongovernmental organizations.

The first of these measures – the *aggregate governance index* – is the average of the six measures of institutions developed in a 1999 study by Daniel Kaufman, Art Kraay and Pablo Zoido-Lobaton. These measures include (1) *voice and accountability* – the extent to which citizens can choose their government and have political rights, civil liberties and an independent press; (2) *political stability and absence of violence* – the likelihood that the government will not be overthrown by unconstitutional or violent means; (3) *government effectiveness* – the quality of public service delivery and competence and political independence of the civil service; (4) *regulatory burden* – the relative absence of government controls on goods markets, banking systems, and international trade; (5) *rule of law* – the protection of persons and property against violence and theft, independent and effective judges, and contract enforcement; and (6) *freedom from graft* – public power is not abused for private gain or corruption.

A second measure focuses on *property rights*. This measure indicates the protection that private property receives. Yet another measure, *constraints on the executive*, reflects institutional and other limits placed on presidents and other political leaders. In a society with appropriate constraints on elites and politicians, there is less fighting between various groups for control of the state, and policies are more sustainable.

Source: H. Edison, 'How Strong are the Links Between Institutional Quality and Economic Performance,' *Finance and Development*, June 2003.

importance of institutions compared with other factors (including geography) in explaining different levels of per capita income across the world, with interesting, but controversial, results. Rodrik *et al.* (2002) take a large sample of developed and developing countries, measuring the quality of institutions mainly by a composite indicator of a number of elements that capture protection afforded by property rights, and conclude 'Our results indicate that the quality of institutions overrides everything else. Controlling for institutions, geography has, at best, weak direct effects on income . . . [s]imilarly trade . . . has no direct positive effect on income.' Easterly and Levine (2002) also test the influence of institutions compared with geography and policy variables across 75 rich and poor countries and find that institutions seem to matter most as the determinant of per capita income. Even countries with 'bad policies' do well with good institutions.

It is recognized, however, that the correlation found between institutions and economic development could reflect reverse causality, or omitted factors. We need to find a source of exogenous variation in institutions where institutions differ or change independently of other factors. Acemoglu *et al.* (2001) argue that the different experience of colonisation is one exogenous source where at one extreme colonizers set up exclusively extractive institutions (to exploit minerals and other primary products) – such as slavery and forced labour – which neither gave property rights to inhabitants nor constrained the power of elites. This was the experience in Africa and Latin America. At the other extreme, colonizers created settler societies, replicating the European form of institutions protecting private property and controlling elites and politicians in countries such as Australia, New Zealand and in North America. But what determined why some countries were settled and others not? Acemoglu *et al.* argued that the major determinant was the mortality rate faced by the early settlers, and that there is both a strong negative correlation between past mortality rates and current institutional quality (because institutions persisted) and between past mortality and the current levels of per capita income. In fact, over 50 per cent of the variation in per capita income across the 75 countries is associated with variation in one particular index of institutional quality which measures 'protection against expropriation'. The authors conclude 'There is a high correlation between mortality rates faced by soldiers, bishops and sailors in the colonies and European settlements; between European settlements and early measures of institutions, and between early institutions and institutions today. We estimate large effects of institutions on income per capita using this source of variation.' They also say that 'this relationship is not driven by outliers, and is robust controlling for latitude, climate, current disease environment, religion, natural resources, soil quality, ethnolinguistic fragmentation, and current racial composition'. But this is where the controversy starts because presumably the mortality rates of the early settlers, which affected the nature of institutions, was strongly influenced by geography as it affects disease. In the same vein Sachs (2003) argues that the finding of Acemoglu *et al.* concerning the negative relation between mortality rates 200 years ago and per capita income today is simply picking up the pernicious effects of malaria (which still persists), not institutions. Development is not simply about good government and institutions. Institutions might make anti-poverty policies more effective, but that is all. Poor countries need resources to fight disease; to provide education and infrastructure, and all the other resource prerequisites of development. Sachs classifies three types of countries combining institutions and geography, which is a sensible approach:

- Countries where institutions, policies and geography are all reasonably favourable, e.g. the coastal regions of East Asia
- Countries with favourable geography, but weak institutions, e.g. many of the transition economies of Eastern Europe and the former Soviet Union
- Countries impoverished by a combination of unfavourable geography – such as landlocked countries and those plagued with disease – and poor governance, e.g. many of the countries of Sub-Saharan Africa.

OTHER DIMENSIONS OF THE DEVELOPMENT GAP

Deprivation in developing countries is not simply a matter of low levels of per capita income. There are many other dimensions to the development gap between rich and poor countries. Developing countries generally experience much higher levels of unemployment – open and disguised – than do developed countries. The levels of education, health and nutrition are often abysmally low, and income distribution tends to be much more inegalitarian. Policy in developing countries is increasingly concerned with these other features of the development gap. The **basic needs approach** to development, pioneered by the World Bank, is a reflection of this switch of emphasis from exclusive concern with per capita income to these wider development issues.

UNEMPLOYMENT

The developing countries contain a huge reservoir of surplus labour. For a long time, poor countries, particularly since the population explosion, have been characterized by underemployment or disguised unemployment in rural areas (see Chapter 5). What has happened in recent years is that disguised rural unemployment has transferred itself into **disguised** and **open unemployment** in the towns. Unemployment in the urban areas of developing countries is another dimension of the development problem and an increasingly serious one. The rationale for rural–urban migration will be considered later, but first let us outline some of the facts on employment and unemployment. According to the International Labour Organisation (ILO) in Geneva, 1 billion people in developing countries are either jobless or underemployed, which amounts to one-third of the total working-age population.[2]

This represents a colossal challenge, particularly as the workforce is expected to grow by another 1.5 billion by the year 2025. The ILO argues for a renewed commitment by developing countries to the goal of employment creation, and not to treat current unemployment levels as natural and the inevitable outcome of market forces, as if nothing can be done. The ILO estimates that at least one billion new jobs need to be created in the next ten years if the proportion of people living in poverty is to be halved by 2015. The World Bank devoted its 1995 *World Development Report* to the conditions of employment in developing countries, and it painted a sombre picture.[3]

To stop unemployment rising there has to be employment growth of at least 2 per cent per annum, which requires output growth of at least 4 per cent per annum. Not many countries are able to grow this rapidly. The statistical evidence across countries tends to suggest that rapid employment growth is associated with the implementation of market-based policies and openness to trade. In particular, employment growth is strongly related to manufacturing export growth, which in turn is closely linked to the skill to land ratio of countries.

All this is very aggregative analysis. The issue still to be addressed is the emergence of increasing urban unemployment. The problem is not so much one of a deficiency of demand for labour in an aggregate demand sense. The causal factors relate to the incentives for labour to migrate from rural to urban areas, and the incapacity of the urban areas to provide employment owing to a lack of other necessary factors of production to work with labour – particularly capital. As far as migration is concerned, there are both push and pull factors at work.

The **push factors** have to do with the limited job opportunities in rural areas and a greater willingness and desire to move, fostered by education and improved communications. The **pull factors** relate to the development of urban industrial activities that offer jobs at a higher real wage than can be earned in rural areas, so that even if a migrant is unemployed for part of the year, he or she may still be better off migrating to the town than working in the rural sector. If there is no work at all in the rural sector, the migrant loses nothing, except perhaps the security of the extended family system. The rate of growth of job opportunities in the rural sector depends on the rate of growth of demand for the output of the rural sector and the rate at which jobs are being 'destroyed' by productivity growth.

As we saw in our previous example (p. 67), if the demand for agricultural output is growing at 1.5 per cent and productivity is growing at 1 per cent, then the growth of labour demand will be 0.5 per cent. But if the labour force is growing at 2 per cent there will be a 1.5 per cent gap between the supply and demand for labour. If the level of disguised unemployment in the rural sector does not increase, this figure constitutes the potential volume of migrants. If the urban labour force is one-quarter of the size of the rural labour force, a 1.5 per cent migration of rural labour would represent a 6 per cent increase in the urban labour force owing to migration.

On average, this is about the extent of the influx from the rural sector into the urban areas of developing countries. On top of this there is the natural increase in the workforce in the urban areas to consider; this is of the order of 2–3 per cent. If job opportunities in the urban areas are increasing at only 5 per cent, then 3–4 per cent of the urban labour force will become unemployed each year, thus raising the amount of urban unemployment year by year, forcing labour into the informal service sector. In that case, unemployment shows up on poverty.

Historically, the process of development has always been associated with, and characterized by, an exodus from the land, continuing over centuries. The uniqueness of the present situation is not the migration itself but its magnitude and speed. And the problem is that the urban sector cannot absorb the numbers involved. For any given technology, the rate at which the urban (industrial) sector can absorb migrants largely depends on the rate of capital formation. If labour and capital must be combined in fixed proportions, and the rate of capital accumulation is only 5 per cent, then the rate of increase in job opportunities can be only 5 per cent also. Unfortunately, however, as we shall show in Chapter 5, the problem is not necessarily solved by a faster rate of capital accumulation in the urban sector, because migration is not simply a function of the actual difference in real remuneration between the two sectors, but also of the level of job opportunities in the urban sector. If the rate of job creation increases, this may merely increase the flow of migrants with no reduction in unemployment. The solution would seem to be to create more job opportunities in the rural sector. This will require, however, not only the redirection of investment but also the extension of education and transport facilities, which in the past few years have themselves become powerful push factors in the migration process. Whereas formerly redundant labour might have remained underemployed on the family farm, nowadays education and easy transportation provide the incentive and the means to seek alternative employment opportunities. While education and improved communications are desirable in themselves, and facilitate development, their provision has augmented the flow of migrants from rural to urban areas.

The **pull factors** behind migration are not hard to identify. The opportunities for work and leisure provided by the industrial, urban environment contrast sharply with the conservatism and stultifying atmosphere of rural village life and naturally act as a magnet for those on low incomes or without work, especially the young. Given the much higher wages in the urban sector, even the prospect of long spells of unemployment in the towns does not detract from the incentive to migrate. Moreover the choice is not necessarily between remaining in the rural sector and migrating to the urban sector with the prospect of long periods of unemployment. The unemployed in the urban sector can often find work, or create work for themselves, on the fringes of the industrial sector – in particular in the **informal services sector** of the urban economy. The wages may be low, but some income is better than no income. In other words, unemployment in urban areas may take the form of underemployment, or become disguised, just as in the case of the rural sector – its manifestation being low income. This has led to the notion of an **income measure of unemployment**, which needs to be added to registered unemployment to obtain a true measure of unemployment and the availability of labour supply.

One way of measuring the extent of unemployment disguised in the form of low-productivity/low-income jobs is to take the difference between the actual labour employed at the sub-standard income and the labour that would be required to produce a given level of output or service at an acceptable level of income per head. Before measurement can take place, of course, the acceptable (standard) level of income has to be defined. It could be that level set as the 'poverty line', below which health and welfare become seriously impaired. The income measure of unemployment would thus be

$$U = L - L^* = \frac{O}{O/L} - \frac{O}{O/L^*}$$

where L is the actual labour employed, L^* is the labour consistent with an acceptable level of income per person employed, O/L is the actual level of productivity, O/L^* is the acceptable level of income per employed person, and O is output.

Let us work an example. Suppose that the annual flow of output of an activity or service is £1 million and that the existing number employed is 10,000, giving a level of productivity of £100. Now suppose that the acceptable level of productivity to produce an acceptable level of income per person employed is £200. The income measure of unemployment is then

$$U = \frac{1,000,000}{100} - \frac{1,000,000}{200} = 5,000$$

that is, one-half of the existing labour force is disguisedly unemployed in the sense that the level of output is not sufficient for those who currently work to maintain an adequate standard of living.

The above analysis of employment and unemployment trends in developing countries points to a number of policy implications that were also highlighted by the ILO in 1969, when it first sponsored missions to several countries to undertake a detailed diagnosis of the employment problem.[4] Certainly an adequate rate of output growth is required to employ workers entering the labour market for the first time and to absorb the effects of productivity growth, but much more is required. There is a case for the use of much more labour-intensive techniques of production (see Chapter 12), and the issue of rural–urban migration needs to be tackled by promoting more employment opportunities outside the urban centres, particularly for young people. Without such measures, unemployment will continue to grow, especially in urban areas.

EDUCATION

Another dimension of the development gap is the difference in educational opportunities between rich and poor countries, which manifests itself in much lower primary, secondary and tertiary enrolment rates in developing countries; much higher levels of illiteracy; and lower levels of human capital formation in general. This has a number of adverse consequences for the growth and development process. Low levels of education and skills make it more difficult for countries to develop new industries and to absorb new technology; it makes people less adaptable and amenable to change; and it impairs the ability to manage and administer enterprises and organizations at all levels. As the famous American economist John Kenneth Galbraith once said: 'Literate people will see the need for getting machines. It is not so clear that machines will see the need for literate people. So under some circumstances, at least, popular education will have a priority over farms, factories and other furniture of capital development' (Galbraith, 1962).

The statistics in Table 3.5 show the relative underprovision of educational facilities and opportunities in many poor countries, and the low rate of literacy in the poorest countries. The first three columns show the percentage of the age group enrolled in primary, secondary and tertiary education. In the primary and secondary sectors, the percentage sometimes exceeds 100 per cent because the gross enrolment ratio is the ratio of *total* enrolment, *regardless of age*, to the population of the age group that official corresponds to that level of education. While primary education is universal in high income countries, one-quarter of children in poor countries still receive no primary education. This amounts to 125 million children, a third of whom live in Africa. In 1990, the world's governments pledged to provide primary education for all by the year 2000, but clearly the commitment has not been met. In 2000, the pledge was renewed (by the so-called 'Dakar Framework') to provide universal primary education in poor countries by the year 2015 (the same date as the poverty reduction target): indeed, this is one of the 'Millennium Goals'. The estimated cost is $10 billion a year. This will require a reorientation of priorities in poor countries (e.g. less expenditure on arms and wasteful subsidies), more aid from donor countries, and more help from the World Bank. The World Bank

Table 3.5 Participation in education

	Gross enrolment ratio			Adult literacy rate	
	% of relevant age group			% ages 15 and older	
	Primary 2001/02	Secondary 2001/02	Tertiary 2001/02	Male 2002	Female 2002
Afghanistan	23	12	–	–	–
Albania	107	78	15	99	98
Algeria	108	72	–	78	60
Angola	–	19	1	–	–
Argentina	120	100	57	97	97
Armenia	96	87	26	100	99
Australia	102	154	65	–	–
Austria	103	99	57	–	–
Azerbaijan	93	80	23	–	–
Bangladesh	98	47	6	50	31
Belarus	110	84	62	100	100
Belgium	105	154	58	–	–
Benin	104	26	4	55	26
Bolivia	114	84	39	93	81
Botswana	103	73	5	76	82
Brazil	148	108	18	86	87
Bulgaria	99	94	40	99	98
Burkina Faso	48	10	–	19	8
Burundi	71	11	2	58	44
Cambodia	123	22	3	81	59
Cameroon	107	33	5	77	60
Canada	100	106	59	–	–
Central African Republic	66	–	2	65	33
Chad	73	12	1	55	38
Chile	103	85	37	96	96
China	114	68	13	95	87
Hong Kong, China	–	–	–	–	–
Colombia	110	65	24	92	92
Congo, Rep.	86	32	4	89	77
Costa Rica	108	67	21	96	96
Côte d'Ivoire	80	23	–	–	–
Croatia	96	88	36	99	97
Cuba	100	89	27	97	97
Czech Republic	104	95	30	–	–
Denmark	102	128	59	–	–
Dominican Republic	126	67	–	84	84
Ecuador	117	59	–	92	90
Egypt, Arab Rep.	97	85	–	67	44
El Salvador	112	56	17	82	77
Eritrea	61	28	2	–	–
Estonia	103	110	59	100	100
Ethiopia	62	17	2	49	34
Finland	102	126	85	–	–
France	105	108	54	–	–
Gabon	134	51	–	–	–
Gambia, The	79	34	–	–	–
Georgia	92	79	36	–	–
Germany	103	99	–	–	–

Table 3.5 continued

	Gross enrolment ratio			Adult literacy rate	
	% of relevant age group			% ages 15 and older	
	Primary 2001/02	Secondary 2001/02	Tertiary 2001/02	Male 2002	Female 2002
Ghana	81	38	3	82	66
Greece	97	96	61	99	96
Guatemala	103	33	–	77	62
Guinea	77	–	–	–	–
Guinea-Bissau	70	18	–	–	–
Honduras	106	–	14	80	80
Hungary	102	98	40	99	99
India	99	48	11	–	–
Indonesia	111	58	15	92	83
Iran, Islamic Rep.	92	81	19	84	70
Iraq	99	38	14	–	–
Ireland	119	–	47	–	–
Israel	114	93	53	97	93
Italy	101	96	50	99	98
Jamaica	101	84	17	84	91
Japan	101	102	48	–	–
Jordan	99	86	31	96	86
Kazakhstan	99	89	39	100	99
Kenya	96	32	4	90	79
Korea, Rep.	100	94	82	–	–
Kuwait	94	85	–	85	81
Kyrgyz Republic	102	85	44	–	–
Lao PDR	115	41	4	77	55
Latvia	99	93	64	100	100
Lebanon	103	77	45	–	–
Lesotho	124	34	2	74	90
Liberia	105	–	–	72	39
Libya	114	105	58	92	71
Lithuania	104	98	59	100	100
Macedonia, FYR	99	85	24	–	–
Madagascar	104	–	2	–	–
Malaysia	95	70	26	92	85
Mali	57	–	2	27	12
Mauritania	86	22	3	51	31
Mauritius	106	80	11	88	81
Mexico	110	73	20	93	89
Moldova	85	72	29	100	99
Mongolia	99	76	35	98	98
Morocco	107	41	10	63	38
Mozambique	99	13	1	62	31
Myanmar	90	39	11	89	81
Namibia	106	61	7	84	83
Nepal	122	44	5	62	26
Netherlands	108	124	55	–	–
New Zealand	99	113	72	–	–
Nicaragua	105	57	–	77	77
Niger	40	6	1	25	9
Nigeria	96	–	–	74	59

Table 3.5 continued

| | Gross enrolment ratio | | | Adult literacy rate | |
| | % of relevant age group | | | % ages 15 and older | |
	Primary 2001/02	Secondary 2001/02	Tertiary 2001/02	Male 2002	Female 2002
Norway	101	115	70	–	–
Oman	83	79	7	82	65
Pakistan	73	–	–	53	29
Panama	110	69	34	93	92
Papua New Guinea	77	23	–	–	
Paraguay	112	64	18	93	90
Peru	121	–	–	91	80
Philippines	112	82	30	93	93
Poland	100	101	55	–	–
Portugal	121	114	50	95	91
Romania	99	82	27	98	96
Russian Federation	114	92	68	100	99
Rwanda	117	14	2	75	63
Saudi Arabia	67	69	22	84	69
Senegal	75	19	–	49	30
Serbia and Montenegro	99	89	36	–	–
Sierra Leone	76	–	2	–	–
Slovak Republic	103	87	30	100	100
Slovenia	100	106	61	100	100
South Africa	105	86	15	87	85
Spain	107	114	57	99	97
Sri Lanka	110	81	–	95	90
Sudan	59	32	–	71	49
Swaziland	100	45	5	82	80
Sweden	110	149	70	–	–
Switzerland	107	100	42	–	–
Syrian Arab Republic	112	45	–	91	74
Tajikistan	107	82	15	100	99
Tanzania	70	6	1	85	69
Thailand	98	83	37	95	91
Togo	124	36	4	74	45
Trinidad and Tobago	105	70	7	99	98
Tunisia	112	79	23	83	63
Turkey	94	76	25	93	75
Uganda	136	–	3	79	59
Ukraine	90	97	57	100	100
United Arab Emirates	92	79	–	76	81
United Kingdom	101	158	59	–	–
United States	100	94	71	–	–
Uruguay	108	101	38	97	98
Uzbekistan	103	99	9	100	99
Venezuela, RB	106	69	18	94	93
Vietnam	103	70	10	94	87
Yemen, Rep.	81	46	–	69	29
Zambia	79	–	2	86	74
Zimbabwe	99	43	4	94	86

Table 3.5 continued

	Gross enrolment ratio			Adult literacy rate	
	% of relevant age group			% ages 15 and older	
	Primary 2001/02	Secondary 2001/02	Tertiary 2001/02	Male 2002	Female 2002
World	**103**	**70**	**24**	**84**	**71**
Low income	94	46	10	72	53
Middle income	111	75	22	92	83
Lower middle income	112	75	20	92	82
Upper middle income	104	81	33	95	92
Low & middle income	103	63	17	83	70
East Asia & Pacific	111	66	14	93	82
Europe & Central Asia	103	89	48	99	96
Latin America & Carib.	129	89	23	90	89
Middle East & N. Africa	96	70	–	76	55
South Asia	95	48	10	67	44
Sub-Saharan Africa	87	–	–	71	56
High income	**102**	**106**	**61**	**–**	**–**

Source: World Bank, *World Development Indicators 2004* (Washington: World Bank)

readily admits that, until the recent past, it has neglected educational (and other social) expenditure in its lending policies.

Notice also the huge discrepancy in the provision of secondary education, with only one-half of the age group in low-income countries receiving any education beyond the age of 11. This basic deficiency in educational provision, compared to rich countries, manifests itself in high levels of adult illiteracy. A huge gender gap is also evident. In low-income countries, 30 per cent of males are illiterate, and almost 50 per cent of females. Among the poor countries, China performs well, but in many of the poorest countries in Africa female illiteracy is way over 50 per cent. The gender gap narrows at higher income levels, but is still evident.

Developing countries neglect educational provision at their peril. Research, which we will discuss in Chapter 4, shows a strong correlation across countries between levels of human capital formation and growth performance.

INEQUALITY: VERTICAL AND HORIZONTAL

As well as the average per capita income being low in developing countries, the distribution of income, wealth and power is also typically very unequal, and much more unequal than in developed countries. All too often, the growth and development that takes place in poor countries benefits the richest few, and the vast mass of the population is left untouched. Rural and urban poverty are still widespread, and if anything the degree of income inequality within many developing countries is increasing. How income is distributed across individuals and households is referred to as **vertical inequality**, and is the traditional measure of inequality that development policy focuses upon. There is also the concept, however, of **horizontal inequality** concerned with how different *groups* in society are treated, based on race, religion, language, class, gender, and so on. The well-being of people can be affected as much by horizontal inequality as vertical inequality. First we will consider vertical inequality and then horizontal inequality.

It should come as no surprise that the transformation of economies from a primitive subsistence state into industrial societies, within a basically capitalist framework, should be accompanied in the early stages by widening disparities in the personal distribution of income. Some people are more industrious than others and more adept at accumulating wealth. Opportunities cannot, in the very nature of things, be equal for all. In the absence of strong redistributive taxation, income inequality will inevitably accompany industrialization because of the inequality of skills and wealth that differences in individual ability and initiative – and industrialization – produce.

The observation that income inequality increases with the level of development and then declines is often called the **Kuznets curve**, named after the famous development economist, Simon Kuznets, who did pioneering research on structural change and income distribution in the 1950s and 1960s (e.g. Kuznets 1955, 1963b) which in 1971 earned him the Nobel Prize for economics. Kuznets showed that in many of the present developed countries, the degree of inequality first increased and then decreased in the later stages of industrialization, giving an inverted U-shaped curve.

For the developing countries, the pioneering work of Adelman and Morris (1971), extended by Paukert (1973), also shows fairly conclusively that inequality increases up to a certain stage of development and then declines, graphically showing an inverted U-shape similar to the work of Kuznets for the developed countries. The average Gini coefficient for 43 developing countries is found to be 0.467 compared with 0.392 for 13 developed countries. The greater degree of inequality in the developing countries appears largely due to the higher share of income received by the richest 5 per cent of income recipients – nearly 30 per cent of income in developing countries compared with 20 per cent in developed countries.

Deininger and Squire (1996) of the World Bank have surveyed 682 studies of income distribution in over 100 countries and calculated average Gini ratios for each country, together with the ratio of the share of income received by the top 20 per cent of income earners (top quintile) to that of the bottom 20 per cent of income earners (bottom quintile). The results are shown by continent in Table 3.6. It can be seen from the Gini ratios (multiplied by 100) that Latin America and the Caribbean, and Africa, have by far the largest degree of income inequality, with the Gini ratio way over 50 in many countries, for example Brazil (57.3), Mexico (53.8) and South Africa (62.3). In contrast, income inequality in Asia and the Pacific, and Eastern Europe, appears to be much less. In the two largest countries in the world measured by population – China and India – the Gini ratio is just over 30, much the same as for the high-income countries. Generally speaking, the higher the Gini ratio, the greater the ratio of income shares between the top and bottom 20 per cent of income earners. In South Africa that ratio is 32:1 and in Brazil 23:1.

There are several formidable barriers to narrowing the income distribution gap. First, there is the dualistic nature of many economies (see Chapter 7), perpetuated by feudal land-tenure systems and urban bias in the allocation of investment resources. Secondly,

Table 3.6 Income inequality, selected economies, 1990s

Region and economy	Number of observations	Average Gini ratio	Ratio of top quintile's share of income to bottom quintile's share
Sub-Saharan Africa	40	44.71	11.61
Botswana	1	54.21	16.36
Cameroon	1	49.00	–
Central African Republic	1	55.00	–
Côte d'Ivoire	4	39.18	7.17
Gabon	2	61.23	19.79
Ghana	4	35.13	5.97
Guinea–Bissau	1	56.12	28.57
Kenya	1	54.39	18.24
Lesotho	1	56.02	20.90
Madagascar	1	43.44	8.52
Mauritania	1	42.53	13.12
Mauritius	3	40.67	6.62
Niger	1	36.10	5.90
Nigeria	3	38.55	8.67
Rwanda	1	28.90	4.01
Senegal	1	54.12	16.75
Seychelles	2	46.50	–
Sierra Leone	1	60.79	22.45
South Africa	1	62.30	32.11
Sudan	1	38.72	5.58
Tanzania	3	40.37	6.63
Uganda	2	36.89	6.01
Zambia	2	47.26	12.11
Zimbabwe	1	56.83	15.66
East Asia and the Pacific	123	36.18	7.15
China	12	32.68	5.17
Fiji	1	42.50	–
Hong Kong	7	41.58	9.46
Indonesia	11	33.49	5.22
Japan	23	34.82	7.06
Korea, Rep. of	14	34.19	6.29
Lao PDR	1	30.40	4.21
Malaysia	6	50.36	14.18
Philippines	7	47.62	12.00
Singapore	6	40.12	6.71
Taiwan (China)	26	29.62	4.67
Thailand	8	45.48	11.65
Vietnam	1	35.71	5.51
South Asia	60	34.06	5.50
Bangladesh	10	34.51	5.72
India	31	32.55	4.98
Nepal	1	30.06	4.34
Pakistan	9	31.50	4.68
Sri Lanka	9	41.71	7.98

▶

Table 3.6 continued

Region and economy	Number of observations	Average Gini ratio	Ratio of top quintile's share of income to bottom quintile's share
Eastern Europe	101	26.01	4.05
Armenia	1	39.39	23.88
Belarus	1	28.53	4.30
Bulgaria	28	23.30	3.24
Czechoslovakia	12	22.25	3.08
Czech Republic	2	27.43	3.75
Estonia	3	34.66	6.62
Hungary	9	24.65	3.61
Kazakhstan	1	32.67	5.39
Kyrgyz Republic	1	35.32	6.31
Latvia	1	26.98	3.83
Lithuania	1	33.64	5.20
Moldova	1	34.43	6.06
Poland	17	25.69	3.75
Romania	3	25.83	3.79
Slovak Republic	2	20.50	2.76
Slovenia	2	27.08	3.77
USSR	5	26.94	4.06
Ukraine	1	25.71	3.71
Yugoslavia	10	32.62	5.63
Middle East and North Africa	20	40.77	7.14
Algeria	1	38.73	6.85
Egypt, Arab Rep. of	4	38.00	4.72
Iran, Islamic Rep. of	5	43.23	–
Jordan	3	39.19	7.39
Morocco	2	39.20	7.03
Tunisia	5	42.51	8.25
Latin America and the Caribbean	100	50.15	16.02
Barbados	2	47.18	17.56
Bolivia	1	42.04	8.58
Brazil	15	57.32	23.07
Chile	5	51.84	14.48
Colombia	7	51.51	13.94
Costa Rica	9	46.00	13.13
Dominican Republic	4	46.94	11.06
Ecuador	1	43.00	9.82
El Salvador	1	48.40	10.64
Guatemala	3	55.68	20.82
Guyana	2	48.19	9.15
Honduras	7	54.49	27.74
Jamaica	9	42.90	8.75
Mexico	9	53.85	17.12
Nicaragua	1	50.32	13.12
Panama	4	52.43	22.64
Peru	4	47.99	9.21
Puerto Rico	3	51.11	22.20
Trinidad	4	46.21	18.31
Venezuela	9	44.42	10.93

▶

Table 3.6 continued

Region and economy	Number of observations	Average Gini ratio	Ratio of top quintile's share of income to bottom quintile's share
Industrial countries and high-income developing countries	238	33.19	6.63
Australia	9	37.88	8.32
Bahamas	11	45.77	14.14
Belgium	4	27.01	4.26
Canada	23	31.27	5.54
Denmark	4	32.09	6.29
Finland	12	29.93	5.35
France	7	43.11	6.31
Germany	7	31.22	5.35
Greece	3	34.53	6.37
Ireland	3	36.31	8.91
Italy	15	34.93	4.94
Luxembourg	1	27.13	4.11
Netherlands	12	28.59	4.43
New Zealand	12	34.36	6.78
Norway	9	34.21	7.39
Portugal	4	37.44	7.44
Spain	8	27.90	4.34
Sweden	15	31.63	5.64
Turkey	3	50.36	15.22
United Kingdom	31	25.98	4.03
United States	45	35.28	8.46
Total	682	36.12	7.80

Source: K. Deininger and L. Squire, 'A New Data Set Measuring Income Inequalities', *World Bank Economic Review*, September 1996.

there is inequality in the distribution of education facilities, and a particular lack of facilities in rural areas where the poorest are concentrated. Third, there is disguised rural unemployment, underemployment and open unemployment in urban areas created by rural–urban migration, a shortage of investment resources and inappropriate technical choices. Until development policy comes to grips with these problems, there will continue to be large pockets of absolute poverty and a marked degree of inequality in income distribution. When deciding on the allocation of investment resources and the choice of projects, a high weight should be given to projects that raise the income of the poorest in the income distribution (see Chapter 10).

Now let us turn to horizontal inequality (HI) which is concerned with how economic differences, social demarcations and political power combine to produce differences in entitlements and capabilities for different groups in society. Groups may be defined in a number of ways, as already mentioned; by race, religion, gender, location, class, language and so on. Stewart (2001) develops the hypothesis that not only is HI responsible for much conflict within societies, but it also affects the development process in a number of ways. For example, some groups may be denied access to public goods such as education and health care. This impoverishes not only the group, but the economy at large. Certain regions may be deprived of infrastructure investment because of particular groups located in these regions, which not only damages the region but the development of the whole economy. To be discriminated against on the basis of a particular group identity has psychological effects, and affects the core goals of development that we discussed in Chapter 1: life sustenance, self esteem, and freedom. Thus HI is an important dimension of well-being, and can have economic and political consequences highly detrimental to development, and yet international development policy is rarely focused on the narrowing of group divisions. HI would not matter so much if there was mobility between groups, or if individuals were free to choose which group they belonged to, but this is rarely the case in often highly stratified developing countries. Stewart (2001) gives examples of several case studies of the basis and consequences of horizontal inequality e.g. in Mexico, Brazil, Fiji, Malaysia and South Africa. The situation in several countries is given in Case Example 3.3. It is clear that development policy needs to tackle horizontal inequality between groups, as well as vertical inequality with respect to the income distribution across individuals.

Case example **3.3**

Inequalities between Groups can Fuel Conflict and Tension

The root causes of violent conflict are rarely simple. But as the examples below show, a common theme is emerging from recent research into conflict: the role that socio-economic and political inequalities between groups can play in causing tensions and violence. Less research has been done on the role that cultural exclusions of groups may play (such as lack of recognition of languages or religious practices), but these are also issues that can lead to mobilization and protests and so may also be important root causes or triggers of conflict.

- Severe rioting against the Chinese in **Malaysia** in the late 1960s has been attributed largely to the animosity felt by the politically dominant but economically sidelined Bumiputera majority towards the economically dominant Chinese minority.
- Civil war in **Sri Lanka** since the early 1980s has been linked to tensions resulting from inequalities between the Tamil minority and Sinhalese majority. Colonial administrators had favoured the Tamil minority economically, but this advantage was sharply reversed once the Sinhalese gained power and increasingly sidelined the Tamil minority in such areas as educational opportunities, civil service recruitment and language policy.
- In **Uganda** the Bantu-speaking people (largely in the centre and south) have been economically dominant but politically sidelined compared with the non-Bantu-speaking people (largely in the north). These economic and political inequities have played a role in major conflicts, including the violence initiated by Idi Amin (1970s) and by the second Obote regime (1983–85).
- Indigenous people in the state of Chiapas, **Mexico**, have long suffered political and socio-economic deprivation. They have demanded greater political autonomy, improved socio-economic conditions and protection of their cultural heritage, culminating in uprisings against the Mexican state in four municipalities.

▶

- In **South Africa** before 1994 the black majority was severely disadvantaged politically and socio-economically. That led to many uprisings between 1976 and the transfer of power in 1993.
- Catholics in **Northern Ireland** have suffered economic and political deprivation since the 16th century. The continuance of Northern Ireland as part of the United Kingdom in the 1920s ensured that Protestants would enjoy permanent political and economic dominance – fuelling demands by northern Catholics to become part of the predominantly Catholic Republic of Ireland. Violent conflict started in the late 1960s and began to ease in the 1990s following systematic efforts to reduce these inequalities.
- Constitutional crises and coups have occurred in **Fiji**, notably in 1987 and 1999, as economically sidelined indigenous Fijians have feared losing political control to the economically dominant Indian-origin Fijians.
- Increasing tensions between Muslims and Christians in Poso, Central Sulawesi, **Indonesia**, began surfacing in the mid-1990s as the Muslim community increasingly gained more than indigenous Christians from new economic policies.
- Since colonial times the indigenous people of **Guatemala** have suffered political and economic discrimination, contributing to the country's ongoing conflicts.
- The Maoist insurgency launched in **Nepal** in 1996 may be attributed to deep grievances stemming from the systematic marginalization and exclusion of certain ethnic groups, castes and women.

Source: UNDP, *Human Development Report 2004* (New York: Oxford University Press, 2004).

GROWTH AND DISTRIBUTION

The observation that income inequality increases with the level of development and then declines is not to say that faster economic growth within a country necessarily worsens the income disribution. Recent international evidence suggests that rapid structural transformation and fast economic growth have benefited the poor as much as the rich. Nor for that matter is inequality a necessary condition for growth because it generates more saving, as sometimes alleged. Naqvi (1995) looked in detail at 40 developing countries and found that high growth rates and distributive justice (as well as macroeconomic stability) have tended to move together. This is also the recent conclusion of Dollar and Kraay (2000) who examine the relation between growth and income distribution across 80 countries over 40 years. They find that the income of the poor (the bottom 20 per cent of the population) rises one-to-one with overall growth, and the relation is no different in poor countries than in rich ones. Nor has the poverty–growth relationship changed much over time. In other words, growth seems to benefit the poor as much as the rich, so that relative inequality (the Gini ratio) stays the same (although *absolute* inequality still widens, of course, because the same growth of income gives more dollars to a rich person than a poor person).

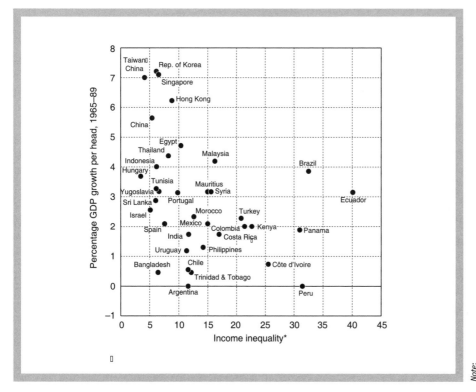

Figure 3.3 Income inequality and economic growth

On the question of whether inequality promotes growth, the answer seems to be 'no'. If the Gini ratio is included in a cross-section equation to explain differences in growth between countries, the coefficient is normally negative, not positive (see Forbes, 2000). In other words, a more equal distribution of income is good for growth. Income equality is probably standing here as a proxy for such growth-inducing factors as good governance, civil society, equal property rights and equality of opportunity. The successful Asian 'tiger economies' have much more equal distributions of income than most other developing economies, and better governance.

The World Bank has also challenged the view that growth and equality necessarily conflict. If anything, countries with a greater degree of equality have grown fastest. This is shown in Figure 3.3, where the growth of income per head is measured on the vertical axis and income inequality is measured on the horizontal axis. It can be seen that many of the fastest-growing countries have a comparatively equal income disribution, while many of the slowest-growing countries have a high degree of income inequality. It appears that income inequality is not necessary for high levels of saving and investment, or other factors that contribute to rapid growth.

POVERTY-WEIGHTED GROWTH RATES

Whether progress is being made towards achieving the twin objectives of faster growth and a more equal distribution of income can be examined simultaneously by constructing **poverty-weighted indices of growth**.

GNP growth as conventionally measured is a weighted average of the growth of income of different groups of people, where the relevant weights are each group's share of total income. The measured growth rate pays no regard to the distribution of income. A high growth rate may be recorded, but this may have only benefited the rich. For example, suppose the bottom third of the population receive 10 per cent of income, the middle third receive 30 per cent of income, and the top third receive 60 per cent of income. GNP growth would be measured as

% growth of GNP = $r_1(0.1) + r_2(0.3) + r_3(0.6)$

where r_1, r_2 and r_3 are the respective rates of growth of income of the three groups. Suppose $r_1 = 1$ per cent, $r_2 = 1$ per cent and $r_3 = 10$ per cent. A GNP growth rate of 6.4 per cent would then be recorded, which looks very respectable but the position of the poorest will hardly have changed.

The idea of constructing poverty-weighted indices of growth is to give at least equal weight to all income groups in society, if not a greater weight to the poor, in order to obtain a better measure of the growth of overall welfare combining the growth of income with its distribution.

In the above example, for instance, if each group is given an equal weight of one-third, the measured growth of welfare becomes

% growth of 'welfare' = $1(0.33) + 1(0.33) + 10(0.33) = 4\%$

which is much less than the rate of growth shown by the conventional measure of GNP growth when distributional considerations are taken into account.

A society could go further and say that it places no value or weight on income growth for the richest third of the population, and places all the weight on the lower-income groups with, say, a 60 per cent weight to the bottom third and a 40 per cent weight to the middle third. The growth of 'welfare' would then look derisory:

% growth of 'welfare' = $1(0.6) + 1(0.4) + 10(0) = 1\%$

This approach has been experimented with by economists from the World Bank (see Ahluwalia et al., 1979) to compare countries, giving a 60 per cent weight to the lowest 40 per cent of the population, a 40 per cent weight to the middle 40 per cent and no weight to the top 20 per cent. In countries where the distribution of income had deteriorated, the poverty-weighted measure of the growth of welfare showed less improvement than GNP growth, and where the distribution of income had improved, the poverty-weighted growth rate showed more improvement than GNP growth.

NUTRITION AND HEALTH

Another dimension of the development gap between rich and poor countries is the poor level of nutrition and health among large sections of the population in developing countries. It has been estimated by the United Nations Food and Agriculture Organisation (FAO) in Rome that over 1 billion people in the world suffer from various types of malnutrition, including over half of the world's 1.5 billion children. One billion people suffer protein–energy malnutrition, 1.3 billion suffer from anaemia (iron deficiency), 1.0 billion people have iodine deficiency, and 30 million children have vitamin A deficiency, causing blindness and death. Over 1 billion people have no reliable access to safe drinking water. Children may suffer several bouts of severe diarrhoea a year. This weakens the body, and the weaker and more undernourished children are, the more prone they are to infection and disease; and the more infections the greater the undernourishment because of loss of appetite, the difficulties of eating and the low absorption rate of food during digestion. Malnutrition among children is particularly serious because it stunts growth and mental development, and adds another twist to the vicious circle of poverty. Malnutrition is also a major cause of infant mortality, the rate of which is ten times higher in developing countries than in developed countries.

In his monumental and pathbreaking book *An Inquiry into Well-Being and Destitution* (1993), the famous Indian economist Partha Dasgupta attempts to understand the common circumstances in which people are born in poor countries and in which they live and die in rural communities in poor countries. He pays a lot of attention to the question of nutrition and its effects on health and work effort. The relation between low income and food intake is, of course, two-way. Low income is the major cause of malnutrition, which in turn is a cause of low income as it impairs work efficiency and productivity. Indices or measures of malnutrition can either be based on **nutritional requirements** in terms of different kinds of food or on **food energy**. Both affect labour productivity. The food requirements that nutritionists consider necessary for efficient working and healthy living are far greater than the levels achieved by the vast mass of the population living in developing countries. Calorie deficiency causes loss of body weight, tiredness, listlessness and a deterioration of mental faculties. Calories are also required for the absorption of protein: if the calorie requirement is met the protein requirement is normally met too, but not always. The condition 'Kwashiorkor' (associated with the bloated stomachs and staring eyes of the starving or malnourished children we see on our television screens) arises from protein deficiency because the calorie intake is in the form of low-protein tubers such as cassavas and yams. Protein is particularly important for brain development in the first three years of life, during which time the brain grows to 90 per cent of its full size. Brain damage due to protein deficiency is irreversible.

When it comes to the relation between nutrition and the capacity for physical effort, nutrition is generally defined in terms of the energy requirement. In this context, Dasgupta (1993) defines undernourishment as 'a state in which the physical functioning of a person is impaired to the point where she cannot maintain an adequate level of performance at physical work, or at resisting or recovering from the effects of any of a . . . variety of diseases'. The minimum amount of energy, or maintenance requirement (r), is the daily calorie requirement when a person is engaged in the minimal activities of eating and maintaining essential hygiene, with no allowance for work and play. According to nutritionists, r is 1.4 times the basal metabolic rate. The relation between productivity and energy intake is shown in Figure 3.4.

The interesting thing here is the slope of the line. In Figure 3.4 it is decreasing, but it could be linear or even increasing over certain ranges. When Bliss and Stern (1978) surveyed the literature they found the line to be linear in the region slightly to the right of r. More recent research confirms this[5] and shows substantial economic and social

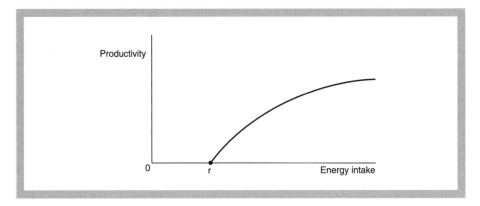

Figure 3.4 Relation between productivity and energy intake

returns to investment in nutrition and health in terms of increased productivity on the job, increased productivity of time spent in school, and cost savings from treating the consequences of malnutrition and poor health. The costs of treating various forms of malnutrition are trivial relative to the tangible benefits, and to the costs of treating the consequences. To prevent malnutrition in children from the age of six months to three years, which is a child's most vulnerable period, can cost as little as $50 at current prices. The annual cost of preventing malnutrition is no more than the daily cost of treating its effects. Vitamin A deficiency is a cause of blindness. The annual cost of supporting a blind person is at least 1000 times the annual ingredient cost of the vitamin A needed for prevention. Iodine deficiency is a cause of hypothyroidism (goitre), which leads to cretinism and deaf-mutism. The cost of iodate to prevent this is less than $0.01 per person per year. And so one could go on. Prevention is better than cure not only for the individual but also in a very real economic sense for the welfare of society as a whole.

The World Bank has calculated that the cost to developing countries of deficiencies of vitamin A, iodine and iron amounts to 5 per cent of GDP owing to disabilities, deaths and reduced productivity. The cost of remedies would be no more than $1 billion. The Bank has now launched **micronutrient projects** in countries such as China to combat nutritional deficiencies that lead to blindness, mental retardation, learning difficulties and low work capacity.

Survival depends not only on nutrition but also freedom from infection and disease. A major investment effort in this field too would yield substantial returns. These major infectious diseases blight the lives of millions of people in developing countries, particularly in Africa. The old enemies, which are still rampant, are tuberculosis and malaria. The new enemy is AIDS, which is starting to have a devastating effect on the economies of Africa.

Tuberculosis kills 3 million people a year. This is controllable. Treatment requires a combined dose of four powerful antibiotics a day for six to eight months. Close monitoring is required to make sure the daily dose is taken, but research in India by the World Health Organisation (WHO) shows that if $200 million a year was spent there on effective control programmes, the economic return would be a colossal $750 million through reduction in the cost of treatment for sufferers and increased productivity.

Malaria kills directly and indirectly 23 million people every year. The social and economic cost is enormous. Since 1970 it has reduced the GDP of Africa by $100 billion. Despite this, malaria control still receives only $130 million a year in aid from the international community. It is estimated that at least $1 billion is needed for effective control in order to distribute mosquito nets and to pay for medical treatment and vaccines. There is, however, hope for the future. Scientists working on the global genome project have unlocked the genetic code of both the malaria parasite and the mosquito species that transmits it. This paves the way for a new generation of vaccines, insecticides and repellents to combat malaria, provided, of course, that it is profitable for the drug companies to develop them.

But fast becoming the biggest killer is AIDS (acquired immune deficiency syndrome). The UN forecasts that 70 million people will have died from AIDs by 2020. Worldwide, 40 million people are currently HIV (human immunodeficiency virus) and AIDS infected, and 30 million of these are in Africa. The numbers infected are increasing by 5 million a year, and nearly 3 million a year are dying. AIDS kills 10 times more Africans than armed conflict. It is not an exaggeration to say that AIDS now poses the foremost threat to development in Africa. The social and economic consequences are manifold. In some of the countries worst affected, such as South Africa, Botswana, Zimbabwe and Zambia, life expectancy has been reduced to less than 40 years (see Case example 3.4). This is denuding countries of skilled and productive labour, including teachers, and leading to high levels of absenteeism at work. It is leaving millions of children orphaned and uneducated. The cost of treatment is putting an enormous strain on the health budget of countries which reduces the resources available to cope with other diseases. The World Bank has estimated that an HIV/AIDS infection rate of 8 per cent reduces annual per capita income growth of countries by 0.4 percentage points, and a 25 per cent infection rate reduces growth by 1 percentage point. This is an enormous cost in lost output. By comparison, the cost of treatment would be easily affordable by the world community. UNAIDS, the joint United Nations programme on HIV/AIDS, estimates $10 billion is needed for prevention, control and community support yet only $3 billion is being spent. Development aid dedicated to health care in Africa is currently only $6 billion to cover all health problems. After some bitter disputes with countries and the WTO over patent protection, most of the world's major drug companies have now agreed to provide anti-retroviral drugs at cost in countries where health programmes are administered efficiently.

Apart from the big killers of tuberculosis, malaria and AIDS, there are four other major tropical diseases that continue to disable tens of millions of people in tropical Asia, Africa and Latin America: leprosy, river blindness, Chagas disease and lymphatic filariasis. With modern medicine and antibiotics there is now the opportunity to eliminate these diseases. There are still 1 million leprosy sufferers, but this was reduced from 5 million as recently as fifteen years ago through a combination of three antibiotics. Over 300,000 people suffer river blindness through a parasite spread by sandflies, but already the drug ivermectin has eliminated the transmission of the disease in eleven West African countries. Chagas disease is spread by bloodsucking bugs and infects 17 million people a year in Africa, killing 45,000 a year. Lymphatic filariasis is transmitted by mosquitos and infects 120 million people in over 70 countries, causing a range of symptoms from elephantiasis to kidney damage. India is the country most affected and the cost of treatment is only $0.05 per person based on an annual dose of the drugs ivermectin and diethylcarbamazine.

AIDS and Life Expectancy

Life expectancy in much of Sub-Saharan Africa will soon fall to levels not seen since the nineteenth century under the weight of the AIDS pandemic, according to research by the American government. Average lifespans will be reduced in 51 countries, mainly in Africa and the Caribbean, and the global catastrophe will become even worse if the disease begins to infect large numbers of people in China, India and South-East Asia, as experts predict. By 2010, people in these regions will be living to 30, instead of perhaps 70, which we would have expected without AIDS.

In Botswana, where 39 per cent of the adult population are HIV positive, life expectancy would have been expected to rise to 74 years and five months in 2010, had there been no AIDS pandemic. It currently stands at 33 years and 11 months. The other countries in which life expectancy will be lower than 40 in 2010 are Angola (35); Lesotho (36.5); Malawi (36.9); Mozambique (27.1); Namibia (33.8); Rwanda (38.7); South Africa (36.5); Swaziland (33.0); Zambia (34.4); and Zimbabwe (34.5).

AIDS has also reversed the decline in infant mortality that was seen across southern Africa in the 1980s and early 1990s, with rates in several countries, such as Swaziland and Zimbabwe, standing at close to double what they would have been without the pandemic. In four countries – Botswana, Zimbabwe, South Africa and Namibia – more infants will die of AIDS than of any other cause by 2010.

Peter Piot, executive director of UNAIDS, the United Nations HIV agency, said that AIDS was now responsible for the worst pandemic in history. 'More money is being spent than ever, but if you look at the number of positive people and treatment in the poorest countries, there is still a long way to go,' he said. 'To a certain extent, we have failed to stop the expansion of the epidemic.'

	Life Expectancy (Age in years)	
	Without AIDS	With AIDS
Angola	41.3	35.0
Botswana	74.4	26.7
Lesotho	67.2	36.5
Malawi	59.4	36.9
Mozambique	42.5	27.1
Namibia	68.8	33.8
Rwanda	54.7	38.7
South Africa	68.5	36.5
Swaziland	74.6	33.0
Zambia	58.6	34.4
Zimbabwe	71.4	34.6

Source: The Times, 8 July 2002.

Disease and malnutrition blight the lives of millions of men, women and children across the developing world. Small investments in nutrition and disease prevention would transform their quality of life and the productive potential of their countries, yet the world prefers to send robots to Mars!

The United Nations and other bodies are calling for an additional $10 billion a year of health aid to fight AIDS and other infectious diseases. This amounts to only $10 per head from the 1 billion citizens of rich countries: not much to improve the health and life-chances of fellow citizens in our so-called 'global community'.

The Sachs Report for the WHO recommends a Global Health Resource Fund with capital of $1.5 billion a year. The report estimates that eight million lives could be saved at a total annual cost of $27 billion by 2007 and $38 billion by 2015 – equal to only 0.1 per cent of the GDP of rich countries.[6]

Poor nutrition and disease, combined with rudimentary health facilities, leads to low life expectancy and a high incidence of infant mortality. Table 3.7 presents some selected health-related statistics, including total expenditure on health as a percentage of GDP; health expenditure per head of the population; the percentage of the population with access to safe water and sanitation, and the rate of infant mortality. Notice that while rich countries spend nearly $3000 per head per year on health, poor countries spend only $23. The lack of access to basic health facilities is reflected in the fact that the infant mortality rate in low-income countries is 79 per 1000 live births compared with only 5 per 1000 in high-income countries.

POVERTY, FAMINE AND ENTITLEMENTS

Malnutrition is caused by a lack of access to food, but this does not only depend on the availability of food; it also depends on people's entitlement to food. Vast sections of the population may go short of food and experience famine conditions, not primarily because food has become scarce, but because their entitlement to food has been impaired. This is the powerful thesis put forward by Sen (1984), who argues that to understand poverty and starvation, and the malnutrition associated with it, it is necessary to understand both ownership patterns and exchange entitlements, which in turn requires an understanding of modes of production and the class structure. He attempts to document the theory, drawing on the experience of major famines such as the Great Bengal famine of 1943, the Ethiopian famine of 1973–5, the famine in the Sahel region of Africa in the early 1970s and the Bangladesh famine of 1974. It seems that some of the worst famines occurred with no significant fall in food availability per head.

What does the entitlement to food depend on? Above all, it depends on the ability of individuals to exchange productive resources and goods for food. This in turn depends on such factors as:

- The ownership and employment status of individuals – for example, whether they are owners of land, labourers, peasant farmers, sharecroppers and so on
- Productivity
- Non-working income in the form of subsidies and transfer payments from government
- The terms of trade (the relative price ratio) between food and other goods.

Table 3.7 Health indicators

	Health expenditure	Health expenditure per capita	Access to an improved water source	Access to improved sanitation facilities	Infant mortality rate
	Total % of GDP (2001)	$ (2001)	% of population (2000)	% of population (2000)	per 1,000 live births (2002)
Afghanistan	5.2	8	13	12	165
Albania	3.7	48	97	91	22
Algeria	4.1	73	89	92	39
Angola	4.4	31	38	44	154
Argentina	9.5	679	–	–	16
Armenia	7.8	28	–	–	30
Australia	9.2	1,741	100	100	6
Austria	8.0	1,866	100	100	5
Azerbaijan	0.9	8	78	81	76
Bangladesh	3.5	12	97	48	48
Belarus	5.6	68	100	–	17
Belgium	8.9	1,983	–	–	5
Benin	4.4	16	63	23	93
Bolivia	5.3	49	83	70	56
Bosnia and Herzegovina	7.5	85	–	–	15
Botswana	6.6	190	95	66	80
Brazil	7.6	222	87	76	33
Bulgaria	4.8	81	100	100	14
Burkina Faso	–	–	42	29	107
Burundi	3.6	4	78	88	123
Cambodia	11.8	30	30	17	96
Cameroon	3.3	20	58	79	95
Canada	9.5	2,163	100	100	5
Central African Republic	4.5	12	70	25	115
Chad	2.6	5	27	29	117
Chile	7.0	296	93	96	10
China	5.5	49	75	40	30
Colombia	5.5	105	91	86	19
Congo, Dem. Rep.	3.5	5	45	21	129
Congo, Rep.	2.1	18	51	–	81
Costa Rica	7.2	293	95	93	9
Côte d'Ivoire	6.2	41	81	52	116
Croatia	9.0	394	–	–	7
Cuba	7.2	185	91	98	7
Czech Republic	7.4	407	–	–	4
Denmark	8.4	2,545	100	–	4
Dominican Republic	6.1	153	86	67	32
Ecuador	4.5	76	85	86	25
Egypt, Arab Rep.	3.9	46	97	98	33
El Salvador	8.0	174	77	82	33
Eritrea	5.7	10	46	13	59
Estonia	5.5	226	–	–	10
Ethiopia	3.6	3	24	12	114
Finland	7.0	1,631	100	100	4
France	9.6	2,109	–	–	4

▶

Table 3.7 continued

	Health expenditure	Health expenditure per capita	Access to an improved water source	Access to improved sanitation facilities	Infant mortality rate
	Total % of GDP (2001)	$ (2001)	% of population (2000)	% of population (2000)	per 1,000 live births (2002)
Gabon	3.6	127	86	53	63
Gambia, The	6.4	19	62	37	91
Georgia	3.6	22	79	100	24
Germany	10.8	2,412	–	–	4
Ghana	4.7	12	73	72	60
Greece	9.4	1,001	–	–	5
Guatemala	4.8	86	92	81	36
Guinea	3.5	13	48	58	106
Guinea-Bissau	5.9	8	56	56	130
Haiti	5.0	22	46	28	79
Honduras	6.1	59	88	75	32
Hungary	6.8	345	99	99	8
India	5.1	24	84	28	65
Indonesia	2.4	16	78	55	32
Iran, Islamic Rep.	6.6	363	92	83	34
Iraq	3.2	225	85	79	102
Ireland	6.5	1,711	–	–	6
Israel	8.7	1,641	–	–	6
Italy	8.4	1,584	–	–	4
Jamaica	6.8	191	92	99	17
Japan	8.0	2,627	–	–	3
Jordan	9.5	163	96	99	27
Kazakhstan	3.1	44	91	99	76
Kenya	7.8	29	57	87	78
Korea, Dem. Rep.	2.5	22	100	99	42
Korea, Rep.	6.0	532	92	63	5
Kuwait	4.3	630	–	–	9
Kyrgyz Republic	4.0	12	77	100	52
Lao PDR	3.1	10	37	30	87
Latvia	6.4	210	–	–	17
Lebanon	12.4	–	100	99	28
Lesotho	5.5	23	78	49	91
Liberia	4.3	1	–	–	157
Libya	2.9	143	72	97	16
Lithuania	6.0	206	–	–	8
Macedonia, FYR	6.8	115	–	–	22
Madagascar	2.0	6	47	42	84
Malawi	7.8	13	57	76	113
Malaysia	3.8	143	–	–	8
Mali	4.3	11	65	69	122
Mauritania	3.6	12	37	33	120
Mauritius	3.4	128	100	99	17
Mexico	6.1	370	88	74	24
Moldova	5.1	18	92	99	27
Mongolia	6.4	25	60	30	58
Morocco	5.1	59	80	68	39
Mozambique	5.9	11	57	43	128

▶

Table 3.7 continued

	Health expenditure	Health expenditure per capita	Access to an improved water source	Access to improved sanitation facilities	Infant mortality rate
	Total % of GDP (2001)	$ (2001)	% of population (2000)	% of population (2000)	per 1,000 live births (2002)
Myanmar	2.1	197	72	64	77
Namibia	7.0	110	77	41	55
Nepal	5.2	12	88	28	62
Netherlands	8.9	2,138	100	100	5
New Zealand	8.3	1,073	–	–	6
Nicaragua	7.8	60	77	85	32
Niger	3.7	6	59	20	155
Nigeria	3.4	15	62	54	100
Norway	8.0	2,981	100	–	4
Oman	3.0	225	39	92	11
Pakistan	3.9	16	90	62	76
Panama	7.0	258	90	92	19
Papua New Guinea	4.4	24	42	82	70
Paraguay	8.0	97	78	94	26
Peru	4.7	97	80	71	30
Philippines	3.3	30	86	83	28
Poland	6.1	289	–	–	8
Portugal	9.2	982	–	–	5
Puerto Rico	–	–	–	–	–
Romania	6.5	117	58	53	19
Russian Federation	5.4	115	99	–	18
Rwanda	5.5	11	41	8	118
Saudi Arabia	4.6	375	95	100	23
Senegal	4.8	22	78	70	79
Serbia and Montenegro	8.2	103	98	100	16
Sierra Leone	4.3	7	57	66	165
Singapore	3.9	81.6	100	100	3
Slovak Republic	5.7	216	100	100	8
Slovenia	8.4	821	100	–	4
Somalia	2.6	6	–	–	133
South Africa	8.6	222	86	87	52
Spain	7.5	1,088	–	–	5
Sri Lanka	3.6	30	77	94	16
Sudan	3.5	14	75	62	64
Swaziland	3.3	41	–	–	106
Sweden	8.7	2,150	100	100	3
Switzerland	11.1	3,779	100	100	5
Syrian Arab Republic	5.4	65	80	90	23
Tajikistan	3.4	6	60	90	90
Tanzania	4.4	12	68	90	104
Thailand	3.7	69	84	96	24
Togo	2.8	8	54	34	87
Trinidad and Tobago	4.0	279	90	99	17
Tunisia	6.4	134	80	84	21
Turkey	6.9	–	82	90	35
Turkmenistan	4.1	57	–	–	70
Uganda	5.9	14	52	79	83

▶

Table 3.7 continued

	Health expenditure	Health expenditure per capita	Access to an improved water source	Access to improved sanitation facilities	Infant mortality rate
	Total % of GDP (2001)	$ (2001)	% of population (2000)	% of population (2000)	per 1,000 live births (2002)
Ukraine	4.3	33	98	99	16
United Arab Emirates	3.5	849	–	–	8
United Kingdom	7.6	1,835	100	100	5
United States	13.9	4,887	100	100	7
Uruguay	10.9	603	98	94	14
Uzbekistan	3.6	17	85	89	55
Venezuela, RB	6.0	307	83	68	19
Vietnam	5.1	21	77	47	20
West Bank and Gaza	–	–	–	–	–
Yemen, Rep.	4.5	20	69	38	83
Zambia	5.7	19	64	78	102
Zimbabwe	6.2	45	83	62	76
World	**9.8**	**500**	**81**	**55**	**55**
Low income	4.4	23	76	43	79
Middle income	6.0	118	82	60	30
Lower middle income	5.8	85	81	58	32
Upper middle income	6.4	357	–	–	19
Low & middle income	5.8	72	79	51	60
East Asia & Pacific	4.9	48	76	46	32
Europe & Central Asia	5.8	123	91	–	31
Latin America & Carib.	7.0	255	86	77	28
Middle East & N. Africa	4.9	166	88	85	44
South Asia	4.8	22	84	34	68
Sub-Saharan Africa	6.0	29	58	53	103
High Income	10.8	2,841	–	–	5
Europe EMU	9.3	1,856	–	–	4

Source: *World Development Indicators 2004* (Washington: World Bank, 2004).

Exchange entitlements may deteriorate independently of a general decline in the supply of food, which raises its price and worsens the terms of trade for other goods. Job opportunities may diminish, real wages or productivity may fall, and other people may become better off and demand more food.

During the Great Bengal famine of 1943, 3 million people died, yet in terms of the total availability of food grain, 1943 was not an abnormal year. Starvation occurred because food entitlements shrank as a result of, first, a rise in the price of food owing to military procurement; second, the price of other commodities falling as more monetary demand was switched to food and, third, a fall in the output of other goods. Because of their ownership position, however, those in rural areas suffered less than the urban poor. The absence of famine in China and other socialist countries is not so much the result of increases in food production per head, but of a shift in the entitlement system through guaranteed employment and social security provisions.

The policy message is that the alleviation of famine requires the establishment and preservation of adequate entitlements to food, not simply the provision of more food – important as that may be. Public action requires programmes of **food security**, which guarantee that people have access to enough food at all times, and **nutrition programmes**, working through clinics targeted particularly at children and pregnant women.[7]

FOOD PRODUCTION

The world food problem is not caused by the world being physically incapable of producing enough food to feed its inhabitants adequately. The pessimism expressed by Thomas Malthus in 1798 that food would grow only arithmetically while the population would grow geometrically (see Chapter 4) has not been borne out in practice. Global food production has kept pace with population growth, and since 1950 has outstripped it by a substantial margin.

The population has increased by 120 per cent while food production has increased by 210 per cent. Since 1970 the world production of cereals has increased from 1000 million tonnes to 2000 million tonnes per annum. Cereal production per head of population has risen from 300kg to 380kg, while food prices relative to industrial goods prices have fallen by over 50 per cent.

The world is probably capable of feeding itself ten times over if need be. There are pessimists, for example Lester Brown of the World Watch Institute in Washington, but there are also more measured assessments, such as that by T. Dyson in his book *Population and Food* (1996). Dyson concludes that it will be perfectly possible to feed the population of 8 billion that is predicted for the year 2020: 'there is fair reason to expect that in the year 2020 world agriculture will be feeding the larger population no worse and probably a little better than it manages to do today'. The green revolution has not entirely run out of steam; genetically modified (GM) technology promises a new dawn; and productivity with the existing technology is way below its potential in many countries, particularly in Africa. For example, India successfully feeds twice as many people as Africa on 13 per cent of its land area, even though the growing conditions are roughly the same. Hunger and malnutrition for a large fraction of the world's population are likely to remain a problem of *distribution* rather than capacity.

The recent past has witnessed food scares, however. Between 1945 and 1975 most of the increase in food production took place in the 'granary' of North America, and to a lesser extent in Europe. Food production in the developing countries barely kept pace with population growth and there was very little margin for safety and very few provisions for improving the distribution of food supplies. In 1972, for the first time since 1945, food production actually fell. Stocks of wheat fell to just four weeks' supply of what was needed for world consumption. In 1973 the world was indeed threatened with a food crisis. A crop failure in just one major producing area would have spelt disaster, but this was averted by reasonably good weather and harvests. Rising prices also stimulated supply. At the first UN World Food Conference in Rome in 1974, the main focus of attention was on food security at the global level.

The year 1996 witnessed a second UN World Food Summit in Rome, where several longer-term issues were addressed:

- The falling growth rate of crop yields as the impact of the green revolution dissipated
- Falling grain stocks while prices begin to rise again
- The demand for food rising faster than population growth in some big countries such as China (the switch to meat consumption actually increases the demand for cereals because it takes 2kg of grain to produce a kg of chicken and 7kg of grain to produce a kg of beef!)
- The effect of reduced agricultural subsidies in developed countries on output and prices
- The environmental costs of agricultural intensification
- The effect of global warming on output and prices
- The implication for agriculture of increased competition for water from the rapidly growing urban areas of developing countries.

Notwithstanding the increased global availability of food, the situation is still precarious for many individuals and countries. The United Nations' **World Food Programme** dispensed emergency relief to millions of people in more than 40 countries in the 1990s, made necessary by poor harvests, political upheaval or a shortage of foreign exchange to pay for imported food. Many developing countries are still far from being self-sufficient in food, even in 'normal' times. In this third millennium it seems incredible (indeed, intolerable) that year in and year out the lives of millions of people should be threatened by the vagaries of the weather or political instability.

There is still an urgent need for agricultural reform in developing countries (see Chapter 5) and for a new world food programme. Technically, it is well within the world's ability to increase agricultural production on an immense scale. What is required is the initiative and political will, on the part of both the international community and the developing countries, to make the necessary radical changes. As far as the international development agencies are concerned, they could increase aid and investment for agricultural projects, especially where this could lead to a significant breakthrough in agricultural production. For example an investment of $4 billion to eliminate the tsetse fly in infected areas of tropical Africa could open up 7 million square kilometres to livestock and crop production. Of the $70 billion of Official Development Assistance to developing countries, only $11 billion goes to agriculture. There must also be genuine international cooperation and agreement to guarantee world food supplies. One possibility would be a system of granaries strategically placed across the world under international supervision, which could store the food surpluses of the rich North and release them in times of need. This need not hinder the fundamental agricultural reforms necessary for achieving a greater degree of self-sufficiency in the long run.

Food availability and security is not only a question of agricultural policy, it is also a question of trade policy. Increased trade liberalization in agriculture, for example, is encouraging many small farmers to produce cash crops for export to the neglect of growing food for their own needs, and the profit from cash crops is not enough to purchase their food requirements. The return from cash crops is often low because so much buying power is concentrated in the hands of large multinational commodity buyers. Also, as the supply of cash crops increases their price falls. Trade liberalization in agriculture can thus have serious consequences for food security in many countries.

BASIC NEEDS

The provision of health services, education, housing, sanitation, water supply and adequate nutrition came to be known in development circles in the 1970s (and supported by the World Bank) as the **basic needs approach** to economic development. The rationale of the approach was that the direct provision of such goods and services was likely to relieve absolute poverty more immediately than alternative strategies that would simply attempt to accelerate growth or would rely on raising the incomes and productivity of the poor. Five arguments were used to support this change in strategy.

- Growth strategies usually fail to benefit those intended
- The productivity and incomes of the poor depend in the first place on the direct provision of health and education facilities
- It may take a long time to increase the incomes of the poor so that they can afford basic needs
- The poor tend not to spend their income wisely, and certain facilities such as water supply and sanitation can be provided only publicly
- It is difficult to help all the poor in a uniform way in the absence of the provision of basic needs.

While these arguments undoubtedly contained an element of truth, when the initiative was first announced, there was some suspicion within the developing countries themselves that the international propagation of this new doctrine was an attack on their sovereignty and would alter the nature of international assistance in such a way as to make the structural transformation of their economies in the direction of industrial development more difficult. There may be a genuine dilemma here, and a trade-off between growth and basic needs. It depends on whether the scale of resource transfer increases as the allocation is changed, and on the degree of complementarity between the two strategies. On the one hand, the provision of basic needs could be regarded as a form of *consumption transfer* – away from investment – so that growth will be retarded and the basic needs strategy will then not be sustainable in the long run. On the other hand, the provision of basic needs could be regarded as a form of investment in *human capital*, which might be as productive as investment in industry.

The International Labour Organisation (ILO) has emphasized in its various publications (see, for example, *Meeting Basic Needs* 1977) that the satisfaction of basic needs depends crucially on the establishment of a new international economic order, the aim of which, according to the Lima Declaration of 1975, was to increase the developing countries' share of world manufacturing output to 25 per cent by the year 2000.

Thus the basic needs strategy and structural transformation in the direction of industry lead to the same conclusion as far as industrial growth is concerned. Whether both objectives are achieved largely depends on the overall economic strategy pursued. The experience of several countries shows that the rapid development of industry and the provision of basic needs are quite compatible. China has achieved remarkable progress in both directions by recognizing the importance of gearing industrial development to the needs of agriculture and the rural sector. It has done this by encouraging the use of modern inputs into agriculture and the development of small-scale rural industries. Other, non-socialist, countries have a good record in the provision of basic needs, judged by the level of life expectancy in relation to per capita income. These tend to be societies where income is more equitably distributed or which make special provisions – for example, Sri Lanka. Countries with a poor performance in the provision of basic needs illustrate that a basic needs strategy must be comprehensive, otherwise failure in one respect will nullify progress in others.[8]

World Bank lending for poverty alleviation programmes rose quite dramatically during the 1970s–1990s. The amount spent on poverty alleviation programmes rose from US$500 million in 1970 to $5000 million in 1998, or from 8 per cent to 30 per cent of the total lending programme. Of the total in 1998, $600 million was spent on basic needs, including education, health and water supply, compared with $340 million in 1970. The rest was spent on infrastructure, rural development and small-scale industrial projects.

STAGES OF DEVELOPMENT AND STRUCTURAL CHANGE

It is often argued that countries pass through certain phases during the course of development and that by identifying these phases, according to certain characteristics, a country can be deemed to have reached a certain stage of development. The simplest stage theory is the sector thesis of Fisher (1939) and Clark (1940), who employed the distinction between primary, secondary and tertiary production as a basis of a theory of development. Countries are assumed to start as **primary** producers and then, as the basic necessities of life are met, resources shift into manufacturing or **secondary** activities. Finally, with rising income, more leisure and an increasingly saturated market for manufactured goods, resources move into **service** or **tertiary** activities producing 'commodities' with a high income elasticity of demand.

Naturally enough in this schema, the less developed countries are identified with primary production, the more developed countries with the production of manufactured goods, and the mature developed economies have a high percentage of their resources in the service sector.

There can be no dispute that resource shifts are an integral part of the development process, and that one of the main determinants of these shifts is a difference in the income elasticity of demand for commodities and changes in elasticity as development proceeds. But just as care must be taken to equate (without qualification) development and welfare with the level of per capita income, caution must be exercised in identifying different degrees of underdevelopment, industrialization and maturity, with some fairly rigid proportion of resources engaged in different types of activity. Such an association would ignore the doctrine of **comparative advantage**, which holds that countries will specialize in the production of those commodities in which they have a relative advantage, as determined by natural or acquired resource endowments. The fact that one country produces predominantly primary products while another produces mainly manufactured goods need not imply that they are at different stages of development, particularly if productivity in the primary sector matches productivity in the industrial sector. Such an association would also ignore the different types of service activities that may exist at different stages of a country's history. There are three broad categories of service activities, and the determinants of resource allocation to service activities accompanying development may operate differently in each in an offsetting manner. Newer service

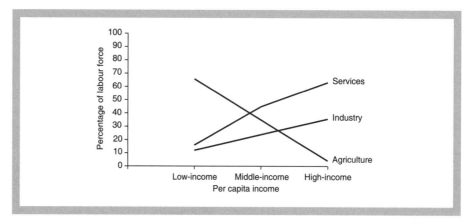

Figure 3.5 Labour force distribution

activities linked with the growth of leisure and high mass consumption tend to have a very high income elasticity of demand; services linked to the growth of manufacturing also grow, but at a declining rate; and traditional services of preindustrial times decline. In short, tertiary production is an aggregation of many dissimilar service activities, some of which are related to low per capita incomes and some to high per capita incomes. Thus the same proportion of total resources devoted to services may be associated with very different levels of development.

Having said all this, however, the fact remains that there is a good deal of empirical support for the Fisher–Clark view that the pattern of development across countries evidences many common characteristics, especially the shift of resources from agriculture to industry. Figure 3.5 shows the proportion of the labour force engaged in agriculture, industry and services between low-income, middle-income and high-income countries. The broad thesis of Fisher and Clark is confirmed: in the low-income countries, on average approximately 65 per cent of the labour force is employed in agriculture, while less than 20 per cent is employed in industry. By contrast, in the high-income economies only 5 per cent on average is employed in agriculture and 30 per cent in industry. The proportion of the labour force in services is also relatively low in low-income countries compared with more mature industrial countries, although there is a wide variation between low-income countries.

Over time there is a noticeable reduction in the proportion of the labour force in agriculture in most countries, but particularly in the high-income economies. There is an increase in the importance of industry in the low- and middle-income countries, but not in the industrial market economies, where on average the shift of resources has been away from both agriculture and industry towards services, which on average employs over 60 per cent of the labour force. Generally speaking the lower the per capita income, the higher the proportion of the labour force in agriculture; and the higher the level of per capita income, the higher the proportion in services.

What is true of the sectoral distribution of the labour force is also true of the sectoral distribution of output, although the magnitude of the proportions differs because productivity differs markedly between sectors. Because productivity tends to be lower in agriculture than in industry, except in some special cases such as Australia and Canada, the proportion of total output generated by agriculture tends to be lower than its share of the labour force, and the proportion generated by industry tends to be higher than its share of the labour force.

For example, it can be seen from the bottom of Table 3.8 that in the low-income countries, agriculture accounts for only 24 per cent of total output in 2002 (compared to approximately 65 per cent of the total labour force in agriculture), while industry accounts for 30 per cent of output, but employs only 20 per cent of the total labour force.

Note also that the process of deindustrialization seems to have already started in the low- and middle-income countries combined, defined as a declining share of industrial output in total output. This fell from 38 per cent to 33 per cent between 1990 and 2002. Only in East Asia and the Pacific has the share increased. Deindustrialization in the developed countries started many years ago (see Rowthorn and Ramswamy, 1999), and it appears from the historical evidence that for most countries, the maximum ratio of industrial output to total GDP is in the range 30–40 per cent. After that, there is a relative shift to services. Many developing countries, although by no means all, seem to be at this point of transition.

As we have already indicated, the changing structure of output and employment is a function of the different income elasticities of demand for different products. It is possible to make estimates of the income elasticity of demand for different commodities by using an estimating equation of the form: $\log V = \log a + b \log Y$, where V is value-added (or output) per capita for good X, Y is per capita income and b is the income elasticity of demand for good X. An income elasticity less than unity would imply that the share of the good in total output declines as income grows. Conversely, an income elasticity greater than unity means that the good's relative importance in total output will increase. To estimate the income elasticities, the equation is applied to data across countries at different stages of development. When this is done, the income elasticity for agricultural products is typically estimated at about 0.5, while the income elasticity for services is significantly above unity. The income elasticity for industries is non-linear. Up to a certain level of income, the elasticity is above unity, and then it falls below unity (consistent with the share of industrial output starting to fall).[9]

Within the industrial sector, there are also differences in the income elasticity of demand for products, which cause the pattern of industry to change as development proceeds. The most notable demand shift is the relative switch from basic necessities and low value-added goods to high value-added consumer durables.

ROSTOW'S STAGES OF GROWTH

Interest in stage theories of development was given new impetus with the publication of Rostow's *The Stages of Economic Growth* (1960), which represents an attempt to provide an alternative to the Marxist interpretation of history – hence its subtitle, 'A Non-Communist Manifesto'. Rostow presents a political theory as well as a descriptive economic study of the pattern of the growth and development of nations.

The essence of Rostow's thesis is that it is logically and practically possible to identify stages of development and to classify societies according to those stages. He distinguishes five such stages: **traditional**, **transitional**, **take-off**, **maturity** and **high mass consumption**.

Table 3.8 Structure of output, 2002

	Agriculture	Industry		Services
		Total	Manufacturing	
	% of GDP	% of GDP	% of GDP	% of GDP
Afghanistan	52	24	18	24
Albania	25	19	10	56
Algeria	10	53	8	37
Angola	8	68	4	24
Argentina	11	32	21	57
Armenia	26	37	23	37
Australia	4	26	12	71
Austria	2	32	22	66
Azerbaijan	16	52	20	32
Bangladesh	23	26	16	51
Belarus	11	37	31	52
Belgium	1	27	19	72
Benin	36	14	9	50
Bolivia	15	33	15	52
Bosnia and Herzegovina	18	37	23	45
Botswana	2	48	4	50
Brazil	6	21	13	73
Bulgaria	13	28	17	59
Burkina Faso	32	18	13	50
Burundi	49	19	–	31
Cambodia	36	28	20	36
Cameroon	43	20	11	38
Central African Republic	57	22	9	21
Chad	38	17	15	45
Chile	9	34	16	57
China	15	51	35	34
Hong Kong, China	0	13	5	87
Colombia	14	30	16	56
Congo, Dem. Rep.	56	19	4	25
Congo, Rep.	6	63	5	30
Costa Rica	8	29	22	62
Côte d'Ivoire	26	20	13	53
Croatia	8	30	21	62
Cuba	7	46	37	47
Czech Republic	4	40	–	57
Denmark	3	27	17	71
Dominican Republic	12	33	16	55
Ecuador	9	28	11	63
Egypt, Arab Rep.	17	33	19	50
El Salvador	9	30	23	61
Eritrea	12	25	12	63
Estonia	5	30	19	65
Ethiopia	40	12	–	48
Finland	3	33	26	64
France	3	25	18	72
Gabon	8	46	5	46
Gambia, The	26	14	5	60
Georgia	21	23	–	56
Germany	1	30	23	69
Ghana	34	24	9	42
Greece	7	22	12	70
Guatemala	22	19	13	58

Table 3.8 continued

	Agriculture	Industry		Services
		Total	Manufacturing	
	% of GDP	% of GDP	% of GDP	% of GDP
Guinea	24	37	4	39
Guinea-Bissau	62	13	10	25
Honduras	13	31	20	56
Hungary	4	31	23	65
India	23	27	16	51
Indonesia	17	44	25	38
Iran, Islamic Rep.	12	39	14	49
Ireland	3	42	33	54
Italy	3	29	21	69
Jamaica	6	31	14	63
Japan	1	31	21	68
Jordan	2	26	16	72
Kazakhstan	9	39	16	53
Kenya	16	19	13	65
Korea, Rep.	4	41	29	55
Kuwait	–	–	–	–
Kyrgyz Republic	39	26	11	35
Lao PDR	51	23	18	26
Latvia	5	25	15	71
Lebanon	12	21	10	67
Lesotho	16	43	20	41
Lithuania	7	31	20	62
Macedonia, FYR	12	30	19	57
Madagascar	32	13	11	55
Malawi	37	15	10	49
Malaysia	9	47	31	44
Mali	34	30	3	36
Mauritania	21	29	9	50
Mauritius	7	31	23	62
Mexico	4	27	19	69
Moldova	24	25	17	51
Mongolia	30	16	5	54
Morocco	16	30	17	54
Mozambique	23	34	13	43
Myanmar	57	10	7	33
Namibia	11	31	11	58
Nepal	41	22	8	38
Netherlands	3	26	16	71
Nicaragua	18	25	14	57
Niger	40	17	7	43
Nigeria	37	29	4	34
Norway	2	38	–	60
Pakistan	23	23	16	53
Panama	6	14	6	80
Papua New Guinea	27	42	9	32
Paraguay	22	29	15	49
Peru	8	28	16	64
Philippines	15	33	23	53
Poland	3	30	18	66
Portugal	4	30	–	66
Puerto Rico	1	43	40	56
Romania	13	38	17	49

Table 3.8 continued

	Agriculture	Industry		Services
		Total	Manufacturing	
	% of GDP	% of GDP	% of GDP	% of GDP
Russian Federation	6	34	–	60
Rwanda	41	21	11	37
Saudi Arabia	5	51	10	44
Senegal	15	22	14	63
Serbia and Montenegro	15	32	–	53
Sierra Leone	53	32	5	16
Singapore	0	36	28	64
Slovak Republic	4	29	21	67
Slovenia	3	36	27	61
South Africa	4	32	19	64
Spain	3	30	18	66
Sri Lanka	20	26	16	54
Sudan	39	18	9	43
Swaziland	16	50	38	35
Sweden	2	28	23	70
Switzerland	1	27	–	72
Syrian Arab Republic	23	28	25	49
Tajikistan	24	24	21	52
Tanzania	44	16	8	39
Thailand	9	43	34	48
Togo	40	22	9	38
Trinidad and Tobago	2	42	7	56
Tunisia	10	29	19	60
Turkey	13	27	17	60
Turkmenistan	29	51	–	20
Uganda	32	22	10	46
Ukraine	15	38	23	47
United Kingdom	1	26	17	73
United States	2	23	15	75
Uruguay	9	27	17	64
Uzbekistan	35	22	9	44
Venezuela, RB	3	43	6	54
Vietnam	23	39	21	38
West Bank and Gaza	6	13	11	80
Yemen, Rep.	15	40	5	44
Zambia	22	26	12	52
Zimbabwe	17	24	13	59
World	**4**	**29**	**19**	**68**
Low income	24	30	17	46
Middle income	9	34	21	57
Lower middle income	10	34	22	56
Upper middle income	6	34	18	60
Low & middle income	11	33	20	55
East Asia & Pacific	15	47	32	38
Europe & Central Asia	9	32	–	59
Latin America & Carib.	7	26	15	67
Middle East & N. Africa	11	41	13	48
South Asia	23	26	16	51
Sub-Saharan Africa	18	29	15	54
High income	**2**	**27**	**19**	**71**

Source: *World Development Indicators 2004* (Washington: World Bank).

All we need say about **traditional societies** is that for Rostow the whole of the pre-Newtonian world consisted of such societies; for example the dynasties of China, the civilizations of the Middle East, the Mediterranean and medieval Europe, and so on. Traditional societies are characterised by a ceiling on productivity imposed by the limitations of science. Traditional societies are thus recognizable by a very high proportion of the workforce in subsistence agriculture (greater than 75 per cent), coupled with very little mobility or social change, great divisions of wealth and decentralized political power. Today there are very few, if any, societies that one would class as traditional. Most societies emerged from the traditional stage some time ago, mainly under the impact of external challenge and aggression or nationalism. The exceptions to the pattern of emergence from the traditional state are those countries which Rostow describes as having been 'born free', such as the United States and certain British dominions. Here the preconditions of 'take-off' were laid in a more simple fashion by the construction of social overhead capital and the introduction of industry from abroad. But for the rest of the world, change was much more basic and fundamental, consisting not only of economic transformation but also a political and social transition from feudalism.

The stage between feudalism and take-off Rostow calls the **transitional stage**. The main economic requirement in the transition phase is that the level of investment should be raised to at least 10 per cent of national income to ensure self-sustaining growth. (On this particular point, as we shall see, there seems to be very little difference between the transition stage and the later stage of take-off.) The main direction of investment must be in transport and other social overhead capital to build up society's infrastructure. The preconditions for a rise in the investment ratio consist of the willingness of people to lend risk capital, the availability of entrepreneurs, and the willingness of society at large to operate an economic system geared to the factory and the principle of the division of labour.

On the social front a new elite must emerge to fabricate the industrial society, and it must supersede in authority the land-based elite of the traditional society. Surpluses must be channelled by the new elite from agriculture to industry, and there must be a willingness to take risks and to respond to material incentives. And because of the enormity of the task of transition, the establishment of an effective modern government is vital. The length of the transition phase depends on the speed with which local talent, energy and resources are devoted to modernization and the overthrow of the old order, and in this respect political leadership has an important part to play.

Then there is the stage of **take-off**. The characteristics of take-off are sometimes difficult to distinguish from the characteristics of the transition stage, and this has been a bone of contention between Rostow and critics. Nonetheless, let us describe the take-off stage as Rostow sees it – a 'stage' to which reference is constantly made in the development literature. Since the preconditions of take-off have been met in the transitional stage, the take-off stage is a short stage of development, during which growth becomes self-sustaining. Investment must rise to a level in excess of 10 per cent of national income in order for per capita income to rise sufficiently to guarantee adequate future levels of saving and investment. Also important is the establishment of what Rostow calls 'leading growth sectors'. Historically, domestic finance for take-off seems to have come from two main sources. The first has been from a diversion of part of the product of agriculture by land reform and other means. The examples of Tsarist Russia and Meiji Japan are quoted, where government bonds were substituted for the landowner's claim to the flow of rent payments. A second source has been from enterprising landlords voluntarily ploughing back rents into commerce and industry.

In practice the development of major export industries has sometimes led to take-off permitting substantial capital imports. Grain in the United States, Russia and Canada, timber in Sweden and, to a lesser extent, textiles in Britain are cited as examples. Countries such as the United States, Russia, Sweden and Canada also benefited during take-off from substantial inflows of foreign capital. The sector or sectors that led to the take-off seem to have varied from country to country, but in many countries railway building seems to have been prominent. Certainly improvement of the internal means of communication is crucial for an expansion of markets and to facilitate exports, apart from any direct impact on such industries as coal, iron and engineering. But Rostow argues that any industry can play the role of leading sector in the take-off stage provided four conditions are met:

- That the market for the product is expanding rapidly to provide a firm basis for the growth of output
- That the leading sector generates secondary expansion
- That the sector has an adequate and continual supply of capital from ploughed-back profits
- That new production functions can be continually introduced into the sector, meaning scope for increased productivity.

Rostow contends that the beginnings of take-off in most countries can be traced to a particular stimulus. This has taken many different forms, such as a technological innovation or, more obviously, political revolution, for example Germany in 1848, the Meiji restoration in Japan in 1868, China in 1949 and Indian independence in 1947. Rostow is at pains to emphasize, however, that there is no one single pattern or sequence of take-off. Thus there is no need for the developing countries today to repeat the course of events in, say, Britain, Russia or America. The crucial requirement is that the preconditions of take-off are met, otherwise take-off, whatever form it takes, will not happen. Investment must rise to over 10 per cent of national income; one or more leading sectors must emerge; and there must exist or emerge a political, social and institutional framework that exploits the impulse to expand. The examples are given of the extensive railway building in Argentina before 1914, and in India, China and Canada before 1895, which failed to initiate take-off because the full transition from a traditional society had not been made. The dates of take-off for some of the present developed countries are given as follows: Britain, 1783–1802; France, 1840–60; the United States, 1843–60; Germany, 1850–73; Sweden, 1868–90; Japan, 1878–1900; Russia, 1890–1914.

Then there is the stage of **maturity**, which Rostow defines as the period when society has effectively applied the range of modern technology to the bulk of its resources. During the period of maturity new leading sectors replace the old, and Rostow sees the development of the steel industry as one of the symbols of maturity. In this respect the United States, Germany, France and Britain entered the stage of maturity roughly together.

Accompanying changes in the industrial structure will be structural changes in society, such as changes in the distribution of the workforce, the growth of an urban population, an increase in the proportion of white-collar workers and a switch in industrial leadership from entrepreneur to manager.

Maturity also has important political features. This is the period when nations grow confident and exert themselves – witness Germany under Bismarck and Russia under Stalin. This is also the period when fundamental political choices have to be made by society on the use to which the greater wealth should be put. Should it be devoted to high mass consumption, the building of a welfare state, or imperialist ends? The balance between these possibilities has varied over time within countries, and between countries. Ultimately, however, every nation will presumably reach the stage of high mass consumption whatever the balance of choices at the stage of maturity. Since the developing countries have no likelihood of reaching this stage in the foreseeable future, however, and only a handful of countries has reached it already, we shall ignore this fifth stage here.

Instead, let us evaluate Rostow's thesis and consider the usefulness of this type of stage theory, apart from it providing a valuable description of the development process and pinpointing some of the key growth variables. Most criticisms have hinged on whether a valid and operationally meaningful distinction can be made between stages of development, especially between the so-called transitional phase and take-off, and between take-off and maturity. Critics have attempted to argue that the characteristics that Rostow distinguishes for his different stages are not unique to those stages. Thus the demarcation between take-off and transition is blurred because the changes that take place in the transition phase also seem to take place in the take-off phase, and similarly with the demarcation between take-off and maturity.

One of the earliest of Rostow's critics was Kuznets (1963a), and some of his criticisms may be quoted as representative of the criticisms that Rostow has received in general. First, there is the difficulty of empirically testing the theory, which Rostow himself makes no attempt to do. For one thing there is a general lack of quantitative evidence for assertions made, and for another Rostow's description of the characteristics of some of the stages are not sufficiently specific to define the relevant empirical evidence even if data were available. With respect to the take-off stage, for example, what is a 'political, social and institutional framework which exploits the impulses to expansion in the modern sector'? Kuznets argues: 'it seems to me that Rostow . . . defines these social phenomena as a complex that produces the effect he wishes to explain and then treats this identification as if it were a meaningful identification.'

With regard to quantitative evidence for testing hypotheses, Kuznets questions Rostow's figures of investment and the incremental capital–output ratio during the take-off period in the countries studied. He says: 'Unless I have completely misunderstood Professor Rostow's definition of take-off, and its statistical characteristics, I can only conclude that the available evidence lends no support to his suggestion.' And on the concept of the take-off stage in general Kuznets concludes that the lack of common experience that typifies countries in the take-off stage, in relation to investment and so on, 'casts serious doubt on the validity of the definition of the take-off as a general stage of modern economic growth, distinct from what Professor Rostow calls the pre-condition, or transition, stage preceding it and the self-sustaining growth stage following it'.

Despite these points of criticism, Rostow's stage theory still offers valuable insights into the development process. While the concept of a stage may be quibbled with, and stage theory dismissed as a blueprint for development, there are certain features of the development process that do follow a well-ordered sequence. Moreover, there are certain development prerequisites that countries neglect at their peril. The importance of agriculture in the early stages of development cannot be overemphasized, together with the provision of infrastructure and political stability, if the preconditions for take-off into self-sustaining growth are to be met. The role of investment is also highlighted: investment must reach a certain ratio of GDP if per capita income growth is to be positive. Finally there is the transition from the rural to the industrial society with growth based on the development of leading sectors and foreign trade, which propels a society from take-off to the stage of maturity and eventually high mass consumption. The process of industrialization is crucial, and we end this chapter by discussing its role as the engine of growth.

INDUSTRIALIZATION AND GROWTH

From a global perspective, there seems to be a close association between living standards and the share of resources devoted to industrial activities, at least up to a certain point. In very poor countries there is virtually no industrial activity at all, while the middle and high-income countries devote 20–40 per cent of resources to industry. Only three countries in the world have become rich on agriculture alone: Australia, New Zealand and Canada. In all other countries, living standards have risen rapidly only as resources have shifted out of agriculture into industry.

Furthermore, research[10] also shows a close association across countries between the growth of industry and the growth of GDP; or more precisely, that GDP growth is the faster the greater the *excess* of industrial growth relative to GDP growth, that is, when the share of industry in total GDP is rising the fastest. Figure 3.6 shows this relationship, with GDP growth measured on the vertical axis and the growth of industry on the horizontal axis. The scatter points represent the individual country observations. A line through the points with a slope less than unity shows that the greater the excess of industrial growth over GDP growth, the faster GDP seems to be. The point where this line cuts the 45° line gives the average growth rate that divides countries into those where the share of industry is falling and are growing slowly, and those where the share of industry is rising and are growing fast.

The question is: what is special about industry, and particularly manufacturing industry, which accounts for these empirical associations, and which makes industry 'the engine of growth'? Since differences in the growth of GDP are largely accounted for by differences in the rate of growth of labour productivity, there must be an association between the growth of industry and the growth of labour productivity. This is to be expected for two main reasons. First, if there are increasing returns to scale in industry, both static and dynamic, a relation is to be expected between the growth of industrial output and the growth of labour productivity in industry. **Static economies of scale** refer to the economies of large-scale production whereby the mass production of commodities allows them to be produced at a lower average cost. **Dynamic economies of scale** refer to the induced effect that output growth has on capital accumulation and the embodiment of new technical progress in capital. Labour productivity also increases as output grows through 'learning by doing'. Second, if activities outside industry are subject to diminishing returns, with the marginal product of labour less than the average product, then if resources are drawn from these activities into industry as industry expands, the average product of labour will rise in non-industrial activities.

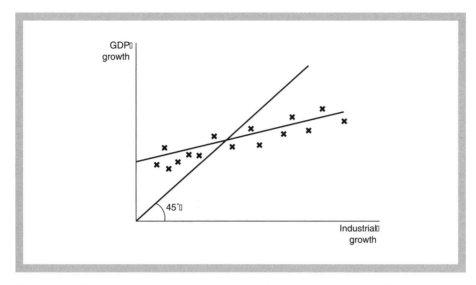

Figure 3.6 Association between growth of industry and growth of GDP

These relationships between industrial growth, productivity growth and GDP growth are known in the growth and development literature as **Kaldor's Growth Laws**, named after the famous Cambridge economist (Lord) Nicholas Kaldor, who first enunciated them in the 1960s (Kaldor, 1966, 1967). Some of the characteristics of China's industrial revolution are outlined in Case example 3.5.

Case example **3.5**

China's Industrial Revolution

Manufacturing growth in China over the past five years has been so rapid that virtually all manufacturers worldwide now have to take the country into account in their strategies.

- Output of factory goods in China has risen 5–10 per cent a year for a decade and China now accounts for an estimated 7 per cent of global manufacturing production, a proportion that is likely to expand greatly in the next few years.
- Since the mid-1990s some $500bn (£274 bn) of foreign investment has gone to China, mostly into manufacturing.
- Foreign enterprises account for 10–15 per cent of the Chinese economy and the proportion is probably bigger in manufacturing.
- In 2003 China was the second most popular country for foreign investment after the US, with telecommunications, automotive, electronics, energy and chemicals among the sectors showing the heaviest spending. Some observers believe that by 2007 a third of the world's electronics industry – in terms of overall output of goods and components – will be based in China.

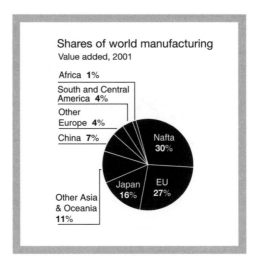

- In some specialized fields of electronics China is already dominant. It is believed to account for about 70 per cent of world production of the 'motherboards' at the heart of personal computers, many of which were made in Taiwan until recently.
- Among the biggest individual manufacturing investors in China are Motorola, Siemens, Philips, General Electric, Nokia and BP. Each company has pumped in more than $1bn.
- While most of China's rapid manufacturing expansion has been based on the availability of low-cost workers (often working for as little as 5 per cent of the wages of those in the main industrialized countries), shortages of highly skilled engineering managers have become a serious problem.
- Chinese universities turn out about 400,000 qualified scientists and engineers a year, although the most pressing skills shortage is among senior engineers with management experience in foreign companies.
- One factor that will help to address this shortage is China's growing share of the world's research and development spending. According to the Organisation for Economic Co-operation and Development, China is the world's third-biggest spender on R&D, behind the US and Japan.

R&D spending in China grew from 0.6 per cent of gross domestic product in 1996 to 1.1 per cent in 2001. About 60 per cent of R&D spending in 2001 came from domestic and foreign companies.

Source: Financial Times, 21 June 2004.

KALDOR'S GROWTH LAWS

There are three basic laws that have been widely tested in developed and developing countries using both cross-section (that is, across countries) and time series data.

The **first law** is that there exists a strong positive correlation between the growth of manufacturing output (g_m) and the growth of GDP (g_{GDP}), that is

$$g_{GDP} = f_1 (g_m) \qquad f_1' > 0 \tag{3.3}$$

where f_1 is the functional relationship that is hypothesised to be positive.

The **second law** is that there exists a strong positive correlation between the growth of manufacturing output and the growth of productivity in manufacturing (p_m), that is

$$p_m = f_2 (g_m) \qquad f_2' > 0 \tag{3.4}$$

where f_2 is the functional relationship assumed to be positive. This law is also known as **Verdoorn's Law** after the Dutch economist P. J. Verdoorn, who in the 1940s first discovered such a relationship for Eastern European countries.

The **third law** is that there exists a strong positive relationship between the growth of manufacturing output and the growth of productivity outside of manufacturing (p_{nm}), that is

$$p_{nm} = f_3 (g_m) \qquad f_3' > 0 \tag{3.5}$$

where f_3 is the functional relationship assumed to be positive.

The most rigorous test of these laws is to take a cross-section of countries, or a cross-section of regions within a country, and to perform correlation and regression analyses for each equation. We will illustrate this with reference to an interesting study that applies the model across 28 regions of China taking average data for the period 1965–91 (Hansen and Zhang, 1996). See also Case example 3.6 for an application of the model to the countries of Africa.

Fitting (3.3) to the Chinese regional data gives the following regression result:

$$g_{GDP} = 1.79 + 0.56 \ (g_m) \qquad r^2 = 0.67$$

The r^2 measures the correlation between the two variables, so this equation says that 67 per cent of the difference in the growth rate of output between the 28 regions in China can be accounted for by variation in the growth of manufacturing output between regions. This is a high degree of explanatory power. The coefficient of 0.56 says that a region with manufacturing output growth of 1 per cent above the average for all regions will grow 0.56 per cent above the average for all regions.

But before using the equation to support the hypothesis of manufacturing industry as the engine of growth, some words of warning are in order. If industrial output is a large fraction of total output, to a certain extent the correlation will be spurious because the same variable appears on both sides of the equation. There are ways, however, to overcome this problem. One is to regress the growth of output on the *difference* between industrial and non-industrial output growth. The other is to regress non-industrial output

Testing Kaldor's Growth Laws Across African Countries

One of the striking features about Africa over the last decades is that there has been virtually no structural change. This is undoubtedly one of the explanations for its poor growth performance. Over the period 1980–96, the average growth of GDP was 2.09 per cent per annum. The growth of manufacturing output was 2.11 per cent, and the growth of agricultural and service output were both 2.07 per cent. On the other hand, some African countries grew faster than others (e.g. Uganda, Botswana, Mauritius, Equatorial Guinea, Swaziland and Cape Verde grew particularly fast). To what extent can this differential growth performance be explained by the differential performance of manufacturing industries?

Regressing GDP growth against the excess of manufacturing growth (g_m) over non-manufacturing growth (g_{nm}) across 45 countries (the side test of Kaldor's first law) gives:

$$g_{GDP} = 0.021 + 0.408 \ (g_m - g_{nm}) \quad r^2 = 0.188.$$

This suggests that a country with excess growth of manufacturing of one percentage point has experienced a GDP growth rate of 0.41 p.p. above average.

When GDP growth is regressed against the excess of agricultural growth over non-agricultural growth, there is a strong *negative* correlation.

Estimating Kaldor's second law gives a Verdoorn coefficient of 0.878 which suggests substantial increasing returns in industry.

Estimating Kaldor's third law gives:

$$p_T = 0.020 + 0.524 \ (g_i) - 1.606 \ (e_{ni}) \quad r^2 = 0.712$$

This shows that overall productivity growth (p_T) across African countries is positively related to the growth of industry (g_i), but negatively related to the growth of employment outside industry (e_{ni}).

These results support Kaldor's structural thesis that there is something special about industrial activity that makes it the 'engine of growth'.

Source: Heather Wells and A.P. Thirlwall, 'Testing Kaldor's Growth Laws Across the Countries of Africa', *African Development Review*, December 2003.

growth on industrial output growth. Also, for manufacturing industry to be regarded as special, it needs to be shown that there is no significant relationship between total output growth and the growth of other major sectors, such as agriculture or services.

Turning to the second law, fitting (3.4) to the regional data for China gave the following result:

$$p_m = -0.009 + 0.71 \ g_m \qquad r^2 = 0.73$$

We see again that the correlation is very high, with 73 per cent of the difference in the growth of labour productivity between regions accounted for by differences in the growth of output. On average, a 1 per cent difference in the growth rate induces a 0.71 difference in the growth of labour productivity. This coefficient is referred to as the **Verdoorn coefficient**. The coefficient here is higher than typically found, which is in the region of 0.5, but this may reflect the large economies of scale to be reaped in the early stages of development. Again, for manufacturing industry to be regarded as special, this second law (or Verdoorn's Law) should be weaker for other activities, which it will be in the absence of scale economies.

The third law is difficult to test directly because it is very difficult to measure productivity growth in many activities outside manufacturing, particularly service activities where output can only be measured by inputs – for example, public services such as teaching, health, defence, the civil service and so on. It can be tested indirectly, however, by taking *overall* productivity growth (p_{GDP}) as the dependent variable to be explained and linking this to employment change in non-industrial activities (e_{nm}) holding constant the effect of output growth in industry. The equation to be estimated is thus

$$p_{GDP} = a_3 + b_3 \ (g_m) + c_3 \ (e_{nm}) \qquad (3.6)$$

with the expectation that $c_3 < 0$.

Fitting (3.6) across the Chinese regions gives:

$$p_{GDP} = 0.02 + 0.49 \ g_m - 0.82 \ (e_{nm}) \qquad r^2 = 0.70$$

The coefficient on e_{nm} is significantly negative so that the slower employment growth outside industry, the faster overall productivity grows.

The complete Kaldor model of the relationship between industrial growth and the development process also contains a number of subsidiary propositions. First, as the scope for absorbing labour from diminishing returns activities dries up, the overall growth of GDP will slow down. The successful newly industrializing countries in South-East Asia will not go on growing at close to 8 per cent per annum for ever! Second, there is the question of what determines the rate at which industry grows in the first place. In the early stages of development, it must be demand coming from the agricultural sector because this is what dominates the economy. In the later stages of development, however, it is export demand that drives the system. The internal market is often too small to reap economies of scale, and selling to the home market does not provide the foreign exchange to pay for necessary imported inputs. The most successful developing countries are those that have geared themselves to export markets. The third proposition is that the fast growth of exports and output can set up a **virtuous circle of growth** that other countries will find difficult to break into without exceptional enterprise or protection. This can lead to polarization between countries, which is the essential feature of the centre–periphery models of growth and development that we shall consider in Chapter 7.

Finally, there is the big policy question of how developing countries bring about structural change in favour of industrial activities if growth and development is to be accelerated. Should everything be left to market forces, or is there a role for government? The Cambridge development economist Ajit Singh tells the story of when he first went to Cambridge as a student of Kaldor that Kaldor taught him three things: first, developing countries must industrialize; second, they can industrialize only by protection, and third, anyone who says otherwise is being dishonest! It is indeed worth remembering that none of today's developed countries, except Britain, which was the first country to industrialize, developed on the basis of free trade. All countries protected and promoted their infant industries in one way or another. And it is a myth, of course, that the highly successful countries of South-East Asia have developed on the basis of minimalist state intervention and simply allowing markets to work freely. In Japan, South Korea, Singapore and other 'Asian Tigers' there has been heavy state involvement in the promotion of industry, often working through the banking system. The issue is not *whether* to protect, but *how* to protect and promote industry while preserving efficiency and international competitiveness. These are issues that will be addressed when we turn to trade and development in Chapter 16.

DISCUSSION QUESTIONS

1 What are the major reasons why some countries are rich and others poor?

2 What is the importance of the distinction between diminishing returns activities and increasing returns activities?

3 Why have economists identified a certain ratio of investment to GDP as a necessary condition for self-sustaining growth?

4 What are the causes of growing urban unemployment in developing countries?

5 What is meant by 'income measure' of unemployment?

6 In what ways does poor education and poor health affect the performance of an economy?

7 Why is the distribution of income more unequal in developing countries than in developed countries?

8 Consider the view that the existence of famine and malnutrition is a distributional problem, not one of food shortage.

9 What do you understand by the 'basic needs approach' to development?

10 What major structural changes take place during the course of development?

11 What accounts for the fact that a close association exists between industrial growth and the growth of GDP?

12 What contribution does Rostow's stage theory make to our understanding of the development process?

NOTES

1. 'Net' in the sense of making an allowance for investment to cover depreciation of worn-out plant and machinery.
2. International Labour Organisation, *Annual Employment Report* (Geneva: ILO, 2002).
3. *World Development Report 1995: Workers in an Integrating World* (Oxford University Press for the World Bank, 1995).
4. See Thorbecke (1973) for a survey of the missions to Colombia, Kenya, Iran and Sri Lanka.
5. For a comprehensive survey, see Behrman (1993).
6. See the Report of the Commission on Macroeconomics and Health chaired by Jeffrey Sachs for the World Health Organisation (2001).
7. See Drèze and Sen (1989) for the Hunger and Poverty project of the World Institute for Development Economics Research (WIDER).
8. For an evaluation of country experience, and of the complementarities and trade-offs in the provision of basic needs, see Streeten *et al.* (1981) and Stewart (1985).
9. For pioneering studies of structural change, see Chenery (1979) and Chenery and Syrquin (1975). For a more recent assessment, see Naqvi (1995).
10. See, for example, the Symposium on Kaldor's growth laws, edited by the present author in the *Journal of Post Keynesian Economics*, Spring 1983; also Bairam (1991), Drakopoulos and Theodossiou (1991) and Hansen and Zhang (1996).

WEBSITES ON HEALTH, NUTRITION, FAMINE, EDUCATION, STRUCTURAL CHANGE AND INCOME DISTRIBUTION

Food production and statistics

Food and Agricultual Organisation (FAO)   www.fao.org

International Food Policy Research Institute   www.ifpri.org

World Hunger Programme at Brown University, USA   www.brown.edu/departments/ world-Hunger-Program

World Food Programme   www.wfp.org/index.html

Health

World Health Organisation   www.who.int

AIDS www.int/emc-hiv;   www.worldbank.org/aidsecon

Pan American Health Organization   www.paho.org

Labour market statistics

International Labour Organisation   http://laborsta.ilo.org

Income distribution

University of Texas Inequality Project   http://utip.gov.utexas.edu

Education

UNESCO   www.unesco.org

World Bank Education Data   www.worldbank.org/education/edstats/

UNICEF Girl's Education   www.unicef.org/girlseducation/

Theories of economic growth: why growth rates differ between countries

Growth and development theory is as old as economics itself. The great classical economists of the eighteenth and nineteenth centuries were all development economists writing about forces determining the progress of nations as the countries of Europe embarked on the process of industrialization. Adam Smith, often thought of as the 'father' of modern economics, entitled his major work, published in 1776, *An Inquiry into the Nature and Causes of the Wealth of Nations*. The question of why the pace of development differs between countries has been at the forefront of economic enquiry ever since. In this chapter we will survey some of the major historical theories and schools of thought that have focused on the growth and development process, starting with the classical economists and then proceeding to Keynesian growth theory, as represented by the Harrod–Domar growth model, to neoclassical growth theory and the use of the production function, and finally to the so-called 'new' growth theory, or endogenous growth theory, and studies of the macrodeterminants of growth. As we go along we shall try to illustrate the contemporary relevance of the theories. We shall in fact discover that the wheel has turned full circle, and that the most recent theories of endogenous growth rehabilitate many of the ideas that were lost in the neoclassical revolution, particularly Adam Smith's emphasis on **increasing returns** associated with investment in manufacturing industry, and the general emphasis in both classical and Keynesian theory on the role of capital accumulation, and the embodiment of the various forms of technical progress associated with it.

CLASSICAL GROWTH THEORY

The macroeconomic issues of the growth of output, and the distribution of income between wages and profits, were the major preoccupation of all the great classical economists, including Adam Smith, Thomas Malthus, David Ricardo and, last but not least, Karl Marx. Let us start the discussion with **Adam Smith**, because while Smith had a generally optimistic vision of the growth and development process, the later classical economists tended to have a more gloomy vision, which led the historian Thomas Carlyle to describe economics as a 'dismal science' – not a sentiment, I hope, that will be shared by students reading this book!

Adam Smith and increasing returns

One of Smith's most important contributions was to introduce into economics the notion of **increasing returns**, based on the **division of labour**. He saw the division of labour (or gains from specialization) as the very basis of a social economy, otherwise everyone might as well be their own Robinson Crusoe producing everything they want for themselves. It is this notion of increasing returns, based on the division of labour, that lay at the heart of his optimistic vision of economic progress as a self-generating process, in contrast to later classical economists who believed that economies would end up in a stationary state owing to diminishing returns in agriculture, and also in contrast to Marx, who believed that capitalism would collapse through its own 'inner contradictions', by which he meant competition between capitalists reducing the rate of profit, and the alienation of workers.

Given the central importance of increasing returns, the essence of Smith's model is basically a very simple one, and many of the features he emphasizes will be a recurring theme in this and other chapters. The growth of output and living standards depends first and foremost on investment and capital accumulation. Investment in turn depends on savings out of profits generated by industry and agriculture and the degree of labour specialization (or division of labour). The division of labour determines the level of labour productivity, but **the division of labour is limited by the extent of the market**. The extent of the market, however, partly depends on the division of labour as the determinant of per capita income. We have here a circular cumulative interactive process, although not without constraints, as we shall see later.

The notion of increasing returns may on the surface appear to be relatively trivial, but it is of profound significance for the way economic processes are viewed. It is not possible to understand divisions in the world economy and so-called 'centre–periphery' models of growth and development (see Chapter 7) without distinguishing between activities that are subject to increasing returns on the one hand, and diminishing returns on the other. Increasing returns means rising labour productivity and per capita income as output and employment expands, while diminishing returns means falling labour productivity and per capita income and a limit to the employment of labour at the point where the marginal product of labour falls to the level of the subsistence wage. Beyond that point there will be no more employment opportunities, and disguised unemployment (see Chapters 3 and 5). Increasing returns are prevalent in most industrial activities, while diminishing returns characterize land-based activities such as agriculture and mining, because land is a fixed factor of production – and one of the incontrovertible laws of economics is that if a variable factor is added to a fixed factor its marginal product will eventually fall (the law of diminishing returns). Poor developing countries tend to specialize in diminishing returns activities, while the rich developed countries tend to specialize in increasing returns activities, and this is one of the basic explanations of the rich country–poor country divide in the world economy. As we shall see later, it is the concept of increasing returns (or more precisely, non-diminishing returns to capital) that lies at the heart of the new endogenous growth theory.

If we go back to Adam Smith, he gives three sources of the increasing returns to be derived from the division of labour:

> This great increase in the quantity of work, which, in consequence of the division of labour, the same number of people are capable of performing, is owing to three different circumstances; first to the increase of dexterity in every particular workman [what we now call **learning by doing**]; secondly, to the saving of time which is commonly lost in passing from one species of work to another; and lastly, to the invention of a great number of machines which facilitate and abridge labour, and enable one man to do the work of many.

That is, specialization provides greater scope for capital accumulation by enabling complex processes to be broken up into simpler processes permitting the use of machinery. But the ability to specialize, or the division of labour, depends on the extent of the market. Smith uses the example of the production of pins. There is no point in installing sophisticated machinery to deal with the different processes of pin production if the market for pins is very small. It is only economical to use cost-saving machinery if the market is large. If the market is small, there would be surplus production. To quote Smith again:

> when the market is very small, no person can have any encouragement to dedicate himself entirely to one employment, for want of power to exchange all that surplus part of the produce of his own labour, which is over and above his own consumption, for such parts of the produce of other men's labour as he has occasion for.

Smith recognized, however, that increasing returns based on the division of labour was much more a feature of industry than agriculture:

> the nature of agriculture, indeed, does not admit of so many subdivisions of labour, nor of so complete a separation of one business from another, as manufactures. It is impossible to separate so entirely the business of the grazier from that of the corn farmer, as the trade of the carpenter is commonly separated from that of the smith.

This does not mean, of course, that agriculture is unimportant in the development process. On the contrary. Even though industry offers more scope for the division of labour, it would be difficult for industry to develop at all without an agricultural surplus, at least in the absence of imports. Smith recognized that an agricultural surplus is necessary to support an industrial population, and labour released by improved productivity in agriculture can be used for the production of non-agricultural goods. So agriculture is certainly important for industrialization from the supply side. On the demand side, it is the agricultural surplus that gives rise to the demand for other goods, which can be purchased with the excess supply of agricultural goods. As Smith put it: 'those, therefore, who have the command of more food than they themselves can consume, are always willing to exchange the surplus – for gratification of this other kind [manufactured goods]'. We have here a model of reciprocal demand between agriculture and industry, with industry demanding food from agriculture to feed workers, and agriculture exchanging its surplus for industrial goods. Balanced growth between agriculture and industry is essential for the growth and development process to proceed without impediment. Many later models of economic development reflect this insight (see Chapters 5 and 9).

The division of labour is limited by the size of the market. This is a central axiom of Smith's model. The size of the market will be partly limited by restrictions on trade; hence Smith's advocacy of free trade and laissez-faire, internally and externally. Goods must be able to be exchanged freely between industry and agriculture. But demand for industrial goods can also come from abroad, and Smith recognized the role of exports in the development process:

> without an extensive foreign market, [manufactures] could not well flourish, either in countries so moderately extensive as to afford but a narrow home market; or in countries where the communication between one province and another was so difficult as to render it impossible for the goods of any particular place to enjoy the whole of that home market which the country could afford.

We shall have a lot to say about trade and growth, and models of export-led growth, in Chapter 16.

Smith's model of development is driven by capital accumulation generated by profits from industry; and the stimulus to invest, as in all classical models, comes from the rate of profit. If the rate of profit falls, the desire to invest diminishes. Smith was somewhat ambiguous about what happens to the rate of profit as development proceeds. On the one hand he recognized that as the economy's capital stock grows, the profit rate will tend to fall due to competition between capitalists and rising wages. On the other hand, new investment opportunities raise the rate of return. Thus the rate of profit may rise or fall in the course of development depending on whether investment is in old or new technology. If there is any tendency towards a stationary state in which the rate of profit falls to zero so that there is no further incentive to invest, it is a long way off in Smith's model, in contrast to the models of Malthus, Ricardo and Marx, in which a fall in the rate of profit is seen as inevitable.

Before turning to these models, however, which focus on some of the more depressing features inherent in the development process, it needs to be mentioned that Smith's vision of development as a cumulative interactive process based on the division of labour and increasing returns in industry lay effectively dormant until an American economist, Allyn Young, revived it in a neglected but profound article in 1928 entitled 'Increasing Returns and Economic Progress'.[1] As Young observed:

> Adam Smith's famous theorem [that the division of labour depends on the extent of the market and the extent of the market depends on the division of labour] amounts to saying that the division of labour depends in large part on the division of labour. [But] this is more than mere tautology. It means that the counter forces which are continually defeating the forces which make for equilibrium are more pervasive and more deeply rooted than we commonly realise . . . Change becomes progressive and propagates itself in a cumulative way.

For Young, increasing returns are not simply confined to factors that raise productivity *within* individual industries, but are related to the output of *all* industries which, he argued, must be viewed as an interrelated whole: what are now sometimes called **macroeconomies of scale**. For example a larger market for product *x* may make it profitable to use more machinery in its production, which reduces the cost of *x and* the cost of the machinery, which then makes the use of machinery more profitable in other industries, and so on. Under certain conditions, change will become progressive and propagate itself in a cumulative way; the precise conditions being increasing returns and an elastic demand for products so that as their relative price falls, proportionately more is bought. Take the example of steel and textiles, both of which are subject to increasing returns and are price elastic. As the supply of steel increases, its relative price (or exchange value) falls. If demand is price elastic, textile producers demand proportionately more steel, and offer proportionately more textiles in exchange. Textile production increases and its exchange value falls. If demand is price elastic, steel producers demand proportionately more textiles, and so on. As Young said, 'under these circumstances there are no limits to the process of expansion except the limits beyond which demand is not elastic and returns do not increase'.

The process described above could not occur with diminishing returns activities with an inelastic price demand, which characterizes most primary products. No wonder rapid development tends to be associated with the process of industrialization. It is true to say, however, that Young's vision was also lost until the 1950s, when economists such as Gunnar Myrdal, Albert Hirschman and Nicholas Kaldor started to challenge equilibrium theory and develop non-equilibrium models of the growth and development process in such books as *Economic Theory and Underdeveloped Regions* (Myrdal, 1957), *Strategy of Economic Development* (Hirschman, 1958), *Strategic Factors in Economic Development* (Kaldor, 1967) and *Economics without Equilibrium* (Kaldor, 1985). Kaldor used to joke that economics went wrong after Chapter 4 of Book I of Smith's *Wealth of Nations*, when Smith abandoned the assumption of increasing returns in favour of constant returns, and the foundations for neoclassical general equilibrium theory were laid. In contrast, it is now Smith and Young's emphasis on increasing returns that lies at the heart of the new endogenous growth theory.

The classical pessimists

The prevailing classical view after Smith was very pessimistic about the process of economic development, focusing on the problems of rapid population growth and the effect exerted on the rate of profit in industry by rising food prices owing to diminishing returns and rising costs in agriculture. One of the foremost pessimists was **Thomas Malthus**, and it might be said that the ghost of Malthus still haunts many developing countries today with respect to his views on population. But there are two strands to Malthus' writing: his theory of population; and his focus on the importance for development of maintaining 'effective demand' – a concept later borrowed by Keynes, who acknowledged a debt to Malthus. In fact Malthus was the only classical economist to emphasize the importance of demand for the determination of output – all others adhered to **Say's Law**: that supply creates its *own* demand, so that the level and growth of output is a function of the supply of physical inputs alone. For Malthus, effective demand must grow in line with productive potential if profitability as the stimulus to investment is to be maintained, but there is nothing to guarantee this. Malthus focused on the savings of landlords and the possible imbalance between the supply of saving and the planned investment of capitalists, which might impede development. Should landlord saving exceed the amount that capitalists wish to borrow, Malthus suggested the taxation of landlords as one solution.

Malthus is best known, however, for his *Essay on the Principle of Population* (1798), in which he claimed that there is a 'constant tendency in all animated life to increase beyond the nourishment prepared for it'. According to Malthus, 'population goes on doubling itself every twenty five years, or increases in a geometrical ratio', whereas 'it may be fairly said . . . that the means of subsistence increase in an arithmetical ratio'. Taking the world as a whole, therefore, Malthus concluded:

> the human species would increase (if unchecked) as the numbers 1, 2, 4, 8, 16, 32, 64, 128, 256, and subsistence as 1, 2, 3, 4, 5, 6, 7, 8, 9. [This would mean that] in two centuries the population would be to the means of subsistence as 256 to 9; in three centuries as 4096 to 13, and in two thousand years the difference would be incalculable.

That food production only grows at an arithmetic rate implies, of course, diminishing returns to agriculture. The imbalance between population growth and growth of the food supply would lead to the per capita income of countries oscillating around the subsistence level, or being caught in what is now sometimes called a '**low-level equilibrium trap**'. Any increases in per capita income brought about by technical progress lead to more births, which then reduces per capita income back to subsistence level. Early development models of the 'big push' were designed to lift economies from this trap (see Chapter 8). Malthus recognized certain checks to the process, which he divided into preventative and positive checks, some of which still operate today in certain countries. Preventative checks with respect to the difficulties of rearing a large family are sexual abstinence or the use of contraception. However, Malthus was opposed to contraception. Where preventative checks are weak, positive checks take over in the form of pestilence, disease and famine. Malthus' solution to the population dilemma was the postponement of marriage in a viceless society!

While Malthusian economics may still have relevance in certain parts of Africa and Asia, Malthus' gloomy prognostications have not materialized for the world as a whole, because preventative checks have become stronger and because food production has not grown at an arithmetic rate but faster than the growth of population (see Chapter 3). Technical progress in agriculture has offset diminishing returns. It is the underestimation of technical progress in agriculture that has confounded all the classical pessimists.

David Ricardo was another of the great classical pessimists. In 1817 he published his *Principles of Political Economy and Taxation*, in which he predicted that capitalist economies would end up in a stationary state, with no growth, also owing to diminishing returns in agriculture. In Ricardo's model, like Smith's, growth and development is a function of capital accumulation, and capital accumulation depends on reinvested profits. However, profits are squeezed between subsistence wages and the payment of rent to landlords, which increases as the price of food rises owing to diminishing returns to land and rising marginal costs. Ricardo thought of the economy as 'one big farm' in which food (or corn) and manufactures are consumed in fixed proportions, so that corn can be used as the unit of account. Figure 4.1 illustrates the model.

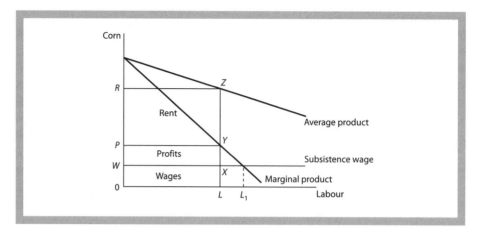

Figure 4.1 Ricardo's model of the economy

With the employment of L amount of labour, the total output is $ORZL$. Rent is determined by the difference between the average and marginal product of labour working on the land and is given by the area $PRZY$. Wages are equal to $OWXL$, and profit is the difference between rent and wages, equal to $WPYX$. As output increases and the marginal product of labour falls to the subsistence wage (L_1), profits disappear. In equilibrium, the rate of profit in agriculture must equal the rate of profit in industry. As the profit rate in agriculture falls, capital will shift to industry, causing the rate of profit to decline there. Profits are also squeezed because wages rise in terms of food. But for Ricardo, unlike Malthus, there was no problem of effective demand. Ricardo saw no limit to the amount of capital that could be employed because he accepted Say's Law that supply creates its own demand. The villain of the piece is wages. He writes: 'there is no limit to demand – no limit to the employment of capital while it yields any profit, and that however abundant capital may become, there is no other adequate reason for a fall in profit but a rise in wages.' As profits fall to zero, capital accumulation ceases, heralding the stationary state. As Ricardo put it:

> a real rise of wages is necessarily followed by a real fall in profits, and, therefore, when the land of a country is brought to the highest state of cultivation, when more labour employed upon it will not yield in return more food than what is necessary to support the labourer so employed, that country has come to the limit of its increase both of capital and population.

As we shall see in Chapter 5, Arthur Lewis's famous development model, 'Economic Development with Unlimited Supplies of Labour', is a classical Ricardian model, but wages are assumed to stay the same until disguised unemployment on the land is absorbed.

Given the central importance of capital accumulation in Ricardo's vision of economic progress, anything that reduces capital accumulation (including rises in wages) will slow economic growth. Ricardo was thus opposed to all forms of taxes, levies and tariffs on inputs into the productive system, including tariffs on imported food. Indeed he believed that the importation of cheap food might delay the predicted stationary state indefinitely by holding down wages measured in terms of food:

> a country could go on for an indefinite time increasing its wealth and population, for the only obstacle to this increase would be the scarcity, and consequent high value, of food and

other raw produce. Let these be supplied from abroad in exchange for manufactured goods, and it is difficult to say where the limit is at which you would cease to accumulate wealth and to derive profits from its employment.

It was for this reason that Ricardo campaigned for the abolition of the Corn Laws in Britain in the nineteenth century, which were eventually repealed in 1846 – to the benefit of industrialists but to the detriment of domestic farmers. In developing countries today, attempts are often made by governments to keep the price of agricultural goods artificially low in order to keep wages low (measured in terms of food). Doing so, however, raises another problem of reducing the incentive of farmers to produce. Determining the equilibrium terms of trade between agriculture and industry, which maximizes the output of both sectors, is a difficult empirical issue.

Finally we turn to **Karl Marx**, famous for his book *Das Kapital* (1867), and his prediction of the collapse of capitalism. All members of the classical school agreed that the rate of profit on capital would fall as the economy grew, but they differed as to the reason for the fall. Adam Smith saw the decline in profits as the result of competition among capitalists. Ricardo saw the fall as the result of diminishing returns to land, and profits being squeezed between rent and wages, leading to a stationary state. For Marx, the economy does not grow for ever, but the end comes not from a stationary state but from 'crises' associated with overproduction and social upheaval. But Marx's model bears many similarities to the other classical economists. The capitalist surplus is the source of capital accumulation and the principal mainspring of growth. Population growth responds to wages in Malthusian fashion, keeping wages down, and the rate of profit has a long-run tendency to fall.

Let us briefly consider Marx's model and his prediction of crisis. Gross output consists of three elements:

- Variable capital or the wage bill (v)
- Constant capital (c), that is, plant and machinery and the raw materials used in production
- Surplus value or profit (s).

The wages of labour are determined by the minimum subsistence level (what Marx called the cost of reproducing the working class), and surplus value (which only labour can create) is the difference between output per worker and minimum wage per worker. The rate of surplus value, or what Marx called the 'degree of exploitation', is given by s/v. The rate of profit is given by the ratio of surplus value to total capital, that is

$$s/(v + c) = (s/v)/(1 + [c/v]) \tag{4.1}$$

where the ratio of constant to variable capital (c/v) is defined as the '**organic composition of capital**'. As techniques of production become more capital-intensive, the organic composition rises through time, and as it does so the rate of profit falls unless surplus value rises. While there is no limit to the rise in c/v, however, there is a limit to s/v. Marx foresaw no major problem as long as surplus labour exists to keep wages down, but he predicted that as capital accumulation takes place, the '**reserve army of labour**', as he called it, would disappear, driving wages up and profits down. The capitalist's response is then either to attempt to keep wages down, leading to the '**immiseration of workers**' and social conflict, or to substitute more capital for labour, which would worsen the problem by raising *c/v*.

For Marx, the desire and necessity to invest are inherent in the psychological makeup of the capitalist. 'To accumulate, is to conquer the world of social wealth, to increase the mass of human beings exploited by him, and then to extend both the direct and indirect sway of the capitalist.' Thus the capitalist's motto is 'Accumulate, accumulate! That is Moses and the Prophets'. But as capital is substituted for labour there is another problem: labour cannot consume all the goods produced, and a '**realization crisis**' is caused by the failure of effective demand. Capitalism eventually collapses through its own 'inner contradictions', and power passes to the working classes because fewer and fewer people benefit from capitalism. Capitalism is replaced by socialism whereby workers own the means of production, distribution and exchange, and ultimately the state withers away.

Marx's analysis contains valuable insights into the functioning of capitalism, but his predictions, like the predictions of his predecessors, have not materialized. Why? There seem to be two basic reasons. The first is that there is a confusion in Marx's work between *money wages* and *real wages*. A rise in money wages as surplus labour disappears does not necessarily mean a rise in real wages; but in any case, any rise in real wages could be offset by a rise in productivity, leaving the rate of profit unchanged. The second and related reason is that just as the other classical economists underestimated the rate of technical progress in agriculture as an offset to diminishing returns, so Marx underestimated the effect of technical progress in industry on the productivity of labour. It can be seen from (4.1) that even if *c/v* is rising, the rate of profit can remain unchanged if technical progress exceeds the rate of wage growth by the same amount. Technical progress also means there is no necessary clash between real wages and the rate of profit. Both can rise.

For nearly sixty years after Marx's death in 1883, growth and development theory lay effectively dormant, as economics came to be dominated by static neoclassical value theory under the influence of Alfred Marshall's *Principles of Economics* (1890). Marshall treated growth and development as a 'natural' phenomenon; an evolutionary process akin to biological developments in the natural world. Modern growth theory started with the classic article by the British economist Roy Harrod, 'An Essay in Dynamic Theory' (1939),[2] which led to the development of what is now called the Harrod–Domar growth model.[3] The model has played a major part in thinking about development issues in the postwar years, and is still widely used in development planning (see Chapter 9).

THE HARROD–DOMAR GROWTH MODEL

Harrod's original model is a dynamic extension of Keynes' static equilibrium analysis. In Keynes' *General Theory*, the condition for income and output to be in equilibrium (in the closed economy) is that plans to invest equal plans to save (or injections into the circular flow of income should equal leakages). The question Harrod asked is: if changes in income induce investment, what must be the *rate of growth of income* for plans to invest to equal plans to save in order to ensure a *moving* equilibrium in a growing economy through time? Moreover, is there any guarantee that this required rate of growth will prevail? If not, what will happen? In static Keynesian theory, if equilibrium between saving and investment is disturbed, the economy corrects itself and a new equilibrium is achieved via the multiplier process. If growth equilibrium is disturbed, will it be self-correcting or self-aggravating? Moreover, will this equilibrium rate be equal to the maximum rate of growth that the economy is able to sustain given the rate of growth of productive capacity? If not, what will happen? These are fundamental questions for the understanding of the growth performance of any country, be it developed or underdeveloped, and Harrod's place in the history of economic thought was guaranteed by the insight and simplicity with which he answered them.

To consider the questions posed, Harrod distinguished three different growth rates: what he called the **actual growth rate** (g), the **warranted growth rate** (g_w) and the **natural growth rate** (g_n). The actual growth rate is defined as

$$g = s/c \qquad (4.2)$$

where s is the ratio of savings to income (S/Y) and c is the *actual* incremental capital–output ratio, that is, the ratio of extra capital accumulation or investment to the flow of output ($\Delta K/\Delta Y = I/\Delta Y$). This expression for the actual growth rate (4.2) is definitionally true since it expresses the accounting identity that savings equals investment. We can see this if we substitute the expressions for s and c into (4.2) – that is, $s/c = (S/Y/(I/\Delta Y)) = \Delta Y/Y$ given $S = I$, where $\Delta Y/Y$ measures the growth of output.

We need more than a definitional equation, however, to know whether the actual growth rate will provide the basis for steady advance in the future in the sense that it keeps plans to invest and plans to save in line with one another at full employment. This is where the concepts of the warranted rate of growth and the natural rate of growth become important.

Harrod defined the warranted rate of growth as

> that rate of growth which, if it occurs, will leave all parties satisfied that they have produced neither more nor less than the right amount. Or, to state matters otherwise, it will put them into a frame of mind which will cause them to give such orders as will maintain the same rate of growth.

In other words, the warranted growth rate is the rate that induces just enough investment to match planned saving and therefore keeps capital fully employed (that is, there is no undercapacity or overcapacity), so that manufacturers are willing to carry on investment in the future at the same rate as in the past. How is this rate determined? Plans to save at any point in time are given by the Keynesian savings function:

$$S = sY \qquad (4.3)$$

where s is the propensity to save. This gives the potential supply of investment goods. The demand for investment is given by the **acceleration principle** (or what Harrod calls 'the relation'), where c_r is the accelerator coefficient measured as the *required* amount of extra capital or investment to produce a unit flow of output at a given rate of interest, determined by technological conditions. Thus:

$$c_r = \Delta K_r/\Delta Y = I/\Delta Y \qquad (4.4)$$

The demand for investment, given by the accelerator principle, is then

$$I = c_r \Delta Y \tag{4.5}$$

For planned saving to equal planned investment, therefore, we have

$$sY = c_r \Delta Y \tag{4.6}$$

and the required rate of growth for a moving equilibrium through time is

$$\Delta Y / Y = s / c_r = g_w \tag{4.7}$$

This is the warranted rate of growth, g_w. For dynamic equilibrium, output must grow at this rate. At this rate, expenditure on consumption goods will equal the production of consumption goods, and this is the only rate at which entrepreneurs will be satisfied with what they are doing, and not cause them to revise their investment plans.

Now suppose there is a departure from this equilibrium rate. What happens? The condition for equilibrium is that $g = g_w$ or, from (4.2) and (4.7), that $gc = g_w c_r$. First suppose that the actual growth rate exceeds the warranted rate. It is easily seen that if $g > g_w$ then $c < c_r$, which means that actual investment falls below the level required to meet the increase in output. There will be a shortage of equipment, a depletion of stocks and an incentive to invest more. The actual growth rate will then depart even further from the warranted rate. Conversely, if the actual growth rate is less than the warranted rate, $g < g_w$, then $c > c_r$, and there will be a surplus of capital goods and investment will be discouraged, causing the actual growth rate to fall even further below the equilibrium rate. Thus, as Harrod points out, we have in the dynamic field a condition opposite to that in the static field. A departure from equilibrium, instead of being self-righting, will be self-aggravating. This is the short-term trade cycle problem in Harrod's growth model.

The American economist **Evesey Domar**, working independently of Harrod, also arrived at Harrod's central conclusion, although by a slightly different route. Domar recognized that investment is a double-edged sword: it both increases demand via the multiplier, and increases supply via its effect on expanding capacity. The question Domar asked, therefore, is what rate of growth of investment must prevail in order for supply to grow in line with demand (at full employment)? The crucial rate of growth of investment can be derived in the following way. A change in the level of investment increases demand by

$$\Delta Y_d = \Delta I / s \tag{4.8}$$

and investment itself increases supply by

$$\Delta Y_s = I\sigma \tag{4.9}$$

where σ is the productivity of capital or the flow of output per unit of investment ($\Delta Y / I$). For $\Delta Y_d = \Delta Y_s$ we must have

$$\Delta I/s = I\sigma \tag{4.10}$$

or

$$\Delta I/I = s\sigma \tag{4.11}$$

In other words, investment must grow at a rate equal to the product of the savings ratio and the productivity of capital. With a constant savings–investment ratio, this also implies output growth at the rate $s\sigma$. If $\sigma = 1/c_r$ (at full employment), then the Harrod–Domar result for equilibrium growth is the same.

But even if growth proceeds at the rate required for full utilization of the capital stock and a moving equilibrium through time, this still does not guarantee the full employment of labour, which depends on the natural rate of growth. The **natural growth rate** is derived from the identity $Y = L\,(Y/L)$, where L is labour and Y/L is the productivity of labour, or taking the rate of growth: $y = l + \dot{q}$. The natural rate of growth is therefore made up of two components: the growth of the labour force (l), and the growth of labour productivity ($\dot{q}$) – both exogenously determined. The natural rate of growth plays an important role in Harrod's growth model in two respects. First it defines the rate of growth of productive capacity or the long-run full employment equilibrium growth rate. Second, it sets the upper limit to the actual growth rate, which brings cumulative expansion in the Harrod (trade cycle) model to a sticky end. If $g > g_w$, g can continue to diverge from g_w only until it hits g_n, when all available labour has been completely absorbed: g cannot be greater than g_n in the long run. The long-run question for an economy, then, is the relation between g_w and g_n; that is, the relation between the growth of capital and the growth of the labour force (measured in efficiency units). With fixed coefficients of production, the full employment of labour clearly requires $g = g_n$. The full employment of labour *and* capital requires

$$g = g_w = g_n \tag{4.12}$$

a state of affairs that the famous Cambridge economist Joan Robinson once called a 'golden age' to emphasize its mythical nature, because there is nothing in the Harrod model that would automatically generate this happy coincidence.

Let us now consider what happens if the warranted growth rate diverges from the natural rate. If $g_w > g_n$ there will be a chronic tendency towards depression because the actual rate of growth will never be sufficient to stimulate investment demand to match the amount of saving at full-employment equilibrium. There is too much capital and too much saving. This was the worry that economists had in the 1930s, particularly when it was predicted that the size of the population would fall in developed countries because the net reproduction rate had fallen below one (that is, females were not replacing themselves). If $g_w < g_n$, there will be a tendency towards demand inflation because there will be a tendency for the actual rate of growth to exceed that necessary to induce investment to match saving. Inflationary pressure, however, will be accompanied by growing unemployment of the structural variety because the growth of capital falls short of the growth of the effective labour force and there is no change in the techniques of production.

Where do the developing countries fit into this picture? In most developing countries the natural growth rate exceeds the warranted rate. If the population growth is, say, 2 per cent and labour productivity is growing at 3 per cent, this gives a rate of growth of the labour force in efficiency units of 5 per cent. If the net savings ratio is, say, 9 per cent and the required incremental capital–output ratio is 3, this gives a warranted growth rate of 3 per cent. This has two main consequences. First it means that the effective labour force is growing faster than capital accumulation, which is part of the explanation for growing unemployment in developing countries. Second, it implies greater plans to invest than plans to save, and therefore inflationary pressure. If g_n = 5 per cent and c_r = 3, there will be profitable investment opportunities for 15 per cent saving, whereas actual saving is only 9 per cent.

The simultaneous existence of inflation and high unemployment in developing countries is therefore not a paradox. It can easily be explained within the framework and assumptions of the Harrod growth model, as can a great deal of development policy. Given the inequality g_n # g_w, or $l + \dot{q}$ # s/c_r, it can be seen that there are basically four ways in which g_n and g_w might be reconciled. If the problem is $g_n > g_w$, the first possibility is to reduce the rate of growth of the labour force. Measures to control population size can be justified on these grounds, as a contribution to solving the problem of structural unemployment. Second, a reduction in the rate of growth of labour productivity would help, but this would of course reduce the growth of living standards of those in work. There is a clash here between employment and efficiency. Third, a rise in the savings ratio could narrow the gap. This is at the heart of monetary and fiscal reform in developing countries (see Chapter 14). Finally, the natural and warranted growth rates might be brought into line by a reduction in the required capital–output ratio through the use of more labour-intensive techniques. There is an active debate in developing countries over the appropriate choice of techniques, and whether developing countries could move towards the use of more labour-intensive techniques without impairing output and sacrificing saving (see Chapter 12).

All of these adjustment mechanisms can be illustrated by a simple diagram (Figure 4.2).

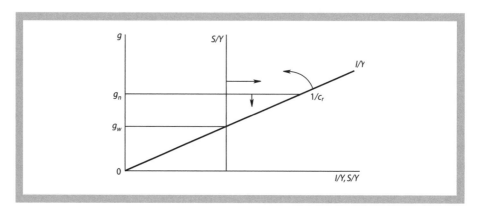

Figure 4.2 Adjustment of g_w and g_n

Growth is measured on the vertical axis, and the investment and savings ratios on the horizontal axis. Growth and the investment ratio are related through c_r the required incremental capital–output ratio. The savings ratio is independent of the growth rate. Figure 4.2 depicts a situation in which the natural growth rate (g_n) exceeds the warranted growth rate (g_w). To equalize g_n and g_w we can bring down g_n to g_w by measures to curb labour force growth; we can shift rightwards the S/Y curve through monetary and fiscal policies (and also by foreign borrowing) to raise g_w to g_n, or we can pivot the I/Y curve inwards by reducing c_r through the use of more labour-intensive techniques of production.

The Harrod framework is not only useful for understanding some of the development difficulties of developing countries, it is also useful for planning purposes. If a country sets a target rate of growth of, say, 5 per cent per annum and the required capital–output ratio is 3, it knows it must save and invest 15 per cent of GDP if the target growth rate is to be achieved. If domestic saving is less than 15 per cent of GDP there is an investment–savings gap to fill, which might be done by foreign borrowing (see Chapter 15).

At a theoretical level, there has been a great deal of discussion in the literature of whether *automatic* adjustment mechanisms might not come into play to reconcile the divergence between g_n and g_w. In the Harrod model, the parameters and variables that make up the model, l, $\dot{q}$, s and c_r, are all independently determined. Harrod himself recognized that in the long run the savings ratio may not be fixed, but will adjust. Specifically, in periods of recession, savings may fall, and in periods of demand inflation, saving may rise. One way this may come about is through a change in the functional distribution of income between wages and profits. This is a possible mechanism of adjustment emphasized by the Keynesian economists of Cambridge, England, represented by Joan Robinson, Nicholas Kaldor, Richard Kahn, Luigi Pasinetti and others. If $g_w > g_n$, and there is a tendency towards depression, this will tend to reduce the share of profits in national income and increase the share of wages, so that if the propensity to save out of profits is higher than the propensity to save out of wages, this change in the distribution of income will lower the overall savings ratio and reduce g_w towards g_n. There is a limit, however, to which the share of profits can fall, given by the minimum rate of profit acceptable to entrepreneurs. Likewise if $g_w < g_n$, and there is a tendency towards demand inflation, the share of profits in national income will tend to rise, increasing the overall savings ratio and raising g_w towards g_n. There is also a limit, however, to the rise in the profit share, set by the degree to which workers are willing to see their real wages reduced – what Joan Robinson called 'the inflation barrier' (see Chapter 14).

In contrast to the Cambridge, England, school of Keynesian (post-Keynesian) economists, in the United States a formidable group of economists in Cambridge, Massachusetts, represented by Robert Solow, Paul Samuelson, Franco Modigliani and others, developed at the same time in the 1950s the so-called neoclassical model of growth as an attack on both Harrod and the post-Keynesian school, pointing out that the gloomy conclusions of Harrod concerning the possibility of achieving steady growth with full employment assume fixed coefficients of production, and that if the capital–labour ratio is allowed to vary there is the possibility of equilibrium growth at the natural rate. In other words, if capital grows faster than labour ($g_w > g_n$), economies will move smoothly via the price mechanism to more capital-intensive techniques, and growth in the long run will proceed at the exogenously given natural rate. Conversely, if labour grows faster than capital ($g_n > g_w$), the wage rate will fall relative to the price of capital, economies will adopt more labour-intensive techniques, and again growth will proceed at the natural rate.

One central feature of this neoclassical model, which has come under sustained attack in recent years from 'new' growth theory, is that investment does not matter for long-run growth. Any increase in the savings or investment ratio is offset by an increase in the capital–output ratio, because of diminishing returns to capital, leaving the long-run growth rate (at the natural rate) unchanged. The argument depends, however, on the productivity of capital falling (or c_r rising) as the capital–labour ratio rises. This is disputed by the 'new' growth theorists. If there are mechanisms to prevent the productivity of capital from falling as investment increases, then investment does matter for long-run growth and growth is *endogenous* in this sense. Before we turn to new growth theory and the important new studies of the macrodeterminants of growth, however, we need to consider the assumptions and predictions of neoclassical growth theory, and see how it has been used empirically for understanding the sources of growth in developed and developing countries.

NEOCLASSICAL GROWTH THEORY

There are three basic propositions of neoclassical growth theory:

- In the long-run steady state, the growth of output is determined by the *rate of growth of the labour force in efficiency units*, that is, by the rate of growth of the labour force plus the rate of growth of labour productivity (exogenously given as in Harrod's natural rate of growth), and is independent of the ratio of saving and investment to GDP. This is so because a higher savings or investment ratio is offset by a higher capital–output ratio or lower productivity of capital, because of the neoclassical assumption of **diminishing returns to capital**.
- The *level* of per capita income (PCY), however, *does* depend on the ratio of saving and investment to GDP. The level of PCY varies positively with the savings–investment ratio and negatively with the rate of growth of the population.
- Given identical tastes (that is, preferences for saving *vis-à-vis* consumption) and technology (production functions) across countries, there will be an *inverse* relation across countries between the capital–labour ratio and the productivity of capital, so that poor countries with a small amount of capital per head should grow faster than rich countries with a lot of capital per head, leading to the *convergence* of per capita incomes and living standards across the world.

Let us now consider how these fundamental propositions are arrived at. The basic **neoclassical growth model** was first developed by Robert Solow[4] and Trevor Swan in 1956, and has been very influential in the analysis of growth ever since – particularly the use of the aggregate production function, as we shall see. The model is based on three key assumptions (ignoring for the moment technical progress).

- The labour force grows at a constant exogenous rate, l
- Output is a function of capital and labour: $Y = F(K, L)$; the production function relating output to inputs exhibits constant returns to scale, diminishing returns to individual factors of production, and has a unitary elasticity of substitution between factors (see later)
- All saving is invested: $S = I = sY$; there is no independent investment function.

What the basic neoclassical growth model is designed to show is that an economy will tend towards a long-run equilibrium capital–labour ratio ($k*$) at which output (or income) per head ($q*$) is also in equilibrium, so that output, capital and labour all grow at the same rate, l. The model therefore predicts long-run growth equilibrium at the natural rate.

The most commonly used neoclassical production function with constant returns to scale is the so-called **Cobb–Douglas production function**:

$$Y = bK^\alpha L^{1-\alpha} \tag{4.13}$$

where α is the elasticity of output with respect to capital, $1-\alpha$ is the elasticity of output with respect to labour, and obviously $\alpha + (1-\alpha) = 1$, that is, a 1 per cent increase in K and L will lead to a 1 per cent increase in Y, which is what is meant by output exhibiting constant returns to scale.

Equation (4.13) can also be written in 'labour-intensive' form by dividing both sides of the equation by L to give output per head as a function of capital per head:

$$\frac{Y}{L} = \frac{bK^\alpha L^{1-\alpha}}{L} = b\left(\frac{K}{L}\right)^\alpha \tag{4.14}$$

or, for short

$$q = b\,(k)^\alpha \tag{4.15}$$

This is the 'labour-intensive' form of the neoclassical production function, and can be drawn as in Figure 4.3. The diminishing slope of the function represents the diminishing marginal product of capital.

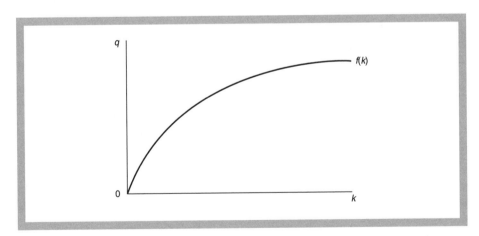

Figure 4.3 The 'labour-intensive' form of the neoclassical production function

Now impose a ray from the origin along which the rate of growth of capital is equal to the rate of growth of labour, so that the capital–labour ratio is constant and the capital–output ratio is constant. This is given by

$$q = (l/s)k \tag{4.16}^5$$

where s is the savings ratio. This straight line from the origin with slope l/s shows the level of q that will keep capital per head constant, and the level of k that will keep output per head constant – given the rate of growth of the labour force, l. Superimposing (4.16) on Figure 4.3 gives Figure 4.4.

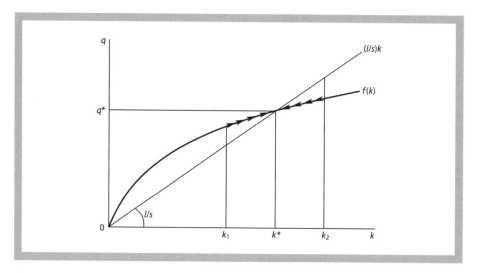

Figure 4.4 Equilibrium capital–labour ratio and output per head

The slope of the ray from the origin to any point on the production function determines the capital–output ratio at that point. It is clear from Figure 4.4 that only where these two lines cross is an equilibrium capital–labour ratio (k^*) and output per head (q^*) defined. To the left of k^* (at k_1), where $q > (l/s)k$, q is greater than necessary to maintain k constant; that is, there is too much saving and capital accumulation relative to the growth of the labour force, and steady growth requires more capital-intensive techniques. There will be a movement from k_1 towards k^*. The capital–output ratio adjusts to bring the rate of growth of capital and labour (or the warranted and natural growth rates) into line. Similarly, to the right of k^* (at k_2), where $q < (l/s)k$, q is less than necessary to maintain k constant; there is too little saving and capital accumulation to keep pace with the rate of growth of the labour force, and steady growth requires more labour-intensive techniques. There will be a movement from k_2 towards k^*. Again, the capital–output ratio adjusts if there is a spectrum of techniques to choose from.

When k reaches an equilibrium, q also reaches an equilibrium, so output must be growing as fast as labour. Thus output, labour and capital must all be growing at the same rate, l, the natural rate of growth, with the capital–output ratio constant. This is the neoclassical story.

We can now see what happens if there is an increase in the ratio of savings and investment to national income (s). If s rises, this lowers the slope of the l/s line in Figure 4.4, *which increases the equilibrium level of per capita income and the capital–labour ratio, but leaves the equilibrium growth rate unchanged*. This demonstrates formally the first two basic propositions of neoclassical growth theory stated on p. 136. The reason a higher savings or investment ratio does not effect the long-run equilibrium growth rate is that a higher savings–investment ratio is offset by a higher capital–output ratio. The capital–output ratio adjusts 'passively' to keep the growth of capital in line with the growth of the labour force.

None of these conclusions is altered if technical progress is introduced into the model. If technical progress augments the productivity of labour only (so-called Harrod neutral technical progress, which leaves the capital–output ratio unchanged), the *effective* labour force now grows at the rate $l + \dot{q}$, where $\dot{q}$ is the rate of growth of labour productivity. Equation (4.16), which defines the relation between q and k that keeps the capital–labour ratio and capital–output ratio constant, now becomes:

$$q = \frac{l + \dot{q}}{s} \, k \tag{4.17}$$

which means that in Figure 4.4 the l/s line becomes *steeper* because output per head must now be higher to provide the saving and capital accumulation required to keep the capital–labour ratio constant with faster growth of the effective labour force. At equilibrium k^* we now have $\Delta K/K = l + \dot{q}$, and at equilibrium q^* we have $\Delta Y/Y = l + \dot{q}$, so that $\Delta Y/Y = \Delta K/K = l + \dot{q}$, and output per head and capital per head grow at rate $\dot{q}$; that is, by the rate of Harrod neutral technical progress:

$$\Delta Y/Y - l = \Delta K/K - l = \dot{q} \tag{4.18}$$

This is, of course, consistent with what we observe in the real world – output and capital grow faster than the rate of growth of the labour force. But a rise in the ratio of savings and investment to GDP still has no effect on the equilibrium growth of output, unless of course a higher level of investment raises the rate of growth of labour-augmenting technical progress, but this is ruled out by assumption in the neoclassical model, because technical progress is assumed to be exogenously determined.

It now only remains to demonstrate the third basic proposition of neoclassical growth theory: that poor countries should grow faster than rich countries, leading to the convergence of per capita incomes because poor countries with a low ratio of capital to labour will have a higher productivity of capital (or lower capital–output ratio). The capital–output ratio may be written as:

$$\frac{K}{Y} = \frac{K}{L} \cdot \frac{L}{Y} \tag{4.19}$$

Given diminishing returns to capital (so that Y/L does not rise in the same proportion as K/L) it can be seen that a higher K/L ratio will be associated with a higher K/Y ratio. This means that if the ratio of savings and investment to GDP is the same across countries, capital-rich countries should grow slower than capital-poor countries. Note, however, that if there are *not* diminishing returns to capital, but, say, constant returns to capital, a higher capital–labour ratio will be exactly offset by a higher output–labour ratio, and the capital–output ratio will not be higher in capital-rich countries than in capital-poor countries, so convergence is not to be expected. If there are not diminishing returns to capital, this also means that the capital–output ratio will not rise as more investment takes place, and therefore *the ratio of saving and investment to GDP does matter for growth. Growth is endogenously determined in this sense*; it is not simply exogenously determined by the rate of growth of the labour force and technical progress. This is the starting point for the 'new' (endogenous) growth theory, which seeks to explain why in practice living standards in the world economy have not converged (see Chapter 2) contrary to the predictions of neoclassical theory. The explanation offered by the new growth theory is that there are forces at work that prevent the marginal product of capital from falling (and the capital–output ratio from rising) as more investment takes place as countries get richer. Before turning to the new growth theory, however, let us first consider how the neoclassical production function can be used to analyse the sources of growth. This requires us to look more closely at the concept of the production function and the properties of the Cobb–Douglas production function, which is still widely used in the analysis of growth in both developed and developing countries.

THE PRODUCTION FUNCTION APPROACH TO THE ANALYSIS OF GROWTH

We have already seen that there are several ways in which the growth of income or output of a country may be expressed, but frequently they consist of identities that tell us very little about the causes or sources of growth. For example, in the Harrod–Domar model, growth can be expressed as the product of the ratio of investment to GDP and the productivity of investment, so that by definition slow growth is the product of a low investment ratio and/or a low productivity of capital, but by itself this does not further our understanding of the growth process in different countries. Why do some countries save and invest more than others, and why does the productivity of capital differ? Likewise we have seen that the growth of output can be expressed as the sum of the rate of growth of the labour force and the rate of growth of labour productivity. By definition, slow growth is attributable to a slow rate of growth of the labour force and/or a slow rate of growth of labour productivity. Again, however, why does growth in labour productivity differ between countries? Is it because of differences in capital accumulation, or is it because of differences in technical progress, broadly defined to include such factors as improvements in the quality of labour, improvements in the quality of capital, economies of scale, advances in knowledge, a better organization of capital and labour in the productive process, and so on? Growth identities cannot distinguish between such competing hypotheses.

The production function approach to the analysis of growth is a response to this challenge. It takes the concept of the aggregate production function and attempts to disaggregate the sources of growth into the contribution of labour, capital, technical progress, and any other variable included in the production function that is thought to influence the growth process. In this sense it is a very versatile approach. It is, however, a **supply orientated** approach. It does not tell us *why* the growth of capital, labour, technical progress and so on differs over time or between countries. The sources of growth are treated as *exogenous*. In practice, however, the supply of most resources to an economic system is endogenous, responding to the demand for them. Capital is a produced means of production and comes from the growth of output itself; labour is very elastic in supply from both internal and external sources (migration), and technical progress is itself partly dependent on the growth of output arising from static and dynamic returns to scale.

Thus while the production function approach can disaggregate any measured growth rate into various constituent growth-inducing sources, and can 'explain' growth rate differences in terms of these sources, it cannot answer the more fundamental question of why labour supply, capital accumulation and technical progress grow at different rates in different countries. The answer to this question must lie in differences in the strength of *demand* for countries' products, which in the early stages of development depends largely on the prosperity of agriculture (see Chapter 5), and in the later stages of development depends largely on the country's export performance relative to its import propensity (see Chapter 17).

Having said this, the production function approach can provide a useful **growth accounting** exercise, which is in fact widely used. Apart from deciding which determinants of growth to specify in the production function, and accurately measuring the independent variables, the main problem is a methodological one of fitting the appropriate production function to the data; that is, specifying the function relating output to inputs.

The production function

A desirable property of any macroeconomic hypothesis, apart from being consistent with the observed facts, is that it should be consistent with and derivable from microeconomic theory. What we call the **production-function approach to the analysis of growth** in the aggregate possesses, in part, this desirable property in that it borrows the concept of the production function from the theory of the firm. Just as it can be said that, for a firm, output is a function of the factors of production – land, labour, capital and the level of technology (or factor efficiency) – so aggregate output can be written as a function of factor inputs and the prevailing technology:

$$Y = f(R, K, L, T) \qquad\qquad (4.20)$$

where R is land, K is capital, L is labour and T is technology.[6]

The question is how to separate empirically the contribution to growth of the growth of factor inputs from other factors that can lead to higher output, included in T, such as economies of scale (due both to technical change and to increases in factor supplies), improvements in the quality of factor inputs, advances in knowledge, better organization of factors and so on. The task is to fit an appropriate, correctly specified production function that, if possible, will not only separate the contribution of factor inputs to growth from the contribution of increases in output per unit of inputs (increases in 'total' factor productivity), but will also distinguish between some of the factors that may contribute to increases in the productivity of factors, such as education, improvements in the quality of capital and economies of scale.

Before going on to discuss the types of function that may be employed, however, let us examine in a little more detail the properties of a production function. We have established so far that the aggregate production function expresses the functional relation between aggregate output and the stock of inputs. If land is subsumed into capital, and technology is held constant, we are left with two factors, and the production function may be drawn on a two-dimensional diagram, as in Figure 4.5. Capital (K) is measured

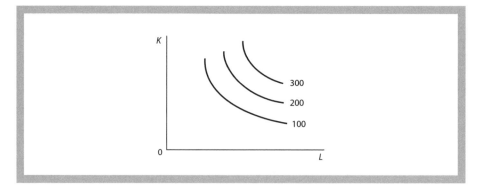

Figure 4.5 The production function

on the vertical axis and labour (L) on the horizontal axis, and each function represents a constant level of output that can be produced with different combinations of capital and labour. The functions slope negatively from left to right on the assumption that marginal additions of either factor will increase total output – that is, factors have positive marginal products – and they are drawn convex to the origin on the assumption that factors have a diminishing marginal productivity as their supply increases, so that if one unit is withdrawn it needs to be substituted by more and more of the other factor to keep output constant. The position of the functions broadly reflects the level of technology. The more 'advanced' the technology, the greater the level of output per unit of total inputs, and the closer to the origin will be the production function representing a *given* output.

From the simple production-function diagram it is easy to see how output may increase. First, there may be a physical increase in factor inputs, L and K, permitting a higher level of production. Either or both factors may increase. If only one factor increases, the movement to a higher production function will involve a change in the combination of factors, and output will not be able to increase for ever, because ultimately the marginal product of the variable factor will fall to zero. This is illustrated in Figure 4.6, where, with a given stock of capital $0K_1$, output cannot increase beyond 300 with increases in the supply of labour ($0L_1$, $0L_2$ and so on) beyond the limit indicated. The diminishing productivity of the variable factor, labour, with capital fixed, is shown by the flatter and

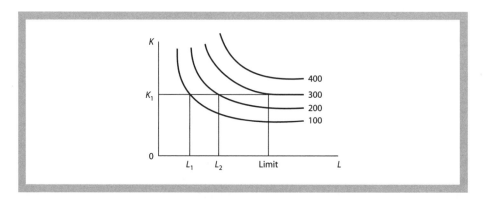

Figure 4.6 Production-function diagram

flatter slope of the production functions at successive points, L_1, L_2, until at the limit the production function is horizontal and the marginal product of labour is zero.

If both factors increase in supply, however, there is no reason why output should not go on increasing indefinitely. In fact, if both factors increase in supply there is a possibility that production may be subject to increasing returns, such that output rises more than proportionately to the increase in combined inputs. If this is the case, output per unit of total inputs will increase and the production functions representing equal additional amounts of production, for example 100, 200, 300 and so on, must be drawn closer and closer together, as in Figure 4.7.

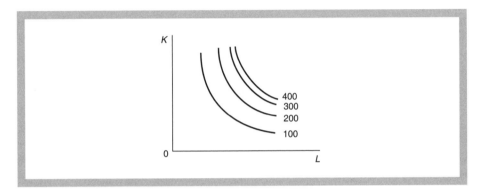

Figure 4.7 The effect of increasing returns

In the opposite case of decreasing returns, the functions would be drawn further and further apart. Finally, in the case of production subject to constant returns, the functions would be drawn equidistant from one another.

Increasing returns may also result from advances in technology, irrespective of increases in factor supplies. These are called **technological economies of scale**. In this case, increases in output per unit of input would have to be represented on a production-function diagram either by relabelling the functions or relabelling the axes. That is, either the same amount of factor inputs, measured on the axes, would have to be shown to be producing a higher output than before, or the same output could be shown to be produced by lesser amounts of inputs. If the functions are relabelled and not the axes, this is tantamount to a shift in all the production functions towards the origin. Shifts in the production function towards the origin are implied by all forms of technical progress or any factor that increases the productivity of the physical inputs.

In short, there are three broad sources of growth that can be distinguished using the production-function framework:

- ■ Increases in factor supplies
- ■ Increasing returns
- ■ Technical progress, interpreted in the wide sense of anything that increases the productivity of factors other than increasing returns.

The Cobb–Douglas production function

The production function most commonly fitted to aggregate data to distinguish empirically between these three broad sources of growth has been the unconstrained form of the **Cobb–Douglas production function**, named after its two American originators, Charles Cobb (a mathematician) and Paul Douglas (an economist), who pioneered research in the area of applied economic growth in the 1920s and 1930s (Cobb and Douglas, 1928). The Cobb–Douglas function may be written as

$$Y_t = T_t K_t^\alpha L_t^\beta \tag{4.21}$$

where Y_t is real output at time, t, T_t is an index of technology, or 'total' productivity, K_t is an index of the capital stock, or capital services, at constant prices, L_t is an index of labour input (preferably man-hours), α is the partial elasticity (responsiveness) of output with respect to capital (holding labour constant), and β is the partial elasticity of output with respect to labour (holding capital constant).

It is assumed that changes in technology are exogenous and independent of changes in factor inputs, and that the effect of technical progress is neutral on the factor intensity of production (see p. 216 for a definition of neutral technical progress). T_t, α and β are constants to be estimated empirically if the function is unconstrained. If α and β are assigned values in advance of the use of the function for estimating purposes, the function is said to be constrained. Normally α and β will be less than unity on the assumption of diminishing marginal productivity of factors. The sum of the partial elasticities of output with respect to the factors of production gives the scale of returns, or the degree of homogeneity, of the function: $\alpha + \beta = 1$ represents constant returns, $\alpha + \beta > 1$ represents increasing returns, and $\alpha + \beta < 1$ represents decreasing returns, and the function is said to be homogeneous of degree one, greater than one, and less than one, respectively.

If α and β are not estimated empirically but are assumed to sum to unity, in which case the function will be constrained to constant returns, then increasing or decreasing returns will be reflected in the value of T_t, which is the index of total factor productivity. The existence of increasing returns would bias the value of T_t upwards, and decreasing returns would bias the value of T_t downwards. These points are made because in practice the Cobb–Douglas function is often employed in this constrained form with the sum of α and β put equal to unity. Then values are assigned to α and β according to the share of capital and labour in the national income. The underlying assumption is the perfectly competitive one that if production is subject to constant returns and factors are paid the value of their marginal products, then factor shares will reflect the elasticity of output with respect to each factor.[7]

In order to use (4.21) to separate the influence of the three broad sources of growth mentioned earlier, we must first make it operational by transforming it into *rate-of-growth* form. This can be done by taking logarithms of the variables and differentiating with respect to time, which gives:[8]

$$\frac{d \log Y_t}{dt} = \frac{d \log T_t}{dt} + \alpha \frac{d \log K_t}{dt} + \beta \frac{d \log L_t}{dt} \tag{4.22}$$

or

$$\frac{dY}{dt} \times \frac{1}{Y} = \left(\frac{dT}{dt} \times \frac{1}{T} \right) + \alpha \left(\frac{dK}{dt} \times \frac{1}{K} \right) + \beta \left(\frac{dL}{dt} \times \frac{1}{L} \right)$$

The above equations are in continuous time. The discrete approximation, taking annual rates of change of the variables, may be written as

$$r_Y = r_T + \alpha r_K + \beta r_L \tag{4.23}$$

where r_Y is the annual rate of growth of output per time period, r_T is the annual rate of growth of total productivity, or technical progress, r_K is the annual rate of growth of capital, r_L is the annual rate of growth of labour, and α and β are the partial elasticities of output with respect to capital and labour, respectively, as before.

In other words, equation (4.23) says that the rate of growth of output is equal to the sum of the rate of growth of 'total' productivity, the rate of growth of capital weighted by the partial elasticity of output with respect to capital and the rate of growth of labour weighted by the partial elasticity of output with respect to labour. With knowledge of r_Y, r_K, r_L, α and β, it becomes possible as a first step to separate out the contribution of factor inputs to growth from increases in output per unit of inputs represented by r_T. Now let us give an illustrative example. Suppose $r_Y = 5$ per cent per annum, $r_K = 5$ per cent per annum, $r_L = 1$ per cent per annum, $\alpha = 0.25$ and $\beta = 0.75$ (decided on the basis of factor shares). Substituting in (4.23) we have

$$5.0 = r_T + 0.25 (5.0) + 0.75 (1.0) \tag{4.24}$$

The contribution of capital to measured growth is $0.25 (5.0) = 1.25$ percentage points; the contribution of labour is $0.75 (1.0) = 0.75$ percentage points; and r_T is left as a residual with a contribution of 3.0 percentage points. If α and β were estimated empirically and there happened to be increasing returns ($\alpha + \beta > 1$), the significance of the factor contribution would be enhanced and r_T would be smaller.

On the assumption of constant returns to scale, the production function can also be estimated in its so-called labour-intensive form to analyse the **growth of output per head** (see (4.14)). If we subtract r_L from both sides of (4.23) and assume $\alpha + \beta = 1$, so that $\beta = 1 - \alpha$, we get

$$r_Y - r_L = r_T + \alpha (r_K - r_L) \tag{4.25}$$

which means that the rate of growth of output per head (or labour productivity) is equal to the sum of the rate of growth of total productivity plus the rate of growth of capital per head times the elasticity of output with respect to capital. Taking the illustrative figures above, if $r_y = 5$ per cent and $r_L = 1$ per cent, then the rate of labour productivity growth is 4 per cent. Therefore

$$4.0 = r_T + 0.25 (5.0 - 1.0) \tag{4.26}$$

The contribution of capital per head (capital deepening) to productivity growth is 1 percentage point, leaving r_T with a contribution of 3 percentage points (as before).

Although r_T has been variously called technical progress, advances in knowledge and so on, definitionally it is that portion of the growth of output not attributable to increases in the factors of production, and includes the effects not only of the multifarious factors that increase the productivity of labour and capital but also any measurement errors in the capital and labour input series . r_T is perhaps best described as a residual, or, perhaps more appropriately still, a 'coefficient of ignorance' if the analysis proceeds no further.

One important component of r_T, which can be considered the result of measurement errors, is likely to be the effect of **resource shifts** from less productive to more productive activities. Since the analysis is aggregative there is bound to be a confounding of changes in actual output with changes in the composition of output unless the weights used for aggregating inputs are continually revised. Resource shifts from agriculture to industry can be expected to figure prominently in any production-function study of developing countries, as they do for studies of many advanced economies.

Limitations of the Cobb-Douglas function

Before considering some of the results of applying the Cobb–Douglas function to empirical data, we must briefly mention some of its limitations. Its use has come under attack on four main counts. First, since only one combination of factor inputs can be observed at any one time, there is an identification problem in attempting to distinguish shifts in the function (technical progress) from movements along the function (changes in factor intensity) unless the assumption of neutral technical progress is made. But technical progress may not be neutral and therefore the effects of technical progress and changing factor intensity become confused, biasing the results of the contribution of factor inputs and technical progress to growth.

Second, the assumption that technical progress is independent of increases in factor inputs has been questioned. This is not a specification error of the function itself, however, and the Cobb–Douglas function can be used, making technical progress a function of the rate of growth of inputs – so-called endogenous models of technical progress.

Third, the Cobb–Douglas function possesses the restrictive property of constant unitary elasticity of substitution between factors, whatever the factor intensity.[9] The assumption of constant elasticity means that the function cannot represent a change in the ease of substitution between capital and labour. The assumption of unitary elasticity may be serious if the elasticity of substitution of factors differs significantly from unity and there are wide discrepancies in the growth rate of factors. For example, if the elasticity of substitution between capital and labour is significantly less than unity, and capital grows faster than labour, this will result in an overestimate of the contribution of capital to growth and an underestimate of the role of other factors. The intuitive explanation of this bias is that the smaller the elasticity of substitution the more difficult it is in practice to obtain increased output just by increasing one factor, because diminishing returns set in strongly. By assuming the elasticity is higher than it is, the importance of the fastest-growing factor is exaggerated. If elasticity is high, diminishing returns are not a problem, and if both capital and labour expand at the same rate, growth is obviously independent of the elasticity of substitution.[10]

A final criticism relates to the measurement of output and inputs. What, argue some, is the meaning of a function that aggregates so many heterogeneous items; in particular, what is the meaning of an aggregation of capital goods built at different times, at different costs and with varying productivities? How are such capital goods to be equated in an aggregate measure of capital?

By and large, most of the above-mentioned criticisms are theoretical worries, the practical significance of which is hard to determine. Studies of the nature of technical progress, at least in advanced countries, suggest that the assumption of neutrality is a fair working hypothesis. The fact that technical progress may be dependent on factor accumulation can be accommodated within the Cobb–Douglas framework. Capital and labour would have to grow at very different rates for the elasticity of substitution to matter very much, but in any case studies show that it is quite close to unity. Finally, although the aggregation of heterogeneous outputs and inputs can present severe problems, especially the aggregation of capital, which cannot be measured directly in physical units, there are techniques of aggregation available that various studies have used with some success.

Application of the Cobb-Douglas function

What have been the results of applying the Cobb–Douglas function to empirical data? First, let us consider its application in developed countries and consider the conclusions that emerge. We can start with the pioneering work of Cobb and Douglas themselves. Ironically, the Cobb–Douglas function, as first conceived, was not intended as a device for distinguishing the sources of growth but as a test of neoclassical marginal productivity theory; that is, to see whether elasticities of output with respect to labour and capital corresponded to factor shares. Douglas had observed that the output curve for US manufacturing industry for the period 1899–1922 lay consistently between the two curves for the factors of production, and he suggested to his mathematician friend, Cobb, that they should seek to develop a formula that could measure the relative effect of labour and capital on the growth of output over the period in question. This story is described by Douglas (1948) in his fascinating review article 'Are There Laws of Production?' As an insight into the inductive method the relevant passage is worth quoting in full:

> Having computed indexes for American manufacturing of the number of workers employed by years from 1899 to 1922 as well as indexes of the amounts of fixed capital in manufacturing deflated to dollars of approximately constant purchasing power, and then plotting these on a log scale, together with the Day index of physical production for manufacturing, I observed that the product curve lay consistently between the two curves for the factors of production and tended to be approximately one-quarter of the relative distance between the curve of the index for labour, which showed the least increase in the period, and that of the index of capital which showed the most. I suggested to my friend Charles Cobb that we seek to develop a formula which could measure the relative effect of labour and capital upon product during this period. At his suggestion the sum of the exponents was tentatively made equal to unity in the formula $Y = TK^{\alpha}L^{1-\alpha}$ [our notation] . . . The fact that on the basis of fairly wide studies there is an appreciable degree of uniformity, and that the sum of the exponents approximates to unity, fairly clearly suggests that there are laws of production which can be approximated by inductive studies and that we are at least approaching them. (Douglas, 1948, p. 20)

The estimated function derived was $Y = 1.01\ K^{0.25}\ L^{0.75}$, which lent support to the neoclassical model of constant returns and marginal product pricing. There was no discussion of the relative importance of factors of production and the T variable in accounting for measured growth. It was not until Abramovitz (1956) and Solow (1957) showed that 80–90 per cent of the growth of output per head in the US economy in the first half of the twentieth century could not be accounted for by increases in capital per head that the production function started to be used in earnest as a technique in the applied economics of growth. Abramovitz remarked that:

> This result is surprising in the lop-sided importance which it appears to give to productivity increase and it should be, in a sense, sobering, if not discouraging to students of economic growth. Since we know little about the causes of productivity increase, the indicated importance of this element may be taken to be some sort of measure of our ignorance about the causes of economic growth in the United States, and some sort of indication of where we need to concentrate our attention. (Abramovitz, 1956, p. 11)

Abramovitz's findings were supported by Solow, who found, when examining the data for the non-farm sector of the US economy for the period 1919–57, that approximately 90 per cent of the growth of output per head could not be accounted for by increases in capital per head; that is, using the notation in (4.25):

$$r_T/(r_y - r_L) = 0.90 \tag{4.27}$$

The findings of Abramovitz and Solow disturbed economists brought up in the belief that investment and capital accumulation played a crucial role in the growth process. Even allowing for the statistical difficulties of computing a series of the capital stock, and the limitations of the function applied to the data (for example, the assumption of constant returns and neutral technical progress, plus the high degree of aggregation), it was difficult to escape from the conclusion that the growth of the capital stock was of relatively minor importance in accounting for the growth of total output. It is true that Abramovitz stressed that his findings did not imply that resources were unimportant for growth, because of the interrelation between the growth of inputs and factors leading to increases in output per unit of inputs, but this caution was not sufficient to counter the initial reaction that capital does not matter.

It would not be misleading to say that much of the subsequent research effort in this field of growth was designed (even before the advent of new growth theory) to reverse this conclusion, or rather to 'assign back' to the factors of production sources of growth that make up the residual factor but are interrelated with, or dependent on, the growth of factor inputs. Work has proceeded on two fronts. On the one hand, attempts have been made to disaggregate the residual factor, measuring factor inputs in the conventional way; on the other hand, attempts have been made to adjust the labour and capital input series for such things as changes in the *quality* of factors and their composition, so that much more measured growth is seen to be attributable to increases in factor inputs in the first place. For example, the labour input series has been adjusted for improvements in its quality due to the growth of education, and for changes in its composition due to age/sex shifts. Likewise the capital stock series has been adjusted to reflect changes in its composition and, more importantly, to allow for the fact that new additions to the capital stock in any line of production are likely to be more productive than the existing capital stock as a result of technical advance. This is the notion of **embodied** or **endogenous technical change** as opposed to the exogenous technical change assumption of the original Cobb–Douglas function, which assumes that all vintages of capital share equally in technical progress.

A distinction is made, therefore, between embodied and disembodied technical progress – embodied technical progress refers to technical improvements that can only be introduced into the productive system by new investment, and disembodied technical progress is exogenous and not dependent on capital accumulation. There are several ways in which embodied technical progress can be isolated from the residual factor by appropriate adjustments to the capital stock series to reflect the greater productivity of the latest investments. The net result is to enhance the role of capital accumulation in the growth process.

Efforts have also been made to overcome one of the problems associated with the aggregation of outputs by taking explicit account of shifts of labour and capital from low-productivity to high-productivity sectors. This, too, reduces the significance of the residual factor and makes the role of labour and capital in the growth process look correspondingly more important.

Since Abramovitz and Solow reported their findings in 1956 and 1957, a substantial body of empirical evidence relating to the sources of growth has accumulated, experimenting with different specifications of the aggregate production function. Unfortunately it is not systematic. The time periods taken, the data used, the sectors of the economy examined and the methodology employed all vary within and between countries. All that can be done here is to draw attention to some of the major findings and let students check the nature of the work for themselves.

Until recently most of the evidence available pertained to fairly advanced economies and it is largely from this evidence, wisely or not, that conclusions have been drawn on development strategy for developing countries. Research in developing countries has been hampered by a lack of researchers, a shortage of reliable empirical data and perhaps an even greater suspicion of the aggregate production function, and its implicit assumptions, than in developed countries. The assumption that factor shares can be used as weights to measure the relative contribution of labour and capital to growth is probably more dubious in developing countries than in developed countries. The price of labour almost certainly exceeds its marginal product, while the price of capital falls short of it so that the share of income going to labour exceeds the elasticity of output with respect to labour and the share of income going to capital understates the elasticity of output with respect to capital. Second, the aggregation of inputs and outputs is generally more difficult, and there are greater problems of resource underutilization to contend with. The recent past, however, has witnessed a number of production-function studies for developing countries.

PRODUCTION FUNCTION STUDIES OF DEVELOPING COUNTRIES

Some of the notable early production function studies of the sources of growth in developing countries are those by Maddison (1970), Bruton (1967), Robinson (1971), Hagen and Hawrylyshyn (1969), Correa (1970), Lampman (1967) (the last two studies, and others, surveyed by Nadiri, 1972). More recent studies include Shaaeldin (1989), World Bank (1991), Young (1995), Hu and Khan (1997), Felipe (1999), Senhadji (2000), and Sala-i-Martin (1997), who surveys other studies. Let us consider these studies and bring out their major conclusions, especially any important contrasts with the conclusions from studies of developed countries.

The major conclusions of the early production function studies of developing countries were:

- Capital accumulation is more important as a source of growth than total productivity growth, and more important than in developed countries.
- Improvements in the *quality* of labour are important through better health, nutrition and education.
- Resource shifts are not so important as might have been expected, perhaps due to the general surplus of labour in developing countries and the low capacity to absorb labour into productive employment in the industrial sector.

Now let us turn to the more recent studies. Shaaeldin (1989) fits equation (4.23) to the industrial sector of four African countries, and shows that between the mid-1960s and the early 1980s total factor productivity growth was *negative* in three of the countries as the result of severe macro-recession. The results are shown in Table 4.1 and confirm the overwhelming importance of the contribution of capital formation to the growth process.

Table 4.2 provides the results of a World Bank study for the period 1960–87, showing the contribution of factor inputs and total productivity growth to the growth of output in various continents. It is clear that the major source of growth is not productivity growth, but the growth of inputs themselves.

Young (1995) has used the production function model to debunk the idea that there has been a 'growth miracle' in the four East Asian countries of Hong Kong, Singapore, South Korea and Taiwan (the so-called 'four little dragons'). Young uses the production-function approach and shows that while the growth of output was spectacular over the 1966–90 period, most of the growth can be accounted for by the rapid growth of factor inputs and there was nothing abnormal about the growth of total factor productivity. Table 4.3 presents the figures. Young describes such calculations as 'the tyranny of numbers', by which he means that there is nothing special to explain. On the basis of Young's calculations, Krugman (1994) has described the 'Asian miracle' as a myth. The spectacular growth of inputs, however, does need explaining. The rapid growth of capital and labour is a function of an internal dynamism fuelled by the relentless and successful drive for export markets, partly engineered by deliberate government intervention. East Asia is not the bastion of free-market enterprise that is often portrayed. The growth of factor inputs may decelerate in the future, but the performance of these four economies up to 1990 was indeed remarkable, notwithstanding the relatively low rate of growth of total factor productivity.

Hu and Khan (1997) use the production function[11] approach to understand the sources of fast growth in China over the period 1953–94, and the acceleration of growth after the economic reforms and 'open door' policy were introduced in 1978. From 1953 to 1978, GDP grew at 5.8 per cent per annum, and then accelerated to 9.3 per cent per annum from 1979 to 1994. Why was this? To estimate the contribution of labour, capital and total factor productivity (TFP) to measured growth over the periods, factor shares of GDP are taken as the elasticities of output with respect to labour and capital, with labour's elasticity approximately 0.4, and capital's elasticity approximately 0.6. The results are shown in Table 4.4.

Table 4.1 Contribution of factor inputs and total productivity growth to industrial growth in Kenya, Tanzania, Zambia and Zimbabwe, 1964–81

	Growth of output (% p.a)	Contribution of labour	Contribution of capital	Total productivity growth
Kenya 1964–83	7.99	1.99	6.89	−0.89
Tanzania 1966–80	8.06	3.16	5.41	−0.51
Zambia 1965–80	4.98	1.20	9.38	−6.60
Zimbabwe 1964–81	5.28	1.88	3.39	+0.03

Source: E. Shaaeldin, 'Sources of Industrial Growth in Kenya, Tanzania, Zambia and Zimbabwe: Some Estimates', *African Development Review*, June 1989.

Table 4.2 Contribution of factor inputs and total productivity growth to economic growth in 68 developing countries, 1960–87

	GDP growth (% p.a)	Contribution of labour	Contribution of capital	TFP
Africa	3.3	1.0	2.3	0.0
East Asia	6.8	1.1	3.8	1.9
Europe, Middle East and North Africa	5.0	0.7	2.9	1.4
Latin America	3.6	1.2	2.4	0.0
South Asia	4.4	0.9	2.9	0.6
68 Economies	4.2	1.0	2.6	0.6

Source: World Bank, *World Development Report 1991* (Washington, DC: World Bank, 1991).

Table 4.3 Growth of output and total factor productivity in the East Asian 'dragons', 1966–90 (per cent)

	Output growth	Total factor productivity growth
Hong Kong	7.3	2.3
Singapore	8.7	0.2
South Korea	8.5	1.7
Taiwan	8.5	2.1

Source: A. Young, 'The Tyranny of Numbers: Confronting the Statistical Realities of the East Asian Growth Experience', *Quarterly Journal of Economics*, August 1995.

Table 4.4 Sources of growth in China, 1953–94 (per cent)

	1953–94	1953–78	1979–94
Output growth	7.2	5.8	9.3
Capital input growth	6.8	6.2	7.7
Labour input growth	2.6	2.5	2.7
TFP growth	2.1	1.1	3.9
Contribution of capital	55.6	65.2	45.6
Contribution of labour	14.9	16.8	12.8
Contribution of productivity growth	29.5	18.0	41.6

Source: Z. F. Hu and M. S. Khan, 'Why is China Growing So Fast?', *IMF Staff Papers*, March 1997.

To give an example, in the pre-reform period 1953–78, the growth of capital was 6.2 per cent per annum. Multiplying 6.2 by 0.6 (capital's elasticity) gives a contribution of capital to growth of 3.72 percentage points which is approximately 65 per cent of the total growth of output of 5.8 per cent. Capital accumulation was by far the most important contributor to growth in this period. In the post-reform period 1979–94, however, it can be seen that the contribution of productivity growth increases considerably to almost equal importance with capital. The rate of growth of TFP more than triples, from 1.1 per cent per annum to 3.9 per cent, contributing over 40 per cent to measured growth. According to Hu and Khan, the process of reform stimulated productivity growth in a number of ways, including the transfer of resources from agriculture to industry; a reallocation of resources from the public to the private sector; the encouragement of foreign direct investment (FDI), and a faster growth of exports.

Felipe (1999) surveys the studies done of TFP growth in the whole of East Asia, most of which use the production-function approach. He is critical of many of them, and shows how estimates of TFP can vary according to the time period taken, the estimates made of the growth of factor inputs and the assumed elasticities of output with respect to labour and capital. Remember that TFP is obtained as a residual after the contribution of the factor inputs has been calculated. The various methodological and conceptual problems associated with the use of production functions discussed earlier are also emphasized, particularly the assumption that technical progress and factor inputs are exogenous and not interrelated.

The latest comprehensive study of the sources of growth using the aggregate production function comes from Senhadji (2000) at the IMF. He estimates production functions for 66 countries over the period 1960–94 (including 46 developing countries) of the form: $Y = TK^\alpha (LH)^{1-\alpha}$ where T is TFP, K is the stock of capital, L is the active population and H is an index of human capital. The function is estimated using levels of the variables (measured in logarithms), and taking first differences of the log level (i.e. in rate of growth form – see (4.22)). The estimates of the elasticity of output with respect to capital (α) varies considerably across countries (and regions) and also according to whether levels or first differences of the variables are used (which is another problem!). Using levels, the estimates of (α) range from 0.43 in sub-Saharan Africa to 0.63 in the Middle East and North Africa. Using first differences, the estimates of α range from 0.30 in East Asia to 0.62 in Latin America. Using the mean value of α from the equations estimated in levels gives the sources of growth in different regions shown in Table 4.5.

Table 4.5 Sources of growth by region of the world, 1960–94

Region	Output growth (%)	Contribution (percentage points) of:			
		Capital	Labour	Human capital	TFP
East Asia	6.49	4.50	1.27	0.44	0.28
South Asia	4.66	2.87	0.99	0.25	0.55
Sub-Saharan Africa	2.83	1.79	1.39	0.22	−0.56
Middle East & North Africa	5.05	3.99	0.84	0.25	−0.03
Latin America	3.42	2.31	1.22	0.28	−0.39

Source: A. Senhadji, 'Sources of Economic Growth: An Extensive Growth Accounting Exercise', *IMF Staff Papers*, 47(1), 2000.

It can be seen again from Table 4.5 that capital accumulation is by far the most important contributor to measured growth in all the regions. The small contribution of TFP in the fastest-growing region of East Asia confirms the conclusions of Young. Notice also, the *negative* contribution of TFP in Africa (which supports Shaaeldin's results), and also in Latin America. Human capital formation makes a positive contribution to growth in all regions, but relatively minor.

It is satisfying that the conclusions from a wide number of studies using different techniques and dubious data should all point in roughly the same direction. First, the major source of growth in developing countries is increased factor inputs, aided by improvements in the quality of labour through health improvement and education. Second, the growth of 'total' factor productivity in developing countries is relatively slow compared with that in developed countries, which may be partly a reflection of the different stage of development reached. Third, resource transfers from agriculture to industry are quite important as a source of growth, but not as important as one might have expected. They will become more important as the ability of the industrial sector to absorb surplus labour increases.

Before ending it should be said again that the aggregate models that produced the above results are rough tools. They do, however, give an important idea of the forces at work and a rough idea of the likely quantitative significance of different factors. The production function approach is also a very versatile tool of analysis. Sala-í-Martin (1997) has surveyed a number of production function studies and found that authors have included at least 62 different variables in the production function to explain growth, in addition to the growth of capital and labour!

'NEW' (ENDOGENOUS) GROWTH THEORY AND THE MACRODETERMINANTS OF GROWTH[12]

Since the mid-1980s there has been an outpouring of literature and research on the applied economics of growth, attempting to understand and explain the differences in the rates of output growth and per capita income growth across the world, many inspired by the so-called 'new' growth theory, or endogenous growth theory. This spate of cross-sectional studies seems to have been prompted by a number of factors:

- Increased concern with the economic performance of the poorer regions of the world, and particularly the striking differences between countries and continents
- The increased availability of standardized data (e.g. Summers and Heston, 1991 and *World Development Indicators* from the World Bank), enabling reliable econometric work
- Pioneering studies (e.g. Baumol, 1986) that could find no convergence of per capita incomes in the world economy, contrary to the prediction of neoclassical growth theory based on the assumption of diminishing returns to capital, which, given identical preferences and technology across countries, should lead to faster growth in poor countries than in rich ones.

It is the latter finding (although hardly new, as outlined in Chapter 2) that has been the major inspiration behind the development of the 'new' growth theory, which relaxes the assumption of diminishing returns to capital and shows that, with constant or increasing returns, there can be no presumption of the convergence of per capita incomes across the world, or of individual countries reaching a long-run steady-state growth equilibrium at the natural rate. If there are not diminishing returns to capital, investment is important for long-run growth and growth is endogenous in this sense. In these 'new' models of endogenous growth, pioneered by Robert Lucas (1988) and Paul Romer (1986, 1990), there are assumed to be positive externalities associated with human capital formation (for example, education and training) and research and development (R&D) that prevent the marginal product of capital from falling and the capital–output ratio from rising. We have a production function in capital of

$$Y = AK^\alpha \tag{4.28}$$

where K is a composite measure of capital (i.e. physical capital plus other types of reproducible capital), and $\alpha = 1$. As Barro and Sala-í-Martin (1995) put it 'the global absence of diminishing returns may seem unrealistic, but the idea becomes more plausible if we think of K in a broad sense to include [for example] human capital'. It can be seen from the expression for the capital–output ratio, that is

$$\frac{K}{Y} = \frac{K}{L} \cdot \frac{L}{Y} \tag{4.29}$$

that anything that raises the productivity of labour (Y/L) in the same proportion as K/L will keep the capital–output ratio constant. Learning by doing and embodied technical progress in the spirit of Arrow (1962) and Kaldor (1957), as well as technological spillovers from trade (Grossman and Helpman, 1990, 1991) and FDI (de Mello, 1996), are additional possibilities to education and research and development.

The first crude test of the 'new' growth theory is to see whether or not poor countries do grow faster than rich ones, or in other words to see whether there is an inverse relation between the growth of output (or output per head) and the *initial* level of per capita income. If there is, this would provide support for the neoclassical model. If there is not, this would support the new growth theory's assertion that the marginal product of capital does not decline. The equation to be estimated is

$$g_i = a + b_1 (PCY)_i \tag{4.30}$$

where g_i is the average growth of output per head of country i over a number of years and PCY_i is its initial level of per capita income. A significantly negative estimate of b_1 would be evidence of **unconditional convergence** or **beta (β) convergence** as it is called in the literature; that is, poor countries growing faster than rich without allowing for any other economic, social or political differences between countries. As we saw in Chapter 2, none of the studies taking large samples of developed and developing countries has been able to find evidence of unconditional convergence. The estimate of b_1 is not significantly negative; in fact it is invariably positive, indicating divergence.[13]

Before jumping to the conclusion that this is a rejection of the neoclassical model, however, it must be remembered that the neoclassical prediction of convergence assumes that the savings or investment ratio, population growth, technology and all factors that affect the productivity of labour are the same across countries. Since these assumptions are manifestly false, there can never be the presumption of unconditional convergence (even if there are diminishing returns to capital), only **conditional convergence**, holding constant all other factors that influence the growth of per capita income, including population growth (p), the investment ratio (I/Y) and variables that affect the productivity of labour, for example education (ED), research and development expenditure ($R + D$), trade (T) and even non-economic variables such as political stability measured by the number of revolutions and coups (PS). The equation to be estimated is therefore

$$g_i = a + b_1 (PCY)_i + b_2 (p)_i + b_3 (I/Y)_i + b_4 (ED)_i$$
$$+ b_5 (R + D)_i + b_6 (T)_i + b_7 (PS)_i + \ldots \qquad (4.31)$$

and the question to be asked is what happens to the sign of the initial per capita income variable (PCY) when these other variables are introduced into the equation? If the sign turns negative ($b_1 < 0$) when allowance is made for these other factors, this is supposed to represent a rehabilitation of the neoclassical model (see Barro, 1991); that is, there *would be* convergence if it were not for differences between rich and poor countries in all these other important variables in the growth process. 'New' growth theory would be supported by finding that education, research and development expenditure and so on matter, and it is these factors that keep the marginal product of capital from falling, producing actual divergence in the world economy. A very good empirical illustration of what we have been talking about is given in Table 2.7 (Chapter 2, p. 59).

Note here that if the model of 'new' growth theory is represented by the AK model, as in (4.35), this can be shown to be equivalent to the Harrod–Domar growth equation. Assuming $\alpha = 1$, totally differentiate (4.28) and divide by Y. This gives

$$dY/Y = A(dK/Y) = A(I/Y) \qquad (4.32)$$

where dY/Y is the growth rate, I/Y is the investment ratio, and A is the productivity of capital (dY/I) which is the reciprocal of the incremental capital–output ratio. This is the same as the Harrod growth equation $g = s/c$, where s is the savings ratio and c is the incremental capital–output ratio, or the Domar equation $g = s\sigma$, where σ is the productivity of capital.

If the productivity of capital was the same across countries, there would be a perfect correlation between the growth rate of countries and the investment ratio where the slope of the relationship is the reciprocal of the incremental capital–output ratio (c). If there is not a perfect correlation, then by definition, the productivity of capital, or the capital–output ratio, must differ between countries. 'New' growth theory equations that attempt to explain growth rate differences between countries (such as (4.31) – and see empirical studies later) are really asking the question (and hopefully answering it!) why does the productivity of capital differ between countries (assuming I/Y is included in the equations)?

We said above that evidence of **conditional convergence** delights the neoclassical economists because it is interpreted as a rehabilitation of the neoclassical growth model with diminishing returns, but this may be a hasty judgement. Outside the neoclassical paradigm there is another distinct body of literature that argues that economic growth *should be* inversely related to the initial level of per capita income because the more backward the country, the greater the scope for '**catch-up**'; that is, for absorbing a back-log of technology (see Gomulka, 1971, 1990; Abramovitz, 1986; Dowrick and Nguyen, 1989; Dowrick and

Gemmell, 1991; Amable, 1993). Thus the negative sign on the per capita income variable could be picking up the effect of catch-up, and the notion of catch-up is conceptually distinct from the *shape* of the production function and whether or not there are diminishing returns to capital. How are the two effects to be distinguished? Also, output growth will be a function of the stage of development because of sectoral differences in the productivity growth rates of agriculture, industry and services, so that convergence may also be partly 'structural', independent of both diminishing returns and catch-up (see Cornwall and Cornwall, 1994). This adds further complications to the interpretation of the coefficient relating country growth rates to the initial level of per capita income.

Now let us turn to the question of the capital–output ratio. Non-diminishing returns to capital, or constancy of the capital–output ratio, lies at the heart of 'new' growth theory, as pioneered by Lucas and Romer who emphasize externalities to education and research. For the historical record, however, it should be mentioned that, many years ago, Nicholas Kaldor pointed out the fact that despite continued capital accumulation and increases in capital per head through time, the capital–output ratio remains broadly the same, implying some form of externalities or constant returns to capital. It is worth quoting Kaldor in full:

> As regards the process of economic change and development in capitalist societies, I suggest the following 'stylised facts' as a starting point for the construction of theoretical models . . . (4) steady capital–output ratios over long periods; at least there are no clear long-term trends, either rising or falling, if differences in the degree of capital utilisation are allowed for. This implies, or reflects, the near identity in the percentage rate of growth of production and of the capital stock i.e. for the economy as a whole, and over long periods, income and capital tend to grow at the same rate. (Kaldor, 1961)

Kaldor's explanation (as a critique of the neoclassical production function) lay in his innovation of the **technical progress function**, which relates the rate of growth of output per worker $(\dot{q})$ to the rate of growth of capital per worker $(\dot{k})$, as depicted in Figure 4.8.

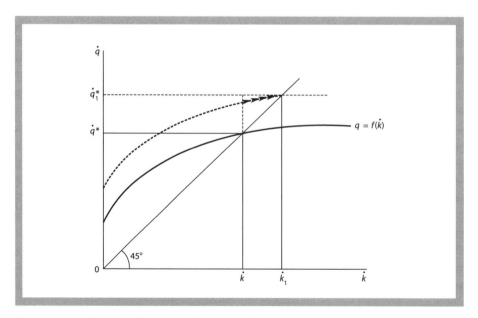

Figure 4.8 Kaldor's technical progress function

The position of the function depends on the exogenous rate of technical progress, and the slope of the function depends on the extent to which technical progress is embodied in capital. Along the 45° line the capital–output ratio is constant, and the equilibrium growth of output per head will be at $\hat{q}*$. An upward shift of the technical progress function – associated, for example, with new discoveries, a technological breakthrough or more education – will shift the curve upwards, causing the growth of output to exceed the growth of capital, raising the rate of profit and inducing more investment to give a new equilibrium growth of output per worker at q_1^*. An increase in capital accumulation *without* an associated upward shift in the schedule will cause the capital–output ratio to rise. 'New' growth theory is precisely anticipated. Kaldor's technical progress function is the true progenitor of endogenous growth theory.

What applies to countries through time applies, *pari passu*, to different countries at a point in time, with differences in growth rates at the same capital–output ratio being associated with different technical progress functions. To quote Kaldor again:

> A lower capital–labour ratio does not necessarily imply a lower capital–output ratio – indeed, the reverse is often the case. The countries with the most highly mechanised industries, such as the United States, do not require a higher ratio of capital to output. The capital–output ratio in the United States has been falling over the past 50 years whilst the capital–labour ratio has been steadily rising; *and it is lower in the United States today than in the manufacturing industries of many underdeveloped countries.* (Kaldor, 1972, emphasis added)

In other words, rich and poor countries are simply not on the same production function.

Empirical studies

In this section we survey six pioneer studies of intercountry growth rate differences that have been inspired by 'new' growth theory. A summary of the studies is given in Table 4.6. Before turning to the individual studies, it may be mentioned from the outset that only four variables seem to be robust in the sense that they remain statistically significant regardless of what other variables are included in the equation. Consider an equation of the form:

$$Y = b_i I + b_m M + b_z Z + \mu \tag{4.33}$$

where I is a set of variables always in the regression, M is the variable of interest, and Z is a subset of variables added to the regression. As a first step, estimate the regression with the I variables (for example, PCY) and the variable of interest (say, investment). Then add up to three other variables and observe the significance of the variable of interest. If the variable remains significant without changing its sign, the variable is regarded as robust. Otherwise it is 'fragile'. The only robust variables found in the majority of studies are the ratio of savings and investment to GDP, population growth, the initial level of per capita income, and investment in human capital measured by the secondary school enrolment rate. All other variables are fragile.

The six studies surveyed are Barro (1991), Mankiw, Romer and Weil (1992), Levine and Renelt (1992), Levine and Zervos (1993), Barro and Wha Lee (1993) and Knight, Loayza and Villanueva (1993).

Table 4.6 The macrodeterminants of growth

Study	Dependent variable	Convergence	Savings–investment ratio	Population growth	Education	Government consumption distortions	Political instability	Monetary and fiscal variables	Trade variables	Inflation
Barro (1991)[1]	Growth of *per capita* income	Conditional	Not considered	Not considered	Significant (+)	Significant (−)	Not considered	Not considered	Not considered	Not considered
Mankiw, Romer and Weil (1992)[2]	Level of *per capita* income	Conditional	Significant (+)	Significant (−)	Significant (+)	Not considered	Not considered	Not considered	Not considered	Not considered
Knight, Loayza and Villanueva (1993)[3]	Growth of output per worker	Conditional	Significant (+)	Significant (−)	Significant (+)	Not considered	Not considered	Not considered	Significant (+)	Not considered
Barro and Wha Lee (1993)[4]	Growth of *per capita* income	Conditional	Significant (+)	Not considered	Significant (+)	Significant (−)	Significant (−)	Not considered	Not considered	Not considered
Levine and Renelt (1992)[5]	Growth of *per capita* income	Conditional	Significant (+)	Not robust	Significant (+)	Not robust	Not robust	Not robust	Not robust	Not robust
Levine and Zervos (1993)[6]	Growth of *per capita* income	Conditional	Not considered	Not considered	Significant (+)	Not considered	Significant (−)	Weak	Weak	Not significant

Notes:
[1] 98 countries, 1960–85.
[2] 98 countries, 1960–85.
[3] 98 countries, 1960–85.
[4] 116 countries, 1965–85.
[5] 119 countries, 1960–89.
[6] 98 countries, 1960–85.

Robert Barro has been one of the major investigators of 'new' growth theory. He examines the growth of per capita income across 98 countries over the period 1960–85. He is basically interested in testing the neoclassical growth model augmented by human capital formation. There is no significant relation between the initial level of *PCY* and the growth rate of *PCY*, which on the surface contradicts the neoclassical model and supports the 'new' models of endogenous growth, which assume non-diminishing returns to capital. In the first instance, however, he does not allow for differences in investment ratios and population growth. Instead he augments the model by allowing for differences in human capital formation, proxied by school enrolment ratios. With this additional variable, *PCY* growth is found to be negatively related to initial levels of *PCY* which, he argues, supports the neoclassical (conditional) convergence hypothesis (although the role of differences in physical capital formation is still unknown).

An interesting difference between 'continents' is apparent. The Pacific Rim countries in 1960 had higher human capital formation than predicted by the level of *PCY* and grew rapidly, while Africa had lower human capital formation than predicted by PCY and grew slowly. Countries with high ratios of human capital formation also seem to have lower fertility rates and higher ratios of physical investment to GDP, which means that the human capital variable is likely to be picking up differences in population growth and investment ratios.

Mankiw, Romer and Weil (1992) take three samples of countries over the period 1960–85: 98 non-oil producing countries, 76 developing countries (excluding small countries and those where data are doubtful), and 22 OECD countries with a population of more than 1 million. First they take the *level* of *PCY* as the dependent variable and find that differences in savings rates and population growth account for over 50 per cent of income differences in the large sample of countries, which is support for the second basic proposition of neoclassical growth theory (see p. 136). However the cross-section regression implies a much higher elasticity of output with respect to capital than capital's share of national income, so that the empirical model overpredicts. The authors thus augment the model for differences in human capital formation, proxied by secondary school enrolment rates, and find that the augmented Solow model 'explains' 80 per cent of differences in *PCY*, and human capital formation is a significant variable in all three samples of countries. Regressing the *growth* of PCY on initial *PCY* levels shows no tendency for convergence (except in the OECD sample), but there is evidence for conditional convergence in all three samples if differences in investment ratios and population growth are allowed for. It is therefore claimed by the authors that the data give support to the Solow neoclassical model against the 'new' endogenous growth models, which, because of the assumption of non-diminishing returns to capital, predict that differences in *PCY* between countries will persist indefinitely or even widen.

Knight, Loayza and Villanueva (1993) extend Mankiw *et al.*'s study in two ways. First, they use panel data (that is, pooled time-series and cross-section data) to look at country-specific effects. Second, they assume that the rate of technical progress is influenced by the 'outwardness' of trade policy and by the stock of infrastructure investment (proxied by the 'flow' variable, government fixed investment as a proportion of GDP). Trade is assumed to influence technical progress in two ways: through technological transfers, and through greater availability of foreign exchange, which enables countries to purchase technologically superior capital goods. Tests of the model, taking two samples (76 developing countries and 22 OECD countries), show that the growth of output per worker is positively related to the savings ratio, and negatively related to the growth of population and the initial level of *PCY*; that is, there is evidence of conditional convergence. Human capital investment is significant and raises the productivity of physical investment. The tests of trade 'openness', and the role of infrastructure investment, also show significant positive effects and enhance the coefficient on physical capital.

Barro and Wha Lee (1993) analyse 116 countries over the period 1965–85 and find that five factors differentiate slowly growing countries reasonably well from rapidly growing countries:

- The initial level of *PCY* (relative to educational and health attainment), which has a negative effect (that is, there is evidence of conditional convergence)
- The investment ratio (+)
- The ratio of government consumption to GDP (–)
- Market distortions measured by the black market rate of foreign exchange (–)
- Political instability measured by the number of political 'revolutions' per year (–).

These five variables 'explain' 80 per cent of the growth rate differences between countries. No trade variables are included in the analysis.

Levine and Renelt (1992) show that cross-country regression results are 'fragile' to model selection and data sets, but at least two 'robust' results stand out: the relation between investment and growth, and the relation between the investment ratio and the ratio of international trade to GDP. The authors first take 119 countries over the period 1960–89 and use the growth of *PCY* as the dependent variable. The *I* (constant) variables used (see (4.33)) are the investment ratio, the initial level of *PCY*, the initial level of secondary school enrolment and population growth. The pool of *Z* variables used includes government expenditure, exports, inflation, the variance of inflation, domestic credit expansion and its variance, political instability and so on. When the *Z* variables are added to the *I* variables, the investment ratio remains robust, the initial *PCY* variable remains robust (that is, there is evidence of conditional convergence), the secondary school enrolment rate is robust, but not population growth. None of the *Z* variables themselves are robust, however; they depend on the conditioning variables, that is, which other *Z* variables are introduced. The authors repeat the Barro (1991) study and find only the investment ratio and the initial level of *PCY* to be robust. No fiscal or monetary indicators are robust, and no trade variables. The authors suggest that the importance of trade probably works through investment (rather than through improved resource allocation).

Levine and Zervos (1993) report new evidence on the 'robustness' of variables, taking a different set of *I* and *Z* variables. The *I* (constant) variables used are the Barro (1991) variables of initial *PCY*, initial secondary school enrolment rate, and the number of revolutions and coups. The results largely support the earlier findings of Levine and Renelt (1992), but no investment variable is included. The authors pay particular attention to financial variables and the role of inflation. Various indicators of financial deepening are robust (which may be standing as a proxy for investment), and apparently there are no *Z* variables that make growth and inflation negatively correlated. They comment that, 'given the uncharacteristically unified view among economists and policy analysts that countries with high inflation rates should adopt policies that lower inflation in order to promote economic prosperity, the inability to find simple cross-country regressions supporting this contention is both surprising and troubling'.[14]

What have we learned?

These studies (and many others not reported here) have revealed a lot about the sources of intercountry growth rate differences. Interestingly, the variables of significance turn out to be those which have traditionally been at the heart of mainstream growth and development theory, particularly the importance of investment and capital accumulation.

On the other hand, it is often the case that studies reach conflicting conclusions, and a large fraction of intercountry growth rate differences remain unexplained (as much as 40 per cent). Why is this? One set of reasons relate to the availability and quality of data, and the econometric procedures used for testing. Often data are weak and unreliable, and the econometric methodology used not only differs but is also questionable because allowance has not been made for lags in the relationship between variables or intercorrelation between variables. A second set of reasons is that countries are much more heterogeneous in their structure and institutions than most studies allow for. As Kenny and Williams (2001) put it 'it is because countries are so heterogenous in their make-up and institutions that cross section studies reach contradictory results and produce a lack of robustness'. They argue 'perhaps more energy should be directed towards understanding the complex and varied inner-workings of actual economies rather than trying to assimilate them into abstract universal models'.

A similar point is made by Putterman (2000), who argues that one of the important reasons why countries have grown at different rates in the last 50 years is that the *preconditions* for development were not equal in terms of institutional structure (the strength of government, for example); the tax system; the state of agriculture; the stock of knowledge and ideas and so on, and these factors are not well captured by the initial level of per capita income. Emphasis on preconditions, and why countries have responded differently to the possibilities of industrialization, goes back to Rostow's ideas of the preconditions for take-off. To put it another way: economic history matters! The question is how to measure the level of 'pre-modern' development? Putterman concentrates on conditions prevailing in agriculture such as cultivatable land per head; population density; and the prevalence of irrigation. When these variables are included in regression equations, along with the investment ratio, population growth, education etc. there is an increase in the proportion of the variance in growth rates that is explained.

Another serious weakness of 'new' growth theory is that many of the models are closed economy models, and there are no demand constraints. It is difficult to imagine how growth rate differences between countries can be explained without reference to trade, and without reference to the balance of payments position of countries, which in most developing economies constitutes the major constraint on the growth of demand and output (see Chapter 17). Where a trade variable is included in the models tested, it is invariably insignificant, or loses its significance when combined with other variables. All this is very puzzling, given the rich theoretical and empirical literature that exists on the relation between trade and growth (see Chapter 16). There are at least two possible explanations. First, it could be that trade works through investment. Indeed in some studies that look directly at the determinants of investment, trade and exports are found to be significant. Second, the measure of trade taken is a very static one, usually measured as the share of trade in GDP. This may pick up the static gains from trade but not the dynamic gains. In a growth model, the most obvious trade variable to focus on is the *growth* of exports, which will favourably influence growth from the demand side (particularly by relaxing a balance of payments constraint on domestic demand), and from the supply side by raising import capacity. A study by the present author (Thirlwall and Sanna, 1996) of 65 countries over the period 1960–88 shows the growth of exports to be a highly significant independent determinant of intercountry growth rate differences, together with the investment ratio, population growth and the initial level of per capita income. So, too, does an interesting study by Pugno (1995), which shows catch-up and convergence to be a function of demand-growth driven by exports.

Finally, a more fundamental issue is raised by Pritchett (2000) who argues that it is difficult to characterize the growth of many developing countries by a single time trend because growth is very volatile. Periods of rapid growth are often followed by plateaus and steep declines. Rapid and slow growth are for the most part transitory. Very few countries see their success or failure persist from decade to decade. Correlations of country growth rates across periods (e.g. 5–10 years) show very low correlations. Taking 111 countries over a 25-year period, Pritchett shows that in 55 of them, growth either accelerated or decelerated by more than 3 percentage points on at least one occasion over the period. In 40 per cent of developing countries, trying to estimate a time trend for the growth of output gives a correlation coefficient of less than 0.5; and volatility around the trend is much higher for developing countries than developed countries. So Pritchett asks the question: what aspects of a country's growth is growth theory trying to explain when growth is so ephemeral and volatile? If growth is so volatile, it is no wonder that the variance of growth explained by traditional variables is relatively low. What is important is to analyse and explain the determinants of *shifts* in growth rates from one period to another.

Macroeconomic instability would be one major explanation of volatility, and monetary, fiscal and exchange rate policies affect investment and demand, as well as external shocks, such as variations in the terms of trade (see Fischer, 1993). 'New' growth theory does not address these issues.

DISCUSSION QUESTIONS

1 What did Adam Smith mean when he said that the 'division of labour is limited by the extent of the market' and 'the extent of the market is limited by the division of labour'? What is the economic significance of these propositions?

2 Why were the classical economists after Adam Smith pessimistic about the growth and development process?

3 How does Harrod define the warranted growth rate and the natural growth rate? What are the implications for a country if the natural growth rate exceeds the warranted rate?

4 What is the mechanism in neoclassical growth theory by which the warranted rate of growth adjusts to the natural rate? Do you think it is a realistic mechanism?

5 What are the essential propositions and predictions of neoclassical growth theory, and how is the conclusion reached that investment does not matter for long-run growth?

6 What are the special properties of the Cobb–Douglas production function, and how might the function be used to calculate the sources of growth?

7 What is the difference between exogenous and endogenous technical progress?

8 What factors does the growth of 'total factor productivity' depend on?

9 What have been the major findings of production function studies of the sources of growth in developing countries?

10 Outline the essential propositions of 'new' (endogenous) growth theory.

11 What have we learnt from the major studies of the macrodeterminants of growth in developing countries?

NOTES

1. *Economic Journal*, December 1928.
2. *Economic Journal*, March 1939.
3. The American economist Evesey Domar arrived at Harrod's result independently in 1947, hence the linking of the two names ('Expansion and Employment', *American Economic Review*, March 1947).
4. Robert Solow from the Massachusetts Institute of Technology (MIT) was awarded the Nobel Prize in economics in 1987, partly for his pioneering contribution to growth theory.
5. This can be seen by rearranging the equation to $qs/k = l$, where $q = Y/L$; $s = S/Y = \Delta K/Y$ (since all saving leads to capital accumulation); $k = K/L$; and $l = \Delta L/L$. Therefore $(Y/L)(\Delta K/Y)(L/K) = \Delta L/L$, or $\Delta K/K = \Delta L/L$.
6. For the time being, the formidable problems associated with an aggregate measure of capital are ignored.
7. The proof is as follows. The elasticity of output with respect to capital, α, is $(dY/Y)/(dK/K) = (dY\ K)/(dK\ Y)$. Now if capital is paid its marginal product, then $dY/dK = r$, where r is the rental on capital. Hence $\alpha = rK/Y$, where rK/Y is capital's share of total output. Thus under perfectly competitive assumptions the elasticity of output with respect to any factor is equal to that factor's share of total output.
8. Alternatively, the total differential of (4.21) can be taken and the result divided by output, which will also convert the equation into rate-of-growth form.
9. The elasticity of substitution (σ) relates the proportional change in relative factor inputs to a proportional change in the marginal rate of substitution between labour and capital (MRS) (or the proportional change in the relative factor-price ratio on the basis of marginal productivity theory). The elasticity of substitution may therefore be written as

$$\sigma = \frac{\partial \log (L/K)}{\partial \log \text{MRS}}$$

The proof that $\sigma = 1$ is very simple:

$$\text{MRS} = \frac{\partial Y}{\partial K} \bigg| \frac{\partial Y}{\partial L} = \frac{\alpha L}{\beta K}$$

$$\log \text{MRS} = \log \frac{\alpha}{\beta} + \log \frac{L}{K}$$

Differentiating with respect to log MRS gives

$$1 = \frac{\partial \log (L/K)}{\partial \log \text{MRS}} = \alpha$$

10. To overcome the restrictive property of the Cobb–Douglas function when the growth rates of factors differ, it is possible to use the more general constant elasticity of substitution production function, of which the Cobb–Douglas is a special case. We cannot discuss the function here except to say that it, too, is not without its specification errors. There is still the assumption of constancy, which has the drawback that one may be ascribing changes in elasticity to changes in technology that are really due to changes in factor proportions. This limitation can be overcome only with a function possessing the property of variable elasticity of substitution.

11. The production function used here is the translog production function which allows for the elasticity of substitution between inputs to vary.

12. For a discussion of the origins of endogenous growth theory, and its relevance to developing countries, see Romer (1994), Pack (1994), Ruttan (1998) and Temple (1999). For an advanced textbook treatment of the topic, see Barro and Sala-í-Martin (1995).

13. For an advanced theoretical discussion of convergence issues, see the Symposium in *Economic Journal*, July 1996; also Islam (2003).

14. See Chapter 14 for a discussion of the relation between inflation and growth.

WEBSITES ON GROWTH THEORY

New School for Social Research (New York)   http://cepa.newschool.edu/het/home.htm

Economic Growth Resources run by Jon Temple, Bristol University, UK   www.bris.ac.uk/Depts/Economics/Growth

Overseas Development Institute   www.odi.org

Foundation for Advanced Studies on International Development   www.fasid.or.jp/english

Institute of Developing Economies Japan-External Trade Organisation   www.ide.go.jp/English/Research/index.html

The Vienna Institute for International Economic Studies   www.wiiw.ac.at

Carnegie Endowment for International Peace   www.ceip.org

Factors in the development process

Land, labour and agriculture

CHAPTER OUTLINE

- Land

- The role of agriculture in development

- Barriers to agricultural development

- The organization of agriculture and land reform

- The supply response of agriculture

- Transforming traditional agriculture

- The growth of the money economy

- Finance for traditional agriculture

- The interdependence of agriculture and industry

- Economic development with unlimited supplies of labour

- A model of the complementarity between agriculture and industry

- Rural–urban migration and urban unemployment

- Disguised unemployment: types and measurement

- Incentives and the costs of labour transfer

The task of a true theory of economic growth and development must be to explain why some societies developed sooner than others; why some societies have experienced such rapid increases in living standards while others have lagged behind, and why development has not spread.

The answer must be that at different stages of development, different constraints on progress operate. While some of these factors are likely to be sociological and political, the major constraints are likely to be economic. One of the most critical factors in the early stages of development is the health of the agricultural sector, because without a surplus of food production over subsistence needs, little else can be done. There would be no surplus labour, no saving and no food to feed labour working in alternative activities.

It is no coincidence that the material progress of mankind started 8000 years ago in the region of Mesopotamia (the cradle of civilization, now Iraq), where for the first time agriculture became settled. Unless agriculture is settled, there is no prospect of agricultural productivity increasing to provide the basis for the development of non-agricultural activities, the building of cities and so on. Where shifting agriculture is practised, as by nomadic tribes in the Kalahari desert of Botswana and Namibia, for example, there is no basis for an agricultural surplus.

In many developing countries today, agriculture is still extremely backward. Low productivity is a major cause of poverty and retards development of the whole economy. In this chapter we shall consider some of the reasons for this agricultural backwardness. Using Arthur Lewis' famous model of 'Economic Development with Unlimited Supplies of Labour' (1954), we shall analyse in detail the key role that agriculture plays in the development process, including the release of labour from the land and the role played by surplus labour in fuelling industrial growth.

LAND

In the production-function approach to the analysis of the sources of growth, land as a separate factor of production tends to be assumed away or subsumed into capital. There are two main reasons for this: the traditional classical notion of land as a fixed factor of production, which in the long run is undoubtedly true; and the practical fact that land without the application of capital is of little use, justifying the treatment of land and capital as one factor.

This is not to deny, however, the importance of land and natural resource endowments as factors in the growth process. The quality of land can markedly affect the level of agricultural productivity in the early stages of economic development, and in turn the importance of agricultural development can be clearly seen within the production-function framework. Rising agricultural productivity permits the release of labour from agriculture to industry, which in turn leads to increasing returns, rising income per head and greater capital accumulation. Given the dominance of the agricultural sector in the economic structure of developing countries, such factors as the physical attributes of land (topography, fertility, and so on), the land-tenure system, the ratio of labour to land and the extent of natural resource endowments are likely to exert a major influence on the speed of development, as determinants of the pace of agricultural advance and the pace of industrialization based on a healthy agricultural sector or the exploitation of indigenous resources. Geographical factors such as the nature of the land, and God-given factors such as the weather, must be included in any list drawn up to answer such questions as: why have some countries developed earlier than others, and why have some countries remained in a traditional or transitional state longer than others? This is the concept of **geographic determinism**, which can be advanced as a hypothesis of underdevelopment in its own right.

In this chapter we shall consider land in relation to agriculture, and discuss in a general way the role of the agricultural sector in the development process. In the course of the discussion we shall elaborate on the progression of an economy from its traditional subsistence state into Rostow's transitional stage, in which the seeds are sown for 'take-off' into self-sustaining growth. The approach to be adopted has a common-sense, pragmatic appeal since land primarily affects the productivity of agriculture, and the development of agriculture, owing to its initial importance in a country's economic structure, must play a crucial role in establishing the framework for industrialization.

THE ROLE OF AGRICULTURE IN DEVELOPMENT

Agriculture makes four major contributions to the process of economic development: a **product contribution**, a **factor contribution**, a **market contribution** and a **foreign exchange contribution**.

Product contribution

The product contribution of agriculture refers to the fact that agriculture must supply food above subsistence needs in order to feed labour working in alternative occupations. If other sectors of the economy are to be developed, labour needs to be fed, and this cannot be done by imports until export activities have been developed to provide foreign exchange to pay for the imports. It will be remembered from Chapter 3 that in Rostow's model of economic growth, the take-off stage of development must be preceded by an agricultural revolution. Indeed, one of the major reasons why Britain was the first country to industrialize was that it was the first to experience a significant agricultural revolution based on the abolition of serfdom and on the enclosure movement, which raised agricultural productivity and provided surplus labour and food to support industrial expansion.

The difference between total agricultural output and subsistence needs is called the **marketable surplus**. Economic progress in the early stages of development requires an increase in the marketable surplus, which in turn requires an increase in labour productivity. If productivity does not increase naturally or 'voluntarily', a marketable surplus can be forcibly extracted, as it was in Japan at the time of the Meiji Restoration (1868), when landowners were compulsorily taxed, and more dramatically in the Soviet Union in the 1920s, when there was mass genocide of the kulaks (small prosperous landowners) during Stalin's collectivization programme.

Marketable surplus is a very important concept in the neoclassical model of the development process, because unless the marketable surplus rises as the demand for food increases, the price of food will tend to rise. This will turn the terms of trade against industry; higher wages will have to be paid to workers in industry, which will eat into profits and capital accumulation. The marketable surplus therefore becomes the major constraint on industrial growth.

Factor contribution

The factor contribution of agriculture consists of two parts: a labour contribution, and a capital contribution. Labour for industry and other activities must come from agriculture, but can be released only if productivity in agriculture rises. The existence of surplus labour (or disguised unemployment) plays a major role in the development process, as we shall see when we consider the famous Lewis model of economic development with unlimited supplies of labour. The lower the cost of industrial labour, the faster the rate of industrial expansion is likely to be, but this depends on the rate at which the agricultural sector is releasing labour. Industrial development today in many of the rapidly growing countries of South-East Asia is being fuelled by cheap labour drawn from agriculture. In this respect, China's industrial potential is enormous.

Secondly, agriculture is a source of saving and capital accumulation for industrial development. The saving can be voluntary or involuntary. Examples of voluntary saving are rich landlords voluntarily investing in industrial activities (the industrial revolution in Britain was partly financed in this way), and peasant farmers investing small savings in rural banks. Involuntary saving could take the form of the government taxing the agricultural sector and using the proceeds for investment, or more drastically, the forced extraction of the agricultural surplus through expropriation or collectivization (as in Stalinist Russia).

Another traditional way in which governments have taxed the agricultural sector is through the pricing policies of **marketing boards**, established to market agricultural produce. The prices paid to farmers are lower than the prices at which the goods are sold on the market – the difference providing net revenue to the government.

The general policy in developing countries of keeping agricultural prices low has been justified on two main grounds: that low prices benefit the industrial sector; and that peasant farmers have limited horizons and do not respond to incentives, so if prices are higher they may actually produce less if all they are interested in is a fixed money income. This is the notion of a **backward-bending supply curve of effort**. It can be said without hesitation that the policy of keeping agricultural prices low has done enormous damage to the agricultural sector in developing countries. As we shall see later, there is ample evidence that peasant farmers do respond to price incentives. They not only increase supply in response to price rises, but also switch crops as relative prices change.

Market contribution

The market contribution of agriculture refers to the fact that the demand from agriculture must be the major source of autonomous demand for industrial goods. If industry is to grow and prosper, it must be able to sell its goods. In the early stages of development the agricultural sector is likely to provide the largest market for industrial goods. There is a *complementarity* between agricultural and industrial growth. This is well documented in the historical experience of developed countries, and in the contemporary world economy. In his classic study of Japanese economic development, Lockwood (1954) wrote:

> The growth of primary production was interrelated with industrialization and urbanization at every point . . . As industry developed, it offered a widening market for the food and raw material surpluses of the countryside . . . On the other hand, the increasing productivity of the primary industries created a growing home market for manufactures and services.

The World Bank's 1979 *World Development Report* remarked that 'a stagnant rural economy with low purchasing power holds back industrial growth in many developing countries'. The 1982 *World Development Report* documented the close correspondence across countries between agricultural development and industrial growth: 'fast growth of industry and sluggish agriculture were evident *only* in countries with oil or mineral-based economies, such as Algeria, Ecuador, Mexico, Morocco and Nigeria . . . These were exceptions but they prove the rule [emphasis in the original].' In other words, a precondition for rapid industrial growth is a rapidly expanding agricultural sector, at least in terms of purchasing power.

This has implications for the pricing of agricultural goods relative to industrial goods, or what is called the agricultural (or industrial) terms of trade. Low farm prices are good for industry from the point of view of supply potential because it means that industry can obtain cheaper raw material inputs and wage goods, which increases profitability. On the other hand, low farm prices are bad for industry from the demand side because this means low farm purchasing power and therefore a lower demand for industrial goods. There needs to be an equilibrium terms of trade between the two sectors to achieve balanced growth between the two sectors, so that industrial growth is not constrained from the supply side by agricultural prices being too high or constrained from the demand side by agricultural prices being too low. Later in the chapter (p. 193) we bring the two sectors together in an equilibrium framework and derive the equilibrium terms of trade that maximises the growth rate of the system as a whole.

Foreign exchange contribution

In the early stages of development, the only source of foreign exchange is likely to be primary commodity exports. Agriculture therefore makes an important foreign exchange contribution. Foreign exchange is a resource just like savings. It provides access to goods that either cannot be produced domestically or can only be produced at enormous cost in an opportunity cost sense. Either way, the imports made possible by exporting agricultural products will be very productive – the more so if they are investment-type goods necessary for the development process. There are not many countries in the world that could not grow faster given the greater availability of foreign exchange. The link between trade, the balance of payments and growth is fully explored in Chapters 16 and 17.

BARRIERS TO AGRICULTURAL DEVELOPMENT

For the agricultural sector to supply food, release labour, provide savings, contribute to the market for industrial goods and earn foreign exchange, it must generate a steadily rising surplus of production in excess of subsistence needs. Since land is relatively fixed in supply, this requires rising agricultural productivity. The 'grass-roots' school of economic development, which came into fashion as a reaction against the emphasis on industrialization at any cost, lays stress on policies to raise the level of productivity in agriculture as the most crucial development priority and an indispensable element of a long-run development strategy. Overall agricultural productivity in developing countries is less than one-twentieth of the level in developed countries, and there are even bigger differences between countries. Table 5.1 gives figures on agricultural productivity in the various countries of the world. In China, productivity is roughly $300 per annum; in India, $400 per annum, and in the United States, $54,000 per annum. In many

Table 5.1 Agricultural output and productivity

	Crop production index	Food production index	Livestock production index	Cereal yield	Agricultural productivity
					Agriculture value added per worker
	1989–91 = 100	1989–91 = 100	1989–91 = 100	kilograms per hectare	1995 $
	2000–02	2000–02	2000–02	2000–02	2000–02
Algeria	128.0	136.2	128.9	1,343	1,919
Angola	195.7	172.5	137.2	606	137
Argentina	165.2	142.5	108.8	3,374	10,317
Armenia	99.8	79.3	67.9	2,049	2,827
Australia	152.2	138.8	116.1	1,758	36,327
Austria	103.6	104.7	103.2	5,589	33,828
Azerbaijan	63.4	83.7	81.8	2,583	1,029
Bangladesh	135.6	138.3	142.1	3,312	318
Belarus	90.3	62.1	58.4	2,369	3,038
Belgium	143.9	113.5	109.8	8,002	57,462
Benin	195.6	173.9	116.7	1,077	621
Bolivia	177.2	151.6	129.7	1,786	754
Botswana	89.8	89.8	89.7	156	575
Brazil	135.8	153.2	169.8	3,081	4,899
Bulgaria	66.9	68.2	62.9	2,961	8,282
Burkina Faso	166.8	157.9	147.8	968	185
Burundi	92.7	93.2	76.1	1,325	151
Cambodia	147.2	152.0	166.9	1,978	422
Cameroon	141.6	138.3	121.8	1,696	1,213
Canada	106.7	123.5	142.2	2,521	43,064
Central African Republic	136.6	146.5	147.4	1,069	502
Chad	160.8	151.2	122.2	697	211
Chile	132.6	140.2	151.4	5,235	6,226
China	155.6	185.9	226.7	4,845	338
Colombia	106.4	120.3	122.4	3,411	3,619
Congo, Dem. Rep.	83.2	86.3	98.3	774	212
Congo, Rep.	127.9	130.3	135.5	779	469
Costa Rica	147.0	150.0	136.6	3,968	5,270
Côte d'Ivoire	133.8	136.5	139.3	1,213	1,046
Croatia	90.6	68.5	55.2	4,748	9,741
Cuba	66.3	70.9	71.6	2,519	–
Czech Republic	88.6	78.0	70.8	4,297	6,382
Denmark	89.9	106.0	118.6	5,912	63,131
Dominican Republic	89.6	107.8	138.2	4,525	3,458
Ecuador	143.2	153.8	170.1	2,122	3,310
Egypt, Arab Rep.	154.9	158.2	165.9	7,244	1,316
El Salvador	98.9	111.7	116.3	2,264	1,678
Eritrea	121.9	116.3	112.0	351	68
Estonia	76.8	39.8	33.8	2,028	3,650
Ethiopia	160.6	152.6	129.8	1,293	154
Finland	99.7	93.7	91.8	3,219	42,306
France	107.0	104.3	105.5	6,796	59,243
Gabon	121.4	116.7	118.9	1,652	2,102
Gambia, The	132.8	127.2	102.7	1,231	307
Georgia	43.7	74.9	93.8	2,004	–
Germany	118.2	97.1	87.7	6,355	33,686
Ghana	190.0	181.2	127.3	1,191	571
Greece	110.6	101.3	94.0	3,555	13,860
Guatemala	131.8	136.2	130.3	1,758	2,115
Guinea	158.7	161.8	188.8	1,403	286
Guinea-Bissau	147.2	142.2	127.2	972	324
Haiti	87.2	101.7	156.2	840	–
Honduras	114.1	121.1	153.8	1,382	1,037

Table 5.1 continued

	Crop production index	Food production index	Livestock production index	Cereal yield	Agricultural productivity
					Agriculture value added per worker
				kilograms per hectare	1995 $
	1989–91 = 100	1989–91 = 100	1989–91 = 100		
	2000–02	2000–02	2000–02	2000–02	2000–02
Hungary	79.7	79.5	73.3	4,026	5,625
India	124.2	131.8	149.8	2,390	401
Indonesia	122.9	123.6	124.7	4,141	748
Iran, Islamic Rep.	151.5	154.8	158.3	2,163	3,737
Iraq	76.7	77.5	67.9	945	–
Ireland	111.3	106.7	107.7	7,053	–
Israel	97.4	115.3	127.6	2,853	–
Italy	101.9	102.3	105.1	4,815	27,064
Jamaica	127.5	125.9	126.2	1,002	1,487
Japan	87.1	91.6	93.2	5,879	33,077
Jordan	132.6	147.4	167.7	1,301	1,145
Kazakhstan	89.5	73.5	46.7	1,149	1,753
Kenya	123.1	122.2	118.0	1,516	213
Korea, Dem. Rep.	–	–	–	3,189	–
Korea, Rep.	114.3	132.3	159.9	6,118	14,251
Kuwait	198.1	229.0	211.2	2,206	–
Kyrgyz Republic	153.2	132.5	80.7	2,742	1,861
Lao PDR	177.5	186.4	188.8	3,140	621
Latvia	78.7	42.4	31.1	2,189	2,773
Lebanon	100.4	108.9	157.0	2,575	29,874
Lesotho	147.9	111.6	87.2	926	575
Libya	129.4	134.1	134.9	631	–
Lithuania	76.5	64.7	52.6	2,807	3,431
Macedonia, FYR	94.9	89.5	89.9	2,642	4,243
Madagascar	108.5	115.8	114.2	2,007	155
Malawi	156.0	174.0	125.4	1,134	124
Malaysia	119.4	142.1	142.1	3,132	6,912
Mali	143.9	128.6	123.2	943	274
Mauritania	126.2	108.3	107.0	860	447
Mauritius	98.1	109.0	145.3	7,577	5,494
Mexico	123.6	135.7	150.1	2,870	1,813
Moldova	61.9	51.1	32.9	2,345	971
Mongolia	29.7	91.9	97.4	751	1,444
Morocco	91.8	103.6	124.6	1,129	1,513
Mozambique	141.1	127.5	103.9	848	136
Myanmar	178.5	176.5	169.4	3,453	–
Namibia	126.9	96.8	93.3	400	1,545
Nepal	137.9	135.8	129.3	2,178	203
Netherlands	111.7	98.4	96.5	7,531	59,476
New Zealand	142.9	135.2	123.9	6,230	28,740
Nicaragua	141.3	154.3	148.1	1,761	1,618
Niger	147.5	140.1	128.9	417	197
Nigeria	156.0	155.8	145.3	1,105	729
Norway	77.6	91.0	97.4	3,760	37,073
Oman	160.3	163.1	144.5	2,319	–
Pakistan	122.8	152.7	171.9	2,266	716
Panama	83.3	105.8	138.6	2,753	2,967
Papua New Guinea	120.7	124.3	146.0	3,919	823
Paraguay	115.5	141.0	136.9	2,034	3,318
Peru	180.3	175.0	159.1	3,302	1,863
Philippines	123.1	137.1	177.8	2,692	1,458
Poland	84.0	86.0	83.3	3,072	1,637
Portugal	91.7	102.2	122.3	2,702	7,567
Puerto Rico	67.9	84.0	89.4	1,731	–

Table 5.1 continued

	Crop production index	Food production index	Livestock production index	Cereal yield	Agricultural productivity
					Agriculture value added per worker
	1989–91 = 100	1989–91 = 100	1989–91 = 100	kilograms per hectare	1995 $
	2000–02	2000–02	2000–02	2000–02	2000–02
Romania	91.0	87.1	80.7	2,562	3,588
Russian Federation	86.1	66.6	52.6	1,846	3,822
Rwanda	115.4	117.3	112.3	1,011	254
Saudi Arabia	84.2	98.5	152.6	3,818	15,796
Senegal	111.0	122.4	147.0	755	354
Serbia and Montenegro	–	–	–	–	–
Sierra Leone	75.4	84.0	126.6	1,234	359
Singapore	48.2	31.9	31.8	–	42,920
Slovenia	81.9	100.9	108.7	5,452	37,671
South Africa	110.1	111.1	104.3	2,633	4,072
Spain	115.8	120.1	134.2	3,091	22,412
Sri Lanka	114.8	117.2	147.7	3,520	725
Sudan	165.9	167.5	161.1	600	–
Swaziland	85.2	99.9	126.4	1,512	1,936
Sweden	89.3	96.0	100.2	4,878	40,368
Switzerland	89.6	98.6	94.9	6,466	–
Syrian Arab Republic	177.2	163.6	136.1	2,114	2,636
Tajikistan	62.2	60.5	41.6	1,561	728
Tanzania	107.7	112.8	126.9	1,438	187
Thailand	124.3	123.5	135.3	2,654	863
Togo	138.0	131.4	115.2	1,008	503
Trinidad and Tobago	87.9	127.8	157.3	2,807	3,034
Tunisia	98.4	115.0	164.4	2,218	3,115
Turkey	118.8	114.6	103.9	2,176	1,848
Turkmenistan	77.7	131.6	138.0	2,621	690
Uganda	138.9	136.7	130.6	1,651	346
Ukraine	71.3	52.4	45.7	2,399	1,576
United Arab Emirates	659.7	549.9	200.6	414	–
United Kingdom	97.2	92.4	93.1	6,841	32,918
United States	118.3	122.5	123.6	5,830	53,907
Uruguay	135.3	124.8	110.4	3,243	8,177
Uzbekistan	89.0	122.3	114.8	3,644	1,449
Venezuela, RB	119.3	135.0	138.8	3,278	5,399
Vietnam	180.3	171.4	193.8	4,375	256
Yemen, Rep.	133.6	142.6	160.4	966	412
Zambia	96.2	107.2	130.2	1,481	194
Zimbabwe	113.9	108.6	121.5	872	355
World	**131.5**	**133.1**	**136.4**	**2,233**	**–**
Low income	134.0	135.1	146.8	1,321	415
Middle income	147.0	150.3	164.4	2,497	820
Lower middle income	154.2	158.0	181.9	2,181	713
Upper middle income	116.2	118.6	114.0	2,926	3,937
Low and middle income	142.7	145.2	159.9	1,966	626
East Asia & Pacific	166.1	170.6	214.6	3,147	–
Europe & Central Asia	–	–	–	2,640	2,353
Latin America & Caribbean	138.6	141.9	144.8	2,804	3,570
Middle East & North Africa	136.4	137.1	145.3	1,726	2,340
South Asia	131.6	133.3	154.3	2,222	412
Sub-Saharan Africa	132.3	133.5	124.4	1,064	360
High income	112.5	113.2	112.5	3,746	–

Source: World Development Indicators 2004 (Washington: World Bank).

countries output per head is barely enough to meet subsistence needs. Some progress has been made in recent years with particular crops in particular countries, but the performance of the agricultural sector is still disappointing, and the lack of a marketable surplus is holding back development on a wide front. So what holds back agricultural productivity? There are several factors, particularly related to geography and land–labour ratios; the existence of urban bias in the treatment of agriculture and the allocation of resources, and unfair competition in world markets, but the most important factors of all are the structure of rural societies, the organization of agriculture, and the land-tenure system that operates.

As far as geographical factors are concerned, climate and terrain determine to a large degree what goods a country can produce, the amount of cultivatable land available per inhabitant and the land's fertility. Table 5.1 shows the enormous difference in arable land per capita between some of the poorest and richest countries, and also differences in the degree of mechanization. To some extent the application of capital to land can compensate for unfavourable natural forces, but there are obvious limits. Mountains cannot be easily flattened or deserts readily watered. Having said this, however, differences in natural conditions and the fertility of the soil can be no more than a partial explanation of low productivity. Poor people are to be found along the highly productive alluvial banks of the Nile, as well as on the barren plateaus of Asia and South America.

Productivity is also affected by land–labour ratios. Low productivity may be associated, for example, with a high population density and a high ratio of labour to land. In this case, productivity might be increased substantially with small applications of capital in the form of drainage schemes, fertilizers and so on. On the other hand, low productivity may be associated with the opposite situation of a high ratio of land to labour, in which case the solution to low productivity is likely to involve much larger doses of capital for labour to work with. Most countries in Asia have high ratios of labour to land, while in Africa the reverse is true, as was the case in many of today's richest countries at an equivalent stage in their economic history, for example the United States, Canada and Australia.

Urban bias against agriculture takes many forms:

- The holding down of agricultural prices to favour the industrial/urban sector
- The concentration of investment in industry
- Tax incentives and subsidies to industry
- Overvalued exchange rates, which keep the price of industrial inputs, and the domestic price of agricultural exports, low
- Tariff and quota protection for industry, which raises the price of fertilizers, seeds and equipment
- Greater spending in urban areas on education, training, housing, nutrition and medical provision, which all affect productivity and the quality of life.

Unfair competition consists of the subsidies that developed countries give to their farmers, and the tariffs that developed countries impose on imported agricultural products from developing countries. The United States and the European Union (EU) alone spend nearly $400 billion a year (or more than $1 billion a day) on farm subsidies. This has two major consequences. First it leads to over-production, and the surpluses are then frequently dumped on the markets of developing countries, impoverishing domestic farmers. Secondly, farmers in developing countries are not able to compete in their own markets, let alone overseas markets. The situation is made worse by developing countries being forced by international agreements to lower their tariffs against imported agricultural produce, while developed countries continue to protect their own agricultural sectors. The average tariff on agricultural commodities into the EU is over 60 per cent, and exceeds 100 per cent for some commodities. The maize growers of Mexico cannot compete with cheap maize from the United States; nor can the cotton growers of West Africa compete against subsidies of $4 billion a year given to the 20,000 cotton growers in the southern states of America. Unfair competition between developed and developing countries in the markets for agricultural goods has become the central issue in world trade talks under the auspices of the World Trade Organisation (WTO); and the unwillingness of the developed countries to make concessions was the major cause of the failure of the Cancún summit meeting in 2003.

Geographic factors, the land–labour ratio, urban bias and competition from developed countries, however, can only explain a small part of the low productivity of agriculture in most developing countries. There are more fundamental forces at work concerned with the structure of rural society, the organization of agriculture, the incentives to produce and the supply of inputs.

In a typical developing country, rural society consists of rich landowners, peasants, sharecroppers, tenants and labourers. Apart from the landowners, most others in the rural sector are extremely poor. Because they live on the margin of subsistence they tend to be **risk averse**. It must be remembered that in all developing countries peasant subsistence farming is a traditional way of life, and attempts to raise productivity will alter that way of life and necessarily involve risk. As Theodore Schultz (1980) perceptively remarked in his Nobel prize-winning lecture:

> Most of the people in the world are poor, so if we knew the economics of being poor we would know much of the economics that really matters. Most of the world's poor people earn their living from agriculture so if we knew the economics of agriculture we would know much of the economics of being poor. People who are rich find it hard to understand the behaviour of poor people. Economists are no exception, for they, too, find it difficult to comprehend the preferences and scarcity constraints that determine the choices that poor people make. We all know that most of the world's people are poor, that they earn a pittance for their labour, that half and more of their meagre income is spent on food, that they reside predominantly in low-income countries and that most of them are earning their livelihood in agriculture. What many economists fail to understand is that poor people are no less concerned about improving their lot and that of their children than rich people are.

Poor people on the margin of subsistence may be reluctant to make the changes necessary to improve productivity because if things go wrong it will spell disaster. But even if poor people wanted to change the traditional ways of doing things, there is the serious constraint of lack of access to credit to finance the purchase of new seeds, fertilizers, pesticides, drainage schemes and so on.

Then there is the question of the incentive to change. Where there are tenant farmers there is little or no security of tenure, and therefore no incentive to invest in improved methods of production. Where there is sharecropping a certain proportion of output must be relinquished to the landowner, which also reduces the incentive to invest. Any serious programme of agrarian reform must provide greater security of tenure for farmers and give incentives to raise agricultural production, coupled with access to credit, water, fertilizers and extension services for advice. This raises the whole question of the organization of agriculture and land reform, to which we now turn.

THE ORGANIZATION OF AGRICULTURE AND LAND REFORM

The system by which land is held and farmed is a serious impediment to increased productivity in many developing countries. The structure of peasant agriculture differs between countries, largely for historical reasons, but the structures have many common characteristics that keep productivity low. In many countries, land-holding tends to be severely concentrated. In many parts of Latin America, for example, agriculture is based on a combination of large estates (*latifundios*), owned by a wealthy few, and small farms (*minifundios*), which are often so small that they cannot support a single family. In Brazil, 90 per cent of the land is owned by 15 per cent of landowners. When land is held and worked in the form of large estates, it is frequently underutilized and farmed inefficiently by peasants, who may have no security of tenure and may have to relinquish to the landowner a large fraction of their output. In these circumstances there is little incentive to increase efficiency and improve productivity.

In Asia the organization of peasant agriculture is also an important determinant of productivity. Because of the high population density, the major problem is that too many small farms are operated by sharecroppers and tenant farmers, the land being owned by absentee landlords. As families multiply and debts rise, land is continually sold and subdivided, leading to a very inefficient structure.

Land reform, involving land rights, and security of tenure for tenants, can contribute both to an increased intensity of land use and to increased efficiency and initiative on the part of the tenant farmer, particularly if they are allowed to reap fully the rewards of their own labour. The scope for land reform remains enormous in Latin America. Still 1 per cent of the landowners own 70 per cent of the land, while 10 per cent of the largest farms occupy 80 per cent of the land.

There is impressive evidence that where a change in the tenure system has permitted the producers themselves to reap the rewards of new techniques, peasant farmers have been ready to break with custom and tradition. The task of persuading producers to adopt more modern methods of production and to purchase improved seed and fertilizer has been much less difficult. In a study of China from 1978, Lin (1992) finds that moving from collective to household farming led to big increases in agricultural productivity related to the acquisition of property and land rights. Likewise, Besley and Burgess (2000) in a study of India find that rural poverty was reduced by land reform, particularly reforms that strengthened property rights over land.

Land reform is not always successful. In Kenya in the 1950s and 1960s, thousands of hectares of land were transferred to Africans through land settlement schemes. But the landless were not the major beneficiaries: the political leaders distributed most of the land among themselves and their friends.

Land reform may be a necessary condition for increased productivity, but it is clearly not a sufficient condition. It needs to be accompanied by other measures of agrarian reform. New landowners must be given access to credit, water, fertilizers and extension services for advice. Farmers must be brought within the organized money market to improve access to credit and to reduce the role of village moneylenders, who charge exorbitant interest rates. Improved farm implements, irrigation and new social infrastructure are likely to be important. There needs to be improved dissemination of agricultural research. Too often the agricultural extension services available are perfunctory and ineffective because the personnel are ill-trained and ill-equipped. Conditions vary from country to country, but in theory at least, agrarian reform coupled with the application of complementary inputs offers substantial scope for increased agricultural productivity.[1]

THE SUPPLY RESPONSE OF AGRICULTURE

What may also be required is a rise in the price of agricultural products relative to industrial products in order to induce extra supply. Traditionally, attempts have been made to 'tax' the agricultural sector by keeping prices low in order to maintain the terms of trade in favour of the industrial sector. This policy was justified by the widespread belief that peasant producers in traditional societies would not respond to price incentives, but this assumption has proved to be wrong. Depressing the agricultural terms of trade has depressed agricultural output and caused problems for the feeding of a growing industrial population.

Many countries have had to introduce a positive price policy to act as a stimulus to agricultural output in general and to alter the composition of agricultural output as circumstances warrant. There is in fact considerable evidence that producers, especially those in close proximity to large markets with good transport facilities, respond positively to price changes, as economic theory would predict. Schultz (1964) gave early warning that 'the doctrine that farmers in poor countries either are indifferent or respond perversely to changes in prices . . . is patently false and harmful. Price policies based on it always impair the efficiency of agriculture'. And Behrman (1968) concludes his pioneering study of four commodities in Thailand by saying that the evidence

> strongly supports the hypothesis that farmers in economically underdeveloped countries respond significantly and substantially to economic incentives . . . The burden of proof thus now lies with those who maintain that the supply behaviour of farmers in underdeveloped agriculture cannot be understood predominantly within the framework of traditional economic analysis.

When discussing the supply response of agricultural output to price, however, a distinction needs to be made between three types of response:

■ A change in the composition of agricultural output to a change in the relative price of individual agricultural commodities

■ An increase in total agricultural output to an improvement in the relative price of agricultural commodities compared with industrial goods

■ An increase in the marketed surplus in response to an increase in the price of agricultural commodities.

Most of the studies on the supply response in peasant agriculture in developing countries relate to how producers respond to changes in the relative price of different agricultural commodities. But of course it would be quite possible for the supply of any individual commodity to be quite elastic with respect to price, yet the total supply of agricultural output and the marketed surplus to be quite inelastic, or even to fall, in response to a rise in price.

Having said this, however, there are reasons for believing that the other two elasticities are likely to be positive if the supply of individual commodities is positive, especially when crops are not just grown for subsistence purposes. For example, for any crop grown commercially the elasticity of marketed supply will be virtually equal to the output elasticity, and unless inputs are withdrawn from the production of other commodities the elasticity of total agricultural supply will also be positive. Only in cases where peasants are content with a fixed money income, or all increased production of a commodity is consumed within the subsistence sector, will the elasticity of marketed supply be negative or zero at the same time as the price elasticity of supply is positive. These conditions are not likely to prevail.

Empirical research on the supply response of agriculture can be divided into four main categories:

- Cross-country studies that look at output differences in relation to price differences across countries
- Time series studies that examine output movements in relation to price movements within countries over time
- Cross-section studies that look at output differences in relation to price differences across farms within a country
- Intersectoral general equilibrium models that examine how the output of agriculture varies in response to changes in the prices of agricultural goods relative to the price of other goods in the economy.

The evidence shows that aggregate supply elasticities of agricultural output range from 0.3 to 0.9 (Chhibber, 1988).[2] Long-run elasticity is obviously higher than short-run elasticity, and elasticity tends to be higher in the more advanced and land-abundant developing countries. The supply response of farmers to price changes depends crucially on the ability of farmers to respond to price signals, which in turn depends on transport, infrastructure and access to agricultural inputs. In poorer countries with inadequate infrastructure, supply elasticity is low (0.2–0.5). In fact, the supply elasticity of agriculture with respect to non-price factors (for example, the provision of public goods and services) is much higher than it is with respect to price, especially in poorer developing countries with inadequate infrastructure and marketing facilities.

The International Monetary Fund (IMF) and the World Bank are naturally concerned with the performance of the agricultural sector in countries to which they lend under various adjustment programmes (see Chapters 15 and 17). Three interrelated issues are typically addressed:

- The terms of trade between agriculture and the rest of the economy
- The efficiency of the agricultural sector
- The supply response of agriculture to price changes.

With regard to the agricultural terms of trade, the IMF normally insists that the prices paid by state marketing boards to producers be increased. Traditionally, governments have 'taxed' the agricultural sector through agricultural marketing boards, driving a large wedge between the prices paid to producers and the market prices of the commodities concerned. One implication, therefore, of raising producer prices is that government revenue may fall. This has implications for government expenditure if there is a budget constraint. Only if the elasticity of the supply of output with respect to producer prices is greater than unity will government revenue not fall, but as we saw above, supply elasticity is typically less than unity.

To achieve efficiency within agriculture, the IMF concentrates on such factors as improving storage and transport facilities, increasing the availability of agricultural inputs and improving extension services, and enhancing the efficiency of public enterprises in agriculture by insisting on the economic pricing of output and inputs, and by privatizing marketing and extension services.

We saw earlier that the supply response of farmers to price changes depends a great deal on the ability to respond, which in turn depends on infrastructure, transport, access to inputs and so on. Governments may be in a dilemma here because raising producer prices and reducing their own revenue may impair their ability to spend on infrastructure and other facilities. Given that the elasticity of supply with respect to non-price factors is higher than with respect to price, it would seem unwise to cut public expenditure as far as it affects the agricultural sector.

TRANSFORMING TRADITIONAL AGRICULTURE

The task of transforming traditional agriculture is not simply a question of land reform or price policy, however. The transformation of traditional agriculture is also dependent on **new inputs**. The policy issue is to determine the form that the new inputs should take if agriculture is to attract an adequate share of investment resources.

It may be argued that the low productivity of farm labour is due more to an absence of specific factor inputs such as research and education, than to a shortage of reproducible capital as such. Thus the most practical and economical approach to achieving sizeable increases in agricultural productivity lies in enhancing the efficiency of the existing agricultural economy through improvements in the quality of inputs, and by the application of advances in knowledge and modern technology on a broad front. Additional quantities of *existing* inputs will achieve nothing because of very low rates of return. Indeed, contrary to the conventional view that a stagnant agricultural sector is the result of the reluctance of peasant producers to respond to incentives, it can be argued that it is traditional agriculture that is the *cause* of the seeming antipathy towards work and investment because of low returns at the margin to existing inputs.

The way to transform traditional agriculture into a relatively cheap source of growth is by investment to produce a supply of new agricultural inputs that will be profitable for farmers to adopt. What is lacking is not so much an unwillingness on the part of the agricultural sector to accept new ideas, but public expenditure and the organization of particular public activities to serve the agricultural sector. Agricultural research, and investment in people to improve human capabilities in agriculture, have been neglected.

The rapid rise of agricultural productivity in Japan and Taiwan in the late nineteenth and early twentieth centuries was due to forms of 'technical progress' that are taken for granted in the developed countries; for example, the application of fertilizers and the selection and cultivation of high-yield crops. In more recent years, parts of Asia and Latin America have experienced a so-called '**Green Revolution**' which has tripled and quadrupled yields of crops such as wheat, rice and maize. Norman Borlaug, working in Mexico, is regarded as the father of the Green Revolution, who in the early 1960s crossed a Japanese dwarf wheat with a disease-resistant local strain to produce a high-yielding hybrid. What came to be known as Mexican dwarf wheat is a prime example of the impact that technology can have on the productivity of agriculture, which at the same time probably saved one billion people from starvation.

Today, **biotechnology (including genetically modified (GM) technology)** has the potential to raise productivity substantially and to reduce the incidence of famine and malnutrition. GM technology can produce crops that are more nutritious, can resist pests, can grow in salty soils, and which store longer. Let us give some examples. Ingo Potrykus, working in Zürich, has genetically engineered a type of rice ('golden rice') to contain beta-carotene, which is the pigment that produces Vitamin A. This is an important breakthrough since Vitamin A deficiency kills 2 million children a year and blinds many more. This research has been funded not by biotechnology companies, concerned with maximizing returns by patenting and the exercise of intellectual property rights, but by the Swiss government and the Rockefeller Foundation. The plan is for growers to be given the new rice free by national research centres supervised by the International Rice Research Institute in Manila. Agricultural innovation cannot flourish without well-resourced agricultural extension services within countries. Research is now underway to cross 'golden rice' with a grain implanted with three genes boosting iron content to combat anaemia, which many people suffer from in developing countries. A quality protein maize has also been developed by Norman Borlaug, containing many important amino acids which could dramatically reduce the number of children that die of malnutrition. GM cotton has increased yields by nearly 100 per cent in India by being more disease resistant.

There is still a suspicion concerning GM technology because in the early days, GM crops were engineered to resist herbicide spray and insect attack and gave rise to fears relating to the effect on the environment. New GM crops that increase yields and help nutrition in developing countries have altered the debate. Malnutrition remains a major scourge in developing countries, and by 2020, there will also be 2 billion more mouths to feed. The application of new technologies is urgently required.

What matters most are the incentives and associated opportunities that farm people have to augment production by means of investments that include the contribution of agricultural research and the improvement of human skills. According to Schultz, 'An integral part of the modernization of the economies of high and low income countries is the decline in the economic importance of farmland and a rise in that of human capital – skills and knowledge' (Schultz, 1980; see also Griffin, 1974, 1979).

We emphasize again that subsistence agriculture is an uncertain activity and therefore risky, particularly when survival is at stake, and this is another factor that breeds conservatism and makes change difficult, even in the face of opportunities. Poor people prefer to be safe than sorry; they tend to prefer an inferior outcome that is relatively certain to the prospect of a higher average return with a greater degree of risk attached. They are **risk averse**. This is clearly not irrational behaviour for poor people living on the margin of subsistence, even if the greater risk is imagined rather than real. To overcome inertia on this score, an integral element of agrarian reform must be policies designed to minimize risk and uncertainty through the provision of various types of insurance (as discussed in Chapter 2). The challenge of agricultural reform in India is highlighted in Case example 5.1.

The Challenge of Agricultural Reform in India

India now exports around 80 per cent of its basmati rice stock. And after China, it is the world's second largest rice producer, highlighting the success story of the country's self-sufficiency in the production of 'foodgrains' (largely wheat and rice), widely seen as one of its greatest economic achievements.

But India's single-minded pursuit of self-sufficiency in food has stalled the development of a modern, efficient, outward-looking agricultural industry.

A potentially world-class export industry in farm products such as organic foods, spices, and flowers is being held back by problems such as poor transport and storage facilities, an absence of agricultural quality standards, inadequate marketing, and a lack of organized production.

Economists, and institutions like the World Bank, blame this crippling paradox on India's defective foodgrain policy, where the government subsidizes grain production, which encourages farmers to overproduce, pushing grain stockpiles higher. The poor are entitled to buy these grains through a food ration system but many cannot because so-called 'Fair Price' food shops overcharge, or sell produce unfit for people to eat.

In another example, in Bihar, one of India's poorest states, only 20 per cent of the foodgrain released through this food ration system reaches poor households, according to Jean Drèze, a leading development economist. The rest is skimmed off and sold on the black market, facilitated by corrupt officials.

Yet these failures of India's foodgrain policy are well known. New Delhi has tried to restrain farm subsidies in favour of more productive investment in rural roads, irrigation, and new technology.

But it has found it tough to resist political pressure from state governments, whose electoral fortunes rely on support from powerful farmer lobbies that fear subsidy reform because they depend on selling their subsidized produce to a state-owned monopoly buyer. With about 75 per cent of India's poor living in rural areas, however, India's government has recognized that raising agricultural productivity is critical to easing poverty.

Agriculture's share of India's GDP has shrunk from around 60 per cent in the 1950s to about 25 per cent today. But farming still offers a livelihood for two-thirds of the country's billion-strong population. Agriculture directly employs around 235m people, or 58 per cent of India's total workforce.

Economists believe that the government must reform agriculture with more urgency, if only to stem a widening gap between India's rural, agriculture-based states, where average incomes per person are about half those of the richest, more urbanized states.

Indian agriculture today is characterized by growing numbers of independent farmers working alongside landless labourers and subsistence farmers, on plots that are not much larger than two football fields.

▶

In many ways, Indian farming still resembles what Mahatma Gandhi described as 'production by the masses, not mass production'. But with such smallscale farms, there are few incentives for farmers to invest in mechanization or crop diversification, which explains why India's rice yields, for example, are about half that of China's.

Economists fear that unless agriculture matches the growth of other sectors, it will shackle the rest of the economy. 'It means we're stuck with a small-farm economy,' says Abhijeet Sen, a senior agricultural economist. 'If you want to have larger farms you have to throw people out. Politically, you're stranded.'

According to Biswajit Dhar, a trade economist, the government should take the initiative to turn agriculture into a 'savvy sector' in the same way that India has focused on developing its information technology and telecommunications industries.

Unless India can modernize agriculture, Dr. Dhar says, rural people's disenchantment cannot be contained. "We'll have social and political discontent and this could lead to insecure life in the cities. We could end up in political turmoil.'

Source: *Financial Times*, 9 December 2003.

THE GROWTH OF THE MONEY ECONOMY

The question of the willingness to change customs and traditions leads naturally to a consideration of how peasant subsistence economies, producing goods for consumption only, typically transform themselves into money economies with an export and industrial sector. From historical experience, two factors would appear to be crucial to expansion of the agricultural sector and the eventual production of goods for exchange at home and abroad:

- The expansion of communications to create outlets and markets for surplus production (and to encourage the production of the surplus itself)
- The emergence of a class of middlemen or export–import merchants acting as agents between world markets and the domestic agricultural sectors.

If these conditions prevail, purely subsistence farming can develop first into mixed agriculture, where part of the crop is retained for subsistence and part is sold in the market, and then into modern agriculture with production entirely for the market, very often based on one crop. In the transition from subsistence agriculture, cash crops can utilize slack labour and land when the subsistence crops are finished; but the transition into mixed farming is possible only if the farmer has the inputs to raise productivity and the credit to purchase those inputs, as well as the marketing facilities.

Modern agriculture, run on strictly commercial lines for profit and based on one crop, must rely on exports since the size of the domestic market will generally be too small. The system of modern commercialized agriculture, upon which so many less developed countries now depend for their export earnings, is often termed **agribusiness**. This is a catch-all phrase referring not only to the production of the commodity in question, but also to the backward and forward linkages associated with the production process;

the provision of finance, machinery, fertilizers, seed and so on at the input end, and the processing, manufacturing and marketing of the product at the output end.

Today, the **multinational corporations** have a powerful position and a strong hold over the production and exportation of major agricultural commodities produced in the developing countries. To give just a few examples: three US firms control over one-half of the global banana trade; five European companies control 90 per cent of the tea sold in the West, and the two largest coffee companies control 20 per cent of the world market.

Both the ability to export and the ability to market internally imply surplus production over subsistence needs, and it is the size of this surplus that will largely determine the speed with which the subsistence sector can be drawn into the money economy. Again we come to the fact that unless productivity in agriculture increases, the expansion of the monetized sector will tend to decelerate as the land for cultivation dries up. When land has been exploited to the full it acts as a constraint on development unless agricultural productivity increases or non-agricultural activities can be established.

The emergence of an export sector provides a powerful stimulus to development and extension of the money economy. Exports create the capacity to import, and the very purchase of foreign products can encourage further export specialization. A population that acquires a taste for imported goods provides the impetus to producers to export more. In the case of new goods, as well as new techniques, there is strong evidence that peasant producers respond to incentives, and are not so dissimilar from 'Western economic man' as is sometimes claimed. Imports also provide a stimulus to industrialization. If a market for a foreign-manufactured good becomes established, it becomes easier and less risky, with the aid of tariff protection, for a domestic manufacturer to set up in business because the market is assured. Imports can also substitute for domestic capital and raise the growth rate directly.

As the distinguished development economist Hla Myint once said (for example Myint, 1958), the introduction of international trade into a hitherto isolated underdeveloped country is not merely a question of allowing countries to allocate resources more efficiently, it also permits the expansion of production possibilities:

> The extension of colonial administration and foreign enterprise were the essential ingredients in [this] process . . . The foreign trading firms played a crucial role in creating trade channels extending deeply into the traditional agricultural sectors, linking the peasant producers with world markets . . . [They] introduced new wants and a wide range of consumer goods to the peasants which provided incentives, spurred the peasant to expand the production of export crops, not by reallocating given resources but by clearing more of the unused land and underemployed labour.

When farmers start to specialize in goods for export, and rely on other producers for goods they previously produced themselves, the money economy will spread from the foreign trade sector to the rest of the domestic economy. This is nothing more than the international division of labour giving rise to the need for a means of exchange within a country as well as between countries.

The transition from a state of total dependence on the production of agricultural goods to a state of dualism, with the coexistence of a subsistence agricultural sector and a commercialized industrial sector, is a significant landmark in the development of an economy. The dual economy sets up incentives which are absent in the purely agrarian economy, and provides a new form of saving (the capitalist surplus). Profit gives the owners of industrial capital the incentive to innovate, and the possibility of acquiring assets in the industrial sector gives an incentive to agricultural producers also. Differences in agricultural productivity are frequently related to the proximity of farms to an industrial–urban complex.

The emergence of an export sector, the spread of the money economy, and the establishment of industries typically occur concurrently. What form industrialization takes will depend, in the first instance, on the initial impetus. One stimulus to industrialization that we have already mentioned is imports creating a market for goods that can be produced domestically without much difficulty. A more obvious factor leading naturally to industrialization is the availability of resources from the land, forming an indigenous industrial base. In this case industrialization takes the form of the processing of raw materials. There are few countries that do not possess some natural resource or other, and every country will have a comparative advantage in the production of one or other raw material that can be processed. These are the agribusinesses mentioned earlier.

In many of the present developing countries, formerly under colonial rule, the initiating force behind industrialization was the foreign exploitation of resources. Industrial activity took the form of mining operations and plantation agriculture. The establishment of foreign enclave activities undoubtedly exerted a development impact, but it is arguable whether development would have been more rapid had the countries been left to their own devices. Some would claim that the long-run development of these countries has been impaired because the availability of cheap labour from the subsistence sector has discouraged the installation of more modern productive machinery, and also that the foreign ownership and exploitation of a country's resources have considerably reduced its potential level of investment through the remittance of profits. The argument raises many important issues concerning development strategy, which are dealt with in some detail in Part IV of this book.

FINANCE FOR TRADITIONAL AGRICULTURE

For many years traditional agriculture has been starved of investment resources. While it accounts for approximately 30 per cent of output and 60 per cent of total employment, it attracts little more than 10 per cent of total investment resources. Private capital has no doubt been deterred by the risks involved, and by the low returns in traditional agriculture. But institutional investment has also been meagre, at least until recently. Of the $4 billion development loans made by the World Bank between 1947 and 1959, only $124 million went into agriculture.

In recent years, however, there has been some reversal of this neglect. Since the global food crisis of the early 1970s, the World Bank has accelerated its lending for agriculture and rural development, and has also reorientated its support towards raising the productivity of low-income groups. Since 1973, the Bank's direct lending for agricultural development in the developing world has grown from $1.4 billion a year to over $3 billion. This represents approximately 20 per cent of all World Bank lending.

Some projects have involved increasing the output of traditional crops through the more effective use of seeds, fertilizer and water. Other projects have involved changing the product mix from subsistence crops to the production of high-value crops, for example the smallholder tea project in Kenya. Irrigation is the largest single component of World Bank lending to agriculture, which permits the expansion of cultivation and makes more intensive cultivation possible by permitting double cropping. Bank-financed irrigation schemes have had a major impact on rice yields and production in Asia.

The World Bank has also become the most important source of financial and technical assistance for the construction of fertilizer plants in developing countries, and these have played an important role in increasing yields and output. The Bank gives credit for rural infrastructure projects such as roads to reduce marketing and supply bottlenecks, and rural electrification schemes. **Agricultural extension** is another important aspect of the Bank's assistance to the rural sector. In India, where 'contact' farmers disseminate knowledge to their neighbours of improved techniques learnt from field agents, over 10 million farm families have been helped. The rural poor now have more extensive and easier access to credit financed by the Bank. In India much of the credit has been used by small farmers to provide supplementary irrigation.

Finally, the World Bank operates various multi-purpose projects that combine a wide range of activities, normally in conjunction with a regional development programme. In Mexico, some 75,000 low-income families have benefited from such a project in about thirty localities through investments in irrigation, soil conservation, electrification, schools, health care, water supplies and marketing services. Each dollar the Bank invests in rural development is supplemented by local investment, and the Bank rightly stresses that its contribution to the total flow of resources can be effective only if appropriate national policies are pursued on pricing, taxation, land reform and so on. The major part of the Bank's programme to reach the rural poor is still in the process of implementation, and is therefore difficult to assess reliably, but indications suggest that a combination of additional resources, institutional reform and national government commitment to improvement in the rural sector can have a major impact.

Apart from the World Bank, other multilateral institutions exist to help traditional agriculture, notably the United Nations International Fund for Agricultural Development (IFAD), which seeks to integrate small farmers and landless people into the development process. IFAD states that its priority is for 'projects which will have a significant impact on improving food production in developing countries, particularly for the benefit of the poorest sections of the rural population'. Up to 2000, over 1 billion dollars had been dispersed.

In the absence of external institutional investment, the sources of capital for the expansion of both agriculture and industry are relatively limited in the early stages of development. In a truly subsistence economy, in the sense of an economy producing only what it needs for itself and no more, everyone is a Robinson Crusoe, supplying their own capital by refraining from present consumption. With specialization in the production of goods for export, and the producer's need for capital to expand productive capacity, mechanisms grow up spontaneously to meet the need for credit. It is a good market maxim that demand will create a supplier at a price. The suppliers are generally village moneylenders, shopkeepers, landlords and, not infrequently, the Church – especially in South America – charging rates of interest that often exceed 50 per cent.

THE INTERDEPENDENCE OF AGRICULTURE AND INDUSTRY

Once agriculture emerges from its stagnatory, subsistence state and starts to specialize and produce goods for export, and industry develops under the impact of growth in the agricultural sector, the two sectors of agriculture and industry become very interdependent. The industrial sector adds to the demand for goods produced by agriculture and absorbs surplus labour, which may raise productivity in agriculture. In turn, the agricultural sector provides a market for industrial goods out of rising real income, and makes a factor contribution to development through the release of resources if productivity rises faster than the demand for commodities. We shall discuss this interaction more fully later in the chapter.

The transfer of resources from agriculture to industry may be capital or labour or both. Since labour is in abundant supply in most low-income countries, there is generally no difficulty in releasing labour for industry, except during harvest time. In any case, labour will tend to migrate naturally in response to seemingly better opportunities in the industrial sector and higher real incomes. The real earnings of labour in the industrial sector may be more than twice as much as the agricultural wage. If the industrial sector is to be guaranteed an adequate supply of labour, some wage differential is inevitably required to offset the higher real living costs in an urban environment, to compensate for the forfeit of non-monetary benefits of rural life, and to compensate for greater job uncertainty in the industrial sector. Real earnings may also be higher because of genuinely higher productivity in the industrial sector, where labour has more factors of production to work with. Most models of rural–urban migration make migration a positive function of the *expected* urban–rural wage differential, which is the difference between the urban wage, adjusted for the proportion of the total urban labour force employed (as a proxy for the probability of finding work), and the agricultural real wage (see later for an outline of the model).

Capital may be less 'mobile' than labour, and if there is considered to be insufficient lending from the agricultural sector on a voluntary basis it may become necessary for a government to extract savings compulsorily from the agricultural sector by taxation. As mentioned already, this method was resorted to in a harsh manner by Japan at the time of the Meiji restoration and by Soviet Russia after the revolution. In Japan between 1880 and 1900 the land tax provided approximately 80 per cent of central government tax revenue, and in Russia forced extraction of the agricultural surplus took the form of expropriation of land and the extermination of labour. Industrialization in Western Europe, and particularly in England, was also financed to a large extent by surpluses generated on the land, but transference of these surpluses was on the whole voluntary through a rapidly expanding banking system. The developing countries today, despite their access to foreign sources of capital, must also rely heavily on extracting the surplus from agriculture to finance industrialization. The difficulty is to decide on the best means of extraction without impairing the incentive to produce, or damaging the growth of productivity, upon which a growing agricultural surplus depends. The financing of economic development will be discussed more fully in Part V of the book.

ECONOMIC DEVELOPMENT WITH UNLIMITED SUPPLIES OF LABOUR

The process of the emergence of a money economy from a subsistence state has been formalized by Sir Arthur Lewis in his classic paper 'Economic Development with Unlimited Supplies of Labour' (1954).[3] There he presents a 'classical' model of a dual economy with the purpose, as he describes it, of seeing what can be made of the classical framework in solving the problems of distribution, accumulation and growth. His ultimate aim is to emphasize the crucial role of the capitalist surplus in the development process.

The Lewis model therefore starts with the assumption of a dual economy with a modern exchange sector and an indigenous subsistence sector, and assumes that there are unlimited supplies of labour in the subsistence sector in the sense that the supply of labour exceeds the demand for labour at the subsistence wage; that is, the marginal product of workers in the subsistence sector is equal to, or less than, the subsistence or institutional wage so that a reduction in the number of workers would not lower the average (subsistence) product of labour and might even raise it.

It has even been argued that the marginal product of labour may be zero or negative in an economy that is still at a fairly low level of development and experiencing a rapid growth of population. One of the distinguishing features of agriculture is that it is an activity that is subject to diminishing returns owing to the fixity of the supply of land. If there is rapid population growth and labour has little employment opportunity other than on the land, a stage may be reached where the land cannot provide further workers with a living unless the existing workers drastically reduce their hours of work. These propositions are illustrated in Figure 5.1. The curve drawn represents the marginal product of successive units of labour added to the land. After the employment of X units of labour the marginal product of labour begins to fall owing to diminishing returns; after X_1 units of labour, labour's marginal contribution to output falls below the subsistence wage; and after X_2 units of labour, labour's contribution to output becomes negative and total product will decline with successive additions of labour beyond X_2.

The same tendencies can also be represented using the type of production-function diagram introduced in Chapter 4, which is reproduced in Figure 5.2. With more than X_2 labour employed with a fixed amount of land, K, the marginal product of labour becomes negative, and further additions to the labour supply, without corresponding increases in the amount of land, will push the economy on to a lower production function, that is, total output will fall from 100 units to, say, 50 units with X_3 units of labour.

There are three main means of escape from the tendency towards diminishing returns and zero marginal product in agriculture: first, by productivity increasing faster than population through the absorption of more and more of the agricultural population into industry; second, by technical progress in the agricultural sector increasing labour's marginal product; and third, by capital accumulation, which can raise productivity directly and can also be the vehicle for technical progress.

In Lewis's model, labour in excess of X_1 in Figure 5.1 is in completely elastic supply to the industrial sector at whatever the industrial wage. The industrial or capitalist sector is represented in Figure 5.3. The curve NR represents the marginal product of labour in the capitalist sector, W is the industrial wage and, on the profit-maximizing assumption, labour is employed in the capitalist sector up to the point where the marginal product

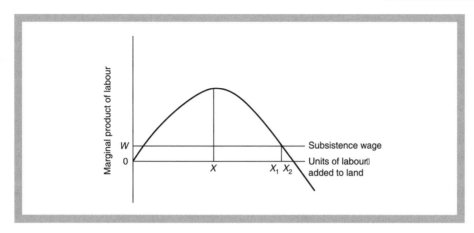

Figure 5.1 Marginal product of successive units of labour added to the land

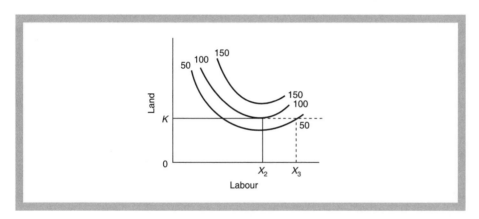

Figure 5.2 Tendency towards diminishing returns

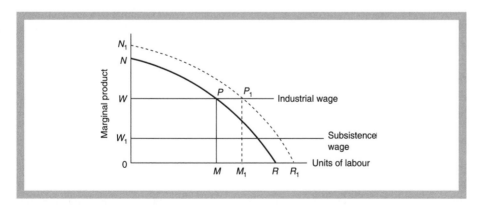

Figure 5.3 Industrial/capitalist sector

is equal to the wage rate. That is, M will be employed. Workers in excess of M earn what they can in the subsistence sector. The industrial wage is assumed to be determined in some relation to the wage that workers can earn in the subsistence sector. The differential (WW_1) between the industrial wage and the subsistence wage will be a function of many factors, some of which were mentioned earlier, for example higher real living costs in the capitalist sector and greater job uncertainty. Given that the industrial wage is based on earnings in the subsistence sector, capitalists have a direct interest in holding down productivity in the subsistence sector, and Lewis comments that the record of every imperial power in Africa in modern times was one of impoverishing the subsistence economy.

The total product of labour, $0NPM$ in Figure 5.3, is split between the payment to labour in the form of wages, $0WPM$, and the capitalist surplus, WNP. The expansion of the capitalist sector and the rate of absorption of labour from the subsistence sector depends on the use made of the capitalist surplus. If the surplus is reinvested, leading to greater capital formation, this will increase the total product of labour. The marginal product curve will shift upwards to the right, say N_1R_1, which means that if wages remain constant the capitalist sector can now afford to employ more labour and will do so by drawing on labour from the subsistence sector to the extent of MM_1 workers. The size of the capitalist surplus will increase from WNP to WN_1P_1, which is available for further reinvestment, and so the process goes on. This for Lewis is the essence of the development process. The stimulus to investment in the capitalist sector comes from the rate of profit, which must rise over time because all the benefits of increased productivity accrue to capital if the real wage is constant.[4]

According to Lewis, the share of profits in the national income ($P/0$) will also rise. First, the share of profits in the capitalist sector (P/C) will increase, and second, the capitalist sector relative to the national income ($C/0$) will tend to expand, that is, if $P/0 = P/C \times C/0$, then $P/0$ will rise as P/C and $C/0$ increase.

Whether the share of profits in national income does rise with development is ultimately an empirical question. At the theoretical level, if the successive marginal product curves are drawn parallel to each other, as in Figure 5.3, the capitalist surplus area does rise more than proportionately to the wage-payment area, so that the surplus and profits as a proportion of capitalist income appear to rise. But is it legitimate to draw the curves parallel? If the capital stock is augmented through reinvestment of the surplus (say, it doubles), then *assuming constant returns to scale*, the marginal product of the nth labourer now becomes that of the $2n$th labourer; that is, what was the marginal product of the first labourer will now be the marginal product of the second labourer, and what was the marginal product of the second labourer will now be the marginal product of the fourth labourer, and so on. It is not strictly correct, therefore, to draw the successive marginal product curves parallel to each other, representing different proportionate increases in product per man. Instead, each curve should be drawn from the same vertical intercept, keeping the proportionate gap between the two curves the same as in Figure 5.4. If the upward shift in the curve NR to NR_1 is proportionately the same over the whole of its range, the capitalist surplus and the payment to labour rise at the same rate, leaving the share of profits in the capitalist sector unchanged, that is, if $Q_2Q/W_2Q = P_2P/WP$, then $WNP/0NPM = WNP_1/0NP_1M_1$.

This technicality does not detract from the usefulness of the Lewis model. For one

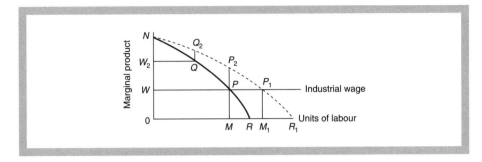

Figure 5.4 Constant returns and marginal product

thing, the main function of Lewis's model is to represent a process, and to contribute to an understanding of the nature of the economic problem in backward economies. Second, Lewis is more concerned with the *size* of the capitalist sector relative to the total economy ($C/0$), an increase in which will also cause the share of profits in national income to rise. The evidence of this comes from Lewis himself: 'If we ask why the less developed countries save so little the answer is not because they are so poor but because their capitalist sector is so small' (Lewis, 1954). Accepting the strict classical assumptions that all wages are consumed and all profits are saved, the savings ratio depends not only on the share of profits in the capitalist sector but also on the size of the capitalist sector.

The process outlined by Lewis comes to an end when capital accumulation has caught up with population, so that there is no surplus labour in the subsistence sector left to absorb. When all surplus labour is absorbed, the supply of labour to the industrial sector becomes less than perfectly elastic. It is now in the interests of producers in the subsistence sector to compete for labour, since the marginal product of labour is no longer below the institutional wage. When this point is reached, the agricultural sector can be said to have become commercialized. This change in producer behaviour in the subsistence sector has also been defined as the end of the take-off stage (Ranis and Fei, 1961).

Implicit in the Lewis model is the assumption that employment growth in the capitalist sector will be proportional to the rate of capital formation. If profits are reinvested in labour-saving technology, however, this will not be so, and the rate of growth of employment in the industrial sector, as well as the rate of absorption from the agricultural sector, may be very low.

It is also possible that the process of absorption may end prematurely before surplus labour in the subsistence sector is fully exhausted, owing to checks to the expansion of the capitalist surplus. First, capital accumulation and labour absorption may be checked for reasons that are related to the expansion of the capitalist sector itself. For example, as the capitalist sector expands, the terms of trade may turn against it. If the demand for food expands faster than agricultural output, the capitalist sector will be forced to pay higher prices for food in exchange for industrial goods, reducing the size of the capitalist surplus. This will have two effects.

First, if the capitalists are forced to pay higher prices for the goods they buy relative to those that they sell, this means less saving for investment. The problem does not arise if productivity in agriculture is expanding rapidly, but Lewis himself recognized that the failure of peasant agriculture to increase its productivity has probably been the chief factor holding back the expansion of the industrial sector in many developing countries. If this is so, argue Lewis's critics, the growth of non-farm employment can be said to depend on the growth of the agricultural surplus. This in fact is the starting point of **neoclassical models of development** (see Jorgenson, 1966), in contrast to classical models with their exclusive stress on the supply of capital.

The second effect arising from the expansion of the capitalist sector if there is a shortage of food is that the real wage may have to rise in industry, further squeezing the capitalist surplus. If labour is needed in agriculture to meet the demand for food, unlimited supplies of labour at a *constant real wage* may be very limited indeed. The assumption of an unlimited supply of labour is the central proposition underlying the classical approach to the theory of development, and Jorgenson has argued that the classical approach stands or falls by this hypothesis. Historically, of course, real wages have risen in agriculture and industry, and the capitalist sector has also expanded rapidly, which lends support to a middle view between the classical and neoclassical approaches. Lewis himself recognized the importance of both capital accumulation and food supply, and it is this consideration that forms the basis of his argument for the balanced growth of the agricultural and industrial sectors.

Capital accumulation in the industrial sector may also be checked for reasons unrelated to the expansion of the capitalist sector and its demand for food. For example, real wages may be forced up directly by trade unions, or indirectly through rising real wages in the subsistence sector due to increased agricultural productivity. Lewis himself states that

> anything which raises the productivity of the subsistence sector (average product per person) will raise real wages in the capitalist sector, and will therefore reduce the capitalist surplus and the rate of capital accumulation, unless it at the same time more than correspondingly moves the terms of trade against the subsistence sector. (Lewis, 1954)

Lewis reaches this conclusion because one of the simplifying assumptions of his classical two-sector model is that the expansion of the capitalist sector is limited *only* by a shortage of capital, so that any increase in prices and purchasing power for farmers is not a stimulus to industrialization but an obstacle to the expansion of the capitalist sector. How does this square with the idea of the agricultural sector providing a market for industrial goods, and the view of the World Bank (*World Development Report 1979*) that 'a stagnant rural economy with low purchasing power holds back industrial growth in many developing countries'? The answer is that there does seem to be a contradiction, because the classical approach emphasizes supply to the exclusion of demand, or rather takes for granted that there will always be a market clearing price for industrial goods. In fact there will be a minimum below which the price of industrial goods cannot fall, set by the subsistence wage in industry.

Johnston and Mellor (1961) recognized this worrying feature of the Lewis model many years ago when they perceptively remarked 'there is clearly a conflict between emphasis on agriculture's essential contribution to the capital requirements for overall development, and emphasis on increased farm purchasing power as a stimulus to industrialization. Nor is there any easy reconciliation of the conflict.' The challenge of reconciliation has never been taken up in a simple way, but there is a resolution of the conflict if the **complementarity** between the two sectors is recognized from the outset, and it is remembered that there must be an equilibrium terms of trade that balances supply and demand in both sectors. The basis of the model originally comes from Kaldor (1979).

A MODEL OF THE COMPLEMENTARITY BETWEEN AGRICULTURE AND INDUSTRY[5]

We have seen that agriculture provides the potential for capital accumulation in industry by providing a marketable surplus. The greater the surplus, the cheaper industry can obtain food and the more saving and capital accumulation can be undertaken. This is the supply side. But industry also needs a market for its industrial goods, which in the early stages of development must largely come from agriculture. This is the demand side, and the higher the price of agricultural goods the greater agricultural purchasing power will be. Given this conflict between low food prices being good for industrial supply and high food prices being good for industrial demand, what is required is a simple model that brings together agriculture and industry in an equilibrium framework, where the terms of trade between agriculture and industry provide the equilibrating mechanism ensuring that supply and demand grow at the same rate in each sector.

Let us first model growth in the agricultural sector in relation to the terms of trade; then growth in the industrial sector; and then bring the two sectors together. Agriculture's growth rate will be a function of how much it invests relative to output and of the productivity of investment. How much investment goods it obtains from industry in exchange for food that it 'saves' depends on the price of industrial goods relative to food, that is, on the terms of trade between industry and agriculture. The higher the price of investment goods, the lower the possible investment for a given amount of food and the lower the growth of supply capacity. This inverse relation between the industrial terms of trade (the price of industrial goods relative to the price of food) and the agricultural growth rate (g_A) is shown in Figure 5.5.

Industry's growth rate will also be a function of its investment ratio and the productivity of investment. But there is a certain minimum to the terms of trade, below which industry would not be able to invest anything because all output would be required to pay for workers' wage goods (food). If all wages are consumed, the cost of food input per unit of output in industry will depend on the real wage rate in industry divided by the productivity of labour, that is $w/(O/L) = (W/O)$, where w is the real wage and W is the wage bill. Industrial prices must cover W/O, and this sets the lower limit to industrial prices relative to food prices. At the other extreme, industrial growth cannot exceed a certain maximum where the price of food is so low relative to industrial goods that all industrial goods are retained for investment in industry. The investment ratio approaches, in effect, 100 per cent, and the upper limit to growth is given by the productivity of investment. The positive relation between the industrial terms of trade and the industrial growth rate (g_I) is shown in Figure 5.6.

If we now assume for simplicity (although without loss of generality) that the income elasticity of demand for agricultural and industrial goods is unity, then at a given terms of trade the rate of growth of agricultural output represents the rate of growth of demand for industrial goods, and the rate of growth of industrial output represents the rate of growth of demand for agricultural output, and where g_A and g_I cross there will be balanced growth of agriculture and industry (g^*) at equilibrium terms of trade (p^*), as shown in Figure 5.7.[6]

In this model of the complementarity between agriculture and industry, we can see the implications of what happens if the terms of trade are not in equilibrium, as well as the checks to the expansion of industry that Lewis mentions.

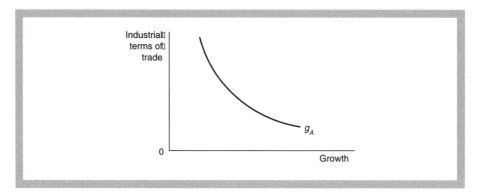

Figure 5.5 Industrial terms of trade and agricultural growth rate

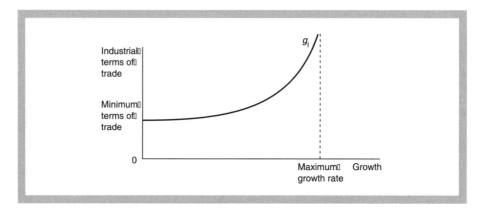

Figure 5.6 Industrial terms of trade and industrial growth rate

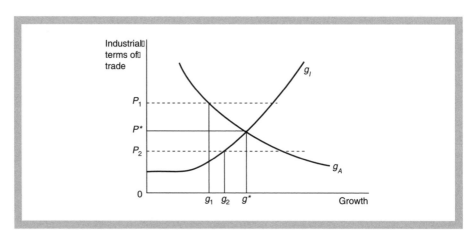

Figure 5.7 Growth equilibrium and disequilibrium

If the terms of trade are not in equilibrium – if the price of food is 'too low' or 'too high' in relation to industrial goods – then industrial growth is either demand constrained or supply constrained. For example, if in Figure 5.7 the terms of trade were at P_1, because the price of food was 'too low', industrial growth would be demand constrained to g_1 by a lack of agricultural purchasing power over industrial goods. Industry could accumulate capital, but it could not sell its goods. Alternatively, if the terms of trade were below equilibrium at P_2, industrial growth would be supply constrained to g_2 because the price of food would be 'too high', impairing capital accumulation in industry. Agriculture could buy, but industry could not supply. Growth is maximized at P^*.

We can now examine what happens if there are shifts in the curves. Clearly shifts in the curves will cause both the growth rates and the equilibrium terms of trade to vary. An improvement in agricultural productivity that shifts g_A outwards will mean both higher industrial growth and an improvement in the industrial terms of trade. The importance of agricultural productivity improvement could not be better illustrated. An improvement in industrial productivity will shift g_I outwards, which will also mean higher industrial growth but at the expense of worse terms of trade for industry. If there is a tendency for real wages in industry to rise commensurately with productivity increases, however, the g_I curve will remain stable and the terms of trade will never move against industry in favour of agriculture unless agricultural productivity falls and the g_A curve shifts inwards.

The checks to industrial expansion in Lewis's model are easily illustrated. A rise in the real wage in industry will shift the g_I curve inwards, which will choke industrial expansion unless an equivalent increase in agricultural productivity shifts the g_A curve outwards (see the quote from Lewis on p. 192).

A final implication of the model is that if through time agriculture is subject to diminishing returns, productivity in agriculture will fall, shifting inwards the g_A curve and reducing the rate of industrial growth. If the g_I curve is relatively stable, industrial growth depends fundamentally on the rate of land-saving innovations (technical progress) in agriculture to offset the effect of diminishing returns.

RURAL–URBAN MIGRATION AND URBAN UNEMPLOYMENT

Lewis spoke of an urban–rural wage differential of approximately 30 per cent to attract labour to the industrial sector. What has happened in recent years, however, is that the urban–rural wage differential has widened considerably beyond this level – there has been rural–urban migration on an unprecedented scale, but the expansion of the industrial sector has not generated sufficient employment for all those available to work. Migration has thus served to transfer unemployment from rural to urban areas, as described in Chapter 3. The **informal economy** of the urban sector harbours the bulk of this labour in transition from the rural sector into industrial employment. The conclusion to be drawn is that the *expected* value of the urban wage, notwithstanding the probability of long spells of unemployment, still exceeds the wage in the rural sector, and as long as it does so the process of migration will continue. In these changed circumstances, development theory has focused its attention in recent years on **urban unemployment** and policies to combat it. Most of the models of the rural–urban migration process are pessimistic about reducing the level of urban unemployment by conventional means such as subsidies to labour or public-works programmes in the urban areas. The reason is that migration from the land is made to be a function not only of the *actual* urban–rural wage differential but also of the level of employment opportunities. More employment opportunities reduce unemployment immediately but encourage more migration. It thus becomes an empirical question whether increasing the rate of growth of employment in urban areas will actually reduce unemployment. The very real possibility exists, however, that urban areas may be caught in a 'high level unemployment equilibrium trap' as long as surplus labour on the land remains and development policy concentrates new activity in established urban (industrial) centres.

One of the earliest and simplest models of the rural–urban migration process, which is also operational in the sense of being testable, is that of Todaro (1971). Let us consider its main features and implications.

The supply of labour to the urban sector is assumed to be a function of the *expected* urban–rural wage differential (d), where the expected urban–rural wage differential is equal to the actual urban wage times the probability of obtaining a job in the urban sector minus the average rural wage. Thus

$$S = f_s(d) \tag{5.1}$$

where S is the supply of labour to the urban sector and

$$d = w\pi - r \tag{5.2}$$

where w is the urban real wage, r is the average rural wage, and π is the probability of obtaining a job in the urban sector.

The probability of obtaining a job in the urban sector is assumed to be directly related to the rate of new job creation and inversely related to the ratio of unemployed job-seekers to the number of existing job opportunities,[7] that is

$$\pi = \frac{\gamma N}{W - N} = \frac{\gamma N}{U} \tag{5.3}$$

where γ is the net rate of new urban job creation, N is the level of urban employment, W is the total urban labour force,[8] and U is the level of urban unemployment. Substituting (5.3) into (5.2) gives

$$d = \frac{w\gamma N}{U} - r \tag{5.4}$$

If it is assumed that migration will come to a stop when the *expected* urban wage equals the rural wage (that is, when $d = 0$), we can derive from (5.4) the equilibrium level of unemployment as

$$U^e = \frac{w\gamma N}{r} \tag{5.5}$$

It can be seen from (5.5) that a reduction in the *actual* urban wage will reduce the equilibrium level of unemployment, and a rise in the rural wage will also reduce it, but (paradoxically) an increase in the rate of new job creation will *raise* the equilibrium level of unemployment by increasing the probability of obtaining a job and encouraging migration. Whether policies such as wage subsidies can reduce unemployment therefore depends on whether the increase in the demand for labour as a result is greater or less than the induced supply.

From (5.5) we can solve for the equilibrium ratio of unemployment to employment and give some quantitative content to the model. Dividing both sides by N gives $U^e/N = w\gamma/r$. Thus, for example, if the industrial wage is twice as high as the rural wage ($w/r = 2$), and $\gamma = 0.05$, the equilibrium ratio of unemployment to employment will be 10 per cent.

To consider the policy implications more fully, and to answer the question 'under what conditions will the actual level of urban unemployment rise?', let us suppose that the rate of urban job creation is a function of the urban wage, w, and a policy parameter, a (for example, a government policy variable to increase employment). Thus

$$\gamma = f_d(w, a) \qquad \frac{\partial \gamma}{\partial a} > 0 \qquad\qquad (5.6)$$

If the growth of urban labour demand is increased, the response of labour supply can be written as

$$\frac{\partial S}{\partial a} = \frac{\partial S}{\partial d}\frac{\partial d}{\partial \gamma}\frac{\partial \gamma}{\partial a} \qquad\qquad (5.7)$$

Now, from (5.4) by partial differentiation, we have

$$\frac{\partial d}{\partial \gamma} = w \frac{N}{U} \qquad\qquad (5.8)$$

Substituting (5.8) into (5.7) gives

$$\frac{\partial S}{\partial a} = \frac{\partial S}{\partial d}\frac{wN}{U}\frac{\partial \gamma}{\partial a} \qquad\qquad (5.9)$$

There will be an increase in the absolute level of urban unemployment if the increase in supply in response to a policy change exceeds the increase in the absolute number of new jobs created, that is, if

$$\frac{\partial S}{\partial d}\frac{wN}{U}\frac{\partial \gamma}{\partial a} > N \frac{\partial \gamma}{\partial a} \qquad\qquad (5.10)$$

Now, cancelling N and $\partial \gamma/\partial a$ from both sides and multiplying both sides by d/w and U/W, the condition for unemployment to increase becomes

$$\frac{\partial S/W}{\partial d/d} > \frac{d}{w}\frac{U}{W} \tag{5.11}$$

or substituting (5.2) into (5.11):

$$\frac{\partial S/W}{\partial d/d} > \frac{w\pi - r}{w}\frac{U}{W} \tag{5.12}$$

In words, (5.12) says that unemployment will increase in the urban sector as a result of a policy change to increase employment if the elasticity of the urban labour supply (by migration) with respect to the urban–rural wage differential exceeds the expected urban–rural wage differential as a proportion of the urban wage times the unemployment rate. Equation (5.12) is obviously testable. It transpires, in fact, that (5.12) is satisfied with a very low elasticity. For example, suppose that the actual urban wage is twice the rural wage,[9] that the probability of obtaining a job in the urban sector is 0.8 and that the unemployment rate is 10 per cent, then the level of unemployment will increase if the elasticity of the urban labour supply with respect to the expected urban–rural wage differential is 0.03.

Note that the growth of total labour supply as a result of migration ($\partial S/W$) is not the same thing as the rate of growth of migration ($\partial S/S$), so that the elasticity of *supply* with respect to a change in job opportunities is not the same thing as the elasticity of *migration* with respect to a change in job opportunities. We could, however, convert (5.12) into the elasticity of migration with respect to $\partial d/d$ by multiplying both sides of (5.10) by U/S instead of U/W. This would give

$$\frac{\partial S/S}{\partial d/d} > \frac{w\pi - r}{w}\frac{U}{S} \tag{5.13}$$

Since the ratio of unemployment to migration (U/S) is much higher than U/W, the elasticity of migration itself would have to be higher than the elasticity of labour supply for unemployment to increase following a job expansion programme. If, as before, we assume that $w/r = 2$, $\pi = 0.8$ and, say, $U/S = 2$, the migration elasticity would have to exceed 0.6 for unemployment to rise. In principle this elasticity is easy to estimate by specifying a migration function in which migration is a function of the expected urban–rural wage differential, holding constant other factors affecting migration. For an interesting case study, see the study of Tanzania by Barnum and Sabot (1977), who estimate an elasticity of migration with respect to the urban wage itself, holding other things constant, of between 0.7 and 2.0.[10]

DISGUISED UNEMPLOYMENT: TYPES AND MEASUREMENT

The higher the marginal product of labour in agriculture, the greater the force of the neoclassical argument that it is the growth of the agricultural surplus that determines the growth of non-farm employment. We must now examine more critically the classical assumption of unlimited supplies of labour, defined as marginal product below the subsistence wage.

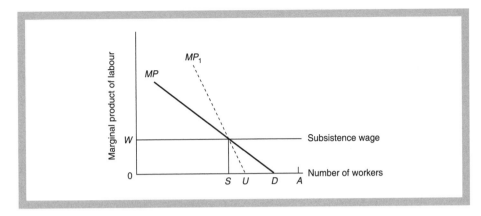

Figure 5.8 Disguised unemployment

If the marginal product of labour in the rural sector is positive (which is not precluded in Lewis's model as long as it is below the subsistence wage), the withdrawal of labour from the subsistence sector will reduce total output. To argue that development via unlimited supplies of labour is feasible and relatively painless one must implicitly assume that the marginal product of labour is virtually zero. The term '**disguised unemployment**' is usually defined loosely in this way. But the question arises of how workers can survive on the land if their marginal product is zero, or even positive but below subsistence. Who would employ such labour? Would output in the subsistence sector really remain unaffected if substantial quantities of labour migrated? In short, what precisely is meant by the term 'disguised unemployment'? Can it be quantified, and what are we to make of the argument that industrial development in surplus-labour economies is a relatively painless process?

Let us redraw Figure 5.1 from the point of diminishing returns and describe more formally three possible interpretations of the concept of disguised unemployment that are commonly found in the literature. Let A in Figure 5.8 be the actual number of workers employable. One possible measure of disguised unemployment is the difference between A and S, or the gap between the number of workers available for work and the amount of employment that equates the marginal product of labour and the subsistence wage. This is the definition of unlimited supplies of labour in Lewis's model where, if the marginal product of labour is below the institutional or subsistence wage, landowners have no interest in retaining these workers and therefore do not compete for them with the industrial sector.

A second possible measure of disguised unemployment is the difference between A and D, or the gap between the actual number of workers available for employment and the level of employment at which the marginal product of labour is zero, which is sometimes referred to as the **static surplus**. This surplus is obviously less than if disguised unemployment is defined as labour with a marginal product below the institutional or subsistence wage.

A third measure of disguised unemployment is the difference between the actual number of workers available and the level of employment at which the marginal product of labour would be zero if some change occurred that enabled the same level of output to be produced with fewer workers. This is represented by a pivoting of the marginal product curve to MP_1. Disguised unemployment is now measured by the difference between A and U, which is sometimes referred to as the **dynamic surplus**. The dynamic surplus clearly embraces many 'types' of disguised unemployment because there are many reasons, particularly in developing countries, why labour may not be fulfilling its potential and why small changes in technique and organization of production may release substantial quantities of labour.

There are three main ways of ascertaining whether surplus labour exists in the sense that labour's marginal product is zero. The first is to examine instances where substantial numbers of the agricultural labour force have been withdrawn from the land, either to work on some industrialization project or as the result of illness, and to observe whether agricultural output falls or not.

This method was followed by Schultz (1964), who examined the effect of the influenza epidemic in India in 1918–19, which killed approximately 8 per cent of the agricultural labour force. He found that acreage and output during the following year declined, and concluded from this that surplus labour in Indian agriculture did not exist. An important criticism of Schultz's study, however, is that he failed to distinguish between the summer and winter season of the year following the epidemic. Mehra (1966) has shown that summer production, which just followed the epidemic, was not in fact reduced and that the decline in agricultural production in 1919–20 found by Schultz was entirely due to a reduction in the winter crop, which could have resulted from low rainfall. Notwithstanding the criticism, this is one method of approach.

A second method of estimating the static surplus is to take the difference between the labour available and the labour required to produce the current level of agricultural output *with given techniques*, making due allowance for the seasonality of production. The estimate of the magnitude of surplus labour in this case will vary with local conditions, and what is regarded as a normal working day.

A third approach is to estimate agricultural production functions (see Chapter 4) to test whether the elasticity of output with respect to labour input is significantly different from zero. This approach indicates whether or not there is surplus labour, but does not measure its magnitude.

When discussing labour's marginal product in agriculture and the extent of disguised unemployment, two important distinctions need to be made: between harvest and non-harvest time; and between farms that hire labour and those that do not. Within the production-function approach this distinction is easily made explicit and is a very fruitful approach for that reason. As far as the distinction between hired and non-hired labour is concerned, the marginal product of family labour can hardly be zero if workers are hired, nor can the marginal product of the hired workers be zero if they are paid.

Desai and Mazumbar (1970) have taken a sample of Indian farms and divided it into those that use hired labour and those that do not. The differences between the two groups are striking. The marginal product of labour on the farms hiring labour is significantly different from zero, while on farms not hiring labour the marginal product is not significantly different from zero. It should be remembered, however, that zero marginal product per man hour or per man day is not a necessary condition for surplus labour. Surplus labour can take the form of a small number of hours or days worked. On the other hand, if the marginal product per man hour or man day is zero, there must be some surplus labour, and presumably it is the tip of the iceberg.

As far as the distinction between harvest and non-harvest labour is concerned, Nath (1974) suggests that busy-season and slack-season labour inputs should be included as separate arguments in the production function. He adopts this approach in a cross-section analysis of 150 farms in the Ferozepur district (Punjab) in India for the period 1967–8, relating annual output to busy-season labour, slack-season labour and other inputs, using a Cobb–Douglas production function (see p. 137). Nath finds, not unexpectedly, that the marginal product of busy-season labour is indeed positive, but that the marginal product of slack-season labour is not significantly different from zero.

The conclusion from all these studies is that the marginal product of labour on family farms with no hired labour in the slack season may well be zero. In this sense a static surplus exists. But where agriculture is partly commercialized, and in the harvest season, the marginal product of labour is positive, and reductions in the agricultural labour force would impair agricultural output. Defenders of the classical model of development claim, however, that no one has ever argued that the withdrawal of labour under *all* circumstances will not affect output. The purpose of the classical model is to draw attention to the fact that the marginal product in industry far exceeds the opportunity cost of labour in agriculture, and those who use the classical model normally stipulate some dynamic change as migration takes place.

This leads to the question of the measurement of the **dynamic surplus**, which is the difference between the actual labour employed and the labour required given some small change in technique (including an increase in the number of hours worked per day).

Unfortunately those investigators who have measured the dynamic surplus have generally not distinguished between the causes of the surplus, or made explicit the assumptions upon which their estimates of labour requirements are based, and this is a major reason why estimates and opinions differ on the extent and existence of disguised unemployment. If the surplus is measured simply by the difference between the amount of labour that, in the investigator's opinion, should be necessary to produce a given output and the amount of labour that there actually is, this does not distinguish between low productivity due to such factors as poor health, lack of incentive, a preference for leisure, primitive technology or the seasonal nature of production.

There may be genuine differences in the extent of disguised unemployment within and between countries; on the other hand, different investigators may have been estimating different things. We have already seen that a large part of the observed labour surplus may result from the seasonal nature of production. Studies that exclude this possibility will certainly overestimate the existence of disguised unemployment. What this also means, however, is that the introduction of small amounts of capital to substitute for labour at times of peak demand could release substantial quantities of workers for the industrial sector without agricultural output falling. If disguised unemployment is seasonal unemployment, the dynamic surplus may be very large indeed.

At least five 'types' of disguised unemployment can be distinguished:

- Unrealized potential output per worker due to low nutritional and health levels of the labour force
- Low levels of output per unit of labour input due to inadequate motivation for the cultivators to pursue maximization
- Low average product due to low aspirations for material income compared with leisure

■ Unemployment due to the lack of cooperating factors ('technological' unemployment)

■ Seasonal unemployment.

Even with a distinct classification of the causes of disguised unemployment, however, measurement will still be arbitrary depending on the investigator's judgement of the potential level of output if the causes of low output were to be removed. Ideally, studies of disguised unemployment should be micro-oriented, based on detailed information of actual and potential labour utilization, and with the assumptions of the analysis explicitly stated.

A reconciliation between those who argue that there is such a phenomenon of disguised unemployment, in the sense of a very low marginal product of labour in agriculture, and those who disagree, is provided by the distinction between **the amount of labour time employed and the number of persons employed**. In a wage-payment system it is extremely unlikely that labour would be used up to the point where its marginal product is zero. If the wage is positive, the marginal product will be positive too. But profit-maximizing behaviour is quite consistent with redundant labour. Labour is employed up to the point where the marginal product of a unit of *labour time* is equal to the wage, and **disguised unemployment takes the form of a small number of hours worked per person**. It is not that there is too much labour time but too many labourers spending it. Total output would fall if workers were drawn from the land unless those remaining worked longer hours to compensate. How much disguised unemployment is estimated to exist depends on what is regarded as a normal working day. Estimates may be subjective, as with the dynamic surplus, but unlimited supplies of labour exist in the classical sense provided those remaining on the land work harder or longer. Let us illustrate these points diagrammatically.

In Figure 5.9 total output is measured on the vertical axis above the origin, and the amount of labour time on the horizontal axis. Let L_1 be the point where the marginal product of labour time is equal to the subsistence wage corresponding to total output, Q. The number of workers is measured on the vertical axis below the origin, so that the tangent of the angle $0YL_1$ (tan a) gives the average number of hours worked by each unit of labour. If the tangent of the angle $0XL_1$ is regarded as the normal length of a working day so that the same output, Q, could be produced by X labour instead of Y, the amount of disguised unemployment would be equal to XY. It can easily be seen that if there was a reduction in the labour force from Y to t and the number of hours worked per worker remained the same (that is, tan $0tS$ = tan $0YL_1$), total output would fall from Q to P. If the normal working day is considered to be longer or shorter than the hours given by tan b, the amount of disguised unemployment will be greater or less than XY. Let us now give a practical example. Suppose a producer employs 10 workers ($Y = 10$), each doing 5 hours' work a day (tan a = 5), and that the marginal product of the 50th hour is equal to the subsistence wage (L_1 = 50). If one worker leaves (say Yt), total output will fall from Q to P unless the nine workers now do the 50 hours' work previously done by 10 workers, that is, the working day must be increased by five-ninths of an hour. The amount of disguised unemployment depends on what is considered to be a full day's work. If 10 hours is considered normal, then only 5 workers would be required to do 50 hours' work and 5 could be regarded as disguised unemployed.

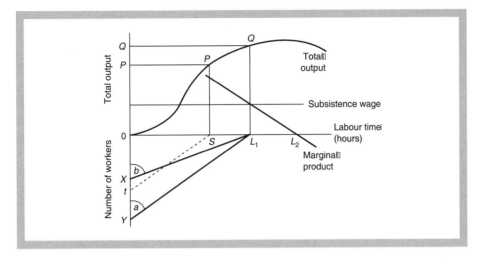

Figure 5.9 The dynamic surplus

The precise conditions under which the remaining labour force would supply more work effort have been formalized by Sen (1966). If workers are rational, they will work up to the point where the marginal utility of income from work (dU/dL) is equal to the marginal disutility of work (dV/dL). Now the marginal utility of income from work can be expressed as

$$\frac{dU}{dL} = \frac{dY}{dL} \cdot \frac{dU}{dY} \tag{5.14}$$

where dY/dL is the marginal product of labour and dU/dY is the marginal utility of income. Welfare maximization therefore implies that

$$\frac{dY}{dL} \cdot \frac{dU}{dY} = \frac{dV}{dL} \tag{5.15}$$

or

$$\frac{dY}{dL} = \frac{dV}{dL} \div \frac{dU}{dY} = \frac{\text{Marginal disutility of work}}{\text{Marginal utility of income}} \tag{5.16}$$

Sen defines the ratio of the marginal disutility of work to the marginal utility of income as the **real cost of labour**. Now consider Figure 5.10.

Equilibrium is at N where the marginal product is equal to the real cost of labour. The removal of one worker reduces total output from $0PXN$ to $0PX_1N_1$, and marginal product rises from X to X_1. Equilibrium will be restored again at N if the real cost of labour remains constant – that is, if the ratio of the marginal disutility of work to the marginal utility of income does not increase. If the real cost of labour rises, there will not be full compensation for output lost. In other words, disguised unemployment in the sense of *zero* marginal product (or full compensation for lost output) implies a **non-increasing marginal disutility of work and a non-diminishing marginal utility**

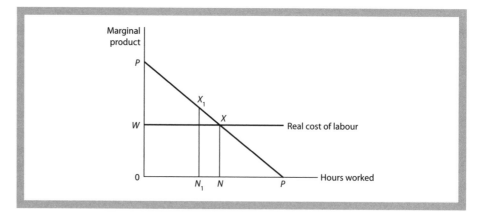

Figure 5.10 Effect of labour withdrawal

of income. Sen gives a number of reasons why this may be the case for people near subsistence with little work and a lot of leisure; for example, rising aspirations and more public expenditure on such things as education may prevent the marginal utility of income from falling, and higher incomes may prevent the marginal disutility of work from increasing if people are better fed.

The amount of underutilized labour is likely to be the greater, the less capitalistic the organization of agriculture. In fact, in the extreme situation of no wage-payment system with no competitive pressure and little desire to maximize, the distinction between a unit of labour and a unit of labour time becomes largely redundant, as in the classical model. It is perhaps this type of environment that the originators of the classical model primarily had in mind. In an extended family-type system, for example, the marginal product of both workers and labour time may be below the subsistence wage. It is the *average* product that matters for the group as a whole, not the product of the last worker or hour, and the average product may still be above the subsistence level when the marginal product of labour time is below it. It is difficult to represent both cases on the same diagram, but if the marginal product of labour is zero, the marginal product of labour time is bound to be zero (and probably negative), so we may continue to illustrate the argument in terms of labour time, as in Figure 5.11.

The basis of Figure 5.11 is the same as Figure 5.9. When the marginal product of labour time is zero at L_2 the average product of labour time is P_1, or PP_1 in excess of the subsistence wage P. The amount of labour time could be extended to L_3 without the average product of labour time falling below subsistence, and the amount of labour time could be made up of any combination of workers and hours worked. If the number of workers was Y_1 they could work hours equal to the tangent of $0Y_1L_3$ without the average product of labour time falling below subsistence. Even though the marginal product of labour time, L_2L_3, is negative, all workers can subsist if the total product is equally shared. A zero or negative marginal product of labour time is not inconsistent with rational worker behaviour if positive utility is attached to work regardless of the effect on output.

Suppose, as in Figure 5.12, that the marginal product of a unit of labour time is zero after four hours' work but the marginal disutility of leisure is still negative at this point. The worker may substitute work for leisure, working, say, 6 hours, despite the fact that the marginal product of labour time is negative after the fourth hour. If such behaviour is observed, the presumption must be that the marginal utility attached to

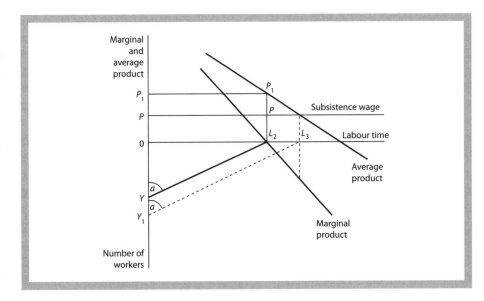

Figure 5.11 Maximum sustainable labour

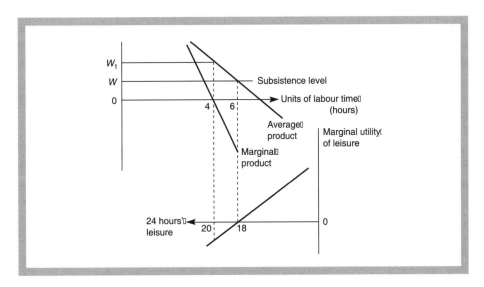

Figure 5.12 The possibility of negative marginal product

working exceeds the loss of utility resulting from a lower average product. The fact that people receive positive utility from work may partly explain why work habits in poor countries seem more leisurely than in advanced countries. What could be done in X hours is done in $X + Y$ hours.

As long as the marginal product of labour is zero, labour could be drawn from the land without total output falling. In fact in our example, with Y_1 workers working tan a hours, labour drawn from the land would increase total output because the marginal product of labour time is negative. Y_1Y labour could be released without the labour that remains working any longer or harder. If negative marginal product can exist in practice, this would be disguised unemployment of an extreme form. If labour time does not extend beyond the point of zero marginal product, however, we should reach our earlier conclusion that disguised unemployment takes the form of a small number of hours worked per person, which is perhaps more accurately described as 'underemployment'.

INCENTIVES AND THE COSTS OF LABOUR TRANSFER

Whether workers are willing to work more intensively to compensate for lost production as labour migrates, or whether capital is substituted for labour to raise productivity, requires some discussion of worker motivation and attitudes towards industrialization in general in a predominantly agricultural economy.

Some economic incentive will almost certainly be required to induce agricultural labour to work extra hours. At the least there will need to be goods with which to exchange their surplus production. It is sometimes argued, however, that peasant producers, accustomed to a traditional way of life, may not respond to such incentives – that their horizons are so limited that they have no desire to increase their surplus either by installing capital or by working longer hours. The corollary of this argument is that as labour productivity increases, workers will ultimately reduce the number of hours they work. This is the notion of the **backward-bending supply curve of effort**, illustrated in Figure 5.13. *SS* is the supply curve of effort relating hours worked to the wage, determined by productivity. Total income is equal to the product of hours worked and the wage. Up to income level *SWZX*, supply responds positively to the wage. Beyond the wage *SW*, however, fewer hours will be offered. This is the point where the positive substitution effect of work for leisure (leisure is more 'expensive' the higher the wage) is offset by a negative income effect because of low aspirations.

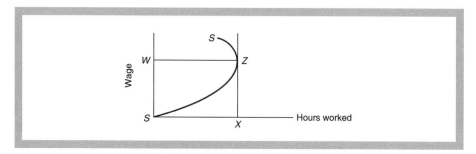

Figure 5.13 Backward-bending supply curve

A backward-bending supply curve of effort is not necessarily indicative, however, that peasants work for a fixed income and no more. The total income from work effort will still increase as long as the number of hours worked falls less than in proportion to the increased wage. But the need for incentives implies a claim on the community's real resources, which creates added difficulties for the argument that a pool of disguised unemployment can be used to build up 'productive' goods and expand the industrial sector in a 'costless' way. Not only may the opportunity cost of agricultural labour not be zero, but resource costs will also be involved in providing incentives to increased effort and productivity in order for resources to be released from agriculture in the first place. The resource costs

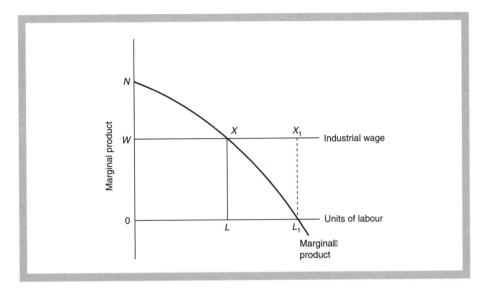

Figure 5.14 The social valuation of labour

will include the provision of investment goods in agriculture, consumer goods for peasant producers to buy and social capital in the industrial sector to cater for migrants.

All this has an important bearing on the question of the valuation of labour in surplus-labour economies when planning the social optimum allocation of resources and deciding on the degree to which activities in the industrial sector should be labour-intensive. Even if labour's opportunity cost is negligible, the resource costs of labour transference must be considered as a cost to the community in expanding the industrial sector.

There is also the question of increased consumption to consider. If the objective of a surplus-labour economy is to maximize growth, as opposed to the level of current consumption, the transference of labour will also involve a further 'cost' in terms of increased consumption because there will be a reduction in the size of the capitalist surplus if labour is valued at its opportunity cost. Consider Figure 5.14.

The diagram represents the capitalist sector of the economy. On the normal assumption of profit maximization, labour will be employed up to the point where the marginal product is equal to the industrial wage. The capitalist surplus is equal to *WNX*. But suppose the supply of labour to the industrial sector is assumed to be 'costless' to society and is given, by the planners, a notional (or shadow) wage of zero. In this planned system labour would be employed up to the point L_1. Given the industrial wage, *W*, and assuming the propensity to consume out of wages is unity, each additional unit of labour employed beyond *L* will involve consumption in excess of production. If LL_1 additional labour is employed, the size of the investible surplus would be reduced by XX_1L_1. It follows that in an economy geared to growth the relationship between the consumption and production of migrant labour must also be taken into account when estimating the costs to society of industrial expansion with surplus labour from agriculture. If at the margin additional saving is valued more than an additional unit of consumption, the cost of a unit of labour transferred from agriculture to industry must include an allowance for increased consumption. These matters are taken up more fully in Chapter 10 in the discussion of social cost-benefit analysis and the determination of the shadow wage.

1 What is the importance to economic development of rapid productivity growth in agriculture?

2 What factors hold back productivity growth in agriculture?

3 How could land reform help to raise agricultural productivity?

4 What is meant by 'marketable surplus'?

5 Explain why poor people tend to be risk-averse and reluctant to innovate.

6 In what sense is there disguised unemployment on the land?

7 Does disguised unemployment on the land mean that development using surplus labour is a relatively painless and costless process?

8 Compare and contrast the main features of Lewis's classical model of development with the neoclassical model.

9 Explain the continued process of rural–urban migration despite growing unemployment in urban areas.

10 In what ways do the agricultural and industrial sectors of an economy complement one another?

NOTES

1. For an excellent survey of the issues, see Dorner (1972). For some detailed case studies, see Lehmann (1974).
2. See also Askari and Cummings (1976) and Schiff and Montenegro (1999).
3. Lewis (1954, 1958). See also the symposium on the Lewis model to celebrate its 25th anniversary in the *Manchester School*, September 1979, and the symposium on the Lewis model after 50 years, *Manchester School*, December 2004.
4. The profit rate can be expressed as

$$P/K = \frac{(0/L - w/p)}{(K/L)}$$

   where P is profits, K is the quantity of capital, $0/L$ is the productivity of labour, w/p is the real wage and K/L is the capital–labour ratio. The profit rate will rise if $0/L$ rises and w/p remains the same (assuming no offsetting rise in K/L).
5. A formal algebraic model, with various extensions, may be found in Thirlwall (1986).
6. If the income elasticity of demand for industrial goods is greater than unity, and for agricultural goods less than unity, then the equilibrium growth rate for industry will exceed that for agriculture.
7. This is not a statistical probability since π is not bounded between zero and unity. The 'chance' of getting a job would be a better word to use.
8. Todaro (1971) uses the same notation, S, for the total urban labour force as for the supply of migrants. This can be confusing. We therefore use W for the total urban labour force and S for the supply of migrants.
9. Any values can be substituted as long as $w/r = 2$.
10. Barnum and Sabot (1977). Other early studies of the rural–urban migration process include Knight (1972). For a survey of studies, see Todaro (1976), Yap (1977) and Stark (1991).

Todaro gives an alternative way of evaluating whether urban unemployment will rise or not. It can be shown that the *level* of unemployment will rise if $\eta > g \times N/S$, where η is the period elasticity of induced migration with respect to the change in modern sector job probabilities, g is the growth of urban employment prior to the increase in job opportunities, N is the level of urban employment and S is the existing level of rural–urban migration. It can also be shown that the *rate* of urban unemployment will rise if $\eta > g \times W/S$, where W is the urban workforce.

WEBSITES ON AGRICULTURE

Food and Agricultural Organization www.fao.org
International Food Policy Research Institute www.ifpri.org
Consultative Group on International Agricultural Research www.cgiar.org
Inter-American Institute for Cooperation on Agriculture www.iicanet.org

6 Capital and technical progress

THE ROLE OF CAPITAL IN DEVELOPMENT

The capital stock of a country increases through the process of net investment (I), which is the difference between the country's net income in an accounting period (that is, gross income minus depreciation) and how much it consumes out of that income in the same period. The essence of capital accumulation is that it enhances a country's capacity to produce goods in the future and enables it to grow faster.

There are many types of capital goods. First, there are **plant and machinery** used in factories and offices, which yield no utility directly but produce consumption goods and services that do. Second, there is **infrastructure investment**, which partly provides goods and services directly, and at the same time makes other forms of investment more productive, for example transport facilities, telecommunications, power generation, the provision of water facilities and so on. Third, there is expenditure on **research and development (R&D)**, which may improve the productivity of labour or capital, or both. R&D can lead to new inventions and then to innovation – either **process**

innovation or **product innovation**. Process innovations make the production of existing products more efficient; product innovations involve the creation of new products that not only add to utility but also enhance productivity by enabling new ways of doing things, for example information technology. Fourth, there is **social expenditure** such as investment in health and education, which also provides some utility directly but at the same time makes individuals and society more productive. Indeed if capital is defined as any asset that generates an additional future stream of measurable income to society, many goods and services that might be thought of as primarily consumption goods ought strictly to be included as part of a country's capital stock. If cars, for example, or other consumer durable goods, save time and make people more efficient, part of the expenditure on them should be considered as an investment. Expenditure on housing is another example where private expenditure may be partly considered as consumption and partly investment, and the public provision of housing might be put in the category of social capital. Similarly if certain types of consumption goods are necessary as incentives to induce peasant producers in the agricultural sector, or workers elsewhere, to increase their productivity, they too ought to be considered as part of the capital stock.

If it is agreed, therefore, that the only way to build up a country's productive potential and raise per capita income is to expand the capacity for producing goods, this need not refer simply to the provision of physical capital such as plant and machinery, but also to roads, railways, power lines, water pipes, schools, hospitals, houses and even 'incentive' consumer goods such as consumer durables – all of which can contribute to increased productivity and higher living standards.

When using the production function approach to the study of the sources of growth or the macrodeterminants of growth, as described in Chapter 4, it is of the utmost importance to define capital as broadly as possible if the relation between capital accumulation and growth is not to be misconstrued. This is in addition to the point, which was also emphasized in Chapter 4, that capital may be the main vehicle for the introduction of technical progress in the productive system. In other words, capital accumulation is not only important in its own right, but is the major conduit for advances in knowledge, which in turn are also a major determinant of productivity growth.

Developing economies lay great emphasis on the importance of capital accumulation, and stress the need to raise the level of investment in relation to output. A glance at any national development plan will testify to this. Development is associated with industrialization and industrialization with capital accumulation. Many famous development economists also see investment as the most important single factor in the growth process. As we saw in Chapter 3, W. W. Rostow (1960) defines the process of 'take-off' into sustained growth in terms of a critical ratio of investment to national product, and Arthur Lewis (1955) has described the process of development as one of transforming a country from being a 5 per cent saver and investor to a 12 per cent saver and investor. It is common, in fact, for countries to calculate fairly precise ratios of investment to national income that will be required either to achieve a particular rate of growth or to prevent per capita income from falling. These calculations involve assumptions about the normal relation between capital and output, a relation that is formally expressed in the concept of the **capital–output ratio** (which we shall consider later). H. G. Johnson (1969) singles out capital accumulation in its widest sense as the distinguishing characteristic of development, and has described the structural transformation of economies as a generalized process of capital accumulation:

> The condition of being 'developed' consists of having accumulated, and having established, efficient social and economic mechanisms for maintaining and increasing large stocks of capital per head in the various forms. Similarly the condition of being 'underdeveloped' is characterised by the possession of relatively small stocks of the various kinds of capital.

The returns to investment in developing countries are potentially much higher than in developed countries, which already have large quantities of capital per head. In countries where specialization (the division of labour) is minimal, the scope for capital to permit more roundabout methods of production and increase productivity will be greater than where specialization has already reached a high level of sophistication. Moreover, in technologically backward countries the rate of growth of capital required to absorb new technology is likely to be greater than in advanced countries. By definition, technologically backward countries also have a backlog of technology to make up. Furthermore, in a labour-abundant economy with a low capital–labour ratio, the very act of *capital deepening* – giving each worker a little more capital to work with – may make a substantial difference to total product, much more so than in countries where the process of capital deepening has been a continuing process for some length of time. All these factors represent important contributions that capital can make to economic progress, which may be relatively more important the smaller is the initial capital stock of a country relative to its population. It is a familiar economic proposition that the scarcer one factor of production is in relation to another, the higher its productivity, all other things being equal.

Capital accumulation is also seen as an escape from the so-called 'vicious circle of poverty' – a circle of low productivity, leading to low per capita income, leading to a low level of saving per head, leading to a low level of capital accumulation per head, leading to low productivity. Low productivity is seen as the source of the 'vicious circle of poverty', and the point where the circle must be broken by capital accumulation.

Since productivity can be raised by other means as well, implicit in the argument is the pessimistic view that no reorganization of the existing factors of production would have much impact on output, and that technical progress is mainly embodied, therefore requiring net additions to the capital stock. Whether this pessimism is justified is an empirical question in the final analysis, but the emphasis placed by developing countries on capital accumulation is very real.[1]

THE CAPITAL–OUTPUT RATIO

The link between capital and output is embodied in the concept of the capital–output ratio, which can measure in physical units, or in value terms, either the average or the marginal relation between capital and output. The **average capital–output ratio** of an economy is the stock of capital divided by the annual flow of output (K/O), while the **marginal or incremental capital–output ratio (ICOR)** measures the relation between increments to the capital stock and increases in output ($\Delta K/\Delta O$ or $I/\Delta O$). If the gross value of a country's stock of capital is £100 billion and its gross annual income is £25 billion, the average capital–output ratio will be 4:1. If the economy is at full capacity, the incremental capital–output ratio will approximate to the average, so that in this example four *extra* units of capital will be required to produce an *additional* unit flow of output (in £).

With fluctuations in income, however, the average capital–output ratio will differ substantially from the ICOR. In periods of recession the average capital–output ratio will tend to be higher than its 'normal' value since the flow of output will be depressed in relation to the size of the capital stock, which is relatively fixed. But while the average ratio is still high at the start of the upturn of the business cycle, the incremental ratio will appear low. If the economy is working below capacity, very little extra capital will be needed to increase output, and substantial growth may be associated with relatively little capital accumulation. In attempting to calculate ICORs, the stage of the business cycle must always be borne in mind.

The dependence of the ICOR on the level of activity raises the question of whether it is legitimate to treat the capital–output ratio as an independent variable in the economic system, and to use the ratio as a parameter in investment planning. Is not the ratio the dependent variable in the system determined by the level of investment and the rate of growth? This is a fairly crucial question to consider, because it is common for countries to use an aggregate ICOR, and also incremental capital–output ratios for sectors of the economy, when deciding on the rate of investment necessary to achieve a particular target rate of growth of income. Yet if the ratio itself is determined by the rate of growth, is this permissible? As we shall come to see, a lot depends on the length of the time period over which investment is being planned.

Taking both time-series and cross-section data, there is substantial empirical evidence of a strong inverse relation between growth and the value of the ICOR and good theoretical reasons for believing that the ICOR is the dependent variable in the relation. Two main reasons can be advanced. First, the investment rate tends to be more stable than other factors, so that growth may increase or decrease while the rate of capital accumulation remains virtually unchanged. The inverse relation would be less marked if capital–output ratios were computed by taking a measure of capital services, rather than the stock of capital, but this is not normally done. Second, if the significance of non-capital inputs in the growth process is greater than that of capital, there will be an inverse relation between the investment rate and the capital–output ratio. This means that if the relation between growth and the investment rate is positive, the relation between growth and the capital–output ratio will be negative.

Let us illustrate these points by making use of the Cobb–Douglas production function. From the equation in its estimating form, $r_Y = r_T + \alpha r_K + \beta r_L$, the ICOR is given by

$$\frac{\Delta K}{\Delta O} = \frac{\Delta K / O}{r_T + \alpha r_K + \beta r_L}$$

where $\Delta K / O$ is the investment ratio. Now if $\Delta K / O$ is stable and r_T and r_L vary more than r_K, $\Delta K / \Delta O$ and r_Y will vary in opposite directions. Likewise, if the growth of the labour force and technical progress contribute more to growth than capital accumulation, $\Delta K / \Delta O$ and r_Y will vary in opposite directions. In the short run, therefore, a low measured ICOR more probably implies that growth has been rapid, and not that relatively rapid growth will be associated with a low ratio of investment to output because the ICOR is low.

The use of the incremental capital–output ratio for estimating the amount of investment required to increase output by a given amount was inspired by the work of **Harrod and Domar** (see Chapter 4 p. 130). Although their work was originally designed to establish the conditions for equilibrium growth, their fundamental equations have been put to various alternative uses. Harrod's basic growth equation is $gc = s$, where g is the rate of growth ($\Delta O/O$), c is the ICOR ($I/\Delta O$) and s is the savings ratio (S/O). By substituting terms it can be seen that the equation merely expresses the *ex post* identity that saving equals investment, which follows from the accounting identities that income equals consumption plus investment, and income equals consumption plus saving. Nonetheless, it is this equation that has been endlessly manipulated to give the savings (or investment) ratio (s) necessary to achieve a particular target rate of growth (g), given the value of c, and to calculate the value of c, given g and s. This is in spite of the fact that no causality is implied by the equation.

The Harrod equation certainly predicts an inverse relation between growth and the ICOR, but since c is assumed constant in Harrod's original model, it is the ICOR that determines growth and not the other way round.

It is not difficult to demonstrate that the exercise of calculating the savings and investment required to achieve a target rate of growth, given c, and the exercise of calculating c, given s and g, are fraught with danger. If the economy has been operating below capacity, there is no telling what is the 'true' value of c, and the investment needed in the short run to produce a given g cannot be calculated with the precision that the equation suggests. Similarly, it would be misleading to calculate c by dividing the savings or investment ratio by the rate of growth of output. Apart from the fact that the economy may not be working at full capacity, the assumption is being made that all increases in output are attributable to increases in capital, which is untrue. The productivity of capital ($\Delta O/I$) is overstated, and, since the ICOR ($I/\Delta O$) is the reciprocal of the productivity of capital, the ICOR is understated.

This latter problem can be overcome by making the distinction between the actual ICOR, as measured above, and the adjusted ICOR, which is the ICOR adjusted for increases in the supply of other factors (for example, an increase in the labour force). The concept of the adjusted capital–output ratio takes care of what otherwise appears to be a conflict between the observed productivity of capital and that implied by the value of the actual ICOR. For example, suppose that a country's investment rate is 15 per cent and its growth rate is 5 per cent, giving an actual capital–output ratio of 3:1. This would suggest a productivity of capital of 33.3 per cent. But, typically, the rate of return on capital is much less than this. The reason is that other factors contribute to growth.

Suppose that the growth of the labour force is such that it contributes 3.5 percentage points to the 5 per cent growth rate, leaving 1.5 percentage points to be 'explained' by capital (assuming no technical progress). In this case, with a 15 per cent investment ratio, the adjusted capital–output ratio is 10:1, giving a rate of return on capital of 10 per cent. The actual capital–output ratio is 3:1, but if there was no growth of the labour force, the adjusted capital–output ratio tells us that an investment ratio of 50 per cent would be required to grow at 5 per cent. In short, if other factors remain unchanged, much more investment is required to achieve a target rate of growth than is implied by calculations of c from the Harrod equation.

The adjusted ICOR is sometimes referred to as the **net incremental capital–output ratio**; that is, the ICOR on the assumption that other factors do not change. Net or adjusted ICORs are difficult to estimate, but clearly the variability of the factors that cooperate with capital in the productive system can play havoc with calculations of the actual ICOR from data on past growth and the investment ratio alone.

When calculations are made of saving and investment requirements to achieve target rates of growth for, say, a 5-year to 10-year planning period, the normal assumption is that the incremental capital–output ratio will approximate to the average and that over the long term the factors that cooperate with capital will be forthcoming, as in the past. For a planning period in excess of 5 years this assumption may not be unreasonable. Criticisms of the use of the incremental capital–output ratio in investment planning relate more to its use in the short run because of its cyclical variability.

On the other hand the ICOR may also be subject to secular change. As countries grow richer, the ratio of capital to labour rises because capital grows faster than labour, and if there are diminishing returns to capital the capital–output ratio will rise. This is the neoclassical story. At the same time, however, various forms of technical progress, economies of scale, and improvements in the quality of labour will tend to raise the productivity of capital, causing the capital–output ratio to fall. There will also be shifts in the pattern of demand and the distribution of resources between sectors with different productivities, which will affect movements in the ratio. Shifts in demand towards service activities requiring less capital per unit of output would reduce the aggregate ICOR. These are all theoretical possibilities. In practice, it seems from the evidence that long-run changes in the capital–output ratio are quite small, and that the factors leading to increases and decreases in the ratio tend to offset one another. This is one of the major conclusions of 'new' growth theory discussed in Chapter 4. The tendency towards diminishing returns to capital as countries become richer is offset by externalities to education and R&D expenditure, which increase the productivity of capital and prevent the capital–output ratio from rising.

If the ratio does stay fairly constant over long periods, capital requirements for growth may be estimated with some accuracy over a long enough time horizon. Planning investment requirements for anything less than a 5-year period on the assumption of a stable capital–output ratio, however, may be asking for trouble.

Finally and briefly, other more obvious dangers may be mentioned of using the capital–output ratio as a basis for investment planning. First, exclusive attention to the capital–output ratio may exaggerate the need for investment when output may be increased by other, simpler means. For example, before calculating the additional capital required to produce a target output, it would be wiser for a developing economy to think first of the output that might reasonably be expected from increased utilization of existing factors and better methods applied to old capital. Second, the accuracy of any calculations of the capital–output ratio may be called into question in backward economies that lack comprehensive and reliable statistics. Third, it must be remembered that the aggregate ICOR is bound to disguise sectoral differences, and when calculating overall investment requirements some allowance should be made for the changing sectoral distribution of resources.

TECHNICAL PROGRESS

The term 'technical progress' is used in several different senses to describe a variety of phenomena; but three in particular can be singled out. First, economists use the term to refer to the *effects* of changes in technology, or more specifically to the role of technical change in the growth process. It is in this sense that we used the term in Chapter 4; that is, as an umbrella term to cover all those factors which contribute to the growth of 'total' productivity. Second, technical progress is used by economists in a narrow specialist sense to describe the *character* of technical improvements, and is often prefaced for this purpose by the adjectives 'labour-saving', 'capital-saving' or 'neutral'. Third, technical progress is used more literally to refer to *changes* in technology itself, defining technology as useful knowledge pertaining to the art of production. Used in this sense, the emphasis is on describing improvements in the design, sophistication and performance of plant and machinery, and the economic activities through which improvements come about – research, invention, development and innovation.

Having already discussed technical progress in the first sense in Chapter 4, we shall concentrate here on the narrow specialist descriptions of technical progress, and on how societies progress technologically.

CAPITAL- AND LABOUR-SAVING TECHNICAL PROGRESS

The classification of technical progress as to whether it is capital-saving, labour-saving or neutral owes its origins primarily to the work of Harrod (1948) and Hicks (1932). Their criteria of classification differ, however. **Harrod's classification of technical progress** employs the concept of the capital–output ratio. Given the rate of profit, technical change is said to be capital-saving if it lowers the capital–output ratio, labour-saving if it raises the capital–output ratio, and neutral if it leaves the capital–output ratio unchanged.

The nature of technical progress by this criterion will be an amalgam of the effect of 'pure' technical change on factor combinations and the effect of the substitution of capital for labour (as, for example, relative factor prices change). As such, Harrod neutrality at the aggregate level is quite consistent with capital-saving technical progress at the industry level. In fact most of the evidence for advanced countries suggests that *if* technical progress is neutral in the aggregate in the Harrod sense, this must be due to substitution of capital for labour because 'pure' technical advance has saved capital. The substitution of capital for labour takes place because as countries become richer the price of labour relative to capital tends to rise, which not only induces a 'pure' substitution effect but also encourages inventive effort towards saving labour, which is becoming relatively expensive (and scarce).

But there is some dispute among economists as to what the aggregate capital–output ratio shows because of potential biases in the estimates. The difficulty stems from the perennial problem of defining capital. If certain expenditures, which ought properly to be regarded as adding to the capital stock, are excluded from the measurement of capital, and these expenditures have grown faster than measured capital, the capital–output ratio will be biased downwards. Thus while technical progress may appear neutral in the Harrod sense (or even capital-saving because of a declining capital–output ratio), it may nevertheless be capital-using, and would appear so if the capital stock were more appropriately measured.

One notable item not conventionally included in the measurement of the capital stock is investment in human capital. In most advanced countries during the last hundred years, investment in human beings has grown faster than physical capital. To the extent that this is true, estimates of the capital–output ratio are biased downwards and would probably show a slight upward trend during the twentieth century if investment in human capital was included in the measurement of capital. We merely stress again the need for defining capital as meaningfully as possible if the relation between factor supplies and growth is to be properly understood.

Hicks' classification of technical progress takes the concept of the marginal rate of substitution between factors, which is the rate at which one factor must be substituted for another, leaving output unchanged. The marginal rate of substitution is given by the ratio of the marginal products of factors. Holding constant the ratio of labour to capital, technical progress is said to be **capital-saving** if it raises the marginal product of labour in greater proportion than the marginal product of capital; **labour-saving** if it raises the marginal product of capital in greater proportion than the marginal product of labour; and **neutral** if it leaves unchanged the ratio of marginal products. These definitions are illustrated in Figures 6.1, 6.2 and 6.3, respectively.

It will be recalled from Chapter 4 that technical progress on a production-function map is represented by shifts in the function towards the origin, showing that the same output can be produced with fewer inputs, or that the same volume of inputs can produce a greater output. According to the shape of the new production function, fewer of either one or both factors will be required to produce the same output. In the case of neutral technical progress, a quantity of both factors can be dispensed with. In the case of non-neutral technical progress, if only one factor is saved technical progress is said to be *absolutely* labour- or capital-saving. If fewer of both factors are required, technical progress is said to be *relatively* labour- or capital-saving.

Consider first **neutral technical progress** (Figure 6.3). The ray from the origin, or expansion path, $0Z$, goes through the minimum-cost point of tangency between the production function YY and the factor–price ratio line KL. With neutral technical progress the production function shifts such that the new point of tangency at the same factor–price ratio lies on the same expansion path. This means that the ratio of marginal products is the same at the same capital–labour ratio, and equal proportionate amounts of the two factors are saved. The condition for neutral technical progress is simply that the new production function is parallel to the old.

With **labour-saving technical change** (Figure 6.2) the ratio of the marginal product of capital to the marginal product of labour rises such as to shift the minimum-cost point of tangency from the old expansion path $0Z$ to a new expansion path $0Z_1$. At P_1, where the new production function cuts the old expansion path, the ratio of the marginal product of labour to capital is lower than at P. P_1 is not an equilibrium point and it will pay producers to move to point Q, substituting capital for labour. The ratio of marginal products has not remained unchanged at a constant labour to capital ratio, and L_2L_3 labour is saved. The isoquants have been so drawn as to keep the volume of capital the same, but this is purely incidental.

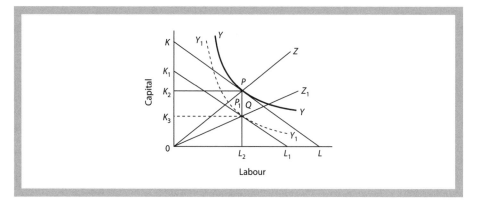

Figure 6.1 Capital-saving technical progress

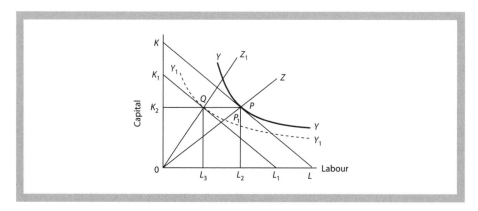

Figure 6.2 Labour-saving technical progress

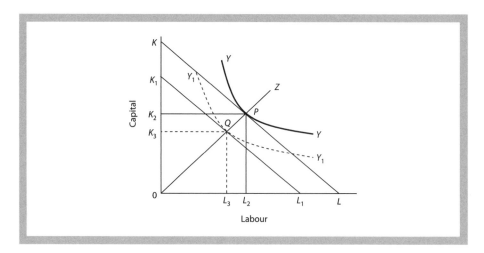

Figure 6.3 Neutral technical progress

Capital-saving technical progress (Figure 6.1) may be described in an exactly analogous fashion. In this case the ratio of the marginal product of labour to the marginal product of capital rises and the shift in the production function is such that the minimum-cost point of tangency now lies to the right of the old expansion path. At P_1, where the new production function cuts the old expansion path, the ratio of the marginal product of labour to capital is higher than at P. Again, P_1 is not an equilibrium point and it will pay producers to move to point Q, substituting labour for capital. The ratio of marginal products has not remained unchanged at a constant labour–capital ratio, and in this case K_2K_3 capital is saved.

As with Harrod technical progress, it is difficult to know what form Hicks technical progress takes in practice, largely because of identification problems. While the classification is analytically distinct, how does one distinguish empirically between a change in factor proportions due to a shift in the production function and a change in factor proportions due to a change in relative prices? Hicks himself seemed to be of the view that technical progress is relatively labour-saving, but the indirect evidence we have for this is slight. For example, given the magnitude of the rise in the price of labour relative to capital and an elasticity of substitution of close to unity, labour could not have maintained or increased its share of the national income (as it has done slightly in some advanced countries) if technical progress was markedly biased in the labour-saving direction. If technical progress is biased in one direction or another, its major impact will be on factor utilization if the price of factors is not flexible. The type of technology employed, and the factor proportions it entails, must bear a major responsibility for the high level of unemployment and underemployment in developing countries, as described in Chapter 3. The case for the use of more labour-intensive techniques is discussed in Chapter 12.

HOW SOCIETIES PROGRESS TECHNOLOGICALLY

Improvements in the art of production, which is the most literal interpretation of technical progress, result from a combination of **research, invention, development** and **innovation**. Research and invention are the activities that 'create' knowledge, and development and innovation are the activities that apply new knowledge to the task of production. These are all basically economic activities. But the study of the way in which societies progress technologically, and the speed of progress, is not only the preserve of the economist.

The economist can identify the mainsprings of progress, but their pervasiveness and acceptance in societies is not a purely economic matter. The spread of new knowledge, for example, depends on its rate of *adoption* and *diffusion* and this raises questions of individual motivation, the willingness to assimilate new ideas and to break with custom and tradition, which impinge heavily on territory occupied by development sociologists. The relative importance of different factors contributing to progress, and the speed of progress itself, will vary from country to country according to its stage of development and a whole complex of social and economic forces. Moreover, many of the mainsprings of technological progress are not mutually exclusive. At the risk of excessive simplification, attention here will be confined to four main sources of progress that are of potential significance to any society.

One major source of improvement in technology and progress is the **inventive and innovative activity** of the native population. All societies are endowed to some degree with a potential supply of inventors, innovators and risk-takers, and in the absence of imported technology and personnel, it is on the emergence of this class of person that technological progress will primarily depend during the early stages of development. Economic backwardness in many countries may quite legitimately be traced back to a relative shortage of inventors, innovators and risk-takers. It is fairly well established that some cultures and some environments are more amenable to change than others, and in the past have produced a greater supply of entrepreneurs. The view is frequently expressed that the major source of growth during Britain's industrial revolution was primarily technological progress fostered by an abundant supply of inventors, innovators, entrepreneurs and risk-takers, with the accumulation of capital playing an essentially secondary role. The great Austrian economist, Joseph Schumpeter (1934, 1943), laid great stress on the role of the entrepreneur and innovation in the development process. Ultimately, however, it is the lag between the creation of knowledge and its adoption, and the rate of dissemination of new knowledge, that most directly affects the rate of measured technical progress between countries; and these two facets of innovation are intimately connected with the attitudes of society at large.

For Schumpeter, progress results from what he calls the 'process of creative destruction', which is bound up with innovation and instigated by competition. Innovation, in turn, is the driving force behind competition. But innovation requires decision-takers and hence his complementary stress on the role of the entrepreneur. A characteristic of many poor countries is a shortage of decision-takers, a relative lack of competitive spirit and a general aversion to risk-taking. These may be partly cultural traits and also partly, if not mainly, a function of the stage of development itself. The characteristics commonly associated with business dynamism are themselves a function of business, and more particularly the form of organization we call 'capitalism'.

There is an enormous technological divide in the world economy which acts as a serious barrier to narrowing the gap between rich and poor countries. A small number of countries (accounting for about 15 per cent of the world's population) produce nearly 50 per cent of the world's technological innovations. A number of other countries (containing 50 per cent of the world's population) are able to adopt some or all of these technologies. The remaining countries (containing one-third of the world's poorest people) are virtually entirely excluded from technological progress. These latter countries are also the areas of the world most affected by low agricultural productivity, malnutrition and disease. They need technology to raise productivity and to improve health, but cannot afford or assimilate it.

To acquire technology, countries can import it embodied in capital and consumer goods; they can obtain it on licence from patent holders, or they can attract foreign direct investment (FDI) which brings technology with it. The spread of technology and ideas may also be expected to come about naturally in the general process of commercial intercourse and the exchange of information through trade. This is one of the dynamic gains from trade (see Chapter 16). But not all countries have equal access to technology. Geography, culture, and the quality of human capital matters. The speed with which modern technology is absorbed by economically backward countries will depend on the same class of factors as the diffusion of knowledge within countries – which in the final analysis amounts to the receptiveness of all sections of the community to change, and the ability to assimilate. Some economists argue that the World Bank should move away from lending money to countries, and instead lend money specifically for knowledge creation and assimilation.

LEARNING

A third means by which societies progress technologically, gradually raising their efficiency and productivity, is through the process of '**learning by doing**', which refers to the accumulation of experience by workers, managers and owners of capital in the course of production, which enables productive efficiency to be improved in the future. It is a learning process that Adam Smith referred to when discussing the **division of labour** (see Chapter 4). Smith stressed the importance of the division of labour for three main reasons: as a means of improving the dexterity of workers; to save the time lost in the absence of specialization; and to encourage the invention of machines that facilitate and abridge labour to improve the productivity of labour. All these advantages of the division of labour are part of a learning process. Labour improves its skill through specialization and work experience, and becomes more adept at the job in hand. Managers see deficiencies in organization, which can subsequently be remedied; and on the basis of accumulated knowledge they are also able to embody more productive techniques in the capital stock.

Learning may be regarded as either endogenous or exogenous, or both, depending on the factor of production considered. If existing labour and existing capital are subject to a learning process, then learning by doing may be regarded as exogenous and part of disembodied technical progress. If, however, it is assumed that learning enters the productive system only through the addition of new factors, then learning by doing must be regarded as endogenous. This is the basis of Arrow's capital model (1962), from which the term 'learning by doing' originates. His hypothesis with respect to capital is that at any moment of time new capital goods incorporate all the knowledge then available, based on accumulated experience, but once built their productive efficiency cannot be altered by subsequent learning.

The endogenous model may be appropriate in the case of capital but is much less relevant in the case of labour. It is in relation to labour that most research into the learning process has been conducted. The notion of the **learning curve**, or progress function, which has been found in many industries, relates direct labour input per unit of output to cumulative output as the measure of experience. Typically, labour input per unit of output is found to decline by between 10 and 20 per cent for each doubling of cumulative output, with a corresponding rise in the productivity of labour. For any one product, of course, learning cannot go on at the same rate for ever, but since product types are constantly changing it is probably safe to conclude that at the aggregate level, over time, there is no limit to the learning process. In production function studies of the sources of growth, there is no easy way of adjusting the labour-input series for learning to include it as part of the contribution of labour to growth. It remains part of the 'residual factor' in the growth process.

INVESTMENT IN HUMAN CAPITAL: EDUCATION

We turn now to the relation between technological progress and improvements in the health, education and skills of the labour force, or what is commonly called **investment in human capital**.

Investment in human capital takes many different forms, including expenditure on health facilities, on-the-job and institutional training and retraining, formally organized education, study programmes and adult education, and so on. Investment in human capital can overcome many of the characteristics of the labour force that act as impediments to greater productivity, such as poor health, illiteracy, unreceptiveness to new knowledge, fear of change, a lack of incentive and immobility. Improvements in the health, education and skill of labour can increase considerably the productivity and earnings of labour and may be preconditions for the introduction of more sophisticated, advanced technology applied to production. The capacity to absorb physical capital may be limited, among other things, by investment in human capital. It is in this respect that there is likely to be a close interrelationship between the mainsprings of technological progress.

We focus here on the relation between education and growth, and the importance of education in the development process. We shall then give some estimates of the rates of return to investment in education in developing countries according to type of education and level of per capita income.

There are three main ways in which education can improve growth performance:

■ Education improves the quality of labour, and also the quality of physical capital through the application of knowledge.
■ Education has spillover effects (externalities) on other sections of society which offset diminishing returns to capital.
■ Education is one of the most important inputs into R&D and for attracting FDI.

There are three main methods of estimating the contribution of education to growth:

■ Measuring the contribution that education makes to the difference in earnings of individuals
■ The production-function approach
■ The use of macrodeterminants of growth equations.

The first method involves constructing a quality-weighted index of the labour force, where quality is measured by the contribution that education makes to the difference in the earnings of individuals as a measure of productivity. The approach, pioneered by Denison (1962), involves two steps. The first involves gathering information on the distribution of the labour force by amounts of schooling at different dates. The second step involves collecting information on income differences between education cohorts with different amounts of schooling embodied in them, which are then used as weights to derive an index of the improvement in the quality of labour due to education on the assumption that a certain percentage of differences in earnings is due to differences in the amount of education.

Suppose, for instance, that the earnings differential between those with 8 years' schooling and those with 10 years' schooling is 20 per cent, that one-half of the difference is assumed to be due to the extra 2 years' schooling, and that a person with 8 years' schooling is treated as one unit; then the person with 10 years' education is counted as $1 + (0.5 \times 0.2) = 1.1$ units. The growth of the quality of labour due to education over a given period can then be estimated and its contribution to measured growth calculated. For example, suppose that the growth in the quality of labour is estimated to be 1 per cent per annum, that the elasticity of output with respect to labour is 0.7, and the annual average growth rate of the economy is 3 per cent. This gives a contribution of education to measured growth of 23 per cent, that is, $(0.7 \times 1.0)/3.0 = 0.23$.

The approach is not without its difficulties. The proportion of earnings differences assumed to be due to differences in the amounts of education between individuals is arbitrary, and if the figure is too high this will give an upward bias to the contribution of education. On the other hand there are other reasons why the approach underestimates the contribution of education:

- The methodology employed ignores the role of education in maintaining the *average* quality of the labour force.
- No allowance is made for improvements in the *quality* of education.
- There are the *'spillovers'* from education to consider, such as the contribution of education to knowledge and its diffusion throughout society.

The second method for estimating the contribution of education to growth, and also the rate of return to educational expenditure, is to use the production-function approach outlined in Chapter 4 (see equation (4.23)). All that is required is a measure of education expansion to be included in the production function. The contribution of education to measured growth is then the rate of growth of the education variable multiplied by the elasticity of output with respect to the education variable. In estimating form, the production function with the growth of education included is written as

$$r_Y = r_T + ar_K + \beta r_L + \gamma r_E \tag{6.1}$$

where r_E is the rate of growth of education, and γ is the elasticity of output with respect to education. The rate of return to education would then be measured as

$$\frac{\Delta Y}{\Delta E} = \gamma \frac{\bar{Y}}{\bar{E}} \tag{6.2}$$

where $\bar{Y}$ and $\bar{E}$ are the mean levels of output and the education variable, respectively.

For example, suppose that the mean level of output over a period was £100 million, that the mean level of expenditure on education was £5 million, and that the elasticity of output with respect to education (γ) was 0.01. The rate of return would then be 0.2 or 20 per cent, that is, $(0.01)(100/5) = 0.2$.

The third method for estimating the contribution of education to growth comes from 'new' growth theory, discussed in Chapter 4, in which the stock of education (measured by enrolment rates, or number of years of schooling) is included as a variable to explain differences in growth rates between countries using large samples of countries. A simple cross-section estimating equation would be of the form:

$$g = a + b(PCY) + c(education) \tag{6.3}$$

where g is the average growth rate of countries over, say, a 20-year period; PCY is the initial level of per capita income of countries, and (*education*) measures the proportion of the age group enrolled in primary or secondary schools in each country, or the average years of schooling. The coefficient, c, then measures the contribution of a 1 percentage point difference in school enrolment rates, or years of schooling, to the difference in growth rates between countries. Barro's (1991) pioneer study using this approach, and adopted by others (see Table 4.7, p. 158), suggested that each additional year of schooling was associated with a 0.3 percentage point faster growth of per capita income over the period 1960–90. These so-called 'macro determinants of growth' studies also include a number of other variables, and the contribution of education to growth sometimes remains a significant variable and sometimes not. The fast growth of the East Asian economies in the last decades is often attributed to their heavy investment in education.

But emphasis on the role of education in the growth process predates 'new' growth theory. In the post-war years, it was Denison, and T. W. Schultz in his Presidential address to the American Economic Association in 1961 (see Schultz, 1961), who first highlighted the importance of education for growth with quantitative evidence. According to Schultz, the stock of education in the United States rose by approximately 850 per cent between 1900 and 1956 compared with an increase in reproducible capital of 450 per cent. He acknowledged the difficulties of estimating the rate of return to education, but argued that even when every conceivable cost is considered, and all expenditure is treated as investment and none as consumption,[2] the return on investment in education is at least as high as, if not higher than, the return on investment in non-human capital. Denison estimated a contribution of education to the growth of per capita income of 40 per cent.

It is the apparent importance of education in the historical growth process of developed countries that has invoked the response that investment in human capital may be as important as investment in physical capital in developing countries. The empirical evidence seems to support this view. In 1980 a World Bank survey concluded that 'studies have shown that economic returns on investment in education seem, in most instances, to exceed returns on alternative kinds of investment, and that developing countries often have higher returns than the developed ones'.[3] Some estimates of the rate of return to education in developing countries are given in Tables 6.1 and 6.2, compiled by Psacharopoulos (1994) from the extensive research done in several developing countries. Table 6.1 shows the social and private returns on investment in primary, secondary and higher education by continent. Table 6.2 gives the same information according to the level of per capita income of countries.

There are several interesting and important conclusions to be derived from the statistics. The first is that the highest rate of return comes from investment in primary education. This is consistent with the observation that one of the strongest associations in developing countries is between the level and rate of growth of per capita income and the proportion of the population in primary education.[4] Traditional customs and attitudes cannot be changed significantly until a large section of the community at a fairly young age is exposed to new ideas and ways of doing things, and there can be very little progress at

Table 6.1 Returns on investment in education, by continent, early 1990s

Country	Social			Private		
	Prim.	Sec.	Higher	Prim.	Sec.	Higher
Sub-Saharan Africa	24.3	18.2	11.2	41.3	26.6	27.8
Asia*	19.9	13.3	11.7	39.0	18.9	19.9
Europe/Middle East/North Africa*	15.5	11.2	10.6	17.4	15.9	21.7
Latin America/Caribbean	17.9	12.8	12.3	26.2	16.8	19.7
OECD	14.4	10.2	8.7	21.7	12.4	12.3
World	18.4	13.1	10.9	29.1	18.1	20.3

* Non-OECD.
Source: G. Psacharopoulos, 'Returns to Investment in Education: A Global Update', *World Development*, September 1994.

Table 6.2 Returns on investment in education, by level of *per capita* income, early 1990s

Country	Mean *per capita* (US$)	Social			Private		
		Prim.	Sec.	Higher	Prim.	Sec.	Higher
Low-income ($610 or less)	299	23.4	15.2	10.6	35.2	19.3	23.5
Lower middle-income (to $2,449)	1,402	18.2	13.4	11.4	29.9	18.7	18.9
Upper middle-income (to $7,619)	4,184	14.3	10.6	9.5	21.3	12.7	14.8
High-income ($7,620 or more)	13,100	n.a.	10.3	8.2	n.a.	12.8	7.7
World	2,020	20.0	13.5	10.7	30.7	17.7	19.0

Source: G. Psacharopoulos, 'Returns to Investment in Education: A Global Update', *World Development*, September 1994.

all without basic literacy and numeracy. The rate of return then declines with the level of schooling. Primary, secondary and tertiary enrolment rates are shown in Table 3.5 (p. 81).

Secondly, it will be noticed that the rate of return on education at all levels tends to decline with the level of development, as measured by per capita income. Since enrolment rates tend to be higher in developed countries than in developing countries, this suggests diminishing returns from expenditure on education at all levels.

A third important observation is that the social return is invariably lower than the private return. This is because most of the costs of education, at least at the primary and secondary level, are not borne by the individual, but by the state. In higher education in high-income countries, however, the private and social returns are close because many of the direct costs are borne by students and there is a high opportunity cost in the form of foregone earnings. The social return on higher education in developed countries is very close to the social discount rate, that is, 8–10 per cent.

Overall, it can be concluded that investment in education in all countries is both privately and socially profitable – the more so, the less developed the country. A social return to investment in primary education in developing countries of 20 per cent or more is very high indeed.

WOMEN'S EDUCATION

This discussion has made no distinction between the education of men and women. In most developing countries, however, there is still an enormous gender gap in the provision of educational opportunities, and in the labour market, with women considerably disadvantaged. This is reflected in the statistics for primary and secondary school enrolment rates, and in levels of literacy, as shown in Table 6.3. One of the major Millennium Development Goals outlined in Chapter 1 is to eliminate gender disparity in primary and secondary education, preferably by 2005 and in all levels of education no later than 2015.

Table 6.3 Educational provision and literacy, males and females, 1997

Country	Prim. school enrolment (%)		Sec. school enrolment (%)		Adult illiteracy (%)	
	Males	Females	Males	Females	Males	Females
All developing countries	88.2	82.9	66.0	54.8	19.8	37.1
Least developed countries	66.0	54.8	37.3	24.6	41.4	61.9
Sub-Saharan Africa	60.9	51.8	47.1	35.8	34.0	50.4
Arab States	90.2	82.1	66.8	56.8	29.7	53.6
East Asia	99.8	99.8	75.5	66.4	9.2	24.6
South-East Asia and Pacific	98.4	97.5	59.8	56.9	7.3	15.6
South Asia	83.8	72.1	65.7	46.0	34.6	61.4
Latin America & Caribbean	94.3	92.4	65.0	65.8	12.1	13.8

Source: UNDP, *Human Development Report 1999* (New York: United Nations, 1999).

The underinvestment in women's education can be explained partly by cultural factors, but also by economic factors. Because women have inferior work opportunities, the costs of educating women are not so easily recouped, and the rate of return is low – at least, the private return. Families see greater returns from investing in the education of boys. From a social point of view, however, the returns to investment in the education of females could be high. The education of women is not only important in its own right for improving the entitlements and capabilities of women, but it has important direct and indirect effects through increasing the supply of skilled labour and leading to reductions in fertility and population growth (see Chapter 8).

To conclude the discussion of education, it needs to be said that the fact that the capacity of a country to absorb physical capital and technological progress may be constrained by the availability of human capital does not necessarily mean it should be given preferential treatment. All types of capital formation need to be considered together and carried out simultaneously. Ultimately, the amount of resources devoted to investment in human capital is an allocative problem that each country must decide for itself on the basis of a number of considerations, of which the rate of return would be one. Other important considerations would be the type of educated workforce that might be required in the future to avoid skill bottlenecks on the one hand, and unemployment on the other, if the pattern of demand and the balance between genders is changing.

INFRASTRUCTURE INVESTMENT

Another major type of investment that is very important to developing countries is infrastructure investment. Just as the productivity of physical capital depends on investment in human capital, so it also depends on the existence of infrastructure investment – for example, in transport and power facilities. Good infrastructure improves productivity and reduces production costs in the private sector. Apart from this obvious benefit, the adequacy of infrastructure can make a crucial difference to a country's development programme in a number of ways, such as diversifying production, expanding trade, improving environmental conditions, coping with population growth and reducing poverty.

The World Bank's *World Development Report 1994* was devoted to the topic of infrastructure for development. Currently, developing countries invest approximately $300 billion a year in new infrastructure – transport, power, water, sanitation, telecommunications, irrigation and so on, equal to 20 per cent of total investment and approximately 4 per cent of GDP – and the need for such investment is still huge. One billion people still lack access to clean water, two billion people lack access to sanitation and electric power, and transport facilities are still very rudimentary in many developing countries.

The need for different types of infrastructure also changes with development. Figure 6.4 shows the composition of infrastructure investment in low-income, middle-income and high-income countries. As development proceeds, the share of power, roads and telecommunications increases relative to basic services such as water and irrigation.

Most infrastructure investment is undertaken by governments. The public sector owns, operates and finances virtually all infrastructure because it is either regarded as a natural monopoly or a public good. Without competition and accountability, however, there can be a great deal of inefficiency and waste. The underutilization of capacity can be a major problem in transport and power because of lack of maintenance. The World Bank calculates that raising operating efficiency to best-practice levels could save over $50 billion a year, and that the greater private provision of infrastructure and the recoupment of costs from users could reduce government subsidies by over $100 billion.

The Bank calls for a shift of emphasis 'from increasing the quantity of infrastructure stocks to improving the quality of infrastructure services', and a change of thinking

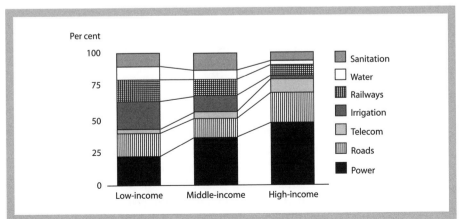

Source: World Bank, World Development Report 1994 (New York: Oxford University Press, 1994).

Figure 6.4 The composition of infrastructure

from the view that infrastructure services can only be provided by government. It makes three major recommendations: the wider application of commercial principles, including managerial autonomy and the setting of performance targets; the introduction of more competition, for example arranging for suppliers to compete for an entire market; and the increased involvement of users so that suppliers respond to user needs.

TECHNOLOGY AND THE DEVELOPING COUNTRIES

Most technological improvement originates from developed countries. The OECD countries spend over $500 billion a year on R&D, which is more than the GDP of Africa, and accounts for more than 90 per cent of patents issued. If developing countries are to develop their own technology, there needs to be the right institutional environment, including an incentive structure through patents, sound infrastructure, political stability to attract investment funds, and the availability of credit. Some of the technological leaders among developing countries include South Korea, Malaysia, China, Mexico, Thailand, Philippines, Brazil and Indonesia.

Technology is currently making a contribution to development in three major fields: agriculture, health and information and communications. In agriculture, the impact of the 'Green Revolution' in the 1960s and 1970s has now diminished, but on the horizon is biotechnology with the potential to end world hunger through the use of genetically modified (GM) foods and crops. The advantage of GM technology is that it allows the transfer of traits between unrelated species. For example, a gene in one species associated with the ability to resist drought can be directly transferred into the genetic code of another species. We now have GM crops more resistant to viruses and insects and more tolerant of herbicides; and in the future we could have food with extra vitamin and protein and even vaccines to combat malnutrition and disease. In the late 1990s China gave 26 approvals for GM crops including transgenic peppers, tomatoes, rice and cotton. China has the advantage of being an authoritarian regime. Other countries – including India, China's main economic rival – have had to deal with public protests against GM technology, with invasion of field trials and burning of GM crops.

In health, new technology has been the biggest single factor in reducing mortality and increasing life expectancy in developing countries. Important discoveries include vaccines against influenza, smallpox, polio, measles, tuberculosis etc; antibiotics (penicillin); and oral rehydration therapy which was originally developed in Bangladesh and has saved millions of babies from dying from diarrhoea. Biotechnology and genomics offer new ways to cure disease by altering genes that contribute to cancer, or boosting genes that might fight it.

Information and communications technology (ICT) can provide enormous benefits to developing countries, both as consumers and producers. Any task that can be digitized can now be done at a distance, which gives the opportunity for low cost countries to develop ICT industries. India's software industry now employs nearly one million people. Call centres are one of the fastest growing industries in the Asian subcontinent. For consumers, access to information through the Internet can be of benefit in almost any field – for weather information in agriculture, for the dissemination of knowledge in health care, and the tracking of diseases, and for distance learning in education.

1 What is meant by the process of capital accumulation?

2 Distinguish between the various forms of investment and capital accumulation that can raise per capita income.

3 Why do developing countries, and many development economists, lay great stress on the role of capital accumulation in the development process?

4 Why did Rostow define 'take-off into sustained growth' in terms of a critical ratio of investment to national income? (See also Chapter 3.)

5 Define the concept of the incremental capital–output ratio. What is the use of the concept in development planning?

6 How will technical progress affect the capital–output ratio?

7 What is meant by the following terms: neutral, capital-saving, and labour-saving technical progress?

8 What are the main means by which societies progress technologically?

9 What is 'learning by doing'?

10 How would you measure the contribution of education to economic growth?

11 Why is the rate of return on investment in education higher in developing countries than in developed countries?

12 In what senses is infrastructure investment complementary to investment in plant and machinery, and does it have to be provided publicly?

NOTES

1. See the discussion by W. B. Reddaway, 'Some Reflections by a Keynesian Economist on the Problems of Developing Countries', in Thirlwall (1987).
2. The greater the proportion of expenditure treated as consumption, the higher the rate of return on the investment component.
3. *Education Sector Policy Paper* (Washington, DC: World Bank, 1980).
4. See Colclough (1982).

WEBSITES ON TECHNOLOGY AND INVESTMENT

Economic Growth Resources run by Jon Temple, Bristol University, UK www.bris.ac.uk/Economics/Growth

International Institute for Communication www.iicd.org

World Intellectual Property Organization www.wipo.int

Obstacles to development

Dualism, centre–periphery models and the process of cumulative causation

It is easy to argue that poverty and backwardness are due to a general shortage and inefficient use of the key factors of production; it is much harder to determine precisely why there should be a dearth of some factors and an abundance of others, and why development may be a slow and lengthy process. It is certainly impossible to explain present-day international discrepancies in the level of development with reference to *initial* differences in factor endowments. The present development gap has arisen largely through industrial development in certain selected areas of the world, which in turn has generated its own factor endowments. The purpose here, however, is not to consider why some countries were able to industrialize sooner than others, but rather to consider some of the potential obstacles to growth in the present developing countries, and the mechanisms through which unequal advantage between developed and developing countries is perpetuated.

First, the **dualistic structure** of developing countries will be considered. Secondly we shall examine Myrdal's model of the process of **circular and cumulative causation**, which can be applied to regions and countries alike (Myrdal, 1957, 1963). We shall see that Myrdal's model is one of many that can be used to understand the perpetuation of the development gap and divergences between North and South or between the 'centre' (industrialized) countries and the 'periphery' (primary producing) countries. The pioneering models of Prebisch and Seers will be examined in this context, and their similarities emphasized. Thirdly, we will discuss the **new economic geography**, which has links with the model of cumulative causation, and the role of geographic factors that seem to be associated with divisions in the world economy. Finally we shall briefly discuss models of **unequal exchange** and **dependency**, which emphasize alternative mechanisms making for international inequality in the world economy. In Chapter 8, we shall elaborate on the so-called population 'problem' in developing countries.

DUALISM

The term 'dualism' describes a condition in which developing countries may find themselves in the early stages of development, the extent of which may have implications for the future pattern and pace of development. There is a number of possible definitions and interpretations of 'dualism', but in the main it refers to economic and social divisions in an economy, such as differences in the level of technology between sectors or regions, differences in the degree of geographic development and differences in social customs and attitudes between an indigenous and an imported social system.

Dualism in all its aspects is a concomitant of the growth of a money economy, which, as we saw in Chapter 5, may either arise naturally as a result of specialization or be imposed from outside by the importation of an alien economic system – typically capitalism. Basically, therefore, a dual economy is characterized by a difference in social customs between the subsistence and exchange sectors of the economy, by a gap between the levels of technology in the rural subsistence sector and the industrial monetized sector, and possibly by a gap in the level of per capita income between regions of a country if the money economy and industrial development are geographically concentrated. In fact it is not unusual for **geographic, social and technological dualism** to occur together, with each type of dualism tending to reinforce the other. Also, the more 'progressive' sectors typically have favourable access to scarce factors of production, which is a major cause of the persistence of dualism. **Urban bias** plays an important part in this process (Lipton, 1977).

If the basic origin of dualism is the introduction of money into a subsistence barter economy, and development depends on the extension of the money economy, development must contend with the existence of dualism in all its aspects. We shall consider here social and technological dualism, leaving geographic dualism until later when we consider Myrdal's hypothesis of cumulative causation.

The first question is, what development problems does the existence of dualism pose for an economy, and how can dualism impede and retard development? As far as **social dualism** is concerned, the obstacles appear to be similar to those presented by a traditional society with no modern exchange sector at all. The task is one of providing incentives in the subsistence sector and drawing the subsistence sector into the money economy. The fact that the indigenous subsistence sector may be reluctant to alter its traditional way of life and respond to incentives is not peculiar to a dual economy. It is therefore true that underdevelopment tends to be associated with social dualism, but it is perhaps misleading to regard social dualism as an underlying *cause* of backwardness and poverty. It would be difficult to argue that development would be more rapid in the absence of a monetary sector, from which the existence of dualism stems. Even if the growth of the exchange sector makes little impact on attitudes in the indigenous sector, it is bound to make some contribution to development by employing labour from the subsistence sector and disseminating knowledge. Without the growth of the money economy it is difficult to envisage any progress at all. In short, it seems more realistic to regard social dualism as an inevitable consequence of development rather than as a basic cause of underdevelopment.

This is not to say that social dualism does not create problems of its own. For example different development strategies will be required to cope with dissimilar conditions in the two sectors, and this may involve real resource costs that are not encountered by the developed economy. It is in this sense that the dual economy is at a comparative disadvantage.

Similar reservations can be raised over whether it is accurate to describe **technological dualism** as a cause of underdevelopment. As with social dualism, it is probably more realistic to regard it as an inevitable feature of the development process. Again, though, the difficulties that may ensue from gaps in technology between the rural and industrial sectors of the economy must be recognized.

Two disadvantages are commonly associated with technological dualism. The first was mentioned earlier: where technological dualism is the result of a foreign enclave, a proportion of the profits generated in the industrial sector will be remitted to the home country, reducing the level of saving and investment below what it might have been. The second disadvantage is more fundamental, but difficult to avoid. If in the rural, or non-monetized, sector of the economy production processes are characterized by labour-intensive techniques and variable technical coefficients of production, while production processes in the industrial, technologically advanced sector are capital-intensive and possess relatively fixed technical coefficients, it is possible that the technology of the industrial sector may impede progress in the agricultural sector, upon which the development of the total economy in part depends. First, relatively fixed technical coefficients (that is, a low elasticity of substitution between factors) means that labour can be absorbed from agriculture into industry only as fast as the growth of capital, and second, capital intensity itself will restrict employment opportunities in the industrial sector, contributing to urban unemployment and perpetuating underdevelopment in the rural sector. Hence productivity growth in the agricultural sector, which is recognized as being necessary to establish a secure basis for take-off into sustained growth, may be slowed down.

It is true that if the technology of the modern sector (imported or otherwise) does embody fixed technological coefficients, it may be difficult for an economy to use the socially optimum combination of factors, but this short-run disadvantage must be weighed against the favourable repercussions on productivity stemming from the advanced technology. If capital accumulation and technical progress, and the development of an industrial sector – in addition to agricultural development – are essential prerequisites to raising the level of per capita income, it is difficult to see how technological dualism can be avoided, at least in the early stages of development. The best that can be done is first to encourage the widespread application and rapid assimilation of technical progress throughout all sectors of the economy, and second to ensure the 'proper' pricing of factors of production to prevent the introduction of a technology that may be profitable to private individuals but does not maximize the returns to society at large because factor prices do not adequately reflect relative factor endowments. But even a technology that is socially optimal in this sense may not be the technology that provides the soundest basis for sustained growth in the long run. The question of the choice of techniques is discussed in detail in Chapter 12.

THE PROCESS OF CUMULATIVE CAUSATION

The hypothesis of cumulative causation as an explanation of the backwardness of developing nations is associated with Gunnar Myrdal (1957, 1963). Basically, it is a hypothesis of **geographic dualism**, applicable to nations and regions within nations, which can be advanced to account for the persistence of spatial differences in a wide variety of development indices, including per capita income, rates of growth of industrialization and trade, employment growth rates and levels of unemployment. As such, the process of cumulative causation is a direct challenge to static equilibrium theory, which predicts that the working of economic forces will cause spatial differences to narrow.

Myrdal contends that in the context of development both economic and social forces produce tendencies towards *disequilibrium*, and that the assumption in economic theory that disequilibrium situations tend towards equilibrium is false. If this were not so, how could the tendency for international differences in living standards to widen be explained? Thus Myrdal replaces the assumption of stable equilibrium with what he calls the hypothesis of **circular and cumulative causation**, arguing that the use of this hypothesis can go a long way towards explaining why international differences in levels of development, and interregional differences in development within nations, may persist and even widen over time.

He first considers the hypothesis in the context of a geographically dual economy, describing how, through the media of labour migration, capital movements and trade, the existence of dualism not only retards the development of backward regions but can also slow up the development of the whole economy. To describe the process of circular and cumulative causation, let us start off with a country in which all regions have attained the same stage of development, as measured by the same level of per capita income, or by similar levels of productivity and wages in the same occupations. Then assume that an exogenous shock produces a disequilibrium situation with development proceeding more rapidly in one region than another. The proposition is that economic and social forces will tend to strengthen the disequilibrium situation by

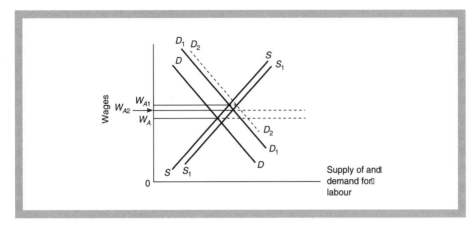

Figure 7.1 Region *A*

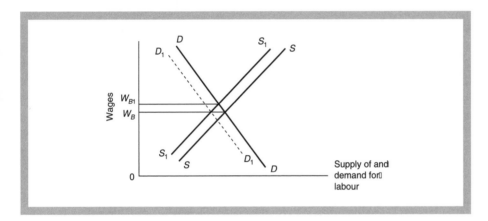

Figure 7.2 Region *B*

leading to cumulative expansion in the favoured region at the expense of other regions, which then become comparatively worse off, retarding their future development.

This contrasts with neoclassical equilibrium theory, which assumes that, through the process of factor mobility, wage rates and the rate of profit will equalize across regions. According to neoclassical theory, in places where labour is scarce and capital is abundant, labour will flow in and capital will flow out, thus reducing wages and raising the rate of profit, while in less prosperous areas where labour is abundant, labour will flow out and capital will flow in, raising wages and reducing the rate of profit.

In contrast, what Myrdal has in mind is a type of multiplier–accelerator mechanism producing increasing returns in the favoured region. Instead of leading to equality, the forces of supply and demand interact with each other to produce cumulative movements away from spatial equilibrium. Since the wage level is the basic determinant of per capita income, let us take the example of wages and wage differences to illustrate the kind of process that Myrdal has in mind. Take two regions, *A* and *B* (for example, northern and southern Italy), and assume that wages are determined by supply and demand, as in Figures 7.1 and 7.2.

Suppose to start with that wage levels are identical in the two regions, that is, $W_A = W_B$. Then assume that a stimulus of some sort causes the demand for labour, and therefore wages, to rise in region A relative to region B; that is, the demand curve for labour in region A shifts to D_1D_1, causing wages to rise to W_{A1}. Since labour tends to respond to differences in economic opportunities of this sort, the wage discrepancy may be assumed to induce labour migration from region B to region A. Equilibrium theory then predicts that there will be a tendency for wage levels to be equalized once more through a *reduction* in labour supply in region B from SS to S_1S_1 and an *increase* in labour supply in region A from SS to S_1S_1, giving a wage in region A of W_{A2}, equal to a wage in B of W_{B1}.

According to the hypothesis of cumulative causation, however, changes in supply may be expected to react on demand in such a way as to counteract the tendency towards equilibrium. Migration from region B denudes the area of human capital and entrepreneurs, and depresses the demand for goods and services and factors of production, while movements into region A, on the other hand, will tend to stimulate enterprise and the demand for products, adding to the demand for factors of production. In short, migration from region B will cause the demand curve for labour to shift to the left, say to D_1D_1, and migration into region A will cause the demand curve for labour to shift further to the right, say to D_2D_2, causing the initial wage discrepancy at least to persist, if not widen (if the shifts in demand are greater than those assumed). Thus once development differences appear, there is set in motion a chain of cumulative expansion in the favoured region, and this has what Myrdal calls a **'backwash' effect** on other regions, causing development differences in general to persist or even diverge.

Capital movements and **trade** also play a part in the process of cumulative causation. In a free market, capital, like labour, will tend to move to where the prospective return is highest, and this will be to the region where demand is buoyant. Capital, labour and entrepreneurship will tend to migrate together. The benefits of trade will also accrue to the host region. Regions within a nation using a common currency cannot have balance-of-payments difficulties in the normal sense, but the maintenance of employment depends on the ability to export, otherwise unemployment will appear. If production is subject to increasing returns, the region experiencing the rapid growth of factor supplies will be able to increase its competitive advantage over the relatively lagging regions containing smaller-scale industries, and increase its real income accordingly. In this same way, the general freeing and widening of international markets and the expansion of world trade will tend to favour the more rapidly growing regions within nation-states.

The impact of immigration into the expanding region is also likely to induce improvements in transport and communications, education and health facilities, and so on, improving efficiency and productivity and widening still further the competitive advantage of the growing region over the lagging regions experiencing emigration of the factors of production.

Such is the potential strength of the backwash effects of the process of circular and cumulative causation, that **Hirschman** (1958) has suggested that the lagging regions may possibly be better off if they became sovereign political states. If a lagging area was an independent 'country', the mobility of factors of production could be more easily controlled, competition between the leading and lagging regions could be lessened, each region could more easily concentrate on producing goods in which it possessed a comparative cost advantage, separate exchange rates could be fixed for the two regions, and resort could be more easily made to protection.

Despite these potential advantages of nationhood for a backward region, however, Hirschman argues against sovereignty because he believes that the forces making for the interregional transmission of growth are likely to be more powerful than those making for 'international' transmission. This presupposes, however, that the forces making for the interregional transmission of growth in sovereign states are lost, and begs the question of whether the differential advantages of being a region within a nation, as distinct from a separate nation, offset the backwash effects that still remain.

Hirschman recognizes the continued existence of backwash effects and argues that, to offset them, a nation that is concerned with developing its backward regions should provide certain equivalents of sovereignty, such as a separate tax system and the right to protect certain activities. Policies must be designed to reduce what he calls the **'polarization' effects** of interregional differences in development and to strengthen the **'trickle down' effects**. The 'trickle down' effects are the favourable repercussions on backward regions emanating from expanding regions, which Myrdal calls **'spread' effects**. These trickle-down or spread effects consist mainly of an increased demand for the backward areas' products and the diffusion of technology and knowledge. In Myrdal's view, the spread effects are weaker than the backwash effects, and if interregional differences are to be narrowed, nations must rely on state intervention through regional policies. The alternative is to wait for a natural end to the process of cumulative causation, which may be a long time coming.

But the time must eventually come when increasing costs in the expanding region will halt expansion. The higher costs of living, and the external diseconomies produced by congestion, will ultimately outweigh the benefits of greater efficiency and higher money returns to the factors of production. The process of migration will then be halted, and possibly reversed. In some developed countries this stage is now beginning to be reached. The question for governments with certain growth and welfare objectives is whether they can afford to let the process take its natural course, and to tolerate the inequalities that may arise before the process ends. In practice, governments in many advanced countries have taken active steps for many years to redress regional imbalances, and this is one reason why regional disparities tend to be less in advanced countries than in developing countries. In the developing countries, however, Myrdal was of the view that, far from lessening regional inequalities, the state has been a positive force in their persistence: 'In many of the poorer countries the natural drift towards inequalities has been supported and magnified by built-in feudal and other inegalitarian institutions and power structures which aid the rich in exploiting the poor' (Myrdal, 1963, p. 40).

REGIONAL INEQUALITIES

The international cross-section evidence on regional inequalities, and time-series evidence for individual countries, suggests that the degree of inequality follows an inverted 'U' shape; that is, regional inequalities first rise with the level of development and then decrease. This pattern is not hard to explain. Very poor countries are uniformly poor. Regional differences then first emerge as a result of some favourable shock to one region or set of regions; for example an export enclave or the development of industrial activities. Once a difference has emerged, it will tend to be widened by the processes already described. Migration from poor to richer regions will tend to be selective in the early stages of development because only those with skills and education will be able to afford to migrate. Capital will tend to locate in the more dynamic region(s). 'Spread' effects emanating from prosperous regions will be weak owing to a general lack of political and economic integration.

The factors that accentuate differences in the early stages of development, however, will tend to weaken with time as countries get richer. Migration will become less selective; the spread effects will become more powerful; industrialization will tend to spread and the size of the agricultural sector shrink; external diseconomies of expansion and congestion in expanding regions will increase, curbing capital and labour migration from poor to rich regions; and governments may also attempt to rectify imbalances through the implementation of regional policies.

The empirical evidence shows that regional disparities in output and income per head are much more unequal in developing countries than in developed countries. Table 7.1 gives the unweighted and weighted (by population) Gini ratios (see Chapter 2, p. 28) for a selection of developed and developing countries estimated by Shankar and Shah (2003), who also distinguish between countries with a federal or unitary political structure. It can be seen that the Gini ratios for developing countries are much higher than for developed countries; also that unitary developing countries are generally more unequal than federal developing countries. Countries with some of the highest measures of regional inequality are large unitary countries such as China, Vietnam, Thailand and Indonesia. There are three main reasons why regional inequalities tend to be lower in federal states: firstly, widening regional disparities pose a greater political risk in federal countries in the sense that disadvantaged regions may decide to break away; secondly, national political parties need to emphasize regional issues more, and thirdly, autonomous regional governments have more concern for their regions than a unitary state.

Shankar and Shah also look at trends in regional inequality over time in 14 developing countries and find inequalities still increasing – or moving up the inverted 'U'. This contrasts to what is happening in most developed countries, including the United States and European Union. In the United States, Barro and Sala-í-Martin (1992) show that a process of regional per capita income convergence has been going on over the last hundred years. Taking personal income data, they find an inverse relation across US states between the average growth of per capita income over the period 1880–1988 and the initial (1880) level of per capita income. Only two subperiods, 1920–30 and 1980–8, show evidence of divergence.

In Europe, the evidence is more mixed. Across the regions of Europe there is some evidence of per capita income convergence in the postwar years up to 1980, but not thereafter. Regional unemployment rate differences, however, both within Europe as a whole and within industrial countries, have remained very stubborn. Fagerberg and Verspagen (1996) take 70 regions in six EU countries and show convergence up to 1980, but not since. The authors argue that the scope for convergence is not exhausted, but other factors in the 1980s pushed towards divergence, particularly differences in unemployment and the research and development (R&D) effort between industrial and agricultural regions.

Table 7.1 Regional disparities within developed and developing countries

Countries	Year	Unweighted Gini ratio	Weighted Gini ratio
Developed countries (federal)			
Canada	1997	0.018	0.067
United States	1997	0.090	0.039
Germany	1997	0.191	0.122
Spain	1997	0.128	0.118
Developed countries (unitary)			
France	1997	0.096	0.126
Italy	1997	0.152	0.145
United Kingdom	1997	0.085	0.083
Developing countries (federal)			
Brazil	1997	0.334	0.267
India	1997	0.226	0.227
Mexico	1997	0.253	0.301
Pakistan	1997	0.113	0.072
Russia	1997	0.283	0.280
Developing countries (unitary)			
Chile	1994	0.267	0.165
China	1997	0.351	0.250
Indonesia	1997	0.378	0.274
Nepal	1996		
Philippines	1997	0.307	0.261
Poland	1996	0.106	0.090
Romania	1996	0.230	0.249
Sri Lanka	1995	0.352	0.341
South Africa	1994		
Thailand	1997	0.438	0.442
Uganda	1997–8		
Uzbekistan	1997	0.155	0.170
Vietnam	1997	0.372	0.410

Source: R. Shankar and A. Shah, 'Bridging the Economic Divide within Countries: A Scorecard on the Performance of Regional Policies in Reducing Income Disparities', *World Development*, August 2003.

Indeed it appears to be the case from a further study by Fagerberg, Verspagen and Caniels (1996) that regional differences in per capita income are systematically related to differences in unemployment rates. They take 64 regions in Germany, France, Italy and Spain over the period 1980–90 and find that growth in poor regions is hampered by unfavourable industrial structure and weak R&D effort. There is evidence of convergence, but only after allowing for differences in industrial structure, R&D effort, population density and migration. Interestingly, labour migration is found to have a strong positive impact on per capita income growth, indicating that migration was disequilibrating during this period. The policy implications are that the predominance of agriculture is a barrier to growth in poor regions, mainly because the scope for scale economies and R&D is less than in industry. Greater regional balance requires structural change in favour of industrial activities, but this in turn requires an appropriate physical infrastructure and the provision of human capital.

Turning to regional unemployment rates across Europe, there is no evidence of global convergence over the last 20 years, as barriers to trade and factor mobility have been reduced. A study by Baddeley, Martin and Tyler (1996), taking 427 regions in Britain,

Germany, France, Spain, Belgium and Italy, shows in fact that the trend dispersion of unemployment rates has been rising. Within the six countries themselves, regional differences have either persisted or widened, except in Britain. The authors argue that the persistence should be interpreted as an equilibrium phenomenon associated with differences in industrial structure and the number of long-term unemployed.

INTERNATIONAL INEQUALITY AND CENTRE–PERIPHERY MODELS

The process of circular and cumulative causation is also used by Myrdal in an attempt to explain widening international differences in the level of development from similar initial conditions. Through the media of labour migration, capital movements and trade, international inequalities are perpetuated in exactly the same way as regional inequalities within nations. Myrdal argues that through trade the developing countries have been forced into the production of goods, notably primary products, with inelastic demand with respect to both price and income. This has put the developing countries at a grave disadvantage compared with the developed countries with respect to the balance of payments and the availability of foreign exchange. Moreover, with the tendency for the efficiency wage (that is, the money wage in relation to productivity) to fall in faster-growing areas relative to other areas, the developed countries have gained a cumulative competitive trading advantage, especially in manufactured commodities. Myrdal, of course, is not alone in this view, and we shall elaborate below on other models that stress the unequal gains and the balance-of-payments effects of trade as the main media through which international differences in development are perpetuated, including the contribution of the new economic geography pioneered by Krugman (1991).

Myrdal argues in the same vein in the case of capital movements. Because the risks associated with investment tend to be higher in developing countries, the natural tendency will be for the developing countries to be net exporters of capital. In practice, because of the large volume of capital from international lending organizations, and the favourable tax treatment of foreign direct investment, the developing countries are generally net importers of long-term capital, although the short-term capital account tends to be adverse. The fact remains, however, as Lucas (1990) points out, that capital flows mainly to regions already rich. With regard to portfolio investment, in 1990 the richest 20 per cent of the world's population received 92 per cent of gross portfolio capital flows, and the poorest 20 per cent received only 0.1 per cent. With regard to foreign direct investment, the richest 20 per cent received 79 per cent of flows, while the poorest 20 per cent received only 0.7 per cent. In total, the richest 20 per cent of the world's population received 88 per cent of private gross capital flows and the poorest 20 per cent received 1 per cent.

The potential weakness of Myrdal's hypothesis at the international level concerns the effects of labour migration. The international migration of labour from developing to developed countries can have beneficial as well as harmful effects on backward economies. The greatest deleterious effect on backward economies is the obvious one of possible loss of human capital, although even here, if the human capital is unemployed, migration may not be a serious loss. But it is not only the skilled and educated that may be induced to leave their native lands. Unskilled labour may also respond to the existence of better employment opportunities elsewhere. If it is argued that developing countries suffer from underemployment, and that productivity is low owing to 'over-population', the emigration of unskilled labour could be a substantial benefit to developing countries. It is possible, for example, that emigration has helped to raise per capita income in some of the poorer European countries such as Greece, Turkey and Spain, and improved the balance of payments at the same time through remittances by emigrants to their home countries. In this important respect, generous immigration policies in advanced countries can provide a valuable means of development assistance.

If there is unrestricted emigration from the developing countries, and unrestricted immigration into the developed countries, it is difficult to know where the balance of advantage lies for the developing countries. In a world that restricts the immigration of unskilled labour, however, but permits the immigration of skilled labour, the developing countries would undoubtedly suffer. While in theory, therefore, certain types of international labour migration could help to narrow international differences in levels of development, in practice the assumptions of such a model are rarely fulfilled.

Even so, any potential gain from unrestricted labour mobility is unlikely to offset the international backwash effects arising from trade and international capital movements. Even with unrestricted migration, therefore, there would still be a tendency for international differences in the level of development to widen through trade and the free movement of capital. The existence of international 'spread' effects gives no cause for modifying this conclusion. International spread effects are relatively weak – certainly weaker than the spread effects within nations.

What, then, should be our verdict on the hypothesis of cumulative causation? Given that the hypothesis assumes free trade and free mobility of the factors of production, it perhaps contains more force with respect to interregional differences in development than international differences. On the other hand it cannot be dismissed lightly when discussing the development gap in the world economy. In view of the fact that there has been no tendency in the recent past for international per capita income levels to converge (see Chapters 2 and 4), the hypothesis is not refuted by the evidence. In particular, the present international trading and payments position of developing countries does not inspire confidence that the total gains from trade between the developed and developing countries are distributed equitably.

The contribution of the hypothesis of cumulative causation to an understanding of development and underdevelopment is its emphasis on development as a cumulative phenomenon and, more important still, its challenge to static equilibrium theory; that is, that regions or nations that gain an initial advantage may maintain that advantage to the detriment of development elsewhere. At its root is the phenomenon of increasing returns, defined broadly as the accumulation of productive advantages of the type discussed in Chapter 6, relating to how societies progress technologically.

MODELS OF 'REGIONAL' GROWTH RATE DIFFERENCES: PREBISCH, SEERS AND KALDOR

While the Myrdal model of centre and periphery emphasizes the process of cumulative causation working through increasing returns and competitiveness in favoured regions, other centre–periphery models stress the balance-of-payments implications of the particular pattern of production and trade between rich and poor countries, which arise from the fact that industrial goods produced and traded by rich countries have a higher income elasticity of demand than goods produced and traded by poor countries. One of the earliest models, powerful in its simplicity, is that of Prebisch.

THE PREBISCH MODEL[1]

Consider a two-country, two-commodity model in which the advanced centre produces and exports manufactured goods with an **income elasticity of demand**[2] greater than unity, and the backward periphery produces and exports primary commodities with an income elasticity of demand less than unity. Let us suppose that the income elasticity of demand for manufactures (e_m) is 1.3, and the income elasticity of demand for primary commodities (e_p) is 0.8. Assume to start with that the growth rates of income of both centre and periphery are equal to 3 per cent, that is, $g_c = g_p = 3.0$. What will be the growth of exports (x) and imports (m) in the centre and periphery? For the centre we have

$$x_c = g_p \times e_m = 3.0 \times 1.3 = 3.9 \text{ per cent}$$

$$m_c = g_c \times e_p = 3.0 \times 0.8 = 2.4 \text{ per cent}$$

For the periphery we have

$$x_p = g_c \times e_p = 3.0 \times 0.8 = 2.4 \text{ per cent}$$

$$m_p = g_p \times e_m = 3.0 \times 1.3 = 3.9 \text{ per cent}$$

With imports growing faster than exports in the periphery, this is not a sustainable position, unless the periphery can finance an ever-growing balance-of-payments deficit on the current account by capital inflows. If it cannot, and balance-of-payments equilibrium on the current account is a requirement, there must be some adjustment to raise the rate of growth of exports or reduce the rate of growth of imports. Now suppose we rule out the possibility that relative prices measured in a common currency can change as an adjustment mechanism, the only adjustment mechanism left (barring protection) is a reduction in the periphery's growth rate to reduce the rate of growth of imports in line with the rate of growth of exports. From the model, we can solve for the necessary growth rate of the periphery to keep trade balanced. On the assumptions outlined, we must have $m_p = x_p$ or $g_p e_m = x_p$ and therefore

$$g_p = \frac{x_p}{e_m} = \frac{2.4}{1.3} = 1.846$$

Thus the growth rate of the periphery is constrained to 1.846 per cent, compared with 3 per cent in the centre. In these circumstances both the relative and the absolute gap in income between periphery and centre will widen. Notice, in fact, that since the growth of the periphery's exports is equal to $g_c \times e_p$, we can write the above equation as

$$g_p = \frac{g_c \times e_p}{e_m}$$

and dividing through by g_c, we reach the interesting result that the relative growth rates of the periphery and centre will equal the ratio of the income elasticity of demand for the two countries' commodities:

$$\frac{g_p}{g_c} = \frac{e_p}{e_m}$$

This result will hold as long as current account equilibrium on the balance of payments is a requirement, and relative price adjustment in international trade is either ruled out as an adjustment mechanism to rectify balance-of-payments disequilibrium or does not work. To avoid the consequences of this model, Prebisch argued the case for protection, which in effect is a policy to reduce e_m, which for the periphery is the propensity to import manufactured goods. We reserve discussion of the relative merits of protection until Chapter 16 on trade policy.

THE SEERS MODEL[3]

A similar model of centre–periphery divergence, in which the crucial source of differences in growth rates and relative income levels is differences in the income elasticity of demand for manufactures and primary commodities, has been developed by Seers. As in the Prebisch model, relative prices between centre and periphery remain unchanged and it is assumed that trade must be balanced. Let the import functions of the centre and periphery be

$$M_c = A + BY_c \tag{7.1}$$

$$M_p = a + bY_p \tag{7.2}$$

where Y is the level of income and B and b are the marginal propensities to import in the centre and periphery, respectively. Balanced trade requires that

$$a + bY_p = A + BY_c \tag{7.3}$$

or

$$\frac{Y_p}{Y_c} = \frac{A - a}{bY_c} + \frac{B}{b} \tag{7.4}$$

Now what will happen to this relative difference in income between periphery and centre through time? Assume that income in the centre grows exponentially through time at some rate, r, so that we can write $Y_{ct} = Y_{co}e^{rt}$, where Y_{co} is the base level of income. We can then rewrite (7.4) with time subscripts as

$$\frac{Y_{pt}}{Y_{ct}} = \frac{A - a}{bY_{co}e^{rt}} + \frac{B}{b} \tag{7.5}$$

Differentiating the above expression with respect to time gives

$$d\frac{Y_{pt}}{Y_{ct}} / dt = \frac{-r(A - a)}{bY_{co}e^{rt}} \tag{7.6}$$

Since the denominator is positive the relative income gap will widen through time (that is, the level of income in the periphery will *fall* relative to that in the centre) if $(A - a) > 0$. Now a is the constant term in the import demand function for the periphery, which will be negative if the income elasticity of demand for imports from the centre is greater than unity.[4] The constant term, A, of the centre's import demand function will be positive if the income elasticity of demand for imports from the periphery is less than unity.[5] Therefore $(A - a) > 0$. Seers notes that the growing disparity will be even greater as far as per capita income is concerned if population growth is faster in the periphery than in the centre. This would be true, of course, in Prebisch's model too. Capital flows could hypothetically stop the relative income gap from widening by allowing unbalanced trade, but no country can go on building up debts for ever. Import substitution is another possibility, but the task is colossal. In terms of the equations of the model, it would mean, in effect, making the import function for the periphery look like that of the centre; or in other words, nothing short of structural change to reduce the periphery's income elasticity of demand for manufactures and to raise the income elasticity of demand for the periphery's exports (to raise the centre's income elasticity of demand for imports).[6]

AN EXPORT GROWTH MODEL OF REGIONAL GROWTH RATE DIFFERENCES

It is possible to combine the ideas of Myrdal with the insights of Prebisch and Seers in a single model, which focuses on the role of export growth in the development process in an open economy and in which the Prebisch result emerges as a special case if relative prices are fixed and trade is balanced. The model is applicable to regions and open developing economies alike.[7] It takes as its starting point the not unreasonable assumption that the output of an open economy is demand-determined, not supply-constrained, and that it is the long-run growth of autonomous demand that governs the long-run rate of growth of output. The main component of autonomous demand in an open economy, in turn, is demand emanating from outside the region, that is, the demand for the region's exports. The model is a variant of export-base models of development, which stress the importance of exports as a leading sector. The hypothesis is that once a region obtains a growth advantage it will tend to sustain it at the expense of other regions because faster growth leads to faster productivity growth (the so-called '**Verdoorn effect**', see Chapter 3, p. 117), which keeps the region competitive in the export of goods that gave the region its growth advantage in the first place. Success breeds success, and failure breeds failure! In this section attention will be confined to outlining the model. An examination of the international evidence of the relation between the growth of exports and the growth of output in developing countries will be left until Chapter 16.

Let

$$g_t = \gamma(x_t) \tag{7.7}$$

where g_t is the rate of growth of output in time t, x_t is the rate of growth of exports in time t, γ is the (constant) elasticity of output with respect to export growth (= 1 if exports are a constant proportion of output), and t is discrete time. Apart from the theoretical considerations underlying the specification of (7.7), that the rate of growth of the economy as a whole will be governed by the rate of growth of autonomous demand, there are a number of practical considerations that make export demand for highly specialized regions (or countries) extremely important for both demand and supply. For most industries in a region, local demand is likely to be trivial compared with the optimum production capacity of the industries. The viability of regional enterprise must largely depend on the strength of demand from outside the region.

There are also a number of important reasons why export demand may be a more potent growth-inducing force than other elements of demand, especially in open, backward areas – regions or countries. The first is that exports allow regional specialization, which may bring dynamic as well as static gains. Second, exports permit imports, and imports may be important in developing areas that lack the capacity to produce development goods themselves. Third, if the exchange of information and technical knowledge is linked to trade, exporting facilitates the flow of technical knowledge, which can improve the area's supply capacity.

Now let us consider the determinants of export demand and the form of the export demand function. It is conventional to specify exports as a multiplicative (or constant elasticity) function of relative prices measured in a common currency and foreign income. Thus

$$X_t = \left(\frac{P_{dt}}{P_{ft}}\right)^{\eta} Z_t^{\varepsilon} \tag{7.8}$$

where X is the quantity of exports in time t, P_d is the domestic price in time t, P_f is the foreign price in time t, Z is foreign income in time t, η is the price elasticity of demand for exports (< 0) and ε is the income elasticity of demand for exports (> 0). Taking discrete rates of change of the variables gives the approximation

$$x_t = \eta(p_{dt} - p_{ft}) + \varepsilon(z_t) \tag{7.9}$$

where the lower-case letters represent the rates of growth of the variables.

The rate of growth of income outside the region (z) and the rate of change of competitors' prices (p_f) may both be taken as exogenous to the region. The rate of growth of domestic (export) prices will be endogenous, however. Let us assume that prices are formed on the basis of a constant 'mark-up' on unit labour costs, so that

$$P_{dt} = \left(\frac{W}{R}\right)_t (T_t) \tag{7.10}$$

where P_d is the domestic price, W is the level of money wages, R is the average product of labour and T is $1 +$ percentage mark-up on unit labour costs. From (7.10) we can write:

$$p_{dt} = w_t - r_t + \tau_t \tag{7.11}$$

where the lower-case letters stand for the discrete rates of change of the variables.

The model becomes 'circular and cumulative' by specifying the growth of labour productivity as partly a function of the growth output itself (Verdoorn's Law). If the function is linear we may write

$$r_t = r_{at} + \lambda(g_t) \tag{7.12}$$

where r_{at} is the rate of autonomous productivity growth at time t, and λ is the Verdoorn coefficient (> 0). Equation (7.12) provides the link between exports and growth via productivity growth and prices. Fast export growth leads to fast output growth, and fast output growth leads to fast export growth by making goods more competitive. Combining (7.7), (7.9), (7.11) and (7.12) to obtain an expression for the equilibrium growth rate gives

$$g_t = \frac{\gamma[\eta(w_t - r_{at} + \tau_t - p_{ft}) + \varepsilon(z_t)]}{1 + \gamma\eta\lambda} \tag{7.13}$$

Remembering that $\eta < 0$, the growth rate is shown to vary positively with r_a, z, ε, p_f and λ, and negatively with w and τ. The effect of η is ambiguous since it appears in both the numerator and the denominator of the equation. It is clear that it is the assumed dependence of productivity growth on the growth rate that gives rise to the possibility that once a region obtains a growth advantage it will keep it. Suppose, for example, that a region obtains an advantage in the production of goods with a high income elasticity of demand (ε), which causes its growth rate to rise above that of another region. Through the so-called Verdoorn effect, productivity growth will be higher, the rate of change of prices lower (other things being the same), and the rate of growth of exports (and hence the rate of growth of output) higher, and so on. Moreover the fact that the region with the initial advantage will obtain a competitive advantage in the production of goods with a high income elasticity of demand will mean that it will be difficult for other regions to establish the same activities. This is the essence of the theory of cumulative causation, of divergence between 'centre' and 'periphery' and between industrial (developed) and agricultural (developing) regions (countries). Figure 7.3 illustrates the model graphically.

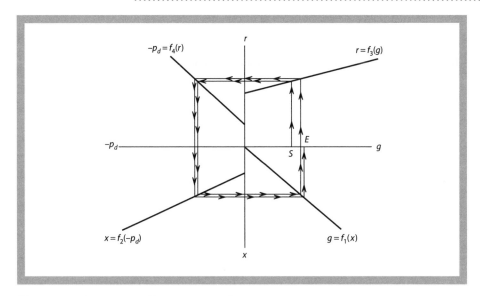

Figure 7.3 Convergent-divergent growth

The distance of each of the linear functions from the origin reflects factors affecting each variable other than the variable specified in the functional relation. From the initial condition, S, the growth rate is shown converging to its equilibrium value E, as determined in (7.13).[8] The link that the Verdoorn relation provides between exports and growth via productivity and prices, and its sustaining influence, is clearly seen. And the greater the dependence of productivity growth on the growth of output (that is, the higher λ), the higher the equilibrium growth rate will be and the greater the divergence between regional growth rates for given differences between regions in the other variables and parameters.

An important implication of the model we have developed is that an autonomous shock will not be sufficient to raise a lagging region's growth rate permanently unless the autonomous shock favourably affects the parameters and variables of the model, or is a sustained shock. On these grounds, the relevance of policies of devaluation in a national context, or wage subsidies in a regional context, for improving a region's growth rate may be called into question. What is likely to be required is structural change, in particular structural change to improve the demand characteristics of exports. It is recognition of this point that accounts, among other things, for the emphasis placed by developing countries on industrialization and the restructuring of world trade to provide their manufactured goods with easier access to world markets (see Chapter 16).

Note that it is also a property of the model that if relative prices measured in a common currency do not change (that is, $p_{dt} - p_{ft} = 0$), then export growth is determined solely by income growth outside the region or country, and 7.13 would reduce to

$$g_t = \gamma \varepsilon \; (z_t) \tag{7.14}$$

and if balanced trade is a requirement so that the growth of imports (m) is equal to the growth of exports ($m = x$) we have

$$g_t\pi = \varepsilon(z_t) \tag{7.15}$$

where π is the income elasticity of demand for imports.

Thus with relative prices fixed, the growth elasticity with respect to exports (γ) must equal the reciprocal of the income elasticity of demand for imports (π) in the balanced trade models of Prebisch and Seers. Again we end up with the simple rule that one country's growth rate (g) relative to that of others (z) depends on the ratio of the income elasticity of demand for the country's exports relative to its imports (or the other country's exports in a two-country model), that is, from (7.15):

$$\frac{g_t}{z_t} = \frac{\varepsilon}{\pi} \tag{7.16}$$

At the country level there is substantial empirical support for this simple growth rule, which is discussed more fully in Chapter 17 in connection with the balance of payments and economic development. This growth rule is also known in the literature as Thirlwall's Law, and Krugman's 45° rule, after the present author first showed how well the model fitted the growth experience of many countries in the postwar years, and Paul Krugman (1989) showed independently that relative price changes have not been an efficient balance-of-payments adjustment mechanism and that countries' growth rates relative to others have been equiproportional to the ratio of the income elasticities of demand for imports and exports.[9]

THE NEW ECONOMIC GEOGRAPHY

The **new economic geography**, pioneered by Krugman (1991, 1998), is also an attempt to explain the geographic pattern of economic development between countries, and between regions within countries, in terms of **centripetal forces** which lead to industrial concentration and **centrifugal forces** which lead to industrial dispersal. In this sense, there is an affinity with the cumulative causation model of Myrdal, but in the new economic geography, distance and transport costs play a key role.

There is always a tug of war going on between centripetal forces which promote geographic concentration of activities and centrifugal forces that oppose it. The centripetal forces, acting as magnets for activity, are mainly the different types of external economies associated with the size of markets and linkages between activities; labour market externalities (pools of skilled labour), and pure externalities such as knowledge spillovers. The centrifugal forces, resisting concentration, are such factors as the immobility of factors of production; high rents in concentrated areas, and pure external diseconomies, such as congestion costs.

Within this framework, the emergence of a 'centre' and 'periphery', and shifts in the geographic pattern of development, can be explained in terms of the changing balance between the pull of the market on the one hand and transport costs on the other. As in the Myrdal model, consider first of all two identical regions. If transport costs are very high, each region will be more or less self-sufficient. Activity will be widely dispersed serving local markets because it is too costly to transport inputs and output elsewhere.

Now suppose that transport costs start to fall. It becomes more economical for some regions to supply the needs of others. Those regions with some small initial advantage, as a result of geography or historical accident, will tend to capitalize on that advantage, exporting to the less favoured region and driving out business. Activity becomes concentrated in a core (or centre), leaving a run-down 'periphery' with only agricultural and service-type activities. A small initial difference between regions leads to a much larger difference in outcomes through the forces of cumulative causation based on external economies associated particularly with market size (**agglomeration economies**). At the regional level, Italy is a good case study. When the railway was introduced and transport costs fell, this made it possible for the factories of northern Italy to supply the needs of the less-competitive south of Italy, causing the heavy concentration of industrial activity in the north and deindustrialization of the south.

The periphery, however, will tend to have low production costs, particularly low wage costs because of high unemployment and underemployment. At some point, if transport costs fall even more, it may become economical to shift production from the centre to the periphery because low production costs now outweigh the cost of transport to the market. This is one important reason why, in recent years, there has been a major shift of the world's manufacturing base from the core of Europe and North America to the periphery of South East Asia.

This set of ideas outlined above helps to explain the historical evolution of divisions between regions and countries of the world which can spontaneously emerge with better communications, and then go into reverse when transport costs fall even lower.

Attempts have been made to quantify the impact of distance and transport costs on the level and growth of per capita income of countries across the world, as well as the effect of other geographic variables (e.g. Gallup, Sachs and Mellinger, 1998). Looking at a map of the world by income, two striking relationships are apparent. The first is that countries located close to the sea have higher per capita incomes (PCY) than landlocked countries. The second is that countries located in the tropics are poorer than countries outside the tropics. A third fact is (although not visible) that the coastal, temperate regions of the northern hemisphere have the highest income per square kilometre (km) of land (i.e. PCY × population density). The regions of North America, Western Europe (and parts of East Asia) that lie within 100 km of the sea contain 13 per cent of the world's population and produce 32 per cent of the world's output of goods and services. The explanation lies in the factors that we discussed above. Regions near the sea have lower transport costs so they can benefit from greater trade and specialization, and the greater densities of population lead to agglomeration economies and increasing returns. Today, the fastest growing developing countries have based their growth on labour-intensive manufactured exports located in coastal regions.

Gallup, Sachs and Mellinger (1998) run regressions across a large sample of countries of the level of PCY, and the growth of PCY from 1965 to 1990, against several geographic variables including the percentage of land in the tropics; the proportion of the population within 100 km of the coast; the minimum distance of a country to one of three core 'regions' (New York, Rotterdam and Tokyo); the incidence of malaria, and transport costs of a country measured (imperfectly) as the difference between the cost of imports free on board (f.o.b.) and their cost including insurance and freight charges (c.i.f.). The level of PCY is found to be negatively related to location in the tropics, malaria, distance, and transport costs; and positively related to the proportion of the population close to the sea. The growth of income (holding other variables constant such as education, trade openness, etc.) is shown to be 0.9 percentage points (p.p.) less in tropical countries than non-tropical countries; 1.2 p.p. less in countries severely affected by malaria; and 1.0 p.p. less in landlocked countries compared to coastal countries. Distance also significantly reduces growth if the trade openness variable is excluded from the equations.

Given these findings, it is hardly surprising that Africa has some of the poorest and most stagnant economies in the world. Geography is stacked against it!

THEORIES OF DEPENDENCE AND UNEQUAL EXCHANGE

Apart from the ideas of circular and cumulative causation and balance-of-payments constrained growth, there is also a number of theories and models in the Marxist tradition (many originating from Latin America and France) concerned with **dependency, exploitation and unequal exchange**. These theories attempt to explain the perpetuation and widening of the differences between centre and periphery, and may be regarded as complementary to, and an integral part of, the mechanisms we have been discussing. For example, part of the dependency and unequal exchange relation is related to the characteristics of trade; but there are many other important dimensions to the argument:

■ The dependence of the periphery on foreign capital and the expropriation of the surplus by the centre
■ The dependence on foreign technology
■ Terms-of-trade deterioration
■ Mechanisms that reduce real wages in developing countries below what they would otherwise be
■ Various socio-cultural aspects of neocolonialism that thwart the drive for independence and self-reliance.

Writers in this tradition include Dos Santos, Baran, Gunder Frank, Amin and Emmanuel. It should be emphasised at the outset that dependency theory cannot easily be tested empirically; rather it is designed to provide a framework of ideas to accommodate the many aspects and features of the functioning of the world capitalist economy and the many types of dominance and dependency.

Dos Santos (1970) defines dependence thus: 'by dependence we mean a situation in which the economy of certain countries is conditioned by the development and expansion of another economy to which the former is subjected'. The relation is such that 'some countries (the dominant ones) can expand and can be self-sustaining, while others (the dependent ones) can do this only as a reflection of expansion, which can have either a positive or a negative effect on their intermediate development'. **Unequal development must be seen as an integral part of the world capitalist system.** Inequality is inevitable because development of some parts of the system occurs at the expense of others. The monopoly power over trade that is exercised by the centre leads to the transfer of the economic surplus from the dependent countries to the centre, and financial relations that are based on loans and the exportation of capital by the centre ultimately lead to reverse flows and strengthen the position of the dominant country in the dependent country.

Different forms of dependence can be distinguished, as they have evolved historically. First, there is **colonial dependence**, based on trade and the exploitation of natural resources. Second, there is **financial–industrial dependence**, which consolidated itself at the end of the nineteenth century and has geared the economic structure of dependent nations to the needs of the centre. Third, a new type of dependence has emerged from 1945 based on multinational corporations, which began to invest in industries geared to the internal market of developing countries. This is **technological–industrial dependence**. Dos Santos argues that each of these forms of dependence has so conditioned the internal structure of peripheral countries, that this itself has become part of the dependency relation; for example the highly dualistic structure, the income inequality and conspicuous consumption of the wealthy classes, a dependency mentality and the ingrained habit of seeking outside help, and the unholy alliance between the domestic ruling elite and foreign interests all conspire to impede internal development. Thus Dos Santos (1973) maintains that dependency is not simply an external phenomenon; it also has to do with the supportive power groups within the poor countries themselves who find the status quo profitable:

> if dependency defines the internal situation and is structurally linked to it, a country cannot break out of it simply by isolating herself from external influence; such action would simply provoke chaos in a society which is of its essence dependent. The only solution therefore would be to change its internal structure; a course which necessarily leads to confrontation with the existing international structure.

Baran (1957), Frank (1967) and Amin (1974) focus their attention more squarely on the traditional Marxist mechanisms by which capitalism in general, and international capitalism in particular, aid the rich in exploiting the poor. Emphasis is placed on the expropriation and transfer of the surplus produced by labour to the owners of capital, which operates at different levels. Think of a cone, the base of which represents the rural poor producing a surplus from their labours in the fields or down the mines. This surplus is first siphoned off by those in the provincial towns, by small employers and merchants. In turn, the wealth of these towns is sapped by the capital cities, and finally, part of this wealth is siphoned away by foreign investors, who repatriate it to the apex of the cone – the rich world. The multinational corporations are seen as the modern instrument for the expropriation of surplus value. Neo-Marxists allow for a residue of surplus, but argue that if it is reinvested in the periphery or left in the hands of local elites, it will not be used appropriately for development purposes. As in Dos Santos' model, the system hinges on the collaboration of the governing elite who live in the capital city, who think like, and identify with, their ex-colonial masters. So poor countries, despite formal political independence, remain locked into an old system of economic dependence that perpetuates underdevelopment.

For Frank, like Dos Santos, underdevelopment is a natural outcome of the world capitalist system since the development of some countries inevitably means the distorted development or underdevelopment of others. Development itself perpetuates underdevelopment, a process that Frank has called '**the development of underdevelopment**'. Frank sees the origins of the process in colonization, which started as a form of economic exploitation and has distorted the economic structure of Third World countries ever since. The developing countries were forced into the position of being suppliers of raw materials to industrial countries, thus effectively blocking industrial development in the primary producing countries themselves. The whole export orientation and foreign dominance of these countries has limited the growth of the domestic market and the establishment of basic national industries for widespread development throughout the whole economy. The international, national and local capitalist systems alike generate economic development for the few and underdevelopment for the many. The solution would appear to be nothing short of social and political revolution.

UNEQUAL EXCHANGE

The theory of unequal exchange owes its name to Emmanuel (1972). Exchange is unequal between rich and poor countries because wages are lower in poor countries, and lower than if the rate of profit in poor countries was not as high as in rich countries. In other words, exchange is unequal in relation to a situation where wages would be equalized: 'Inequality of wages as such, all other things being equal, is alone the cause of the inequality of exchange.' Let us illustrate the model diagrammatically and show its affinity with the ideas of those who stress the terms of trade as the main mechanism through which the gains from exchange are unequally distributed. Let us take two countries and call them 'centre' (c) and 'periphery' (p). Assume that prices in the two countries are based on a percentage mark-up (r) on unit labour costs, so that

$$P_c = w_c \left(\frac{L}{O}\right)_c (1 + r_c)$$

and

$$P_p = w_p \left(\frac{L}{O}\right)_p (1 + r_p)$$

where w is the money wage rate, and wL/O is wage costs per unit of output. Now assume that for institutional reasons $w_c > w_p$ and that the mark-up or rate of profit equalizes between the two countries. The theory of unequal exchange says that because of this, the terms of trade will be worse for the periphery than if wages in the periphery were higher and the rate of profit lower. This can be illustrated diagrammatically, taking the price of the centre's goods as the *numéraire*, so that $P_c = 1$ (Figure 7.4).

In the centre, the given rate of profit ($\bar{r}$) and wage rate (w_c) gives a constant price (P_c) which acts as *numéraire* (hence the horizontal line, w_c). In the periphery, at a given wage (w_p), there is a positive relation between the rate of profit and terms of trade (P), given by the upward-sloping line w_p. The equilibrium terms of trade is given at P_1. An increase in periphery wages shifts the periphery curve rightwards to w_p^1, giving a new terms of trade, P_2, at the same rate of profit. Unequal exchange is measured as the difference between the actual terms of trade (P_1) and what it would be if wages were higher in the periphery and the rate of profit was lower at r^1. The 'explanation' of unequal exchange is unequal wage rates.

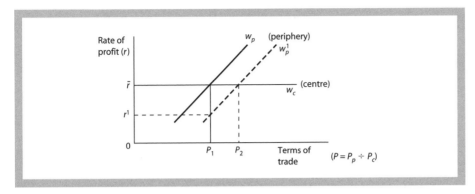

Figure 7.4 The theory of unequal exchange

The model does not get us very far, however, without understanding why there are wage differences between centre and periphery. In Emmanuel's model, the wage differences are institutionally determined outside the model, whereas in practice there are many factors that impinge on wage differences within the model itself that need consideration. Moreover, money wage differences may not be the only factor leading to unequal exchange. If money wage differences between centre and periphery reflect differences in labour productivity, the terms of trade between periphery and centre will not be nearly as bad as suggested by money wage differences alone. Indeed, if differences in money wages are exactly matched by differences in productivity, there will be no difference in money wage costs per unit of output and no difference in relative prices 'caused' by differences in money wages. There can still be unequal exchange in the Emmanuel sense by virtue of the way Emmanuel defines the concept, but if the cause of low wages is low productivity it is not a simple institutional matter to raise them.[10]

On the other side of the coin, if there is no good reason why the rate of profit should equalize between the two countries, a higher rate of profit in the centre could be an independent source of unequal exchange between centre and periphery, and also an explanation of why wages are depressed in the periphery. If account is taken of the characteristics of the goods produced by the centre and periphery – manufactured goods in the centre subject to decreasing costs, and primary commodities in the periphery subject to increasing costs – we can predict that oligopolistic structures will develop in the centre, while competitive structures will prevail in the periphery, with a tendency, therefore, for the rate of profit to be higher in the centre. The lower rate of profit in the periphery, and the attempt by capitalists to keep up the rate of profit in the face of competition, leads to the depression of wages in classic Marxist style.

DISCUSSION QUESTIONS

1 What do you understand by the terms technological dualism, social dualism and geographic dualism?

2 Is dualism avoidable in the development process?

3 In what ways might dualism impede the functioning of the total economy?

4 In what senses is Myrdal's theory of circular and cumulative causation a challenge to static equilibrium theory?

5 What are the media through which the process of circular and cumulative causation work?

6 If backward regions suffer 'backwash' effects from regions of expansion, would they be better off as sovereign states?

7 What is the so-called 'Verdoorn effect' and its importance in the process of circular and cumulative causation?

8 What do the centre–periphery (or North–South) models by Prebisch, Seers, Dixon and Thirlwall, and Kaldor all have in common?

9 How does distance and geography affect the geographical pattern of economic development?

10 What are the various 'Marxist' explanations of the growing divergence between rich and poor countries?

11 What do you understand by the theory of unequal exchange?

NOTES

1. First hinted at in Prebisch, *The Economic Development of Latin America and its Principal Problems* (1950), and developed in 'Commercial Policy in the Underdeveloped Countries', *American Economic Review, Papers and Proceedings*, May 1959.
2. The income elasticity of demand for goods measures the proportionate change in demand for a good with respect to a proportionate change in income, holding other things constant.
3. D. Seers, 'A Model of Comparative Rates of Growth of the World Economy', *Economic Journal*, March 1962.
4. In other words, with a linear import demand function, the intercept of the function must be negative for the ratio of imports to income to increase as income rises, which is what is implied if the income elasticity of demand for imports exceeds unity.
5. By analogous reasoning to the above.
6. A fuller discussion of balance-of-payments constrained growth, and the role of various adjustment mechanisms, is given in Chapter 17.
7. The model is discussed more fully in Dixon and Thirlwall (1975).
8. Under certain circumstances the growth rate may not converge to its equilibrium level. This depends on the behaviour of the model out of equilibrium. See Dixon and Thirlwall (1975).
9. For a comprehensive review and discussion of the models, see McCombie and Thirlwall (1994).
10. Within this framework, movements in the terms of trade can be seen as the outcome of differences in the movement of productivity on the one hand and whether money wage changes fully match productivity changes on the other. If money wage increases fail to match productivity increases in the periphery, for example, so that real wages do not rise as fast as productivity, whereas they do in the centre, there will be a steady deterioration in the terms of trade of the periphery. This is the essence of the Prebisch argument (see Chapter 16).

Population and development

INTRODUCTION

The relation between population growth and economic development is a complex one and the historical quantitative evidence is ambiguous, particularly concerning what is cause and what is effect. Does economic development precede population growth, or is population growth a necessary condition for economic development to take place? Is population growth an impediment or a stimulus to economic development? Many people consider rapid population growth in the Third World to be a major obstacle to development, yet there are several ways in which population growth may be a stimulus to progress, and there are several rational reasons why families in developing countries choose to have many children.

The complexity of the subject is compounded by the fact that, as we saw in Chapter 1, economic development is a multidimensional concept, and if the measure of development is to be translated into a measure of welfare, complex philosophical questions are involved that relate to the meaning of welfare maximization and the concept of an optimum population, which have preoccupied welfare economists for centuries. If it could be shown, for example, that slower population growth leads to a higher rate of growth of per capita income, or that fewer people means higher living standards, would this mean that if a society adopted successful population control policies it would be better off? The utilitarian approach to welfare would say 'not necessarily'. Utilitarians adopt a total welfare criterion, as Sidgwick did in his *Methods of Ethics* (1874):

> if the additional population enjoy on the whole positive happiness, we ought to weigh the amount of happiness gained by the extra number against the amount lost by the remainder. So that, strictly conceived, the point up to which, on utilitarian principles, population ought to be encouraged to increase is not that at which *average* happiness is the greatest possible – as appears to be often assumed by political economists of the school of Malthus – but at which the product formed by multiplying the number of persons living into the amount of average happiness reaches its maximum. (emphasis added)

On the other hand, instinctively and intuitively, most people are not utilitarian.

In conditions of poverty, if increments to population reduce the average standard of living still further, most people would no doubt think it perverse to call this an improvement in welfare simply because the number of people 'enjoying' such an impoverished state had risen. As Cassen (1976) has put it: 'concern for the never born (as opposed to those actually born, past and future) may be something of a luxury.' Rawls (1972), in *A Theory of Justice*, invites us to think of a rational observer having to choose membership of one or other society from behind a veil of ignorance as to where in each society he would find himself placed. With a moderate degree of self-interest, Rawls argues, he would probably choose the society that rejects utilitarianism and adheres to the per capita criterion. And yet a population policy based on maximizing per capita income has frightening implications (not entirely fanciful) for all sub-marginal groups in society that may be deemed to be depressing the average standard of life (see the later discussion on optimum population).

Where does all this leave the welfare basis for population control programmes? A surer basis lies not in diminishing returns to population (indeed there may be increasing returns, in which case the utilitarian debate becomes irrelevant), but in the divergences between the private and social benefits to be had from large numbers of children. For example, individual families may prefer to have fewer children if they know that all other families will have fewer children, but in isolation they are not willing to limit the number of children they have. This is an example of what is known in welfare economics as '**the isolation paradox**', and it establishes a case for public intervention. It is the young who suffer from there being more children because most of the costs arise in the future. Present parents may enjoy their children, but their children may wish their parents had had fewer, and they probably would have had fewer if they could have been sure that everybody else would have had fewer too. A further reason for public intervention in the field of population control may be market failure, if it can be shown that families have more children than they actually want and that there is an unmet need for family planning services.

It is interesting to note that surveys of desired family size in developing countries have consistently put the figure at one or two lower than the actual family size. Apart from this, it could be argued that it is a basic human right to be able to choose freely and responsibly the number of children to have and how far apart to have them. This indeed was the resolution endorsed by the Bucharest World Population Conference in 1974, which laid the foundation for the World Bank's increased support for population control programmes throughout the Third World, and reiterated by the UN Conference on Population and Development in Cairo in 1994. The Cairo Conference emphasized the right of women to control the number and timing of their children and urged countries to provide universal access to family planning services. It is estimated that only 50 per cent of married women in developing countries use any form of birth control. As we shall see later, however, the education of women is the major determinant of fertility, and a necessary condition for a reduction in fertility is the expansion of educational and work opportunities for women.

First, however, let us outline the facts on the world population and then consider in more detail the determinants of fertility, followed by an analysis of the conflicting role of population growth in the growth and development process.

FACTS ABOUT WORLD POPULATION

The pertinent facts about the level and growth of the populations of individual countries and for the world as a whole are shown in Table 8.1. At the present time the world's population is just over 6300 million, of which more than two-thirds live in the developing countries, and nearly one-half reside in Asia. This level compares with approximately 179 million at the time of Christ, and less than 1000 million as recently as 1800 AD. The current rate of growth of the world population is 1.2 per cent per annum, which has no precedent historically. From AD 1 to 1750 the rate was no more than 0.05 per cent per annum; from 1750 to 1850 it was 0.5 per cent per annum; and even between 1900 and 1950 it was only 0.8 per cent per annum.[1]

At the present rate of increase the world population will double every 65 years. The current projection from the United Nations is that by the year 2050 the population will rise to 8 billion if birth rates continue to fall dramatically, or 12 billion if birth rates come down only slowly. The explosive growth of the world population is illustrated in Figure 8.1, which also shows the crude birth and death rates for the developed and developing countries. The gap between the two rates gives the rate of population growth. The past and projected population growth rates are shown in Figure 8.2.

The rates of population growth in developing countries in the recent past have been substantially in excess of the rate of growth for the world as a whole, and they look like continuing in the foreseeable future. The average rate of growth for the low- and middle-income countries since 1980 has been 1.7 per cent per annum, compared with 0.7 per cent in the developed countries. By continent, Africa has experienced the most rapid population growth (2.7 per cent), followed by Latin America (1.8 per cent) and Asia (1.4 per cent).

The country with the largest population is China, with an estimated current population of 1300 million, followed by India, the United States, Indonesia, Japan, Russia, Brazil, Bangladesh, Nigeria, Pakistan and Mexico, all with populations of over 100 million. China and India alone currently add 25 million people to the world's population every year. In the last minute, approximately 300 babies have been born and 150 people have died, increasing the world's population by 150 persons, giving a yearly increase of 80 million.

The rate of growth of population is the difference between the number of live births

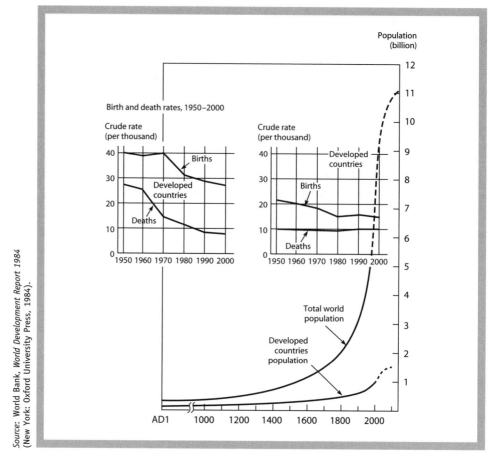

Source: World Bank, *World Development Report 1984* (New York: Oxford University Press, 1984).

Figure 8.1 Past and projected world population, AD 1–2150

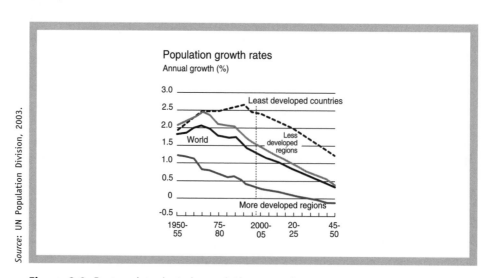

Source: UN Population Division, 2003.

Figure 8.2 Past and projected population growth rates

Table 8.1 Population dynamics

	Total population (millions)		Average annual population growth rate (%)		Dependency ratio — dependents as proportion of working-age population		Crude death rate per 1,000 people	Crude birth rate per 1,000 people
	2002	2015	1980–2002	2002–15	Young 2002	Old 2002	2002	2002
Afghanistan	28.0[a]	38.8	2.6	2.5	0.8	0.1	21	49
Albania	3.2	3.5	0.7	0.8	0.4	0.1	6	17
Algeria	31.3	38.3	2.4	1.5	0.6	0.1	5	22
Angola	13.1	18.9	2.8	2.8	1.0	0.1	19	50
Argentina	36.5	42.9	1.2	1.2	0.4	0.2	8	19
Armenia	3.1	3.0	0.0	−0.1	0.3	0.1	8	9
Australia	19.7	21.7	1.3	0.8	0.3	0.2	7	13
Austria	8.0	8.0	0.3	−0.1	0.2	0.2	10	9
Azerbaijan	8.2	9.0	1.3	0.7	0.4	0.1	7	16
Bangladesh	135.7	166	2.1	1.5	0.6	0.1	8	28
Belarus	9.9	9.3	0.1	−0.5	0.3	0.2	14	9
Belgium	10.3	10.4	0.2	0.1	0.3	0.3	10	11
Benin	6.6	9.0	2.9	2.4	0.9	0.1	13	38
Bolivia	8.8	10.9	2.3	1.7	0.7	0.1	8	29
Bosnia and Herzegovina	4.1	4.2	0.0	0.2	0.2	0.1	8	12
Bostwana	1.7	1.8	2.9	0.4	0.7	0.0	23	30
Brazil	174.5	201	1.6	1.1	0.4	0.1	7	19
Bulgaria	8.0	7.3	−0.5	−0.7	0.2	0.2	14	9
Burkina Faso	11.8	15.6	2.4	2.1	0.9	0.1	19	43
Burundi	7.1	8.8	2.4	1.7	0.9	0.0	20	39
Cambodia	12.5	15.1	2.8	1.5	0.8	0.1	12	27
Cameroon	15.8	19.7	2.7	1.7	0.8	0.1	16	36
Canada	31.4	33.5	1.1	0.5	0.3	0.2	7	11
Central African Republic	3.8	4.6	2.3	1.5	0.8	0.1	20	36
Chad	8.3	12.1	2.8	2.8	1.0	0.1	16	45
Chile	15.6	17.8	1.5	1.0	0.4	0.1	5	17
China	1 280.4	1 389.5	1.2	0.6	0.4	0.1	8	15
Hong Kong, China	6.8	7.0	1.4	0.2	0.2	0.2	5	7
Colombia	43.7	51.4	2.0	1.2	0.5	0.1	6	21
Congo, Dem. Rep.	51.6	75.2	2.8	2.9	1.0	0.1	18	45
Congo, Rep.	3.7	5.1	3.2	2.8	0.9	0.1	14	44
Costa Rica	3.9	4.7	2.5	1.4	0.5	0.1	4	20
Côte d'Ivoire	16.5	20.2	3.2	1.6	0.8	0.0	17	37
Croatia	4.5	4.3	−0.1	−0.3	0.2	0.2	12	10
Cuba	11.3	11.7	0.7	0.3	0.3	0.1	8	12
Czech Republic	10.2	9.9	0.0	−0.2	0.2	0.2	11	9
Denmark	5.4	5.4	0.2	0.1	0.3	0.2	11	12
Dominican Republic	8.6	10.1	1.9	1.2	0.5	0.1	7	23
Ecuador	12.8	15.4	2.2	1.4	0.5	0.1	6	23
Egypt, Arab Rep.	66.4	80.9	2.2	1.5	0.6	0.1	6	24
El Salvador	6.4	7.9	1.5	1.6	0.6	0.1	6	26
Eritrea	4.3	5.6	2.7	2.0	0.8	0.1	13	38
Estonia	1.4	1.3	−0.4	−0.6	0.2	0.2	14	9
Ethiopia	67.2	87.3	2.6	2.0	0.9	0.1	20	40
Finland	5.2	5.3	0.4	0.1	0.3	0.2	10	11
France	59.5	61.8	0.4	0.3	0.3	0.2	10	13
Gabon	1.3	1.7	2.9	2.2	0.7	0.1	15	35
Gambia, The	1.4	1.8	3.5	1.9	0.7	0.1	14	37
Georgia	5.2	4.7	0.1	−0.8	0.3	0.2	10	8
Germany	82.5	80.3	0.2	−0.2	0.2	0.2	10	9
Ghana	20.3	25.2	2.8	1.7	0.8	0.1	13	29
Greece	10.6	11	0.4	0.3	0.2	0.3	11	9

Table 8.1 continued

	Total population (millions)		Average annual population growth rate (%)		Dependency ratio — dependents as proportion of working-age population		Crude death rate per 1,000 people	Crude birth rate per 1,000 people
	2002	2015	1980–2002	2002–15	Young 2002	Old 2002	2002	2002
Guatemala	12.0	16.3	2.6	2.3	0.8	0.1	7	33
Guinea	7.7	9.8	2.5	1.8	0.8	0.0	17	38
Guinea-Bissau	1.4	2.0	2.7	2.6	0.8	0.1	20	49
Haiti	8.3	10.3	2.0	1.7	0.7	0.1	14	32
Honduras	6.8	8.9	2.9	2.1	0.7	0.1	6	30
Hungary	10.2	9.6	−0.2	−0.4	0.2	0.2	13	10
India	1 048.6	1 231.6	1.9	1.2	0.5	0.1	9	24
Indonesia	211.7	245.5	1.6	1.1	0.5	0.1	7	20
Iran, Islamic Rep.	65.5	77.5	2.3	1.3	0.5	0.1	6	18
Iraq	24.2	31.1	2.8	1.9	0.7	0.1	8	29
Ireland	3.9	4.3	0.6	0.8	0.3	0.2	8	15
Israel	6.6	7.9	2.4	1.4	0.4	0.2	6	20
Italy	57.7	55.1	0.1	−0.3	0.2	0.3	11	9
Jamaica	2.6	3.0	0.9	1.0	0.5	0.1	6	20
Japan	127.2	124.6	0.4	−0.2	0.2	0.3	8	9
Jordan	5.2	6.8	3.9	2.2	0.6	0.1	4	28
Kazakhstan	14.9	15.5	0.0	0.3	0.4	0.1	12	15
Kenya	31.3	37.5	2.9	1.4	0.8	0.0	16	35
Korea, Dem. Rep.	22.5	24.0	1.2	0.5	0.4	0.1	11	17
Korea, Rep.	47.6	50.0	1.0	0.4	0.3	0.1	7	12
Kuwait	2.3	3.0	2.4	1.9	0.3	0.0	3	20
Kyrgyz Republic	5.0	5.8	1.5	1.1	0.5	0.1	7	20
Lao PDR	5.5	7.3	2.5	2.1	0.8	0.1	12	36
Latvia	2.3	2.1	−0.4	−0.7	0.2	0.2	14	8
Lebanon	4.4	5.2	1.8	1.2	0.5	0.1	6	19
Lesotho	1.8	2.0	1.5	0.9	0.8	0.1	23	33
Liberia	3.3	4.4	2.6	2.2	0.8	0.1	20	43
Libya	5.4	6.9	2.6	1.8	0.5	0.1	4	27
Lithuania	3.5	3.3	0.1	−0.4	0.3	0.2	12	9
Macedonia, FYR	2.0	2.2	0.3	0.5	0.3	0.2	9	14
Madagascar	16.4	22.5	2.8	2.4	0.8	0.1	12	39
Malawi	10.7	13.6	2.5	1.8	0.9	0.1	25	45
Malaysia	24.3	29.6	2.6	1.5	0.5	0.1	5	22
Mali	11.4	15.6	2.5	2.4	0.9	0.1	22	48
Mauritania	2.8	3.6	2.5	2.0	0.8	0.1	15	35
Mauritius	1.2	1.4	1.0	0.9	0.4	0.1	7	17
Mexico	100.8	120.6	1.8	1.4	0.5	0.1	4	20
Moldova	4.3	4.1	0.3	−0.2	0.3	0.2	13	11
Mongolia	2.4	2.9	1.8	1.3	0.5	0.1	6	23
Morocco	29.6	35.4	1.9	1.4	0.5	0.1	6	21
Mozambique	18.4	22.7	1.9	1.6	0.8	0.1	21	40
Myanmar	48.8	55.7	1.7	1.0	0.5	0.1	12	23
Namibia	2.0	2.3	3.0	1.1	0.8	0.1	21	35
Nepal	24.1	31.1	2.3	2.0	0.7	0.1	10	32
Netherlands	16.1	16.7	0.6	0.3	0.3	0.2	9	12
New Zealand	3.9	4.4	1.1	0.8	0.3	0.2	7	14
Nicaragua	5.3	7.0	2.7	2.0	0.7	0.1	5	29
Niger	11.4	16.3	3.3	2.7	1.0	0.0	20	49
Nigeria	132.8	169.4	2.8	1.9	0.8	0.0	17	39
Norway	4.5	4.7	0.5	0.3	0.3	0.2	10	12
Oman	2.5	3.4	3.8	2.2	0.8	0.0	3	26
Pakistan	144.9	192.8	2.5	2.2	0.7	0.1	8	33

Table 8.1 continued

	Total population (millions)		Average annual population growth rate (%)		Dependency ratio — dependents as proportion of working-age population		Crude death rate per 1,000 people	Crude birth rate per 1,000 people
	2002	2015	1980–2002	2002–15	Young 2002	Old 2002	2002	2002
Panama	2.9	3.5	1.9	1.2	0.5	0.1	5	20
Papua New Guinea	5.4	6.9	2.5	1.9	0.7	0.0	10	33
Paraguay	5.5	7.2	2.6	2.0	0.7	0.1	5	30
Peru	26.7	31.5	2.0	1.3	0.5	0.1	6	22
Philippines	79.9	98.2	2.3	1.6	0.6	0.1	6	26
Poland	38.6	38.4	0.4	0.0	0.3	0.2	9	9
Portugal	10.2	10.2	0.2	0.0	0.3	0.2	11	12
Puerto Rico	3.9	4.2	0.9	0.7	0.4	0.2	8	15
Romania	22.3	21.4	0.0	-0.3	0.2	0.2	13	10
Russian Federation	144.1	134.5	0.2	-0.5	0.2	0.2	15	10
Rwanda	8.2	10.0	2.1	1.6	0.9	0.1	22	44
Saudi Arabia	21.9	30.8	3.9	2.6	0.7	0.1	4	31
Senegal	10.0	12.8	2.7	1.9	0.8	0.1	13	35
Serbia and Montenegro	8.2	10.7	0.4c	2.1	0.3	0.2	12	12
Sierra Leone	5.2	6.7	2.2	1.9	0.8	0.0	25	44
Singapore	4.2	4.8	2.5	1.1	0.3	0.1	5	11
Slovak Republic	5.4	5.4	0.3	0.0	0.3	0.2	10	11
Slovenia	2.0	1.9	0.1	-0.2	0.2	0.2	10	9
Somalia	9.3	14.0	1.6	3.1	1.0	0.0	18	50
South Africa	45.3	47.0	2.3	0.3	0.5	0.1	20	25
Spain	40.9	41.5	0.4	0.1	0.2	0.2	9	10
Sri Lanka	19.0	21.9	1.2	1.1	0.4	0.1	6	18
Sudan	32.8	42.6	2.4	2.0	0.7	0.1	10	33
Swaziland	1.1	1.3	3.0	1.2	0.8	0.1	18	35
Sweden	8.9	9.0	0.3	0.1	0.3	0.3	11	11
Switzerland	7.3	7.5	0.6	0.2	0.2	0.2	9	10
Syrian Arab Republic	17.0	22.0	3.0	2.0	0.7	0.1	4	29
Tajikistan	6.3	7.2	2.1	1.0	0.6	0.1	7	23
Tanzania	35.2	43.9	2.9	1.7	0.9	0.0	18	38
Thailand	61.6	66.3	1.3	0.6	0.3	0.1	8	15
Togo	4.8	6.2	2.9	2.0	0.8	0.1	15	36
Trinidad and Tobago	1.3	1.4	0.8	0.8	0.4	0.1	7	16
Tunisia	9.8	11.5	1.9	1.3	0.4	0.1	6	18
Turkey	69.6	81.3	2.0	1.2	0.4	0.1	7	22
Turkmenistan	4.8	5.7	2.3	1.3	0.6	0.1	8	22
Uganda	24.6	33.6	3.0	2.4	1.0	0.0	18	44
Ukraine	48.7	44.7	-0.1	-0.7	0.2	0.2	15	9
United Arab Emirates	3.2	3.7	5.1	1.1	0.4	0.0	4	17
United Kingdom	59.2	59.6	0.2	0.0	0.3	0.2	10	11
United States	288.4	319.9	1.1	0.8	0.3	0.2	9	14
Uruguay	3.4	3.6	0.6	0.6	0.4	0.2	10	16
Uzbekistan	25.3	30.0	2.1	1.3	0.6	0.1	6	20
Venezuela, RB	25.1	30.3	2.3	1.4	0.5	0.1	5	23
Vietnam	80.4	92.4	1.8	1.1	0.5	0.1	6	19
West Bank and Gaza	3.2	4.9	–	3.2	0.9	0.1	4	35
Yemen, Rep.	18.6	27.3	3.5	2.9	0.9	0.1	10	41
Zambia	10.2	11.9	2.6	1.2	0.8	0.0	23	39
Zimbabwe	13.0	14.1	2.7	0.6	0.8	0.1	21	29

Table 8.1 continued

	Total population (millions)		Average annual population growth rate (%)		Dependency ratio (dependents as proportion of working-age population) Young Old		Crude death rate (per 1,000 people)	Crude birth rate (per 1,000 people)
	2002	2015	1980–2002	2002–15	2002	2002	2002	2002
World	6 198.5	7 090.7	1.5	1.0	0.5	0.1	9	21
Low income	2 494.6	3 044.0	2.1	1.5	0.6	0.1	11	29
Middle income	2 737.8	3 039.0	1.3	0.8	0.4	0.1	8	17
Lower middle income	2 408.5	2 658.4	1.3	0.8	0.4	0.1	8	17
Upper middle income	329.3	380.6	1.5	1.1	0.5	0.1	6	19
Low & middle income	5 232.4	6 083.0	1.7	1.2	0.5	0.1	9	22
East Asia & Pacific	1 838.3	2 036.9	1.4	0.8	0.4	0.1	8	16
Europe & Central Asia	472.9	478.2	0.5	0.1	0.3	0.2	12	13
Latin America & Carib.	524.9	619.4	1.8	1.3	0.5	0.1	6	21
Middle East & N. Africa	305.8	382.7	2.6	1.7	0.6	0.1	6	24
South Asia	1 401.5	1 683.7	2.0	1.4	0.6	0.1	9	26
Sub-Saharan Africa	688.9	882.1	2.7	1.9	0.8	0.1	18	39
High income	966.2	1 007.7	0.7	0.3	0.3	0.2	9	12

Source: World Bank, *World Development Indicators 2004* (Washington: World Bank).

per thousand of the population and the number of deaths per thousand. In a country where the birth rate is 40 per 1000 and the death rate is 20 per 1000, the rate of population growth will therefore be (40 − 20)/1000 = 20 per 1000, or 2 per cent per annum. If (in normal circumstances) a birth rate of 60 per 1000 is considered to be a 'biological' maximum, and a death rate of 10 per 1000 is considered a 'medical' minimum, the maximum possible growth rate of population, ignoring immigration, would be about 5 per cent per annum. These birth and death rates are in fact extremes, and are rarely found in practice. The current maximum birth rates recorded are 45 per 1000 in some African countries. For the low income countries the average birth rate is about 29 per 1000 and the average death rate is now about 11 per 1000, giving an average rate of population increase of approximately 1.8 per cent annum (see Table 8.1). This rapid rate of population growth, compared with advanced countries (and also in relation to the growth of national income), is the result of relatively high birth rates coupled with death rates that are almost as low as in advanced countries. If population growth is a 'problem' in developing countries, this is the simple source of the difficulty and the long-run solution is plain: there must be a reduction in fertility.

THE DETERMINANTS OF FERTILITY

The vital questions are, can high birth rates be expected to fall naturally with development, and if so, what is the crucial level of development and per capita income at which the adjustment will take place and how long will the process take? The conventional wisdom used to be that fertility decline would come only with rising levels of per capita income, urbanisation and industrialization. This is the theory of **demographic transition**.

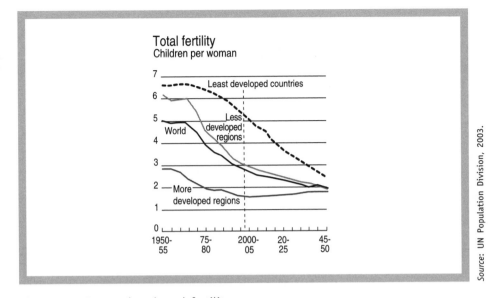

Source: UN Population Division, 2003.

Figure 8.3 Past and projected fertility

If the fertility rate of countries (i.e. the number of children per woman) is plotted against the level of per capita income, a definite negative relationship is observable. It is also true that through time the fertility rate decreases at a given level of per capita income, and that there are big differences in the fertility rate between countries at the same level of income. Clearly there are important factors, other than the level of per capita income, that affect the level of fertility through time and across countries.

The past and projected fertility rates are shown in Figure 8.3.

The data show fertility declining in all regions of the world, with the world fertility rate falling to two children per woman by the year 2050. The number of children per woman required for the population to replace itself is 2.1. Notice that in the developed countries, fertility has already fallen below this critical level with an average of 1.6 children per woman.

Reductions in fertility can occur with improvement in a wide range of socioeconomic conditions, such as access to family planning services, the provision of health care and a reduction in child mortality, greater employment opportunities for women, and above all the education of women and the promotion of female literacy. Where women are excluded from secondary education the average number of children per woman is seven. In countries where half of women go to secondary school, the average number of children is three. Figure 8.4 shows the strong negative relationship between female literacy and the reduction in fertility across 93 countries.

There are a number of reasons why women's education lowers fertility:

■ Education improves work opportunities for women, which makes having children more costly in terms of income forgone

■ Educated women want their own children to be educated, which raises the cost of having children

■ Education and literacy make women more receptive to information about contraception

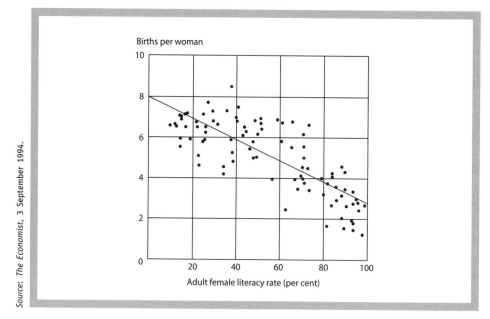

Source: The Economist, 3 September 1994.

Figure 8.4 Fertility rate and female literacy, 1990

- Education and employment delay marriage and the time available to rear children
- Education improves the status, bargaining power and independence of women, encouraging and enabling them to make their own choices.

From a vicious circle of no education, high fertility, poor health of children and low productivity, the education of women can lead to a virtuous circle of lower fertility, better care of children, more educational opportunity and higher productivity. The countries where fertility is declining most rapidly are those with the highest levels of female schooling, the lowest levels of child mortality and the widest availability of family planning services.

The reductions in fertility in different parts of the world over the last two decades are shown in Table 8.2. In developing countries as a whole the reduction has been 40 per cent from five children per fertile woman in 1975 to three in 1997. In the least developed countries, however, the number of children is still five. Africa has the highest fertility rate and East Asia the lowest.

The birth rate of a country is equal to its fertility rate multiplied by the ratio of fertile women to the total population. Even though fertility rates decline, birth rates do not necessarily decline in the same proportion because of the young age structure of the population produced by high fertility levels in the past. Thus, even if fertility continues to decline substantially, it will still take decades for the population level to stabilize because of the sheer number of couples having families. There is a **population momentum** built into the present age structure of the population of most developing countries. It is estimated that even if fertility rates were reduced immediately to the level of replacement (that is, one daughter per woman, which means approximately 2.1 children per family), the population of the developing countries will not stabilize until 2050, at a level of about 9 billion.

Table 8.2 Total fertility rate (births per woman)

Country	1970–5	2000–5
Developing countries	5.4	2.9
Least developed countries	6.6	5.1
Arab States	6.7	3.8
East Asia and the Pacific	5.0	2.0
Latin America and the Caribbean	5.1	2.5
South Asia	5.6	3.3
Sub-Saharan Africa	6.8	5.4
Central & Eastern Europe & CIS	2.5	1.4
OECD	2.5	1.8
High-income OECD	2.2	1.7
High human development	2.5	1.8
Medium human development	4.9	2.4
Low human development	6.8	5.6
High income	2.2	1.7
Middle income	4.5	2.1
Low income	5.9	3.7
World	4.5	2.7

Source: UNDP, *Human Development Report 2004* (New York: Oxford University Press, 2004).

Given that there may be a lag between the death rate falling and a subsequent decline in the birth rate, rapid population growth may be considered a transitional or more enduring 'problem' for a country depending on the currently prevailing level of the rate of births and deaths. This proposition is best illustrated by means of a simple diagram (Figure 8.5).

The curves *RB* and *RD* represent the time paths of the birth rate and death rate, respectively. Population growth is determined by the gap between the two curves. To save drawing more diagrams, let us suppose that points *X* and *Y* in Figure 8.5 represent two countries with the same current rate of population growth (*Pq* = *St*). In the case of country *Y*, population growth will soon slow down since the death rate has reached its minimum and the birth rate is falling. In the case of country *X*, however, which has the same *current* population growth, the population growth rate can be expected to increase in the future as the gap between the birth and death rates widens. The

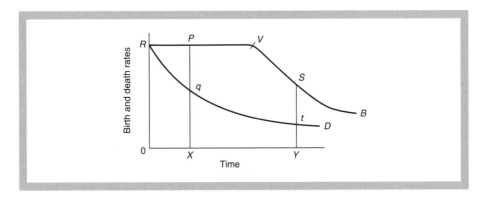

Figure 8.5 Population momentum

death rate is falling but the birth rate remains constant to the point V; only after this point will population growth decrease. Here, then, are two countries with the same observed population growth at present but with radically different future prospects. When comparing countries, and their population 'problems', the time profile of countries must be borne in mind. But the crucial questions, as we suggested earlier, are what is the length of the time lag between the death rate falling and the downturn of the birth rate? What is the length of the **demographic transition**? It is the length of this lag that determines the short-run prospects of countries emerging from a transitional state and attempting to 'take-off' into self-sustaining growth.

The experience of the developing countries today has no historical parallel, at least in Western Europe. In nineteenth-century Europe the birth and death rates tended to fall together and population growth never exceeded 1 per cent per annum. It could almost be argued that the 'balance of nature' has been upset in the present developing countries. The introduction of public-health measures and medical advances reduced death rates suddenly and dramatically, but the means and know-how to effect an equally dramatic fall in the birth rate were not provided at the same time. Modern science and public health administration have contributed to the ending of premature death, but have not until recently exerted a significant impact on births.

THE COSTS AND BENEFITS OF POPULATION GROWTH

Population growth plays a conflicting role in the development process. It can act as both a stimulus and an impediment to growth and development. The question, to which there is no easy answer, is at what point do the economic disadvantages begin to outweigh the advantages? Where does the balance lie?

The conventional view is that high levels and rates of growth of population constitute a problem for the world as a whole and for the developing countries in particular. Population growth, it is argued, depresses human welfare because it:

- Uses up scarce (non-renewable) resources and causes environmental degradation
- Puts pressure on food supplies
- Leads to overcrowding and congestion in cities
- Adds to the employment problem
- Reduces the savings ratio and dilutes the quantity of capital per person employed.

There are elements of truth in all these arguments, especially in parts of the world where there are particularly heavy concentrations of population in relation to habitable land. Asia, for example, contains over one-half of the world's population and over 1 billion people live in big cities which already suffer the highest levels of air pollution in the world, not to mention the congestion. Asia will be the biggest source of greenhouse gases by the year 2015 (on present trends). As we shall see, however, there are arguments to be put on the other side.

The pessimistic view of population originated with Malthus (see Chapter 4, p. 126), and in recent years it has been revived by ecologists, environmentalists and various ecodoomsters of different persuasions. The pessimism of Malthus stemmed from the pervasive classical belief in the law of diminishing returns, and the underestimation of humankind's response to the challenge of diminishing productivity with the expansion of numbers through invention and innovation. According to Malthus there is a 'constant tendency in all animated life to increase beyond the nourishment prepared for it'. Thus every mouth is accompanied by a pair of hands, but every pair of hands produces less and less additional output. Technological progress (always grossly underestimated by pessimists in general and by the classical economists in particular) would not be rapid enough, it was thought, to offset the tendency. However, Malthus became much less pessimistic between the first and fifth editions of his book, and conceded at one point that if it were not for population increase, 'no motive would be sufficiently strong to overcome the acknowledged indolence of man and make him proceed to the cultivation of the soil'.

A fairly typical remark, representative of the modern pessimistic school of population economists, is that by Enke (1971):

> The economic danger of rapid population growth lies in the consequent inability of a country both to increase its stock of capital and to improve its state of art rapidly enough for its *per capita* income not to be less than it otherwise would be. If the rate of technological innovation cannot be forced, and is not advanced by faster population growth, a rapid proportionate growth in population can cause an actual reduction in income per capita. Rapid population growth inhibits an increase in capital per worker, especially if associated with high crude birth rates that make for a young age distribution.

Hoover and Coale (1958), in their classic study of population growth and development based on the Indian experience, remark that:

> While greater numbers in the labour force add to the total product, faster growth of the labour force implies a lower output per worker than slower growth. The reason for this result is that with a faster growing labour force more capital must be directed to provide tools and equipment for the extra workers so that they will be as productive as the existing labour force, and thus less will be available, *ceteris paribus*, for increasing output per worker.

The arguments made do not sound unreasonable but they are rarely backed by direct empirical evidence. There are some early simulation studies for individual countries (see Enke, 1966, 1971) showing a negative relation between population growth and capital accumulation, but these studies invariably hold total factor productivity growth constant, which may be mistaken if population growth and total factor productivity growth are positively correlated.

The effect of population growth on savings is also a good deal more theoretically complex than the above arguments suggest. The traditional argument is that population growth reduces the community's savings ratio by leading to a high dependency ratio of children who consume but do not produce. Ignoring the fact that many young children in developing countries do in fact work, the implication of the argument would seem to be that a reduction in population growth would increase the savings ratio by raising the age structure of the population. In the process, however, it must be remembered that many of the older members of a community also consume without producing and that the proportion of retired members of the community to total population will rise as population growth slows. Thus what happens to the aggregate savings ratio as the population growth rate changes will depend on how the composition of the *total* dependency ratio alters, and on the propensity to save (dissave) of the two groups of dependents. For example, if the propensity to dissave of the retired was greater than that of the inactive young, the aggregate savings ratio might fall with a reduction in the birth rate as the retired dependency ratio rose.

Thus while it is certainly true that both groups of dependants dissave, it would be wrong to conclude that countries with high rates of population growth will necessarily have lower savings ratios, all other things being equal, than countries with lower rates of population growth. On the contrary, in fact, in the very long term the savings ratio will tend to rise with the rate of population growth owing to the increase in the ratio of active to non-active households. This is one of the predictions of the life-cycle hypothesis of saving (see Modigliani, 1970). In the long term, when the population is in balanced growth, the age structure of the population will be uniquely related to the rate of population growth, and the same effect on the savings ratio can be expected from population growth as from the increase in income due to productivity growth.

It should also be remembered that the effect of children on a society's total savings works primarily through the family as a unit and depends on how the family reacts to the increase in the number of children. There may just be a substitution of one form of expenditure (on children) for another. Alternatively the family may work harder to provide for the children, in which case there will be no adverse effect on saving at all. Saving in some families may even increase if there is a sufficient increase in output and a high degree of substitution. The degree of substitution between one form of expenditure and another will depend on the ability to substitute, determined by living standards, and the level of saving already achieved.

The question of an output response to population pressure comes back to the point made earlier of the possibility of a positive relation between population growth and total productivity growth. The argument that a slow-down of population growth would raise the savings ratio assumes that the factors that determine output are independent of the number of dependents for whom provision has to be made. But it may well be that the sheer increase in numbers creates work and production incentives that favourably affect output and productivity. In fact there is a good deal of theory and empirical evidence to suggest a positive relation between population growth and the growth of output per unit of labour, especially in the manufacturing sector, assuming some growth in the labour force as the population expands. This is **Verdoorn's Law** (discussed in Chapter 3, p. 117), which hypothesises a positive relation between the growth of the population, employment and output on the one hand and the growth of production per head on the other.

The possible explanations for such a relation are numerous. First, it has been argued (see Chapter 6, p. 221) that an economy with a faster rate of growth of employment and output may be able to learn more quickly and hence raise its rate of technical progress. Second, if there are internal and external economies of scale in production, increased employment and output will lead to a faster rate of growth of labour productivity. Third, there are likely to be economies of scale in the use of capital. Capital requirements, in most cases, do not increase in the same proportion as population. There are many important indivisibilities in the provision of capital, especially in the field of transport and other social-overhead capital. There may even be capital deepening if the life-cycle hypothesis of saving holds – which predicts a positive relation between the savings ratio and population growth, provided the population is in balanced growth.

It is also possible that population pressure can favourably affect individual motivation and lead to changes in production techniques that can overcome the negative consequences of population growth. In this connection it has been argued that a major stimulus to the 'Green Revolution' in the 1970s came from the pressure of population on food supply. The young age structure of a country also makes it more amenable to change, more receptive to new ideas, more willing to shift resources from low-productivity to high-productivity sectors, and so on, all of which may raise income per head. In Hirschman's model of development (see Chapter 9), population growth increases the supply of potential decision makers, expands markets and leads to development via shortages.

It must not be forgotten that the world as a whole has grown progressively richer while the population has expanded. Would the world be as rich today if the population had remained static? Would Britain have been the first country to industrialize if the size of its population had been static? Would the United States have become the richest country in the world without the great influx of people from beyond its shores to exploit its abundant natural resources?

All that has really been said so far is that population growth presents a paradox. On the one hand increases in population may reduce living standards owing to the adverse effect of population growth on savings and capital per head. On the other hand increases in population and the labour force can raise living standards through the learning, specialization and scale economies that larger numbers, wider markets and a higher volume of output make possible. What may be called the '**paradox of labour**' can be seen more easily by taking the identity $O = P(O/P)$, or in differential form, $(\Delta O/O) = \Delta P/P + \Delta(O/P)/(O/P)$, where O is output, P is population and O/P is output per head of population (and a constant fraction of the population is assumed to work). Decreasing amounts of capital per worker (and possibly diminishing returns to land) imply a negative relation between the terms on the right-hand side of the equations, so that output per head is lower than it would otherwise be as the population increases. On the other hand the possibility of increasing returns, due to the factors mentioned, implies a positive relation between the two terms, so that living standards rise as the population increases. The question is, which forces predominate? The debate as to whether population growth acts as a stimulus or an impediment to the growth of living standards is largely a question of whether the relation between $\Delta P/P$ and $\Delta(O/P)/(O/P)$ is significantly positive or negative. If the relation is negative, then population growth is an impediment to rising living standards, and the growth of output itself may also be impaired. If the relation is positive then the effect of population growth on the growth of output and output per head is unambiguously favourable. Evidence across countries suggests that population growth and the rate of capital accumulation are inversely related which decreases the growth of labour productivity, but population growth and technical progress are positively related which increases the growth of labour productivity. The two effects offset each other leaving the total effect of population growth on the growth of per capita income roughly neutral.[2]

This indeed is the conclusion of studies that examine *directly* the relation between population growth and the growth of living standards by correlating the two variables for a cross-section of countries to see whether the relation is positive or negative. When this is done, there is very little systematic relation to be found between intercountry rates of population growth and rates of growth of per capita income. As an exercise, students might like to take their own sample of countries and correlate the rate of growth of population with the rate of growth of per capita income, to see what results emerge.

The fact that the international cross-section evidence lends very little support to the notion that curbing population growth will have much impact, if any, on the growth of income per head is not to deny, of course, that curbing population growth may be desirable for other reasons, such as to relieve overcrowding, to relieve pressure on food supplies and, in general, to improve the distribution of income. To be sceptical of an inverse relation between population growth and per capita income growth is not to pour cold water on population-control programmes. On the contrary, given the uncertainty of the population-growth/living-standards relation, and the force of other arguments for limiting numbers, the most sensible strategy is to pursue programmes on the hypothesis that population control increases per capita income. In simulation studies of the gains from population control that use the effect on per capita income as the criterion for success, however, it is important that explicit account should be taken of the positive relation between population growth and technical progress if the gains are not to be exaggerated. This leads us to the work of **Simon**.

SIMON'S CHALLENGE

The most recent concerted challenge to the view that population growth is uniformly depressing for the material well-being of mankind, has come from Julian Simon (1992, 1996). Simon's major thesis is that 'the ultimate resource is people – skilled, spirited and hopeful people – who will exert their wills and imaginations for their own benefit, and so, inevitably, for the benefit of us all'. The English political economist of the seventeenth century, William Petty, was making the same point when he said 'it is more likely that one ingenious, curious man may rather be found among 4 million than among 400 persons' (Petty, 1682). Simon brings together both the theoretical arguments and empirical evidence on both sides of the population debate and presents his own simulation results on the relation between population growth and living standards. He finds that the initial effects of population increase on per capita income are negative, but that in the longer term the positive feedback effects that result from the stimulus of population growth to technological progress and other factors that improve the rate of growth of productivity outweigh the negative effects. Simulations suggest that for countries already industrialized the initial negative effect of population is offset within 50 years. For less developed countries the conclusion is that moderate population growth is more favourable to the growth of living standards than either a stationary population or very rapid population growth.

An overall judgement on population growth, and whether it is beneficial or not, therefore depends very much on a weighing of the balance between the present and the future. In economic analysis the present and the future are made comparable using the concept of a discount rate. Whether the positive long-run benefits of population growth are considered to outweigh the short-run negative effects depends on the discount rate and the time period taken. The less future benefits are discounted and the longer the time period taken, the more beneficial (less detrimental) population growth appears, and the shorter the time period considered and the more future benefits are discounted, the less beneficial (more detrimental) population growth appears. There will be some time period and some discount rate at which additional population is exactly on the borderline of having a negative or positive value.

What are the positive feedback effects that population increase can have on economic progress that vitiate the classical prediction that population growth is uniformly depressing on living standards? In his simulation model of the relationship between population growth and per capita income in advanced countries, Simon attempts to capture the effect of additional children on such factors as the savings ratio, labour supplied by the parents, scale economies and technical progress. In his simulation model for developing countries Simon considers the following important feedback mechanisms:

- The stimulus to new methods in agriculture
- The supply response of families
- The provision of social infrastructure (particularly transport)
- Scale economies
- Demand-induced investment.

Let us briefly consider some of these factors.

A society under pressure from population growth may be expected to respond by finding new and more efficient ways of meeting given needs. In agriculture, the Malthusian view would be that improvement in agricultural techniques is independent of population and that improvements simply induce population expansion. Others would argue that even if population pressure does not induce the production of new techniques it certainly induces the adoption of new techniques. It is difficult to see how the Green Revolution would have occurred without the pressure of numbers on food supply.

Agricultural families may respond to the needs of additional children by changing methods, working harder and producing more. Studies suggest that the elasticity of output to increases in the number of children is about 0.5; that is, an increase in family size, say, from four to five (25 per cent) would result in a 12.5 per cent increase in output. Simon argues that population growth also has a large positive effect on agricultural saving, which tends to be overlooked because a large fraction is non-monetized.

Population pressure provides a stimulus to develop social infrastructure, transport and communication facilities, which have far-reaching external repercussions, extending beyond the additional numbers they were designed to serve. Population growth also makes these facilities more economical to provide because of the scale economies involved in their provision. Simon argues 'if there is a single key element in economic development other than culture and institutions and psychological make-up, that single key element is transportation together with communications'. Adam Smith, an early contemporary of Malthus and much more optimistic about the development process, was impressed by the benefits of communications:

> good roads, canals and navigable rivers, by diminishing the expense of carriage, put the remote parts of the country more nearly upon a level with those in the neighbourhood of the town. They are upon that account the greatest of all improvements – they break down monopolies . . . they open new markets.

To the extent that population growth exerts pressure for these facilities to be provided, a significant output response is to be expected.

Increased population has many other productivity effects that are subtle and indirect, yet nonetheless very important. It is very difficult, for example, to improve health and sanitation in sparsely populated areas, but once sanitation and health improvement become feasible and economical with greater numbers, enormous benefits may result – more than in proportion to the increase in population. A growing population also facilitates change without disrupting the organization and positions of those already established. Thus government and administration may be expected to improve and become more in keeping with the needs of development. Youth itself has positive advantages. Young people are more receptive to change and modernization than older people. The younger a population the more education (or human capital) per head of the population. Young people tend to be more mobile, which is an asset when structural change is required. With a growing population, investment is less risky. Many economists are of the view that one of the major obstacles to development is not a shortage of savings but a lack of willingness to invest. An expanding market resulting from population growth provides an incentive to investment.

The great difference between the results of Simon and those of the pessimists is that all the beneficial feedback effects of population on output mentioned above are not considered. But any of the feedback factors referred to may partially or fully offset the capital-dilution effect of greater numbers in the short run, which is the factor that the predictions of conventional models reflect. A complete analysis of the relation between population and living standards must have due regard to the longer-term benefits that population expansion can confer on societies, as well as the short-term costs. Indeed only when the benefits are considered is it possible to comprehend why societies are infinitely wealthier today than centuries ago, despite population expansion.

THE 'OPTIMUM' POPULATION

What is the 'optimum' population? The term 'optimum population' is used in several different senses, but four in particular are commonly employed. First, it is sometimes used to refer to the size of population that *maximizes the average product or income per head*. It is in this situation that a society's savings ratio is likely to be maximized. Thus if the total product curve for an economy is drawn as in Figure 8.6, the optimum population is P, where a ray from the origin is tangential to the total product curve. At P, total product (Y) divided by population (P), or average product per head of population, is at its maximum. The condition for maximum average product per head is that the marginal and average product per head should be equal. If the marginal product of an addition to the population is above the average, the average product could be increased by an expansion of the population. Conversely, if the marginal product is below the average, a further increase in population will reduce the average product and the population will exceed the optimum level in the way defined. If there was no saving, the maximization of product per head would maximize welfare per head because consumption per head would then be at a maximum.

On the surface, this concept of optimum population seems an attractive one upon which to base a population policy. It provides the greatest scope for maximizing savings per head if desired or, in the absence of forced or compulsory saving, it will lead to

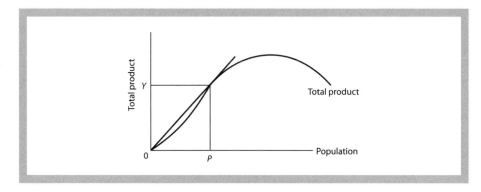

Figure 8.6 Maximization of average product

the maximization of welfare per head. Yet a population policy based on maximizing per capita income has frightening implications (not entirely fanciful) for all submarginal groups in society that may be deemed to be depressing the average standard of life.

A second approach to the concept of optimum population adopts the criterion of *total welfare maximization*. This is the utilitarian approach, adopted by the English economist cum philosopher Henry Sidgwick, whom we quoted earlier (p. 258):

> the point up to which, on utilitarian principles, population ought to be encouraged to increase is not that at which *average* happiness is the greatest possible – as appears to be often assumed by political economists of the school of Malthus – but at which the product formed by multiplying the number of persons living into the amount of average happiness reaches its maximum (Sidgwick, 1907, emphasis added)

On this criterion, the population would be suboptimal as long as the marginal product of labour was above some notional welfare subsistence level, and would reach the optimum when all incomes were equalized at the welfare subsistence level (assuming a diminishing marginal utility of income). But in conditions of poverty, if increments to population reduce the average standard of living still further, it seems perverse to call this an improvement in welfare simply because the number of people 'enjoying' such an impoverished state has risen.

A third definition of optimum population refers to the level of population beyond which the average product in an economy falls below the level of production necessary for subsistence, on the assumption that the total product is equally shared. In this case the term 'optimum' simply refers to the maximum population that can be supported with existing resources, and is the point of Malthusian equilibrium. In Figure 8.7 a population beyond P_1 could not be supported because the average product of the population would be below the level of subsistence. If total product was not equally shared, a total population of P_1 would not be supportable, for some would have more income than necessary for subsistence and others less. But note that if the product is equally shared, a much larger population can be maintained than the population at which the marginal product falls below subsistence, that is, P. In fact the optimum population, P_1, is consistent with a negative marginal product.

This last point leads us to the fourth sense in which the term 'optimum' population is sometimes used, which is to describe a state of affairs where a country's population is so large that increases in it can only be detrimental to growth – not only detrimental

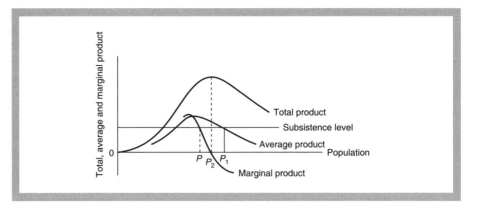

Figure 8.7 The 'optimum' population

to a country's long-run growth prospects but also to growth in the short run, implying zero or negative marginal product. The population is optimal in this sense when total product is maximized, at P_2 in Figure 8.7. This definition of optimum population is closely linked with the notion of population density, and attempts to define under-population and overpopulation in terms of the relation between population and resources, and, in particular, land. Since resources such as land vary considerably in quality, however, intercountry comparisons of ratios of population to resources must be treated with great care. A country may be regarded as 'underpopulated' in relation to another even though it has a higher population–resource ratio, simply because the technology it uses to exploit its resources is superior. Technology will influence the position and shape of the total product curve – and hence the optimum population – for any given ratio of population to resources. In view of the variety of interpretations of the concept of optimum population, the claim that a country is 'overpopulated' or 'underpopulated' needs to be viewed with some scepticism unless a precise definition of the terms is given.

A MODEL OF THE LOW-LEVEL EQUILIBRIUM TRAP

To repeat, there are two main interrelated reasons why rapid population growth may be regarded as a retarding influence on development. First, rapid population growth may not permit a sufficiently large rise in per capita incomes to provide the savings necessary for the required amount of capital formation for growth. Second, if population growth outstrips the capacity of industry to absorb new labour, either urban unemployment will develop or rural underemployment will be exacerbated, depressing productivity in the agricultural sector. It is not inconceivable, moreover, that rises in per capita income in the early stages of development may be accompanied by, or even induce, population growth in excess of income growth, holding down per capita incomes to a subsistence level. Today's falling death rates (associated with development) are contributing to population pressure; and presumably for centuries past the population of most countries has been oscillating around the subsistence level, with small gains in living standards (due to 'technical progress') being wiped out either by higher birth rates or such factors as disease, famine and war.

One vital question that a theory of economic development must answer is, at what level of per capita income can income growth be expected to exceed population growth permanently, thus sustaining further rises in per capita income indefinitely? This question cannot be answered at a certain point in time by the casual observation that income growth exceeds population growth, because the very rise in per capita income may induce greater population growth than income growth in the future. A full behavioural model is required, as well as a population theory that is able to explain the pattern of population growth during the course of development. What happens to population as per capita income rises, and what happens to national income, and therefore per capita income, as the population rises?

Models of the **low-level equilibrium trap** attempt to integrate population and development theory by recognizing the interdependence between population growth, per capita income and national income growth. This type of model, which originated in the 1950s, is designed first to demonstrate the difficulties that developing countries may face in achieving a self-sustaining rise in living standards, and secondly to provide pointers to policy action. One such model by Nelson (1956), upon which we shall concentrate, contains three basic equations that deal with the determination of net capital formation, population growth and income growth. Let us consider these equations separately before examining the simple workings of the model.

Capital formation

Capital formation takes place through saving and new land brought into cultivation, that is, $dk = dk' + dR$, where k is capital, k' is savings-created capital and R is land. We shall ignore new land as a part of capital and concentrate on savings-created capital. It is assumed that all saving is invested.

The rate of savings per capita (dk'/P) is related to income per capita (O/P) in the way shown in Figure 8.8. In equation form:

$$dk'/P = b([O/P] - X)$$

where $(O/P) > (O/P)'$ (8.1)

and $= -C$

where $(O/P) \leq (O/P)'$

Per capita income is so low up to the level $(O/P)'$ that there is disinvestment (dissaving), assumed to be at a constant rate, C. Beyond $(O/P)'$ the rate of savings per capita rises linearly with per capita income.

Population growth

With rising per capita income, population growth (dP/P) is first assumed to increase owing to falling death rates. Then at a critical level of per capita income $(O/P)''$, population growth reaches the maximum $(dP/P)^*$ when the death rate has fallen to the minimum. Since

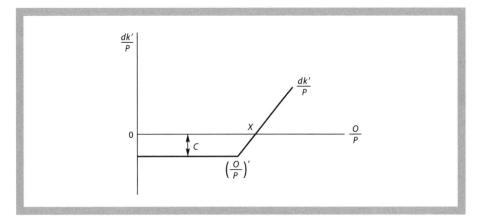

Figure 8.8 Rate of savings and per capita income

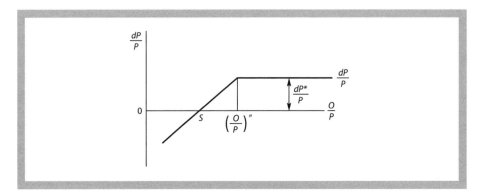

Figure 8.9 Population growth and per capita income

Nelson's model is short run, the effect of per capita income on the birth rate is ignored, but the relation can easily be accommodated if desired. The relation between population growth and per capita income can be represented as in Figure 8.9. In equation form:

$dP/P = P\ ([O/P] - S)$.

where $(O/P) < (O/P)''$ (8.2)

and $= dP*/P$,

where $(O/P) \geq (O/P)''$

S is the subsistence level of per capita income. At per capita income levels below S, dP/P is negative since the death rate would exceed the birth rate.

Growth of national income

Income (or output) is assumed to be a linear homogeneous function of factor inputs, $O = Tf(K, L)$ where K is capital, L is labour (as a constant proportion of the population)

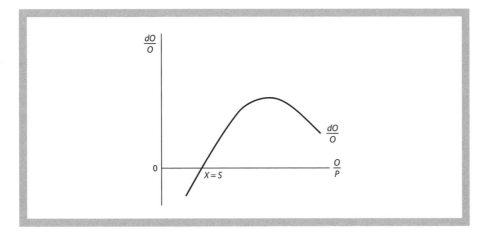

Figure 8.10 Income growth curve

and T is an index of 'total' productivity. Technology and the social structure are assumed constant. From the assumptions of the model, the income growth curve can be drawn as in Figure 8.10. Where $S = X$ (taken from Figures 8.8 and 8.9), population is stationary, the rate of savings-created capital per head is zero, and therefore income will be stationary ($dO/O = 0$). With rising per capita income beyond this stationary equilibrium, growth increases because of increases in the labour force and capital per head. As population growth reaches a maximum, however, and savings as a percentage of national income approach a constant, income growth will level off. In the absence of technical progress, growth will ultimately decrease owing to the law of variable proportions, in this case due to a fall in the capital–labour ratio.

Combining Figures 8.9 and 8.10, we have a diagrammatic representation of the possibility of a low-level equilibrium trap situation in which per capita income is permanently depressed. Figure 8.11 shows this. Any level of per capita income between the subsistence point ($S = X$) and a will be accompanied by a growth of population faster than the growth of income, forcing down per capita income. The equilibrium level of per capita income will be where the population growth curve cuts the income curve from below. One such point is to the left of a, where $S = X$, and this point represents the low-level equilibrium trap. Any level of per capita income below a will force per capita income down to this subsistence level. Conversely, any per capita income level beyond a will mean a sustained rise in per capita income until the two curves cross again at q. This would be a new stable equilibrium with the population growth curve again cutting the income growth curve from below.

To escape from the low-level equilibrium trap, per capita income must either be raised to a, or the dO/O and dP/P curves must be shifted favourably. The origin of '**big push**' theories of development (see Chapter 9 and below), and the concept of a '**critical minimum effort**', was the belief that to escape from the 'trap' it would be necessary to raise per capita income to a in one go. If countries are in a trap situation, however, much greater hope probably lies in the dO/O curve drifting upwards over time, through technical progress, or in a sudden drop in the dP/P curve from a reduction in the birth rate. Capital from abroad, raising the dO/O curve, and emigration, lowering the dP/P curve, could also free an economy from such a trap.

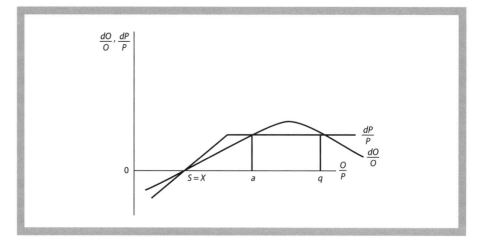

Figure 8.11 Low-level equilibrium trap

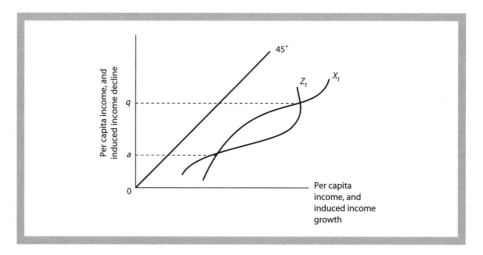

Figure 8.12 Leibenstein's approach

To take account of factors other than population growth that may depress per capita income, and factors other than increases in capital per head that may raise per capita income, the low-level equilibrium trap model can be extended and generalized by adopting Leibenstein's terminology of income-depressing forces and income-raising forces (Leibenstein, 1957). Leibenstein's approach is illustrated in Figure 8.12. The curve representing income-depressing forces, Z_t, is measured horizontally from the 45° line, and the curve representing income-raising forces, X_t, is measured vertically from the 45° line. Per capita income level a is the only point of stable equilibrium. Between a and q income-depressing forces are greater than income-raising forces and per capita income will slip back to a. Only beyond q are income-raising forces greater than income-depressing forces such that a sustained increase in per capita income becomes possible. q is the critical per capita income level necessary to escape the low-level equilibrium trap.

THE CRITICAL MINIMUM EFFORT THESIS

It has been argued that *if* a low-level equilibrium trap exists, a critical minimum effort will be required to escape from it. This is the so-called **critical minimum effort thesis**, which refers to the effort needed, normally measured by investment requirements, to raise per capita income to that level beyond which the further growth of per capita income will not be associated with income-depressing forces exceeding income-raising forces. But as soon as one begins to calculate the amount of extra investment required to raise per capita income in one go, by even a modest amount, it becomes all too obvious that a critical minimum effort, or a 'big push' as it is sometimes called, is not feasible. But in any case it is doubtful whether a critical minimum effort or 'big push' is necessary in practice.

While it is important to recognize the interdependence between population growth, per capita income and income growth, models of the low-level equilibrium trap tend to be unduly pessimistic and restrictive in their assumptions. Furthermore the prediction of a low-level trap in the absence of a critical minimum effort does not wholly accord with historical experience. In Western Europe income-induced population growth did not prevent substantial rises in per capita income from taking place. On the contrary, it was not *until* the population started to grow rapidly that per capita income started to rise, and population growth preceded income growth rather than the other way round.[3] We hinted earlier that one of the most likely escapes from a Malthusian situation is a permanent fall in the birth rate due to a standard-of-living effect. It is this effect that prevented a Malthusian situation in nineteenth-century Europe. Birth rates followed death rates downwards long before the maximum possible population growth rate had been reached.

What happened in Europe was not the experience of the present developing countries until recently. There are now signs, however, that the birth rate is falling faster than the death rate, and most countries may be out of the trap. There are other potent forces at work that also offer an escape from Malthusianism. The most significant of these forces are technical progress and 'irreversible' additions to the capital stock (especially in the form of social and human capital), the consequence of which is to shift the income growth curve upwards over time so that the level of per capita income representing stable equilibrium is continually rising over time. Technical progress was an important source of economic progress in nineteenth-century Europe; it is, potentially, an even greater force in the present developing nations, given their ready access to ideas and technology from developed countries.

The way in which rising living standards may be regarded as a natural phenomenon, obviating the need for a critical minimum effort, is shown diagrammatically in Figure 8.13. Consider a small rise in the per capita income level from X (the subsistence level) to X_1. The traditional argument is that this will be accompanied by population growth in excess of income growth, causing per capita income to fall back to the subsistence level. If time is not abstracted from the analysis, however, it is possible to argue that the increase in per capita income from X to X_1 will be accompanied by permanent changes in the quality of the capital stock, skills and so on, such that per capita income will not fall back to X but to some higher level, say X_2. Income growth in the range of per capita income X to X_2 is now permanently higher, represented by the curve dO/O'. If X_2 becomes the new stable equilibrium, and the sequence of events is repeated, per

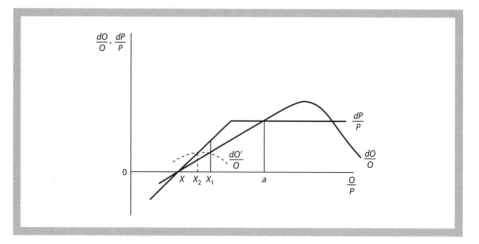

Figure 8.13 Escape from the 'trap'

capita income will reach *a* in a series of steps. No critical minimum effort will be needed. With continuous productivity growth due to all forms of technical progress, a 'ratchet' mechanism of the type described is quite feasible, and it is probably by this mechanism that, in practice, countries typically 'take off'.

Most developing countries in the world today are experiencing income growth that is faster than the rate of population growth. Whether income growth would be faster if population growth was reduced is an open question. It is possible to conceive of a low-level equilibrium trap, but its level almost certainly rises over time owing largely to technical progress before a reduction in birth rates sets in.[4]

DISCUSSION QUESTIONS

1 What accounts for the population explosion in developing countries since the 1970s?

2 Why do poor people have large families?

3 What are the major determinants of fertility?

4 It has been said that 'affluence is its own prophylactic'. Does this mean that it is futile to attempt to control the size of the population before living standards rise?

5 Why will the population continue to grow rapidly even if fertility rates in developing countries fall rapidly?

6 In what ways may rapid population growth impair development?

7 What are the stimuli that rapid population growth might give to development?

8 How would you do a cost-benefit analysis of population growth?

9 What do you understand by the concept of the 'low-level equilibrium trap'?

10 Is it possible to define an 'optimum' population?

NOTES

1. For a history of world population, see Kremer (1993).
2. For an early study, see Thirlwall (1972).
3. French economic historians have blamed their country's comparatively late industrialization on lack of population pressure.
4. For good surveys of many of the issues discussed in this chapter, see Cassen (1976), Kelley (1988) and Simon (1997).

WEBSITES ON POPULATION

World Bank, World Development Indicators   www.worldbank.org/data/onlinedatabases/onlinedatabases.html

United Nations   www.un.org/popin/wdtrends

UNDP   www.undp.org/popin.htm

UN Population Division   www.un.org/esa/population/unpop.htm

UN Population Fund   www.unfpa.org

UN Population Information Network   www.un.org/popin/

The role of the state, the allocation of resources, sustainable development and the choice of techniques

Resource allocation in developing countries: the market mechanism and the role of the state

The central issue facing all economies is how to allocate resources among competing uses. This question takes on more significance in developing countries than in developed countries as resources are scarcer and the basic needs of people are greater. In Part IV of this book we turn to some of the major topics of development strategy concerning the use of investment criteria for the allocation of resources (and particularly the use of social cost-benefit analysis for the appraisal of public sector projects), the concept of sustainable development, the choice of techniques of production, and the use of the technique of input–output analysis for planning and forecasting purposes. Separate chapters are devoted to each of these subjects.

In this preliminary chapter we shall first review the role of the market mechanism as an efficient device for resource allocation and then the role of the state in promoting economic development, after which we shall discuss some of the broader policy issues confronting decision-makers, including the balance between agriculture and industry; consumption today versus consumption tomorrow; the law of comparative advantage, and the choice of techniques of production.

THE MARKET MECHANISM AND MARKET FAILURES

In free-enterprise market economies, resources are allocated by Adam Smith's 'invisible hand' of the market in accordance with consumer demand. The market is the organizational framework that brings together those who supply and those who demand a product, who then trade at an agreed price. In a completely free market, the price will completely clear the market so there are no unsatisfied buyers and sellers. Decision-making about what is produced is completely decentralized and left to the market, comprising the decisions of a myriad of private individuals. If the demand for a good increases, the price will rise and producers will be induced to supply more; if demand falls, the price will fall and producers will supply less. Market prices act as **signals** to producers to supply more or less of a commodity according to the changing profitability of production. The efficiency of markets relies on prices acting as signals, on suppliers responding, and on the mobility of the factors of production enabling supply to be forthcoming.

We now come to one of the most important theorems in welfare economics: if consumers consume to the point where the marginal utility of consumption is equal to the price of a good, and producers produce to the point where the marginal cost of production is equal to price, then resources will be optimally allocated since the marginal utility of production will just equal the marginal cost. Society will have reached its highest level of utility consistent with its production possibilities. This is illustrated in Figure 9.1.

The curve I_1I_1 is society's indifference curve between two goods, A and B, representing the highest utility attainable, and X_1X_1 is a country's production possibility curve between the two goods, A and B. Point 1 represents the optimum allocation of resources between the two goods. Any point to the left or right of point 1, or inside the production possibility curve, would represent a lower level of utility.

The allocation role of markets, however, is only one of the functions of the market mechanism. To use a distinction introduced by Kaldor (1972), the market also has a *creative* function, to provide an environment for change that expands production possibilities, that is, which shifts the production possibility curve outwards to X_2X_2, enabling a higher level of utility at point 2. Change means all the dynamic forces that lead to technical progress, innovation and ultimately investment. In the early stages of development, the creative function of markets, producing new opportunities for growth, may be just as important as the allocative function of markets.

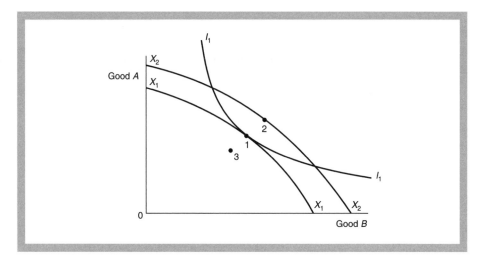

Figure 9.1 Welfare maximization

The conditions required for markets to perform their allocative and creative functions in an optimal manner are very stringent, and are unlikely to be satisfied in any economy, let alone developing countries. The true benefit of output may not be reflected in price because of **externalities**; price may not reflect marginal cost because of **market imperfections**; and many developmental goods and services may not be produced at all because **markets are incomplete or missing** entirely, and therefore cannot perform their creative function. In other words, there are likely to be **market failures**.

In addition, there is the problem that there is nothing in the market mechanism that guarantees an equitable distribution of income in society, or that will direct adequate resources away from present consumption to build up the means of production for a higher level of consumption in the future.

It is all these types of market failure that in the past have led development economists to argue for government intervention in the development process, as well as causing most developing countries to interfere with the market mechanism and to adopt various forms of planning for the allocation of resources. In the former Soviet Union and the countries of Eastern Europe, planning superseded the market mechanism entirely, and output and resource allocation was decided by bureaucrats, not by consumers. In other countries, governments produced plans for the sectoral allocation of resources, and took on more and more functions. In the latter half of the twentieth century there was an explosion of government expenditure in developing countries, rising to over 30 per cent of national income on average and over 50 per cent in some countries.[1]

In recent years, however, there has been disillusion with planning, and the role of the state has come under increased scrutiny for a number of reasons. First, there has been the collapse of the former state-planned, communist countries of the Soviet Union and Eastern Europe. What to put in their place? Most of these former command economies have swung to the other extreme, embracing the market mechanism almost unconditionally, with other damaging consequences. There is surely a middle way. Second, the state has failed in many developing countries to deliver properly even the most fundamental public goods such as law and order and property rights, and essential social capital and infrastructure such as education, health facilities and transport. Third, civil strife has caused the collapse of the state in a number of countries, particularly in Africa, with markets left to operate in an institutional vacuum. Fourth, many countries have found themselves in fiscal crisis – associated with mounting expenditure on the welfare state in developed countries, and huge public enterprise deficits in developing countries. Finally, there is a fascination with the role that the state has played in the successful developing countries of South-East Asia – in Japan and the Asian Tigers of Hong Kong, Singapore, Taiwan and South Korea. Can the East Asian model be copied?

Surveying the experience of the developed and developing countries in the years since 1945, the message would seem to be that the state has a vital role to play in economic development, but not so much as a direct provider of goods and services; rather as the agency through which market failures can be rectified and as the architect of a framework in which markets can flourish and evolve. History shows that markets do come into existence without government intervention, but markets work incrementally. It takes time for price signals to be recognized, for people to respond to incentives and for resources to be (re)allocated. This does not mean that the state should step in and do everything. There is a middle way between state-led, central planning on the one hand, and the minimal state espoused by extreme free-marketeers on the other. The bad experience of government planning in Eastern Europe should not blind us to the market failures mentioned earlier. The way forward in most developing countries must be a judicious mix of market capitalism combined with state intervention. Let us now consider in more detail the role of the state in correcting these market failures.

THE ROLE OF THE STATE

The state has four key roles to play in the development process:

- To provide public goods
- To correct market imperfections
- To protect the vulnerable and ensure an equitable distribution of income, both intra-temporally (between people at a point in time) and intertemporally (between generations over time)
- To provide an institutional environment in which markets can flourish (including the maintenance of macroeconomic stability).

Public goods are goods that have certain characteristics that make it difficult, if not impossible, to charge for them, and therefore private suppliers will not provide them. These characteristics are (1) consumption by one user does not reduce the supply available for others (the good is **non-rival**), and (2) users cannot be prevented from consuming the good (the good is **non-excludable**). There are not many *pure* public goods (air is perhaps the purest of all) but there are others that come close and are important for economic development, such as defence, law and order, and the provision of basic infrastructure such as roads, sewers, clean water and so on. A market in defence, or laws governing property rights which benefit the whole nation, is not conceivable. Markets in some infrastructural facilities are conceivable, but not very likely because of the high fixed costs. Also the providers might have difficulty in charging for, and capturing, the externalities. The market would either not provide at all, or it would underprovide.

Market imperfections refer to three important phenomena. First, market prices may provide a very imperfect guide to the *social* optimum allocation of resources because they do not reflect the opportunity costs to society of using factors of production, or the value to society of the production of commodities. The price of labour may be above its opportunity cost and therefore used too little. The price of capital and foreign exchange may be below the opportunity cost and therefore used too much from a social point of view. Likewise the price of goods may not reflect the marginal cost of production. Monopolies, tariffs, subsidies and other imperfections in the market all distort free market prices, upon which private producers base their production decisions. There is a lot more on this topic in Chapter 10, where we shall discuss social cost-benefit analysis.

Second, there is the existence of **externalities**, both positive and negative, which means that some goods may be underprovided and others overprovided from a social point of view because the positive or negative externality is not reflected in the price. Most infrastructure projects, such as transport facilities, power generation, irrigation schemes and so on, and social capital, such as education and health facilities, will have greater social returns than the private return and will therefore be underprovided from a social point of view unless private suppliers in the market are compensated or subsidized. Other activities may confer negative externalities by imposing costs on society that are not paid for by the provider, and therefore the market oversupplies from a social point of view. Governments can curb negative externalities through regulation or taxation, and promote positive externalities through subsidies or providing the output itself, as with education and health care.

Third, markets may be incomplete or missing altogether. One good reason why markets may be missing in the case of public goods is the inability of suppliers to exclude '**free-riders**', that is, to exclude people from consuming the good once it is provided. But there are other important reasons for incomplete or missing markets, for example high transaction costs can prevent markets from developing, particularly in developing countries, where poor communications make information costs high and there is an absence of futures markets to compensate for risk in conditions of uncertainty. The actual cost of providing a good or service may be less than individuals are willing to pay, but imperfect information on the part of consumers leads to an undervaluation of the product and therefore restricted supply; for example, preventive health care. In this sense the market is incomplete.

Asymmetric information, adverse selection and **moral hazard** can also lead to market inefficiency. 'Asymmetric information' refers to the imbalance of knowledge in a market between buyers and sellers. In the market for bank loans, for example, the borrowers know more about their own circumstances than the lenders. Banks could make bad loans (adverse selection), which makes them cautious and leads to credit rationing. It would be very costly for banks to obtain all the information they require on high-risk customers. The informal money market compensates by charging very high interest rates for all. Another example would be the health insurance market, where individuals know more about their health than the suppliers of insurance. Those who know they are prone to illness are more likely to take out insurance, and more likely to be turned down. 'Moral hazard' is present when the possession of insurance encourages the activity that is insured against, leading to resource waste and higher costs (and higher insurance premiums for all). Governments may step in by regulating private insurance, or providing the service themselves at lower cost.

As far as **equity** is concerned, the state has an important role to play in protecting the vulnerable and ensuring an equitable distribution of income between people, between groups in society, between regions and across generations. There is not only a moral case for the state to help those in absolute poverty, but also a strong political and economic one. Poor, vulnerable and disaffected people can be a major cause of civil unrest and political instability (Stewart, 2001). This deters investment and growth. It is also important for the state to keep an eye on the welfare of future generations, which may require altering the balance between consumption and investment in the present. There are a number of ways in which governments can intervene to discourage present consumption and raise the level of investment for higher future consumption; for example, taxation, subsidized interest rates and public investment on society's behalf. We shall talk more about altering the balance between consumption and investment in Chapter 10.

Finally, the state is essential for providing the appropriate **institutional environment** for markets to flourish and operate efficiently. In this sense, markets and government intervention are complementary. The World Bank devoted its *World Development Report 1997* to the topic of 'The State in a Changing World'. It conveys three principal messages:

- Development (economic, social and sustainable) without an effective state is impossible. It is increasingly recognized that an effective state – not a minimal one – is central to economic and social development, but more as partner and facilitator than director. States should work to complement markets, not replace them.
- A rich body of evidence shows the importance of good economic policies (including the promotion of macroeconomic stability), well-developed human capital and openness to the world economy for broad-based, sustainable growth and the reduction of poverty. But as our understanding of the ingredients of development improves, a deeper set of questions emerges: why have some societies pursued these actions with greater success than others, and how precisely did the state contribute to these differing outcomes?
- The historical record suggests the importance of building on the relative strengths of the market, the state, and civil society to improve the state's effectiveness. This suggests a two-part strategy of matching the role of the state to its capability, and then improving that capability.

The *World Development Report 1997* argues that many developing countries are not performing their core functions properly. They are failing to protect property, to ensure law and order, and to protect the vulnerable, all of which causes unrest and leads to a lack of government **credibility**. A survey of 69 countries shows that government credibility is highest in South and South-East Asia, and lowest in Sub-Saharan Africa and the states of the former Soviet Union. Investment and growth are positively related to credibility. The report says of Africa that many countries are 'trapped in a vicious circle of declining State capability and thus declining credibility in the eyes of their citizens – leading to increased crime and an absence of security affecting investment and growth'. It refers to a 'crisis of statehood' in Africa, and a lower 'state capability' than fifty years ago. In contrast, it praises the countries of South-East Asia because they have paid attention to the institutional framework for markets to fulfil their various roles in allocating and augmenting resources. State credibility is particularly important if developing countries are to attract private foreign investment. The statistical evidence shows that in countries with sound policies and good governance, real per capita income grew at 3 per cent per annum on average over the period 1964–93; in countries with reasonable policies but poor governance, per capita growth was only 1.4 per cent; and in countries with bad policies and bad governance, per capita growth was a mere 0.4 per cent. The World Bank concludes that without an improvement in the effectiveness of the state, there is no prospect of significant improvement in economic and social welfare.

The World Bank outlines a two-pronged strategy for governments to increase both their credibility and the effectiveness of the state: first, governments must match the role of the state to its capabilities and not try to do too much, and second, they must try to improve capabilities by reinvigorating state institutions.

With regard to the first prong of the strategy, the state should concentrate on getting the basics right, such as safeguarding property rights and guaranteeing the rule of law, rather than trying to do too much. In many countries there is overregulation and excessive state consumption. Governments should decide more carefully what to do and how to do it. The basics should be:

- Law and order
- Maintaining macroeconomic stability
- Investing in basic social services and infrastructure
- Protecting the vulnerable
- Protecting the environment.

But the state does not have to be the *sole* provider of all infrastructure and social services. It can contract out to the private sector and introduce competition into their provision, coupled with a regulatory framework to protect consumers and workers. Neither does the state have to be the monopoly supplier of public utilities such as electricity, gas, telecommunications and so on. These activities can be **privatized** with state supervision. Privatization has gathered pace throughout the world in recent years. In total there have been over 1500 divestitures of state companies in developing countries, and over 3000 in the former communist countries of Eastern Europe. The motivation has been the generally poor economic performance of state-owned companies, the large deficits of public enterprises, and the promotion of competition to improve the delivery of services.

Beyond the basics, the state may want to intervene strategically – in industrial policy, for example, if it has the capability, as the successful Asian Tiger economies have done. The past success of Hong Kong, Singapore, Taiwan and South Korea has depended on the state and the private sector working in harmony with each other, with the state providing the economic and legal environment for markets to flourish but with the government taking an entrepreneurial role and intervening where it thought necessary. In Hong Kong the state took a leading role in planning infrastructure and providing subsidized housing to maintain social stability and to reduce the cost of labour. Singapore, Taiwan and South Korea targeted financial assistance to specific industries and even specific companies (with an emphasis on exports), with spectacular success.

On the second strategy of improving the capabilities of the state and reinvigorating state institutions, the task is to provide incentives for public officials to perform better and reduce the scope for arbitrary action that could lead to bad decision-making and corruption.

CORRUPTION

Corruption is a serious issue in many developing countries. An organization based in Germany called Transparency International publishes a corruption perception index based on surveys of business people, risk analysts and perceptions of the general public, ranked on a scale 0 to 10 (the lower the index, the more corrupt). The results for 89 countries in 2000 are shown in Table 9.1.

Developing countries appear to be the most corrupt, although the same level of income (or development) is often associated with different levels of corruption. In general, poverty breeds corruption, and corruption can lead to severe inefficiencies in the functioning of economies.[2]

The World Bank defines corruption as 'the abuse of public office for private gain', including bribery, threats and 'kickbacks'. These are all aspects of **rent-seeking** behaviour that arise primarily because decisions over the allocation of resources are in the hands of politicians and government officials. The existence of licences, permits, regulations, subsidies and, of course, taxes all offer scope for corruption. Corruption not only leads to inefficiency – particularly the discouragement of investment – but can undermine

Table 9.1 Transparency International's corruption perception index, 2000

Country	Rank	Index	Country	Rank	Index	Country	Rank	Index
Finland	1	10.0	Hungary	31	5.2	Thailand	59	3.2
Denmark	2	9.8	Tunisia	31	5.2	China	62	3.1
New Zealand	3	9.4	South Africa	33	5.0	Egypt	62	3.1
Canada	4	9.2	Greece	34	4.9	Burkina Faso	64	3.0
Iceland	5	9.1	Malaysia	35	4.8	Kazakhstan	64	3.0
Norway	5	9.1	Mauritius	36	4.7	Zimbabwe	64	3.0
Singapore	5	9.1	Morocco	36	4.7	Romania	67	2.9
Netherlands	8	8.9	Italy	38	4.6	India	68	2.8
United Kingdom	9	8.7	Jordan	38	4.6	Philippines	68	2.8
Luxembourg	10	8.6	Peru	40	4.4	Bolivia	70	2.7
Switzerland	10	8.6	Czech Republic	41	4.3	Cote d'Ivoire	70	2.7
Australia	12	8.3	Belarus	42	4.1	Venezuela	70	2.7
United States	13	7.8	El Salvador	42	4.1	Ecuador	73	2.6
Austria	14	7.7	Lithuania	42	4.1	Moldova	73	2.6
Hong Kong	14	7.7	Malawi	42	4.1	Armenia	75	2.5
Germany	16	7.6	Poland	42	4.1	Tanzania	75	2.5
Chile	17	7.4	South Korea	47	4.0	Vietnam	75	2.5
Ireland	18	7.2	Brazil	48	3.9	Uzbekistan	78	2.4
Spain	19	7.0	Turkey	49	3.8	Uganda	79	2.3
France	20	6.7	Croatia	50	3.7	Mozambique	80	2.2
Israel	21	6.6	Argentina	51	3.5	Kenya	81	2.1
Japan	22	6.4	Bulgaria	51	3.5	Russia	81	2.1
Portugal	22	6.4	Ghana	51	3.5	Cameroon	83	2.0
Belgium	24	6.1	Senegal	51	3.5	Angola	84	1.7
Botswana	25	6.0	Slovak Rep.	51	3.5	Indonesia	84	1.7
Estonia	26	5.7	Latvia	56	3.4	Azerbaijan	86	1.5
Slovenia	27	5.5	Zambia	56	3.4	Ukraine	86	1.5
Taiwan	28	5.5	Mexico	58	3.3	Yugoslavia	88	1.3
Costa Rica	29	5.4	Colombia	59	3.2	Nigeria	89	1.2
Namibia	29	5.4	Ethiopia	59	3.2			

Source: Transparency International, as taken from their website <transparency.org>, 3 November 2000.

the legitimacy of government itself. Where corruption is endemic it makes it much more difficult for governments to enforce laws in such areas as taxation or control of environmental damage.[3]

The IMF now specifies anti-corruption measures as one of the conditions for loan support. For example, the IMF got tough with the Kenyan government, insisting first on a 'wealth declaration law' that all government ministers and senior civil servants declare the full range of their assets and liabilities every year, and secondly on a weekly inspection by IMF officials in Washington of the Kenyan Central Bank's balance sheet to prevent foreign aid being used for private gain.

Economic reform, and liberalizing markets, reduces the scope for corruption, but vested interests involved in corruption make the reform process more difficult. The *World Development Report 1997* outlines three essential ingredients for improving the capabilities of the state (and rooting out corruption):

- There must be effective rules and restraints to check public authority and prevent corruption. Independence of the judiciary is important, and an independent Commission against corruption would be helpful.
- Public officials should be appointed on merit, not on the basis of political patronage, and can be encouraged to perform effectively through a merit-based promotion system and adequate remuneration. Opening up competition in employment in the delivery of services is necessary to reduce the discretionary power of state officials to minimize **rent-seeking** behaviour, which is the basis of bribery and corruption.
- Decision-making needs to be brought closer to the people so that they have more confidence in the state. All government programmes are likely to work better if there is democracy, if power is devolved, and users are consulted.

Figure 9.2 shows the functions of the state in tabular form, distinguishing between the roles of addressing market failure and improving equity on the one hand, and the provision of minimal functions through to activist functions on the other, according to capability.

Countries with a low state capability should concentrate first on basic functions such as the provision of pure public goods, macroeconomic stability and anti-poverty programmes. Going beyond these basic services are intermediate functions such as the management of externalities, regulating monopoly, improving information and providing social insurance. Finally, states with a strong capability can take on more active functions, as mentioned above in the case of the Asian Tigers, particularly promoting new markets through active industrial and financial policy.

The state also has a duty to reduce bureucracy and regulation to allow markets to flourish. According to a World Bank (2004) study of laws and regulations in 133 countries, the costs in time, effort and money in setting up businesses in developing countries are colossal compared to developed countries because of bureaucratic delays and institutional inefficiencies. In Indonesia it takes 168 days to set up a business; in Brazil 152 days, and only 2 days in New Zealand. In some developing countries, the average bureaucratic cost of setting up a business can be four times average income per head; in developed countries, it is as little as 1 per cent of average income per head. The consequences of poor and inappropriate regulations are that business is discouraged; a higher proportion of businesses operate outside the law, so the tax base is lower, and corruption is more widespread.

Addressing market failure

			Improving equity
Minimal functions		*Providing pure public goods:* Defence Law and order Property rights Macroeconomic management Public health	*Protecting the poor:* Antipoverty programmes Disaster relief
Intermediate functions	*Addressing externalities:* Basic education Environmental protection	*Regulating monopoly:* Utility regulation Antitrust policy	*Overcoming imperfect information:* Insurance (health, life, pensions) Financial regulation Consumer protection	*Providing social insurance:* Redistributive pensions Family allowances Unemployment insurance
Activist functions		*Coordinating private activity:* Fostering markets Cluster initiatives		*Redistribution:* Asset redistribution

Figure 9.2 Functions of the state

Source: World Bank, *World Development Report 1997* (New York: Oxford University Press, 1997).

The following extract from the *World Development Report 1997* outlines the challenge that various regions in the world currently face with regard to the role of the state (World Bank, 1997):

■ Many countries in **Sub-Saharan Africa** are suffering from a crisis of statehood – a crisis of capability. An urgent priority is to rebuild state effectiveness through an overhaul of public institutions, reassertion of the rule of law, and credible checks on abuse of state power. Where the links between the state, the private sector, and civil society are fragile and underdeveloped, improving the delivery of public and collective services will require closer partnerships with the private sector and civil society.

■ The capability of the state in most **East Asian** countries may not be considered a problem. But states' ability to change in response to the new challenges facing the region will play a critical role in their continued economic success.

■ The main issue in **South Asia** is overregulation, both a cause and an effect of bloated public employment and the surest route to corruption. Regulatory simplification and public enterprise reform, and the resulting contraction of the role of the state, will be complex and politically difficult.

■ The job of reorienting the state towards the task of 'steering, not rowing' is far from complete in **Central and Eastern Europe**. But most countries have made progress and are on the way to improving capability and accountability.

■ Low state capability in many countries of the **Commonwealth of Independent States** *(CIS)* is a serious and mounting obstacle to further progress in most areas of economic and social policy. Reorientation of the state is still at an early stage, and a host of severe problems has emerged from a general lack of accountability and transparency.

■ In **Latin America**, decentralization of power and of spending, coupled with demo-cratization, has dramatically transformed the local political landscape, in what some have called a 'quiet revolution.' A new model of government is emerging in the region. But greater emphasis is also needed on reform of the legal system, the civil service, and social policies.

■ In the **Middle East and North Africa**, unemployment is by far the greatest economic and social problem and makes government downsizing especially difficult. Because the political and social difficulties of reform are considerable, although not insurmountable, a promising approach might be to begin decentralizing selected services, and focus on reforming state enterprises, while preparing the ground for wider-ranging reforms.

DEVELOPMENT PLANS

In its *World Development Report 1997*, the World Bank does not address the role of development planning, but almost all developing countries, whatever their political ideology, publish development plans.[4] A **development plan** is an ideal way for a government to set out its development objectives and demonstrate initiative in tackling the country's development problems. A development plan can serve to stimulate effort throughout the country, and also act as a catalyst for foreign investment and loans from international institutions.

As an example, the Tongan 6th Development Plan (1991–5) stated that:

The ultimate aim of government policy is to induce improvements in the standard of living of Tongans in an equitable manner with a view to protecting natural resources and preserving cultural assets – Government policy will also pursue an equitable distribution of public investment and services between rural and urban areas, and between the capital, islands and outer regions.

Four economic and social objectives were set out:

- To achieve sustainable economic growth conducive to higher per capita income
- To achieve a more equitable distribution of income
- To generate more employment opportunities
- To restore and control external financial imbalances.

Depending on the politics of a country and its available expertise, a development plan will vary in its ambitiousness from a mere statement of aims to detailed calculations (and proposals for action) of the resources needed, and the amount of output that each sector of the economy must generate in order to achieve a stipulated rate of growth of output or per capita income. Anything more than a statement of aims inevitably involves some form of model building, if only to delineate the relationship between sectors of the economy and between the key variables in the growth process.

Four basic types of model are typically used in development planning:

- **Macro or aggregate models** of the economy, which may either be of the simple Harrod–Domar type (see Chapter 4) or of a more econometric nature, consisting of a series of equations that represent the basic structural relations in an economy between, say, factor inputs and product outputs, saving and income, imports and expenditure, and so on.
- **Sector models**, which isolate the major sectors of an economy and give the structural relations within each sector, and perhaps also specify the interrelationships between sectors, for example between agriculture and industry, between capital- and consumer-goods industries, and between the government and the rest of the economy.
- **Inter-industry models**, which show the transactions and interrelationships between producing sectors of an economy, normally in the form of an input–output table (see Chapter 13).
- Models and techniques for **project appraisal** and the allocation of resources between industries (see Chapter 10).

Models such as these serve a twofold purpose. In the first place they enable planners to reach decisions on how to achieve specified goals. They highlight the strategic choices open to the policy-maker in the knowledge that not all desirable goals are achievable simultaneously. Only with an understanding of the interrelationship between the different parts of the economy, and a knowledge of the parameters of the economic system, is it possible for meaningful and consistent policy decisions to be reached. Without detailed information upon which to base planning (or what has been called 'planning without facts'), the case for decentralized decision-making becomes overwhelming.

Second, models of the type described above can perform an equally valuable function from the point of view of enabling the future to be projected with a greater degree of certainty than would otherwise be possible, thereby providing some knowledge of what resources are likely to be available in relation to requirements within a stipulated planning period. Various types of model may be classified, therefore, according to whether they are required for policy or decision purposes or for the purpose of projection and forecasting. The necessary constituents of a plan containing both types of model are a statement of economic goals, a specification of policy instruments or instrumental variables, an estimation of structural relationships, historical data, the recognition of exogenous variables, and last but not least, a set of national accounts for national income and expenditure, foreign trade and even manpower to ensure consistency between demand and the supply of resources available.

POLICY MODELS

The essence of a policy model is that a certain set of objectives is specified and the model is then used to determine the most appropriate measures to achieve those objectives within certain constraints. In most development plans the primary objective is the achievement of a target rate of growth of output or per capita income within the planning period, or some terminal level of consumption, subject to constraints on the composition of output, the distribution of income and the availability of factor supplies. Given the time horizon of the plan and the objective function, an optimum strategy can be worked out from the initial conditions. One of the big dangers of planning in developing countries is that planners and policy makers are prone to choose targets based on needs and aspirations rather than on the basis of available resources, with the inevitable consequence that the targets are not achieved. It is incumbent on the planner to specify the constraints as accurately and honestly as possible to avoid disillusion with the planning process.

The solution to a policy model of this kind is somewhat different from one designed to find the value of certain instrumental variables that will achieve a particular target rate of growth. The difference can be illustrated with reference to the simple Harrod model of growth, which gives the level of savings necessary to achieve a particular growth rate assuming some value of the capital–output ratio. The level of savings required to achieve a target rate of growth may be very different from the level of savings available when the problem is posed as one of maximizing growth subject to constraints. The level of savings necessary to achieve the target rate of growth may conflict with society's wish for present rather than future consumption; it may be incompatible with the supplies of skilled labour necessary to work with capital; and the level of savings may not even be achievable because of a limit to the capacity to tax or to 'force' saving through inflation.

It is clear from what we have said so far that the first step in the formulation of a policy model must be the construction of an aggregate model of the economy (incorporating, if need be, a sector model and an interindustry model) to highlight and check the implications of the target rate of growth. If it is possible to formulate a reasonably sound set of structural equations for the economy, this exercise should not be too difficult.

The structural relations given by the structural equations are the restrictions on the instrumental variables that the policy-makers must consider as datum. They represent, as we have said already, such things as technological relations in industry, income–

consumption relations, foreign-trade relations and other behavioural and institutional relations that, in the short run at any rate, are outside the influence of the policy-maker. In the long run, certain structural relations may of course change with changes in the economy, induced by the planning process itself. The capital–output ratio, for example, may change under the influence of education expansion and the development of infrastructure. Other, more basic, structural relations, however, must be contended with in the planning process, even in the long run. Some of the important questions that need to be answered with the help of the structural equations are as follows:

- Can capital be guaranteed in the quantities required?
- Will exports and foreign assistance keep pace with the imports required?
- Will the future demand for consumption goods, out of increases in per capita income, exceed the supply and cause inflation?
- Can the required interrelationships between industries be maintained so that bottlenecks do not arise?

If the objective function or goals of a plan require a certain degree of balance between supply and demand in various markets and sectors of the economy, then clearly the objective function must be maximized subject to this general requirement of avoiding shortages of capital, labour and foreign exchange. The basic structural relations required can be found or determined by drawing on economic theory and econometric research, or by intuitive 'feel' in the case of behavioural and institutional relations.

Next, the instrumental variables must be specified. These are the variables that the planners intend to influence in some way in order to achieve the objectives specified within the constraints laid down. If the basic objective is a higher rate of growth, one obvious instrumental variable is the level of savings and investment in relation to national income. This can be influenced by tax policy, monetary policy and assistance from abroad. If the structural relations are given, and the constraints are outlined, a solution to a policy model will give a set of values for the instrumental variables that satisfies all the structural (and behavioural) equations in the model, consistent with the constraints imposed. In the case of savings, for example, the solution to a policy model would give the level of possible saving that would be compatible with the balance between the agricultural and industrial sectors of the economy, foreign borrowing of no more than a certain amount, a consumer desire for present rather than future consumption, and so on.

It should be emphasized at this point that the planners ought not to lay down rigid policy prescriptions for more than a very short length of time. Planning itself may alter circumstances in the future in an unforeseen way and planners must be ready to adapt to the new situation. The means by which to achieve the plan's goals must be flexible, and so too must the planning period. The term 'rolling plan' is used to describe planning of a flexible nature, where plans are continually being reviewed and revised in the light of new developments. If plans need to be revised, however, it is important that they are modified cautiously to avoid erosion of confidence. One of the purposes of planning is to imbue confidence, especially among the private decision-making class who are most susceptible to uncertainty, and it is vital that this confidence is not upset and uncertainty increased by sudden changes in policy. There are three typical planning horizons: one-year plans corresponding to a normal budget and accounting period; medium-term plans stretching over 4 to 7 years; and 10- to 20-year plans (which is probably the maximum length of time for which it is possible to make meaningful projections).

Because of computational limitations, separate decision models will probably have to be constructed for distinct policy purposes, for example the choice of techniques, the structure of trade, the pattern of final demand, the allocation of resources and so on. The application of aggregate macro models based on interconnections between income, consumption, investment, employment and foreign trade is also likely to run into the problem of sectoral differences in structural relations such that if the structure or pattern of production changes over time within the plan period, the use of average structural coefficients may give rise to misleading results. This is where sectoral models become important. If the economy can be conveniently divided into two or three sectors, the average coefficients can be adjusted for expected changes in the expansion or contraction of the different sectors over the period of the plan. Ultimately, any macro model must be consistent with the models and predictions for various sectors of the total economy.

Despite the potential use of decision models, they are not so widely used as might be expected in developing countries, especially decision models that attempt to optimize one thing or another. In practice, planning tends to be much more *ad hoc*. The reason is very often the difficulty of arriving at an agreement on the objective function. It is extremely difficult to balance the conflicting aims of different parts of the community and to reach a consensus over conflicting economic objectives.

PROJECTION MODELS

Any of the first three of the basic types of model mentioned at the outset may be used for projection or forecasting purposes. Typically, aggregate models for projection are of the Harrod–Domar type and are used to indicate the amount of investment required, either to achieve a particular target rate of growth or to keep the labour force fully employed (or both), assuming the labour force is exogenously determined. Sector models, on the other hand, are designed to project the output of various sectors and, if balanced growth is required, to allocate resources accordingly. Finally, interindustry models are designed to estimate the output requirements of industries as a result of a projection of expansion of the final demand for goods and services over a future period of time (see Chapter 13).

It would be wrong, of course, to think of forecasting models as entirely distinct and divorced from decision models. Forecasting models, especially of the econometric type, are often used, and are designed to be used, as decision models, with current choices and decisions depending on the future the models portray. Indeed there is little use for *pure* forecasting models as such without using them as a guide to policy.

THE ALLOCATION OF RESOURCES: THE BROAD POLICY CHOICES

Given the scarcity of resources in developing countries in relation to development needs, one of the central issues in development economics is the allocation of resources among competing ends. For most developing countries the two major constraints on the growth of output are the ability to invest and to import, and most theories of resource allocation and most public investment criteria reflect this fact. A common starting point in the consideration of resource allocation is how to maximize the level or growth of output with the domestic resources available, and how to minimize the use of foreign exchange.

Apart from the decision of how much to invest, three broad types of allocation decision may be distinguished:

- Which sectors to invest in
- Which projects should receive priority given the factor endowments of a country and its development goals
- Which combination of factors of production should be used to produce a given vector of goods and services, which will determine the technology of production.

While these decisions may look independent, in fact they are not. In practice, interdependence between decisions on output and decisions on technology is inevitable. Deciding which goods to produce will, to a certain extent, dictate factor proportions if technical coefficients are relatively fixed, and decisions about technology are bound to influence the types of goods and services that are produced, insofar as factor proportions cannot be varied. Some goods and services are obviously more labour-intensive than others. The choice of technology, in turn, will be particularly influenced by the price of factors of production, and by the relative valuation given to present versus future consumption and welfare.

Because of the interdependence between the choice of goods and the choice of technology, a country that decides to use relatively labour-intensive techniques within the framework of goods chosen may nonetheless have a greater capital intensity than another country using relatively capital-intensive techniques with a different mix of goods. When discussing resource allocation and the choice of techniques a sharp distinction needs to be made between investment criteria that relate to the pattern of output on the one hand, and the choice of technology to produce the given vector of outputs on the other.

Investment decisions of the micro type outlined above will also be influenced to a certain degree by the nature of the development strategy intended; that is, by broader policy issues such as whether emphasis is to be given to agriculture or industry, whether resources are to be used to build up complementary activities or whether imbalances are to be deliberately created in order to induce investment and decision making, and whether emphasis is to be on static short-term efficiency in the allocation of resources or on laying the foundations for faster growth in the future. And in an open economy, the potential clash between efficiency and growth also requires a consideration of the implications of adherence to different versions of the comparative cost doctrine. In short, the question of resource allocation between projects cannot be divorced from consideration of the wider policy issues of industry versus agriculture, balanced versus unbalanced growth, foreign trade strategy and so on. And influencing all these decisions will be the underlying objectives of the development strategy: whether the aim is to maximize *current welfare* or to maximize consumption at *some future point in time*.

The choice of development strategy itself will be subject to political, social and economic constraints. A particular strategy, for example, may conflict with the desired income distribution or other social objectives. Other strategies may involve political repercussions inimical to development. One factor that cannot be ignored is the regional distribution of political power. Spatial considerations of this sort add a further dimension to the allocation problem. The pursuit of balanced growth or massive investment in social-overhead capital may imply a large public sector in the economy, which may not be politically tolerable. Certain development plans may antagonize foreign investors or multilateral aid-giving agencies such that if the plans are carried out foreign capital or 'agency' capital dries up. Bearing in mind these constraints, let us first consider some of the broader aspects of development strategy and briefly discuss development goals, before examining a number of specific investment criteria that have been recommended for determining the allocation of resources and the pattern of output.

INDUSTRY VERSUS AGRICULTURE

The issue of the choice between industry and agriculture, and where the emphasis should lie, can be discussed very quickly because, as we saw in Chapter 5, the two sectors are very much complementary to each other. In practice the fortunes of agriculture and industry are closely interwoven in that the expansion of industry depends to a large extent on improvements in agricultural productivity, and improvements in agricultural productivity depend on adequate supplies of industrial 'inputs', including the provision of consumer goods to act as incentives to peasant farmers to increase the agricultural surplus. It is worth mentioning, however, that the emphasis on *balance* between industry and agriculture is of fairly recent origin. On the one hand it represents a shift of emphasis away from the 'modern' view of an all-out drive for industrialization by developing countries, and at the same time it represents a reaction against the traditional doctrine of comparative cost advantage which, when applied to developing countries, almost certainly dictates the production of primary commodities and a pattern of trade that puts these countries at a relative development disadvantage.

THE COMPARATIVE COST DOCTRINE

Whether the comparative cost doctrine should be adhered to is itself a question of development strategy, which is closely bound up with the goals of developing countries (that is, what they are trying to maximize), and with the controversy over whether trade should be looked at more from the point of view of the balance of payments than from that of the allocation of real resources. Assuming the full employment of resources, and that the price of a commodity reflects its opportunity cost (admittedly bold assumptions in any country), adherence to the comparative cost doctrine will produce the optimum pattern of production and trade for a country (see Chapter 16). Efficiency will be maximized when no commodity is produced that could be imported at a lower cost, measured by the resources that would have to be sacrificed to produce it at home. In a free-trade world this would rule out the production of a wide range of industrial commodities in developing countries.

If the objective is *growth*, however, as opposed to static efficiency, the theory of growth suggests investment criteria that are quite different from those derived from the theory of comparative advantage. If growth depends on increases in per capita investment, for example, it may be unwise to channel resources into activities that are too labour-intensive, where the income generated is all consumed and none is saved, or where there is no scope for increasing returns. Similarly, if growth is constrained by the balance of payments, it may be equally misplaced to develop activities producing goods with a low price and income elasticity of demand in world markets. A low price elasticity of demand can cause fluctuations in export earnings with shifts in supply, and cause the terms of trade to move adversely. A low income elasticity of demand will mean that for any given growth of world income countries producing these commodities will be put at a permanent balance-of-payments disadvantage compared with other countries producing goods with a higher income elasticity of demand (see Chapter 14).

The question ultimately boils down to one of the relative valuation of present versus future output and consumption (or welfare) – between consumption today and consumption tomorrow. Efficiency in resource allocation will maximize present output and consumption from a given amount of resources, but may impair growth and future consumption. Striving for growth may lower present welfare but provide greater output in the future.

PRESENT VERSUS FUTURE CONSUMPTION

The choice between present and future consumption is the same as the choice between consumption and investment in the present. How much investment should be undertaken in the present depends on the time interval over which society wants to maximize consumption and what value it places on consumption in the future compared with consumption in the present; that is, on the rate at which it discounts future consumption gains. Time affects both the accumulation of consumption gains and the effect that discounting has. Investment should take place so as to maximize consumption over the planning period. The investment ratio that maximizes consumption will vary according to the planning period, with and without discounting.

Let us illustrate this with a numerical example. Consider three different investment ratios – 0 per cent, 10 per cent and 50 per cent – and three different planning periods – 3 years, 6 years and 10 years. Further assume that the capital–output ratio is 2, and that, for simplicity, there is no depreciation and no discounting. Let the initial capital stock equal 200, producing 100 units of output. The time paths of output, consumption, investment and the capital stock for the three different investment strategies and three different planning horizons can now be shown, as in Table 9.2. Over the three-year planning period, the first policy of no investment maximizes consumption. Over the six-year planning period, the second policy of a 10 per cent investment ratio maximizes consumption, and over the ten-year planning period the third policy of a 50 per cent investment ratio maximizes consumption.

The calculations in Table 9.2, and the conclusions drawn from them about the time period over which consumption will be maximized, will be affected by discounting and the discount rate chosen, because the present value of future consumption gains becomes less and less the further into the future they accrue, and their value is also lower the higher the discount rate chosen. What we illustrate, then, is that the answer to the

Table 9.2 Consumption benefits with different investment ratios over different planning horizons

Time	Policy 1 (no investment)			Policy 2 (10 per cent investment)			Policy 3 (50 per cent investment)		
	K	Y	I	C	K	Y	I	C	K	Y	I	C
1	200	100	0	100	200.00	100.00	10.00	90.00	200.00	100.00	50.00	50.00
2	200	100	0	100	210.00	105.00	10.50	94.50	250.00	125.00	62.50	62.50
3	200	100	0	100	220.50	110.25	11.03	99.22	312.50	156.25	78.12	78.12
4	200	100	0	100	231.53	115.76	11.57	104.19	390.62	195.31	97.65	97.65
5	200	100	0	100	243.10	121.55	12.15	109.40	488.27	244.13	122.07	122.07
6	200	100	0	100	255.25	127.62	12.76	114.86	610.34	305.17	152.58	152.58
7	200	100	0	100	268.01	134.00	13.40	120.60	762.92	381.46	190.73	190.73
8	200	100	0	100	281.41	140.70	14.07	126.61	953.65	476.82	238.41	238.41
9	200	100	0	100	295.48	147.74	14.77	132.97	1192.06	596.03	298.01	298.01
10	200	100	0	100	310.25	155.12	15.51	139.61	1490.07	745.03	372.51	372.51

Key: K = capital stock; Y = output; I = the level of investment; C = consumption.

question of how much to invest depends crucially on the *planning horizon* taken and the *discount rate* chosen. The longer the planning horizon and the less the stream of future consumption benefits is discounted, the more the investment. The shorter the planning horizon and the higher the discount rate, the less investment there will be.

We also illustrate that countries with low initial stocks of capital and low levels of consumption must invest heavily if high future living standards are to be attained. But to invest heavily they must have long planning horizons. One of the arguments for planning is, in fact, to lengthen the planning horizon beyond that chosen by individuals maximizing privately. Any finite planning horizon, however, only takes care of the people living within the planning period. To take account of generations living beyond the horizon, certain constraints must be built into the investment model such that, for example, the level of consumption at the end of the period should not be above a specified level, otherwise maximization of consumption within the horizon would mean consuming all income at the end of the horizon, leaving no saving for future investment and consumption.

CHOICE OF TECHNIQUES

In a planning framework, the valuation of present versus future welfare is also the central issue regarding the choice of technology – whether techniques should be capital- or labour-intensive. At first sight it would seem sensible, in a labour-abundant economy, to use labour-intensive techniques of production, and to encourage activities that use factors of production that are in abundance. Doing so, however, may lead to a conflict between efficiency and growth; a clash between the maximization of present consumption and the level of consumption in the future. The problem is that if the wage rate is given, and invariant with respect to the technique of production, the more labour-intensive the technique the less saving that is likely to be generated for future reinvestment. Specifically, if the workers' propensity to consume is higher than that of the owners of capital, the total surplus, and the surplus per unit of capital invested, left for reinvestment will be smaller than if the technology were more capital-intensive. On the other hand, the more capital-intensive the technology, the lower the level of consumption and employment in the present.[5]

In general, we reach the conclusion that the higher the valuation placed on raising the present level of employment and consumption as compared with future output, the more that labour-intensive techniques should be favoured. On the other hand, the greater the valuation placed on future output in relation to present welfare, the more that capital-intensive methods of production should be favoured. It is capital-intensive techniques that are capable of yielding the largest surplus of income over wage costs for a given capital outlay, making possible a higher rate of reinvestment for the future. The choice between projects of different degrees of capital intensity, therefore – insofar as there is a choice – boils down to the relative weights to be attached to an additional increment of investment compared with an additional increment of consumption. If saving is regarded as 'suboptimal', then at the margin an extra unit of investment must be regarded as more valuable than an extra unit of consumption and there is a case for more capital-intensive techniques that will generate this extra investment potential at the margin. As we said in Chapter 5, the fact that the social opportunity cost of labour is zero makes no difference to the argument because even 'costless' labour will consume if employed in industry, and the object is to minimize consumption. As long as the wage in industry is higher than the marginal product in alternative uses, there will be an increase in consumption with the employment of more labour in industry. This has important implications for the valuation of labour in resource allocation, which we take up when we discuss social cost-benefit analysis and shadow wages in Chapter 10.

There is not only a potential conflict between employment and saving in the choice of techniques, but also a conflict between employment and output. The conflict arises not in the utilization of existing equipment but in the choice of *new* techniques. Techniques of production that are labour-intensive may have higher capital–output ratios than techniques that are more capital-intensive. A simple example will illustrate the point. Assume a fixed amount of capital to be invested of £1000. One technique of production could employ 100 units of labour with £1000 of capital, but the capital–output ratio is 5. This would give a flow of output of 200 with the employment of 100 persons. A second technique of production employs 50 units of labour but has a capital–output ratio of 4. This would give a flow of output of 250 with the employment of 50 persons. Thus maximizing both the current level of employment and output are consistent only if the more labour-intensive techniques also have the lowest capital–output ratios. We discuss these conflicts more fully, as well as the choice of techniques in practice, in Chapter 12.

BALANCED VERSUS UNBALANCED GROWTH

Another broad choice of development strategy is between so-called balanced and unbalanced growth. Whether or not there exists a low-level equilibrium trap, which needs a 'critical minimum effort' to overcome it (see Chapter 8), sound economic reasons can be advanced in support of a 'big push', taking the form of a planned large-scale expansion of a wide range of economic activities. The economic rationale for a 'big push' forms part of what is known as the doctrine of **balanced growth**. Opposed to this thesis, however, is a school of thought that argues that a 'big push' is not feasible, and that in any case development is best stimulated in developing countries by the deliberate creation of imbalance. In this respect balanced versus unbalanced growth is an issue of development strategy that may constrain the application of investment criteria.

The term 'balanced growth' is used in many different senses, but the original exponents of the balanced growth doctrine had in mind the scale of investment necessary to overcome indivisibilities on both the supply and the demand side of the development process (see, for example, Rosenstein-Rodan, 1943). Indivisibilities on the supply side refer to the 'lumpiness' of capital (especially social-overhead capital), and the fact that only investment in a large number of activities simultaneously can take advantage of various external economies of scale. Indivisibilities on the demand side refer to the limitations imposed by the size of the market on the profitability, and hence feasibility, of economic activities. This was the original interpretation of the doctrine of balanced growth: the large-scale expansion of activities to overcome divergences between the private and social return.

The doctrine was later extended, however, to refer to the *path* of economic development and the *pattern* of investment necessary to keep the different sectors of the economy in balance, so that lack of development in one sector does not impede development in others. This does not mean, of course, that output in all sectors should grow at the same rate, but rather in accordance with the income elasticity of demand for products, so that supply equals demand. The notion of equilibrium is implied, and an absence of shortages and bottlenecks.

Balanced growth, therefore, has a *horizontal* and *vertical* aspect. On the one hand it recognizes indivisibilities in supply and complementarities of demand, and on the other it stresses the importance of achieving balance between such sectors as agriculture and industry, between the capital-goods and consumer-goods industries, and between social capital and directly productive activities.

Thus there are two fairly distinct versions of the balanced growth doctrine that need considering: one referring to the path of development and the pattern of investment necessary for the smooth functioning of the economy, and the other referring to the scale of investment necessary to overcome indivisibilities in the productive process on both sides of the market. Nurkse's (1953) original exposition of balanced growth tends to embrace both versions of the theory of balanced growth, while Rosenstein-Rodan concentrates on the necessity for a 'big push' to overcome the existence of indivisibilities. We shall first consider the economic arguments for a large-scale investment programme and then discuss the desirability of achieving balance between different sectors of the economy.

On the demand side, the argument amounts to little more than Adam Smith's famous dictum that specialization, or the division of labour, is limited by the extent of the market, and that if the market is limited certain activities may not be economically viable (see Chapter 4). If, however, several activities are established simultaneously, each could provide a market for the other's products, so that activities that are not profitable when considered in isolation would become profitable when considered in the context of a large-scale development programme. It is true that industrial enterprises may have to be of a certain minimum size to be profitable, if only to compete in international markets, but there are also other ways in which markets can be widened. The improvement of transport facilities in developing countries, and of communications in general, offers tremendous scope for the expansion of markets. Also, the need for a large-scale development programme loses much of its force in the context of an open economy. Restrictions on imported commodities could immediately expand the market for home-produced substitutes, and export promotion could provide a similar stimulus.

On the supply side, the argument for a 'big push' is bound up with the existence of **external economies of scale**. The external economies referred to in this context go beyond the external economies of the traditional theory of the firm. Whereas in traditional equilibrium theory external economies refer to the fact that the nature of the production function in one activity may be altered by the existence of other activities (for example those in close proximity), in the context of development theory they refer mainly to the impact of a large investment programme on the profit functions of participating firms. If there exist external economies in either sense, the social return of an activity will exceed the private return. It is argued that the way to eliminate this divergence is to make each activity part of an overall programme of investment expansion.

Enterprises that are not, or do not appear to be, profitable in isolation become profitable when considered as part of a comprehensive plan for industrial expansion embracing several activities. As several commentators have pointed out, however, while the expansion of several activities may improve the profitability of each activity – assuming there are interindustry linkages – the cost of factor inputs may rise, offsetting the benefit of these external economies.

The second version of the balanced growth doctrine, lays emphasis on the path of development and the pattern of investment. This version of the balanced growth doctrine stresses the necessity of balance between sectors of the economy to prevent bottlenecks developing in some sectors, which may be a hindrance to development, and excess capacity in others, which would be wasteful. Among the foremost, early proponents of this version of the balanced growth doctrine were Nurkse (1953) and Arthur Lewis (1955). Particular emphasis is placed by these two economists on achieving a balance between the agricultural and industrial sectors of developing economies. This is for two main reasons, both of which recognize the interdependence between the two sectors and the mutual assistance and stimulus that each can give the other:

- If agricultural productivity is to improve, there must be incentives for farmers to expand their marketable surplus, and this requires a balance between the agricultural and consumer-goods sectors of the economy
- Agriculture requires capital inputs and this requires a balance between agriculture and the production of capital goods and the provision of social-overhead capital.

This is in addition to the fact that agricultural output can provide a basis for the development of local industries and that the industrial sector relies on the agricultural sector for food. Furthermore, in the absence of increasing exports the agricultural sector must rely on the industrial sector for a substantial proportion of the increased demand for its products. The doctrine of balanced growth in this form, especially the stress on the balance between agriculture and industry, steers a middle course between the traditional comparative cost doctrine that developing countries should confine themselves to the production of primary commodities, and the view that developing countries ought to industrialize as intensively and quickly as possible.

UNBALANCED GROWTH

A major criticism of the balanced growth doctrine is that it fails to come to grips with one of the fundamental obstacles to development in developing countries, namely a shortage of resources of all kinds. Critics of balanced growth do not deny the importance of a large-scale investment programme and the expansion of complementary activities. Their argument is that in the absence of sufficient resources, especially capital, entrepreneurs and decision makers, the striving for balanced growth may not provide a sufficient stimulus to the spontaneous mobilization of resources or the inducement to invest, and will certainly not economize on decision-taking if planning is required.

One of the most provocative books ever written on development strategy is that by Hirschman (1958), whose argument is along the above lines. Hirschman was then the foremost exponent of the doctrine of **unbalanced growth**, and we must briefly consider his views as these are still relevant today. The question he attempts to answer is this: given a limited amount of investment resources and a series of proposed investment projects whose total cost exceeds the available resources, how do we pick out the projects that will make the greatest contribution to development relative to their cost? And how should 'contribution' be measured?

First of all he distinguishes two types of investment choices – *substitution choices* and *postponement choices*. Substitution choices are those which involve a decision as to whether project *A* or *B* should be undertaken. Postponement choices are those which involve a decision as to the sequence of projects *A* and *B* – that is, which should precede the other. Hirschman is mainly concerned with postponement choices and how they are made. His fundamental thesis is that the question of priority must be resolved on the basis of a comparative appraisal of the strength with which progress in one area will induce progress in another. The efficient sequence of projects will necessarily vary from region to region and from country to country, depending on the nature of the obstacles to development, but the basic case for the approach remains the same; that is, to economize on decision-making. In Hirschman's view, the real scarcity in developing countries is not the resources themselves but the means and ability to bring them into play. Preference should be given to that sequence of projects which maximizes **'induced' decision-making**.

He illustrates his argument by considering the relation between social capital (SC) and directly productive activities (DPA). The case in which SC precedes DPA he calls 'development via excess capacity', and the case in which DPA precedes SC he labels 'development via shortages'. Both sequences create inducements and pressures conducive to development; but which sequence should be adopted, if it is not possible to pursue a 'balanced' growth path, to produce DPA output at minimum cost in terms of inputs into both DPA and SC? The question can be made clearer with the aid of a diagram (Figure 9.3).

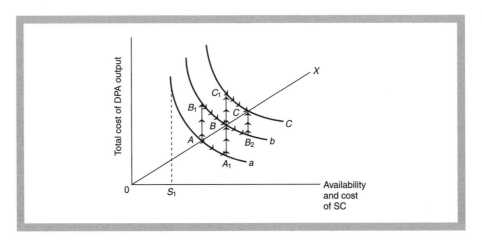

Figure 9.3 Induced decision-making

If the total cost of DPA output is measured on the vertical axis, and the availability and cost of SC is measured on the horizontal axis, curves can be drawn (*a, b, c*) showing the cost of producing a given full-capacity output of DPA from a given amount of investment in DPA, as a function of the availability of SC. The successive curves, *a, b, c*, represent different levels of DPA output from successively higher investment in DPA. The curves are negatively sloped and convex to the origin because DPA costs will decrease the greater the availability of social capital, but there is a minimum amount of SC necessary for any level of DPA output (for example $0S_1$, corresponding to curve *a*), and as SC increases its impact on the cost of DPA output becomes less and less.

Now assume that the objective of the economy is to obtain increasing outputs of DPA with the minimum use of resources devoted to both DPA and SC. On each curve, *a, b, c*, the point where the sum of the coordinates is smallest will represent the most desirable combination of DPA and SC on this criterion. The line $0X$ connects the optimal points on the different curves and this represents the most 'efficient' expansion path, or 'balanced' growth path, between SC and DPA.

But suppose that 'optimal' amounts of SC and DPA cannot be expanded simultaneously to keep in balance with one another. On what criteria is that postponement choice made? One possibility is the sequence AA_1BB_2C, where the initial expansionary step is always taken by social capital. This sequence is called 'development via excess capacity'. The other (opposite) possibility is the sequence AB_1BC_1C, where the initial expansionary step is taken by DPA. This sequence is called 'development via shortages'. According to Hirschman, the preference should go to the sequence of expansion that maximizes 'induced' decision-making. It is difficult to tell *a priori* which sequence this is likely to be. If SC is expanded, existing DPA becomes less costly, encouraging further DPA. If DPA is expanded first, costs will rise but pressures will arise for SC facilities to be provided. Both sequences set up incentives and pressures, and ultimately, in Hirschman's view, the sequence chosen must depend on the relative strength of entrepreneurial motivations on the one hand, and on the response to public pressure of the authorities responsible for social capital on the other.

In general, however, Hirschman has some harsh things to say about the traditional view that SC must precede, or even be kept in balance with, DPA if development is to progress smoothly. While he admits that a certain minimum of social capital is a prerequisite to the establishment of DPA, he argues that development via excess capacity is purely permissive, and that to strive for balance is equally dangerous because there will be no incentive to induced investment (or induced decision-making). On the other hand, development via shortages will compel further investment, and hence the most 'efficient' sequence as far as 'induced' decision-making is concerned is likely to be that where DPA precedes SC.

It is true that where there is strong social and economic resistance to change, 'permissive' acts such as the construction of social-overhead capital are not likely to provide much impetus to development. On the other hand Hirschman's analysis leaves several questions unanswered. He concedes that the objective must be to obtain increasing outputs of directly productive activities at minimum cost in terms of resources devoted to both DPA and SC, and that the cost of producing any given output of DPA will be higher the more inadequate is SC, but what is the *minimum* amount of SC required in a developing economy? Is this minimum so high as to contradict the argument that DPA should precede SC, at least in the earlier stages of development? Furthermore, what is the guarantee that SC will subsequently be provided once DPA has been established? Indivisibilities with respect to social capital may be so large that private investors are not induced to supply at any price. Reliance would then be on the government. Hirschman does not pay adequate attention to the government's crucial responsibility in this connection. It looks suspiciously as if unbalanced growth via shortages, like the 'big push', may not be economically feasible (albeit for different reasons).

Hirschman would apply the same criterion of 'induced decision-making' to the choice and sequence of projects *within* the directly productive sector. Here inducements stem from interdependencies between activities, or what Hirschman calls **'backward' and 'forward' linkage effects**. Backward linkages measure the proportion of an activity's output that represents purchases from other domestic activities. Forward linkages measure the proportion of an activity's output that does not go to meet final demand but is used as an input into other activities. With knowledge of interindustry flows in an economy, with the help of an input–output table (see Chapter 13), it is possible to rank activities according to the magnitude of their combined linkage effects. Hirschman is suggesting that within the directly productive sector a useful development strategy would be to encourage those activities with the potentially highest combined linkages, because this will provide the greatest inducement and incentive to other activities to develop.

Unfortunately, one of the typical characteristics of developing countries is a lack of interdependence between activities. Primary product production has very limited backward linkages with other activities, while forward linkages, although potentially greater, also tend to be limited in practice. Agriculture's demands on other sectors are minimal, and only a comparatively small fraction of total agricultural output in developing countries is processed domestically; most is exported. The fact that manufacturing activities possess greater backward and forward linkages, strengthening the cumulative nature of development, is another powerful reason for industrialization. Hirschman advocates the expansion of industry through the transformation of semi-manufactures into goods required for final demand, or what he calls 'enclave import' industries.

In general he lays great stress on the role of imports in the development process, seeing imports as part of the inducement mechanism. For not only can semi-manufactured imports be processed into goods for final demand, but final-demand imports themselves can then be readily produced at home once the market has attained a certain size (or production threshold). If one of the major obstacles to development is a shortage of decision-makers, coupled with uncertainty and a limited market, the existence of imports provides conclusive proof that the market is there. As imports increase, so too do the chances that domestic production will one day be profitable. Hirschman criticizes developing countries for restricting imports prematurely, and argues that infant industry protection should only be given after imports have reached such a level as to guarantee domestic producers a market for their goods.

It is not easy to evaluate the balanced versus unbalanced growth debate. For one thing, the theories cannot easily be tested empirically, and for another the strategies are politically contentious. From the purely economic point of view, however, there is really no reason at all why balanced and unbalanced growth should be presented as alternatives. Several attempts have in fact been made to present a reconciliatory view. One step towards this reconciliatory approach, which both Hirschman and Nurkse mention themselves, is to treat unbalanced growth as a means of achieving the ultimate objective of balanced growth. A further step is to look for compatibilities in the two approaches. Since balanced growth is consistent with sectors growing at different rates, provided supply and demand are in balance, the distinctive feature of the alternative strategies must be the imbalance between supply and demand. Unbalanced growth would concentrate resources in a few selected areas, creating shortages elsewhere. But this is consistent with the 'big push' version of the balanced growth doctrine, provided the scale of investment is sufficient to overcome indivisibilities and complementarities. If unbalanced growth is defined not so much in terms of shortages as in terms of concentration on certain activities, according to comparative advantage or the existence of increasing returns, balanced and unbalanced growth can be complementary strategies.

There is no reason why development strategy should not draw on the strong points of both doctrines so that an optimum strategy of development combines some elements of balance as well as imbalance. The gain of real resources from concentration and specialization must be weighed against the potential disadvantages, and perhaps a saving of resources through maintaining balance between sectors. Historically, growth has been unbalanced, and this is implicit in classical trade theory, with balance being restored through imports. By and large, the present developing countries are following the same route and pursuing a combination of strategies. Resources tend to be concentrated in a limited number of sectors, but within these sectors the investment programme attempts to maintain vertical balance. Concentration of effort is feasible in an open economy with the capacity to buy imports, and at the same time investment is on a large enough scale for complementary activities to be established, recognizing interdependencies in production and consumption.

INVESTMENT CRITERIA

Traditional micro theory teaches that under perfect competition, resources will be optimally allocated when each factor of production is employed up to the point where its marginal product is equal to its price, and that society's output (welfare) will be maximized when the marginal products of factors are equated in all their uses. This is the so-called 'marginal rule' for resource allocation, and implies 'efficiency' in the sense that a society's total output of goods and services could not be increased by any redistribution of resources between activities because each factor of production is equally productive in existing activities. In static analysis, therefore, 'efficiency' in resource allocation implies maximizing the national product, and this is achieved when the marginal products of factors are equated in their different uses.

If the application of the marginal rule leads to an efficient allocation of resources, what is the allocation 'problem' in developing countries? Why seek other criteria to decide on the allocation of resources? One good reason is that the assumptions of traditional micro theory accord neither with the realities nor with the aspirations of developing countries. Two major drawbacks of the application of the marginal rule may be cited. One is that the marginal rule is a static criterion, and as we have said before it is by no means certain that the aim of developing countries is, or ought to be, the maximization of the *present* level of output, consumption or welfare. Second, traditional static theory ignores a host of factors that may have a bearing on the *social* optimum allocation of resources. In countries characterized by fundamental structural disequilibria and extreme imperfections in the market, it may not be assumed that the market prices of goods and factors of production reflect the social costs and benefits of production. The application of the marginal rule will only lead to a *socially* optimal allocation of resources in the absence of divergences between market prices and social costs and benefits, or if market prices are corrected to reflect social values.

Several factors may lead to divergences between market prices and the social valuation of goods and factors of production. First, if external economies and increasing returns are attached to some projects, their social value will exceed their private value, and the application of the marginal rule must make allowances for this if output is to be maximized from a given endowment of factors.

Second, if perfect competition does not prevail in the product market, product prices will not reflect society's valuation of those products, and market prices must somehow be adjusted to achieve a social optimum. Similarly, if perfect competition does not prevail in the factor market, the price of factors will not reflect their opportunity cost to society so that employing factors up to the point where their marginal product equals their price will not produce a social optimum. Idle resources such as labour will be overvalued, and scarce resources such as capital and foreign exchange will be undervalued, and market prices must therefore be corrected to reflect the value of these resources to society.

Third, static analysis ignores the future structure of product and factor prices arising from the choice of projects in the present. An optimum resource allocation in the present may not produce an optimal allocation of resources in the future. The only way of coping with this difficulty is through what is called the programming approach to resource allocation, by which the repercussions of one activity on others are explicitly considered and due allowance is made for time.

Finally, the application of the marginal rule can only lead to optimal resource allocation if income distribution is 'optimal' and remains unaffected by whatever programme is decided on. If a new pattern of resource allocation alters income distribution, output may be maximized but welfare diminished because of 'undesirable' changes in the distribution of income gains. To say anything concrete on this score requires an explicit statement of societal objectives if interpersonal comparisons of utility are to be avoided. Presumably there might be a fair degree of consensus that an income distribution that leaves half the population unemployed and starving is 'inferior' to one that does not. Only the conditions for Pareto optimality would deny it![6]

For all the above reasons, there has been a prolonged debate for many years over the most appropriate criterion for resource allocation in the light of the development obstacles of developing countries and their aspirations. The different criteria that have been suggested reflect, by and large, differences of opinion as to what developing countries ought to attempt to maximize, the broad choice being between present and future levels of output and consumption. Most of the criteria discussed by early writers in this field refer to the allocation of capital, reflecting the view of domestic capital as the primary scarce resource. Increasingly, however, attention has been paid to the effects of resource allocation decisions on the balance of payments in recognition of foreign exchange as an equally scarce resource. This leads us to Chapter 10 on social cost-benefit analysis.

1 What is the role of markets in the development process?

2 Distinguish the different types of market failure, and the role that governments can play in rectifying market failures.

3 According to the World Bank (1997), what are the key roles of the state in developing countries, and how can the role of the state be made more effective?

4 What causes corruption, and how can it be reduced?

5 What are the major causes of divergences between the market prices of goods and the value of those goods to society?

6 What are the major causes of divergences between the market prices of factors of production and their cost to society?

7 Why do developing countries construct development plans?

8 What do you understand by the concept of 'balanced growth'?

9 What is Hirschman's major criticism of the doctrine of balanced growth?

NOTES

1. In many developed countries the state is even more pervasive in terms of expenditure, although a much higher proportion represents social security transfer payments, not expenditure on real resources.
2. For a comprehensive survey, see Abed and Gupta (2002).
3. For a collection of case studies on corruption see Elliott (1997); also Tanzi (1998) and Bardhan (1997).
4. Students should familiarize themselves with a plan for a country of their choosing.
5. This conclusion depends, among other things, on the wage rate being invariant with respect to the technique of production. If the wage is higher the more capital-intensive the technique, this conclusion would have to be modified. For a discussion of this point, and other considerations that may lessen the conflict between employment and saving in the choice of techniques, see Chapter 12.
6. A situation is said to be Pareto optimal only if a change that benefits some does not harm others.

WEBSITES ON GOVERNMENT AND CORRUPTION

Role of the state

World Bank   www.worldbank.org/publicsector

The International Development Department Research (University of Birmingham) www.idd.bham.ac.uk/research/Projects/Role_of_gov/role_of_gov.htm

Corruption

Transparency International   www.transparency.org

Internet Centre for Corruption Research   www.gwdg.de/ruwvw/icr.htm

10 Project appraisal, social cost-benefit analysis and shadow wages

The literature and discussion about project choice and the allocation of resources has been dominated since the 1970s by **social cost-benefit analysis**. Social cost-benefit analysis is really the public analogue or equivalent of the **present value method** of private investment appraisal, but it has to take many things into account, which adds to its complexity. The technique is recommended for the appraisal of publicly financed investment projects in order to allocate resources in a way that is most profitable to society, recognizing that the market prices of goods and factors of production do not necessarily reflect their social value and costs, respectively, and, given that society is concerned with the *future* level of consumption as well as the present, the level of current saving may be suboptimal.

PROJECT APPRAISAL

When we talk about 'public investment' we are talking mainly about *public infrastructure projects* (such as roads and water supplies) and *public enterprise projects* (such as steel mills, power plants and so on). But there are other categories of state-supported investment where social cost-benefit analysis may be applied, such as private sector projects financed by public credit (for example, small-scale industries financed through state development banks) and private sector projects subject to public control (for example, transport and mining ventures).

When discussing project appraisal there is a distinction to be made between financial, economic and social appraisal.

- **Financial appraisal** has to do with the financial flows generated by the project itself and the direct costs of the project measured at market prices.
- **Economic appraisal** has to do with adjusting costs and benefits to take account of costs and benefits to the economy at large, including the indirect effects of projects that are not captured by the price mechanism.
- **Social appraisal** has to do with the distributional consequences of project choices, both intertemporal (that is, over time) and intratemporal (that is, between groups in society at a point in time).

A typical **project appraisal report** would consist of the following:

- The terms of reference
- An engineering study to see whether the project is technically feasible
- A financial study to ascertain how much the project will cost in budgetary terms, at market prices
- An appraisal of the economic costs and benefits, valuing outputs and inputs at social prices and including secondary impacts on the economy and the effect on the distribution of income
- Details of the administrative requirements of the project
- Conclusions and recommendations.

Project appraisal or project planning must be thought of as a process of decision-making over time, starting with the **identification** of projects (in relation to the planning process, which may have set a target growth rate), and going through **stages** of various

feasibility studies (for example engineering, financial and so on), then the **investment** phase, and finally **evaluation**. This is the notion of the **project cycle**.

FINANCIAL APPRAISAL

We first turn to financial appraisal and consider how to calculate the **net present value** of an investment. The first step in project (investment) appraisal is always to identify the *flows* involved. First there is the investment cost in the initial period. Second, there are the operating costs, for example labour and raw materials. Third, there is the value of the output (sales volume multiplied by price). Fourth, there is the question of the life of the project. The value of the flows must then be **discounted** to obtain their **present value** because everything has an opportunity cost. To have £100 next year is not the same as having £100 at the present, because £100 now could be invested at a rate of interest, say 10 per cent, to give £110 next year. The future and the present are made equivalent by discounting future sums by the rate of interest. The present value (PV) of any future value (FV) in period t is $FV_t/(1 + r)^t$, where r is the rate of interest (or discount rate). We can show this with a simple algebraic example: The value of a present sum after 1 year invested at rate, r, is $FV_1 = PV(1 + r)$. After 2 years the sum is worth $FV_2 = [PV(1 + r)] (1 + r) = PV(1 + r)^2$ and so on. Therefore $FV_t = PV(1 + r)^t$, and hence $PV = FV_t/(1 + r)^t$.

The NPV formula is then

$$\text{NPV} = \sum_{t=0}^{T} \left(\frac{V_t - C_t}{(1 + r)^t} \right) - K_0 \tag{10.1}$$

where K_0 is the initial cost of the project in the base period, V_t is the value of output at time t, C_t are the operating costs at time t, r is the rate of discount and T is the life of the project. If NPV > 0, the project yields a positive return.

Let us give a numerical example of a small shoe factory, the initial cost of which is £5 million and which yields a net cash flow over 5 years of £2 million per annum, with a rate of interest of 8 per cent. Table 10.1 gives the calculation of net present value. The project yields a net present value of £2.98 million.

Table 10.1 Numerical example of the calculation of NPV

Year (t)	Net cash flow ($V_t - C_t$)		Discount factor $1/(1 + 0.08)^t$	Discounted cash flow
0	−5		–	−5.00
1	2	×	0.926	+1.85
2	2	×	0.857	+1.71
3	2	×	0.794	+1.59
4	2	×	0.735	+1.47
5	2	×	0.681	+1.36
				NPV = +2.98

ECONOMIC APPRAISAL

First of all, let us consider the secondary (or indirect) costs and benefits that may arise from public projects, and then consider how to adjust the market prices of goods and services and factors of production in order to take account of their **economic** value to society at large. There are three major indirect effects to consider:

- First there is the economic impact of the project on the immediate vicinity of the project. Some projects, of course, such as an irrigation scheme, are designed to have an impact on the immediate vicinity, and their benefits would be counted as direct benefits, but other projects will have incidental indirect effects, both positive and negative. A new road, for example, which is designed to cut travel time, may raise output in the immediate vicinity. This is a positive benefit. On the other hand a new dam to generate electricity may flood arable land and reduce agricultural production. This is a negative indirect effect.

- Second, there are the price effects upon local markets. If, for example, prices fall as a result of a project, this represents a gain in consumer surplus, and this needs to be added to the value of the project. A new road that reduces supply costs will reduce the price of local supplies and represent an indirect benefit of the road.

- Third, there are the consequences of a project for other sectors that supply inputs to the project. If a project demands more inputs, this is income to the supplier. For example a new dam will require local materials; a new factory will demand steel, and so on. These repercussions need to be taken account of.

Beyond the secondary (or indirect) effects of projects, the market prices of goods produced and the factors of production used may not reflect their value to the economy as a whole. The prices need adjusting to reflect their true economic value to society.

In **economic** appraisal (as opposed to financial appraisal), we now have to redefine the variables in the net present value formula in (10.1) to ascertain whether a project is profitable to society at large.

- V_t is the flow of social benefit **measured at economic (or efficiency) prices**.
- C_t is the **social** cost of inputs (measured by opportunity cost).
- r is the **social** rate of discount.
- K_0 is the **social** cost of the investment.

A project will be profitable to society if the social benefits of the project exceed the social costs – or, to put it another way, if the net present value of the project to society is greater than zero.

The question is, how should a project's social benefits and costs be measured, and what common unit of account (or *numéraire*) should the benefits and costs be expressed in, given a society's objectives and the fact that it has trading opportunities with the rest of the world so that it can sell and buy outputs and inputs abroad (so that domestic and foreign goods need to be made comparable)? There are two broad approaches to this question.

First, benefits and costs may be measured at domestic market prices using consumption as the *numéraire*, with adjustments made for divergences between market prices and social values, and making domestic and foreign resources comparable using a shadow exchange rate. This is sometimes referred to as the **UNIDO approach** (see Dasgupta, Marglin and Sen, 1972).

Second, benefits and costs may be measured at **world prices** to reflect the true opportunity cost of outputs and inputs (also obviating the need to use a shadow foreign exchange rate), using public saving measured in foreign exchange as the *numéraire* (that is, converting everything into its foreign exchange equivalent). This is referred to as the **Little–Mirrlees approach** (see Little and Mirrlees, 1969, 1974). The fact that foreign exchange is taken as the *numéraire* does not mean that project accounts are necessarily expressed in foreign currency. The unit of account can remain the domestic currency, but the values recorded are the foreign exchange equivalent – that is, how much net foreign exchange is earned.

Before proceeding to contrast the approaches and to look at the problems of measurement, let us consider the important divergences that require correction between the market prices of goods and factors of production and their value to society.

DIVERGENCES BETWEEN MARKET PRICES AND SOCIAL VALUES

The market prices of goods may not reflect their social value for a number of reasons:

- First, government-imposed taxes, subsidies, tariffs and controls of various kinds distort free market prices. Opportunity cost must be measured *net* of taxes and subsidies.
- Second, imperfections in the market will raise prices above the marginal cost of production. Prices set by private monopolists and public utilities may be particularly distorted.
- Third, the existence of externalities, both positive and negative, will mean that the prices of goods do not reflect their true value to society.

The market prices of factors of production may not reflect their true cost to society – that is, the opportunity cost of using them measured by their marginal product in alternative uses – because:

- Labour's market price in the industrial sector (that is, the industrial wage) is likely to exceed the cost to society of using labour if there is disguised unemployment on the land or in the petty service sector.
- Capital's market price will be below its social cost if it is subsidized.
- Foreign exchange may also be too cheap from a social point of view if the exchange rate (measured as the domestic price of foreign currency) is kept artificially low by exchange controls of one form or another.

The existence of external economies and diseconomies may also cause divergences between the market price of inputs and their social cost. If, for example, a project purchases inputs from decreasing cost industries, the social cost is not equal to the price based on average cost but to the lesser figure of marginal cost.

It is also possible that aggregate saving and investment in an economy is less than socially desirable, but the market does not allow individuals to express a preference for a higher rate of investment and capital accumulation for growth and future welfare. This is another example of the **isolation paradox** – one solution to which is for the government to use a lower social discount rate than the market rate of interest to encourage more investment than if the market rate of interest was used for calculating net present value.

Market prices adjusted for these various divergences and distortions are called **shadow, social**, **economic** or **accounting** prices. Adjusted market prices for goods we shall call 'economic prices', and adjusted market prices for factors of production (including foreign exchange) we shall call 'shadow prices'.

ECONOMIC PRICES FOR GOODS

The first divergence mentioned above requires the economic prices for goods to be found. As already stated, either domestic market prices may be corrected for the various distortions and imperfections, with domestic and foreign goods made comparable using a shadow price of foreign exchange (the UNIDO approach), or goods may be valued at world prices, as recommended by Little and Mirrlees. Doing the latter, it is argued, will give a truer measure of the social valuation of goods than the first alternative of measuring some goods at domestic prices (with adjustments), traded goods at their international price, and then making domestic and foreign goods comparable using a shadow foreign exchange rate that may itself be subject to distortions.

The stimulus to valuing output (and inputs) at world prices (as a measure of true economic benefit) originally came in the context of **import substitution policies** pursued by many developing countries in the 1950s and 1960s, when it became clear that a large number of commercially profitable industries were producing goods at a much higher price than the alternatives available on the international market. At the same time, these industries were high cost, devoting more resources to new investment than embodied in alternative sources of supply on the world market. It was thought that if a project was analysed at world prices, this would give an indication first of whether it could survive in the long term in the face of international competition, and secondly of whether its output could be obtained more cheaply from international sources.

If world prices are used, the economic price at which to value a project's output is its export price if it adds to exports, or its import price if domestic production leads to a saving in imports. Similarly, on the cost side, the price at which to value a project input is its import price if it has to be imported, or its export price if greater domestic use leads to a reduction in exports.

To give a simple example: suppose the purpose of a project to produce more wheat for domestic use is to reduce wheat imports. The true economic value of wheat output is the border price of imports whatever the domestic price is (that is, what is saved in foreign exchange). The same argument applies if the wheat is exported; its true economic value is its border price, that is, what the foreign exchange will buy in world markets.

For imports, the **border price** corresponds to the amount of foreign currency needed to pay for the good at the border, including cost, insurance and freight (c.i.f.). For exports, the **border price** corresponds to the amount of foreign currency received at the border, free on board (f.o.b.).

However, since projects are not usually located at the border, the prices must be adjusted for handling and transport costs between project locations and the border. This is called **border parity pricing**.

Thus the **economic price of imports** is the c.i.f. price of imports *plus* transport and handling costs, and the **economic price of exports** is the f.o.b. price of exports *minus* transport and handling costs.

The Little–Mirrlees approach of using world prices for measurement presents no major problems when goods are tradeable. The problem comes with **non-traded goods**, which by definition do not have world prices. Some method has to be found of converting non-traded goods prices into their foreign exchange equivalent.

NON-TRADED GOODS AND CONVERSION FACTORS

The method used for converting non-traded goods prices into world prices is to use **conversion factors**. A conversion factor (CF) is the ratio of the economic (or shadow) price to the market price, that is

$$CF = \frac{\text{economic price}}{\text{market price}} \tag{10.2}$$

so that the economic price for a non-traded good is its market price multiplied by the conversion factor.

How are conversion factors derived? The true economic cost of any good is its *marginal cost to society*. In principle, to find the world price of non-traded goods, each good could be decomposed into its traded and non-traded components in successive rounds – backwards through the chain of production. A detailed input–output table would be required for the job to be done properly. By this method, each good would be treated separately and have a specific conversion factor. In practice, however, only special outputs (and inputs) are treated in this way because the procedure is difficult, time consuming and costly. Major non-traded outputs and inputs include roads and railways, electricity and water supplies, buildings, and labour.

For most goods, it is convenient to have a **standard conversion factor** (**SCF**) to convert non-traded goods prices into border (world) prices. What we can show is that the standard conversion factor is equal to the reciprocal of the shadow price of foreign exchange, and if this is so, the Little–Mirrlees and UNIDO approaches to project appraisal amount to the same thing.

The SCF translates domestic prices into border prices (measured at the official exchange rate), that is

$$(SCF)P_d = P_w(OER) \tag{10.3}$$

where P_d is domestic prices, P_w is world prices, and OER is the official exchange rate measured as the domestic price of foreign currency. In this sense, the standard conversion factor (SCF) is the reciprocal of the shadow price of foreign exchange (P_F). To show this, from (10.3) we have

$$SCF = \frac{P_w}{P_d}(OER) \tag{10.4}$$

or

$$SCF = \frac{1}{P_d/P_w(OER)} \tag{10.5}$$

where P_d/P_w is the shadow exchange rate (SER), that is, the price of goods in domestic currency relative to their world prices:

$$SCF = \frac{1}{SER/OER} = \frac{1}{P_F} \tag{10.6}$$

where SER/OER is the shadow price of foreign exchange (P_F). This means that the standard conversion factor is effectively measured by estimating the shadow price of foreign exchange.

To calculate the shadow price of foreign exchange let us do a simple numerical example for one commodity: a bicycle. Suppose that in India the official exchange rate is 2 rupees per US dollar, and that the world price of a bicycle is $100. Therefore in India the border price of a bicycle costing $100 is 200 rupees. But suppose the price of the bicycle in India is 250 rupees. According to the formula in (10.5), the standard conversion factor will be $1/(250/200) = 0.8$. Also, the fact that a bicycle for 200 rupees at the official exchange rate sells for 250 rupees indicates that the domestic price of foreign exchange is too low (that is, the currency is overvalued). In other words, the shadow exchange rate is higher than the official exchange rate. For bicycles alone it is 2.5 rupees per dollar. The shadow price of foreign exchange (P_F) is therefore $2.5/2.0 = 1.25$, and we know that the SCF is the reciprocal of P_F, that is, $SCF = 1/P_F = 1/1.25 = 0.8$.

Extending this line of argument to many commodities, the shadow price of foreign exchange may be written as

$$P_F = \sum_{i=1}^{n} f_i \left(\frac{P_{di}}{P_{wi}(OER)} \right) \tag{10.7}$$

where i is the ith good and f_i are the weights. The SCF is the reciprocal of (10.7).

We can now show that if the SCF is the reciprocal of the shadow price of foreign exchange, the Little–Mirrlees and UNIDO approaches to the social profitability of projects amount to the same thing. Let us give a simple illustration. Suppose we have a project producing exports that uses both foreign and domestic inputs. Using the UNIDO methodology, the net benefit (ignoring discounting) would be estimated as

$$\text{Net benefit} = (SER)(X - M) - D \tag{10.8}$$

where X is the border price of exports, M is the border price of imported inputs, D is domestic inputs and SER is the shadow exchange rate (assuming the official exchange rate does not accurately reflect the true value of foreign exchange to the economy).

Goods are all valued at domestic prices, but revalued by the shadow exchange rate. If the net benefit is greater than zero the project will be acceptable.

In contrast, Little and Mirrlees use world prices so that

$$\text{Net benefit} = (OER)(X - M) - (SCF)D \tag{10.9}$$

where OER is the official exchange rate, and SCF is the standard conversion factor which converts the value of domestic inputs into their foreign exchange equivalent and is defined as the ratio of OER/SER.

It is clear that the two approaches are equivalent since multiplying (10.8) by OER/SER yields (10.9).

Note that if OER is less than SER because the currency is overvalued, then the standard conversion factor will always be less than unity, and the foreign exchange equivalent of using domestic inputs will be less than their value in domestic prices. This will favour the use of domestic inputs and save foreign exchange.[1]

TRADED GOODS

As far as traded goods are concerned, Little and Mirrlees distinguish three categories:

- Commodities that are being exported and imported with infinite elasticities of demand and supply, respectively
- Commodities traded with less than infinitely elastic demand and supply
- Commodities that are not currently traded but which are potentially tradeable if the country adopts optimal trade policies.

For commodities in the first category, in principle the valuation is straightforward. Exports and imports should be valued at border prices, *net* of taxes, tariffs, transport and distribution costs, and so on. If import supply is infinite (the small country assumption), the foreign price of imports will not change as import demand rises. Likewise, if the demand for exports is infinite, export price will not be affected if more exports are supplied.

For commodities in the second category, the supply of imports can be assumed to be infinite, but the demand for exports may be less than infinite. In this case the foreign exchange impact will be less than the border price times the quantity sold. In other words, marginal revenue is less than price. In this case the economic price of the good is the border price multiplied by $(1 - 1/\eta)$, where η is the price elasticity of demand. If $\eta = \infty$, the economic price is the border price; if $\eta = 1$, the economic price is zero, and if $\eta < 1$, the economic price is negative.

Commodities in the third category that are potentially tradeable can be treated as traded goods for all practical purposes.

SHADOW PRICES FOR FACTORS OF PRODUCTION

The second divergence mentioned above between market prices and social values requires the shadow prices of the factors of production to be found. We shall spend some time below considering the Little–Mirrlees derivation of the shadow price of labour, which in many ways is the most important price to calculate. It is through the valuation of labour that projects using domestic inputs as opposed to foreign inputs are encouraged or discouraged. Moreover, as we shall see, the shadow price of labour can take into account *both* the opportunity cost of labour *and* the effect of new projects on saving, if saving is suboptimal. It can thus incorporate distributional considerations over time and between social groups. **In this way, the shadow price of labour bridges economic and social appraisal**. The output forgone from the employment of additional labour on projects and the increased consumption (or lost saving) must, of course, be valued at world prices using the Little–Mirrlees methodology.

THE SOCIAL RATE OF DISCOUNT

The choice of discount rate depends on the *numéraire* taken. If consumption is taken as the *numéraire*, the appropriate discount rate is the **consumption rate of interest** (**CRI**), measured as the rate at which the marginal utility of income declines, which may be approximated by the market rate of interest.

If public saving (measured by foreign exchange) is taken as the *numéraire*, the appropriate discount rate is the rate at which the marginal utility of public saving falls. This rate is termed the **accounting rate of interest** (**ARI**), which should equal the rate of return on public money. In practice the ARI is determined by trial and error, such that its value does not pass more projects as profitable than the investment budget allows. The alternative would be to take the marginal rate of return on private capital as a measure of opportunity cost, on the grounds that public investment ought to produce benefits at least equal to the rate of return forgone if the resources had been invested privately. This assumes, however, that public and private investment compete for funds.

For the UNIDO and Little–Mirrlees approaches to project appraisal to give the same result, clearly the CRI and the ARI must be equal, which will be the case if the relative valuation of saving compared with consumption stays unchanged. This can be shown as follows. Let U_I be the utility weight of public money (saving) and V_c be the utility weight of consumption. Thus $S = U_I/V_c$ is the relative valuation of saving compared with consumption. It then follows that (taking small rates of change):

$$\frac{dS}{S} = \frac{dU_I}{U_I} - \frac{dV_c}{V_c} = ARI - CRI \tag{10.10}$$

If S is constant (so that $dS/S = 0$), the accounting rate of interest will equal the consumption rate of interest. If S is falling through time, however, which seems likely as countries get richer, then $dS/S < 0$ and $ARI < CRI$.

THE SOCIAL COST OF INVESTMENT

If investment is wholly at the expense of consumption, the social cost of the investment may be measured by the current sacrifice of consumption, if consumption is the *numéraire*. If investment in one project is partly at the expense of another investment, part of the costs of the sacrifice of consumption is deferred until the time at which the displaced investment would itself have yielded consumption.

If saving expressed in foreign exchange is taken as the *numéraire*, the cost of the investment must be valued at world prices.

A numerical example comparing the Little–Mirrlees and UNIDO approaches, applying (10.1), will be given after we have considered the economic cost of the variable inputs (C_t), the chief input being that of labour. We turn now, therefore, to the important topic of the valuation of labour and determination of the shadow wage rate.

THE SHADOW WAGE RATE[2]

In a dual economy, such as the typical developing country, where the marginal product of labour differs between sectors and in which saving is suboptimal, there are two aspects to the measurement of the social cost of the use of more labour in projects:

- The **opportunity cost of the labour in alternative uses**, which could be the marginal product in agriculture, or perhaps the earnings to be had on the fringe of the industrial sector in the informal service sector (P_A).
- The **present value of the sacrificed saving** that results if an attempt is made to maximize present output by equating the marginal products in the different sectors.

Consider Figure 10.1, which depicts the industrial sector of the economy.

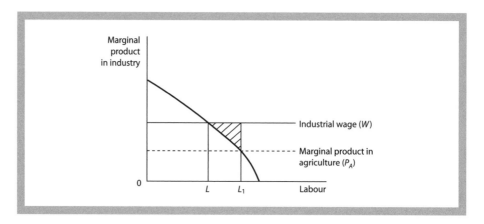

Figure 10.1 The optimal shadow wage

Total output in the economy will be maximized when labour is employed in industry up to the point where the marginal product in industry is equal to that in alternative uses (say, agriculture), that is, up to L_1 in Figure 10.1. But at this employment level the industrial wage exceeds the marginal product of labour, and if all wages are consumed there will be a loss of saving equal to the shaded area. If saving is suboptimal, the optimal shadow wage cannot be the marginal product of labour in alternative uses. Savings will be maximized at employment level, L, where the marginal product of labour in industry is exactly equal to the industrial wage, but at the expense of employment and present consumption. No society places an infinite value on saving at the margin. Thus the optimal shadow wage cannot be the industrial wage. Clearly the shadow wage is going to lie somewhere between the limits of the opportunity cost of labour on the one hand, and the industrial wage on the other, depending on the relative valuation of saving and consumption. We may derive the optimal shadow wage by making the cost of using an additional unit of labour equal to the benefits. The social cost of the labour is

$$P_A + (C - m) \tag{10.11}$$

where P_A is the opportunity cost of labour and $(C - m)$ is the *total* net increase in consumption (C is the increase in consumption in industry and $-m$ is the fall in consumption in agriculture as labour migrates).

The social benefit of the labour used on the project is its marginal product (P_I), plus that part of the increase in consumption that is valued, which we may write as $(C - m)/S_o$, where S_o is the valuation of saving (or future consumption) relative to present consumption. The total social benefit is thus

$$P_I + \frac{(C - m)}{S_o} \tag{10.12}$$

Labour should be employed up to the point where the social benefit is equal to the social cost, that is, up to the point where

$$P_I + \frac{(C - m)}{S_o} = P_A + (C - m) \tag{10.13}$$

or

$$P_I = P_A + (C - m)\left(1 - \frac{1}{S_o}\right) \tag{10.14}$$

This defines the optimum shadow wage rate (W^*). That is, the shadow wage is equal to the loss of agricultural output (P_A), plus the increase in consumption ($C - m$) less that part of the increase in consumption that is treated as a benefit $(C - m)/S_o$.

Within this framework we can see the two bounds between which the shadow wage will lie. If societies are indifferent between the present and the future, the valuation coefficient of saving relative to consumption will equal unity ($S_o = 1$) and the shadow wage from (10.14) will be

$$W^* = P_A \tag{10.15}$$

which is the opportunity cost of labour in alternative uses. This is the standard, static result. If the opportunity cost of labour is zero, the shadow wage would be zero. If it is positive, as in Figure 10.1, the shadow wage would give employment level, L_1.

At the other extreme, if societies place an infinite value on the future and none on the present, then the valuation coefficient of saving relative to present consumption would be infinite ($S_o = \infty$) and the shadow wage from (10.14) will be

$$W^* = P_A + (C - m) \tag{10.16}$$

If workers' consumption in agriculture (m) is equal to their marginal product (P_A), and the increased consumption in industry (C) represents increased workers' consumption out of the wage (W),[3] so that $C = W$, then the shadow wage is equal to the industrial wage:

$$W^* = W \tag{10.17}$$

In Figure 10.1, this would give employment level, L, where savings are maximized.

In practice the shadow wage will lie somewhere between P_A and W, depending on the value of S_o. How do we measure the relative value of future versus present consumption? An approach originally suggested by Sen (1968), and embraced by Little and Mirrlees, is to take a time horizon acceptable to society and to calculate the present value of the future consumption gains arising from investment now, relative to the current consumption sacrifice. Thus

$$
\begin{aligned}
S_o &= \frac{\dfrac{C_1}{(1 + i)} + \dfrac{C_2}{(1 + i)^2} + \ldots + \dfrac{C_t}{(1 + i)^t}}{C_o} \\[2em]
&= \frac{\displaystyle\sum_{t=1}^{T} \dfrac{C_t}{(1 + i)^t}}{C_o}
\end{aligned}
\tag{10.18}
$$

The value of S_o will depend on the marginal product of capital, the length of the time horizon (T) taken and the discount rate (i) chosen. The longer the time horizon and the lower the discount rate, the higher S_o and the higher the shadow wage rate. If S_o = 3, for example, then assuming P_A and m to be very small, the shadow wage would be approximately two- thirds of the industrial wage. In the Little–Mirrlees approach to project appraisal, the shadow wage is the principal means by which the scarcity of foreign exchange is allowed for. The lower the shadow wage, the greater the use of domestic resources.

A CLOSER EXAMINATION OF THE CHANGE IN CONSUMPTION IN INDUSTRY AND AGRICULTURE

Up to now it has been assumed that the marginal propensity to consume out of wages is unity and that all 'profits' are saved. It has also been assumed that consumption falls in agriculture to the extent of the migrants' consumption. In practice the marginal propensity to consume out of wages may be less than unity; the marginal propensity to save out of 'profits' may be less than unity; and consumption in agriculture may not fall by the extent of the migrant's consumption. A more general formulation of the shadow wage is required to allow for these possibilities.

The change in consumption in industry as more labour is employed may be written as

$$C = Wc + c* (P_I - W) \qquad (10.19)$$

where W is the industrial wage, $(P_I - W)$ is 'profit' per worker, c is the marginal propensity to consume out of wages, and $c*$ is the marginal propensity to consume out of profits (or government income).

The change in consumption in agriculture as labour is drawn away may be written as

$$m = d(1 - c') \qquad (10.20)$$

where d is the consumption of the migrants from agriculture and c' is the propensity to consume of those remaining in agriculture. Clearly if those remaining increase their consumption by as much consumption as the migrants 'release', so that $c' = 1$, agricultural consumption will not fall as labour migrates.

Substituting for C and m in the standard formulation for the shadow wage in (10.14), we obtain

$$P_I = P_A + [Wc + c* (P_I - W)$$
$$- d (1 - c')] [1 - (1/S_o)] \qquad (10.21)$$

as the optimal shadow wage ($W*$).

THE VALUATION OF PRODUCTION FORGONE AND THE INCREASE IN CONSUMPTION

Using the Little–Mirrlees approach, the value of agricultural production forgone (P_A) and increased consumption ($C - m$) must be measured at world prices. To value agricultural production forgone, a bundle of goods must be taken to represent the marginal physical product, which must then be priced according to whether they are traded or non-traded, as described earlier. To value the increased consumption also requires taking a bundle of goods, distinguishing between traded and non-traded goods. To recap, **standard conversion factors** are recommended to reprice non-traded goods, which are calculated as the ratio of the weighted average of the world prices of all exports and imports to the value of their domestic prices (see p. 323).

As we saw earlier, it is generally accepted in the comparison of the Little–Mirrlees and UNIDO approaches to project evaluation that the standard conversion factor (SCF) should be the inverse of the shadow price of foreign exchange (P_F). The reason is that both approaches advocate the use of border prices to value traded goods, so while in the Little–Mirrlees method they are automatically expressed in the *numéraire*, in the

UNIDO approach they need to be converted into domestic prices using a shadow exchange rate. The opposite is the case with non-traded goods, and the Little–Mirrlees approach must convert the domestic prices of these goods into border prices using the standard conversion factor. As the one process is the reverse of the other, it is accepted by both methodologies that SCF = $1/P_F$ (see p. 323).

A NUMERICAL CALCULATION OF THE SHADOW WAGE

Now let us do a simple numerical example of the calculation of the shadow wage using the simple formula in (10.14) for illustration:

$$W^* = P_A + (C - m)(1 - 1/S_o)$$

Consider a project in India where the market wage is 70 rupees and all wages are consumed ($C = 70$). The marginal product in agriculture is 10 rupees ($P_A = 10$), and the worker consumed 10 rupees of output in agriculture before working on the project ($m = 10$). All goods are non-traded and the standard conversion factor is 0.8. The relative valuation of future to present consumption is 4 ($S_o = 4$). Therefore, the shadow wage is:

$$W^* = [10 + (70 - 10)(1 - ¼)] \, 0.8 = 44 \text{ rupees}$$

Note that all the values for the lost output in agriculture and net increases in consumption are multiplied by the standard conversion factor of 0.8 to measure the foreign exchange equivalent of using more labour. The market price of labour is 70 rupees but the shadow price is only 44 rupees. This will encourage the use of more domestic labour on projects and save foreign exchange.

There are two additional considerations. The first is that more employment on projects in urban areas may bring additional migration from the rural sector, so that the loss of output in alternative uses is greater than the marginal product of the person employed. For example, if five extra jobs pulled in ten extra people, the loss of output would be $2P_A$ – double the marginal product of labour in agriculture. In this case, the shadow wage would be 52 rupees.

The second consideration is the distributional consequences of project choice to which we now turn. We will see that the formula for the shadow wage changes when distributional weights are included to take account of who gains from the project – the rich or the poor.

SOCIAL APPRAISAL

Distributional considerations in project appraisal[4]

So far, we have ignored the effect of project choice on the distribution of income. The distributional consequences of projects can be included in the estimation of the shadow wage by altering the valuation of present to future consumption ($1/S_o$) – increasing the value if the consumption gain is to the poor, and decreasing the value if the consumption gain is to the rich. **The distribution-weighted relative valuation of**

present to future consumption may be thought of as being composed of two parts. The first is the value of a marginal increase in consumption to someone at a level of consumption, C, divided by the value of a marginal increase in consumption accruing to someone at the average level of consumption, $\bar{C}$. Let us denote this as

$$\frac{W_C}{W_{\bar{C}}} \quad (= d) \tag{10.22}$$

The second part is the value of a marginal increase in consumption to someone at the average level of consumption divided by the value of a marginal increase in public income (saving). Let us denote this as

$$\frac{W_{\bar{C}}}{W_g} = \frac{1}{S_o} \tag{10.23}$$

Therefore the distribution-weighted relative valuation of present versus future consumption is

$$\frac{W_C}{W_{\bar{C}}} \cdot \frac{W_{\bar{C}}}{W_g} = \frac{d}{S_o} \tag{10.24}$$

The ratio d/S_o can be thought of as the trade-off between raising the consumption levels of the poor and accelerating economic growth.

Up to now it has been implicitly assumed that $d = 1$, as if it is the average person who always gains from projects or that the gains to all individuals are valued equally. If greater weight is given to the consumption gains of the poor ($d > 1$) than to the rich ($d < 1$), however, it can be seen from (10.21) or (10.14) that the substitution of d/S_o for $1/S_o$ will alter the shadow wage. A high d will lower the shadow price of labour and favour projects that provide consumption gains to the poor, and a low d will raise the shadow price of labour and favour projects that benefit the wealthy.

The question is, how is d determined? To derive distribution weights, a utility function must be specified. One possible utility function, with the underlying assumption of diminishing marginal utility of consumption, is

$$U_c = C^{-n} = \frac{1}{C^n} \tag{10.25}$$

where C is consumption and n is a parameter of the utility function. n is a reflection of the rate at which the marginal utility of consumption decreases, and is measured as the intertemporal elasticity of substitution between present and future consumption. The higher that n is, the higher the rate of diminishing marginal utility.

The question is, how should the value of n be decided? This is not an easy question to answer. Squire and Van der Tak (1975) say that for most governments, n would probably centre around 1. One justification for this would be to make the simple assumption that if a poor person's income is only one-half of the average level of income, then a dollar increase in income to the poor person is twice more valuable. It can be seen from (10.25) that if the utility of the consumption of a person with twice as much

Table 10.2 Values of the consumption distribution weight (d) for marginal changes in consumption

At existing consumption level (C)	At relative consumption level $(\bar{C}/C)$	And when n equals				
		0	0.5	1.0	1.5	2
10	10.00	1.00	3.16	10.00	31.62	100.00
25	4.00	1.00	2.00	4.00	8.00	16.00
50	2.00	1.00	1.41	2.00	2.83	4.00
75	1.33	1.00	1.15	1.33	1.53	1.77
100	1.00	1.00	1.00	1.00	1.00	1.00
150	0.66	1.00	0.81	0.66	0.54	0.44
300	0.33	1.00	0.57	0.33	0.19	0.11
600	0.17	1.00	0.41	0.17	0.07	0.03
1000	0.10	1.00	0.32	0.10	0.03	0.01

Source: L. Squire and H. G. Van der Tak, *Economic Analysis of Projects* (Baltimore, Md.: Johns Hopkins University Press, 1975).

consumption as another person is only one-half, then $n = 1$. So, if n = 1, the utility of consumption for a person with double consumption of another $(C = 2)$ is one-half. If $n = 2$, the utility of consumption for a person with double the consumption of another is one-quarter, and so on. To compare the value of consumption to different people (or groups), some standard needs to be taken, and it makes sense to take the average. Thus

$$d = \frac{U_c}{U_{\bar{c}}} = \left(\frac{\bar{C}}{C}\right)^n \tag{10.26}$$

where $\bar{C}$ is the average level of consumption (and utility and consumption at the margin are inversely related).

Equation (10.26) says, for example, that the marginal utility of consumption to someone with a level of consumption of half the average $(0.5\bar{C})$ is $(2)^n$. If $n = 1$, $d = 2$. The lower the level of consumption relative to the average, and the higher that n is, the higher the distributional weight will be, and the greater the egalitarian bias in project selection. Table 10.2 shows how the value of the distribution weight changes with n and $\bar{C}/C$, for representative values of n and $\bar{C}/C$ with $(\bar{C} = 100)$. The values of $\bar{C}$ and n are not project-specific, but country-specific, and must be provided by the planning office.

Having discussed the determination of d in (10.24), we must return to the valuation of S_o. We have already discussed one method of valuing S_o (see (10.18)). We now have some independent check of whether the value of S_o is plausible. One test is to estimate, at the chosen value of S_o, the value of $\bar{C}/C$ at which the government is indifferent between its own income (saving) and consumption, so that the costs and benefits of increased consumption are assumed to be equal and the shadow price of labour is measured simply as the efficiency price or opportunity cost. In other words, what is the value of $\bar{C}/C$ at which $d/S_o = 1$, so that $1 - d/S_o = 0$?

If S_o is assumed to be 4, then d must equal 4. With $n = 1$ (say), this required value for d implies an existing level of consumption equal to one-quarter of the average (see Table 10.2). In this case the value of S_o used by the planners would imply that the government is indifferent between additions to its own income and additions to the consumption of those currently consuming one quarter of the average level. This may not seem plausible in the light of other policies. For example the government may be distributing various forms of subsidies at this level of consumption, which suggests it values consumption more highly than public income or saving. In this case it should lower S_o and put a higher value on present consumption to give a lower shadow wage. An S_o that implied some starvation level of consumption could be immediately ruled out.

If we go to our numerical calculation of the shadow wage, we can now replace $1/S_o$ with d/S_o. If $d = 4$ and $S_o = 4$, then the shadow wage becomes simply $W* = 10 \times 0.8 = 8$ rupees compared with a market wage of 70 rupees. Attaching a high value to the benefit of the project to the poor has made the social use of labour virtually costless and therefore much more profitable to undertake from society's point of view.

THE EQUIVALENCE OF THE LITTLE–MIRRLEES FORMULATION OF THE SHADOW WAGE AND THE UNIDO APPROACH

In the UNIDO approach, the optimal shadow wage is given by

$$W* = P_A + s* (P^{INV} - 1)\ W \tag{10.27}$$

where $s*$ is the propensity to save out of public income, W is the wage and P^{INV} measures the price of investment in terms of consumption. Assuming that the propensity to save out of public income is unity ($s* = 1$) and all wages are consumed, (10.27) may be written as

$$W* = P_A + (P^{INV} - 1)\ C \tag{10.28}$$

where $(P^{INV} - 1)\ C$ represents the *present* value of aggregate consumption lost (assuming $P^{INV} > 1$) because of the increased consumption of workers, which reduces saving for future consumption.

Now, for the two approaches to give equivalent cash flows, whichever *numéraire* is taken, P^{INV} must equal S_o so that (10.28) may be written as

$$W* = P_A + (S_o - 1)\ C \tag{10.29}$$

Now the Little–Mirrlees formulation of the shadow wage from (10.14) is

$$W* = P_A + (C - m) \left(1 - \frac{1}{S_o}\right)$$

which, assuming that $P_A = m$, may be written as

$$W* = \frac{P_A}{S_o} + C \left(1 - \frac{1}{S_o}\right) \tag{10.30}$$

Comparing (10.30) with the UNIDO (10.29), it can be seen that the UNIDO formula is S_o times the Little–Mirrlees formula because the UNIDO *numéraire* is $1/S_o$ times as valuable as the Little–Mirrlees *numéraire*.

The calculation of the shadow wage will be different according to the two approaches (assuming that $P^{INV} = S_o$) only to the extent that they classify goods into traded and non-traded in a different way and that the standard conversion factor (SCF) to convert non-traded goods into world prices is not the reciprocal of the shadow price of foreign exchange (P_F) to convert traded goods prices into domestic prices.

IS IT WORTH VALUING ALL GOODS AT WORLD PRICES?

The justification in the Little–Mirrlees approach for valuing all goods at world prices is that it avoids the use of a shadow exchange rate in order to value in a single currency goods that are measured at world prices (traded goods) and others that are measured at domestic prices (non-traded goods). The question is how much trouble is it worth to avoid using a shadow foreign exchange rate? Some economists feel it is a lot of trouble for doubtful accuracy because of the need to disaggregate non-traded goods into their traded and non-traded inputs, which requires input–output data that do not exist in many cases. It may be just as accurate, it is argued, to convert the prices of non-traded goods into a single currency by the exchange rate appropriately adjusted for under- or overvaluation. Baldwin (1972) concludes his layman's guide to Little–Mirrlees by saying that 'their essential ideas are not new and their new ideas are not essential . . . the world pricing of non-traded inputs that has caused so much argument is a tempest in a teapot. I doubt it will catch on and it will not matter much if it doesn't'! Baldwin's first prediction has not proved accurate. There are now many case studies that have used the Little–Mirrlees methodology and students are encouraged to read some for themselves.[5] In his second prediction, Baldwin may be right. Below we give a simple hypothetical example of the application of the UNIDO and Little–Mirrlees approaches, assuming that the standard conversion factor and the shadow price of foreign exchange are the reciprocal of each other.

THE APPLICATION OF THE LITTLE–MIRRLEES AND UNIDO APPROACHES TO PROJECT APPRAISAL

Assume that world prices are measured in dollars and domestic prices in rupees (R), that the official exchange rate is 1 rupee per dollar, that the shadow exchange rate is 1.25 rupees per dollar, that the shadow price of foreign exchange (P_F) = 1.25 and that the standard conversion factor for converting non-traded goods prices into world prices is 0.8, that is, 1/1.25. Assume further that:

- All output is exported with an annual value of $3000
- The cost of the investment has a foreign component of $1000 and a local (non-traded) component of 1000 rupees
- There are traded inputs of $1000 and non-traded inputs of 1000 rupees
- The accounting rate of interest is equal to the consumption rate of interest.

We can now apply our net present value formula in (10.1) using the two approaches. Remember that with the Little–Mirrlees approach we convert world prices into domestic prices at the official exchange rate and the prices of non-traded goods into world prices using the standard conversion factor of 0.8. With the UNIDO approach we convert all values at world prices ($) into domestic prices using the shadow exchange rate of 1.25. We shall do the analysis for three periods only (see Table 10.3).

We can see that the results obtained using the Little–Mirrlees approach and those obtained using the UNIDO approach differ only to the extent that the shadow exchange rate is different from the actual exchange rate. To obtain NPV the net benefit streams in years 1 and 2 must be discounted by the appropriate discount factors, which we assume here to be the same in both approaches. Assuming a discount rate of 10 per cent we have the following:

Using Little–Mirrlees $\quad$ NPV $= \dfrac{R1,200}{(1.1)} + \dfrac{R1,200}{(1.1)^2} - R1,800 = R282.6$

Using UNIDO $\quad$ NPV $= \dfrac{R1,500}{(1.1)} + \dfrac{R1,500}{(1.1)^2} - R2,250 = R353.2$

The Little–Mirrlees result would yield the same rupee value if the actual exchange rate of dollars into rupees was equal to the shadow exchange rate of 1.25.

Little and Mirrlees conclude their own evaluation of the two approaches by saying:

> there is no doubt that the two works adopt basically the same approach to project evaluation. Both treatments single out the values of foreign exchange, savings and unskilled labour, as crucial sources of a distorted price mechanism. Both go on to calculate accounting prices which will correct these distortions, and both carry out these corrections in an essentially similar manner. Both advocate DCF (Discounted Cash Flow) analysis and the use of PSVs (Present Social Values) (Little and Mirrlees, 1974)

Finally, both works advocate making explicit allowance for inequality and distributional considerations in project choice through manipulation of the shadow wage. In the UNIDO approach this is done by giving greater weight to the increased consumption of the poor than of the rich, which reduces the present value of lost consumption. In the Little–Mirrlees approach distributional considerations are taken account of by working out the value of S_o taking account of the standard of living of the particular extra workers employed, as described above.

Table 10.3 Comparison of the Little–Mirrlees and UNIDO approaches to project appraisal

	Little–Mirrlees			UNIDO			
	Year 0	Year 1	Year 2		Year 0	Year 1	Year 2
Cost of investment (K)							
1. Foreign component	R1,000			1. Foreign cost converted into rupees at shadow exchange rate of 1.25	R1,250		
2. Local component = 1,000 rupees × conversion factor of 0.8	R800			2. Local component	R1,000		
Input costs (C)							
1. Traded inputs		R1,000	R1,000	1. Traded inputs converted into rupees at shadow exchange rate of 1.25		R1,250	R1,250
2. Non-traded inputs = 1,000 rupees × conversion factor of 0.8		R800	R800	2. Non-traded inputs		R1,000	R1,000
Benefit flow (V)		R3,000	R3,000	Benefit flow in rupees		R3,750	R3,750
Net benefit	R−1,800	R1,200	R1,200	Net benefit	R−2,250	R1,500	R1,500

1 What is the meaning of social cost-benefit analysis?

2 Explain how the costs and benefits of a project to society may differ from the costs and benefits to the private entrepreneur.

3 Why are the future net benefits of a project discounted?

4 Why do Little and Mirrlees choose to measure the net benefits of a project in terms of saving rather than consumption?

5 Why do Little and Mirrlees measure benefits and costs of a project using world prices rather than domestic prices?

6 How is it possible to measure non-traded goods at world prices?

7 What is the relationship between the standard conversion factor and the shadow price of foreign exchange?

8 What factors need to be taken into account when measuring the shadow wage (or the social opportunity cost) of labour?

9 Evaluate the relative merits of the Little–Mirrlees and UNIDO approaches to social cost-benefit analysis.

10 How would you measure the relative value of investment (or future consumption) compared with present consumption?

NOTES

1. The domestic inputs referred to are goods not labour. We shall consider the valuation of labour later.
2. The discussion here takes the approach of Little and Mirrlees, the origin of which can be found in Sen (1968) and Little (1961). See also Little and Mirrlees (1974) and Squire and Van der Tak (1975). See later for the equivalence of the Little–Mirrlees and UNIDO approaches.
3. Implicitly assuming for the time being that the propensity to consume out of profits is zero and the propensity to consume of workers out of wages is unity. We shall relax this assumption later.
4. This section relies heavily on the exposition given in Squire and Van der Tak (1975) and Brent (1998).
5. See, for example, Lal (1980), Scott, MacArthur and Newbery (1976), Stewart (1978) and the Symposium in the *Oxford Bulletin of Economics and Statistics*, February 1972.

WEBSITES ON PROJECT APPRAISAL

OECD Development Centre   www.oecd.org/department

UNIDO   www.unido.org

11 Development and the environment*

* This chapter has been written by my colleague Dr John Peirson. He is grateful to Michael Common and Douglas Peirson for helpful comments.

INTRODUCTION

The environment is vital to supporting life, absorbing waste and providing inputs for production. Since the 1960s, there has been increasing concern about the effects of economic activity on the environment. In particular it has been argued that economic growth has caused serious environmental damage and that the current state of the environment will constrain future economic development. The poor in developing countries are often dependent on the natural environment for their livelihood, and even their continued existence. Thus damage to the environment and the relationship between the environment and the economy are often thought to be of more importance to developing than to developed countries. Figure 11.1 shows how selected environmental indicators vary with economic development, as measured by per capita income. This chapter provides an introduction to the economic analysis of the relationship between the environment, development and the economy.

First, a simple model is developed that explains the services the environment provides for economic activity and the effects of the economy on the environment.

Second, the market-based approach to analysing the interactions of the environment and the economy is examined. This approach emphasizes the efficient use of the environment and considers market failures to be the main, and perhaps the only, cause of market economies' difficulties in allowing for environmental concerns in economic development. Drawing on the material on social cost-benefit analysis in Chapter 10, it is shown how this approach can be used to provide valuations of environmental services and to improve the efficiency of the use of the environment. The neoclassical analysis

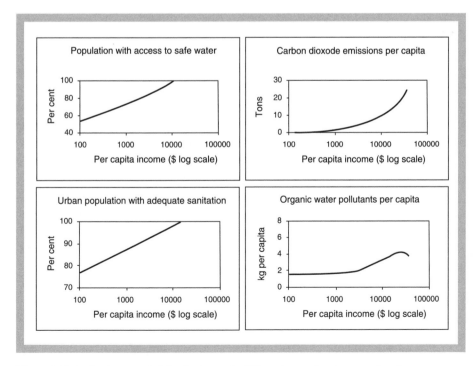

Note: The estimates are based on cross-country data for the year 2000.
Source: World Bank, *World Development Indicators 2004* (Washington: World Bank).

Figure 11.1 Environmental indicators at different country income levels

of equity within and between generations is considered and its importance in the context of the environment is examined.

Third, the concept of **sustainable development** is explained. This idea defines forms of development that meet the needs of the present generation whilst maintaining the potential to meet the needs of future generations.

Fourth, a brief review is given of how environmentalists, economists and international agencies have approached the analysis of the environment and the economy.

A MODEL OF THE ENVIRONMENT AND ECONOMIC ACTIVITY

There are many different models of the relationship between the environment and the economy. The simple model depicted in Figure 11.2 illustrates the four functions of the environment in supporting economic activity and the effects of this activity on the environment.[1] These four functions are life-support, supply of natural resources, absorption of waste products and supply of amenity services. The economy is represented in Figure 11.2 by households consuming goods and services, and firms producing with natural resources provided by the environment, with labour and man-made capital provided by households.

The environment provides a **biological, chemical and physical system** that enables human life to exist. This system includes, for example, the atmosphere, river systems, the fertility of the soil and the diversity of plant and animal life. These environmental services are consumed by households and are essential to life. Large reductions in these services, for example through major damage to the ozone layer, could have catastrophic consequences for life.

The environment provides **raw materials and energy** for economic production and household activity. These natural resources are either renewable, for example forests and fisheries, or non-renewable, for example minerals. Renewable resources can be used in a sustainable manner, though excessive use or mismanagement can result in the complete loss of the resources, for example desertification following deforestation. The ability to use renewable resources sustainably and to increase the stock of renewable resources is represented in Figure 11.2 by the flow from firms to natural resources. However, the use of a non-renewable resource reduces the finite stock of the resource forever.

The **waste products** of economic and household activity are absorbed by the environment. This sink function allows much of such waste to be disposed of safely. However, there are certain wastes that are difficult or impossible for the environment to dispose of safely, for example long-lived radioactive materials and heavy metals. Other arrangements should be made for such waste. The ability of the environment to absorb waste is not infinite. For example the natural breakdown of effluents in the sea and rivers will not give rise to serious pollution as long as the discharges are below threshold levels, but above these levels discharges will give rise to rapid increases in pollution.

The environment also provides **amenity services**: for example, natural beauty and space for outdoor pursuits, which are consumed, but are not crucial to the continued existence of life.

Parts of the environment may serve more than one function: for example the oceans are important in determining the life-support systems of the global and micro climates;

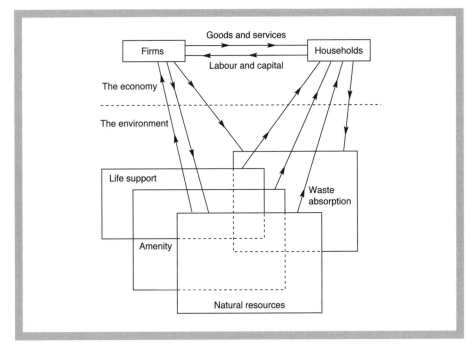

Figure 11.2 A simple model of the relationships between the economy and the environment

they are sources of many minerals and other resources; they assimilate many different wastes; and they provide the space and opportunity for marine pastimes. Thus in Figure 11.2 the four blocks representing the different functions of the environment overlap. The functions of the environment may be competitive. For example, excessive discharges of waste materials into the oceans will reduce their capacity to provide a habitat for fish stocks. Alternatively, environmental functions can be complementary. For example, appropriate forestry policies can provide a sustainable source of timber (a natural resource function) and reduce soil erosion (an improvement in the life-support function).

THE MARKET-BASED APPROACH TO ENVIRONMENTAL ANALYSIS

The market-based approach to environmental analysis has probably been the dominant view of the relationship between the environment and the economy.[2] In particular, many environmental policies and much analysis are based on the view that markets may not function efficiently with regard to the environment and that the state has a duty to intervene and correct market failures. The underlying assumptions of the market-based approach are examined and various applications to the environment are considered.

The market or neoclassical approach to economics is concerned with how scarce resources are allocated in a market economy.[3] Allocation is assumed to take place on the basis of consumers' preferences, the distribution of economic assets and the costs of production. It is assumed that each consumer is rational and decides to purchase goods and services on the basis of prices and economic assets, which include labour income. It is assumed that the value a consumer places on additional consumption of a good declines with increasing consumption. Economic rationality dictates that consumption of a good continues up to the point at which the value placed on an additional unit is just equal to the price. Further expenditure on the good would be inefficient as greater value could be obtained from using the additional expenditure to purchase more preferred goods and services. Similarly, less expenditure is inefficient, as greater value could be obtained by purchasing more of the good and fewer less preferred goods and services. Thus the neoclassical model assumes that economic rationality gives efficiency in consumption.

The neoclassical view assumes that firms are profit maximizers. This implies that firms minimize costs. This gives efficiency in production.

Finally, it is assumed that competition among firms forces them to charge prices that are equal to their marginal costs of production. As consumption decisions are based on prices, the equality between prices and marginal costs means that these decisions are based upon the marginal costs of production. This ensures efficiency between consumption and production.

The neoclassical view has various important implications for the analysis of the relationship between the environment and the economy. First, it is implicitly assumed that the value of consumption is determined by the individual consuming the good. The value of consumption is not determined by the state or some higher authority. Additionally, it is assumed that individual consumers and producers do not consider the effects of their decisions on other economic agents. Second, economic rationality implies that the value of marginal consumption of a good or service can be measured by price. Third, the neoclassical analysis of the market is based upon considering small changes in consumption and production. This view extends to the neoclassical view of the environment. Fourth, the outcome of a market economy, in terms of prices, quantities and the distribution of economic welfare, depends on the initial distribution of economic assets. Different distributions or reallocations of assets give different outcomes. It is frequently pointed out that under certain conditions the operation of the market may be efficient, but it may not be equitable. It may be possible to assess the efficiency of a market economy in an objective manner, but evaluation of the equity of a market outcome is a value judgement.

EXTERNALITIES

The idea of externalities can be used to analyse many, but not all, types of environmental degradation. Externalities occur when the actions of one economic agent affect other economic agents and the actions are not controlled through the operation of the market. Externalities have two related causes: lack of individual property rights, and jointness in either production or consumption (Baumol and Oates, 1988). Individual property rights are exercised over goods, services and factors of production and allow markets to function efficiently. With a complete set of individual property rights, all the effects of an action are controlled by the market, since consumption of a good or service and use of a factor require payment to the owner. Beneficial or positive externalities are likely to be undersupplied by a market, and negative externalities are likely to be

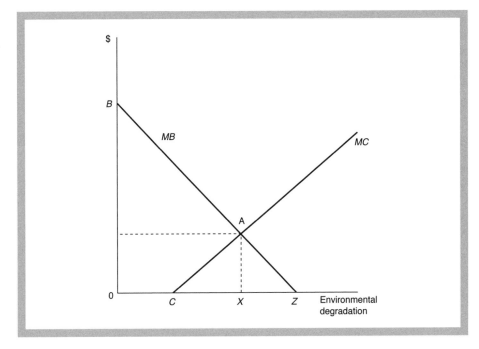

Figure 11.3 Marginal benefits and environmental costs of a dam

oversupplied. For an externality to continue to exist, it is usually presumed that jointness in either production or consumption is involved.

An example of environmental externalities and economic development can be seen in the building and operation of the Manantali and Diama hydroelectric dams in Mali.[4] These dams generate cheap electricity which is distributed to the countries of Mali, Senegal and Mauritania. Downstream from the dams, the annual floods have been reduced and this has decreased agricultural productivity. Additionally, the elimination of salt water intrusion through the building of these dams has led to an increased incidence of bilharzia and other health problems. Thus, the building and operation of these hydroelectric dams has imposed external costs on those living and working downstream of the dams.

These (negative) externalities are caused by jointness in production of electricity. At the same time as electricity is being generated, the water system is being altered and this causes health and productivity effects. The economic cause of the externalities is that no markets exist in the management of water systems. In particular, there are not clear, legally enforceable rights to the ownership and services of the water system downstream. A simple model is developed in Figure 11.3 of the interests of the electricity generators and the downstream population. The downstream environmental degradation by the generators produces a benefit to them as it allows the production of electricity. This is denoted by the marginal benefit curve *MB* (measured in dollars) and is assumed to be downward sloping. The downward slope can be justified by a lower price being obtained for the sale of electricity as more is produced.

The environmental effects are mostly negative and are represented by an upward sloping marginal cost of environmental degradation curve (*MC*). There is a threshold effect below which there is no environmental damage as the environment can absorb a minor change in the water system without any cost. The curve then slopes upwards as the environment has difficulty in coping with the increased environmental degradation.

The neoclassical view is that there is an optimal level of environmental degradation at which the marginal benefit is equal to the marginal cost, point X in Figure 11.3. Whether this level of degradation is small or large depends on the shape of the marginal benefit and cost functions. This conclusion considers environmental effects purely from the point of view of efficiency. However, it should be remembered that outcome X may be efficient, but if the costs imposed on the inhabitants are relatively large, the resulting distribution of welfare may not be desirable.

The operation of a market economy is unlikely to lead to an efficient outcome. The downstream inhabitants' environment is being degraded by the actions of the generators. In an economy with a complete set of individual property rights over all economic assets, the inhabitants or the generators would own the property rights to the environment. If the inhabitants owned the rights, the generators would have to pay to be allowed to degrade the environment. In the case of the generators owning the rights, the inhabitants would have to pay the generators to restrict environmental degradation. In reality, such property rights are likely to be ill-defined, particularly across national boundaries. It might be expected that no market controls this environmental degradation. Generators are likely to continue to degrade the environment until the marginal benefit to them of degradation is zero, point Z in Figure 11.3.

This analysis is one of market failure. A conventional reaction to market failure is to suggest the intervention of the state to secure a more efficient outcome. There are four feasible policies that have been suggested as solutions to this type of externality problem: **Pigovian taxes and subsidies** (named after the famous Cambridge economist A. C. Pigou); **Coasian bargains** (named after the Nobel Prize winning economist Ronald Coase); **marketable permits**; and **administrative action and legislation** (see Perman *et al.*, 2003).

The **Pigovian tax solution** imposes an environmental-use tax on the generators of the value of the marginal cost of degradation at the point of the optimal outcome X. This forces the generators to take account of the costs they impose on the inhabitants. This is shown in Figure 11.4, where the generators face a new marginal benefit of environmental degradation schedule (MB') that includes the tax. Generators will, out of self-interest, choose the efficient level of degradation. A Pigovian subsidy could be given to generators to reduce environmental degradation and a similar solution occurs.

However, the Pigovian solution suffers from a number of problems. First, it is very difficult to quantify and value the costs and benefits of environmental degradation (this point is returned to later). The benefits and costs are not likely to be uniform across the two dams and this implies the complication of different tax rates. Second, many of the downstream inhabitants are not part of the cash economy and the state is unlikely to be able to tax and regulate generators or afford the cost of subsidies.

The **Coasian bargain solution** assumes that individual property rights are established and economic agents bargain an efficient outcome. If individual property rights over the environment are given to the inhabitants, then generators have an incentive to bargain and pay to be allowed the right to degrade the environment, as their marginal benefit exceeds the inhabitants' marginal cost at the origin in Figure 11.3. The potential efficiency gains of this bargaining are represented by the area ABC. Similarly, if the generators are given the property right, there are incentives for the inhabitants to pay

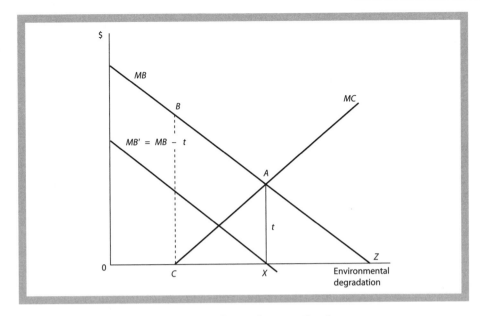

Figure 11.4 Taxation, marginal benefits and costs of a dam

the generators to reduce degradation from the point Z. The Coasian solution suffers from the major problem of how property rights are established. Additionally, there are incentives for individuals to **free ride** on the contributions that others make to reduce externalities. It is difficult to see how bargains can be enforced when there are many inhabitants. Finally, in many cases the transactions costs of negotiating a Coasian bargain may be high and are likely to prevent such solutions from emerging.

In the real world, it may be rare for Coasian bargains to occur as solutions to environmental problems. The Global Environment Facility could be interpreted as such an example (see Sjöberg, 1996). This facility is controlled jointly by the World Bank, UNDP and UNEP and receives donations from many countries. The Facility provides grants to countries to address such global problems as ozone depletion and pollution of international waters. The Global Environment Facility was charged with funding mechanisms to help achieve the Climate Change and Biodiversity Conventions of the 1992 Rio Earth Summit.

The issuing of **marketable permits** that give the bearers the right to pollute is a potentially elegant and efficient means of solving the problem of pollution. The size of the issue of permits directly controls the level of total pollution. Potential polluters have to decide whether to reduce their pollution or use their own or purchased permits. This should result in the set level of pollution being obtained at the least cost. Schmalensee *et al.* (1998) conclude that tradeable permits are a very valuable policy tool for dealing with acid rain and that they are likely to be used more extensively in the future. However, it is difficult to imagine such sophisticated and complex schemes operating in many developing countries. (For developed countries, see the OECD (1999) survey).

The fourth solution to the externality problem is **administrative/legal action**. This approach takes action to ensure that the externality is reduced to a lower level. The usual examples of this solution are fixed standards backed up by legal sanctions, for example maximum allowable levels of environmental degradation. The actions taken by the government to deal with the environmental problems caused by the Manantali Energy Scheme have taken many forms. The government enforced standards and monitored the building of the project. A reservoir management plan was developed to help irrigate downstream areas; affected land was purchased; people were resettled, and health programmes were implemented. These measures are practical, but do not have the theoretical elegance of the three previous solutions.

The one major problem facing all solutions to the problem of dealing with externalities is assessing their physical nature and calculating their economic value. The uncertainty surrounding environmental effects and their economic value is discussed later.

COMMON PROPERTY RIGHTS

The common ownership of a renewable resource is likely to lead to an important externality. Such circumstances are frequently referred to as **the tragedy of the commons**. However, Dasgupta has forcefully argued that there has been considerable confusion over the economic analysis of this problem.[5] The analysis is considered in terms of the example of cattle farmers grazing their animals on commonly owned land. The rational individual farmer will use common land without regard to the cost this use imposes on other farmers. This behaviour is a negative externality and is inefficient. The cost imposed on other farmers is the exhaustion of the fertility of the soil. This effect will decrease the future value of the resource to farmers. In this sense, the problem of the commons is an **intertemporal externality**. However, it is not the case that use of the common property resource of grazing land necessarily destroys the usefulness of the land. The extent of overgrazing depends on the private cost of rearing animals, their market value and the ability of the land to support a large number of animals. However, appropriate cooperative action by farmers to reduce overgrazing would increase the economic welfare of farmers as a group.

THE DISCOUNT RATE

Degradation of the environment reduces the supply of environmental services in the future. Economic analysis of the environment requires a means of comparing the benefits and costs of environmental effects in the present and the future. This comparison is usually made through a weighting device called **the discount factor** (see Chapter 10). The practice of discounting environmental costs and benefits has caused much confusion and dispute.

In a neoclassical model of the behaviour of individual economic agents with finite lives, the discount rate is simply the market rate of interest. The level of the market rate of interest is the outcome of the preferences of individuals for present consumption over future consumption and the physical possibilities of transforming present consumption into future consumption. However, even with a set of perfect capital markets, the resulting intertemporal allocation of resources is unlikely to be socially efficient for a number of reasons.

First, the outcome of perfect capital markets reflects the preferences and actions of those presently alive. All individuals will eventually die and presumably value their own consumption more highly than that of their descendants. This implies the market outcome may underweight the consumption of future generations. It might be argued that the state should decide upon a distribution of economic welfare over time that favours future generations more. Alternatively, it has been argued that technical progress will increase future incomes and fairness requires redistribution from future generations to the present. However, it is unclear how the state can easily decide which distribution should be preferred (see Hanley and Spash, 1993).

Second, even with regard to the preferences of the present generation, the market outcome may be inefficient. The present generation may wish to save for the benefit of future generations. This can lead to two types of market failure, called the **assurance problem** and the **isolation paradox** (Sen, 1967). Both phenomena are examples of externalities. The assurance problem concerns saving by one individual for future generations, which benefits all other individuals in the present who place a value on the consumption of future generations. Thus the market aggregate level of saving is inefficient and the market rate of interest undervalues future consumption. Aggregate saving would be increased if individuals were assured that their additional savings would be matched by other altruistic individuals.

The isolation paradox concerns the value individuals place on their descendants' consumption compared with that of the rest of future generations. If the return from saving for the benefit of future generations cannot be captured entirely by an individual's descendants, then it is likely that even perfect capital markets will provide an inefficient level of saving.

Imperfections in the capital market are widespread and there is no unique interest rate or discount rate. Instead of the use of an observed market interest rate, the social opportunity cost of capital has been used as a measure to discount the future. The social opportunity cost of capital measures the social value of a loss of one unit of capital in the economy to fund the proposed investment. If resources to fund a project displace other investments, rather than consumption, the social opportunity cost of capital is the correct measure of the cost of capital. However, there are practical difficulties in calculating the social opportunity cost of capital.

The effect of the discount rate on environmental degradation is unclear. A low discount rate weights future consumption more heavily and might be thought to give a better future environment than a higher rate. However, most investments have costs at the beginning of their life and benefits thereafter. Thus a lower discount rate will make these investments appear more attractive as weighted future benefits will increase relative to present costs (see 10.1) (p. 318). Increased investment and the consequent economic growth may lead to more environmental degradation.

THE HARVESTING OF RENEWABLE RESOURCES

Renewable resources are those whose stock is capable of growth as well as depletion. Renewable resources are usually thought of as experiencing growth and regeneration through a biological process. Fisheries, forests and the previous example of common pasture land are all examples of renewable resources. The neoclassical analysis of renewable resources considers efficient harvesting, whilst biologists are often concerned

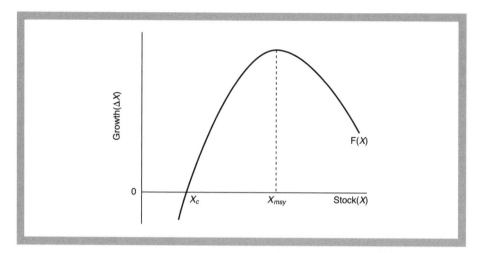

Figure 11.5 Relation between the growth and stock of a renewable resource

with the **maximum sustainable yield** (MSY) that can be obtained from the resource. These two ideas are examined in the context of a fisheries example.

The growth of the stock of fish, ΔX, depends on the stock, X. This relationship is shown in Figure 11.5. Below a critical level, X_c, the stock is in danger of terminal decline as it is not capable of replication. The existence of a critical level may be explained by difficulties in reproduction. Above this level, growth is positive. Eventually the growth declines because of competition for food supplies or the effects of predators. The MSY occurs at the point of greatest absolute growth.

The efficient use of the fish stock is examined by considering a simple model in which harvesting is costless. The objective is to maximize the social value of the stock over time. The social gain is examined in connection with reducing the harvesting of fish and allowing the present stock to increase by one unit. The present marginal social value of one unit of fish is denoted by v. The marginal productivity of the stock, $F'(X)$, represents the change in growth from increasing the stock by one unit. The social value of this gain is $v F'(X)$. The marginal social value of an additional unit of fish in the second period is $(v + \Delta v)$, where Δv is the change in social value between the first and second periods. With a discount rate of r, the present value of an additional unit of stock in the next period is

$$\frac{v F'(X) + (v + \Delta v)}{1 + r} \tag{11.1}$$

The marginal social value of consuming one unit of fish in the present period is v. Thus if (11.1) exceeds v, an increase in social welfare can be obtained by reducing the level of harvesting. This condition can be written more simply as

$$F'(X) + \Delta v/v > r \tag{11.2}$$

This condition has a simple interpretation. If the marginal productivity of the stock plus the proportionate gain in the value of the stock over time exceeds the discount rate, then it is efficient to reduce harvesting. A reduction in the harvest increases the stock, which is likely to decrease $F'(X)$ (see Figure 11.5). A reduction in the harvest means consumption will fall and the marginal social value of present compared with future consumption will increase. These two effects may be expected eventually to give equality in (11.2), and thus efficiency.

Equation (11.2) has two important implications. First, the efficient outcome is not the same as the MSY, as the latter is given by $F'(X) = 0$. Second, for species that have a low marginal productivity of stock and whose value does not increase appreciably with decreasing stock, extinction may be an efficient outcome!

The present analysis is concerned with maximizing the social value of the fishery stock over time. It is appropriate to consider whether the efficient outcome can be achieved through a market system. The fisheries example is another case of common property rights. In the discussion of common property rights, it was seen that it can be difficult to establish individual property rights for renewable resources such as fisheries, forests and pasture land. Thus the market use of such renewable resources is likely to be inefficient.

If the property rights for the resource are given to a few individuals, this will affect the distribution of economic welfare and will result in monopoly power. Private monopoly control of a renewable resource may result in its inefficient use, as marginal (private) revenue rather than social value would appear in (11.2) and, in order to maximize profits, the monopolist may restrict the use of the resource below the efficient level (see Hanley, Shogren and White, 1997).

NON-RENEWABLE RESOURCES

Non-renewable resources cannot be regenerated over time. The present use of one unit of such a resource prevents it from being used in the future. The finite levels of these resources means that they are often referred to as exhaustible resources. This suggests that non-renewable resources should be used with care.

There are many estimates of the stocks of non-renewable resources. Calculation of the known reserves of a non-renewable resource has to be made in the context of the extraction cost and the price of the resource. It is considered inappropriate to include in estimates of reserves sources for which the cost of recovery exceeds the current price or for which there is no proven extraction technology. Proven reserves refer to those sources that are presently known. It is likely that there are sources yet to be discovered. However, uncertainty means that it is difficult to calculate meaningful estimates for unproven reserves.

The depletion of a non-renewable resource can be analysed in terms of the objective of maximizing the social value of the stock. Figure 11.6 considers a one-period model and the maximization of the economic rent from extracting a mineral that has a price P. The economic rent is the area between the price and the marginal cost curve. If the price is equal to the marginal social value of consumption, a perfectly competitive industry will extract the resource up to the point Q_0 and this is a socially efficient outcome. A monopoly faced with a downward sloping demand curve would restrict output below Q_0, which is inefficient.

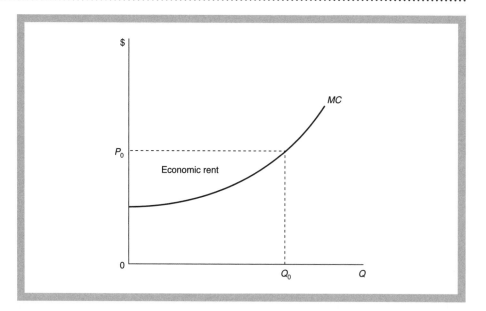

Figure 11.6 Economic rent and the use of a non-renewable resource

The **optimal depletion** of a non-renewable resource over time can be analyzed in a very similar manner to the harvesting of a renewable resource. Again the objective is maximization of the social value of the stock over time. The decision to extract a non-renewable resource is simpler in that there is no marginal productivity of the stock to consider. It is assumed that the extraction of the resource is costless. The resource should be further conserved if

$$\frac{\Delta v}{v} > r \tag{11.3}$$

Equation (11.3) has a simple interpretation. If the relative appreciation of the social value of the resource is greater than the discount rate, then more of the resource should be saved for the future.

For an efficient outcome, the social value of marginal consumption should be increasing at the rate r. This implies (through integration) that v is given by the function $v_0 e^{rt}$, where v_0 is the social value at time zero. If a constant marginal cost of extraction (mc) is introduced into the analysis, the efficient outcome gives a final equation:

$$v(t) = mc + v_0 e^{rt} \tag{11.4}$$

Equation (11.4) reflects the optimal depletion path. It is possible for a perfect market to give this outcome. In this case, the optimal price path is given by

$$p(t) = mc + r_0 e^{rt} \tag{11.5}$$

The $r_0 e^{rt}$ term is referred to as the **discounted rental premium**. It may be interpreted as the social cost of consuming the resource in the present rather than in the future.

As before, if the price is equal to the marginal social value of consumption, a perfectly competitive market will maximize social welfare across time. A monopoly may restrict the use of the resource below the efficient level and the price path will be inefficient (see Hanley, Shogren and White, 1997).

It has been pointed out by Kay and Mirrlees (1975) that, for reasonable discount rates, one would expect the optimal price to be close to marginal cost for most of the lifetime of a non-renewable resource.

OTHER ENVIRONMENTAL VALUES

It is a central tenet of neoclassical economics that prices should reflect the marginal costs of production. In a competitive economy, prices may reflect private marginal costs, but there is a number of other types of social costs that should be taken into consideration (see Pearce and Turner, 1990). First, the external costs imposed on other individuals should be taken into account.[6]

Second, the economic rent in the use of non-renewable resources should be included in social marginal costs. As noted before, the economic rent may be regarded as a premium that has to be paid for the use of the resource in the present rather than in the future.

There are four other types of value that have not yet been considered: **option**, **quasi-option**, **existence** and **bequest values**. An option value is the value placed on an option that allows use to be made of the environment in the future. Option values depend on attitudes to uncertainty, e.g. risk averseness. The option is not necessarily taken up, but it gives value. An example of an option value is **biodiversity**. Protection of species of animals and plants may be desired in order to allow possible future uses of these species as inputs to production, and because many individuals may wish to have the opportunity of seeing these species in the future. **Quasi-option values** are the values placed on an option given an expectation that there will be increases in knowledge. For example the value of certain plant species may depend on the development of knowledge of new uses of the plants.

Existence value is the value placed on a good or service independent of any actual or possible future consumption. This value is different from the other types of value in that it is unrelated to use. An example of existence value is the concern expressed by many individuals for the preservation of elephants, even though they are unlikely ever to see them at first hand, or use this resource.

The final type of value is the self-explanatory **bequest value**, when an economic agent wishes to pass on resources to members of future generations.

Thus the total social cost is composed of seven components:

$$
\begin{aligned}
\text{Social cost} = \ & \text{private cost} \\
& + \text{external cost} \\
& + \text{rental premium} \\
& + \text{option value} \\
& + \text{quasi-option value} \\
& + \text{existence value} \\
& + \text{bequest value}
\end{aligned}
\tag{11.6}
$$

Efficient allocation requires consideration of all seven components of social costs.

MEASURING ENVIRONMENTAL VALUES

The analysis of this chapter suggests that a market economy will not value all aspects of the environment appropriately. This view is widely held and has led to much intellectual and practical effort being applied to the problem of how to introduce appropriate environmental values into economic decision-making. The following discussion considers the introduction of environmental considerations into social cost-benefit analysis and national income accounting.

Appraisals of many investment projects in developing countries now include **environmental impact assessments** (EIAs) that estimate the environmental effects of the projects. This should be the first stage of the introduction of the environmental effects of a project into social cost-benefit analysis. Often it is very difficult to assess a project's physical effects on the environment. For example models of the effects of emissions of carbon dioxide on global warming have given quite different predictions (see for example Hanley and Owen, 2004). EIAs can rarely firmly establish the type and extent of environmental effects of projects. Thus the introduction of previously unconsidered environmental effects into economic decision-making should take account of this uncertainty.

Once the environmental effects of a project have been estimated, there are three approaches to placing economic values on the effects.[7] First, the basic valuation technique in social cost-benefit analysis is to use market prices. This is justified by the neoclassical assumption that prices reflect the value of goods and services. In the case of environmental effects in developing countries, markets and prices may not exist for many of the effects that require valuation. For large environmental effects, the project may actually alter prices. In this case, the changes in the values placed on environmental effects should be modelled. In practice, this is often impossible.

The second approach calculates the value of environmental effects indirectly through observed economic behaviour. Within this approach, there is a number of different techniques. One is the **preventive expenditure technique**, which takes the expenditure that people are prepared to undertake to prevent degradation as a measure of the value of the environmental effects. Another is the **replacement cost technique**, which estimates the expenditure people are prepared to undertake to restore the environment to its previous state after degradation has occurred.[8] These techniques can be very similar. The full long-term consequences of environmental effects may not be understood. Not all environmental effects can be fully offset by preventive expenditure and the environment cannot always be restored after degradation. Such problems may be particularly important for large changes in the environment, for example changes in the ecology of a large watershed and global warming. The ability of individuals to fund these expenditures may be limited by imperfect capital markets. For these reasons, it is usually thought that the two techniques may underestimate environmental costs.

In the absence of a market for an environmental effect, it is sometimes possible to derive the value placed on the effect by the prices paid for other goods and services that implicitly value the effect. For example property values vary with location, and this may in part reflect differences in the environment. The method of **hedonic prices** can produce estimates of the contribution of differences in the environment to the prices of property. This can be used to give an estimate of the implied value of certain environmental qualities. In developing countries, there are often significant imperfections in markets, for example rent controls, which affect the validity of the technique. The hedonic price method requires large amounts of data. It is often difficult to measure the environmental quality that is being considered. The importance of the environmental variable may not be properly understood by individuals. These problems limit the usefulness of this technique, particularly in developing countries.

The production function approach values environmental impacts by their effects on production. Thus part of the environmental impact of a change in climate conditions could be valued through the effects on agricultural output. Another example is the valuation of environmental health effects by estimating changes in the productivity of affected individuals. This implies that the value of life is only determined by production and there are no psychic costs to ill-health and early death.

The **travel cost method** values the time and costs that people are willing to incur in travelling to areas with more pleasant environments. Thus the method gives an implied value of environmental quality. The formal assumptions of the model and its applicability to developing countries have been criticized (see Winpenny, 1995). The method implicitly considers the environment in terms of the provision of recreational services rather than basic life-support services.

The third approach to valuing environmental effects is that of **contingent valuation**. A subset of the population is surveyed and asked for their valuation of the environment. There are two ways in which this question can be asked. Individuals can be asked either about their willingness to pay for an environmental benefit or about their willingness to accept compensation for a loss of environmental quality. Economic theory suggests that the answers to the two types of question should be similar. In many surveys, willingness to accept compensation questions receive much higher responses. The questions asked are hypothetical and those surveyed may not be familiar with the environmental effect/resource being surveyed. Respondents may respond to questions strategically, and there is evidence of other forms of bias in the replies to surveys. The responses of individuals may reflect the context of the survey question. Thus, for example, individuals could, with appropriate questions, be induced to respond as citizens concerned with the public interest rather than as consumers pursuing their own self-interest. It is not always clear how to gross up the response from a survey to represent the general population's valuation of an environmental effect.

In Chapter 10, the importance to social cost-benefit analysis of the distribution of costs and benefits was considered. There are many environmental effects that imply major changes in the distribution of economic welfare, for example, the resettlement of an indigenous population following the construction of a dam. The distribution of environmental benefits and costs can affect the desirability of a project. Simple social cost-benefit analysis is concerned with improving the efficiency of economic decision-making. The prices used in social cost-benefit analysis reflect the distribution of welfare. If this distribution is unfair, the use of the resulting prices may be inappropriate. The introduction of distributional issues means that value judgements have to be made explicitly.

The valuation of environmental costs is essential to improving economic decision-making on the environment, and social cost-benefit analysis has developed various techniques to this end. However there remain theoretical and practical problems with the use of these techniques.

NATIONAL INCOME ACCOUNTING

The neoclassical approach to economic analysis assumes that consumption in its widest sense is, and should be, the objective of economic activity. The ethical issues concerning whose consumption should be considered were examined in Chapter 8 on population. The conventional approach is to measure economic welfare in terms of per capita income. This approach has been widely criticized and alternative measures have been proposed, many of which emphasize the importance of accounting for the environment.

Measures of economic welfare have to be judged in terms of their theoretical definition and practical application. The most obvious measure of current economic welfare is per capita current consumption. Current consumption can be increased by reducing investment, and thus future consumption. This suggests that economic welfare in one period should be defined relative to a fixed capital stock. Thus additions to capital stock, though not increasing current consumption, should be reflected in a measure of economic welfare as they allow increases in future consumption. This idea underlies the conventional definition of income (see Hicks, 1946).

There are many conceptual and practical problems with the definition of income (see Anderson, 1991; Masu, 1997). Only those directly concerned with accounting for the environment are examined here. Environmental degradation can be mitigated by the actions of economic agents, for example soil erosion can be reduced by planting forests. In national income accounts, such **defensive expenditures** are taken as giving rise to increases in economic welfare rather than as attempts to maintain the environment. It is commonly argued that these expenditures should be excluded from measures of economic welfare and account be taken of the environmental effects that give rise to these expenditures.

Environmental degradation affects economic welfare as individuals directly consume environmental services, for example unpolluted air. As there is not always a market in such services, or only an indirect one, they are not recorded in national income accounts. Degradation also reduces the productive potential of the environment, for example non-natural causes of soil erosion and reductions in the ability of the environment to absorb waste products. Reductions in the productive potential of the environment are examples of the depreciation of the stock of natural capital. These types of change are not recorded in national income accounts.

The use of non-renewable resources, for example fossil fuels, is not allowed for in a correct manner in national income accounts. These resources are part of the natural capital of the environment. Their use in the present reduces the supply available for future generations. National income accounts consider the use of non-renewable resources as a simple productive activity. It should also be considered as a depreciation of natural capital.[9]

There have been three responses to the failure of national income measures to account for the environment. The first method follows Nordhaus and Tobin's (1972) calculations of **measures of economic welfare** which attempt to recalculate national income accounts allowing for environmental effects. A study (Repetto *et al.*, 1989) for Indonesia estimated an environmentally adjusted annual economic growth rate of 4 per cent for the period 1971–84 compared with the measured GDP growth rate of 7.1 per cent. The environmental adjustment allowed for various changes in petroleum, forest and soil natural capital. Thus allowing for the environment can give quite different estimates of economic welfare and economic growth.

The second method of accounting for the environment follows the weak sustainability view that total capital should be at least maintained. In this approach, the level of saving is calculated and the depreciation of natural, manmade and other forms of capital is deducted. If the resulting number is negative, this may be taken as evidence of unsustainable development. The method is explained in Pearce and Atkinson (1998) and the World Bank (1997 and 2004) has estimated such measures of the sustainability of the development of a number of developing countries.

A third method of accounting for the environment in economic growth is to construct *physical*, rather than monetary, accounts of the environment. These accounts divide up the environment into different sectors and estimate the changes that have taken place over time. For example, the use and discovery of mineral and energy resources would be recorded. The OECD (1994) has argued for the collection of indicators across time of the effect of human activities on the environment and of the effect of the environment on human activities.

The three methods of accounting for the environment are not substitutes. The monetary approach of the first of the two methods requires the calculation of physical accounts. Physical environmental accounts are useful for considering ecological and environmental issues. Monetary environmental accounts are useful as they reduce all effects to a common measure and estimate a net figure for the use of the environment. However, because of the difficulty of doing this, they have been criticized on theoretical and practical grounds (see Perman *et. al.*, 2003, and Hanley and Atkinson, 2003).

RISK AND UNCERTAINTY

Risk exists where there is doubt about a future outcome and it is possible to estimate objective probabilities of the occurrence of different possible future outcomes. The outcome of a throw of a dice is an example of risk. Uncertainty exists where there is doubt about the outcome and it is not possible to estimate probabilities of the occurrence of the different possible future outcomes. It is difficult to analyze uncertain events and most environmental analysis that considers risk and uncertainty assumes, either explicitly or implicitly, that it is possible to estimate probabilities with some degree of objectivity – that is, the circumstances are assumed to be those of risk rather than uncertainty.

Uncertainty about the relationship between the environment and the economy complicates analysis. As previous examples have shown, there is scientific dispute about many important environmental effects. In the analysis of environmental policies, it is possible to distinguish two approaches to managing this uncertainty.

First, the different possible outcomes of a policy are predicted. Then probabilities are estimated for these different outcomes, though these probabilities are necessarily subjective. It can be argued that the notion of estimating probabilities for events such as global warming is not appropriate, as they cannot be considered as repeated probabilistic events like the throwing of a dice. Notwithstanding this, policy analysis could proceed by selecting the most preferred policy on the basis of the probabilities of the different outcomes of the policies. If society is averse to taking risks, it can be shown that uncertain costs should be given more weight than the expected value of costs, and uncertain benefits should be given less weight than their expected value.

The alternative procedure is to select the mean estimates of the effects of different environmental policies. These estimates are then used to decide the most preferred policy. This procedure is the more commonly used. The choice of the best estimates is highly subjective. More importantly, this approach estimates only the expected effect and, in this sense, does not take account of either risk or uncertainty.

ECONOMIC GROWTH AND THE ENVIRONMENT

Figure 11.2 (p. 341) indicates that the environment is essential for economic activity and growth, and shows the importance of the effects of economic growth on the environment. Environmentalists have argued that unconstrained economic growth will lead to the exhaustion of non-renewable resources and to levels of environmental degradation that will seriously affect economic production and the quality and existence of life (Meadows *et al*, 1972; Forrester, 1971). Economists who believe in the effectiveness of the market have responded to these arguments (see Barbier, 1989).

If markets operate effectively, increased scarcity of non-renewable resources will increase their prices. These higher prices will give incentives for changes in economic behaviour:

- The direct consumption of these resources may fall – for example lower consumption of scarce fossil fuels
- The use of higher-priced non-renewable resources in production will decline through substitution towards techniques of production that are less intensive in these inputs – for example production will become less fossil-fuel-intensive
- There will be incentives to search for new supplies of these resources – for example the level of exploration for new oil fields will increase
- Higher prices will encourage the development of new technologies that provide substitutes for the scarce resources – for example non-fossil fuels such as 'biomass' or wind power – or utilize it more efficiently – for example, fuel-efficient cars.

Thus efficient markets may provide a solution to the running down of non-renewable resources.

Supporters of economic growth argue that its contribution to environmental pollution has been overestimated. They suggest that economic growth, particularly in developing countries, will release more resources that can then be used to reduce environmental degradation, for example to improve water supplies and reduce urban congestion. This view of the existence of opportunities for simultaneous economic development and improvement in the environment is supported by the World Bank. However, the pursuit of these twin goals is usually assumed to require the state to intervene and improve the operation of markets with regard to the environment.

It has been suggested by Grossman and Krueger (1995) that in the early stages of economic development the level of environmental degradation increases, but after this phase the environment improves with economic development. This proposition is in line with the World Bank (1992) and the results that are reported at the beginning of this chapter. However, there is an extensive debate on the relationship between the environment and economic development (see *Environment and Development Economics* (1998); de Bruyn (2001); and Cole (2003)). This relation between the environment and economic development could be explained by changes in the mix of output at different levels of development, changes in the demand for the environment at different levels of income and the policy responses to these demands, and the availability and use of more environmentally friendly technologies in developed countries.

All the different views of economic growth and environmental degradation considered here are likely to be true in part. It is unlikely that the debates on the relationships between the environment and the economy can be resolved through exhaustive scientific and economic investigation. Economic and environmental policies have to be formulated and carried out on the basis of existing uncertain and disputed evidence.

SUSTAINABLE DEVELOPMENT

Much of the vast literature on the environment and the economy could be interpreted as a response to the concern that present patterns of economic growth may seriously degrade the environment and may be unsustainable, as the environment cannot support economic growth forever. This proposition may or may not be substantially true. At its heart lies the view that past and present economic policies have usually been concerned with providing the conditions for equilibrium economic growth, as measured by standard national accounting methods. Many environmentalists are concerned that these policies have not attempted to ensure 'the existence of ecological conditions necessary to support human life at a specified level of well-being through future generations' (Lele, 1991). This concern is of major importance in the concept of **sustainable development**. Sustainable development has become perhaps the most important approach to considering the environment and development.

There is a wide range of definitions and interpretations of the meaning of 'sustainable development'. The term first came to prominence in the *World Conservation Strategy*, presented in 1980 by the International Union for the Conservation of Nature and Natural Resources. It was popularized by the World Commission on the Environment and Development's study *Our Common Future* (1987), which is also known as the Brundtland Report, named in honour of its chairperson, the Norwegian prime minister. These and other studies have defined sustainable development in different ways. The most frequently quoted definition comes from the latter study:

> Sustainable development seeks to meet the needs and aspirations of the present without compromising the ability of future generations to meet their own needs.

This definition would appear uncontroversial and is remarkably similar to the neoclassical definition of income. Hicks (1946) has given a frequently quoted definition of income:

> A person's income is what he can consume during the week and still be as well off at the end of the week as he was at the beginning.

However, the interpretation differs in that *Our Common Future* examined how sustainable development can be achieved. This inevitably requires the making of value judgements that link the definition and the operational objectives that it has been suggested will result in the attainment of sustainable development. For this reason, there has been criticism of the connection between the definition and the operational objectives. The objectives are increasing economic growth, meeting basic needs, involving more of the population in decision-making and development, controlling population growth, conserving and improving the environment, accounting for the environment in economic decision making, changing technology, managing risk and changing international economic relationships (see Pearce and Atkinson, 1998).

The concept of sustainable development has gained very wide acceptance and has become a standard model for thinking about the environment, development and the economy. Most countries attending the Rio Earth Summit in 1992 accepted the general idea of sustainable development, for example as enshrined in the *Agenda 21* process agreed at this summit (United Nations, 1993a). However, as suggested above, what the concept of sustainable development should imply for economic and environmental policies is disputed. In particular, the concern for equity between and within generations is central to most interpretations of the concept, but it is unclear how the welfare of individuals can be compared. This is a central problem in neoclassical economics and the concept of sustainable development does not appear to provide a solution to the problem.

NATURAL CAPITAL, EQUITY AND ENVIRONMENTAL VALUES

In defining the notion of sustainable development, it is common to require that the stock of capital be non-declining through time. A constant or increasing stock of capital allows consumption levels to be maintained or increased. However, there are major differences of opinion over the capital stock that must be held constant or increased. The weak sustainability view considers all the different forms of capital (for example, manmade, human, natural and social capital) to be substitutes and that they can be aggregated into total capital. Thus, for example, degrading the natural fertility of the soil can be compensated for through using fertilizers and the methods of agricultural science to maintain crop yields. In this example, human and manmade capital are used to substitute for natural capital.

The alternative view of strong sustainability takes the position that it is only natural capital that needs to be held constant or increased. In this view, the focus is often on critical natural capital which is either required for human survival or cannot be substituted for with other forms of capital. Thus, one might take atmospheric carbon dioxide levels as critical natural capital as higher levels cannot be offset by other capital. For an economic comparison and analysis of weak and strong sustainability, see Hanley and Atkinson (2003).

Underlying the analysis of the environment and development, and the importance of natural capital, are views about environmental values. The study of environmental values suggests three possible ways in which these values could be generated. First, the preferences of individuals give rise to values that with a complete set of perfect markets are reflected in the prices of goods and services. This is the neoclassical approach to valuation and examples of market failure have already been examined. Market failures suggest that the environment will not be adequately accounted for in the operation of market economies.

The second source of environmental values is that of social preferences. Sagoff (1988) has suggested that individuals are capable of considering issues, in particular those concerning the environment, from the point of society. It is not clear how such values could be established in the psyche of individuals. A possible explanation is a sociobiological one in that individuals behave as social organisms for the benefit of the species (Dawkins, 1976). Environmental choices are so complex that even if social preferences exist it is difficult to assume that, apart from in a tautological sense, they will result in decisions that improve social welfare. However, it has been suggested that the poor in developing countries are the most dependent on the environment. Thus if social preferences are to give weight to the circumstances of the poor, the environment should be given greater weight than would occur from simple aggregation of the individual values placed on the environment.

The third source of environmental values follows from the belief that ecological systems have an intrinsic value independent of any value placed on them by humans (see Norton, 1987; Common, 1995). The individual-preferences basis for values considers only human beings to have rights. The ecological view represents the extension of rights to other species. How these rights can be measured is a difficult problem. The ecological-values view suggests that greater weight should be attached to the environment than would be given by taking just social values or simple aggregation of individual values.

Preserving or increasing the stock of natural capital has important effects on intergenerational equity. If it is believed that present levels of environmental degradation and resource use will substantially alter future human economic welfare, then inter-generational equity may be improved by the constraint that the stock of natural capital should be preserved. This is the strong sustainability view. However, the substitution of this constraint by a more flexible approach that allows some use of natural capital could conceivably increase economic welfare measured across all present and future generations. This is the weak sustainability view.

The use of a positive discount rate weights future environmental effects less heavily than those occurring in the present. This has been criticized as underestimating the importance of environmental degradation and resource use. This criticism is misplaced. If the arguments are accepted for the social preference of the present compared with the future, then discounting is appropriate. If it is felt that too little weight is being attached to future environmental effects, their estimated values should be adjusted, but not the discount rate.

Many environmental effects are irreversible, for example the extinction of a species. Irreversibility has been used as an argument for maintaining the natural capital stock. However, the dislike of irreversible losses in natural capital can be captured by the concepts of option, quasi-option and existence values.

The resilience of an ecosystem is its ability to maintain its normal functions after an external disturbance (Common, 1995). It has been suggested that the larger the stock of natural capital, the more resilient an ecosystem is likely to be. This argument is justified on the basis of the idea that the diversity of the ecosystem increases its resilience. However, the notion of resilience and the related concept of stability have been criticized, as no ecosystem is likely to be globally stable and constant through time. This implies that the size of the external disturbance is important (Norton, 1987).

As discussed previously, uncertainty is crucial to the analysis of the relation between the environment and the economy. A possible policy response to such uncertainty is to adopt policies that provide insurance against possibly disastrous future outcomes. This risk-averse strategy of emphasizing the worst possible outcome might be justified by, say, the worst forecasts of the disastrous outcomes of global warming. This argument supports the setting of a constraint that keeps the stock of natural capital fixed. Alternatively, it has been argued (for example, see Beckerman, 1992) that the vast expenditure necessary to reduce global warming, the long period before such effects become important and the lack of absolutely clear scientific proof of the size of these effects suggest that a conservative approach ought to be adopted. It is unclear how uncertainty should be included in environmental decision-making, but it *is* clear that the treatment of uncertainty has a very important effect on the actual decisions that have been or will be taken.

Arguments about weak and strong sustainability, sources of environmental values, discounting, irreversibility, uncertainty and resilience suggest a higher value should perhaps be placed on the environment than the operation of a market economy would give. Strictly, this is not the same as suggesting that the stock of natural capital should be maintained. However, the complexity of decision-making on the environment might require a very approximate constraint on the use of environment such as preserving the stock of natural capital.

This critical discussion of the concept of sustainable development suggests that the environment has an important role in economic development and this may not have been fully understood in the past. The concept of sustainable development has won many academic and political adherents. However there are differences in opinion whether natural capital deserves special protection in economic development or whether it can be traded off against manmade and human capital.[10] These differences are important in determining how the environment enters into economic decision-making.

There are also practical difficulties with the implementation of a constraint that keeps the stock of natural capital fixed. The environment is made up of many different resources and services. Constancy of the stock of natural capital could be interpreted as constancy of all types of natural capital. This interpretation implies that any positive use of non-renewable resources would not be compatible with sustainable development and is difficult to justify.

The alternative interpretation is to consider a single measure of natural capital that appropriately weights the different types of natural capital. The obvious weights are the values of the various types of natural capital. These values may not only reflect the ideas considered in (11.6), but also the distributional views that are often associated with the idea of sustainable development. However, placing values on the different types of natural capital would appear to deny the special role of such capital. If different forms of natural capital can be valued so as to give a single measure, this suggests that it can be traded off against manmade and human capital and requires no special protection in the process of development.

It may be the case that a single measure of most types of natural capital would be desirable, with individual measures for the remaining and critical types of natural capital, for example the ozone layer.

If the view is taken that the environment must be preserved, then social cost-benefit analysis of a project should be carried out subject to the additional constraint that the net effects on the environment are zero or positive. The strength of this additional constraint can be weakened by adding environmentally friendly investments to the project that allow the constraint to be met. If it is considered necessary to preserve the different types of natural stock, then there must be an additional constraint for each type of natural capital.

The constraint of preservation of all aspects of the environment implies that national income accounting methods cannot be altered to allow the calculation of one measure of economic welfare that includes environmental effects. Thus it has been suggested that measures of economic welfare be presented alongside a set of indicators of the state of the environment.

The less restrictive interpretation of the concept of sustainable development allows substitution between different forms of capital and the simple inclusion of the environment in social cost-benefit analysis and national income accounting (see Pearce and Atkinson, 1995). The inclusion of the environment simply requires the correct valuation of environmental effects.

ECONOMIC THOUGHT AND THE ENVIRONMENT[11]

Classical economists such as Malthus, Ricardo and Mill were generally pessimistic about the possibility of continued economic progress.[12] These economists assumed that there were diminishing returns to factors of production and the supply of land was fixed. The growth in population, and thus the labour force, would lead to reductions in the marginal product of labour and a declining average product of labour. Malthus and Ricardo assumed a constant technology, with the inevitable result that average agricultural production per unit of labour would decline. Mill considered that technical progress could offset the effect of diminishing returns to a factor, but was unlikely to do so in the long run.

Marshall (1890) invented the idea of an externality and it was developed by Pigou (1920). However, in general, environmental externalities were considered to be unimportant (see, for example, Little and Mirrlees, 1969).

The start of the debate about the environment and the economy is usually attributed to Rachel Carson and her book *Silent Spring* (1962). Other early contributions to the environmental debate were made by Boulding (1966), the Ehrlichs (1970), Goldsmith *et al.* (1972), Forrester (1971), Schumacher (1973) and Commoner (1972). A most influential environmental publication was *The Limits to Growth* by Meadows *et al.* (1972). The basic point of this study was that there is a number of non-renewable resources whose present levels of consumption are such that the known reserves will be exhausted in the not so distant future. The study was heavily criticized for not allowing for the effects of the price mechanism to reduce consumption and provide incentives to explore for new reserves and develop new technologies.

These environmental contributions to the debate stimulated economic interest in the relation between the environment and the economy. Barnett and Morse (1963) could find little evidence of resource scarcity in the US economy in the period 1850–1957. Dasgupta and Heal (1979) provided a rigorous neoclassical analysis of the depletion of exhaustible natural resources. Kneese, Ayres and D'Arge's (1970) development of the **materials balance approach** changed the view that some economists had of how the economic system dealt with the environment's waste absorption function. This simple principle states that all resources that flow into an economic system must eventually end up as waste products.

The debate about the environment and the economy has changed public views, and in particular the views of international agencies have changed.

INTERNATIONAL AGENCIES AND THE ENVIRONMENT[13]

Since 1990, international agencies have begun to accept the importance of allowing for the environment in economic development and have started to change their practices.

The World Bank has accepted that the environment is directly relevant to the Bank's mission of supporting development (see Conable, 1989; Lutz, 1993; World Bank, 1992). The World Bank supports the sustainable development view. There are various aspects to the Bank's new policy view. First, it is accepted that there is a need for appropriate valuation of environmental effects. Since 1989, the World Bank has formally required environmental assessments of all projects that are expected to have a significant adverse environmental impact. However, there have been criticisms of whether these assessments contribute to actual project decision-making (see Horta, 1996).

Second, poverty is seen as a major cause of environmental damage and the poor are regarded as being heavily dependent on the environment (for example, see Wunder, 2001). Third, it is argued that high-income countries must accept the financial responsibility and take the initiative for dealing with major worldwide environmental problems. However, it is also clear that the World Bank disagrees with the view that economic development should take place under the constraint that the stock of natural capital should not be depleted. The Bank does now lend explicitly for environmental projects, and through the Global Environment Fund makes grants to protect the environment. By 2001, the World Bank provided $US5 billion of capital for active environmental projects and funded many other projects with clear environmental objectives (see Stokke and Thommessen, 2003). However, the benefits to the environment and native peoples of this lending have been disputed (Horta, 1996; Sjöberg, 1996).

Similarly, the IMF has slowly begun to recognize the need to take account of the environment in its structural adjustment programmes (SAPs) (IMF, 1993). The IMF has been criticized for only making token and superficial changes in policy (see Reed, 1996). Both the World Bank and the IMF are large international agencies where change is difficult to implement, and whether there is a commitment to implement changes in policies properly to protect the environment and the most disadvantaged persons in developing countries remains to be seen.

The World Trade Organization (WTO) (and its predecessor, the General Agreement on Tariffs and Trade, GATT) exists to promote the liberalization of world trade.[14] The WTO's position is that there may be a trade-off between trade and the environment and that environmental concerns could turn into trade protectionism. The WTO upholds the benefits of a multilateral non-discriminatory world trading system. They believe that it is not appropriate for the WTO to set environmental policies and standards. They believe that such issues should be considered by specialized agencies and international negotiation. However, the WTO supports the objective of sustainable development and has been involved in assisting multilateral environmental agreements and increasing the awareness of links between trade and the environment (see Stokke and Thommessen, 2003).

The United Nations has been responsible for the two reports – *World Conservation Strategy* and *Our Common Future* – that have greatly influenced world opinion in favour of sustainable development. The UN Development Programme (UNDP) and the World Bank, as we have seen, set up the Global Environment Facility in 1991.

The UN Conference on Environment and Development in June 1992 – the Rio Earth Summit – reached agreements on various issues. A convention to reduce global warming was signed by 150 countries (the United States signed in 1993), most of which agreed to limit atmospheric emissions by the year 2000 to their 1990 levels. At the 1997 Kyoto Conference, outline agreement was given to a market in greenhouse gas emission targets. In this market, countries exceeding and more than meeting their agreed targets can trade so that the overall target is met at a minimum cost. The market is very similar to the marketable permits system discussed earlier in the chapter. The subsequent negotiations of the arrangements for the trading system have been very difficult and it is not clear how effective the present proposals will be in reducing global warming. At this Conference, a Biodiversity Convention to protect plants and animals was signed.

There was agreement on the Rio Declaration's support of sustainable global development, and *Agenda 21* considers specific programmes to achieve sustainable development in the twenty-first century (United Nations, 1993a). The United Nations Commission on Sustainable Development was set up with the objective of promoting, investigating and monitoring sustainable development (see Mensah, 1996).

The Rio Earth Summit was criticized for its failure to secure a binding commitment to increase aid, reduce debt and fundamentally shift resources from rich to poor countries (Rogers, 1993). One of the underlying assumptions of the concept of sustainable development is that poverty is an important cause of environmental degradation. Though there appears to be general acceptance that there is a problem with the present sustainability of economic activity, there is little commitment at the level of national governments to incur the potentially major costs associated with policies of sustainable development.

DISCUSSION QUESTIONS

1 What are the functions of the environment in supporting economic activity?

2 What is an externality, and why are externalities considered to be a problem?

3 What are the different possible solutions to externalities?

4 Explain the causes of 'the tragedy of the commons'.

5 What conditions determine the efficient use of renewable and non-renewable resources?

6 What are the different types of value that should be included in social costs?

7 How might one allow for environmental effects in social cost-benefit analysis and national income accounting practices?

8 Define and explain the idea of sustainable development.

9 What are the arguments for and against keeping the stock of natural capital fixed?

10 How have international organizations responded to the ideas of sustainable development and the economic importance of the environment?

NOTES

1. This discussion of the relationships between the environment and the economy is very general and simple. Specific examples of the interaction of the environment and the economy in developing countries can be found in Winpenny (1995); Hanley and Spash (1993); Turner (1993); Grossman and Krueger (1995); Blowers and Glasbergen (1996); special issue of *Environment and Development Economics* (1998); de Bruyn (2001); and Cole (2003).
2. For a good introduction to this subject, see Common (1996).
3. Explanations of the neoclassical approach to economics can be found in most intermediate microeconomics textbooks: see Varian (2002).
4. See Bond *et al.* (2001) for details and evaluation of the external effects of this hydroelectric facility.
5. See the discussion of 'the problem of the commons' in Dasgupta (1982).
6. The remaining values could strictly be classified as private or external costs, but for the purpose of exposition they are separated into different categories.
7. More precise details and discussion of economic valuation can be found in Hanley and Spash (1993) and Winpenny (1995).
8. These expenditures and costs may be difficult to observe and both techniques often require experts to estimate them.
9. A similar analysis applies in the case of renewable resources, as regeneration can require time and investment, and thus present consumption of renewable resources can impose costs on future generations.
10. For examples see Common (1995), World Bank (1992), and Hanley and Atkinson (2003).
11. See Barbier (1989) for a good survey of the history of economic thought on the environment and development.
12. Malthus (1798); Ricardo (1817); Mill (1856). See also Chapter 4 above.
13. For a good clear summary of the objectives and activities of most international agencies that work in the environmental and development fields see Stokke and Thommessen (2003).
14. See Makuch (1996) and Runge (1995) for a discussion of the organization of the WTO and possible future developments.

WEBSITES ON THE ENVIRONMENT

Amazing Environmental Organisation Web Directory www.webdirectory.com

International Institute for Environment and Development www.iied.org

World Watch Institute www.worldwatch.org

World Resources Institute www.wri.org

United Nations Environmental Program www.unep.org

UN Commission on Sustainable Development www.un.org/esa/sustdev

The choice of 12
techniques

THE CAPITAL INTENSITY OF TECHNIQUES IN DEVELOPING COUNTRIES

If labour is more abundant and capital is scarcer in developing countries than in developed countries, we might expect to observe the use of more labour-intensive techniques of production in the industrial sector of developing countries, reflecting a lower price of labour relative to capital. Figure 12.1 shows this. Assuming the same production function in the two sets of countries, labelled '1', and holding everything else constant, the lower relative price of labour in the developing country, given by the price line (or isocost curve), *cb*, gives a more labour-intensive choice of technique than in the developed country, where the relative price of labour is given by the steeper line *ad*.

In the developed country the capital–labour ratio is given by the ray from the origin, *DC*, while in the less-developed country the capital–labour ratio is given by the ray *LDC*;

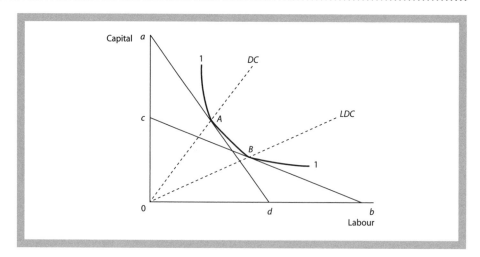

Figure 12.1 Optimal choice of technique

both rays pass through the point of tangency between the price line and production function – A and B, respectively.

In practice, however, it is often the case that for the same outputs produced, the capital intensity of techniques is not very different between the two sets of countries, and that the capital–labour ratio differs between developed and less-developed countries in the aggregate only to the extent that the composition of output differs; that is, because there are large sectors in developing countries' economies where very little capital is employed at all, as in subsistence farming and petty service activities. In the modern sectors of developing countries, however, techniques are much more capital-intensive than would be predicted on the basis of knowledge of factor endowments. Given the supply of labour available, and given the rate of investment, the more capital-intensive the techniques, the less employment and the more unemployment there will be.

Unemployment and underemployment are major preoccupations in developing countries, and are one reason why the prevailing techniques of production might be regarded as 'inappropriate'.

But what accounts for this relative capital intensity of modern sector techniques, and would the developing countries be better off using more labour-intensive techniques? There is a number of reasons why technological choice sometimes appears to be little different in developing countries than in technologically advanced societies.

First, for a large number of commodities there may not be a spectrum of techniques to choose from; that is, in practice the production function in Figure 12.1 may not be smooth, and a country cannot move from point A to B in accordance with differences in relative factor endowments and relative factor prices. We are talking here, of course, about techniques that are profitable. There may always be more labour-intensive techniques using both more labour and capital, but then the output would not be competitively saleable. If there is not a spectrum of profitable techniques of production, and the coefficients of production are fixed, the production function is L-shaped (sometimes called a **Leontief production function** after Wassily Leontief, the 'father' of input–output analysis, which assumes no substitutability between capital and labour – see Chapter 13). Whether world technology is such that there is only one profitable technique, or whether there are many but developing countries are denied access to them, is an empirical question that we shall consider later.

A second reason for the relative capital intensity of production in developing countries is that the market prices of factors of production frequently do not reflect relative abundance or scarcity. This tendency is often exacerbated by developing countries themselves, which give generous subsidies to scarce capital and encourage high wages in the modern manufacturing sector by the government paying high wages to its own employees. The old justification for using capital-intensive techniques, which governments used to believe in and still do to a great extent, was that they are necessary to maximize output and saving, and that more labour-intensive techniques would reduce the level of output and saving because of their relative inefficiency and higher wage bills. Later in the chapter we shall examine these contentions thoroughly, but clearly the cheaper that capital is made by subsidies and the higher wages are above their 'shadow' price, the more capital-intensive the techniques will tend to be.

A third factor to bear in mind is that although labour may be abundant and the money wage may be lower than in developed countries, it is not necessarily 'cheaper' or less 'costly' to employ, because its productivity may be lower. In other words, the so-called **efficiency wage** (that is, the wage rate divided by the productivity of labour), or wage costs per unit of output, may differ very little between the developing and developed countries. This means that the production function for the developing country in Figure 12.1 will lie outside the production function for the developed country in such a way that even if the relative money wage of labour is lower in the developing country, it is profitable to choose a relatively capital-intensive technique. Figure 12.2 shows this. The production function for the developing country is labelled '2'. Even though labour is cheaper relative to capital in the developing country (slope of cb < slope of ad), nonetheless the most profitable capital–labour ratio will be the same in both countries (given by the ray from the origin, $DC = LDC$). It is probably because abundant labour is not necessarily 'cheap', in a cost per unit of output sense, that accounts for the observation that in trade developing countries' exports are sometimes as capital-intensive as in developed countries, contrary to the prediction of certain trade theories. This apparent paradox (sometimes called the **Leontief Paradox**) could be explained by the fact that it is the 'efficiency' wage that matters, not the money wage, and while the

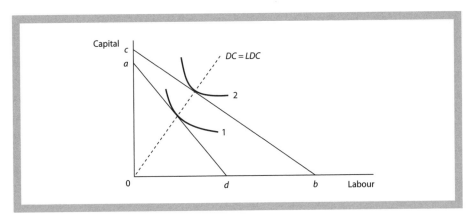

Figure 12.2 Different wages: same technique

money wage may be low in developing countries, the 'efficiency' wage is relatively high.

Fourthly, we may mention the fact that in certain instances capital intensity may be explained by a skill constraint. Typically, labour-intensive techniques require a great deal of skilled labour, compared with capital-intensive techniques which mainly require a preponderance of semi-skilled labour to undertake routine tasks. In developing countries that are short of skilled manpower, capital may substitute for skills and constitute a rational response on the part of decision makers, whoever they may be.

But perhaps the overriding factor that accounts for the relative capital intensity of the modern sector of developing countries is the fact that many, if not most, of the techniques of production are imported from abroad, with a heavy bias in the labour-saving direction. The techniques may either be employed by indigenous firms or, as increasingly seems to be the case, by large foreign-owned **multinational corporations**, which invest in the country and bring their technology with them. In this case the technology may be 'inappropriate' not because there is not a spectrum of techniques or an inappropriate selection is made, but because the technology available is circumscribed by the global profit-maximizing motives of the companies investing in the less-developed country concerned. The labour-saving bias of the technology is to be explained by the labour-saving bias of technical progress in advanced countries where labour is relatively scarce and expensive. As we saw in Chapter 6 (Figure 6.2, p. 218), labour-saving bias on a production-function diagram is represented by a non-uniform inward shift in the production function, causing capital to be substituted for labour at the same ratio of relative factor prices.

If developed countries have designed labour-saving technologies that, through the process of international investment, are now being widely used in developing countries, it might well be asked: why have developing countries not invented capital-saving technologies to economize on scarce capital? The answer is that if a country is to develop technology to save capital, it must have a capital goods industry, but typically the capital goods sector of developing countries is rudimentary or non-existent. With a large fraction of investment goods coming from abroad, coupled with a lack of domestic know-how, there has been very little incentive for developing countries to establish their own capital goods industries.

Capital goods production is characterized by the ability to specialize, but to do this economically requires a large market: a much larger market than for homogeneous consumer products that can reap economies of scale. Capital saving also comes from improvement in the efficiency of capital goods production itself, but without a capital goods sector there cannot be innovations and an important source of capital saving and technical progress in the economy as a whole is lost. It is widely recognized that a capital goods sector is essential for innovatory activity in the economy as a whole, and if developing countries are to reduce their dependence on imported technology, priority must be given to the establishment and nurture of an indigenous capital goods sector.[1]

The empirical evidence on multinational corporations and the choice of techniques is mixed. Lall (1978) distinguishes three separate issues:

■ Whether the technologies used by multinationals are adaptable to abundant labour and low wage conditions in developing countries

- Whether multinationals do adapt the technologies they transfer
- Whether multinationals adapt better or worse than local firms.

Regarding the first question, the technologies used by multinationals are unlikely to be very flexible because the companies tend to predominate in modern industries where processes are complex, continuous and, by their very nature, capital intensive. Outside processing, however, ancillary activities, such as the handling of materials and packaging, may be amenable to substitution. On the second issue, it is unlikely that multinationals will undertake major, expensive alterations to technology simply to suit local conditions, and there is not much evidence that they do so.

With regard to the third matter, however, in comparison with local firms, the experience of the multinationals seems to be very mixed. The problem here is that when making comparisons, like must be compared with like; that is, local and foreign firms must be compared in the same market, producing similar products with equal access to technology. Studies must therefore be treated with caution. It is easy to reach the conclusion that multinationals are more capital-intensive than local firms if they operate in different industries producing different products. This in fact is often the case; being concentrated in activities that are intrinsically more capital- intensive such as heavy industries and extractive industries. We shall say more about the empirical evidence below, and more about multinational corporations in Chapter 15, where we consider the role of private foreign investment in the development process.

We turn now, to the potential conflict between moving towards the use of more labour-intensive techniques of production and output on the one hand, and saving on the other.

THE CONFLICT BETWEEN EMPLOYMENT AND OUTPUT AND EMPLOYMENT AND SAVING IN THE CHOICE OF TECHNIQUES

Developing countries have three broad objectives: to raise the level of *present* consumption, to raise the level of *future* consumption (by saving now), and to raise the level of *employment*. In the choice of *new* techniques, a conflict between objectives may arise. First, a technique that maximizes employment *may* involve a sacrifice of output. Second, a technique that maximizes employment *may* involve a sacrifice of saving. As we have mentioned already, certainly one of the justifications for the use of modern capital-intensive technology used to be that labour-intensive techniques would reduce output and the investible surplus. We need to look at this matter theoretically and empirically. We shall argue that while in theory there may be a conflict, the assumptions upon which a potential conflict is based are either invalid or too extreme, and that in practice developing countries could move towards the use of more labour-intensive techniques without sacrificing the level of present or future consumption. Some of the empirical evidence would seem to bear this out.

EMPLOYMENT VERSUS OUTPUT

A potential conflict between employment and output exists in the choice of new techniques because methods that employ high labour–capital ratios may involve high

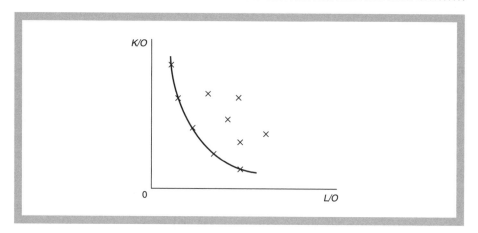

Figure 12.3 Efficiency frontier

capital–output ratios because labour productivity is lower.[2] We may use again the illustration of this in Chapter 9 (p. 307). Assume that a fixed amount of capital, £1000, is to be invested. Technique I employs 100 persons with an incremental capital–output ratio of 5, giving an annual flow of output of £200. Technique II employs 50 persons with an incremental capital–output ratio of 4, giving an annual flow of output of £250. Therefore the technique that maximizes employment has a lower flow of current output.

It should be said straight away that there is very little evidence, if any, to support the view that labour-intensive techniques have higher capital–output ratios than capital-intensive techniques. On the contrary, there is growing evidence that labour can be substituted for capital, provided cooperating factors are available, without the level of output being impaired. One interesting pioneer study is that by Pack (1974), using UN data on capital per unit of output (K/O) and labour per unit of output (L/O) for six commodities in 16 firms across 10 countries. Pack plots the observations of (K/O) and (L/O) (as in Figure 12.3) for each commodity from the cross-section data, and then defines the efficiency frontier to estimate the elasticity of substitution along it.

Each scatter point in Figure 12.3 represents country observations for one industry, say cotton textiles, of the relative amounts of capital and labour employed per unit of output. The **efficiency frontier** (or unit isoquant) is drawn through the points closest to the origin and the elasticity of substitution is calculated as

$$\frac{(K/L)_i}{(K/L)_j} = \left[\frac{(w/r)_i}{(w/r)_j}\right]^{\sigma}$$

where w/r is the wage-rental ratio, i and j are the two observations closest to the origin, and σ is the elasticity of substitution. For five of the six commodities there is a large difference in the amount of capital per worker year used by countries on the efficiency frontier and a fairly high elasticity of substitution. The results are shown in Table 12.1. The results suggest that for countries using large amounts of capital per unit of labour there are more labour-intensive techniques available (as used by other countries) that could be adopted without sacrificing output unless the cooperating factors associated with the increased labour intensity are not available. One interesting observation from

Table 12.1 Capital–labour-substitution possibilities

Industry	Countries on the efficiency frontier	Capital per worker year ($)	Elasticity of substitution (σ)
Bicycles }	India	400	0.24
	Japan	520	
Grain milling }	Japan	280	3.70
	Israel	6,410	
Paints }	India	214	1.60
	Middle Europe	2,790	
Tyres }	Iran	6,240	1.50
	Mexico	10,600	
Cotton textiles }	India	1,100	2.00
	Mexico	8,240	
Woollen textiles }	India	260	1.20
	Japan	4,600	

Pack's work is that India is invariably either on or close to the efficiency frontier, and hence is using labour-intensive techniques effectively.

Pack's study (1976) of 42 plants in Kenyan manufacturing also suggests that there appears to be considerable *ex ante* choice of capital intensity in most industries, particularly outside the processing sector in the auxiliary activities of material receiving, material handling among processes, packaging and storage of the finished products. In fact many auxiliary activities are already very labour-intensive, and contrary to the conventional wisdom it was found that foreign-owned firms generally used more labour-intensive techniques than indigenous firms. Pack ascribes this to the better managerial expertise and technical training of personnel in foreign firms. Forsyth and Solomon (1977) in a study of Ghana, also find scope for capital–labour substitution and can find no overwhelming evidence that foreign firms are more capital intensive than resident expatriate or private indigenous firms. The situation varies from industry to industry. Helleiner (1975) concludes his survey of multinational corporations and technological choice by saying: 'In particular industrial sectors, the multinational firm has often proven more responsive and adaptable in its factor and input use, especially in the ancillary activities associated with the basic production processes, than local firms, and so it perhaps should be with its wide range of experience on which to draw.'

▌ AGGREGATIVE IMPLICATIONS OF FACTOR SUBSTITUTION

Pack (1982) has taken nine industrial sectors from studies that have examined choice of techniques and has worked out the aggregative effects on employment, wage income, non-wage income and value-added of $100 million investment in each sector, using the most capital-intensive technique and the most appropriate technology, defined as that which yields the highest present discounted value per unit of capital. The results are very revealing, although Pack pinpoints many obstacles to the adoption of more labour-intensive technology. The industrial sectors concerned are shown in Table 12.2, which gives data on investment and employment in relation to output for the two

Table 12.2 Fixed investment and employment associated with capital-intensive and appropriate technologies

Sector	Annual output of plant	Capital-intensive technology			Appropriate technology		
		Investment in 000 dollars	Number of workers	000 dollars per worker	Investment in 000 dollars	Number of workers	000 dollars per worker
Shoes	300,000 pairs	334	155	2.2	165	218	0.8
Cotton weaving	40 000,000 square yards	9,779	260	37.6	4,715	544	8.7
Cotton spinning	2,000 tons	1,440	98	14.7	480	240	2.0
Brickmaking	16 000,000 bricks	3,437	75	45.8	796	238	3.3
Maize milling	36,000 tons	613	63	9.7	219	96	2.9
Sugar processing	50,000 tons	6,386	1,030	6.2	3,882	4,986	0.8
Beer brewing	200,000 hectolitres	4,512	246	18.3	2,809	233	12.1
Leather processing	600,000 hides	6,692	185	36.2	4,832	311	15.5
Fertilizer	528,000 tons of urea	34,132	248	137.6	29,597	242	122.3

Table 12.3 Annual employment, wage and non-labour income and value-added under alternative technologies

Sector	Employment[1]		Wage income[2]		Non-labour income[2]		Value-added[2]	
	Appropriate	Capital-intensive	Appropriate	Capital-intensive	Appropriate	Capital-intensive	Appropriate	Capital-intensive
Shoes	31,589	18,158	15.79	9.08	73.19	59.04	88.99	68.12
Cotton weaving	10,488	2,538	5.24	1.27	18.20	3.61	23.44	4.80
Cotton spinning	10,747	4,525	5.37	2.26	52.61	32.00	57.98	34.26
Brickmaking	29,909	2,182	14.95	1.09	40.72	−5.50	55.67	−4.41
Maize milling	19,231	7,574	9.62	3.79	13.48	8.30	23.10	12.09
Sugar processing	123,980	15,925	61.99	7.96	185.68	154.84	247.66	162.80
Beer brewing	7,460	4,316	3.73	2.16	48.66	21.73	52.39	23.89
Leather processing	4,502	2,108	2.25	1.05	17.49	10.72	19.74	11.77
Fertilizer	772	691	0.39	0.35	54.57	49.76	54.95	50.11
Total	238,678	58,017	119.33	29.01	504.60	334.50	623.92	363.51

Notes:
1. All workers in the industry.
2. Million dollars.
Source for Tables 12.2 and 12.3: H. Pack, 'Aggregate Implications of Factor Substitution in Industrial Processes', *Journal of Development Economics*, II (1982).

technologies compared. For most sectors there are wide differences in the capital–output ratio and the capital–labour ratio.

To derive the aggregative implications of factor substitution, each sector is assumed to have invested $100 million, either on the most capital-intensive process or on the most appropriate technology, from which employment, wage income (assuming an annual average wage of $500 per worker), non-labour income and value-added can be calculated for the two technologies. The results are shown in Table 12.3.

Focusing on the aggregate totals, it can be seen that value-added on the appropriate technology is nearly twice as high as on the most capital-intensive technology, and that the aggregate level of employment is four times higher. Note also that while labour's share of value-added is higher on the more labour-intensive technology and the share of profits is lower, the absolute level of non-labour income is higher. There is no clash between employment and output, or employment and the reinvestible surplus. However, value-added per worker on the more labour-intensive techniques is less than half that on the most capital-intensive techniques. What is also clear from the Table 12.3 is that there are large differences between sectors in the capital–labour ratio using more appropriate technology, so that the actual sectoral composition of investment will affect the aggregate calculations of employment effects. To increase employment, therefore, it is possible to exploit the scope for factor substitution *between* sectors as well as *within* sectors. The obstacles identified by Pack to the adoption of more labour-intensive technology include:

- The costs of information
- The problems associated with the use of second-hand machinery
- The fact that technical change may be slowed down
- The shortages of skilled manpower.

Pack shows high benefit–cost ratios to training in skills; and to overcome the problems arising from the adoption of more labour-intensive technologies he suggests an **industrial extension service** equivalent to the extension services commonly available for the agricultural sector in developing countries.

Even if more labour-intensive techniques can be used without a sacrifice of output, there is still the question of whether the investible surplus, and therefore future output, will be impaired. Pack's work suggests otherwise, but let us now consider in more detail the potential conflict between employment and saving, as the traditional argument has it.

EMPLOYMENT VERSUS SAVING

The potential conflict between employment and saving can be illustrated in its starkest form using a simple production function diagram first used in this context by Dobb (1955) and Sen (1968).

Consider the use of a given amount of investible resources, K, and the possibility of employing those resources with varying amounts of labour to produce output. In Figure 12.4, $0O$ is the production function in the consumption sector, exhibiting diminishing returns to labour. Now take the standard traditional (though not necessarily correct!) assumption that in the industrial sector labour is paid a fixed wage that is all consumed, so that a ray from the origin ($0C$) with a constant slope (w) shows the level of the wage bill and consumption at each level of employment. The difference between $0O$ and $0C$ is profit; and if all profits are saved the difference also shows the level of saving at each capital–labour ratio. Saving is maximized where a line drawn parallel to $0C$ is tangential to the production function – at employment level L in Figure 12.4. Beyond this point further employment generation would diminish the level of saving and investible surplus. If the production function in Figure 12.4 is denoted algebraically as

$$O = aL - bL^2 \tag{12.1}$$

and the savings function as

$$S = aL - bL^2 - wL \tag{12.2}$$

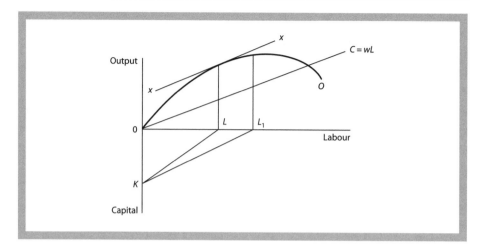

Figure 12.4 Employment versus saving

the level of employment that maximizes saving is obtained by differentiating (12.2) with respect to L and setting equal to zero which gives:

$$\frac{\partial S}{\partial L} = a - 2bL - w = 0 \tag{12.3}$$

Therefore the level of employment that maximizes saving is

$$L = (a - w)/2b \tag{12.4}$$

and the level of employment that maximizes output is

$$L_1 = a/2b \tag{12.5}$$

Since $L < L_1$, there is a conflict between savings and employment maximization. The more labour-intensive technique maximizes output and consumption in the short run; but the more capital-intensive technique provides a greater surplus for reinvestment for growth and future output and consumption. As Dobb (1955) puts it:

> The choice between more or less capital-intensive forms of investment has nothing to do with existing factor proportions. It depends, not on the existing ratio of available labour to capital (treated as a stock), but on precisely the same considerations as those which determine the choice between a high and a low rate of investment – namely the importance to be attached to raising consumption in the immediate future compared with the potential increase of consumption in the more distant future which a particular rate of investment or form of investment will make possible. In other words, the same grounds which would justify a high rate of investment . . . would justify also a high degree of capital intensity in the choice of investment forms, and vice versa!

The potential clash between increasing employment and maximizing saving, represented by the difference between L_1 and L in Figure 12.4, can be seen, however, to be based on several assumptions, the validity of which may be questioned.

- That the wage rate is given and invariant with respect to the technique of production. This assumption would seem to be a hangover from Lewis's influential model of the development process (discussed in Chapter 5), which assumes an elastic supply of labour to the industrial sector at a *constant* wage. If this wage is above the minimum necessary, however, several implications ensue.
- That all profits are saved and all wages are consumed.
- That unemployment resulting from the use of capital-intensive techniques does not reduce community saving to the level of saving that would prevail with more employment and a higher wage bill.
- That consumption is not productive (that is, has no investment component), or that present consumption is no more productive than future consumption.
- That governments lack the ability to tax and to subsidize labour to reconcile the potential conflict.

Let us relax these assumptions and see what difference is made.

WAGES AND THE CAPITAL INTENSITY OF PRODUCTION

Let us first relax the assumption that the wage rate is given and the same for all techniques, regardless of the capital intensity. There are two fundamental points to be made here in the context of a developing country. The first is that a great deal of the technology, at least in the modern industrial sector, is not indigenous but imported. In this case the wage structure is set by the *skill mix* demanded by the technology and the need to keep the labour force well nourished and contented if the capital equipment is to be worked productively and profitably. By and large it may be expected that the greater the degree of capital intensity the higher the average wage paid.

The second point is that with large amounts of disguised and open unemployment in the urban sector of developing countries there is likely to be a big difference between the wage that is being paid with the use of existing technology (imported or indigenous) and the wage at which labour would be willing to work, given the opportunity, with the use of more labour-intensive technology. If more labour-intensive technology could be developed and applied, there is no reason why the wage rate should not be lower with the use of these techniques, unless there is strong trade union resistance in certain sectors.

If the wage is not assumed to be given but may vary with the technique of production for the reasons outlined above, the conclusion of a conflict between employment and saving in the choice of new techniques is affected considerably. Indeed if the marginal product of labour declines with the labour intensity of production, and the wage is equal to the marginal product, the conflict disappears entirely. The surplus increases in line with increases in the amount of employment.

This is obvious since under these conditions the surplus on *intramarginal* units of labour increases. The formal proof is as follows. From the production function in (12.1) the marginal product of labour is $(a - 2bL)$. Setting the wage equal to the marginal product and substituting for w in the savings function in (12.2) gives

$$S = aL - bL^2 - (a - 2bL)L \qquad (12.6)$$

Partially differentiating (12.6) with respect to L gives

$$\frac{\partial S}{\partial L} = 2bL > 0 \tag{12.7}$$

Thus there is no conflict between saving and employment at positive levels of employment if the wage rate equals the marginal product of labour, both of which fall with the labour intensity of production.

We need not assume that the wage is equal to the marginal product of labour. We can simply assume that the wage falls with the labour intensity of techniques, that is, $w = f(L)$, where $f' < 0$. Now rewrite the savings function as

$$S = aL - bL^2 - f(L)L \tag{12.8}$$

differentiate with respect to L, and set equal to zero:

$$\frac{\partial S}{\partial L} = a - 2bL - [f'(L)L + f(L)] = 0 \tag{12.9}$$

The employment level that maximizes saving is now

$$L* = \frac{a - f(L)}{2b + f'(L)} \tag{12.10}$$

Since $f'(L) < 0$, $L* > L$, and the conflict between employment generation and savings maximization is narrowed. (Compare (12.4) with (12.10)).

Presumably wages cannot fall to zero, however – there must be some minimum below which wages cannot fall. This gives the conclusion that there is no necessary conflict between employment and saving up to the point where the marginal product equals the *minimum* wage, or where $f'(L) = 0$. Beyond that point there will be a conflict. Let us denote the minimum wage as $\bar{w}$. Then, using (12.2) or (12.8) we can find the level of employment at which a conflict sets in by differentiating with respect to L and setting the result equal to zero. This gives

$$L** = (a - \bar{w})/2b \tag{12.11}$$

$L**$ is obviously less than L_1 in Figure 12.4, where w is assumed to be zero, but will probably be much greater than L if the market wage is considerably in excess of the minimum wage at which workers would be willing to work, given the opportunity.

DIFFERENT CLASSES' PROPENSITY TO CONSUME

The alleged conflict between employment and saving also depends on the assumption that the propensity to save out of profits is higher than the propensity to save out of wages. In Figure 12.4 the difference between employment levels L and L_1 depends on the extreme assumption that all profits are saved and all wages are spent. No one would dispute that the propensity to save out of profits is higher than the propensity to save out of wages (indeed there is plenty of empirical evidence to support the assertion), but it is somewhat extreme to argue that there is no saving out of wages and no consumption out of profits. Both consumption out of profits and saving out of wages will reduce the conflict between employment and saving and move the point of maximum surplus away from L towards L_1. To show this, we rewrite the savings function as

$$S = s_p \, (aL - bL^2 - wL) + s_w(wL) \qquad (12.12)$$

where s_p is the propensity to save out of profits and s_w is the propensity to save out of wages. Partially differentiating (12.12) with respect to L and setting it equal to zero gives the level of employment consistent with savings maximization of

$$L^{***} = \frac{s_p a + w(s_w - s_p)}{s_p 2b} \qquad (12.13)$$

If $1 > s_p > s_w > 0$ it can be seen that L^{***} represents a higher level of employment than L in (12.4) or L^{**} in (12.11) if w is replaced by $\bar{w}$. The narrower the difference between s_w and s_p the higher the level of employment before a conflict sets in, until at the limit, when $s_w = s_p$, there is no conflict as long as the marginal product of labour is non-negative. The level of employment at which a conflict sets in will be the same, in other words, as if the wage rate were zero (L_1 in Figure 12.4) and (12.5):

$$L^{***} = L_1 = a/2b$$

Bhalla (1964) has shown how the assumption that workers save alters the marginal calculation of the reinvestible surplus per unit of capital between techniques. His interesting case study is of three cotton spinning techniques in India – two hand spinning techniques and one (relatively capital-intensive) factory spinning technique. Assuming workers do not save, Bhalla finds that the most labour-intensive hand spinning technique has the lowest K/O ratio but that the factory spinning technique has the highest reinvestment ratio. On the assumption that hand spinners do save, however, the most labour-intensive techniques are also shown to have the highest rate of reinvestment per unit of capital.

SUPPORT OF THE UNEMPLOYED

If a particular choice of technology, which is designed to maximize the reinvestible surplus, causes unemployment and the unemployed make claims on society's investible resources, the surplus may ultimately be less than if more labour-intensive techniques had been chosen. There are three main ways in which the unemployed may reduce the investible surplus:

■ If the unemployed remain in the agricultural sector they may depress average product and consume more than they produce, thus reducing the agricultural surplus.

■ If the unemployed remain in the industrial sector they will absorb family savings to support themselves.

■ There may be public support for the unemployed through unemployment insurance programmes, in which case public saving will be reduced below what it otherwise might be.

If 'compensation' to the unemployed in any of the forms outlined above exceeds the difference between the industrial wage and the marginal product using more labour-intensive techniques, it would pay to create extra employment because the difference between consumption and production as a result of expanding employment would be less than the reduction in saving caused by the unemployment. At the limit, of course, if the unemployed 'consumed' resources equal to the value of the industrial wage, it would make no difference if labour was employed up to the point where the marginal product of labour is zero. There is clearly no difference from the point of view of saving between an unemployed man consuming the equivalent of an industrial wage and an employed man with zero marginal product receiving an industrial wage. As long as unemployment absorbs saving, therefore, in whatever form, employment can be higher without reducing the investible surplus to below what it would otherwise have been. Thus as a general proposition it may be said that the extent of the conflict between employment and saving will also depend on the amount of compensation to the unemployed out of the total investible surplus.

ARE CONSUMPTION AND INVESTMENT DISTINCT?

The alleged conflict between employment and saving also assumes either that consumption has no investment component or that present and future consumption are equally productive. Those who argue for techniques to maximize the investible surplus at the expense of employment place no value on present consumption at the margin, and those who argue for techniques to maximize employment are indifferent at the margin between an extra unit of consumption and saving (investment). It can be shown, however, that if consumption has an investment content, and that the productivity of consumption falls as the level of consumption increases, the relative valuation of present consumption increases, favouring more labour-intensive techniques (Thirlwall, 1977). By 'productive' consumption we mean consumption that improves the efficiency of labour, thereby raising the level of income in the same way as normal additions to the capital stock. As long as consumption is productive, therefore, an increase in employment and consumption need not be at the expense of 'investment' for future output.

All too little is known about the precise extent to which low levels of consumption, and particularly food intake, impair working efficiency and productivity. But we do know that the food requirements considered by nutritionists to be necessary for efficient working and healthy living are far greater than the levels achieved by a large minority of the population in developing countries (see Dasgupta, 1993). Calorie deficiency causes loss of body weight, tiredness, listlessness and a deterioration of mental faculties. Protein deficiency causes such conditions as kwashiorkor, and may cause death in children. Vitamin A deficiency causes blindness, and iodine deficiency is a cause of goitre, which leads to cretinism and deaf-mutism. Altogether it has been estimated by the UN Food and Agriculture Organization that at least one billion people in the world suffer from various degrees of malnutrition (see Chaper 3). To the extent that this impairs efficiency and output, and is caused by a lack of consumption, an increase in present consumption may be as valuable at the margin as an extra unit of saving from the point of view of future welfare. The more equal the relative valuation of consumption and saving at the margin, the less the conflict between employment generation in the present and the level of future output.

TAXES AND SUBSIDIES

It has been assumed so far that savings and employment depend exclusively on the choice of technique. In practice, of course, governments can tax and subsidize to achieve desired ends, and this they can do to reconcile the conflict between employment and saving. As Sen (1969) has remarked:

> the total amount of income to be saved can be determined by the planner in any way he likes . . . If this is true then the link snaps between the choice of techniques and the proportion of income saved. The technical choice may be made with the main purpose of maximising the amount of output, and the proportion of the output to be invested can be decided at a separate stage.

Consider again Figure 12.4, which is redrawn here as Figure 12.5. By the choice of techniques alone, maximization of the surplus XY means a sacrifice of employment L_1L. Or employment L_1 means a sacrifice of savings equal to Y_1Y_2. Now suppose that the government possesses the power to tax and subsidize. To employ L_1 requires a shadow wage of zero: that is, a subsidy to employers equal to the full value of the wage. The employers' surplus will now be X_1L_1, but since workers receive the market wage and all wages are consumed, consumption will still be, Y_1L_1, and the investible surplus, X_1Y_1. The question is, can tax policy in the new situation preserve the level of the surplus XY generated by the more capital-intensive technology? The answer must be yes, provided the propensity to consume is greater than zero. The total wage bill is Y_1L_1 and it is desired to reduce consumption out of the wage bill by Y_1Y_2. Consumption will fall by

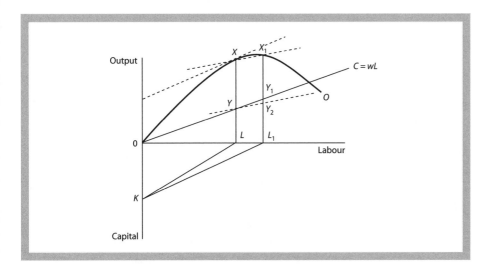

Figure 12.5 Preserving the level of saving through taxation

the amount of tax times the propensity to consume (c). Hence the level of tax raised must be $T = (Y_1 Y_2)/c$. If the wage bill is, say, £1,000, $Y_1 Y_2$ is £100 and c is 0.8, then the tax raised must be £100/0.8 = £125.

In this example the preservation of the level of saving is quite easily accomplished while moving from the more capital-intensive to labour-intensive techniques. If, of course, a fairly high level of taxation already exists, and there is no scope for further taxation, subsidization and taxation will not be a feasible means of reconciliation. In practice, however, the presumption must be that developing countries are not yet at their taxable capacity, and that the subsidization of labour, coupled with appropriate tax policy, is a possible policy.

Some care must be taken, however, over the form of taxation. For example if the wage is fixed in real terms, indirect taxes that raise prices will reduce the real wage, and the money wage will have to rise to compensate. Since the money wage is the cost to the employer, subsidies will then have to be increased. The imposition of indirect taxes to finance subsidies may lead to a spiral of increased taxation, inflation and subsidization. Direct taxes on workers' incomes may also be counterproductive if workers bid for money-wage increases to maintain disposable income. The only feasible taxes to finance subsidies may be on exports or luxury consumption goods, which will not affect the real income of the broad mass of the working class. While theoretically, therefore, a policy of labour subsidization financed by taxation may reconcile the conflict between employment and saving, it may run into a number of practical difficulties.

All of the factors discussed that may lead to an increase in the labour intensity of production without impairing the investible surplus may either be thought of as additive, or any one of them by itself may be powerful enough to push employment close to L_1 in Figure 12.4 without loss of saving or its benefits.

CONCLUSION

It has become part of conventional wisdom, and there may be a good deal of truth in the assertion, that a major cause of the growth of urban unemployment in developing countries lies in the application of 'inappropriate' production techniques because of the limited choice of techniques available, both from within the countries and from outside. The choice is limited from within owing to the absence of a domestic capital goods sector, and it is limited from without because the techniques imported reflect the labour-saving bias of technical progress in the developed countries from which they come. The application of 'inappropriate' technology not only exacerbates unemployment, but perpetuates the dualistic structure of developing countries, increases income inequality, may worsen the foreign exchange position, and in general produces a distorted economy, while at the same time increasing the dependence of developing countries on developed countries.

There is now a strong movement throughout the developing countries in support of the creation of an **intermediate technology** using more labour per unit of capital and fewer foreign inputs. What is required is a whole spectrum of techniques to suit different circumstances, from which developing countries can choose. For this to transpire, developing countries need to encourage the establishment of their own capital goods industries; and more R&D is required both within, and on behalf of, poor countries. An **international technology bank** would be a useful starting point, giving countries access to technological blueprints from different sources.

The capital intensity of production is also a function of the composition of output. There are often many ways of meeting a given need, some of which may be more labour-intensive than others. Where this is so, such as in transport, nutrition, housing and so on, serious consideration should be given to the most labour-intensive way of meeting such needs, consistent with other objectives.

Finally, the location of activity needs to be considered. Whatever technology is applied in the modern sector, it will have implications for the rural sector that will rebound on the modern sector. We saw in Chapter 5 that the creation of more modern sector jobs may encourage more migrants than the number of jobs created, thus increasing urban unemployment. This would seem to call for the location of new labour-intensive industries in the rural sector, to curb the flow of migrants and ease urban unemployment.

To conclude our analysis, we have seen that there are many reasons for believing that the potential conflicts inherent in the choice of new techniques between employment and saving on the one hand, and between employment and output on the other, have been exaggerated, and that techniques can be more labour-intensive without impairing the level of the investible surplus or the level of output. It is in the direction of more rural-based labour-intensive projects that development strategy ought to move for maximization of the general welfare.

DISCUSSION QUESTIONS

1 What are the major factors that dictate the choice of techniques in the industrial sector in developing countries?

2 Why did early development theory tend to stress the importance of capital-intensive techniques for rapid economic development?

3 Would the use of more labour-intensive techniques necessarily reduce the size of the investible surplus?

4 Outline the importance for developing countries of promoting their own indigenous capital-goods sector.

5 To what extent are multinational corporations responsible for the relatively high degree of capital intensity of production in the manufacturing sector of developing countries?

6 Outline how a change in the product mix could help to create more employment?

7 Would the use of more labour-intensive technology in the industrial sector in urban areas necessarily reduce the level of urban unemployment?

8 What do you understand by the 'efficiency wage' of labour, and how does this concept help to explain the relative capital intensity of production and goods traded?

9 How can governments help to reconcile the potential conflict between increasing employment by the use of more labour-intensive techniques and raising the level of saving for investment?

10 What would be the best way of encouraging the use of more labour-intensive techniques in developing countries?

NOTES

1. For a lucid discussion of these issues, see Stewart (1977), especially Chapter 6.
2. The capital–output ratio (K/O) may be expressed as the product of the capital–labour ratio and labour requirements per unit of output, that is, $K/O = (K/L)(L/O)$. Techniques with a low K/L may nonetheless have a high K/O because L/O is high – that is, the productivity of labour is low.

WEBSITE ON CHOICE OF TECHNIQUES

UNIDO   www.unido.org

Input–output analysis

Input–output analysis is a planning and forecasting technique with a wide variety of applications. The purpose here is to present the basic elements of the technique without going into its refinements, and to illustrate some of its uses.

An input–output table provides a descriptive set of social accounts, recording purchases by and sales from different sectors of the economy. It provides a snapshot picture at a point in time of the interdependencies between activities in an economy. Tables may be constructed for a whole economy, for a region within an economy or to show flows between regions. They may vary in size and ambitiousness according to the number of sectors identified and the purposes for which they are constructed. The most common type of input–output table at the national and regional level is that recording interindustry transactions showing, in Hirschman's terms, backward and forward linkages in an economy (see Chapter 9).

THE USES OF INPUT–OUTPUT ANALYSIS

Input–output analysis has many uses:

- For **projection and forecasting** purposes: after some manipulation (which we shall consider shortly), an interindustry transactions matrix can provide information to the planner on how much of commodities X_1, X_2, X_3, and so on will be required at some future date, assuming a certain growth rate of national income or final demand. Information of this nature is important if planning is to achieve consistency and future bottlenecks in the productive process are to be avoided.

- For **simulation** purposes: the simulation of development is concerned with what is economically feasible, as opposed to forecasting, which is concerned with what one expects to happen on the basis of a certain set of assumptions. In the case of simulation there is no presumption that the simulated changes in the economy are actually going to occur. If they are economically feasible the changes could occur, but whether they do or do not may depend on a variety of prior changes of an economic or institutional nature that may be outside the planner's control. Using an input–output table for simulation purposes requires first that the feasible changes (for example new activities such as import substitutes) be identified, and then the input–output table can be used to estimate the impact of the changes on the rest of the economy. Again, with some manipulation, the interindustry transactions matrix can then be used to provide answers to such questions as: how will the production requirements of the economy be altered if a new steel mill is introduced, or what will be the repercussions on the economy if a series of import-saving schemes are introduced?

- To **forecast import requirements** and the balance-of-payments effects of given changes in final demand.

- To **forecast labour requirements** consistent with a given growth target.

- To **forecast investment requirements** consistent with a given growth target if information is available on incremental capital–output ratios sector by sector.

- To calculate the **matrix multiplier** attached to different activities; that is, the direct and indirect effects on the total output of *all* activities in the system from a unit change in the demand for the output of any *one* activity.

- To show the strength of **linkages** between activities in an economy.

- To portray the **technology** of an economy.

Three major stages must be gone through before knowledge of input–output relations can be put to practical use in the planning field in the manner described above. The first step must be the **construction of the input–output table** itself, recording the relevant transactions. The second stage involves the derivation of what are called **input–output coefficients** (or input coefficients for short). The third task is the inversion of the so-called **Leontief matrix** to obtain a **general solution.** The content of these stages, and the underlying assumptions of input–output analysis, will become clear as we examine the three stages in turn. We shall wait until the end, however, to spell out the assumptions explicitly, and to discuss the shortcomings of input–output analysis for planning purposes.

Table 13.1 Input–output table

Purchases by / Sales by		Intermediate users — Industries					Final demand — Consumption		Investment (I)	Exports (E)	Total demand
		1	2	3	j	n	Private (C)	Government (G)			
Processing Industries	1	X_{11}	X_{12}	X_{13}	X_{1j}	X_{1n}	X_{1C}	X_{1G}	X_{1I}	X_{1E}	X_1
	2	X_{21}	X_{22}	X_{23}	X_{2j}	X_{2n}	X_{2C}	X_{2G}	X_{2I}	X_{2E}	X_2
	3	X_{31}	X_{32}	X_{33}	X_{3j}	X_{3n}	X_{3C}	X_{3G}	X_{3I}	X_{3E}	X_3
	i	X_{i1}	X_{i2}	X_{i3}	X_{ij}	X_{in}	X_{iC}	X_{iG}	X_{iI}	X_{iE}	X_i
	n	X_{n1}	X_{n2}	X_{n3}	X_{nj}	X_{nn}	X_{nC}	X_{nG}	X_{nI}	X_{nE}	X_n
Payments Wages		W_1	W_2	W_3	W_j	W_n	W_C	W_G			W
Rent		R_1	R_2	R_3	R_j	R_n	R_C	R_G			R
Interest		D_1	D_2	D_3	D_j	D_n	D_C	D_G			D
Profits		P_1	P_2	P_3	P_j	P_n	P_C	P_G			P
Imports		M_1	M_2	M_3	M_j	M_n	M_C	M_G	M_I	M_E	M
Total supply		X_1	X_2	X_3	X_j	X_n	C	G	I	E	

THE INPUT–OUTPUT TABLE

The layout of a typical input–output table, and the sectors and transactions distinguished, are shown in Table 13.1. The table is divided horizontally into a **processing** and **payments** sector, and vertically to distinguish between **intermediate users** of goods and factors of production, and **final users.** Thus the upper left-hand quadrant of the table records interindustry transactions; the lower left-hand quadrant gives the payments by industries to the factors of production and to foreigners for the purchase of imports; the upper right-hand quadrant gives the final demand for goods and services produced (including exports); and the lower right-hand quadrant gives the direct sales of factors of production and imports to final users, for example the private consumption sector buys domestic help, and the government sector 'consumes' civil servants!

The notation used in Table 13.1 to denote the various transactions should be easy to follow. Take first the processing sector. X stands for the value of output, and the two subscripts denote the origin of the output and its destination, respectively. Generalizing, X_{ij} denotes sales by industry i to industry j or inputs into industry j from industry i, where $i = 1, \ldots, n$, and $j = 1, \ldots, n$. The disposal of outputs to final users can be represented in exactly the same way.

In the payments sector, the subscript simply refers to the industry or final demand sector making the factor payment, and the same for imports.

We can see, then, that in the processing half of the table each row shows how the output of each industry is disposed of, and each column shows the origins of inputs into each sector. The sum of each row gives the total demand for each industry's output.

In the payments half of the table, the sum of each row gives the value of the various factor payments, and the sum of each column in the bottom left-hand quadrant gives the total value-added (in the form of factor payments) to the inputs bought by the different industries.

In the intermediate sector, the sum of the columns gives the value of the total output of each industry, that is, the sum of the value of inputs in the processing half plus the sum of value-added in the payments half plus imported inputs. Thus the columns in the intermediate sector and the rows in the processing sector both add up to the total value of domestic production. Let us demonstrate this proposition using the notation of our table. Call industry (1) the coal industry. The (domestic) output of coal must equal all its intermediate uses $X_{11}, \ldots, X_{1n}$ plus all its final uses. We thus have a row for the coal industry of the form:

$$X_1 = \sum_{j=1}^{n} X_{1j} + X_{1C} + X_{1G} + X_{1I} + X_{1E} \qquad (13.1)$$

But the (domestic) output of coal must also equal the value of inputs into the coal industry, plus the value added to those inputs by employing factors of production to work on them, plus imports. We thus have a column for the coal industry of the form:

$$X_1 = \sum_{i=1}^{n} X_{i1} + W_1 + R_1 + D_1 + P_1 + M_1 \qquad (13.2)$$

INPUT COEFFICIENTS

The second stage in the practical use of input–output analysis is to derive input coefficients from the interindustry section of the transactions table. This is done very simply by dividing each column entry in the matrix by the sum of the column. If we denote the input coefficient by a_{ij} then $a_{ij} = X_{ij}/X_j$. The input coefficient a_{ij} thus gives the amount of purchases from each industry to support one unit of output of industry j. If output is measured in pounds sterling and a_{ij} equals 0.1, this means that every pound's worth of output of industry j will require 10p worth of input from industry i.

$X_{ij} = a_{ij}X_j$, and our (13.1) in general form can now be written as

$$X_i = \sum_{j=1}^{n} a_{ij}X_j + X_{iC} + X_{iG} + X_{iI} + X_{iE} \qquad (13.3)$$

With a series of equations of this nature for each sector, representing the rows in the processing sector of the transactions matrix, it is possible, through the use of the input coefficients and with the aid of matrix algebra, to work out what the effect will be of changes in demand for the output of one sector on the output of all other sectors. Equation (13.3) for all industries, $i = 1, \ldots, n$, becomes a system of n simultaneous equations in n unknown variables, which can be solved if certain conditions are satisfied. The technique is to specify the final demands for each industry, i, and then to determine X_i from the new values of the input requirements, which give both the *direct* and the *indirect* requirements from each industry.

In specifying the final demands for each industry, one obtains from (13.3) the following set of relations for each industry:

$$X_i - \sum_{j=1}^{n} a_{ij} X_j = Y_i \quad i = 1, \ldots, n \tag{13.4}$$

where Y_i is total final demand, X_i is total output, and $\sum_{j=1}^{n} a_{ij} X_j$ is the sum of intermediate demands. The solution to the problem of finding all the values of X_i which satisfy all the final demands may be written in the form

$$X_i = b_{i1} Y_1 + b_{i2} Y_2 + \ldots + b_{in} Y_n \quad (i = 1 \ldots, n) \tag{13.5}$$

The coefficients $b_{i1}, \ldots, n$ give – per pound of delivery to final demand made by the industries listed along the top of the interindustry matrix – the total output directly and indirectly required from the industries listed at the left of the matrix. Equation (13.5) therefore gives the total output (X) of industry (i) consistent with the final demands for all other industries' products ($Y_1, \ldots, Y_n$).

These equations for each industry represent a transformation of the original (13.4), in which a new set of constants, b_{ij}s, are derived from the original parameters (a_{ij}s). The new equations are referred to as the **general solution** and can be found, in normal cases involving more than two or three equations with two or three unknowns, by the technique called **inversion of the matrix,** that is, the inversion of the set of (13.4) in matrix form.

Let us now express our input–output system in matrix form and, using a little elementary matrix algebra, show how a general solution is arrived at by matrix inversion. For ease of exposition, and also to compare our results using a simple iterative procedure, we shall take two sectors and two outputs only.

With two industries the equations of type (13.4) become:

$$\begin{aligned} X_1 - a_{11} X_1 - a_{12} X_2 &= Y_1 \\ X_2 - a_{21} X_1 - a_{22} X_2 &= Y_2 \end{aligned} \tag{13.6}$$

Or in matrix form:

$$\begin{bmatrix} 1 - a_{11} & - a_{12} \\ - a_{21} & 1 - a_{22} \end{bmatrix} \begin{bmatrix} X_1 \\ X_2 \end{bmatrix} = \begin{bmatrix} Y_1 \\ Y_2 \end{bmatrix} \tag{13.7}[1]$$

The system in (13.7) may also be written as

$$\left(\begin{bmatrix} 1 & 0 \\ 0 & 1 \end{bmatrix} - \begin{bmatrix} a_{11} & a_{12} \\ a_{21} & a_{22} \end{bmatrix} \right) \begin{bmatrix} X_1 \\ X_2 \end{bmatrix} = \begin{bmatrix} Y_1 \\ Y_2 \end{bmatrix} \tag{13.8}$$

where $\begin{bmatrix} 1 & 0 \\ 0 & 1 \end{bmatrix}$ is an identity matrix $(I)^2$ and $\begin{bmatrix} a_{11} & a_{12} \\ a_{21} & a_{22} \end{bmatrix}$ is the matrix of input–output coefficients (A). In matrix notation our input–output system in (13.8) may be written as

$$(I - A)X = Y \tag{13.9}$$

$I - A$ is often called the **Leontief matrix**, named after the 'father' of input–output analysis, Wassily Leontief. It follows that

$$X = (I - A)^{-1}Y \tag{13.10}$$

that is, to solve for X, given Y, we need to find the inverse of the Leontief matrix, $I - A$.

A DIGRESSION ON MATRIX INVERSION

The inverse of a matrix, Z, is another matrix, B, which when multiplied by Z gives the identity matrix, I. This corresponds to the inversion of real numbers in ordinary algebra, where b is the inverse of a if $ab = 1$. Similarly, in matrix algebra B is the inverse of Z if $ZB = I$. Thus the identity matrix in matrix algebra plays a similar role to the number 1 in ordinary algebra. Hence B is the inverse of Z if

$$\begin{bmatrix} z_{11} & z_{12} \\ z_{21} & z_{22} \end{bmatrix} \begin{bmatrix} b_{11} & b_{12} \\ b_{21} & b_{22} \end{bmatrix} = \begin{bmatrix} 1 & 0 \\ 0 & 1 \end{bmatrix} \tag{13.11}$$

By multiplying the matrices, (13.11) would give four equations in four unknowns, and it would then be possible to solve for the elements in the inverse matrix, b_{11}, b_{12}, b_{21}, b_{22}. By simple arithmetic:

$$b_{11} = \frac{z_{22}}{z_{11}z_{22} - z_{12}z_{21}}$$

$$b_{12} = \frac{-z_{12}}{z_{11}z_{22} - z_{12}z_{21}}$$

$$b_{21} = \frac{-z_{21}}{z_{11}z_{22} - z_{12}z_{21}}$$

$$b_{22} = \frac{z_{11}}{z_{11}z_{22} - z_{12}z_{21}}$$

Note that the denominator of the elements of the inverse matrix is the same in all cases, namely the product of the elements of the principal diagonal in the Z matrix minus the product of the other diagonal. This is called the **determinant** of the matrix.

In the language of matrix algebra, **the inverse of a matrix is the adjoint of the matrix divided by the determinant,** that is

$$Z^{-1} = \frac{1}{|Z|} \quad \text{adjoint } Z \tag{13.12}$$

where $|\ |$ denotes determinant. In general (for a square matrix of any dimension) we can write the determinant as

$$|Z| = z_{11}|M_{11}| - z_{12}|M_{12}| + \ldots - z_{1j}|M_{1j}| \qquad (13.13)$$

where $|M_{11}|, |M_{12}|$ and so on are subdeterminants of Z – called **minors.** Each element in Z has a minor. For example, in the 2×2 case the minor of the element z_{11} is denoted by $|M_{11}|$ and is obtained by deleting the first row and first column of the Z matrix. Thus the $|M_{11}|$ of Z is z_{22}. Similarly the $|M_{12}|$ of Z is z_{21}.

It follows from (13.13) in the 2×2 case that

$$|Z| = \begin{bmatrix} z_{11} & z_{12} \\ z_{21} & z_{22} \end{bmatrix} = z_{11}z_{22} - z_{12}z_{21} \qquad (13.14)$$

which is the denominator of the elements of the inverse matrix $b_{11}, b_{12}, b_{21}, b_{22}$ above. In the 3×3 case we would have, using (13.13) and the rules for obtaining minors:

$$|Z| = \begin{bmatrix} z_{11} & z_{12} & z_{13} \\ z_{21} & z_{22} & z_{23} \\ z_{31} & z_{32} & z_{33} \end{bmatrix} = z_{11}\begin{bmatrix} z_{22} & z_{23} \\ z_{32} & z_{33} \end{bmatrix} - z_{12}\begin{bmatrix} z_{21} & z_{23} \\ z_{31} & z_{33} \end{bmatrix} + z_{13}\begin{bmatrix} z_{21} & z_{22} \\ z_{31} & z_{32} \end{bmatrix}$$

$$= z_{11}(z_{22}z_{33} - z_{32}z_{23}) - z_{12}(z_{21}z_{33} - z_{23}z_{31}) + z_{13}(z_{21}z_{32} - z_{22}z_{31})$$

and similarly for matrices of higher dimensions.

The adjoint of Z is defined as the transpose of all the cofactors of the matrix. The cofactor of an element is that element's minor with the appropriate sign attached. If the sum of the subscripts (*ij*) of the minor is an even number (for example M_{11}) the cofactor will have a positive sign. If the sum of the subscripts is an odd number (for example M_{12}), the cofactor will have a negative sign. In the 2×2 case the minors of the matrix Z will be

$$M = \begin{bmatrix} z_{22} & z_{21} \\ z_{12} & z_{11} \end{bmatrix}$$

The cofactor matrix will therefore be

$$C = \begin{bmatrix} z_{22} & -z_{21} \\ -z_{12} & z_{11} \end{bmatrix}$$

Now the transpose of a matrix C is another matrix, C', with the rows and columns interchanged. Hence

$$C' = \begin{bmatrix} z_{22} & -z_{12} \\ -z_{21} & z_{11} \end{bmatrix} \qquad (13.15)$$

Thus from our definition of an inverse matrix in (13.12) we have in the 2×2 case from (13.14) and (13.15):

$$Z^{-1} = \frac{1}{|Z|} \times \text{adjoint } Z = \frac{1}{z_{11}z_{22} - z_{12}z_{21}} \times \begin{bmatrix} z_{22} & -z_{12} \\ -z_{21} & z_{11} \end{bmatrix} \tag{13.16}$$

If B is the inverse of Z, then the elements of the inverse $b_{11}, b_{12}, b_{21}, b_{22}$ can be seen to be the same as those derived by simple arithmetic from the system in (13.11).

THE GENERAL SOLUTION TO THE INPUT–OUTPUT MODEL

It is clear from (13.10) that once the Leontief matrix $(I - A)$ has been inverted it is possible to obtain a general solution to the simultaneous equation system of n unknown outputs (the Xs). From what we have said above about matrix inversion, $(I - A)^{-1}$ is some matrix that we can call B, which when multiplied by $I - A$ gives the identity matrix I. We now have

$$X = BY \tag{13.17}$$

In other words, each industry's output is equal to the sum of the elements of the final demand matrix Y (which is a column vector $n \times 1$) times the coefficients of the inverse of the matrix $(I - A)$. In the 2×2 case:

$$\begin{bmatrix} X_1 \\ X_2 \end{bmatrix} = \begin{bmatrix} b_{11} & b_{12} \\ b_{21} & b_{22} \end{bmatrix} \begin{bmatrix} Y_1 \\ Y_2 \end{bmatrix} \tag{13.18}$$

This is exactly what is stated in equation form in (13.5). By matrix multiplication:

$$X_1 = b_{11}Y_1 + b_{12}Y_2$$

$$X_2 = b_{21}Y_1 + b_{22}Y_2$$

In summary notation:

$$X_i = \sum_{j=1}^{n} b_{ij}Y_j \ (i = 1, \ldots n) \tag{13.19}$$

and for changes in Y:

$$\Delta X_i = \sum_{j=1}^{n} b_{ij}\Delta Y_j \ (i = 1, \ldots n) \tag{13.20}$$

The outputs of all industries will be consistent with the final demand for the products of all industries. b_{ij} gives the direct and indirect requirements from industries $1, \ldots, n$ per pound of final demand for the products of industries $1, \ldots, n$. The b_{ij} column sum gives the so-called **matrix multiplier** of each of the industries listed at the top of the columns. For example the matrix multiplier attached to industry 1 is $b_{11} + b_{21}$. The matrix multiplier is a useful concept in planning because it gives a measure of the impact

Table 13.2 Input-output coefficients

Sales	Purchases	Coal	Steel
Coal		0.1	0.4
Steel		0.3	0.2

of the expansion of one activity on the level of output of all other activities in the system. It is therefore possible to identify which activities may give the greatest stimulus to others through the linkages in the system.

Now let us consider a simple arithmetical example. Suppose that the direct input–output coefficients (a_{ij}) for the steel and coal industries of a country are as given in Table 13.2. We wish to show what the output of coal and steel must be to satisfy certain final demands for steel and coal:

$$A = \begin{bmatrix} 0.1 & 0.4 \\ 0.3 & 0.2 \end{bmatrix}$$

$$I - A = \begin{bmatrix} 1 & 0 \\ 0 & 1 \end{bmatrix} - \begin{bmatrix} 0.1 & 0.4 \\ 0.3 & 0.2 \end{bmatrix}$$

$$= \begin{bmatrix} 0.9 & -0.4 \\ -0.3 & 0.8 \end{bmatrix}$$

By matrix inversion to derive the elements of the inverse matrix:

$b_{11} = 1\frac{1}{3}$
$b_{12} = \frac{2}{3}$
$b_{21} = \frac{1}{2}$
$b_{22} = 1\frac{1}{2}$

Thus

$$(I - A)^{-1} = \begin{bmatrix} 1\frac{1}{3} & \frac{2}{3} \\ \frac{1}{2} & 1\frac{1}{2} \end{bmatrix} = B$$

If final demands are

$$Y = \begin{bmatrix} 15 \\ 10 \end{bmatrix}$$

then total industry outputs consistent with this final demand for both products would be

$$X = \begin{bmatrix} 1\frac{1}{3} & \frac{2}{3} \\ \frac{1}{2} & 1\frac{1}{2} \end{bmatrix} \begin{bmatrix} 15 \\ 10 \end{bmatrix}$$

$$= \begin{bmatrix} 1\frac{1}{3} \times 15 + \frac{2}{3} \times 10 \\ \frac{1}{2} \times 15 + 1\frac{1}{2} \times 10 \end{bmatrix} = \begin{bmatrix} 26\frac{2}{3} \\ 22\frac{1}{2} \end{bmatrix}$$

or coal output $= 1\frac{1}{3} \times 15 + \frac{2}{3} \times 10 = 26\frac{2}{3}$, and steel output $= \frac{1}{2} \times 15 + 1\frac{1}{2} \times 10 = 22\frac{1}{2}$.

We can also solve for the *change* in each sector's output following a change in final demand. Suppose, for instance, the final demand for steel is projected to rise from 10 to 15. From our inverse matrix we can work out by how much coal and steel output will have to increase in order to meet this increase in final demand. The new final demand vector is

$$Y = \begin{bmatrix} 15 \\ 15 \end{bmatrix}$$

and the output of the two industries consistent with this new demand vector is

$$X = \begin{bmatrix} 1\frac{1}{3} & \frac{2}{3} \\ \frac{1}{2} & 1\frac{1}{2} \end{bmatrix} \begin{bmatrix} 15 \\ 15 \end{bmatrix} = \begin{bmatrix} 30 \\ 30 \end{bmatrix}$$

Therefore coal output must rise by $3\frac{1}{3}$ from $26\frac{2}{3}$, and steel output must rise by $7\frac{1}{2}$ from $22\frac{1}{2}$ to 30. Given the inverse matrix, any manipulation of the final demand vector is possible and a general solution can be reached.

Our result using matrix methods can now be checked by going back to the original 2×2 matrix of direct input coefficients given in Table 13.2 and calculating step by step the direct and indirect demands made upon the steel and coal industries as a result of the increase in final demand for steel. The task is laborious, but let us proceed if only to underline the beauty and usefulness of matrix methods.

We use an iterative procedure analogous to that used to solve a single-equation national income model with a given propensity to consume and a postulated change in autonomous demand. In interindustry analysis, however, there is more than one 'multiplier' coefficient to contend with and there may be several changes in final demands.

The ultimate change in output must equal the sum of the direct and indirect effects of the change in final demand. We assume that the first increment of production of commodity X_i is equal to the increase in final demand for X_i. The first-round effects on production in each sector are then given by the input–output coefficients. The second-round effects are given by derived demands in the first round multiplied by the input–output coefficients, and so on.

In our two-sector example, the primary effect of an increase in demand for steel of 5 is an increment of steel production of the same amount, that is, the primary effect on steel is 5:

The first-round effect on steel is
$0.2 \times 5 = 1$

The first-round effect on coal is
$0.4 \times 5 = 2$

These derived demands, following the initial increase in demand, are then multiplied by their respective input coefficients. Thus

$$\left.\begin{array}{l}\text{the second-round effect}\\\text{on steel is } 0.2 \times 1 = 0.2\\\text{and } 0.3 \times 2 = 0.6\end{array}\right\} = 0.8$$

and

$$\left.\begin{array}{l}\text{the second-round effect on}\\\text{coal is } 0.4 \times 1 = 0.4\\\text{and } 0.1 \times 2 = 0.2\end{array}\right\} = 0.6$$

The second-round derived demand figures are further multiplied by their respective input coefficients. Thus

$$\left.\begin{array}{l}\text{the third-round effect on}\\\text{steel is } 0.2 \times 0.8 = 0.16\\\text{and } 0.3 \times 0.6 = 0.18\end{array}\right\} = 0.34$$

and

$$\left.\begin{array}{l}\text{the third-round effect on}\\\text{coal is } 0.4 \times 0.8 = 0.32\\\text{and } 0.1 \times 0.6 = 0.06\end{array}\right\} = 0.38$$

and so on,
Summing after three rounds, we have

Change in steel output $= 5 + 1 + 0.8 + 0.34 = 7.14.$

Change in coal output $= 2 + 0.6 + 0.38 = 2.98.$

These compare with our *final* results by matrix methods of $7\frac{1}{2}$ and $3\frac{1}{3}$ for steel and coal, respectively.

Calculation by this iterative procedure is clearly tedious and becomes impossibly complicated with more than five or six sectors to cope with. Similarly, matrix inversion by hand is laborious and complicated, but fortunately there is recourse to the computer. When it comes to input–output work for practical policy-making purposes, a computer is indispensable. To be of much practical use, the degree of disaggregation required in input–output analysis is such that work would be impossible without mechanical aids. A regular computer can invert a 30 × 30 matrix in less than a second.

FORECASTING IMPORT REQUIREMENTS

What happens to imports and the balance of payments when there is a change in final demand can also be estimated from the general solution to the input–output model. Exports are assumed to be determined exogenously, but imports are endogenous. The changes in the import requirements of industries (intermediate imports) may be calculated by multiplying the required change in each industry's output by the industry's import coefficient (defined as $m_i = M_i/X_i$), and summing. Imports to meet the new final demand directly may be calculated in the same way by multiplying the change in each component of final demand by the import-content coefficient of final demand, for example where m_c is defined as the ratio of consumption imports to total consumption, m_I is the import coefficient attached to investment and so on.

If imports into each industry are disaggregated by the column cells showing which activity they belong to, then total intermediate imports may be written as

$$MX = M[I - A]^{-1}Y = M*Y \tag{13.21}$$

where M is the matrix of direct import coefficients, and $M*$ is the matrix of direct plus indirect import coefficients. In the 2 × 2 case we have

$$\begin{bmatrix} m_{11} & m_{12} \\ m_{21} & m_{22} \end{bmatrix} \begin{bmatrix} X_1 \\ X_2 \end{bmatrix} = \begin{bmatrix} \begin{bmatrix} m_{11} & m_{12} \\ m_{21} & m_{22} \end{bmatrix} \begin{bmatrix} b_{11} & b_{12} \\ b_{21} & b_{22} \end{bmatrix} \end{bmatrix} \begin{bmatrix} Y_1 \\ Y_2 \end{bmatrix} \tag{13.22}$$

Therefore

$$M_1 = m_{11}X_1 + m_{12}X_2 = (m_{11}b_{11} + m_{12}b_{21})\ Y_1 + (m_{11}b_{12} + m_{12}b_{22})\ Y_2$$

and

$$M_2 = m_{21}X_1 + m_{22}X_2 = (m_{21}b_{11} + m_{22}b_{21})\ Y_1 + (m_{21}b_{12} + m_{22}b_{22})\ Y_2$$

If imports also go directly into final demand we have

$$\begin{bmatrix} M_1 \\ M_2 \end{bmatrix} = \begin{bmatrix} m_{1I} & m_{1C} \\ m_{2I} & m_{2C} \end{bmatrix} \begin{bmatrix} I \\ C \end{bmatrix} = M^D Y^D \tag{13.23}$$

(assuming just two components of final demand: investment [I] and consumption [C]). Therefore

$$M_1 = m_{1I}I + m_{1C}C$$

and

$$M_2 = m_{2I}I + m_{2C}C$$

Total imports $= M*Y + M^D Y^D$

Changes in import requirements may then be calculated by specifying the changes in final demand, ΔY and ΔY^D, and assuming that the average and marginal import coefficients are the same.

Some imports will be competitive with domestic production; others not. In either case the input–output model may be simulated to calculate the effects throughout the system of import substitution. In the case of replacing competitive imports, each of the column entries would have to be adjusted and the input–output coefficients recalculated. In the case of non-competitive imports, a new row and column would have to be added to the interindustry matrix, and the Leontief inverse recalculated to ascertain the likely impact.

If imports into each industry remain aggregated, as in Table 13.1 (p. 385), we may simply write the aggregate level of imports as

$$M = \sum_{i=1}^{n} m_i X_i + m_C C + m_G G + m_I I + m_E E \tag{13.24}$$

Since $\Delta X_i = \sum_{i=1}^{n} b_{ij} \Delta Y_j$ (from (13.20)), changes in import requirements may be calculated as

$$\Delta M = \sum_{i=1}^{n} \sum_{j=1}^{n} m_i b_{ij} \Delta Y_j + m_C \Delta C + m_G \Delta G + m_I \Delta I + m_E \Delta E \tag{13.25}$$

In the 2 × 2 case:

$$\Delta M = m_1(b_{11}\Delta Y_1 + b_{12}\Delta Y_2) + m_2(b_{21}\Delta Y_1 + b_{22}\Delta Y_2) + m_C \Delta C \\ + m_G \Delta G + m_I \Delta I + m_E \Delta E \tag{13.26}$$

FORECASTING LABOUR REQUIREMENTS

If we have estimates of employment coefficients industry by industry, defined as $1_i = L_i/X_i$, we can estimate labour requirements from the input–output model, given specified changes in final demand. Total labour requirements can be expressed as

$$L = \sum_{i=1}^{n} 1_i X_i + 1_y Y \tag{13.27}$$

where 1_y is the employment coefficient of the final demand sector, for example of government employment of civil servants.

Assuming the marginal employment coefficient is equal to the average, the change in labour requirements is

$$\Delta L = \sum_{i=1}^{n} 1_i \Delta X_i + 1_y \Delta Y \tag{13.28}$$

and since $\Delta X_i = \sum_{j=1}^{n} b_{ij} \Delta Y_j$

$$\Delta L = \sum_{i=1}^{n} \sum_{j=1}^{n} 1_i b_{ij} \Delta Y_j + 1_y \Delta Y \tag{13.29}$$

Thus given the specified changes in final demand for each industry's output (ΔY_j), and given the elements of the Leontief inverse (b_{ij}), the change in total labour requirements can be forecast.

FORECASTING INVESTMENT REQUIREMENTS

Changes in output to meet specified changes in final demand over a plan period will require additions to the capital stock. In a normal input–output table such as Table 13.1, all that is usually specified is the total amount of each sector's output that is allocated for the purpose of investment, without specifying the activities it goes into. In principle, however, a table of investment flows or capital transactions could be prepared, just as for current inputs, as in Table 13.3.

From this table the incremental capital–output ratios (ICORs) for each sector can be calculated by dividing each column entry by the *change* in output of the industry concerned over an accounting period. We would then have a matrix of incremental capital–output coefficients, with the sum of the sector coefficients adding up to the incremental capital–output ratio (c_i) for the industry as a whole, as in Table 13.4. In practice, with a number of sectors the subsectoral ratios will all be very small.

Table 13.4 says that industry 1 needs four units of extra capital from industry 2 to produce a unit flow of output, and one unit of extra capital from itself. Likewise for industry 2, 0.75 units of capital are needed from industry 1 and 2.25 units from itself to produce a unit flow of output.

The total investment requirements may then be written as

$$I = \Delta K = \sum_{i=1}^{n} c_i \Delta X_i \qquad (13.30)$$

where $c_i = \Delta K_i / \Delta X_i$ is the aggregate ICOR for industry i.

Since $\Delta X_i = \sum_{j=1}^{n} b_{ij} \Delta Y_j$, we have

$$I = \Delta K = \sum_{i=1}^{n} \sum_{j=1}^{n} c_i b_{ij} \Delta Y_j \qquad (13.31)$$

Table 13.3 Interindustry capital transactions

Industries	1	2
1	I_{11}	I_{12}
2	I_{21}	I_{22}

Table 13.4 Matrix of capital–output coefficients

Industries	1	2
1	1.0	0.75
2	4.0	2.25
Aggregate ICOR (c_i)	5.0	3.00

Thus, given the specified changes in final demand, the elements of the Leontief inverse and information on investment flows and capital–output ratios, investment requirements industry by industry, and in total, can be forecast.

BACKWARD AND FORWARD LINKAGES

The essence of the interindustry transactions table is that it shows linkages between industries. Backward linkages refer to where an industry obtains its inputs and forward linkages refer to where an industry's output goes. A precise numerical measure of the extent of an industry's backward and forward linkages is possible. The **backward linkages** of any jth sector (L_{Bj}) can be measured as the ratio of purchased intermediate inputs to the total value of production, that is:

$$L_{Bj} = \frac{\sum_i X_{ij}}{X_j} = \sum_i a_{ij}$$

The **forward linkages** of any ith sector (L_{Fi}) can be measured as the ratio of interindustry demand to total demand, that is:

$$L_{Fi} = \frac{\sum_j X_{ij}}{X_i}$$

where X_i is the sum of interindustry (ΣX_{ij}) and final demand (Y_i) for industry i. Industries can be ranked according to their backward or forward linkages, or their sum. Both give a measure of the stimulus that one industry may give to others.

TRIANGULARIZED INPUT–OUTPUT TABLES

A visual impression of the structural interdependence of different industries can be obtained by triangularizing the interindustry transactions matrix to show interdependence on both the input and output sides. Two criteria may be applied in triangularizing matrices, or a combination of both. One is to list the sector with the largest number of zero-output entries at the top of the table and the others in descending order. The second is to order rows so that final demand as a proportion of total output declines as one reads down the table. Either way a line drawn from the top left-hand corner of the table to the bottom right should reveal a big difference in the magnitude of the cell entries, and the number of zeros between the 'bottom' and 'top' triangles, as illustrated in Table 13.5. In real life the triangularized matrix would not look quite so symmetrical, but it illustrates the principle. In this example it can be seen at a glance that industry 5 has high backward linkages but no forward linkages, while industry 4 has strong forward linkages but no backward linkages. One useful thing about triangularizing matrices for different countries is that other countries can see at a glance what industries they might encourage if the prevailing economic conditions are similar.

Table 13.5 Hypothetical triangularized interindustry transactions matrix

Industries	5	2	3	1	4
5	3	0	0	0	0
2	8	1	0	0	0
3	6	2	3	0	0
1	12	4	4	2	0
4	9	8	6	2	2

THE ASSUMPTIONS OF INPUT–OUTPUT ANALYSIS[3]

Now let us briefly turn to the assumptions underlying input–output analysis and consider their validity. The basic assumptions of traditional (Leontief-type) input–output models are fourfold:

- There are no joint products, which means that each commodity is produced by only one industry and each industry produces only one product.
- The technical coefficients are fixed, that is, there is no substitutability between inputs, so that input functions are linear and the marginal input coefficient is equal to the average.
- The total effect of carrying on several activities is the sum of the separate effects, ruling out external economies and diseconomies.
- Technical progress is static and production is subject to constant returns.

All these assumptions are necessary if the input–output coefficients are to be constant and the estimated inputs and outputs are to balance at the aggregate level.

The validity of these assumptions is of course open to question, especially over the long run. Indeed, we know that changes do occur of a type that input–output analysis denies. The question is essentially an empirical one: how large are the errors associated with sacrificing accuracy for convenience? In the short run they may not be substantial, and the use of input–output relations for forecasting and simulation within periods of five years may not yield results that are too far wide of the mark. There may not be much substitutability between inputs in the short run owing to the nature of technology or the comparative stability of relative factor prices. In the long run, however, changes in the ratio of factor prices and technical progress may alter the input–output coefficients substantially in physical terms.[4] Similarly, the composition of demand may be assumed to be fairly static in the short run, but is liable to change considerably in the longer run. If commodities with different input coefficients are grouped together in the same sectors, a changing pattern of demand will alter a sector's input–output coefficient automatically. To overcome this problem it is advisable to use the similarity of input structures as a criterion for the aggregation of activities in the original input–output table.

The most serious criticism of input–output analysis for projection, forecasting and simulation purposes is the fact that the marginal or incremental input coefficient may differ substantially from the average relationship embodied in the matrix. With technical change, increasing returns to scale and the changing structure of international trade, marginal input coefficients may diverge substantially from average coefficients over time. Needless to say, this possibility could lead to inaccurate forecasts of the need for certain commodities on the basis of projections of final demand. But there are ways of overcoming this inherent weakness of traditional input–output economics. The problem is lessened if the transactions table from which the input coefficients are derived can be produced at regular and frequent intervals. With better methods of data collection, this is more feasible. The problem can also be overcome to a certain extent if some satisfactory adjustment can be made to 'out-of-date' coefficients to allow for such factors as changes in technology and the pattern of trade. It is fairly common practice, for instance, to adjust out-of-date national coefficients for a sector by the coefficients prevailing in the best-practice techniques in the sector. And for developing countries, or backward regions within a nation, it may be assumed that within a certain time period they will have the coefficients prevailing at the present in other, more advanced countries or regions.

In growth and planning exercises, knowledge of input–output relationships is of greatest use when growth is based on the expansion of domestic demand and where there is considerable interdependence between activities. As we noted earlier, however, in developing countries the backward and forward linkages between sectors are typically quite weak. Unless there is a great deal of consolidation of sectors, many of the cells in the interindustry transactions matrix are likely to be empty. The reason is that a great deal of output goes directly to meet final demand, particularly into exports. If growth is primarily based on exports, the traditional input–output table is of limited use, although there are a number of ways in which it may be modified for the general purpose of assisting the achievement of balance within the economy.

DISCUSSION QUESTIONS

1 What does an input–output table show?

2 What are the major purposes of input–output analysis?

3 What are 'input–output coefficients', and what conditions must be fulfilled if they are to be stable through time?

4 What is the 'Leontief inverse matrix' and what does it show?

5 How would you derive the matrix multiplier for each industry from the Leontief inverse matrix?

6 Define the backward and forward linkages of each industry, and consider how linkage analysis might be used when planning economic development.

7 Give examples of how you would use an input–output table for 'simulation' purposes.

8 What information would be required if input–output analysis is used to forecast investment requirements?

9 Show how the balance-of-payments implications of a given growth in final demand can be forecast by using input–output analysis.

10 How indispensable is input–output analysis as a planning technique?

NOTES

1. Equation (13.7) is equivalent to (13.6) by multiplying each element in the rows of the 2×2 matrix by the equivalent element in the column vector of Xs.
2. An identity matrix is a square matrix with the number 1 down its principal diagonal and zeros everywhere else. The importance of the identity matrix in matrix algebra is discussed below.
3. For an excellent account of the practical problems of constructing input–output tables in developing countries, see Bulmer-Thomas (1982).
4. If the coefficients from one time period to the next are calculated at current prices, then changes in relative prices will not change the value of the coefficients if the elasticity of substitution between inputs is unity.

Financing economic development

Financing development from domestic resources

INTRODUCTION

The topic of financing development from domestic resources has two major aspects. The first concerns the ways in which **savings** can be encouraged in developing countries, because only if society is willing to save can resources be devoted to the production of capital goods. Saving is necessary to *fund* investment. In a primitive subsistence economy, without money or monetary assets, saving and investment will tend to be simultaneous acts, in the sense that saving and investment will be done by the same people, and saving will be invested in the sector in which the saving takes place. Those who sacrifice time and resources that would otherwise be used for consumption purposes do so to develop the means of production. They do not hold money or interest-bearing assets. In a more sophisticated money exchange economy, however, there is no guarantee that saving will necessarily be converted into investment. With the existence of money and monetary assets, the act of saving becomes divorced from the act of investing. Those who want to do the investing may be different from those who want to do the saving, and the process of capital accumulation is likely to require financial and credit mechanisms to 'redistribute' resources from savers to investors. Indeed, with a banking system with the power to create credit, investment can take place *without* prior saving through the process of borrowing. In other words, saving funds investment, but does not necessarily *finance* it. Investment generates its own saving through increases in output and profits. In fact, in the early stages of development, savings may not be the major barrier to capital formation but rather an unwillingness or inability to invest.

Unwillingness to invest may stem from cultural attitudes or simply from a realistic assessment of the risks involved. We analysed in Chapter 5 why poor people may be risk averse. The inability to invest, on the other hand, may result from shortages of cooperating factors of production (including foreign exchange), or lack of access to credit because of the underdeveloped nature of the financial system. The second important aspect of financing development from domestic resources, therefore, has to do with the role of the banking and financial system in promoting and financing investment. **The financial system is important for encouraging saving, financing investment and allocating savings in the most productive manner**.

In this chapter we focus primarily on the determinants of saving, the role of the financial system and financial liberalization in promoting savings, investment and growth, and also on the process of credit-financed growth initiated by the government, which may be inflationary. This leads us to consider the relation between inflation and economic development.

FORMS OF SAVING

There are three broad groups in society that save: the household sector, the business sector and the government. The household sector saves out of personal disposable income (personal saving), the business sector saves out of profits, and the government can save out of tax revenues if it spends less than it receives (that is, runs a budget surplus on current account). Household and business saving is sometimes referred to as **private saving**, while government saving is **public saving**. Each of the sectors' motives for saving will differ, and we shall consider the determinants of saving later.

As far as the nature of saving is concerned, three broad 'types' may be distinguished: voluntary, involuntary and 'forced'. The nature of these 'types' of saving is fairly self-explanatory:

■ **Voluntary savings** are savings that arise through voluntary reductions in consumption out of disposable income. Both the household and the business sector may be a source of voluntary savings.

■ **Involuntary savings** are savings brought about through involuntary reductions in consumption. All forms of taxation and schemes for compulsory lending to governments are traditional measures involving involuntary reductions in consumption.

■ Consumption may be reduced because of rising prices. This is referred to as **'forced' saving**[1] and may happen for a number of reasons. People may spend the same amount in money terms, but because prices have risen this means they spend less in *real* terms (money illusion). People may want to keep the *real* value of their holdings of money constant, so they accumulate more money as prices rise (**the real balance effect**). Also inflation may redistribute income to those with a higher propensity to save, such as profit earners.

For a variety of reasons, which will be considered later, inflation is likely to be a natural concomitant of development, but it can also be deliberately induced by governments financing budget deficits at full employment by monetary expansion. This is the idea of **'inflation as a tax on money'**. It should also be remembered that if an economy is at less than full employment, there can always be more saving by activating unemployed or underemployed resources, provided not all of the increase in output is consumed.

Domestic savings for investment can also be supplemented from abroad. Private foreign investment is a direct source of capital formation and provides a direct addition to domestic investment. It can also be a source of savings by stimulating income and employing previously underutilized resources. Second, borrowing from abroad provides resources for investment by enabling imports to exceed exports, which in the national accounts shows up as investment in excess of domestic saving. Foreign assistance may be from multilateral or bilateral sources and may take a variety of forms, ranging from loans at commercial rates of interest to outright gifts of goods and services and technical assistance (see Chapter 15).

Finally, a country's commercial policy can stimulate savings and release resources for investment purposes. Trade itself, and an improvement in a country's terms of trade, can provide additional resources for investment if the resulting increase in real income is not fully consumed. Likewise policies to restrict imports of consumption goods can release additional resources for investment, provided that domestic saving is not reduced by the purchasing power released being switched to home consumption goods.

The amount that countries save and invest as a proportion of their gross domestic product (GDP) differs enormously, affected by differences in the ability and willingness to save and invest. Some countries dissave, consuming more than they produce. Some countries save more than they invest domestically, which means they are investing abroad, and other countries invest more than they save, which means they are net importers of capital. The experience by country and by continent for 2002 is shown in Table 14.1. The first thing to note is that the savings ratio is much lower in poor

Table 14.1 Savings and investment as a percentage of GDP

	Gross capital formation % of GDP 2002	Gross domestic savings % of GDP 2002
Afghanistan	16	−16
Albania	23	−1
Algeria	31	40
Angola	32	39
Argentina	12	27
Armenia	21	3
Australia	24	22
Austria	22	23
Azerbaijan	33	25
Bangladesh	23	18
Belarus	22	18
Belgium	19	23
Benin	18	6
Bolivia	15	10
Bosnia and Herzegovina	20	−13
Botswana	25	38
Brazil	20	22
Bulgaria	20	13
Burkina Faso	18	5
Burundi	8	−4
Cambodia	22	14
Cameroon	19	18
Canada	20	25
Central African Republic	15	10
Chad	59	6
Chile	23	27
China	40	43
Hong Kong, China	23	32
Colombia	15	14
Congo, Dem. Rep.	7	4
Congo, Rep.	23	50
Costa Rica	22	17
Côte d'Ivoire	10	28
Croatia	27	18
Cuba	10	7
Czech Republic	28	26
Denmark	20	26
Dominican Republic	23	15
Ecuador	28	20
Egypt, Arab Rep.	17	10
El Salvador	16	2
Eritrea	26	−30
Estonia	31	22
Ethiopia	21	2
Finland	20	28
France	19	21
Gabon	28	48
Gambia, The	21	4
Georgia	21	9
Germany	18	22
Ghana	20	7
Greece	23	17
Guatemala	19	7
Guinea	17	11

Table 14.1 continued

	Gross capital formation % of GDP 2002	Gross domestic savings % of GDP 2002
Guinea-Bissau	15	–17
Haiti	21	–3
Honduras	28	12
Hungary	24	22
India	23	22
Indonesia	14	21
Iran, Islamic Rep.	35	37
Ireland	24	38
Israel	18	9
Italy	20	21
Jamaica	34	13
Japan	26	26
Jordan	23	3
Kazakhstan	27	28
Kenya	14	10
Korea, Rep.	26	27
Kuwait	9	18
Kyrgyz Republic	19	15
Lao PDR	22	–
Latvia	27	17
Lebanon	18	–9
Lesotho	40	–15
Libya	14	26
Lithuania	22	17
Macedonia, FYR	20	0
Madagascar	14	8
Malawi	12	–6
Malaysia	24	42
Mali	20	12
Mauritania	31	2
Mauritius	22	26
Mexico	20	18
Moldova	23	–3
Mongolia	31	16
Morocco	23	18
Mozambique	45	30
Myanmar	12	12
Namibia	24	23
Nepal	25	12
Netherlands	20	26
New Zealand	20	22
Nicaragua	32	6
Niger	13	4
Nigeria	23	17
Norway	19	33
Oman	13	34
Pakistan	15	14
Panama	25	24
Paraguay	20	8
Peru	18	18
Philippines	19	19
Poland	19	16
Portugal	28	18
Romania	23	17

Table 14.1 continued

	Gross capital formation % of GDP 2002	Gross domestic savings % of GDP 2002
Russian Federation	21	32
Rwanda	19	1
Saudi Arabia	20	37
Senegal	20	10
Serbia and Montenegro	16	−7
Sierra Leone	9	−14
Singapore	21	45
Slovak Republic	31	24
Slovenia	23	25
South Africa	16	19
Spain	26	24
Sri Lanka	21	14
Sudan	20	21
Swaziland	18	9
Sweden	17	23
Switzerland	17	24
Syrian Arab Republic	22	30
Tajikistan	23	10
Tanzania	17	10
Thailand	24	31
Togo	22	5
Trinidad and Tobago	16	20
Tunisia	25	21
Turkey	16	16
Turkmenistan	37	36
Uganda	22	6
Ukraine	19	24
United Kingdom	16	14
United States	18	14
Uruguay	12	14
Uzbekistan	20	24
Venezuela, RB	17	29
Vietnam	32	28
West Bank and Gaza	4	−31
Yemen, Rep.	17	16
Zambia	17	4
Zimbabwe	8	11
World	**20**	**20**
Low income	20	19
Middle income	23	27
Lower middle income	25	28
Upper middle income	19	25
Low and middle income	23	26
East Asia and Pacific	32	37
Europe and Central Asia	21	23
Latin America and Caribbean	19	22
Middle East and North Africa	23	29
South Asia	22	20
Sub-Saharan Africa	18	17
High income	19	19

Source: World Bank, *World Development Indicators 2004* (Washington: World Bank).

countries than in rich ones, but that the savings ratio does not continue to rise for ever as countries grow richer. It tends to level off in the middle-income group of countries and then stabilize. The weighted average savings ratio in the low-income countries is 19 per cent of GDP compared with 27 per cent in the middle-income countries and 19 per cent in high-income countries.[2] Some countries in the low-income category dissave, for example Sierra Leone and Malawi. Most of the low-income countries also have investment ratios that are higher than their domestic savings ratios, indicating that they are net capital importers.

The second important observation is the enormous disparity in saving performance between continents, particularly between the high savings ratios of the highly successful East Asian countries and the much lower savings ratios in the less successful economies of Latin America and Sub-Saharan Africa. The ratio in East Asia (37 per cent) is nearly double that of Latin America (22 per cent), and more than double that of Sub-Saharan Africa (17 per cent). The question that naturally arises is: did high savings precede rapid growth in East Asia, or did rapid growth generate its own high savings ratio? Some might argue that it was policies to stimulate saving that were important, including financial liberalization. Some might say it was policies to stimulate investment, partly through control of the banking system, that generated growth and therefore saving. Others might say it was the deliberate involvement of the government in generating and reallocating new resources.

There is no easy answer to the question, but the different replies that might be given highlight the differences in the three broad analytical approaches to the study of financing development from domestic resources, which we will use as the organizing framework for the rest of the chapter. The three approaches are as follows:

- The **prior-savings approach** to the financing of development, which stresses the importance of prior savings for investment and the need for policies to raise the level of savings either voluntarily or involuntarily, or both. The approach is very classical in conception, emphasizing saving as a prerequisite of investment. The approach is also characterized by a strong aversion to inflation and a belief that saving will readily find investment outlets.
- The **Keynesian approach**, which rejects the idea that saving determines investment and argues instead that the encouragement of investment will generate its own saving, either through increases in output if resources are unemployed, or through income redistribution from groups with a low propensity to save to groups with a high propensity to save as a result of inflation if resources are fully employed.
- The so-called **quantity theory approach**, which emphasizes the role of government monetary expansion in appropriating resources for development through forced saving or the inflation tax.[3]

If developing countries are characterized as fully employed in the Keynesian sense (with no spare capacity in the consumption-goods industries), both the Keynesian and the quantity theory approach to the financing of development will involve inflation. Plans to invest in excess of plans to save at full employment will drive up the price level, and so will monetary expansion by government. In this sense there is an important practical, as well as a theoretical, difference between the prior-savings approach and the other two approaches. In the prior-savings approach the resources released for investment come from voluntary and involuntary saving and no inflation is involved. In the Keynesian and quantity theory approaches the resources are partly released through the process of inflation, by income redistribution from classes with low propensities to save to those with higher propensities to save, and by inflation as a 'tax' on money.

THE PRIOR-SAVINGS APPROACH

In classical theory saving and investment are one and the same thing. All saving finds investment outlets through variations in the rate of interest. Investment and the development process are led by savings. It is this classical view of the development process that underlies such phrases in the development literature as the 'mobilization of savings for development' and also underlies the policy recommendation of high interest rates to encourage voluntary saving. Lewis's influential model of the development process, which we considered in Chapter 5, is a classical model stressing the importance for development of reinvesting the capitalist surplus.

The level of saving and the ratio of saving to national income in developing countries are likely to be a function of many variables affecting the ability and willingness to save. The main determinants of the **capacity or ability to save** are the average level of per capita income, the rate of growth of income, the distribution of income between rich and poor and the age composition of the population (or dependency ratio). In turn, the **willingness to save** depends mainly on monetary factors such as the rate of interest, the range and availability of financial institutions and assets (financial deepening), and the rate of inflation. Differences in cultural attitudes towards saving may also be important, but are not easily measured.

THE CAPACITY TO SAVE

Income is the major determinant of the capacity or the ability to save. It was Keynes who first introduced into economics the idea of the consumption function (and therefore savings function), making consumption and saving primarily a function of income rather than a function of the rate of interest as in classical theory. Saving as a function of income is known as the Keynesian **absolute income hypothesis**. We can derive the savings ratio as a function of the level of per capita income (PCY) in the following way: If we write the Keynesian savings function as $S = -a_0 + b_0 (Y)$ and divide by the population level (N) we have:

$$S/N = -a_1 + b_1(Y/N) \tag{14.1}$$

Then to obtain an expression for the savings ratio, multiply (14.1) by N and divide by Y:

$$S/Y = b_1 - a_1 (Y/N)^{-1} \tag{14.2}$$

The Keynesian absolute income hypothesis therefore predicts that savings per head (S/N) is a linear (but non-proportional) function of income per head (Y/N), and that the savings

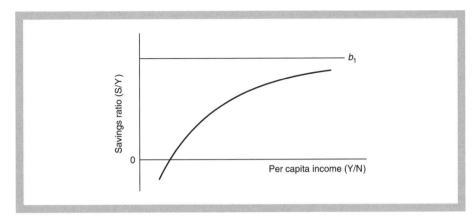

Figure 14.1 The Keynesian absolute income hypothesis

ratio (S/Y) is a hyperbolic function of the level of income per head; that is, that the savings ratio will rise with the level of per capita income but at a decreasing rate. As $Y/N \to \infty$, $S/Y \to$ to the asymptote b_1. This is shown in Figure 14.1.

The data on the savings ratio in Table 14.1 suggest this type of relation, as already discussed. The savings ratio is lower in poor countries than in richer countries, but the ratio does not continue rising linearly (for ever) as PCY rises. It increases at a diminishing rate and then levels off. Indeed, there is even some indication that it starts falling at high levels of income, as we shall see when we come to examine the empirical evidence.

The reason why the savings ratio should rise as per capita income increases and then level off is not clear-cut. It is as if saving is a luxury good in the early stages of development but then loses its appeal. Part of the reason may be purely 'statistical,' arising from the way saving is normally defined in developing countries as the difference between investment and foreign capital inflows. As investment expenditure becomes more faithfully and accurately recorded as development proceeds (as per capita income rises) the savings ratio is also shown to increase. But there are also a number of economic factors that probably play a contributory role in explaining the relation. One is the growth of the money economy. As money replaces barter for transactions, the public will wish to hold a higher proportion of their income in the form of money, which they can do only by giving up command over real resources. This hypothesis is supported by what we know about the income elasticity of demand for money in developing countries, which exceeds unity.

A second possible explanation is that population growth decreases with increases in the level of per capita income, so that population growth absorbs household saving to a lesser and lesser extent. Another plausible hypothesis is that in the early stages of development the distribution of income, both personal and functional, grows more unequal but at a decreasing rate. If higher-income groups have higher propensities to save than lower-income groups, and profit earners have a higher propensity to save than wage earners, the savings ratio will be positively related to the degree of inequality in income distribution (personal income distribution) and to the share of profits in total income (functional income distribution). Some evidence of the widening distribution of income in the early stages of development was given in Chapter 3.

A second major determinant of the capacity of a country to save is the growth of income as suggested by the **life-cycle hypothesis of saving**. The basis of the hypothesis, as originally formulated by Modigliani and Brumberg (1954), is that individuals and households attempt to spread out consumption evenly over their lifetime so that decisions to save are assumed to be a function of total lifetime earnings and the stage reached in the earnings cycle. A typical pattern of behaviour would be dissaving in youth, positive saving in middle-age and dissaving in retirement. Consider now the effect of income growth within this framework. If income is rising over time, this means that the life earnings and consumption of each successive age group will be higher than the preceding one. If each successive age group is aiming for a higher level of consumption in retirement, the volume of saving of the active households will exceed the dissaving of the currently retired households with a lower level of lifetime consumption. The saving ratio will then tend to rise with the rate of growth of income because the higher the growth rate, the greater the gap between the target consumption level of the current generation of working households and the dissaving of retired people from a less prosperous generation. Thus countries with higher growth rates might be expected to have at least higher personal savings ratios than countries with lower growth rates.

But income growth comprises two components: the growth of income per head (PCY) and the growth of population. Income growth due to population growth will affect the savings ratio according to how population growth affects the ratio of active to non-active households. Thus a third major determinant of the savings ratio is the **dependency ratio**. If population growth rises suddenly this will lead to a higher ratio of young dependants who consume but do not produce and this will tend to reduce saving. Equally, however, if population growth slows for a long period this will lead to a higher ratio of retired people who also consume but do not produce. Thus, both high and low population growth may be associated with a low savings ratio. To test the life-cycle hypothesis of saving it is best to relate the savings ratio to the growth of per capita income and to include the age structure of the population, or dependency ratio, as a separate variable (see Hussein and Thirlwall, 1999).

Finally, we have already mentioned the distribution of income as a determinant of the capacity to save. If the propensity to save of the rich is higher than that of the poor, the aggregate savings ratio will be positively related to the degree of inequality both in the personal income distribution (between individuals), and also in the functional distribution (between wages and profits) on the assumption that the propensity to save out of profits is higher than out of wages. It will be remembered from Chapter 5 that in Lewis's model of development with unlimited supplies of labour, it is not the absolute level of per capita income that is the prime determinant of the savings ratio but the size of the capitalist surplus and the distribution of income between entrepreneurial profits and other income. According to Lewis (1955): 'if we ask why the less developed countries save so little the answer is not because they are so poor but because their capitalist sector is so small.' Lewis also expressed the view that no nation is so poor that it could not save and invest at least 12 per cent of its national income if it so wished. Investment as a proportion of national income is not small because of an incapacity to save but because the surplus generated in developing countries is used to maintain 'unproductive hoards of retainers' and for conspicuous consumption in general.

Empirical studies

There have been four major recent studies of the determinants of saving across countries which include all or some of the variables discussed above, and also other variables measuring the willingness to save that we will discuss later. These are Edwards (1996); Masson, Bayoumi and Samiei (1998); Hussein and Thirlwall (1999); and Loayza, Schmidt-Hebbel and Serven (2000). Edwards takes panel data for 36 countries over the period 1970–92, distinguishing between private and government savings. Masson *et al.* use panel data for 21 developed countries (1971–93) and 40 less developed countries (1982–93) to explain the ratio of private saving to GDP. Hussein and Thirlwall take 62 countries over the period 1967–95, taking the domestic savings ratio as the dependent variable. Finally, Loayza *et al.* use a data set of 160 countries from 1964–94 taking four different measures of private saving (all highly correlated). All the studies find the level and growth of per capita income highly significant as determinants of intercountry differences in the savings ratio. Masson *et al.* and Hussein and Thirlwall use a non-linear specification for the level of PCY, as discussed above, and find it more significant than the linear specification, thus supporting the shape of the curve in Figure 14.1. Indeed, in the Masson study, a quadratic term for PCY is used so that the savings ratio is first assumed to rise and then fall. For both developed and developing countries the quadratic term turned out to be significantly negative with the savings ratio peaking at 60 per cent of the US level of PCY. The Loayza *et al.* study does separate analyses of developing countries and OECD countries and finds the impact of PCY on the savings ratio larger in developing countries than in developed countries, which is also evidence of non-linearity. For the sample as a whole, the authors find that a 10 per cent difference in PCY is associated with a 0.47 percentage point difference in the savings ratio. The authors conclude that 'policies that spur development are an indirect but most effective way to raise saving' and 'successful growth policies may be able to set in motion a virtuous cycle of saving, capital accumulation and growth'. The question is how to get this cumulative process started of rising income, more saving, faster growth, leading to more saving, etc. Monetary and fiscal policy, and the sophistication of the financial system, are likely to play an important part in this process. This leads us on to the topic of the willingness to save and the role of the financial system in promoting saving and allocating resources in the most efficient manner. All of the studies mentioned above include financial variables in their equations.

THE WILLINGNESS TO SAVE

Saving represents an intertemporal choice between consumption today and consumption tomorrow. It might be expected, therefore, that the price of present consumption, namely the real rate of interest, will affect saving positively. The higher the rate of interest, the greater the amount of saving. This assumed positive relation also reflects the classical idea of the rate of interest as the reward for waiting, and lies behind the financial liberalization programmes in developing countries which seek to raise the real interest rate in order to maximize saving, investment and growth. For the last 30 years or so there has been extensive testing of the **financial liberalization hypothesis**, and the role of the **interest rate**, in promoting saving, with mixed and largely inconclusive results. Perhaps this is not surprising since the financial liberalization argument largely refers to *financial* saving, but financial saving is only one component of total saving. If interest rates rise, financial saving may rise but at the expense of other assets, leaving total saving unchanged (see Warman and Thirlwall, 1994). It is also standard theory that any price change has both *income* and *substitution* effects. The substitution effect promotes saving, but the income effect reduces saving and the two effects may cancel each other out.

Probably a more important determinant of the willingness to save is the existence of financial institutions and the range and availability of financial assets to suit savers. There is no *single* measure that can capture those institutional determinants of the willingness to save. The number, proximity and diversity of financial institutions serving the different needs of savers could be important. Equally, the volume and range of financial assets might matter as a measure of financial deepening. Such measures include: money and quasi-money as a percentage of GDP; money and quasi-money growth, and quasi-liquid liabilities as a percentage of GDP. Domestic credit provided by the banking system as a percentage of GDP is also a measure of financial deepening, but the effect on saving is ambiguous. On the one hand, if bank credit finances investment and growth, this will have a positive effect on saving. On the other hand, an increase in bank credit will relax a liquidity constraint on consumption resulting in a decline in saving.

Finally, the rate of inflation can be expected to affect the willingness to save, but the effect is ambiguous. On the one hand, inflation acts as a tax on money balance holdings. If individuals wish to restore the real value of their money balance holdings (the so-called **real balance effect**), saving will rise with the rate of inflation. On the other hand, it is natural to expect individuals to avoid the tax if it becomes burdensome in relation to the convenience of holding money. Even if private saving does increase, however, total saving may not increase if the government fully consumes the proceeds of the inflation tax. Inflation will also redistribute income from wages to profits within the private sector if the wage–price coefficient is less than unity. This will increase saving if the propensity to save out of profits is higher than out of wages (as discussed already), but this process can last only as long as there is money illusion and workers do not bid for wage increase to match price increases. The most likely relation between inflation and the savings ratio is an inverted U-shape (quadratic function) showing saving rising with mild inflation and then falling as inflation becomes excessive. This type of non-linear relation is also suggested by the evidence available on the relation between inflation and growth (see later).

The evidence that we have from the four studies cited above (and others) is that financial variables matter for the performance of saving, but financial deepening and credit availability are much more significant than interest rates. Edwards, and Masson *et al.*, find that the level of financial development is an important determinant of private saving. Hussein and Thirlwall experiment with different measures of financial deepening and find a strong positive relation between the domestic savings ratio of countries and the ratio of quasi-liquid liabilities of the banking system to GDP. Loayza *et al.* take the ratio of M_2 money to GNP as a measure of financial deepening but find it only weakly significant. More interesting, they find that both higher interest rates and larger private domestic credit flows exert a *negative* effect on the private savings ratio. The authors

Table 14.2 Interest sensitivity of saving under alternative scenarios

Country groupings	Initial real interest rate		
	3%	4%	5%
Low-income			
Average for group	0.312[1]	0.306	0.300
Average for 10			
poorest	0.177	0.174	0.171
Lower-middle-income	0.532	0.522	0.512
Upper-middle-income	0.560	0.549	0.539
High-income	0.584	0.573	0.562

Note:
1. The data refer to the change (in percentage points) in the saving rate owing to a 1 percentage point increase in the real interest rate. For example, in high-income countries with a real interest rate of 3 per cent, a 1 percentage point rise in the real interest rate would raise the saving rate by nearly two-thirds of a percentage point (0.584 of a percentage point). At higher baseline levels of the real interest rate, the saving response diminishes slightly.
Source: M. Ogaki, J. D. Ostry and C. M. Reinhart, 'Savings Behaviour in Low and Middle Income Developing Countries', *IMF Staff* Papers, March 1996.

conclude 'these results provide a bleaker view of the savings effects of financial liberalization than previous studies suggested'. We will discuss the process and effects of financial liberalization later.

The overall conclusion would be that while financial variables may not be as important as income variables in determining savings behaviour, economic development itself is dependent on the sophistication of the financial system, and there is evidence that saving may be more responsive to interest rates when the level of income rises above subsistence. Research on this topic by Ogaki, Ostry and Reinhart (1996) is reported in Table 14.2.

It appears that saving is very unresponsive to interest rates in low-income countries where there is little margin of income over subsistence needs, but its responsiveness increases as consumption rises above subsistence needs and people can exercise choice about increasing their present or future consumption.

This leads us to the extensive topic of financial systems, financial policy and economic development.

FINANCIAL SYSTEMS AND ECONOMIC DEVELOPMENT

One of the characteristic features of developing countries is that large sections of the economy are either non-monetized or transactions take place outside the formal financial sector. In other words, the economies of developing countries have a large sector where money is not used as the primary means of exchange, as well as having a large **informal financial sector** or **unorganized money market**. This has a number of consequences that are not conducive to development:

■ If transactions take the form of barter, this is both costly in time and wasteful of resources. Sellers must spend time and effort finding buyers who have things they want. Money as a means of exchange avoids the problem of the double coincidence of wants. In this sense money is a resource and its introduction into an economy can be highly productive.

■ Without a convenient and acceptable means of payment, the division of labour or specialization is impeded, which hinders the process of capital accumulation and reduces productivity. Remember that for Adam Smith (see Chapter 4) it is the division of labour that is the source of increasing returns by allowing complex processes to be broken up into simpler operations that permit the use of machinery and mass production. Specialization is not worthwhile if the market is limited by the difficulty of exchanging goods.

■ Saving takes the form of the acquisition of real assets – for example land, cattle, gold, jewellery and so on – as opposed to monetary assets, which absorb resources and may not be used productively.

■ Without the existence of financial institutions issuing monetary assets, investment will tend to take place in the sector in which the savings take place, and this may not be the most productive sector.

■ Much of the lending in the informal sector is for consumption purposes and interest rates are very high, both of which can adversely affect total investment. The informal financial sector has an important role to play in the development process, but its integration with the formal financial sector is desirable on a number of grounds.

THE INFORMAL FINANCIAL SECTOR

The **informal financial sector** refers to all institutions and transactions that take place outside a country's authorized banking system. The sector plays a significant role in the financing of economic development, although exactly how important no one really knows. Within the informal sector there exist a wide variety of institutions and multifarious arrangements between depositors, lenders and borrowers, some dating back for centuries, rooted in custom and tradition. Others are constantly evolving in response to changing economic and social conditions. The sector is characterized by a high degree of spontaneity and flexibility, with demand creating its own supply. The major participants are money lenders, merchants, loan brokers, savings groups, and friends and relatives.

Money lenders have a long tradition in the rural areas of developing countries. They may be landlords, merchants, storekeepers and pawnbrokers. Loans are typically for short periods at high rates of interest, reflecting the scarcity of funds and the high demand for short-period loans to finance both consumption and investment, for example the holding of stocks. Merchants often provide loans to clients based on the future sale or purchase of commodities. Loan brokers act as intermediaries between agents who have surplus funds and those who require credit. The loans tend to be larger and the duration longer than for other sectors in the informal market.

Savings groups take different forms and have different names in various countries, and are also important sources of finance and credit in rural areas. In some cases the savings group consists of individuals who deposit money on a regular basis with a group leader or treasurer, sometimes for special purposes such as tax payments, investment or paying for festivities. If the savings are invested, the returns may be shared by the members. Rules and regulations are shaped by local conditions and traditions. In other cases, members of the savings group take turns to borrow the collected sums of money. One particular type of savings group with a long history in Africa is the 'Rotating savings and credit association' (ROSCA). ROSCAs operate like miniature credit unions based on the 'mutuality' principle, whereby members of the association make a fixed contribution to the savings fund on a periodic basis and are entitled to withdraw money on a rotational basis. Individuals can decide on the cycle of payments and withdrawals that suit their needs. The advantage is that large expenditures can be undertaken by members sooner than if they had to rely on their own personal savings.

Finally, friends and relatives are major providers of credit. The credit is flexible and interest-free, and repayment is open-ended.

Despite the growth of the formal financial sector in the majority of developing countries, the informal financial sector continues to flourish because it fulfils needs that are not met elsewhere. First, many rural areas have no ready access to financial institutions, either because they are non-existent or because they are not within the immediate vicinity. The formal financial sector is predominantly urban-based. Second, where banks do exist, there are a number of institutional barriers to their use, in the form of rules of procedure for obtaining financial assistance. The conditions for obtaining loans can be stringent and hard to satisfy for a number of people. It is difficult, for instance, for the poor and illiterate to provide collateral for loans, which is usually required by the formal sector. In practice the formal financial sector tends to be out of reach of peasant farmers, small-scale entrepreneurs and ordinary households, so the informal financial sector fills the gap in the market. Third, the informal sector sometimes acts as a complement to the formal sector. Individuals may borrow from the formal sector but find such credits inadequate and therefore resort to the informal sector to augment their borrowing. In recent years the World Bank Structural Adjustment Programmes, implemented in several countries, have reduced the flow of credit from the formal sector and demand has switched to the informal sector.

A well-developed financial system serving the whole community has five main requisites, each of which can contribute to the process of **financial deepening**, as well as to raising the level of saving and investment, the productivity of capital and the growth of output:

- Full monetization of the economy and the replacement of barter as a means of exchange
- Integration of the informal and formal money markets
- Development of a commercial banking system with central bank supervision
- The creation of development banks and micro-credit facilities for small-scale borrowing
- Development of financial markets and financial intermediaries, issuing and dealing in financial assets.

MONETIZATION AND MONEY MARKET INTEGRATION

Monetization of an economy provides the potential to generate a real investible surplus in several ways. As fiat money replaces barter in transactions, the demand for money relative to income rises, which releases real resources of equivalent value. The increase in real saving is equal to the increase in the real stock of money held. The issuer of money can appropriate the released resources and increase the level of investment accordingly. In a growing economy monetary expansion is also required to allow an increased volume of transactions to take place. Monetary expansion for this purpose, too, can be appropriated by governments for development purposes.

The increased use of money not only releases resources, but it also saves and generates resources. It saves resources by replacing barter objects, or commodity money, which may be costly to produce, with money which is virtually costless to produce. It also saves time – which is a resource if the marginal product of labour time is positive – by avoiding the double coincidence of wants necessitated by barter. Money generates resources by facilitating exchange and thereby permitting the greater division of labour (and specialization).

Historically, the growth of the money economy has also been a powerful stimulus to the development of banking and credit mechanisms, which can themselves act as a stimulus to saving and investment. When the range of financial assets is narrow, saving tends to take the form of the acquisition of physical assets. While in principle this should not mean that the level of saving is reduced to below what it might otherwise be, in practice it depends on how sellers of physical assets dispose of the sale proceeds. If a portion of the proceeds is consumed, the saving of one person is offset by the dissaving of another, and less resources are released for investment than if financial assets had been acquired, issued by financial institutions with an investment function.

For a number of reasons, there is also the need to promote links between the informal and formal financial sectors. The high interest rates charged in the informal sector add to costs and add to household debt, and these could be reduced if the informal sector was exposed to greater competition from the formal sector. This could be done by transforming informal institutions into more formal ones, or using the informal sector as a conduit for formal funds, taking advantage of the low transactions costs, local knowledge and greater flexibility in the informal sector. There could also be support mechanisms to guarantee loans from the informal sector.

It is also important that the capital market should be integrated, in the sense that the interest-rate structure is unified. The consequence of a fragmented capital market in which interest rates vary from one sector to another because of a lack of information and factor immobility is that some sectors of the economy may be able to borrow funds far below the rate of interest prevailing in other sectors where the productivity of capital is higher. The allocation of capital is distorted and inefficient and the capital–output ratio is higher than it would otherwise be: the solution is to encourage funds into the organized money market, and to extend the provision of financial institutions into sectors of the economy that lack them.

Paradoxically (on a classical view of the world), development of the organized money market can both *lower* average interest rates in the economy at large and *raise* the level of saving because the unorganized money market charges very high interest rates and lends mainly for consumption purposes, whereas in the organized money market interest rates are lower and lending is more for investment purposes.

DEVELOPING A BANKING SYSTEM

Developing a national banking system, comprising a central bank, a commercial banking system and special development banks, is one of the first priorities of development strategy. The functions of **a central bank** include the following:

- Issuing currency and lending to government, whereby real resources are transferred to the government in the manner described earlier (with a strong central bank it is very much easier to give priority to the needs of the government and the public sector).
- Developing a fractional reserve banking system through which it can provide liquidity and control credit (a central bank can require member banks to hold reserves in government bonds, and the growth of the bond market itself can aid development without excessive monetary expansion).
- Developing other financial institutions, especially institutions that provide long-term loan finance for development and a market for government securities.
- Maintaining a high level of demand to achieve capacity growth.
- Applying selective credit controls when necessary, in the interests of developing particular sectors of the economy.

The **commercial banking system** has two important functions: to create credit, and to encourage thrift and allocate saving in the most socially productive manner. The ability of an economic system to create credit is important for two main reasons. First, it can compensate for the failure of the economic system to equalize planned saving and investment. Second, it provides the means by which growth is financed. This is the real significance of the invention of paper money and credit – permitting the economic system to expand in response to the continual opportunities for growth provided by technical progress, which a barter system or a purely metallic currency do not allow.

Banks can encourage thrift and allocate savings more productively than would otherwise be the case by offering a return on savings and enabling savings to be used outside the sector in which they originate. Banks can help to break down sectoral bottlenecks and to unify interest rates. But commercial banking is still rudimentary in many developing economies. The ratio of bank deposits to national income averages approximately 15 per cent and the proportion of demand deposits to the total money supply averages between 25 and 30 per cent. In developed countries, in contrast, the ratio of bank deposits to national income usually exceeds 30 per cent and the money supply consists largely of the deposits of commercial banks. The number of banks relative to population size is also small. In the developing countries as a whole, the average number of banks per million of the population is about ten compared with 180 in developed countries. Banks need to be numerous and dispersed if they are to act as catalysts for small savings. The case for **branch banking** is that it can tap small savings. If savings institutions are pushed under people's noses they will save more than if the nearest savings institution is some distance away! Case example 14.1 describes Vietnam's Bank on Wheels, which is also an example of micro-credit as discussed in the next section.

Vietnam's Bank on Wheels

Ma Seo Sang, a Hmong widow living on less than 25 cents a day in the mountainous region of Vietnam, needed help. She had sold a pig to pay for her husband's funeral, paid a fine incurred by her son by selling one of her buffalo, and redeemed a debt with the other. She had borrowed all she could from relatives. Moneylenders, if they would even lend to her, would charge exorbitant interest (up to 10 per cent per month). She needed money to survive.

Sang's plight raises many issues related to extreme poverty, of which lack of access to credit is one. Part of the solution is microfinance – the provision of basic financial services to the poor. Microfinance can offer a path out of poverty. But how long is the path, and can it be shortened? Vietnam's experiment with the Mobile Banking Programme under the World Bank's Rural Finance Project provides a partial answer to those questions. It suggests that creative ways can be found not only for lenders to reach out to the poor but also for the poor to 'reach in' to lenders.

In 1998 the Vietnam Bank for Agriculture and Rural Development (Agribank) initiated a mobile banking programme modelled after similar programme in Bangladesh and Malaysia. It procured 159 vehicles equipped to travel on dirt roads and hilly pathways, enabling loan officers to reach remote areas to process loan applications, disburse money, collect payments, and mobilize savings deposits. The visits followed a fixed calendar and were announced in advance.

Once the programme was launched, it became clear that more than just difficult access prevented the poorest from taking advantage of its services. Their isolation caused them to have feelings of helplessness and fear. In the upland ethnic group, the higher up a mountain people lived and the longer their isolation, the more they seemed to believe that they could not get credit. Suspicion was another issue. What if the lender offered a loan and then, if a payment were late, took a farmer's buffalo, as had happened to Sang?

Above all, the poorest people lacked confidence and self-esteem. For example, the illiterate poor would wonder how they could fill in applications and receipts. Others felt they could do nothing to earn extra income to repay a loan. Many were afraid to venture into activities other than cultivation and animal husbandry, even though opportunities existed.

For mobile banking to work for borrowers, the following services had to be made available: **offering appropriate loan products; linking lending and saving; combining credit and human asset building.**

For lenders, it was necessary that the mobile banking experiment be financially self-sustaining. It thus required the following ingredients: **group-based lending; linking formal and informal credit; reasonable interest rates.**

Barely five years in operation, the Mobile Banking Programme has proved to be relatively cost-effective, providing financial services to 315,000 poor households.

Preliminary data show that, on average, each mobile bank disbursed 1921 loans, collected 1387 payments, and transported cash on 75 occasions to 16 local points monthly. The excellent repayment rate suggests that the poor are good credit risks. The programme also mobilized 1983 small savings accounts every month, showing that the poor can be good savers.

As for Ma Seo Sang, she received a loan of about $300 and used the money to buy some chickens and pigs to raise. The income she made from selling her animals helped her earn a living.

Source: G. Nguyen Tien Hung (2004), 'Bank on Wheels', *Finance and Development*, June.

SPECIAL DEVELOPMENT BANKS AND MICRO-CREDIT

Special development banks and **micro-credit institutions** play a particularly important role in the development process because it is not the explicit function of the commercial banking system to have development priorities in mind when making loans, unless directed by the government. The function of the commercial banks is to make a profit for their shareholders. This means that commercial banks are generally risk averse and have short time horizons. It also means that they are only interested in their own cash flows and have no interest in the *social* profitability of the projects that they lend for. Development banks can afford to have longer time horizons, take more risks, pursue development objectives and focus on the social profitability of lending, as well as encouraging saving.

The activities of the Tonga Development Bank provide an interesting case study.[4] The bank was established in 1977 'to promote the expansion of Tonga for the economic advancement of the people of Tonga'. The bank's lending policy gives priority to projects that have the potential to increase exports or reduce imports, involve local entrepreneurship, use local inputs, contribute to increased employment opportunities, particularly for women, and increase income for the poorer sections of the community in rural areas and the outer islands. On the question of exports, if economic growth is constrained by a shortage of foreign exchange, any project financed by the bank that earns net foreign exchange will give a higher social return than private return because the growth of output will be higher than would otherwise have been the case. In Tonga, the commercial banking system would not lend to producers wishing to grow squash because the venture was regarded as too risky. However the Tonga Development Bank lent nearly $10 million to squash producers, and squash now accounts for 80 per cent of the country's export earnings. The bank reaches out to nearly 50 per cent of households in Tonga, and 70 per cent of all loans to the private sector are funded by the bank. The bank fills an important gap in the market for small loans because commercial banks will not lend for projects of less than $5000. There can be little doubt that the Tonga Development Bank is playing a pivotal role in the development of the economy of Tonga and is able to do things that the private sector would not contemplate. The positive externalities conferred fully justify interest rate subsidies.

All development banks have a role to play in stimulating the capital market. They can do this by selling their own stocks and bonds to raise finance, by helping enterprises to float or place their own securities, and by selling from their own portfolio of investments.

Micro-credit institutions can also play a crucial role in helping the poor and fostering the growth of small businesses, where potential entrepreneurs are precluded from borrowing from the banking system because they are too poor and lack collateral. It is estimated that about 20 million poor people worldwide borrow from micro-credit organizations with each borrower on average supporting five family members. The lobby group, Microcredit Summit Campaign, wants to see 100 million borrowers by the year 2005, with more support from the commercial banking system.[5]

It was the Grameen (meaning 'village') Bank that pioneered the concept of micro-credit in developing countries, and there now exist several schemes throughout the world that enable poor people without collateral to borrow. The Grameen Bank was formally established in 1983 (seven years after the initial idea) by Muhammad Yunus, an economics professor at Chittagong University in Bangladesh, who instead of teaching the economics of poverty from an ivory tower decided to do something practical about it, based on the philosophy that everyone has the right to credit, but the poor are excluded from the conventional banking system. But the best way for people to help themselves out of poverty is to be able to borrow to set up small businesses. Thus, the Grameen Bank was founded as a micro-credit organization to lend to the rural poor, especially women, without collateral – sums as little as $10. A poor woman may obtain a micro-loan to buy an oven in order to sell hot food. She repays the loan with interest; others can borrow; she can borrow more to buy another oven and ultimately becomes a prosperous trader. Another poor woman uses her micro-loan to buy chickens; starts selling eggs; repays the loan; borrows more and becomes a chicken farmer. These are simple, real-life stories of what is possible. Lending and repayment takes place within a group context (usually five people) where each member of the group agrees to monitor each other, so that there is peer pressure to use loans wisely and to repay. Each member of the group comes from the same village with a similar economic and social background. Loans are first given to two of the group who are closely observed for two months and must repay the loan in weekly instalments. If the repayments are made, then two others can borrow. If any member defaults, the whole group becomes ineligible to borrow. Loan use is monitored by the staff of the Grameen Bank and groups meet collectively to discuss the choice of new projects. All credit transactions are discussed openly, so there is complete transparency concerning what is going on. There can be no 'cover-ups' and no corruption. Such is the pressure that the record of repayment to the Grameen Bank is close to 98 per cent of loans; far better than the record of repayment to the commercial banking system where bad debts are rife. The Grameen Bank also involves itself in social development programmes in the villages to improve the quality of life, such as encouraging members to build houses and sanitation facilities, planting trees and kitchen gardens, etc. There is also a comprehensive training programme in maternal health, nutrition and child care. In Bangladesh alone there are over 1000 branches of the bank serving 36,000 villages employing 12,000 people and lending to over 2 million people.

The Grameen idea has now spread to over 60 countries. Not all micro-credit banks operate in the same way, but all are designed to lend to poor people denied access to credit because they have no collateral. The first commercial micro-credit bank in Latin America was Banco Sol in Bolivia established in 1992 and has an enviable record of lending. Kenya's Rural Enterprise Programme (K – Rep) was established in 1999 intending to replicate the success of Banco Sol, lending to groups of 20–40 people, with loans taken out on a staggered basis. Acción Internacional based in the United States has affiliates in 13 Latin American countries including Mibanco in Peru, the first wholly privately funded micro-enterprise bank in that country.

Generally, schemes need to be subsidized for up to 5 years before they become self-sufficient because overhead costs are high. It is possible, however, to design schemes that minimize costs and the risk of default, and where the element of subsidy is very small. One such scheme is the Start-up Fund located near Cape Town in South Africa, as described by Reinke (1998). It is a highly successful scheme that relies on the self-selection of potential borrowers and the self-motivation of existing borrowers. Participants must first undergo a training programme (funded separately), and loan accessibility increases with good behaviour. Thus there are built-in structures and incentives to ensure good performance and repayment. Two years after starting in 1993, the fund was already in surplus, and by the end of 1996 had dispersed 6 million rand to over 5000 borrowers. Reinke concludes that 'the Start-up Fund has assisted poor people in becoming economically self-reliant, and it has done so in a cost effective way'. This is a model scheme that could be usefully copied elsewhere.

FINANCIAL INTERMEDIARIES

The importance of having a wide variety of financial intermediaries is that they can offer a diversity of financial assets with different yields, maturities, divisibilities and so on to suit savers and investors with different requirements and different time horizons. This can increase the level of both saving and investment, and also improve the efficiency of resource allocation.

As far as the level of saving and investment is concerned, financial intermediaries offer four major advantages:

- In general, savers wish to lend for only a short period of time (to remain liquid), while investors wish to borrow for a longer period of time. Direct lending from savers to investors, without financial intermediation, would involve savers committing themselves for longer periods than they really would like because investment does not generally generate returns immediately. Financial intermediaries, however, are able to pool risks and can borrow short and lend long, thus suiting both savers and investors.
- The use of financial intermediaries reduces transaction costs. Direct lending, whereby savers have to find suitable borrowers or investors have to find suitable lenders, is both time consuming and costly. Reduced transaction costs encourage both saving and investment.
- Financial intermediaries can specialize in particular areas of business, which reduces information costs by accumulating knowledge of various markets. This lessens the credit risks associated with lending, and also encourages greater saving and investment.

■ Investment projects are invariably larger than the savings of any one individual or group of individuals. The existence of financial intermediaries overcomes the problem of indivisibilities.

As far as the *efficiency* of resource allocation is concerned, the great advantage of financial intermediaries is that the creation of financial assets and liabilities allows savers to hold part of their wealth in financial form. This means that investment is no longer confined to the sector where the saving takes place, thereby facilitating the allocation of resources to the most productive sectors of the economy.

FINANCIAL LIBERALIZATION

The formal financial sector, consisting of a central bank, a commercial banking system and various other financial intermediaries, typically suffers from various forms of **financial repression**, which may thwart the development process. For example, the government may have a monopoly over the banking system and restrict the growth of financial institutions. Private sector banks may have to keep high reserve requirements and lend compulsorily to the government to finance its deficits. The central bank may impose credit rationing on the commercial banks, or insist that the banks lend to certain priority sectors. Nominal interest rates may be kept artificially low, so that with inflation the real rate of interest is negative, discouraging the acquisition of interest-bearing financial assets. These are all examples of financial repression.

The argument for **financial liberalization** is that the various forms of financial repression impede the development of financial markets. The consequences, it is argued, are a reduction of the flow of funds to the formal financial sector and distortion of the allocation of resources, leading to lower levels of saving, investment and output growth than otherwise would be the case.

The importance of the growth of the money economy and financial deepening for economic development along the lines indicated above has been stressed in the development literature for a long time,[6] but it was McKinnon (1973) and Shaw (1973) who independently in 1973 first highlighted the dangers of financial repression in a rigorous way, and argued the case for maximum financial liberalization. Their views became highly influential in the thinking of the IMF and the World Bank in the design of programmes for the financial restructuring of countries as part of Structural Adjustment Programmes. Their arguments, however, emphasize different points:

■ **McKinnon's argument** is that money holdings and capital accumulation are complementary in the development process. Because of the lumpiness of investment expenditure and the reliance on self-financing, agents need to accumulate money balances before investment takes place. Positive (and high) real interest rates are necessary to encourage agents to accumulate money balances, and investment will take place as long as the real rate of return on investment exceeds the real rate of interest.

■ **Shaw's argument**, on the other hand, stresses the importance of financial liberalization for financial deepening, and the beneficial effect of high interest rates on encouragement to save and discouragement to invest in low-yielding projects.

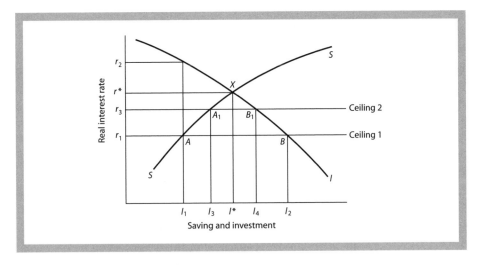

Figure 14.2 The McKinnon–Shaw argument

The increased liabilities of the banking system, resulting from higher real interest rates, enable the banking system to lend more resources for productive investment in a more efficient way.

A simple diagram (Figure 14.2) can illustrate the McKinnon–Shaw argument.

Figure 14.2 is a standard classical savings and investment diagram showing saving as a positive function of the real interest rate (reflecting the idea of time preference and the interest rate as the reward for abstaining from present consumption), and investment as a negative function of the real interest rate (reflecting the diminishing marginal efficiency of investment). With no interest rate controls, the equilibrium rate of interest would be r^* and the level of saving and investment would be I^*.

Now suppose that the government imposes a ceiling on the *nominal deposit rate* for savers, giving a *real* rate of interest of r_1. This would mean that saving is I_1, and on classical assumptions that prior saving is necessary for investment, this also constrains investment to I_1. If there was no ceiling on the *loan* rate of interest, the banks could charge interest rate r_2 to investors and the gap between r_1 and r_2 would give substantial profits to banks, which they could use for various forms of non-price competition. At r_2 there is no unsatisfied demand for investment funds.

Suppose, however, that the interest rate ceiling applies to loans as well as deposits. This means that saving is still I_1, but investment demand is now I_2 and there is an unsatisfied demand for investment funds equal to AB. Credit will have to be rationed. There will be a tendency for banks to favour less risky projects with lower rates of return. This will lower the overall productivity of investment.

If the interest rate ceiling is raised so that real interest rates rise to r_3, this encourages saving from I_1 to I_3. This leads to more investment, credit rationing is reduced and the productivity of investment rises. From this argument, it would seem to follow that saving and investment will be optimal and credit rationing will disappear when the market is fully liberalised and the real rate of interest is left to find its market clearing level at r^*.

CRITICS OF FINANCIAL LIBERALIZATION AND EMPIRICAL EVIDENCE

Many of the arguments for financial liberalization sound convincing on the surface, but a number of qualifications needs to be made. The experience of financial liberalization across the globe has been very mixed, and we shall consider some of the empirical evidence relating to the effect of liberalization on saving, investment and growth as we examine some of the major criticisms of the financial liberalization argument.[7]

First, the argument refers to *financial* saving, but financial saving is only one type of saving. Financial saving may increase as interest rates are liberalized, but there may simply be a substitution between financial assets and other assets, leaving total saving unchanged. It is also well known that any price change (in this case the interest rate) has income as well as substitution effects. The substitution effect promotes saving by making current consumption more 'expensive', but the income effect deters saving because at higher interest rates the same income can be obtained with less saving, and the two effects may cancel each other out. This being so, it is perhaps surprising, as Dornbusch and Reynoso (1989) have remarked, 'to find so strong a belief in the ability of higher interest rates to mobilise saving'.

In fact many of the empirical studies and surveys of the results of financial liberalization in various countries are extremely cautious in their conclusions. Research by Gupta (1987) on 22 Asian and Latin American countries over the period of 1967–76 suggests that there is little support for the 'repressionist' hypothesis that the positive substitution effect of real interest rates on savings dominates the negative income effect. The most important determinant of saving is real income. Giovannini (1983) concludes from his research on eight Asian countries that his results 'cast serious doubts on the view that the interest elasticity of savings is significantly positive and easy to detect in developing countries'. Similarly, a study by two World Bank economists (Cho and Khatkhate, 1990) of the financial liberalization experience of five Asian countries concluded that:

> financial reform, whether comprehensive and sweeping or measured and gradual, does not seem to have made any significant difference to the saving and investment activities in the liberalised countries. It was believed until recently that removal of the repressive polices would boost saving. The survey in this paper of the consequences of reform does not reveal any systematic trend or pattern in regard to saving . . . it lends support to the conclusion that decisions to save are determined by several factors and the relationship between saving and real interest rates is at best ambiguous.

Bandiera *et al.* (2000) examine the liberalization experience of eight countries (Chile, Ghana, Indonesia, South Korea, Malaysia, Mexico, Turkey and Zimbabwe) over 25 years and conclude 'our results cannot offer support for the hypothesis that financial liberalization will increase saving. On the contrary, the indications are that liberalization overall – and in particular those elements that relax liquidity constraints – may be associated with a fall in saving'. Maxwell Fry (1995), a leading authority on finance and development and an ardent advocate of financial liberalization, has conceded that 'what is agreed . . . is that if an effect [on saving] exists at all, it is relatively small' and that 'positive interest effects are easier to find in Asia than in other parts of the world, but even in Asia the effects appear to have diminished over the past two decades'.

If financial liberalization does not increase aggregate saving, its positive impact on development must come through a more efficient allocation of resources, which raises the productivity of investment. In other words, as stressed by Shaw, financial liberalization should concentrate on the quality of investment rather than the quantity. There is not much evidence on this point, but the World Bank, which devoted its *World Development Report 1989* to the topic of financial systems and economic development, claims that in countries with positive real interest rates, the average productivity of investment (as measured by the incremental output–capital ratio) was four times higher than in countries with strongly negative real interest rates. Bandiera *et al.* also conclude their study by saying that even if financial liberalization does not increase private saving, it does not follow that the process contracts the volume of funds applied to productive investment. For one thing, financial liberalization can increase the flow of capital from abroad, and secondly the reform process can have the effect of eliminating less productive uses of loanable funds. This is an area where more research needs to be done.

A second major criticism of the financial liberalization argument is that the model seems to treat banks simply as savings depositories, with the presumption that the supply of loans from the banking system depends on deposits held by the banks, and if deposits increase, loans will automatically increase. In short, the supply of credit is treated as exogenously determined. However if banks have the power to create credit (which they do), backed by a central bank acting as lender of last resort, the supply of loans will depend on the demand for loans, not on the supply of deposits. The supply of loans becomes endogenous. Within this framework, what is important is not so much incentives for saving, but incentives for investment, which may require lower interest rates. This is part of the **Keynesian and post-Keynesian** critique of the financial liberalization school. The work of the foremost post-Keynesian, Paul Davidson (1986), is representative of this line of argument. Davidson argues that all that is needed to initiate additional real investment is finance provided by an increase in total bank loans and there is no need for increased savings, 'as long as the banks can create new finance via acceptable bank accounting practices'.

How the supply of credit responds to the interest rate, and how investment is affected by the supply of credit and the rate of interest, becomes very much an empirical matter that can only be settled by an appeal to the facts. The present author and Fanny Warman of the Bank of Mexico (Warman and Thirlwall, 1994) found that, for Mexico over the period 1960–90, financial saving had responded positively to the rate of interest, and this had led to an increase in the supply of credit from the banking system to the private sector. However, while the increased supply of credit affects investment positively, there is a strong negative effect of interest rates on the level of investment, holding the supply of credit constant, and the *net* effect of higher real interest rates on investment is adverse. This is also the central conclusion of Demetriades and Devereux (1992) from research on 63 developing countries over the period 1961–90. They find that the negative effect of a high cost of capital on investment outweighs the effect of a greater supply of investible funds. Greene and Villanueva (1991), in a sample of 23 developing countries over the period 1975–87, likewise show a negative effect of real interest rates on investment.

This leads to a third worry about the financial liberalization model, which is that it ignores the adverse effect that high real interest rates can have on costs and the level of demand in an economy, which may lead to stagflation (a combination of cost inflation and rising unemployment). This is another aspect of the post-Keynesian critique of the financial liberalization model (see Dutt, 1990–1). High interest rates not only discourage investment, but may also lead to currency overvaluation by attracting capital from overseas, which leads to a fall in exports, and also increases the cost of servicing government debt, which leads to cuts in government expenditure. This has occurred in Africa (see *African Development Report, 1994*). Currency overvaluation and cuts in government expenditure are both deflationary. In Latin America in the 1970s, financial liberalization went wrong because there was an explosion of government debt, economic instability and excessively high real interest rates, which led to bankruptcies, bank failures and prolonged recession. In the immortal words of Diaz-Alejandro (1985): 'Goodbye financial repression, hello financial crash'! Financial liberalization programmes were abandoned (temporarily).

A fourth critique of the financial liberalization school concerns the relationship between the formal and the informal financial sectors. Higher real interest rates are likely to attract funds away from the informal money market, or **curb market**, where there is no regulation over the use of funds. If banks are subject to reserve requirements and are forced to lend compulsorily to governments, the diversion of funds away from the informal sector may lead to the total supply of loans to the private sector being reduced. This is part of the argument of the **neostructuralist school** (see Buffie, 1984). The hypothesis is very difficult to test directly without information on the supply and composition of credit from the curb market. To the extent that curb loans are mainly for consumption purposes and the government uses the reserve requirements of the banks for productive investment, the problem may not be serious. If, however, the curb loans are for investment and the government uses the banks to finance current account budget deficits, the reallocation of funds between the sectors will adversely affect the total level of saving and investment.

A final point to make is that it does not follow that credit rationing will necessarily be eliminated and resources allocated more 'efficiently' if interest rates are not controlled and are allowed to reach their market clearing level. As Stiglitz[8] and Weiss (1981) showed in a classic paper, banks suffer from the problem of **adverse selection** because of **asymmetric information** on the part of borrowers and lenders. Borrowers know more than lenders about the risks involved in a loan transaction. A rational profit-maximizing bank may therefore be expected to practise credit rationing to reduce risk, and not simply lend to those projects that seem to offer the highest return but with more risk attached.

Where do these various criticisms leave the financial liberalization argument? Clearly, the existence of financial repression has to be taken seriously, but it does not follow that the more liberalization there is the better, when we know that financial markets have many imperfections, and that competition between banks and other financial institutions can lead to **financial distress** if there are not institutional structures in place with adequate standards of accounting and auditing to prevent bad loans. Financial liberalization does not mean 'free banking'. Governments will always need to intervene for prudential reasons, and also for strategic reasons either as a major borrower or to direct credit. Particular care needs to be exercised in the liberalization of interest rates because of their impact on costs, investment demand, the exchange rate and the cost of financing government deficits. This raises the intriguing question of what is the 'optimum' real rate of interest for a country? This is virtually impossible to answer (see Clarke, 1996), but even in classical terms it is not clear that the optimum real interest rate (r^* in Figure 14.2) is necessarily positive. The savings and investment curves could cut below the horizontal axis if liquidity preference is very high and investment demand is very weak.

Ultimately, financial liberalization has to be judged by its impact on economic growth and development, and here the evidence is very mixed. In a major cross-section study of 80 countries over the period 1960–89, King and Levine (1993) conclude that 'higher levels of financial development are significantly and robustly correlated with faster current and future rates of economic growth, physical capital accumulation and economic efficiency improvements'. Using cross-section analysis, however, it is difficult to test for causality. It could be that financial development is itself the product of growth and economic development. In fact Demetriades and Hussein (1996), taking time-series data for 16 countries, find considerable evidence of bi-directional causality between levels of financial deepening and economic development, and conclude that different countries exhibit different causality patterns, reflecting differences in financial sector policies and institutional structures. Arestis and Demetriades (1997) find that in South Korea the real interest rate and growth performance have been negatively related, and South Korea, despite financial liberalization, has deliberately pursued a policy of keeping real interest rates low in order to encourage investment. This is also the message from the World Bank's analysis of the *East Asian Miracle* (1993). It says 'a policy of moderate financial repression at positive real interest rates may have boosted aggregate investment and growth in the HPAEs [high performing Asian economies] by transferring income from depositors, primarily households, to borrowers, primarily firms'.

De Gregorio and Guidotti (1995) suggest that the relationship between real interest rates and growth is likely to be an inverted U-shape because negative real interest rates are not conducive to financial development and growth, and very high real interest rates are also likely to reduce growth by adversely affecting investment and leading to a concentration on risky projects. Somewhere in between, growth is likely to be maximized. Fry (1997) tests this hypothesis across 85 countries for the period 1971–95 and finds broad support for the idea, with the growth rate maximized with the real interest rate at zero!

What is clear from all the evidence across countries and continents is that if financial reforms are to succeed, they must be implemented in an appropriate macroeconomic, financial and institutional framework, with proper sequencing between internal and external liberalization. Sequencing is important because if countries liberalize their external sector before or at the same time as internal liberalization, it could have severe repercussions for the exchange rate. If there is no confidence in the country, the relaxation of capital controls could lead to capital flight and downward pressure on the exchange rate. On the other hand, higher real interest rates could attract massive capital inflows, leading to excessive currency appreciation. Either way, exchange rate instability is not conducive to macroeconomic stability.

Liberalization has been more successful in Asia than in Latin America and Africa because it has taken place in an environment of greater macroeconomic stability with a sounder institutional framework of regulation and supervision of the banking system. Macroeconomic stability means manageable fiscal and balance-of-payments deficits and low inflation to encourage the holding of financial assets and to allow funds to be devoted to the private sector. Confidence in the banking system is also important and requires the restructuring of bank balance sheets, the removal of bad debts and a strengthening of the management and risk evaluation capabilities of bank managers in order to avoid bankruptcies. Governments need to strengthen banking regulation and supervision at the same time that liberalization takes place. For successful liberalization, Fry (1997) outlines the following five prerequisites:

- Adequate prudential regulation and supervision of commercial banks, implying some minimal levels of accounting and legal infrastructure
- A reasonable degree of price stability
- Fiscal discipline
- Profit maximizing, competitive behaviour by the commercial banks
- A tax system that does not impose discriminatory explicit or implicit taxes on financial intermediation.

Two brief contrasting case studies of financial liberalization are presented in Case example 14.2.

Case example 14.2

Financial liberalization in Indonesia and Kenya, mid-1990s

Indonesia

Foreign exchange controls were eliminated in Indonesia in 1971, partly at the urging of the IMF but also because these controls reduced the efficiency of international trade and payments, and were extremely difficult to enforce given Indonesia's proximity to an open international financial centre in Singapore. However, extensive controls on the domestic financial system remained in place until 1983. Only then were interest rates liberalized and controls on credit allocation relaxed. Prudential supervision was strengthened in 1984, after the initial liberalization of the banking system. Similarly, after relaxing controls on the entry of new banks and easing restrictions on the extension of bank branches in 1988–9, stricter prudential regulations were introduced by the central bank to constrain the explosion of bank credit that followed deregulation.

Indonesia's experience is therefore characterized by the implementation of several large reforms, each followed by retrenchment and consolidation. Although problems have emerged because institutional development, especially in the area of prudential supervision, has tended to lag behind deregulation measures, the overall success of reform has been considerable. Real interest rates have been positive since 1983, and financial deepening has been extensive. Privately owned banks now constitute a much larger proportion of the banking sector, as the relative importance of publicly owned banks has declined, and securities markets, especially the Jakarta Stock Exchange, have become more important. Although there have been occasional setbacks, and institutional weaknesses in the accounting and legal systems remain, overall

▶

the financial liberalization strategy pursued in Indonesia has been supportive of wider economic development.

Kenya

Financial liberalization in Kenya is much more recent. Ceilings on bank lending rates were not removed until July 1991. The central bank continued to announce guidelines for the sectoral composition of bank credit expansion, although these were not strictly enforced after interest rate liberalization. International financial liberalization is even more recent. Offshore borrowing by domestic residents has been permitted only since early 1994, and portfolio capital inflows from abroad were restricted until January 1995. Supporting structural and institutional reforms have yet to be fully implemented. Many banks remain publicly owned and competition among them is limited.

Deregulation of interest rates in this monopolistic environment permitted banks to widen their margins such that real interest rates on bank deposits fell substantially. Partly in consequence, financial deepening has been modest, especially when measured by the ratio of private sector credit to national income. Although it is too early to evaluate the success of financial liberalization, the lack of accompanying institutional and structural reforms suggests that financial sector reforms will provide only modest benefits to the overall Kenyan development strategy.

Source: *Finance and Development*, June 1997.

FISCAL POLICY AND TAXATION[9]

There is another arm of the prior-savings approach to the financing of development from domestic resources that needs to be considered, and that is the use of fiscal policy and taxation. Fiscal policy has two major roles in the financing of development. The first is to maintain the economy at full employment so that the savings capacity of the economy is not impaired. The second is to design a tax policy to raise the marginal propensity to save of the economy as far above the average as possible without discouraging work effort and consistent with an equitable distribution of the tax burden.

Using fiscal policy to maintain full employment will involve deficit finance if unemployed or underused real resources exist in the Keynesian sense. While deficit finance is likely to be inflationary in the short run until supply has had time to adjust, there is an important analytical distinction between the means by which resources are made available for investment through deficit finance at less than full employment and the means by which savings are generated by inflation. In the former case savings are generated by an increase in real output; in the latter case by a reduction in real consumption through a combination of factors, including a real balance effect on outside money,[10] income redistribution from low savers to high savers, and money illusion.

Fiscal policy to raise the marginal propensity to save above the average is concerned with the implementation of taxes to reduce consumption in the private sector. Saving brought about by taxation is **involuntary saving**. How much taxation a country raises as a proportion of national income depends on two major factors: the **taxable capacity** of the country, and the **tax effort** made by the country in relation to its taxable capacity. The taxable capacity of a country depends on such factors as the overall level of per capita income of the country, the distribution of income, the level of literacy and urbanization, the size of the industrial sector, the importance of trade, whether the country has mineral resources, and the amount of foreign investment. In turn, the tax effort depends on the extent to which a country exploits these various tax bases and on the rates of tax applied to the bases.

The overall **buoyancy** of a tax system is measured by the proportional change in total tax revenue ($\Delta T/T$) with respect to the proportional change in national income ($\Delta Y/Y$), and is composed of two parts: the elasticity of tax revenue ($\Delta T/T$) with respect to the tax base ($\Delta B/B$); and the elasticity of the base ($\Delta B/B$) with respect to income ($\Delta Y/Y$), that is

$$(\Delta T/T)/(\Delta Y/Y) = (\Delta T/T)/(\Delta B/B) \times (\Delta B/B)/(\Delta Y/Y) \tag{14.3}$$

If the tax system is progressive (with higher tax rates applied to higher levels of income or expenditure), then the elasticity of tax revenue with respect to the base will be greater than unity, and buoyancy will be greater than unity provided the elasticity of the base with respect to income is at least unity. If buoyancy is greater than unity, then tax revenue as a proportion of national income will rise as national income rises. The buoyancy of the tax system can be increased by increasing the rates of tax or extending the base.

Any measured change in tax revenue with respect to income is likely to consist both of an automatic increase in tax revenue as income increases if the rate structure is progressive, and the effect of discretionary changes in tax rates and extension of the tax base. The **elasticity** of a tax system is measured as buoyancy minus the effect of discretionary tax changes. There are techniques for estimating the elasticity of the tax system but we will not describe them here – suffice it to say that the greater the elasticity, the more that tax revenue and saving can increase without the need for discretionary changes. This is a desirable feature of tax systems in circumstances where it may be difficult to implement discretionary changes.

Tax effort depends on the elasticity of the system and overall buoyancy, and needs to be measured in relation to capacity. One way of doing this, pioneered by the IMF (see Tait *et al.*, 1979), is to take a cross-section of countries and relate their ratios of tax revenue to national income to the various measures of tax capacity mentioned earlier, namely per capita income, the importance of trade and industry and so on. Estimating such an international tax function gives an equation of the form:

$$T/GDP = a + b_1(PCY) + b_2(X/GDP) + b_3(I/GDP) + \text{other variables} \tag{14.4}$$

where T/GDP is a country's ratio of tax revenue to national income, PCY is per capita income, X/GDP is the ratio of trade to GDP, I/GDP is the ratio of industrial output to GDP, and the coefficients b_1, b_2, b_3 etc. measure the *average* effect of each of the variables on the tax ratio across countries. For example, if b_2 was estimated as 0.5, this would mean that a country with a trade ratio that is 1 per cent above the average for all countries will have a tax ratio that is 0.5 percentage points above the average for all countries, other things remaining the same.

By this method, a country's tax effort can be measured by substituting its values for PCY, X/GDP, I/GDP and so on in (14.4), predicting what the tax ratio *should be* and then comparing the predicted value with the actual value of the tax ratio. If the actual value is greater than predicted, the country can be said to be making a good effort; if it is less, then the tax effort can be regarded as weak. A study of this nature has been made by Piancastelli (2001) for 75 developed and developing countries over the period 1985–95, and the results are shown in Table 14.3. Any country with a tax effort index greater than 1 has a tax ratio greater than predicted. It can be seen from Table 14.3 that there are several developing countries making a good tax effort, including some of the largest and poorest such as India, Pakistan and Ghana. Equally, however, there are other developing countries making a very poor effort, including many countries in Latin America, notably Mexico, Argentina, Venezuela, Colombia, Bolivia and Peru.

The facts on tax revenue in developing countries are that tax revenue as a percentage of national income is typically low, averaging less than 20 per cent compared with nearly 30 per cent in high-income countries, and taxes on income are a minor source of tax revenue compared with indirect taxes, as can be seen in Table 14.4. The proportion of the population that pays income tax in developing countries is correspondingly low, averaging about 20 per cent, compared with the vast majority of the working population in developed countries, who constitute over 40 per cent of the total population.

On the surface there would appear to be a great deal of scope for using tax policy to raise the level of community saving relative to income. Two important points must be borne in mind, however. The first is that the rudimentary nature of the tax system in developing countries is partly a reflection of the stage of development itself. Thus the scope for increasing tax revenue as a proportion of income may in practice be severely circumscribed. There are the difficulties of defining and measuring the tax base and of assessing and collecting taxes in circumstances where the population is dispersed and primarily engaged in producing for subsistence, and where illiteracy is also rife. And there is also the fact that, as far as income tax is concerned, the income of the majority of the population is so low anyway that it falls outside the scope of the tax system. Whereas 70 per cent of national income is subject to income tax in developed countries, only about 30 per cent is subject to income tax in developing countries.

Even if there is scope for raising considerably more revenue by means of taxation, whether the *total* level of saving will rise depends on how tax payments are financed – whether out of consumption or saving – and how income (output) is affected. It is often the case that taxes that make tax revenue highly elastic with respect to income are taxes that are met mainly out of saving or have the most discouraging effect on incentives. For example, very progressive income tax will discourage work effort if the substitution effect of the tax outweighs the income effect; and to the extent that high marginal rates of tax fall primarily on the upper-income groups with a low propensity to consume, saving may fall by nearly as much as tax revenue rises.

To avoid such large reductions in private saving, an **expenditure tax** on upper-income groups, which exempts saving from taxation, is an alternative to a progressive income tax, but the disincentive effect on work effort is not necessarily avoided. This

Table 14.3 Tax effort indices estimated over 1985–95

Countries	Actual tax ratio (a)	Predicted tax ratio (b)	Tax effort index ((c)=(a)/(b))	Countries	Actual tax ratio (a)	Predicted tax ratio (b)	Tax effort index ((c)=(a)/(b))	Countries	Actual tax ratio (a)	Predicted tax ratio (b)	Tax effort index ((c)=(a)/(b))
Fiji	20.595	9.023	2.283	Botswana	26.766	22.224	1.204	Peru	10.728	12.223	0.878
Kenya	19.991	10.497	1.908	PN Guinea	18.825	15.774	1.193	Jordan	17.733	20.938	0.847
Belgium	42.357	23.774	1.782	UK	32.752	27.542	1.189	Panama	17.881	22.197	0.806
South Africa	25.182	15.297	1.646	Luxembourg	39.923	33.653	1.186	Philippines	13.696	17.218	0.795
Netherlands	44.273	27.228	1.626	Portugal	28.667	24.307	1.179	Madagascar	9.174	11.641	0.788
Ethiopia	11.665	7.502	1.555	Sweden	34.721	29.484	1.178	Japan	15.856	20.236	0.784
Ghana	11.760	7.776	1.512	Costa Rica	20.903	17.913	1.167	Dominican R	12.677	16.432	0.772
France	37.808	25.785	1.466	Cameroon	12.784	11.011	1.161	Colombia	11.895	15.431	0.771
India	10.645	7.279	1.462	Spain	28.326	24.437	1.159	El Salvador	12.265	15.979	0.768
Lesotho	23.370	16.058	1.455	Belize	21.649	18.685	1.159	Mexico	13.752	18.431	0.746
Italy	37.482	26.176	1.432	Finland	28.219	24.777	1.139	USA	18.020	24.251	0.743
Zimbabwe	21.449	15.062	1.424	Austria	32.210	28.559	1.128	Turkey	12.452	16.899	0.737
Uruguay	25.515	18.089	1.411	Syria	16.334	14.576	1.121	Congo (Dem. Rep.)	6.885	9.379	0.734
Morocco	22.534	16.027	1.406	Iceland	24.347	22.018	1.106	Switzerland	19.878	28.015	0.710
Namibia	27.595	19.957	1.383	Indonesia	15.737	14.533	1.083	Nepal	7.160	10.387	0.689
Egypt	20.704	15.121	1.369	Greece	23.093	21.862	1.056	Venezuela	16.119	23.675	0.681
Romania	21.053	15.797	1.333	Brazil	17.103	16.273	1.051	Argentina	11.401	17.434	0.654
Tunisia	24.165	18.171	1.330	Malaysia	20.016	20.417	0.980	Canada	18.008	27.743	0.649
New Zealand	32.996	24.815	1.330	Chile	18.801	19.451	0.967	Bolivia	9.451	14.620	0.646
Ireland	34.487	26.496	1.302	Thailand	15.620	16.450	0.950	Sierra Leone	6.789	10.772	0.630
Norway	32.860	25.263	1.301	Mauritius	19.667	20.720	0.949	South Korea	15.619	25.678	0.608
Pakistan	12.999	10.058	1.292	Malta	25.688	27.647	0.929	Paraguay	9.139	15.754	0.580
Denmark	33.840	26.369	1.283	Germany	23.485	26.413	0.889	Guatemala	8.024	14.269	0.562
Sri Lanka	17.886	14.422	1.240	Australia	22.017	24.904	0.884	Iran	7.423	13.702	0.542
Zambia	18.286	15.133	1.208	Ecuador	14.836	16.819	0.882	Singapore	15.672	38.905	0.403

Source: M. Piancastelli, 'Measuring the Tax Effort of Developed and Developing Countries: Cross Country Panel Data Analysis', mimeo, University of Kent, 2001.

Table 14.4 Composition of tax systems, by major type of tax, 1992

	Total taxes share of GNP (%)	Composition of taxes (%)				
		Taxes on international trade	Domestic commodity taxes	Domestic income taxes	Social security taxes	Other taxes
Low-income countries	16.0	25.2	32.9	18.8	0.1	23.0
Lower-middle-income countries	19.0	17.8	28.3	31.5	1.7	20.7
Upper-middle-income countries	21.0	9.3	29.1	25.2	14.8	21.6
High-income countries	27.0	1.1	18.2	42.5	27.9	10.3

Source: M. Gillis, D. Perkins, M. Roemer and D. Snodgrass, *Economics of Development* (New York: W. W. Norton, 1996).

is so because if the expenditure tax encourages saving, the tax rate must be higher to yield the same revenue as the income tax. If people work to consume and the price of consumption is raised, work effort will be curtailed if the substitution effect of the change outweighs the income effect. The more successful the expenditure tax is in stimulating saving out of a given income, the higher must be the rate of tax to keep the yields from the two taxes equal, and the greater the disincentive to work effort is likely to be. If the expenditure tax is in addition to the income tax, however, there is no reason to expect any substitution effect in favour of private saving, so that whether aggregate community saving increases depends on how much work effort is discouraged and on the relative propensities to consume and save of those who pay the tax compared with those of the government. In general the most effective tax policy to raise the level of saving relative to income is to impose taxes on those with a high marginal propensity to consume, namely the poor, but there are obvious considerations of equity to bear in mind in pursuing such a policy, as well as the practical consideration of political feasibility.

The predominant importance of agriculture in developing countries makes agricultural taxation a potentially significant source of tax revenue and a means of transferring resources into investment. There is a great variety of tax instruments for taxing agriculture, including taxes on land area, on land value, on net income, marketing taxes, export taxes, land transfer taxes and so on. If revenue is the aim, then marketing and export taxes are probably the most efficient and the easiest to collect. As far as exports are concerned, two main systems may be adopted. Either the state-controlled marketing board may pay the producer a price that is lower than the international price received, or the government may require that all foreign exchange receipts be surrendered, with compensation given in local currency at an exchange rate that overvalues the local currency.

Export taxes may, however, have disincentive effects. The substitution effect of export taxes will be to discourage production, or to switch production to the home market if the home market is not saturated. Either way, the yield from tax will fall if the tax base (the level of exports) falls more than in proportion to the rise in the export tax. Trade taxes have also been shown to be very unstable because of the volatility of primary product exports (and of imports), which can lead to severe budgetary problems for countries that rely on them (see Bleaney *et al.*, 1995).

In theory, land taxes are probably the most desirable way to transfer resources from agriculture, but in practice land taxes are not important as a source of tax revenue. It is also worth mentioning that no developing country has yet successfully applied a conventional income tax to agricultural income. The nearest that countries have come to this is to tax the value of land, the imputed income from land or the potential physical yield from land.

The balance between direct taxes on income and indirect taxation on expenditures and trade in the economy at large is heavily weighted in the direction of the latter, particularly in the form of import duties and sales taxes. The emphasis on indirect taxes originates from the difficulties already mentioned of levying direct taxes, and the disincentive effects that direct taxes can have. This is not to say that indirect taxes are totally devoid of disincentive effects, but they are probably less, especially if taxes such as sales taxes and import duties can be levied on necessities without too much social hardship. Indirect taxes on luxuries will raise revenue, the more so the more price inelastic the demand, but the taxes may largely be paid out of saving to the extent that luxuries are consumed by upper-income groups with a low propensity to consume. The equity grounds for such taxation, however, are still strong.

Taxes on business are relatively easy to collect and administer, but again business taxation may merely replace one form of saving with another. The marginal propensity to save out of profits is typically high. The main justification for company taxation must be to retain control of resources that might otherwise leave the country if the business is foreign-owned, or to substitute public for private investment on the ground that public investment is more socially productive than its private counterpart.

TAX REFORM IN DEVELOPING COUNTRIES[11]

Efficient utilization of the tax potential of developing countries raises problems that vary with the circumstances of each country, but there are certain fundamental changes in most of these countries that if adopted would make it possible to increase public revenue and reduce some of the inequities that now exist. In particular, if a tax system is to be accepted by a poor community it must be seen to be administered honestly and efficiently, which means that every attempt must be made to minimize the scope for avoidance (legal) and evasion (illegal).

According to the classical canons of taxation, a tax system is to be judged by the standards of equity, efficiency and administrative convenience. In most developing countries the tax system is neither equitable nor efficient and is administratively cumbersome. Avoidance and evasion are rife.

Equity requires a comprehensive definition of income and non-discrimination between income sources. A major deficiency of tax systems all over the world, and particularly in developing countries, is that there is no single comprehensive tax on all income. Typically there is a 'cedular' system, with separate taxes on different sources of income. Wage and salary earners ('earned' incomes) tend to be discriminated against *vis-à-vis* the owners of property and capital and the self-employed (professional people and small traders). An equitable system should also be such that it discourages luxury consumption and makes it difficult to avoid and evade taxation.

Taxable capacity is not measured by income alone, but also by wealth. Equity therefore also requires the taxation of wealth. The ownership of wealth endows the owner with an inherent taxable capacity, irrespective of the money income that the asset yields. Consider the case of a beggar with nothing and a rich man who holds all his wealth in the form of jewellery and gold, which yields no money income. Judged by income their taxable capacity is the same: nil! No one could claim, however, that their ability to pay was the same, and that for tax purposes they should be treated equally.

Income tax is not only inequitable between those with property and those without, but also *between* property holders. For example two property holders may derive the same income from property but the value of their property may differ greatly. One has a greater taxable capacity than the other. Only a combination of income and property taxes can achieve equity according to ability to pay. This is the case for a **wealth tax**.

Equity also requires that gifts between individuals be taxed, on death and *inter-vivos*.

Efficiency requires that the entire tax system be self-reinforcing and self-checking so that the attempt to escape one tax increases the liability to other taxes. The system should also, as far as possible, be based on a comprehensive annual return.

The above considerations suggest at least four major reforms of the tax system in developing countries, which at the same time would release resources for investment and act as an incentive to effort:

- That *all* income (including capital gains) be aggregated and taxed in the same way, at a progressive rate but not exceeding a maximum marginal rate of, say, 50 per cent. Marginal rates above this level may not only discourage incentive but may also be counterproductive by encouraging evasion and avoidance.
- The institution of a progressive personal expenditure tax levied on rich individuals who reach the maximum marginal rate of income tax.
- The institution of a wealth tax.
- The institution of a gifts tax.

INFLATION, SAVING AND GROWTH

If voluntary and involuntary saving are inadequate, inflationary policies that 'force' saving by 'taxing' money and redistributing income between classes within the private sector are an alternative possibility. The price of financial conservatism may well be economic stagnation. The potential benefits of inflationary finance, which embrace both the Keynesian and the quantity theory approach to development finance, have been discussed by economists[12] at least since David Hume in the eighteenth century; and several economic historians (including Keynes) claim to have discerned a relationship in history between periods of inflation and rapid economic development. Hamilton (1952) claims that inflation was a powerful stimulant to growth in a wide number of historical contexts through the favourable effect of excess demand on profits, saving and investment; for example in England and France in the sixteenth and seventeenth centuries and in England in the latter half of the eighteenth century. Rostow (1960) also claims that inflation was important for several industrial take-offs.

Keynes, in his *Treatise on Money* (1930), similarly remarked on the apparent extraordinary correspondence in history between periods of inflation and deflation and national rise and decline, respectively. Keynes was certainly more predisposed to inflation than to deflation. He described inflation as unjust and deflation as inexpedient, but of the two inflation is to be preferred because 'it is worse in an impoverished world to provoke unemployment than to disappoint the rentier' (Keynes, 1931). While recognizing that inflation to increase capital accumulation may have regressive distributional consequences, he further argued that the long-run gains to wage earners can outweigh the short-term losses:

> the working class may benefit far more in the long run from the forced abstinence which a profit inflation imposes on them than they lose in the first instance in the shape of diminished consumption so long as wealth and its fruits are not consumed by the nominal owner but are accumulated. (Keynes, 1930)

THE KEYNESIAN APPROACH TO THE FINANCING OF DEVELOPMENT

The Keynesian approach to the financing of development by inflationary means stresses, first, that investment can generate its own saving by raising the level of income when the economy is operating below capacity, and by redistributing income from wage earners with a low propensity to save to profit earners with a high propensity to save when the economy is working at full capacity. Second, inflation itself can encourage investment by raising the nominal rate of return on investment and reducing the real rate of interest. Only the first of these two aspects of the Keynesian approach will be considered here.

Unemployed resources provide the classic argument for Keynesian policies of inflationary finance. If resources are unemployed or underused, real output and real savings can be increased by governments running budget deficits financed either by printing money or by issuing government bonds to the banking system and the public.

In a situation of genuine 'Keynesian' unemployment, any tendency towards inflation, whatever method of deficit finance is used, should burn itself out as the supply of goods rises to meet the additional purchasing power created. Some economists have questioned, however, whether the observed unemployment of labour in developing countries is strictly of the Keynesian variety, and whether the supply of output would respond very much to increased demand. It is probably true that most unemployment in developing countries results not from a shortage of demand, but from a lack of cooperating factors of production to work with (mainly capital); and the direct multiplier effects of government expenditure may be low, but some deficit-financed projects may have considerable secondary repercussions on output if they eliminate production bottlenecks at the same time.

In the agricultural sector of developing countries, and in the production of consumer goods in the industrial sector, there are many opportunities for investment that can yield outputs several times the money value of capital invested in a very short space of time. In agriculture, the use of fertilizers and the provision of transport facilities are good examples. Credit expansion for these activities can soon generate sufficient output to absorb the demand-creating effects of the new money in circulation.

Thus while it may be true that much of the unemployment in developing countries is not of the Keynesian variety, it does not follow that monetary expansion in conditions of unemployment cannot generate secondary employment and output effects. The capacity-generating effects need to be considered in conjunction with the emphasis on demand in Keynesian static multiplier theory.

Let us now turn to the Keynesian full-employment case. At full employment, inflation is the inevitable result of the Keynesian approach to development. In contrast to classical and neoclassical theory, Keynesian theory specifies independent saving and investment functions and allows price changes in response to excess demand in the goods market to raise saving by redistributing income. Inflation is the means by which resources are redistributed between consumption and investment. In Keynesian models, investment is not constrained by saving, but by the inflation rate willing to be tolerated by wage earners who have had their real wages cut.

If plans to invest exceed plans to save it is reasonable to suppose that both investors and consumers will have their plans thwarted. Investment is less than firms desire, but greater than consumers plan to save. Let us assume, therefore, that the actual growth of capital is a linear combination of planned saving and planned investment:

$$\frac{dK}{K} = \alpha \frac{I}{K} + (1 - \alpha) \frac{S}{K} \qquad \alpha < 1 \tag{14.5}$$

where K is the quantity of capital, I is planned investment and S is planned saving. Now assume that the rate of inflation is proportional to the degree of excess demand as measured by the difference between plans to invest and save:

$$\frac{dP}{P} = \lambda \left(\frac{I}{K} - \frac{S}{K} \right) \qquad \lambda > 0 \tag{14.6}$$

where P is the price level. Substituting the expression for I/K into (14.5) gives

$$\frac{dK}{K} = \frac{\alpha(dP/P)}{\lambda} + \frac{S}{K} \tag{14.7}$$

S/K is planned saving and $\alpha(dP/P)/\lambda$ is forced saving per unit of capital. Forced saving results from the inability of consumers to fulfil their planned consumption in conditions of excess demand. The underlying mechanism that thwarts the plans of consumers is inflation, which redistributes income from wage earners to profits. Other things remaining the same, if prices rise faster than wages, real consumption will fall and real saving increase as long as the propensity to save out of profits is higher than the propensity to save out of wages.

In Keynesian models, therefore, the effect of inflation on saving depends on two factors: the extent to which income is redistributed between wages and profits; and the extent of the difference in the propensity to save out of wages and profits. The relation between wages, prices and profits, and the consequent effect of income redistribution on saving, is best illustrated using simple algebra. Let Z be labour's share of national income so that

$$Z = \frac{W}{PY} = \frac{wL}{PY} = \frac{w}{Pr} \tag{14.8}$$

where W is the wage bill, w is the wage rate, P is price per unit of output, Y is income and $r = Y/L$ is the productivity of labour. Hence the rate of change of labour's share may be written as

$$\frac{dZ}{Z} = \left(\frac{dw}{w} - \frac{dP}{P}\right) - \frac{dr}{r} \tag{14.9}$$

From this equation a number of interesting propositions can be established. First, given a positive rate of growth of productivity, a sufficient condition for a redistribution of income from wages to profits is that prices rise faster than wages. Note, however, that in a growing economy (with positive productivity growth) it is not a necessary condition. Labour's share will fall and the share of profits rise as long as $(dw/w - dP/P) < dr/r$; that is, as long as the real wage rises less than the growth of labour productivity. In a growing economy, therefore, there is no necessary clash between the real wage and profits. The real wage can rise and the share of profits in income can also rise as long as some of the gains in labour productivity are appropriated by the capitalists.

Second, it can be shown that, on the classical savings assumption that the propensity to save out of profits is unity and the propensity to save out of wages is zero, the rise in the aggregate savings ratio will be equal to the fall in labour's share of income. If all wages are consumed and all profits are saved, (14.9) may be written as

$$\frac{dZ}{Z} = \frac{dc}{c} - \frac{dr}{r} \tag{14.10}$$

where c is real consumption per worker. Hence

$$\frac{dZ}{Z} = \frac{dC}{C} - \frac{dY}{Y} = \frac{d(C/Y)}{C/Y}$$

where C is aggregate consumption, Y is income and C/Y is the consumption–income ratio. Since $d(C/Y)/(C/Y) = - d(S/Y)/(C/Y)$ and $dZ = d(C/Y)$, we have the result that $- d(S/Y) = dZ$, that is, labour's share and the aggregate savings ratio change by exactly the same amount (in opposite directions).

The basic Keynesian notion that investment determines saving forms the backbone of **neo-Keynesian growth theory**, as originally expounded by Robinson (1962) and Kaldor (1955–6). Variations in the savings ratio resulting from inflation and income redistribution is one of the many possible adjustment mechanisms for raising the warranted growth rate towards the natural rate (see Chapter 4). As Robinson used to argue, in response to the neoclassical adjustment mechanisms of variations in interest rates and the capital–output ratio, there is nothing in the laws of nature to guarantee growth at the natural rate, but if entrepreneurs wish to invest sufficient to grow at the natural rate then saving will adapt, subject to an **inflation barrier**.[13] When a steady rate of growth is going on, the share of savings adapts to it. In effect, the actual growth rate pulls up the warranted growth rate by forcing saving. Saving adapts to investment through the dependence of saving on the share of profits in income, which rises with the level of investment relative to income in the way that has already been described.

Profits in turn depend on what happens to real wages when the system is out of equilibrium. The basic equation of Robinson's model is the distribution equation:

$$PY = wL + \pi PK \tag{14.11}$$

where π is the gross profit rate R/K, and P, Y, w, L and K are as before. Dividing by P and rearranging to obtain an expression for the profit rate, gives

$$\pi = \frac{(Y/L) - (w/P)}{(K/L)} = \frac{R/L}{K/L} = \frac{R}{K} \tag{14.12}$$

Given the capital–labour ratio (K/L), the rate of profit depends on the relationship between output per head and the real wage. If all wages are consumed and all profits are saved, the rate of profit gives the rate of capital accumulation and the rate of growth. This follows since $S = I = \pi K$, and $\Delta K = \pi K$; therefore $\Delta K/K = \pi$. And if the capital–output ratio is fixed, $\Delta K/K = \Delta Y/Y$; hence $\pi = \Delta K/K = \Delta Y/Y$.

Variations in the rate of profit and corresponding variations in the real wage provide the mechanism that equilibrates plans to save and invest and the actual and warranted growth rates. If the actual growth rate equals the natural rate, the warranted and natural growth rates will also be equalized. If the real wage remains unchanged as investment takes place, however, saving cannot adapt and a greater volume of real investment cannot be funded. This is the inflation barrier in a static model. It appears, in fact, that in a static context the growth rate can only be raised at the expense of the real wage, which comes close to the pessimistic development theories of Ricardo and Marx. In a growing economy, however, such pessimism would be unfounded because it can be seen from (14.12) that the rate of profit and capital accumulation can rise even if the real wage is rising, as long as the growth in labour productivity exceeds the increase in the real wage.

Kaldor's model also makes saving adjust to the desired level of investment through a rise in the share of profits in national income. The model consists of three basic equations:

$$Y = W + R \tag{14.13}$$

$$I = S \tag{14.14}$$

$$S = s_w W + s_r R \tag{14.15}$$

where R is profits, W is wages, s_w is the propensity to save out of wages and s_r is the propensity to save out of profits. Using the three equations we can write

$$\begin{aligned} I &= s_w(Y - R) + s_r R \\ &= (s_r - s_w) R + s_w Y \end{aligned} \tag{14.16}$$

Making investment the independent variable in the system, and dividing by Y gives

$$\frac{R}{Y} = \left(\frac{1}{s_r - s_w}\right)\frac{I}{Y} - \frac{s_w}{(s_r - s_w)} \tag{14.17}$$

The ratio of profits to income and the investment ratio are positively related as long as the propensity to save out of profits exceeds the propensity to save out of wages. The investment ratio must clearly be the independent variable in the system. Capitalists can decide how much they are going to consume and invest but they cannot decide how much profit they are going to make. If $s_r = 1$ and $s_w = 0$, then $I/Y = R/Y$, and, multiplying both sides of (14.17) by Y/K we have Robinson's result that the rate of profit, the rate of capital accumulation and the rate of growth are all equal. A higher level of investment can raise the rate of capital accumulation by raising the profit rate and the share of saving in total income, subject, of course, to the inflation barrier. The mechanism that gives this result is rising prices relative to wages.

It is interesting to consider, using a model like Kaldor's, how much inflation is necessary to raise the savings ratio by a given amount. There are two ways of approaching this, and both can be considered using the same model. One is to consider the redistributive effects of inflation through time and ask how much inflation there would have to be within a certain time period for the savings target to be achieved, holding the parameters of the model constant. The second approach is to consider what increase in the rate of inflation is required for a once-and-for-all increase in the savings ratio of a given amount. Both methods of approach can be considered if Kaldor's model is formulated in continuous time. Taking a savings function of the Kaldor type, $S = s_w W + s_r R$, let

$$S_t = s_w W_0 e^{wt} + s_r(Y_0 e^{pt} - W_0 e^{wt}) \tag{14.18}$$

where W_0 is the initial wage bill, Y_0 is the initial income level, w is the rate of growth of wages and p is the rate of growth of money income (= the rate of inflation). Dividing by $Y_0 e^{pt}$ to obtain an expression for the savings ratio at time t, and rearranging, gives

$$\left(\frac{S}{Y}\right)_t = \left(\frac{W_0}{Y_0}\right)e^{wt-pt}(s_w - s_r) + s_r \tag{14.19}$$

Now let $w = a + \alpha(p)$, where a is the rate of autonomous wage change and α is the wage–price coefficient. Equation (14.19) may then be written as

$$\left(\frac{S}{Y}\right)_t = \left(\frac{W_0}{Y_0}\right)e^{p(\alpha-1)t+at}(s_w - s_r) + s_r \tag{14.20}$$

The effect of inflation on the savings ratio through time can be ascertained by differentiating (14.20) with respect to time:

$$\frac{\partial(S/Y)_t}{\partial t} = [a + p(\alpha - 1)]\left(\frac{W_0}{Y_0}\right)e^{p(\alpha-1)t+at}(s_w - s_r) \tag{14.21}$$

Given the target rise in the savings ratio required during a particular time period, an approximate solution to p can be obtained given the parameter values of the model.

To consider the increase needed in the inflation rate to raise the savings ratio by a given amount, differentiate (14.20) with respect to p:

$$\frac{\partial (S/Y)_t}{\partial p} = (\alpha - 1)t \left(\frac{W_0}{Y_0}\right) e^{p(\alpha-1)+at}(s_w - s_r) \tag{14.22}$$

The reciprocal of (14.22) then gives the extra inflation required to raise the savings ratio by one percentage point. The change in the savings ratio with respect to a change in the inflation rate can be seen to depend on four factors:

- The difference in the propensity to save out of wages and profits $(s_w - s_r)$
- The wage–price coefficient (α)
- Labour's initial share of income (W_0/Y_0)
- The rates of inflation and autonomous wage increases already prevailing (p and a).

It is clear from (14.22) that if $\alpha = 1$ and/or $s_w = s_r$, there can be no redistribution effects on saving by generating extra inflation.

The extra inflation required to raise the savings ratio is very sensitive to the parameter values taken. On classical assumptions that $s_w = 0$ and $s_r = 1$, the extra inflation required to raise the savings ratio by one percentage point is relatively mild, regardless of the value of the wage–price coefficient and the initial share of wages in income.

If it is assumed that the initial share of wages in national income is 70 per cent and that the wage–price coefficient is 0.5, then only 2.85 per cent inflation would produce a 1 percentage point increase in the savings ratio.[14] This might be regarded as a small price to pay for extra growth. The narrower the difference in saving propensities, however, and the higher the wage–price coefficient, the more extra inflation would be required. For example if W/Y is 0.7, the wage–price coefficient is 0.9 and the difference between s_w and s_r is only 0.1, then 142 per cent inflation would be required to raise the savings ratio by 1 percentage point. Even Keynesians might regard such a rate as a high price to pay for extra growth.[15]

RECONCILING THE PRIOR-SAVING AND FORCED-SAVING APPROACHES TO DEVELOPMENT

There can be little doubt that the traditional development literature and the governments of most developing countries have veered towards the classical view of development when making policy prescriptions and formulating plans. But there is scope for a more eclectic approach. It is not necessary to be a classicist to recognize the importance of voluntary saving in capital-scarce economies, and it should not be necessary to be a Keynesian to admit that investors may lay claim on real resources in excess of the community's plans to save. Keynesians welcome prior saving. What they dispute is that saving is necessary for investment; that investment is constrained by saving. As Robinson (1960, Vol. II) said when discussing the relation between savings and investment at full employment: 'We cannot return to the pre-Keynesian view that savings governs investment. The essential point of Keynes' teaching remains. It is decisions about how much investment is to be made that governs the rate at which wealth will accumulate, not decisions about savings.' A start at reconciliation would be for the prior-savings school to admit the possibility of forced saving and to reduce their aversion to demand inflation. Equally, the Keynesians could admit that saving depends on factors other than the functional distribution of income, and that for any desired savings–investment ratio, inflation will fall as voluntary saving rises.

THE QUANTITY THEORY APPROACH TO THE FINANCING OF DEVELOPMENT

The quantity theory approach to the financing of development stresses the effect of inflation as a tax on real money balances. Suppose a government wishes to divert more of a country's resources to investment, one of the ways it can do so is to invest on society's behalf, financing the investment by expanding the money supply. In conditions where capital is already fully employed, monetary expansion will be inflationary.

Inflation is the means by which resources are effectively transferred to government. Inflation imposes a **tax on money holdings** and consists of a reduction in the real purchasing power of money and of the real resources that the holders of money must forgo to restore the real value of their money holdings. The base of the tax is the level of real cash balances (M/P), and the tax rate is the rate at which the real value of money is deteriorating, which is equal to the rate of inflation (dP/P). The real yield from the tax is the product of the tax base and the tax rate, that is, (M/P) (dP/P), which will be maximized (as in standard tax theory) when the elasticity of the base with respect to the rate of tax is equal to -1. If the rate of inflation is equal to the rate of monetary expansion, the real tax yield (R) will equal the real value of the new money issued, that is, (M/P) (dM/M) $= dM/P$. If $dP/P > dM/M$, some of the potential tax yield will be lost owing to a reduction in the tax base.

The inflation tax can be illustrated diagrammatically, as in Figure 14.3. DD is the demand for real money balances in relation to the rate of inflation. When prices are stable, the demand for real balances is D. At inflation rate P, however, which is expected to continue, the demand for real balances falls to M. The area $0PXM$ thus represents the amount of real income that holders of real money balances must substitute for money balances to keep real balances intact at level M. Since money balances must be accumulated and real income forgone at the same rate as the rate of inflation, the rate of tax is equal to the rate of inflation.

Inflation as a tax on money redistributes resources from the private sector to the government as the issuer of money – resources that are just as real as those obtained by more conventional means of taxation. Keynes was fully aware of this aspect of inflation, as well as the tendency for demand inflation to transfer income from wages to profits. In his *Tract on Monetary Reform* (1923) he describes inflation as 'a form of taxation that the public finds hard to evade and even the weakest government can enforce when it can enforce nothing else'.

The real yield from the inflation tax available for investment as a proportion of income (R_I/Y) will be the product of the money–income ratio, (M/P)/Y, the rate of inflation,

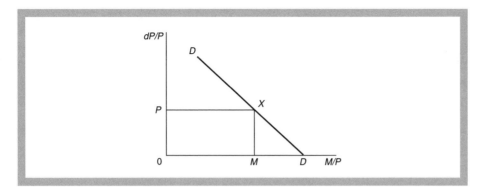

Figure 14.3 Inflation tax

$dP/P = dM/M$, and the proportion of the increase in the real money supply captured for investment $(R_I)/(dM/P)$, that is

$$\frac{R_I}{Y} = \left(\frac{M}{PY}\right)\left(\frac{dM}{M}\right)\left(\frac{R_I}{dM/P}\right) \tag{14.23}$$

Suppose that the money–income ratio is 0.4 and 50 per cent of new money issued is used for investment purposes, then a 10 per cent expansion of the money supply leading to a 10 per cent rate of inflation would yield 2 per cent of the national income for the development programme. If all the new money is used for investment purposes, the real yield from the tax is simply the ratio of the real value of the new money issued to income (our earlier result), which in this example would be 2.5 per cent. These calculations assume, however, that the desired ratio of money holdings to income remains unchanged regardless of the rate of inflation. In practice the ratio is likely to be a decreasing function of the rate of inflation because the opportunity cost of holding real money balances rises. Only if the base of the tax falls more than in proportion to the inflation rate, however, will the yield from the inflation tax actually decline.

From the limited evidence available, it appears that the elasticity of the money–income ratio with respect to the rate of inflation is quite low even in high-inflation countries. This suggests that inflation can operate effectively as a tax on money even in countries that have been experiencing high rates of inflation for many years. It should also be remembered that while inflation may reduce the desired ratio of money holdings to income, the ratio will have a continual tendency to rise with the gradual monetization and development of the economy. On balance the ratio may be very little affected by monetary expansion.

It should also be added that government investment projects financed by monetary expansion can reduce an economy's capital–output ratio (if the projects have high output–labour ratios and low capital–labour ratios), enabling a higher rate of capital accumulation for any given investment ratio, and therefore a higher rate of employment growth.

NON-INFLATIONARY FINANCING OF INVESTMENT

Up to now it has been assumed that the rate of inflation is equal to the rate of monetary expansion. If output is growing, however, and/or the demand to hold money relative to income is rising, a proportion of the expansion of the money supply will be non-inflationary, enabling some government investment to be financed without any increase in the general price level. This is easily seen taking the fundamental equation of exchange:

$$MV = PY$$

or

$$M = K_d PY \tag{14.24}$$

where M is the nominal money supply, V is the income velocity of circulation of money, K_d ($= 1/V$) is the demand to hold money per unit of money income, P is the average price of final goods and services and Y is real income.

Taking rates of growth of the variables, denoted by lower-case letters, gives

$$m = k_d + p + y \tag{14.25}$$

It can be seen that if the demand for money per unit of income is increasing ($k_d > 0$), m can be positive without the price level rising. Similarly, if the economy is growing ($y > 0$), m can also be positive without the price level rising. The government's proceeds from monetary expansion will equal $m - p$. In several developing countries the rate of growth of the demand for money per unit of income seems to be of the order of 5 per cent per annum. This, combined with a growth rate of output of 5 per cent per annum, would mean that the non-inflationary growth of the money supply would be of the order of 10 per cent per annum.

To calculate the fraction of investment requirements to sustain a given rate of growth that can be financed without inflation, we assume for simplicity that the banks operate a 100 per cent reserve system.[16] Setting $p = 0$, the approximate increase in the demand for money is equal to the product of the money stock and the rate of growth of the money stock:

$$dM = Mm = M(k_d + y) \tag{14.26}$$

Dividing by Y gives

$$\frac{dM}{Y} = \frac{M}{Y}(k_d + y) = K_d(k_d + y) \tag{14.27}$$

If y is the target growth rate and c_r is the required capital–output ratio, the investment ratio to achieve the growth rate is

$$\frac{I}{Y} = c_r y \tag{14.28}$$

Dividing (14.27) by (14.28) gives

$$\frac{dM}{I} = \frac{K_d(k_d + y)}{c_r y} \tag{14.29}$$

Equation (14.29) gives the proportion of total investment that can be financed by newly created money without leading to a rise in the price level. If $K_d = 0.3$, $k_d = 0.04$, $y = 0.03$ and $c_r = 3$, then $dM/I = 0.23$; that is, 23 per cent of total investment could be financed without inflation. The estimate is high because of the 100 per cent reserve ratio assumption, but the model is a good illustration of the potential that exists for the non-inflationary financing of development that results from the increased demand for money balances as the economy grows, and from the rise in the money–income ratio during the process of monetization of the economy.

THE DANGERS OF INFLATION

Some of the benefits of inflation have been considered, especially the ability of inflation to release resources for development by redistributing income between classes within the private sector and from the private sector to the government. Inflation is not without its dangers, however, and these must be emphasized.

First, a distinction needs to be made between the different types of inflation that may be experienced by a developing country: **demand inflation**, **cost inflation** and **structural inflation**. The argument for inflationary finance is an argument for demand inflation. Cost inflation, by reducing profits, will not be conducive to development. Structural inflation may be the inevitable price of development, but there is nothing in the process of structural inflation itself that will necessarily accelerate the development process.

There are also certain dangers and costs involved in deliberately pursuing an inflationary policy to stimulate development. The most serious threats to growth from inflation come from the effect on the balance of payments if foreign exchange is a scarce resource, and from the possibility that voluntary saving, productive investment and the use of money as a medium of exchange may be discouraged if inflation becomes excessive. If one country inflates at a faster rate than others its balance of payments may suffer severely, leading to protection and exchange controls, and hence inefficiency in resource allocation. As far as investment is concerned, if inflation becomes excessive, investment in physical plant and equipment may become unattractive relative to speculative investment in inventories, overseas assets, property and artefacts that absorb a society's real resources. If the real rate of interest becomes negative (that is, the rate of inflation exceeds the nominal rate of interest) it may even become attractive to claim real resources and not to use them.

Inflation clearly reduces the purchasing power of money. If inflation becomes excessive, not only may voluntary saving be discouraged but the use of money as a medium of exchange may be discouraged, involving society in real resource costs and welfare losses. Since inflation reduces the purchasing power of money, holders may be expected to avoid losses by cutting down their holdings of money for transactions purposes. The cost of inflation arises from the fact that cash balances yield utility and contribute to production, and inflation causes energy, time and resources to be devoted to minimizing the use of cash balances that are costless to produce; for example the frequency of trips to the bank may increase, which absorbs labour time, and credit mechanisms may be resorted to, which absorb society's resources.

There are also the distributional consequences of inflation to consider. These are difficult to assess, but the following can be said with some confidence:

- Debtors benefit at the expense of creditors
- Profit earners gain at the expense of wage earners in times of demand inflation and lose at the expense of wage earners in times of wage inflation
- Real-asset holders probably gain relative to money-asset holders
- The strong (in a bargaining sense) probably gain relative to the weak; and the young gain relative to the old, who tend to live on fixed contractual incomes.

In developing countries the possible inegalitarian distributional consequences of demand inflation should not be allowed, however, to constitute an argument against the use of mildly inflationary policies if one of the objects of the policies is to create additional employment. The major beneficiaries of inflationary finance should be the unemployed and the underemployed, which represents a move towards a more egalitarian structure of household incomes.

Having considered some of the potential dangers of inflation it can be seen that there is plenty of room for disagreement over whether inflation is a help or a hindrance to development. We have seen that it can help to raise the level of real saving and encourage investment; on the other hand it may stimulate the 'wrong' type of investment, and inflation may get out of control and retard development through its adverse effects on productive investment and the balance of payments. A lot clearly depends on the type of inflation under discussion and its rate. We now turn to the empirical evidence.

INFLATION AND GROWTH: THE EMPIRICAL EVIDENCE

The discussion above suggests that the relation between inflation and growth is likely to be non-linear, with growth positively related to inflation up to a certain rate of inflation and then negatively related as the disadvantages of inflation outweigh the advantages. This is in line with recent empirical evidence from large data sets across developing and developed countries.

A study by Bruno (1995) at the World Bank, taking pooled annual observations for 127 countries over the years 1960–92, produced the pattern depicted in Figure 14.4. Inflation and growth are positively related up to 5 per cent inflation, and then 'diminishing returns' to inflation set in. Inflation and growth are strongly negative once inflation rises above 30 per cent.

A study by Sarel (1996) at the IMF has produced a similar result. He takes 87 countries over the period 1970–90 and divides the observations into twelve inflation groupings using the inflation rate of group 6 as the standard of reference. He then estimates the effect that differential inflation has on the growth rate in the other groups. The results are shown in Figure 14.5. It can be seen that inflation has a generally positive effect on growth up to group 7, with inflation averaging 8 per cent. Thereafter, inflation and

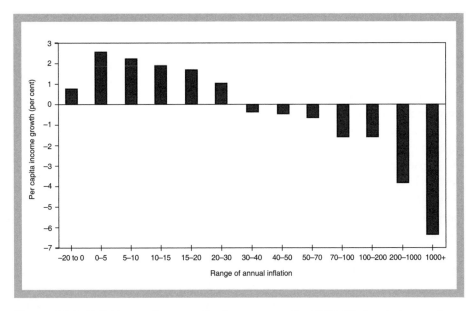

Figure 14.4 Inflation and per capita income growth, 1960–92 (pooled annual observations, 127 countries)

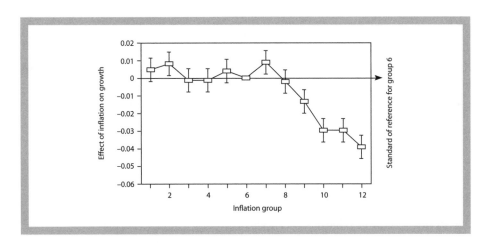

Figure 14.5 Effects of different inflation rates on growth

growth are negatively related. When inflation is very high (in group 12) the difference in the effect of inflation on growth compared with group 6 is close to 4 percentage points (holding all other factors constant).

Ghosh and Phillips (1998), also at the IMF, show the growth of GDP to be highest in the range of inflation 3–5 per cent for developed countries, and in the range 5–10 per cent for developing countries (no doubt reflecting greater structural inflation).

Evidence of non-linearity between inflation and growth is also found by Stanners (1993) in a study of nine countries over the period 1948–86 and 44 countries over the period 1980–88. First he divides the 44 countries into four groups according to the rate of inflation and shows that the highest growth occurred in the second group of countries, with an average rate of inflation of 8.2 per cent. He then takes a scatter of 342 points for nine countries over 38 years and shows a positive correlation between inflation and growth up to 8 per cent.

These recent results support early work by the present author (Thirlwall and Barton 1971; Thirlwall, 1974) which also showed a non-linear relation between inflation and the savings ratio and inflation and the investment ratio.[17]

It is not surprising from this evidence that Temple (2000) concludes his survey of inflation by saying 'since there is not yet robust evidence that moderate inflation has an adverse impact on growth, any case for price stability which relies on a positive growth effect should continue to be regarded with considerable suspicion'. Similarly, Levine and Zervos (1993), in a review of studies of the macrodeterminants of growth, conclude that 'given the uncharacteristically unified view among economists and policy analysts that countries with high inflation rates should adopt policies that lower inflation in order to promote economic prosperity, the inability to find simple cross-country regressions supporting this contention is both surprising and troubling'. Indeed we can be more categorical and say that there is *no* scientific evidence to suggest that a necessary condition for faster growth is that inflation should be as low as possible. The evidence suggests that mild inflation, up to 5–8 per cent, is positively beneficial for growth. After that, however, the effects of inflation can be seriously damaging.

THE INFLATIONARY EXPERIENCE

Having discussed the advantages of inflation and warned of the dangers of excessive inflation, the fact is that the inflationary experience of most developing countries outside Latin America, at least until the recent past, has been relatively mild. It is a myth that developing countries have been typically prone to high rates of inflation. Out of a sample of 48 developing countries over the period 1958–68, 38 recorded average rates of inflation of less than 6 per cent per annum (see Thirlwall, 1974, p. 35 and Appendix 1). Historically, most developing countries have been very financially conservative.

From the mid-1970s, however, there was a marked acceleration of inflation world-wide, and this continued into the 1980s and 1990s in many countries. The average rate of inflation in developed and developing countries over the period 1990–2002 is shown in Table 14.5. There is a wide variety of experience between countries, but on balance the developing countries have been more prone to inflation than the developed countries. In the developed countries, the average rate of inflation has been less than 10 per cent, whereas in the low- and middle-income countries it has averaged well over 20 per cent, even excluding the higher inflation countries (with rates over 100 per cent) and the inflation-prone countries of Latin America. In Latin America, inflation has been endemic for many years, almost from the start of the industrialization process, and we conclude this chapter with a brief discussion of the Latin American experience and of the 'structuralist–monetarist' controversy over the causes of rapid inflation.

Table 14.5 Inflation

	GDP implicit deflator average annual % growth 1990–2002		GDP implicit deflator average annual % growth 1990–2002		GDP implicit deflator average annual % growth 1990–2002
Albania	28.6	Germany	1.7	Oman	2.0
Algeria	15.7	Ghana	26.4	Pakistan	9.1
Angola	584.3	Greece	8.0	Panama	3.2
Argentina	4.5	Guatemala	9.6	Papua New Guinea	7.4
Armenia	142.2	Guinea	5.0	Paraguay	11.3
Australia	1.8	Guinea-Bissau	25.6	Peru	20.4
Austria	1.8	Haiti	20.1	Philippines	8.0
Azerbaijan	78.6	Honduras	17.1	Poland	19.8
Bangladesh	3.8	Hungary	17.4	Portugal	4.9
Belarus	283.6	India	7.2	Puerto Rico	3.1
Belgium	1.9	Indonesia	15.6	Romania	84.3
Benin	7.5	Iran, Islamic Rep.	25.0	Russian Federation	121.1
Bolivia	7.5	Ireland	3.8	Rwanda	11.7
Bosnia and		Israel	8.9	Saudi Arabia	1.7
Herzegovina	3.4	Italy	3.5	Senegal	4.0
Botswana	9.0	Jamaica	19.7	Serbia and Montenegro	57.1
Brazil	139.8	Japan	-0.3	Sierra Leone	26.7
Bulgaria	83.8	Jordan	2.7	Singapore	0.7
Burkina Paso	4.8	Kazakhstan	141.0	Slovak Republic	9.7
Burundi	12.8	Kenya	12.8	Slovenia	10.2
Cambodia	3.7	Korea, Rep.	4.2	South Africa	9.1
Cameroon	4.5	Kuwait	2.6	Spain	3.8
Canada	1.5	Kyrgyz Republic	82.5	Sri Lanka	9.1
Central African		Lao PDR	28.8	Sudan	51.9
Republic	4.1	Latvia	36.1	Swaziland	12.1
Chad	7.1	Lebanon	13.4	Sweden	1.9
Chile	7.1	Lesotho	9.6	Switzerland	1.1
China	5.5	Liberia	53.8	Syrian Arab Republic	6.9
Hong Kong, China	2.5	Lithuania	53.1	Tajikistan	175.2
Colombia	19.0	Macedonia, FYR	56.4	Tanzania	18.6
Congo, Dem. Rep.	731.4	Madagascar	17.0	Thailand	3.6
Congo, Rep.	8.5	Malawi	32.2	Togo	6.3
Costa Rica	15.6	Malaysia	3.5	Trinidad and Tobago	5.9
Côte d'Ivoire	7.8	Mali	6.7	Tunisia	4.1
Croatia	61.3	Mauritania	5.6	Turkey	71.8
Cuba	1.1	Mauritius	6.0	Turkmenistan	266.6
Czech Republic	9.9	Mexico	17.3	Uganda	9.5
Denmark	2.0	Moldova	89.4	Ukraine	183.4
Dominican Republic	8.9	Mongolia	45.4	United Arab Emirates	2.8
Ecuador	3.8	Morocco	2.5	United Kingdom	2.8
Egypt, Arab Rep.	7.4	Mozambique	26.8	United States	2.0
El Salvador	6.3	Myanmar	24.6	Uruguay	25.5
Eritrea	9.6	Namibia	10.3	Uzbekistan	184.2
Estonia	40.3	Nepal	7.2	Venezuela, RB	40.8
Ethiopia	5.6	Netherlands	2.3	Vietnam	12.5
Finland	2.0	New Zealand	1.7	West Bank and Gaza	8.8
France	1.5	Nicaragua	30.7	Yemen, Rep.	19.8
Gabon	5.3	Niger	5.5	Zambia	44.7
Gambia, The	4.6	Nigeria	25.0	Zimbabwe	32.3
Georgia	225.2	Norway	3.2		

Source: *World Development Indicators 2004* (Washington: World Bank).

THE STRUCTURALIST–MONETARIST DEBATE IN LATIN AMERICA

The inflation rate in countries such as Argentina, Brazil, Peru, Bolivia, Chile and Uruguay has averaged over 100 per cent in the last 40 years. In the early postwar years a heated debate developed, that still smoulders today, over the primary impetus behind rapid price increases. The participants in the debate polarized into two schools, frequently referred to as the 'structuralists' and the 'monetarists'. Although the debate is set in the Latin American context, it is nonetheless of general interest and in many ways has been analogous to the Keynesian–monetarist debate over the causes of inflation in developed countries. It might also be said that the two debates have been equally sterile and inconclusive.

The essence of the structuralist argument is that price stability can only be attained through selective and managed policies for economic growth. It is claimed that the basic forces of inflation are structural in nature, that inflation is a supply phenomenon, and as such can only be remedied by monetary and fiscal means at the expense of intolerable underutilization of resources. Structuralists do not deny that inflation cannot persist for long without monetary expansion, but they regard this as irrelevant because price stability can only be achieved by monetary means at the cost of stagnation and under-employed resources. Thus the role of financial factors in propagating inflation is not denied; what is disputed is that inflation has its *origins* in monetary factors. In the structuralists' view, monetary policy can only attack the symptoms of inflation, not its root causes.

In support of their case that inflation emanates from the supply side, the structuralists point to the characteristic features of developing countries: the rapid structural changes taking place in the economy, the supply inelasticities leading to bottlenecks, and so on, and refer back to the pre-industrialization era in Latin America when inflation was much less severe than it has been in the recent past. The main plank of the argument, and on which blame for inflation is placed, seems to be the lack of preparedness for industrialization. Prior to 1930 there was relative price stability due to fairly elastic supplies of agricultural output and low population growth. It is claimed, however, that Latin America entered the industrialization era burdened with a capitalist class that was unwilling to invest, in addition to growing population pressure on food supplies, which together contributed to bottlenecks and the beginnings of inflation, subsequently exacerbated by a wage–price spiral.

However there is some dispute about whether this picture is accurate for the whole of Latin America. According to some observers the sequence of events described by the structuralist school is more a description of a particular country, Chile. Indeed Campos (1961) went as far as to say that any visitor to the Economic Commission for Latin America in Santiago could not help but feel that the thinking of the structuralist school had been affected by the peculiarities of Chilean inflation. But Campos was a confessed monetarist! For even in the Chilean case he claims that the bottlenecks observed were induced by inflation itself and were not causal elements in the process. This is a more general claim of the monetarist school. They argue that supply bottlenecks are created by policies that discourage investment, for example price controls. Thus they maintain that the act of repressing inflation, instead of tackling the root causes of inflation, creates bottlenecks that subsequently feed the inflation. But in the first instance inflation is caused by excess demand due to monetary expansion. And balance-of-payments difficulties are also ascribed to monetary irresponsibility. In summary, the monetarists hold that the only way to curb inflation is through monetary and fiscal policy to dampen demand, and that most of the alleged supply inelasticities and bottlenecks are not autonomous or structural, but result from price and exchange rate distortions generated in the inflationary process. And on the broader question of whether or not inflation is desirable in the interests of development, the answer of the monetarists is an unequivocal 'no'.

It is true that it is hard to find a systematic relation between the rate of inflation and the rate of development in Latin America. If anything, the relation may be negative. It also seems to be the case that in countries where prices have risen the fastest the money supply has also grown most rapidly. Neither of these observations, however, answers the question of whether monetary expansion initiates inflation or simply stokes inflationary tendencies already present on the supply side. Moreover, if monetary expansion were curtailed, would it be output or prices that would fall the most? There is no consensus, but a majority of observers seem to pinpoint supply factors as the main contributors to rising prices. In many cases there seems to be a fair degree of unanimity that inflation has resulted from a combination of policies to foster high-priced import-substitution activities and exchange rate depreciation due to balance-of-payments difficulties. It is of course possible to argue that all balance-of-payments deficits are a monetary phenomenon, but the more relevant question is, what is the cost of balance-of-payments stability in terms of growth? If the cost is high, inflation may be regarded as the price paid for the worthy goal of attempting to maintain growth in the face of balance-of-payments deficits. There is a case, at least for policy-making purposes, for regarding inflation as primarily a supply phenomenon if a reasonable rate of growth is incompatible with a balance on the international account, or if price stability is only compatible with a massive underutilization of resources.[18]

What, then, are we to make of these two schools of thought on inflation in Latin America? The best solution is undoubtedly to play safe and steer a middle course. Indeed it would not be difficult to defend the view, even without much knowledge of individual situations, that inflation has probably resulted from a combination of both demand and supply factors; all inflations, other than hyperinflations, usually are!

DISCUSSION QUESTIONS

1 What is the difference between voluntary saving, compulsory saving and 'forced' saving?

2 What are the main determinants of voluntary saving?

3 How can 'monetization' of the economy help to raise the level and productivity of capital accumulation in developing economies?

4 What are the essential features of the informal financial sector in developing countries?

5 Outline the main requisites of a well-developed financial system.

6 What forms does financial repression take in developing countries?

7 What are the dangers of financial liberalization, and on what factors does the success of liberalization depend?

8 What role do special development banks and micro-credit play in financing development?

9 Suggest reforms to the tax system in developing countries that would promote both equity and capital accumulation.

10 What is meant by 'inflation as a tax on money'?

11 In what ways is demand inflation conducive to growth and development?

12 What conclusions would you draw from the recent empirical evidence on the relation between inflation and growth?

NOTES

1. Some inflation-induced saving may be voluntary, some involuntary.
2. Excluding China and India from the low-income countries, the savings ratio is only 10 per cent.
3. The approach gets its name from the quantity theory of money, which predicts that increases in the quantity of money will always lead eventually to increases in the price level.
4. The author was a consultant to the Tonga Development Bank in 1995.
5. For a survey of micro-credit, see Morduch (1999).
6. See, for example, Schumpeter (1911), Gurley and Shaw (1960) and Tun Wai (1972).
7. For an excellent comprehensive survey of the issues involved, see Gibson and Tsakolotos (1994).
8. A Nobel Prize winner in 2001.
9. For a comprehensive discussion of the general issues in this field, see Bird (1991) and Burgess and Stern (1993).
10. The 'real balance effect on outside money' refers to the attempt by holders of money assets to restore the real value of their money balances, eroded by inflation, by reducing their consumption. For a fuller discussion, see below.
11. For an excellent discussion of general issues, and with specific reference to Pakistan, see Ahmad and Stern (1991).
12. Including Malthus, Bentham, Thornton, Robertson and, more recently, Kaldor.
13. In a static economy the inflation barrier means a real wage so low that wage earners react to price increases to prevent the real wage from falling further. In a growing economy, it is the point at which labour resists any further reduction in its share of national income, that is, where labour appropriates all increases in labour productivity itself in the form of increased real wages.
14. The initial values of p and a can be ignored because for reasonable values the expression $e^{p(a-1)+at}$ is approximately unity.
15. For a full range of estimates see Thirlwall (1974).
16. Using a fractional reserve system lowers the capacity to finance government investment without inflation.
17. For a survey of models of inflation and growth, and some of the early empirical evidence, see Johnson (1984). For an up-to-date overview, see Temple (2000).
18. For a 'structural' interpretation of Bolivian hyperinflation, see Pastor (1991).

WEBSITES ON BANKING AND FINANCE

Micro-credit

Grameen Development Bank   www.grameen-info.org

Banking statistics

Search engine for central banks of countries   www.directhit.com

Foreign assistance, debt and development

CHAPTER OUTLINE

- Introduction
- Dual-gap analysis and foreign borrowing
- Models of capital imports and growth
- Capital imports, domestic saving and the capital–output ratio
- Types of international capital flows
- The debate over international assistance to developing countries
- The motives for official assistance
- Assessing the impact of aid
- The total net flow of financial resources to developing countries
- Official development assistance (ODA)
- Total net flow of financial resources from DAC countries
- UK assistance to developing countries
- The recipients of official assistance
- Aid tying
- Multilateral assistance
- World Bank activities
- Structural adjustment lending
- Poverty Reduction Strategy Papers
- Estimating the aid component of international assistance
- The distribution of international assistance
- Schemes for increasing the flow of revenue
- Foreign direct investment and multinational corporations
- International debt and debt-service problems
- Optimal borrowing and sustainable debt
- The debt crisis of the 1980s
- Debt relief
- The highly indebted poor country initiative (HIPC)
- Debt rescheduling
- Debt service capping
- Debt buy-backs and debt-swaps
- Long-term solutions

INTRODUCTION

In an open economy, domestic savings can be supplemented by many kinds of external assistance. In this chapter the role of foreign borrowing in the development process is considered, together with the debt-servicing problems associated with it, and particularly the debt crisis of the 1980s, which still lingers today in many developing countries, blighting the lives of millions of poor people. We shall consider the various types of foreign assistance, including bilateral assistance from developed countries, multilateral assistance from the World Bank, and foreign direct investment, which in recent years has come to dominate financial flows to developing countries. The motives for foreign assistance, and the problems to which it may give rise, will come under close scrutiny. In this chapter the emphasis is on longer-term resource flows to developing countries rather than on the provision of short-term balance-of-payments support, which is the traditional function of the International Monetary Fund (IMF) (we shall consider this in Chapter 17).

It is important to understand that lending and borrowing are natural features of capitalist economic activity, and without them capital accumulation would be confined to sectors of economic activity that have a surplus of income over current requirements, which would be inefficient and suboptimal from a growth point of view. Very often the factors that cause the supply of capital to increase create their own demand. The most obvious example of this, at the international level, was the increase in the price of oil in 1973 and 1979, which created large surpluses for oil-exporting countries and the need to borrow by oil-importing countries to maintain economic growth without curtailing imports. Going back into history, sovereign lending (and the problems associated with it) has been a feature of international economic life at least since the Medicis of Florence started to make loans to the English and Spanish monarchs in the fourteenth century. Historically, the international lending and borrowing process has played an integral part in the development of most major industrialized countries, and continues to play a significant role in the economic transformation of today's developing countries.

Traditionally, the role of foreign borrowing has been seen by countries as a supplement to domestic saving to bridge an investment–savings gap and achieve faster growth. The concept of **dual-gap analysis**, however, pioneered by Hollis Chenery and his collaborators (see later), shows that foreign borrowing may also be viewed as a supplement to foreign exchange if, to achieve a faster rate of growth and development, the gap between foreign exchange earnings from exports and necessary imports is larger than the domestic investment–savings gap, and domestic and foreign resources are not easily substitutable for one another. Foreign borrowing must fill the larger of the two gaps if the target growth rate is to be achieved. The historical sequence of experience originally suggested by Chenery was that countries in the pre-take-off stage of development would have a dominant investment–savings gap, followed by a dominant foreign exchange gap, with the possibility of a skill constraint at any stage. Most of today's developing countries, apart from the oil-producing and -exporting countries, have a dominant foreign exchange gap, which manifests itself in a chronic balance-of-payments deficit on the current account, while domestic resources lie idle. These deficits require financing not only in the interests of the countries themselves, but for the sake of the growth momentum of the whole world economy. There is an interdependence in the world economic system because countries are linked through trade. The alternative to the financing of deficits is adjustment by deflation to reduce imports, which means slower growth in the world economy as a whole.

If the historical experience of the developed countries is considered, in cases where borrowing took place (mainly from Britain as the major creditor) the borrowing was ultimately converted into an export surplus, which enabled the borrowing country to redeem its debt and become a net creditor. The condition for this to happen is that the marginal savings ratio should exceed the average in order to eliminate the investment–savings gap, if that is the dominant constraint, or that the marginal propensity to export should exceed the marginal propensity to import if foreign exchange is the dominant constraint. For most developing countries today there is little evidence that they have either the desire or the option to reduce the level of net resource inflows without a major disruption of their economies. The need for resources is as acute as ever, because of a dominant foreign exchange gap to meet development requirements and to pay interest and amortization on past borrowing. The countries find it difficult to convert domestic resources into foreign exchange in adequate quantities, not only cyclically when the world economy is depressed, but also secularly owing to their economic structure, that is, they produce goods whose demand tends to be both price and income inelastic in world trade.

In the first edition of this book (1972) I predicted that 'unless something is done the debt servicing problem arising from mounting resource flows may well become unmanageable in the not too distant future. It will certainly be a long time before these countries become net exporters of capital even in the absence of a investment–savings gap.' This prediction was made even before the Organization of Petroleum Exporting Countries (OPEC) first exerted its influence on the world economy in that fateful month of December 1973. Third World debt stands at $2300 billion in 2005, and over $200 billion flows out of the developing countries each year to service the debts.

DUAL-GAP ANALYSIS AND FOREIGN BORROWING

In national income accounting an excess of investment over domestic saving is equivalent to a surplus of imports over exports. The national income equation can be written from the expenditure side as

Income = Consumption + Investment + Exports − Imports

Since saving is equal to income minus consumption, we have

Saving = Investment + Exports − Imports

or

Investment − Savings = Imports − Exports

A surplus of imports over exports financed by foreign borrowing allows a country to spend more than it produces or to invest more than it saves.

Note that in accounting terms the amount of foreign borrowing required to supplement domestic savings is the same whether the need is just for more resources for capital formation or for imports as well. The identity between the two gaps, the investment–savings (I–S) gap and the import–export (M–X) gap, follows from the nature of the accounting procedures. It is a matter of arithmetic that if a country invests more than it saves this will show up in the national accounts as a balance-of-payments deficit. Or to put it another way, an excess of imports over exports necessarily implies an excess of the resources used by an economy over the resources supplied by it, or an excess of investment over saving. There is no reason in principle, however, why the two gaps should be equal *ex ante* (in a planned sense), that is, that *plans* to invest in excess of *planned* saving should exactly equal *plans* to import in excess of *plans* to export. This is the starting point of dual-gap analysis.

Before going into dual-gap analysis in more detail, a reminder of elementary growth theory is in order. Growth requires investment goods, which may either be provided domestically or be purchased from abroad. The domestic provision requires saving; the foreign provision requires foreign exchange. If it is assumed that some investment goods for growth can be provided only from abroad, a minimum amount of foreign exchange is always required to sustain the growth process. In the Harrod model of growth (see Chapter 4), it will be remembered, the relation between growth and saving is given by the incremental capital–output ratio (c), which is the reciprocal of the productivity of capital (p) that is, $g = s/c$ or $g = sp$, where g is the growth rate and s is the saving ratio. Likewise the growth rate can be expressed as the product of the incremental output–import ratio ($\Delta Y/M = m'$) and the ratio of investment-good imports to income ($[M/Y] = i$), that is, $g = im'$.

If there is a lack of substitutability between domestic and foreign resources, growth will be constrained by whatever factor is the most limiting – domestic saving or foreign exchange. Suppose, for example, that the growth rate permitted by domestic saving is less than the growth rate permitted by the availability of foreign exchange. In this case, **growth will be savings-limited** and if the constraint is not lifted a proportion of foreign exchange will go unused. For example, suppose that the product of the savings ratio (s) and the productivity of capital (p) gives a permissible growth rate of 5 per cent, and the product of the import ratio (i) and the productivity of imports (m') gives a permissible growth rate of 6 per cent. Growth is constrained to 5 per cent, and for a given m' a proportion of the foreign exchange available cannot be absorbed (at least for the purposes of growth). Some oil-exporting countries fall into this category. Conversely, suppose that the growth rate permitted by domestic savings is higher than that permitted by the availability of foreign exchange. In this case the country will be **foreign-exchange constrained** and a proportion of domestic saving will go unused. Most developing countries fall into this category. The policy implications are clear: there will be *resource waste* as long as one resource constraint is dominant. If foreign exchange is the dominant constraint, ways must be found of using unused domestic resources to earn more foreign exchange and/or raise the productivity of imports. If domestic saving is the dominant constraint, ways must be found of using foreign exchange to augment domestic saving and/or raise the productivity of domestic resources (by relaxing a skill constraint, for example).

Suppose now a country sets a target rate of growth, r. From our simple growth equations (identities), the required savings ratio ($s*$) to achieve the target is $s* = r/p$, and the required import ratio ($i*$) is $i* = r/m'$. If domestic saving is calculated to be less than the level required to achieve the target rate of growth, there is said to exist an investment–savings gap equal at time t to

$$I_t - S_t = s*Y_t - sY_t = (r/p)\ Y_t - sY_t \tag{15.1}$$

Similarly, if minimum import requirements to achieve the growth target are calculated to be greater than the maximum level of export earnings available for investment purposes, there is said to exist an import–export gap, or foreign exchange gap, equal at time t to

$$M_t - X_t = i*Y_t - iY_t = (r/m')\ Y_t - iY_t, \tag{15.2}$$

where i is the ratio of imports to output that is permitted by export earnings. If the target growth rate is to be achieved, foreign capital flows must fill the largest of the two gaps. The two gaps are not additive. If the import–export gap is the larger, then foreign borrowing to fill it will also fill the investment–savings gap. If the investment–savings gap is the larger, foreign borrowing to fill it will obviously cover the smaller foreign exchange gap.

The distinctive contribution of dual-gap analysis to development theory is that if foreign exchange is the dominant constraint, it points to the dual role of foreign borrowing in supplementing not only deficient domestic saving but also foreign exchange. Dual-gap theory thus performs the valuable service of emphasizing the role of imports and foreign exchange in the development process. It synthesizes traditional and more modern views concerning aid, trade and development. On the one hand it embraces the traditional view of foreign assistance as merely a boost to domestic saving; on the other hand it takes the more modern view that many of the goods necessary for growth cannot be produced by the developing countries themselves and must therefore be imported with the aid of foreign assistance. Indeed if foreign exchange is truly the dominant constraint, it can be argued that dual-gap analysis also presents a more relevant theory of trade for developing countries that justifies selective protection and import substitution. If growth is constrained by a lack of foreign exchange, free trade cannot guarantee simultaneous internal and external equilibrium, and the efficiency gains from trade may be offset by the underutilization of domestic resources. We shall take up this matter in Chapter 16.

A practical example of dual-gap analysis[1]

Now let us give a practical example of how dual-gap analysis may be applied with reference to an imaginary country, Padania. We shall be applying (15.1) to estimate the investment–savings gap, and (15.2) to estimate the import–export gap. Suppose that the target rate of growth (r) set by the government of Padania over the six-year planning period 2005–11 is 7.5 per cent per annum and the capital–output ratio is 3. The investment requirements in time t may be written as

$$I_t = crY_t = (3)\ (0.075)Y_t$$

Table 15.1 Estimates of investment–savings and import–export gaps assuming a 7.5 per cent growth of GDP, 2005–11 (£ million)

	$\begin{pmatrix} Y_0 \\ \text{Base year} \\ \text{2005} \end{pmatrix}$	Y_1 2006	Y_2 2007	Y_3 2008	Y_4 2009	Y_5 2010	Y_6 2011
GDP	1,822	1,958.7	2,105.5	2,263.4	2,433.2	2,615.7	2,811.8
Savings	161	172.9	185.3	198.6	212.9	228.2	244.7
Investment	319	440.7	473.7	509.3	547.4	588.5	632.7
Investment–savings gap	158	267.8	288.4	310.7	334.5	360.3	388.0
Exports	214	228.2	243.3	259.9	276.5	294.9	314.4
Imports	378	506.5	544.5	585.3	629.2	676.4	727.1
Import–export gap	164	278.3	301.2	325.4	352.7	381.5	412.7

Now let us assume that the following savings function has been empirically estimated:

$$S_t = 8.5 + 0.084 \, (Y_t)$$

Given this information and the target level of income, Y_t, for each year ($t = 1$–6), obtained from applying the target rate of growth to the base level of income (Y_0), the *I–S* gap can be estimated for each year in the future. The results are shown in Table 15.1. All values are in Padanian pounds at constant (base year) prices.

For import requirements, Padania's historical incremental output–import ratio (m') is 0.29. Therefore

$$M_t = \frac{r}{m'} \, Y_t = \frac{0.075}{0.29} \, Y_t$$

Exports in time t are calculated on the basis of an exponential trend rate of growth of 6.4 per cent per annum, that is

$$X_t = X_0 e^{0.064t}$$

The calculated import–export gap is also shown in Table 15.1. The results indicate that while, *ex post*, the two gaps were equal in the 2005 base year from the national accounts, the forecast gaps, *ex ante*, diverge through time, with the import–export gap dominant. For the target rate of growth to be achieved there would have to be foreign borrowing each year to fill the biggest of the two gaps. The analysis here is brief and mechanistic, but it illustrates the principle and what can be done in a simple way as a first approach.

The assumptions of dual-gap analysis

The basic underlying assumption of dual-gap analysis is a lack of substitutability between foreign and domestic resources. This may seem a stringent assumption, but nonetheless may be valid particularly in the short term.[2] If foreign exchange is scarce, it is not easy in the short run to use domestic resources to earn more foreign exchange, or to save foreign exchange by dispensing with imports. If it were easy, the question might well be posed: why do most developing countries suffer chronic balance-of-payments deficits over long periods despite vast reserves of unemployed resources? If domestic saving is scarce, it is probably easier to find ways of using foreign exchange to substitute, raising the domestic savings ratio and the productivity of capital. The Arab oil-producing countries are prime examples of countries with a surplus of foreign exchange and a dominant investment–savings gap that use their foreign exchange to buy imported capital equipment and manpower. In most, if not all, the oil-producing countries there is a **skill constraint** that prevents full utilization of the foreign resources available.

The pioneering dual-gap studies were undertaken by Chenery and his collaborators.[3] In the countries studied the typical sequence seemed to be an investment–savings gap followed by an import–export gap in the 'take-off' stage of development, sometimes of considerable stubbornness. In the past, before the oil price increases of 1973 and 1979, there was no tendency for one gap to predominate as the major constraint, taking the developing countries as a whole. Now almost every non-oil-producing developing country is confronted with a dominant foreign exchange gap. How temporary or permanent this dominant constraint will be depends on the future price of oil, the future export performance of the developing countries and the import requirements for growth.

MODELS OF CAPITAL IMPORTS AND GROWTH

It has been established that capital imports can raise the growth rate, but we have not considered how capital imports are financed and how the terms of borrowing may affect the growth rate. A model that incorporates these considerations is developed below. It is shown that:

- **The rate of growth of output** will be faster with capital imports, provided new inflows of foreign capital exceed the loss of domestic saving to pay interest – if, however, interest charges are met by new borrowing, capital imports must always have a favourable effect on the growth rate of output.
- **The rate of growth of income** will be faster as long as the productivity of capital imports exceeds the rate of interest.

The model is as follows. Let

$$O = Y + rD \tag{15.3}$$

where O is output, Y is income, r is the interest rate and D is debt. The difference between domestic output and national income is net factor payments abroad (including interest, profits and dividends). From (15.3) we have

$$\Delta O = \Delta Y + r\Delta D \tag{15.4}$$

Now

$$\Delta O = \sigma I \tag{15.5}$$

where σ is the productivity of capital, and

$$I = sO + \Delta D - srD \tag{15.6}$$

where s is the propensity to save. Substituting (15.6) into (15.5) and dividing by O gives an expression for output growth of

$$\frac{\Delta O}{O} = \sigma \left(s + \frac{\Delta D - srD}{O} \right)$$

(15.7)

Equation (15.7) shows that the growth of output will be higher than the rate obtainable from domestic saving alone as long a $\Delta D > srD$, that is, as long as new inflows of capital exceed the amount of outflow on past loans that would otherwise have been saved. This is a fairly stringent condition unless it is assumed that the interest payments due are met by creating new debt. It can be seen from (15.7) that if $rD = \Delta D$, the rate of growth of output with capital imports will always be higher than without capital imports as long as $s < 1$ (which is the normal case to consider). It may be concluded, then, that if interest payments on past loans can be borrowed in perpetuity, there is a permanent gain to be had from running an import surplus. In practice, however, a country that continually reschedules its debts might ultimately be classified by the international community as uncreditworthy and therefore not be able to borrow continually.

Now let us consider the rate of growth of income as the dependent variable. From (15.3):

$$\Delta Y = \Delta O - r\Delta D$$

(15.8)

Substituting (15.6) into (15.5) and the result into (15.8) gives

$$\Delta Y = \sigma(sO + \Delta D - srD) - r\Delta D$$

(15.9)

Now since $Y = O - rD$, we can also write (15.9) as

$$\Delta Y = \sigma sY + \Delta D(\sigma - r)$$

(15.10)

and dividing by Y we have the following expression for the rate of growth of income:

$$\frac{\Delta Y}{Y} = \sigma s + (\sigma - r) \frac{\Delta D}{Y}$$

(15.11)

Equation (15.11) shows that the growth rate of income with capital imports will be higher than that obtained from domestic saving alone as long as the productivity of capital imports (σ) exceeds the rate of interest on foreign borrowing (r). This is a standard result showing that investment is profitable as long as the rate of return exceeds the rate of interest. In some circumstances, however, this condition may also be a fairly stringent one.

CAPITAL IMPORTS, DOMESTIC SAVING AND THE CAPITAL–OUTPUT RATIO

From the discussion above it would appear that import surpluses have great potential in the development process. It is sometimes argued, however, that import surpluses financed by foreign capital inflows increase the capital–output ratio (that is, reduce the productivity of capital) and discourage domestic saving; and that a large fraction of capital inflows is consumed rather than invested. The net result may be no extra growth at all or even a reduction in the growth rate.[4] In terms of (15.7) and (15.11), the inflow of capital ΔD may reduce s and σ and only a fraction of ΔD may be invested.

As far as the relation between capital imports and domestic saving is concerned, many studies find a negative relation. Care must be taken in interpreting the relation, however, because owing to the way saving is defined, a negative relation is bound to be found as long as a proportion of capital imports is consumed. As we said before, domestic saving is normally defined in developing countries as investment minus foreign capital inflows: $S = I - F$. If F rises and I rises by less than F, S must fall for the equality to hold. Thus, a negative statistical relation between foreign capital inflows and domestic saving cannot necessarily be interpreted as a weakening of the development effort; it may simply reflect the fact that a proportion of foreign capital inflows is consumed. The important point is that no studies find a negative relation between capital inflows and the investment ratio. This means that capital inflows must finance some additional growth unless the productivity of capital falls drastically.

Some economists argue that foreign capital inflows do lower the productivity of capital and raise the capital–output ratio because of the tendency for international assistance to be used for prestige projects and because of a bias towards the use of international resource flows for infrastructure projects and social-overhead capital. It should be remembered, however, that there is an important distinction to be made between the capital–output ratio of a particular project on the one hand and the capital–output ratio for the economy as a whole, which is the ratio relevant to the model. It is quite possible for the overall capital–output ratio to fall even if projects financed by capital inflows are relatively capital-intensive. This could happen in at least two ways.

First, the greater availability of foreign exchange could enable a more productive use to be made of capital resources as a whole, for example if output is depressed because foreign exchange is the dominant constraint. Capital inflows also allow a change in the product mix towards more labour-intensive commodities which can reduce the overall capital–output ratio of the economy.

The second point is that the particular projects undertaken could have external effects on the output of other sectors. This is the 'externalities' argument for the public provision of infrastructure projects that themselves may have very high capital–output ratios. There is no convincing evidence that countries with a high ratio of capital inflows to national income have a higher capital–output ratio than other countries, and there is no convincing evidence that the productivity of foreign resource inflows is lower than the productivity of domestic savings.

TYPES OF INTERNATIONAL CAPITAL FLOWS

The main forms of international capital flows to developing countries consist of:

- Official flows from **bilateral** sources and **multilateral** sources (such as the World Bank and its two affiliates, the International Development Association, IDA, and the International Finance Corporation, IFC) on concessional and non-concessional terms
- Foreign direct investment (FDI)
- Commercial bank loans (including export credits).

Because of the different types of capital flow and the different terms of borrowing, there is an important distinction between the nominal value of capital flows and their worth in terms of the increased command over goods and services that they represent to the recipient. There is also a distinction between the **return** to international assistance, the **benefit** of international assistance (in a cost-benefit sense) and the **value** of international assistance.

The **return** to international assistance is the difference between the nominal value of assistance and the repayments discounted by the productivity of the assistance in the recipient country. In other words, the rate of return to assistance is measured in the same way as the return to any other investment.

The **benefit** of assistance is the difference between the nominal value of assistance and repayments discounted by the rate of interest at which the country would have had to borrow in the capital market. The benefit of assistance is measured as a differential, as in cost-benefit analysis. It is this calculation that we shall refer to subsequently as the '**grant element**' or '**aid component**' of the capital flow, representing 'something for nothing' to the recipient country. Clearly, if the terms on which the country borrows from the donor are no different from those prevailing in the free market, there is no grant element or aid attached to the capital transfer and the benefit of assistance in this sense is zero.

The **value** of the assistance may in turn differ from its benefit if the assistance is tied to the purchase of donor goods that differ in price from the world market price. If the prices are higher, this reduces the value of the grant element of assistance to below what it would otherwise have been.[5]

Looked at from the point of view of the donor, a positive benefit to the recipient does not necessarily mean a cost or sacrifice to the donor. There is a sacrifice to the donor only to the extent that the opportunity cost of capital – or the rate at which the donor would have had to borrow from another source in order to provide the loan – exceeds the rate of interest charged. Nor is any real resource transfer from the donor country necessarily implied. This depends on whether the donor country provides the real counterpart of the financial flow in terms of an export surplus. It is quite possible that the real transfer is provided by a different set of countries. For example, the United States gives aid to developing countries, but absorbs resources from the rest of the world by running huge balance-of-payments deficits on current account financed by foreign borrowing. Before going into the measurement of these concepts in greater detail, however, let us first consider the motives for international assistance to developing countries and give some idea of the magnitude of the nominal flows involved.

THE DEBATE OVER INTERNATIONAL ASSISTANCE TO DEVELOPING COUNTRIES

As indicated above, capital flows to developing countries come in many different forms: from grants or pure aid, to loans, to portfolio investment and foreign direct investment by multinational companies. The magnitude of these various flows will be given later in the chapter. Donor countries and institutions provide aid, loans and investment, and the developing countries accept the flows, for a mixture of reasons. But the motives and the wider interests of the developing countries as a whole may not always coincide. The rationale and relevance of financial assistance to developing countries are very much a matter of subjective assessment, depending on the meaning and vision of the development process held by the protagonists. There is a substantial body of opinion on both the right and the left of the political spectrum that argues that not only are financial resource transfers unnecessary for development, but may even be inimical to development by fostering dependence, weakening the domestic development effort and leading to a distorted structure of consumption and production (as well as to debt-servicing problems and profit outflows). These criticisms are levelled both at official assistance and at private investment, particularly at the activities of multinational companies. We shall consider some of these concerns later, but first let us examine the motives for assistance and why developing countries accept the transfers.

THE MOTIVES FOR OFFICIAL ASSISTANCE

There are several motives that inspire financial assistance from bilateral and multilateral sources on concessionary terms, but they can be grouped under three headings.

- The **moral, humanitarian motive** to assist poor countries, and particularly poor people in poor countries (see Opeskin, 1996). The same arguments that provide the basis for income redistribution within nations can also be applied at the global level, namely that absolute poverty is morally unacceptable and that if the marginal utility of income diminishes, total welfare will be increased by a redistribution of income from rich to poor. From a moral and welfare point of view, national boundaries are quite artificial constructions. Developing countries accept assistance with this concern in mind not only from national governments and international organizations as part of their regular aid programmes, but also from many voluntary and charitable organizations, and from emergency and disaster relief funds.

- The **political, military and historical motives** for granting assistance. A large part of the US aid programme was originally designed as a bulwark against the spread of communism, and the regional and country distribution of international assistance can still be partly explained in these terms. British and French assistance tends to be concentrated on ex-colonial territories, reflecting strong historical ties and perhaps some recompense for former colonial neglect. Most developing countries are willing to accept assistance on this basis to assist their development effort, particularly when governments are threatened by hostile forces from within or without.

- The **economic motives** of developed countries to invest in developing countries are not only to raise the growth rate of the developing countries, but also to improve their own welfare. Hence international assistance can be mutually profitable. If the rate of interest on loans is higher than the productivity of capital in the developed donor country and lower than the productivity of capital in the developing recipient country, both parties will gain. If there are underutilized resources in the developed country that could not otherwise be activated because of balance-of-payments constraints, international assistance will be mutually profitable by adding to the resources in the developing country and enabling fuller utilization of the resources in the developed country. This is the strong Keynesian argument for international assistance, and forcefully recommended in the Brandt Report (discussed in Chapter 1). Developing countries accept these financial flows because most are desperately short of foreign exchange (see Chapter 17), and judge the benefits of the international programmes and the projects that they finance to be greater than the costs of servicing the borrowing and any unfavourable side-effects.

The critics of official assistance dispute the alleged advantages of international assistance but weaken their case by confusing the operation of the system itself with its use as a potential instrument for the improvement of material well-being in developing countries, and by arguing from the particular to the general case. For example, aid antagonists argue that assistance is maldistributed and does not reach the poorest people in the poorest countries. If true this would partly undermine the humanitarian objective of aid. However, this is not a criticism of aid as such, but of its administration.

Secondly, critics argue that assistance has not helped economic development. The evidence brought to bear on this contention is that many countries are still desperately poor after 50 years of assistance, and that many parts of the Third World – South-East Asia, West Africa, and Latin America – made rapid progress long before the advent of official assistance. But clearly this is not conclusive evidence. In the first place, the per capita levels of annual assistance are trivial; in the second place, the countries in question might have been worse off without assistance; and thirdly, it does not logically follow that because some countries have progressed without official assistance, such assistance is unproductive. The capital that went into South-East Asia, West Africa and Latin America before the Second World War was mainly commercial capital, but there is no reason to believe that official capital from bilateral or multilateral sources would have been any less productive.

The critics of official resource flows are on much stronger ground when they argue that international assistance may help to support governments that are pursuing policies that are obstructing development, and that by increasing the power of government, assistance breeds corruption, inefficiency and tensions in society, which retards development. Assistance may also encourage irresponsible financial policies, and if the assistance is free (pure aid) there may be no incentive to use resources productively. There are elements of truth in these arguments, but it is not clear that the same policies would not be pursued without aid. Indeed the alternatives might be worse, because with assistance comes a certain amount of 'leverage', which can be used for the promotion of good governance.

A distinction also needs to be made between **programme aid** and **project aid**. Programme aid is much more open to abuse than supervised project aid. No one who has seen infrastructure projects the world over, financed on concessional terms by donor countries and multilateral agencies, could possibly claim that developing countries cannot benefit from aid.

ASSESSING THE IMPACT OF AID

History is littered with examples where aid to countries has been disastrous, but also of where it has been successful. Case example 15.1 on the successes and failures of aid gives a flavour of the contrast in experience. What accounts for the difference in outcomes can be summed up in two words 'good governance'.

Successes and Failures of Aid, 1970–1990s

Foreign aid has at times been a spectacular success. Botswana and the Republic of Korea in the 1960s, Indonesia in the 1970s, Bolivia and Ghana in the late 1980s, and Uganda and Vietnam in the 1990s are all examples of countries that have gone from crisis to rapid development. Foreign aid played a significant role in each transformation, contributing ideas about development policy, training for public policy-makers, and finance to support reform and an expansion of public services. Foreign aid has also transformed entire sectors. The agricultural innovations, investments and policies that created the 'Green Revolution' – improving the lives of millions of poor people around the world – were financed, supported and disseminated through alliances of bilateral and multilateral donors. Internationally funded and coordinated programmes have dramatically reduced such diseases as river blindness and vastly expanded immunization against key childhood diseases. Hundreds of millions of people have had their lives touched, if not transformed, by access to schools, clean water, sanitation, electric power, health clinics, roads and irrigation – all financed by foreign aid.

On the flip side, foreign aid has also been, at times, an unmitigated failure. While the former Zaire's Mobutu Sese Seko was reportedly amassing one of the world's largest personal fortunes (invested, naturally, outside his own country), decades of large-scale foreign assistance left not a trace of progress. Zaire (now the Democratic Republic of Congo) is just one of several examples where a steady flow of aid ignored, if not encouraged, incompetence, corruption and misguided policies. Consider Tanzania, where donors poured a colossal $2 billion into building roads over 20 years. Did the road network improve? No. For lack of maintenance, roads often deteriorated faster than they were built.

Sadly, experience has long since undermined the rosy optimism of aid-financed, government-led, accumulationist strategies for development. Suppose that development aid only financed investment and investment really played the crucial role projected by early models. In that case aid to Zambia should have financed rapid growth that would have pushed per capita income above $20,000, while in reality per capita income stagnated at around $600.

Foreign aid in different times and different places has thus been highly effective, totally ineffective, and everything in between. The chequered history of assistance has already led to improvements in foreign aid, and there is scope for further reform.

Source: World Bank Policy and Research Bulletin, October–December 1998.

There are two main approaches that can be used for assessing the impact of aid on economic development. The first, traditional approach is to do detailed case studies. As representative of this approach, a study by Cassen (1994) of seven countries (Bangladesh, Colombia, India, Kenya, Korea, Malawi and Mali) shows that most aid achieves its development objectives, although in several instances the performance could have been improved. The provision of aid played a major part in the 'Green Revolution' in South-East Asia, in the building of infrastructure in southern Africa and in the direct provision of basic needs and the relief of poverty in many countries. The study also found, however, that aid performance appears to be least satisfactory where it is most needed, and that, above all, improved performance requires better collaboration between aid agencies.

The second approach to assessing the impact of aid is to conduct a detailed statistical analysis of the relation between the growth of GDP or living standards and the amount of aid (as a proportion of GDP) received by each country, controlling for other variables. A typical estimating equation, taking a large sample of developing countries, would be:

$$y = a + b \, (\text{AID}) + (V_i)$$

where y is the growth of per capita income; AID is the ratio of official development assistance (ODA) to GDP and V_i is a vector of control variables ($i = 1 \cdots n$). Hansen and Tarp (2001) show that aid has a positive effect on growth with a coefficient (b) of approximately 0.25, but not when investment is included in the equations as one of the control variables. The implication is that aid promotes growth by encouraging investment, and this is confirmed by equations relating the ratio of investment to GDP with the ratio of aid to GDP. Dalgaard, Hansen and Tarp (2004) also show that aid has a positive effect on the growth of living standards with a one percentage point difference in the aid variable leading to (approximately) a 0.5 percentage point difference in the growth of per capita income. The impact is lower, however, in tropical countries. The authors conclude 'we have confidence . . . that aid has a positive impact on growth, and that the impact depends on climate-related differences'.

The World Bank has been heavily involved in work of this kind and one of its major researchers is David Dollar. The World Bank (1998) and Burnside and Dollar (2000) take a panel of 56 developing countries over the period 1970–93 and try to disentangle the circumstances in which aid 'works' and in which it does not. The major findings are that, on average, aid has had only a minor impact on the growth of GDP per head (partly because aid as a per cent of GDP is so small – not more than 0.5 per cent on average), but that it can be extremely effective in promoting growth and reducing poverty in the right economic and political environment where there are democratic governments pursuing sensible macroeconomic policies. In countries with good economic management, a one percentage point increase in aid raises the growth rate by 0.5 per cent and reduces poverty by 1 per cent. The Bank calculates that an extra $10 billion of aid could lift 25 million people out of poverty if the aid is directed to countries that manage their economies well. In countries with poor management, aid is entirely wasted. There are also diminishing returns to aid. Even in good environments, the returns to aid peak when aid reaches about 10 per cent of GDP.

The Bank emphasizes five major points from its analysis, and indicates five policy reforms for making aid more effective:

- ◼ Analysis
  - – Financial aid works in a good policy environment.
  - – Improvements in economic institutions and policies are the key to reducing poverty.
  - – Effective aid and private investment are complementary.
  - – The value of development projects is to strengthen institutions and policies so that services can be delivered effectively.
  - – Aid can nurture reform even in the most distorted environments – but it requires patience and a focus on ideas, not money.
- ◼ Reforms
  - – Financial assistance must be targeted more effectively to low-income countries with sound economic management.
  - – Policy-based aid should be provided to nurture policy reform where needed.
  - – The mix of aid activities should be tailored to suit the needs of the country and sectoral conditions.
  - – Projects need to focus on creating and transmitting knowledge and capacity.
  - – Aid agencies need to find alternative approaches to helping highly distorted countries.

Research also shows that uncertainty over the flow of aid also affects the impact of aid on growth because uncertainty deters investment and constrains fiscal management. Lensink and Morrissey (2000) take 75 countries over the period 1970–95 and find that aid uncertainty (measured by the standard deviation of aid flows) negatively affects growth performance, but when uncertainty is controlled for, aid itself has a positive and significant effect on growth performance.

Since the fundamental purpose of international aid is the relief of primary poverty, there is a strong case for arguing (as part of the reform of aid programmes) that assistance should be given only to countries that are committed to poverty reduction programmes and make progress towards certain targets, such as literacy, basic health care provision, reducing infant mortality and so on. As incentives for governments to embark on and continue the programmes, donor countries could, in turn, commit themselves to funding as long as the recipients continue to support them. This would improve the certainty of aid flows.

The World Bank is moving in these directions. In its *World Development Report 2000/ 2001* it refers to the new consensus on how aid can be made more effective: by linking aid to policy reforms; by improving coordination between donors, and by, above all, getting people in the recipient countries to believe that the projects or reforms will bring benefits, so that countries feel they 'own' the programmes (see also later on the reform of World Bank lending). The Bank now has a **Comprehensive Development Framework** which addresses these various issues. One new approach is the sectorwide approach where donors sign on to finance a *sector* (not individual projects), and the country itself does the work. An example is given in Case example 15.2.

Sectorwide Development Cooperation, mid-1990s

To address problems of ownership, donor coordination, and fungibility, donors are experimenting with pooling their resources to support sectorwide strategies designed and implemented by the recipient government. The country, in consultation with key stakeholders, designs a sector strategy and a budget framework extending several years forward, and donors put their money into the central expenditure pool for the sector. The approach encourages country ownership of sector strategies and programmes. It also links sector expenditure with the overall macroeconomic framework. And it ensures coordination of donor and recipient activities.

Some benefits of a sectorwide programme are evident in the Zambian health sector. In 1994 the government presented its national health policy and strategy to donors and – to ensure equitable distribution of services and coherent implementation of the strategy – asked them not to fund specific provinces or projects but to fund the Ministry of Health centrally. Hesitant at first, donors began to comply. An independent evaluation in 1997 found that 'health workers are better motivated; clinics are functioning; funds are flowing to the districts; some modicum of decentralization is in place; [and] an important part of the private sector has become formally involved'.

The approach ensures full ownership by the country and eliminates problems of donor coordination. With the country having more ownership and control over what happens, the use of resources can be much more efficient. But it also means great changes in donor–recipient relations and perhaps greater difficulties in implementation. Several sectorwide programmes have stumbled because of the recipient country's inadequate institutional capacity. Lack of consistency with the macroeconomic programme has been another problem. And donors often have too many requirements and thus too much of a problem (or too little interest) in harmonizing them. . . . Furthermore, these arrangements greatly diminish donor control and monitoring of exactly how money is spent.

The changes required imply that gaining support for the approach will be difficult. The recipient government has to be very confident, because strict adherence to a sectorwide approach means donors that do not participate in common implementation arrangements are not allowed to act in the sector (that is, they do not have their own projects). The result may be less donor funding for a sector. Governments might therefore opt for less strict sectorwide programmes choosing instead to allow donors to implement projects as long as they fit into the overall sector strategy.

Source: World Bank, World Development Report 2000/2001: Attacking Poverty (New York: Oxford University Press, 2000).

THE TOTAL NET FLOW OF FINANCIAL RESOURCES TO DEVELOPING COUNTRIES

The total net flow of financial resources to developing countries is the total of all official and private flows to developing countries *net* of repayments of past loans (amortisation). It includes flows given **bilaterally** by individual donor countries and **multilaterally** through international organizations, and includes flows both with and without concessionary terms. Most official flows are given on concessionary terms and are referred to as **official development assistance**. To qualify as such, the concessional (or grant) element of the flow must be at least 25 per cent. Only the concessional element of international financial flows really qualifies for the term 'aid'. The major donors of official development assistance are the 22 developed countries that form the **Development Assistance Committee (DAC)** of the OECD, and the various multilateral agencies. In addition, the OPEC countries have lent substantial sums on concessional terms in recent years.

Non-concessional flows are primarily bilateral, and consist mainly of foreign direct investment (FDI), export credits and syndicated bank loans.

The magnitude of all these various types of flow for 1991–2 and from 1999 to 2002 is shown in Table 15.2. The total net flows of financial resources from DAC countries to developing countries and multilateral institutions in 2002 was $86 billion, of which

Table 15.2 Total net flow of financial resources from DAC countries to developing countries and multilateral organizations, by type of flow ($ million)

	1991–2 average	1999	2000	2001	2002
I. Official development assistance	58,453	53,233	53,749	52,335	58,274
1. Bilateral grants and grant-like flows	35,678	33,931	33,040	33,410	39,793
of which: Technical co-operation	12,945	13,036	12,767	13,602	15,452
Developmental food aid (a)	1,707	1,045	1,180	1,007	1,086
Emergency and distress relief (a)	2,502	4,414	3,574	3,276	3,869
Debt forgiveness	4,508	2,277	1,989	2,271	4,534
Administrative costs	2,314	3,049	3,083	2,964	3,027
2. Bilateral loans	7,139	3,912	3,024	1,613	941
3. Contributions to multilateral institutions	17,513	15,390	17,685	17,311	17,540
of which: UN (b)	4,550	3,654	5,185	5,233	4,634
EC (b)	4,350	5,017	4,950	4,946	5,695
IDA (b)	5,505	2,834	3,672	3,599	3,279
Regional development banks (b)	1,503	1,860	2,187	1,491	1,813
II. Other official flows	8,097	15,589	−4,326	−1,443	−45
1. Bilateral	7,474	14,640	−4,303	−651	2,401
2. Multilateral	622	949	−23	−792	−2,446
III. Private flows at market terms	29,996	115,999	78,128	49,745	18,899
1. Direct investment	25,495	94,314	71,729	66,041	48,844
2. Bilateral portfolio investment	4,692	25,575	2,416	−14,946	−26,835
3. Multilateral portfolio investment	−1,075	−5,786	−3,369	−4,086	−3,124
4. Export credits	884	1,896	7,352	2,736	14
IV. Net grants by NGOs	5,704	6,715	6,934	7,289	8,765
Total net flows	**102,252**	**191,536**	**134,485**	**107,926**	**85,893**

Source: OECD, *DAC Journal Development Cooperation 2003 Report* (Paris: OECD).

$58 billion was official development assistance, and $28 billion consisted of non-concessional flows, largely FDI. Notice that official development assistance in money terms is no higher today than it was in 1991–2, which implies a large decline in *real* terms since prices have risen by at least 50 per cent.

The aid targets set for the developed countries of 1 per cent of their national incomes refer to the total net flow of financial resources, while the target for official development assistance alone is 0.7 per cent of donor countries' national incomes. It must also be remembered that the net flow of financial resources is not the same thing as the flow of *real resources*, since the former excludes interest payments and profit repatriation. If the terms of lending are steady over time, the net transfer of resources in any one year (that is, the gross capital inflow net of amortization *and* interest and profit payments) will be approximately equal to the estimated grant equivalent or aid component of assistance, the measurement of which is discussed later (see p. 486).

OFFICIAL DEVELOPMENT ASSISTANCE (ODA)

The total flow of ODA from the DAC countries in 2002 was $58 billion, of which approximately $40 billion consisted of grants, including $15 billion for technical assistance. $17 billion was disbursed to multilateral institutions. The recent record of individual DAC countries as providers of official development assistance is shown in Table 15.3,

Table 15.3 ODA and total net flow

	ODA		Total net flow of resources	
	$ million	% GNP	$ million	% GDP
Australia	989	0.26	834	0.22
Austria	520	0.26	1,866	0.92
Belgium	1,072	0.43	1,337	0.54
Canada	2,006	0.28	2,046	0.28
Denmark	1,643	0.96	1,577	0.93
Finland	462	0.35	−200	−0.15
France	5,486	0.38	4,729	0.33
Germany	5,324	0.27	8,733	0.44
Greece	276	0.21	322	0.24
Ireland	398	0.40	1,469	1.49
Italy	2,332	0.20	1,399	0.12
Japan	9,283	0.23	4,659	0.11
Luxembourg	147	0.77	148	0.78
Netherlands	3,338	0.81	−1,487	−0.36
New Zealand	122	0.22	164	0.30
Norway	1,696	0.89	2,279	1.19
Portugal	323	0.27	171	0.14
Spain	1,712	0.26	8,171	1.25
Sweden	1,991	0.83	2,211	0.93
Switzerland	939	0.32	2,234	0.75
United Kingdom	4,924	0.31	18,820	1.18
United States	13,290	0.13	24,410	0.23
Total DAC	**58,274**	**0.23**	**85,893**	**0.35**

Source: OECD, *DAC Journal Development Cooperation 2003 Report* (Paris: OECD).

together with the flow measured as a proportion of the donor's GNP. It can be seen that only the Netherlands, Denmark, Norway, Luxembourg and Sweden met the aid target of 0.7 per cent of GNP. The United States is the richest country but contributes the lowest proportion of GNP. The ratio for all DAC countries fell during the 1990s and now averages only 0.23 per cent.

TOTAL NET FLOW OF FINANCIAL RESOURCES FROM DAC COUNTRIES

As well as providing official development assistance, there are other official flows on non-concessional terms from the DAC countries to the developing countries, and the DAC countries are the major source of the various private flows. Table 15.3 also shows the total net flow of financial resources by DAC countries to developing countries and multilateral agencies, together with the total flow as a proportion of the donor's GNP. It can be seen that some of the countries that failed to meet the official development assistance target managed to meet the total net financial flow target of 1 per cent of GNP by virtue of large volumes of private lending, e.g. Ireland, Spain and the UK.

UK ASSISTANCE TO DEVELOPING COUNTRIES

The total net flow of ODA from the United Kingdom to developing countries and multilateral agencies in 2002 was $4924 million – a rise in money terms since the 1980s but a fall in real terms and as a proportion of GNP from 0.33 per cent in the mid-1980s to 0.31 per cent in 2002. This was way below the UN target of 0.7 per cent.

Most of the bilateral development assistance is now given in the form of grants. This represents a dramatic softening of the terms of assistance over the years, when in the past assistance was largely in the form of loans at near market rates of interest. Two-thirds of assistance is bilateral and the remainder multilateral. Of total bilateral aid, most is financial aid, of which approximately 25 per cent represents technical assistance. Technical assistance is an integral part of the British aid programme, and expenditure on it rose from $100 million in 1970 to $874 million in 2000. Over 60 per cent of bilateral aid goes to those poorest countries with a per capita income of less than $1000 at 1995 prices. The recent levels of total official and private flows are shown in Table 15.4.

As far as the geographical distribution of total official bilateral assistance is concerned, nearly one-third was disbursed to Sub-Saharan Africa in 2002, 20 per cent to Asia and the remainder to South America, Oceania and Europe. Over 130 countries received assistance, varying in amount from as little as $5000 to $271 million in the case of India, the largest recipient. To put the Indian sum in perspective, however, this total represents only 25 cents per head of India's population. This compares with the average per capita assistance from the UK to all developing countries of 90 cents. For further details on the distribution of UK aid see Case example 15.3.

In 1995 there was a major review of British aid policy. The new mission statement of the Overseas Development Administration (now the Department for International Development, DFID) was to 'improve the quality of life of people in poorer countries

Table 15.4 Total net flow of financial resources from the United Kingdom to developing countries and multilateral agencies, 2002

	$ million
NET DISBURSEMENTS	
I Official Development Assistance (ODA) (A + B)	4,924
ODA as % of GNP	**0.31**
A Bilateral Official Development Assistance (1 + 2)	3,506
1 Grants and grant-like contributions	3,384
of which: Technical cooperation	874
Developmental food aid	–
Emergency and distress relief	400
Contributions to NGOs	226
Administrative costs	279
2 Development lending and capital	121
of which: New development lending	–25
B Contributions to multilateral institutions	1,419
Grants and capital subscriptions, total	1,455
of which: EC	925
IDA	–
Regional development banks	103
II Other official flows (OOF) net (C + D)	–4
C Bilateral other official flows (1 + 2)	–4
1 Official export credits	97
2 Equities and other bilateral assets	–101
D Multilateral Institutions	–
III Grants by private voluntary agencies	353
IV Private flows at market terms (long-term) (1–4)	13,547
1 Direct investment	13,940
2 Private export credits	–1,237
3 Securities of multilateral agencies	–
4 Bilateral portfolio investment	840
V Total resource flows (long-term) (I–IV)	**18,820**
Total resource flows as a % of GNP	**1.18**

Source: OECD, *DAC Journal Development Cooperation 2003 Report* (Paris: OECD, 2003).

Case example **15.3**

UK Aid Policy

The United Kingdom's ODA was stable in 2002 and totalled US$ 4.9 billion. Its ODA/GNI ratio fell slightly from 0.32 per cent in 2001 to 0.31 per cent in 2002 but there are plans to increase ODA to reach 0.40 per cent of GNI by 2005.

Partnership approaches

The United Kingdom is commited to developing its partnership approaches. The Department for International Development (DFID) has established more offices in partner countries.

Poverty reduction policies

Taking poverty reduction as the overarching aim, DFID gives close attention to its development strategy and encourages other donors to target funds towards low-income countries. DFID focuses spending in sectors that contribute to poverty reduction, including those that promote pro-poor economic growth.

Policy coherence

The United Kingdom is committed to promoting coherence in government policy on all issues affecting developing countries. To make such coherence a reality, DFID works closely with other government departments on a range of issues including trade, conflict prevention, debt, the environment and child labour.

Performance measurement

DFID supports international efforts to develop a more results-based approach, through the development of indicators and joint evaluations. The Millennium Development Goals are an important point of reference for DFID. Its Public Service Agreement, strengthened by a detailed Service Delivery Agreement, provides the means for showing how DFID activities contributed towards achieving these longer-term international objectives while monitoring shorter-term performance.

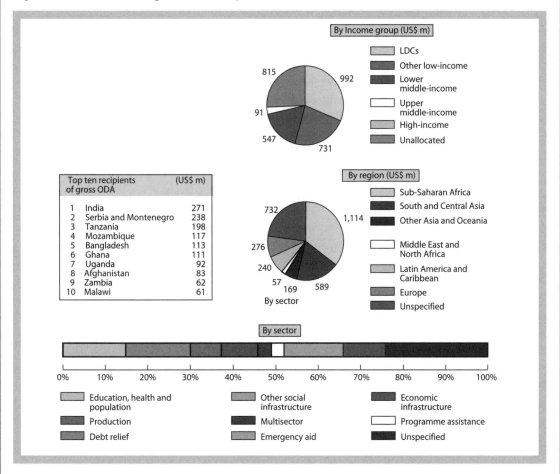

Source: OECD, *DAC Journal Development Corporation 2003 Report* (Paris: OECD, 2003).

by contributing to sustainable development and reducing poverty and suffering'. Four major aims were outlined:

- ■ To encourage sound development policies, efficient markets and good government
- ■ To help people achieve better education and health and to widen opportunities – particularly for women
- ■ To enhance productive capacity and conserve the environment
- ■ To promote international development and enhance the effectiveness of multilateral development institutions.

These aims now provide the basis of the DFID's approach to overseas development, with a renewed focus on aid to the poorest countries. A major White Paper in 1997 officially announced a new aid strategy of redirecting UK aid to the world's poorest countries, and abolishing at the same time the 'aid and trade provision' which gave money to exporters to compete internationally for big infrastructure projects abroad. Some aid, however, is still tied to the purchase of UK goods, which means that the foreign exchange cost of the UK aid programme is less than the budgetary cost or financial flow. See Case example 15.3 on UK aid policy for further details on the overall UK aid strategy.

The level of net private flows to developing countries from the United Kingdom fluctuates widely from year to year. During the 1970s there was a colossal increase in the amount of bank lending and portfolio investment in developing countries, largely consisting of the recycling of OPEC oil revenues deposited in London. The 1990s witnessed a big increase in FDI and portfolio investment. In 2002, the total was over $14 billion. Because of these private flows, the UN target for total flows of 1 per cent of national income is sometimes met, while the target for official development assistance has never been met.

THE RECIPIENTS OF OFFICIAL ASSISTANCE

We end this statistical section by showing the distribution of external capital by country for 2001 (the latest year available at the time of writing). It is well to remember that while ODA in 2002 amounted to approximately $58 billion, it was spread over more than 4 billion people in developing countries, giving an average annual per capita receipt of a little over $10. In India, the largest developing country in receipt of ODA from the DAC, assistance per head is approximately $2 per annum. The aggregate amounts of net official development assistance and ODA per head, and aid as a percentage of recipient's GNP, are shown in Table 15.5. It can be seen that in several poor countries, the amount of ODA per head is paltry and in the low-income countries as a whole ODA represents only 2.5 per cent of their GNP.

Table 15.5 The recipients of aid

	Net official development assistance $ millions 2001	Aid per capita $ 2001	Aid as % of GNI 2001		Net official development assistance $ millions 2001	Aid per capita $ 2001	Aid as % of GNI 2001
Albania	269	85	6.3	Mali	350	32	13.9
Algeria	182	6	0.3	Mauritania	262	95	26.6
Angola	268	20	3.4	Mexico	75	1	0.0
Argentina	151	4	0.1	Moldova	119	28	7.5
Armenia	212	69	9.7	Mongolia	212	88	20.5
Azerbaijan	226	28	4.2	Morocco	517	18	1.6
Bangladesh	1,024	8	2.1	Mozambique	935	52	28.2
Belarus	39	4	0.3	Myanmar	127	3	–
Benin	273	42	11.6	Namibia	109	61	3.4
Bolivia	729	86	9.4	Nepal	388	16	6.7
Bosnia & Herzegovina	639	157	12.7	Nicaragua	928	178	–
Botswana	29	17	0.6	Niger	249	22	12.9
Brazil	349	2	0.1	Nigeria	185	1	0.5
Bulgaria	346	44	2.6	Pakistan	1,938	14	3.4
Burkina Faso	389	34	15.7	Panama	28	10	0.2
Burundi	131	19	19.3	Papua New Guinea	203	39	7.2
Cambodia	409	33	12.4	Paraguay	61	11	0.9
Cameroon	398	26	4.9	Peru	451	17	0.9
Central African Rep.	76	20	7.9	Philippines	577	7	0.8
Chad	179	23	11.3	Poland	966	25	0.5
Chile	58	4	0.1	Romania	648	29	1.6
China	1,460	1	0.1	Russian Fed.	1,110	8	0.4
Hong Kong, China	4	1	0.0	Rwanda	291	37	17.3
Colombia	380	9	0.5	Saudi Arabia	27	1	0.0
Congo, Dem. Rep.	251	5	5.3	Senegal	419	43	9.2
Congo, Rep.	75	24	3.8	Serbia & Montenegro[a]	1,306	123	11.3
Costa Rica	2	1	0.0	Sierra Leone	334	65	45.8
Côte d'Ivoire	187	11	1.9	Singapore	1	0	0.0
Croatia	113	26	0.6	Slovak Rep.	164	30	0.8
Czech Rep.	314	31	0.6	Slovenia	126	63	0.7
Dominican Rep.	105	12	0.5	South Africa	428	10	0.4
Ecuador	171	13	0.9	Sri Lanka	330	18	2.1
Egypt, Arab Rep.	1,255	19	1.3	Syrian Arab Rep.	153	9	0.8
El Salvador	234	37	1.7	Tajikistan	159	25	15.5
Eritrea	280	67	40.9	Tanzania	1,233	36	13.3
Estonia	69	50	1.3	Thailand	281	5	0.2
Ethiopia	1,080	16	17.5	Togo	47	10	3.8
Georgia	290	55	9.0	Tunisia	378	39	2.0
Ghana	652	33	12.6	Turkey	167	2	0.1
Guatemala	225	19	1.1	Turkmenistan	72	13	1.2
Guinea	272	36	9.2	Uganda	783	34	14.1
Haiti	166	20	4.4	Ukraine	519	11	1.4
Honduras	678	103	10.8	Uruguay	15	5	0.1
Hungary	418	41	0.8	Uzbekistan	153	6	1.4
India	1,705	2	0.4	Venezuela, RB	45	2	0.0
Indonesia	1,501	7	1.1	Vietnam	1,435	18	4.4
Iran, Islamic Rep.	115	2	0.1	Yemen, Rep.	426	24	5.0
Israel	172	27	0.8	Zambia	374	36	10.7
Jamaica	54	21	0.7	Zimbabwe	159	12	1.8
Jordan	432	86	4.9	**World**	**58,244**	**10**	**0.2**
Kazakhstan	148	10	0.7	**Low income**	24,611	10	2.5
Kenya	453	15	4.0				
Korea, Rep.	−111	−2	0.0	**Middle income**	21,006	8	0.4
Kuwait	4	2	0.0	Lower middle income	17,145	7	0.5
Kyrgyz Rep.	188	38	12.9	Upper middle income	3,336	10	0.2
Lao PDR	243	45	14.6	**Low & middle income**	**57,208**	**11**	**0.9**
Latvia	106	45	1.4	East Asia & Pacific	7,394	4	0.5
Lebanon	241	55	1.4	Europe & Central Asia	9,783	21	1.0
Lesotho	54	26	5.5	Latin America & Caribbean	5,985	12	0.3
Lithuania	130	37	1.1	Middle East & North Africa	4,836	16	0.7
Macedonia, FYR	248	122	7.3	South Asia	5,871	4	1.0
Madagascar	354	22	7.8	Sub-Saharan Africa	13,933	21	4.6
Malawi	402	38	23.4	**High income**	1,036	1	0.0
Malaysia	27	1	0.0				

Source: World Bank, *World Development Report 2004* (Washington: World Bank, 2003).

AID TYING

About $20 billion of DAC aid to developing countries (or roughly one-half of total bilateral aid) is tied to the purchase of donors' goods. In this sense, capital inflows are not worth as much as they might be as the recipients have to pay higher prices for goods and services bought with aid money than the prices prevailing in the free market. Tying tends to be of two kinds: restrictions on where the recipients can spend the aid money; and restrictions on how the aid is used. Spending restrictions take the form of tying assistance to purchases in the donor country – so-called 'procurement tying'. This reduces the real worth of aid because it prevents recipients from shopping around to find the precise goods they want in the cheapest markets. Use restrictions normally mean that the aid must be used to cover the foreign exchange costs of a defined project. Restricting the use of aid to particular projects as well as to the donor country's goods amounts to double tying. Tying can be expensive.

The price of tied goods can be 20 per cent or more above the price of the same goods in the free market (see Jepma, 1991; Morrissey and White, 1993). Moreover there are other costs of tying apart from the inability of the recipient to buy in the cheapest market. If there is double tying, the project for which assistance is given might not fit perfectly into the recipient's development programme, the technology might be inappropriate, the donor may raise the import content unnecessarily, the suppliers may engage in exploitation, knowing that they have a captive consumer, and servicing over the life of the investment may be expensive.

The excess cost of imported goods from the tied source represents a form of export subsidy to suppliers in the donor country in the sense that if the aid was not tied and the suppliers had to remain competitive, the subsidy would have to be paid by the donor country itself. This subsidy to exporters in DAC countries through aid-tying amounts to about $2 billion a year, or 5 per cent of DAC assistance.

It seems unfair that developing countries should have to pay interest on export subsidies to developed countries' exporters. These excess costs should be deducted from the amount of the loans to be repaid, which at the same time would also reduce interest payments and bring the measure of aid closer to its real worth. Equally unfair is requiring loans to be repaid in scarce foreign currency. If tying is necessary to protect the balance of payments of donors, it would be helpful if the donors would accept loan repayments in the recipient's currency, saving the recipient's scarce foreign exchange and possibly promoting trade at the same time.

The one mitigating factor in all this is that the project for which assistance is given in tied form may have been undertaken anyway using the same source of supplies, in which case the assistance releases resources for another purpose. In other words, assistance to a certain extent is fungible because of resource switching. The fungibility of assistance also means that the balance-of-payments gain to the donor from tying may be quite small in practice because one form of purchase is substituted for another. This could be used as a bargaining weapon to reduce the extent of tying, the major reason for which seems to be balance-of-payments protection.

Several proposals have been put forward in recent years aimed at mitigating the disadvantages to the developing countries of aid tying without straining the balance of payments of the donor countries. One possibility is to institute bilateral purchasing arrangements between donor countries, whereby assistance from one donor to developing countries could be swapped for assistance from another donor country, leaving tying levels intact but increasing the competitive opportunities open to the recipient countries. Another possibility is a multilateral purchasing arrangement that would allow recipients to buy in the cheapest markets within a group of countries so chosen that the gains and losses from untying assistance would cancel out. To avoid any one donor being involved in a foreign exchange loss through untying, all the donors would have to untie at a different rate, depending on their relative share of exports to developing (recipient) countries and their relative share of the aid disbursed.

MULTILATERAL ASSISTANCE

The major sources of multilateral assistance to developing countries are the World Bank (the International Bank for Reconstruction and Development, IBRD) and its two affiliates, the International Development Association (IDA) and the International Finance Corporation (IFC), as well as the United Nations and various regional development banks. The total disbursement in 2002 was $43 billion, of which $23 billion was on concessional terms. A detailed breakdown of the lending by the various multilateral agencies from 1991/92 to 2002 is shown in Table 15.6.

The disbursements by multilateral agencies to developing countries consist not only of the contributions of developed countries but also of funds raised on the international capital market and repayments of previous loans. As can be seen from Table 15.6 the World Bank is essentially a commercial institution lending on non-concessional terms, and it raises large sums of money on the world's capital markets.

The IDA is the 'soft' loan affiliate of the World Bank and dispenses loans at very low rates of interest with long repayment periods. It is the most important provider of concessional multilateral assistance. Since 1960 it has lent over $100 billion to 90 countries. Only countries with less than a certain level of per capita income are eligible to receive assistance ($9000 in 1995), but this currently includes 79 countries with over 3 billion people.

The European Union (EU) has also become a major provider of concessional assistance through the European Development Fund (EDF). In 2002 it dispensed $6831 million – almost as much as the IDA.

The major providers of non-concessional assistance in recent years (apart from the World Bank) have been the two regional development banks – the IDB (the Inter-American Development Bank, lending to Latin America) and the ADB (Asian Development Bank).

WORLD BANK ACTIVITIES

The activities of the World Bank since its creation in 1946 have broadly reflected changes in thinking about development policy and development priorities – changes that the World Bank itself has played a large part in promoting. In the early years, and throughout the 1960s, the major emphasis of the Bank was on financing infrastructure projects in the field of power generation and distribution, transportation, ports, telecommunications and irrigation. There was very little support for agriculture and rural development, or industry and tourism; and programme loans (as opposed to project assistance)

Table 15.6 Concessional and non-concessional flows by multilateral organizations

	Gross disbursements				
	1991–1992 average	1999	2000	2001	2002
CONCESSIONAL FLOWS					
International Financial Institutions					
African Dev. Fund	679	516	360	464	741
Asian Dev. Fund	1,048	1,114	1,135	1,031	1,168
Caribbean Dev. Bank	33	33	36	50	113
Council of Europe	1	–	–	–	–
EBRD	–	11	5	17	44
IBRD	–	–	–	–	–
IDA	4,896	6,135	5,468	6,160	6,923
IDB	250	512	442	545	425
IFAD	171	231	250	254	250
IMF	904	1,471	1,131	1,683	2,936
Nordic Dev. Fund	–	38	39	33	35
Total IFIs	**7,981**	**10,060**	**8,865**	**10,235**	**12,635**
United Nations					
UNDP	866	508	390	282	275
UNFPA	149	185	133	311	310
UNHCR	909	253	493	545	633
UNICEF	665	564	576	600	567
UNRWA	307	286	301	359	392
UNTA	259	428	454	410	466
WFP	1,455	354	357	379	351
Other UN	653	161	568	574	614
Total UN	**5,263**	**2,741**	**3,272**	**3,462**	**3,608**
EC	3,904	5,238	4,763	5,908	6,831
Global Environment Facility	–	66	86	101	109
Montreal Protocol Fund	–	44	56	72	60
Arab Funds	461	227	215	381	298
Total concessional	**17,610**	**18,376**	**17,257**	**20,159**	**23,541**
NON-CONCESSIONAL FLOWS					
International Financial Institutions					
African Dev. Bank	1,466	723	506	614	679
Asian Dev. Bank	1,973	3,710	2,884	2,850	3,067
Caribbean Dev. Bank	24	77	65	50	108
Council of Europe	548	–	–	–	–
EBRD	–	366	439	548	627
IBRD	10,243	13,256	11,778	10,729	8,381
IFC	932	1,596	1,276	1,061	1,409
IDB	2,420	7,934	6,662	6,016	5,508
IFAD	–	–	40	33	20
Total IFIs	**17,606**	**27,703**	**23,643**	**21,902**	**19,799**
EC	386	855	608	662	109
Arab Funds	35	–	–	–	–
Total non-concessional	**18,027**	**28,559**	**24,251**	**22,564**	**19,908**

Source: OECD, *DAC Journal Development Cooperation 2003 Report* (Paris: OECD).

were largely confined to countries outside those classified as less developed.

The Bank began to realize, however, that investment in infrastructure was not enough; that it had a role to play in lending to support directly productive activities. It also recognized inadequacies in education and managerial skills, and became increasingly aware that the development taking place in the countries it was supporting was not trickling down to the vast masses of the poor. In the late 1960s and throughout the 1970s, the Bank began to play a more active role in agriculture and in helping both the rural and urban poor. Robert McNamara, the President of the Bank from 1968 to 1981, inaugurated this radical change of emphasis in his annual address to the Bank in Nairobi in 1973. He defined absolute poverty as 'a condition of life so degraded by disease, illiteracy, malnutrition and squalor as to deny its victims basic human necessities', and he pledged that the Bank would make a concerted attack on rural poverty in order to raise the productivity of the poor and improve the incomes of small farmers. The objective was to provide most of the benefits of lending to those in the bottom 40 per cent of income groups. In 1975 the Bank announced that it would also attempt to deal with the problems of the urban poor by promoting productive employment opportunities on labour-intensive projects, and by developing basic services to serve the poor at low cost, for example water supplies, sanitation, family planning and so on.

Successive Presidents of the World Bank have reiterated the Bank's commitment to helping the poor. It was mentioned in Chapter 2 that Lewis Preston announced in May 1992 that poverty reduction will be the 'benchmark by which our performance as a development institution will be measured', and this was reaffirmed by his successor James Wolfensohn who wrote in the *World Development Report 2000/2001*: 'poverty amidst plenty is the world's greatest challenge. We at the Bank have made it our mission to fight poverty with passion and professionalism, putting it at the centre of all the work that we do.' The Bank is committed to the Millennium Goal of halving the proportion of people living in poverty by 2015 compared to the level in 1990.

The distribution of World Bank assistance for various purposes is shown in Table 15.7. Apart from programme assistance, the majority of lending goes to transport and communications, and education.

Table 15.7 Distribution of World Bank lending, 2002

Area	% of total
Social and administrative infrastructure	25.8
Education	9.9
Health and population	4.1
Water supply and sanitation	3.9
Government and civil society	4.2
Other social infrastructures	3.8
Economic infrastructure	23.9
Transport and communications	13.4
Energy	7.3
Other	3.1
Production	3.3
Agriculture	2.9
Industry	0.2
Trade and tourism	0.2
Programme assistance, including emergency relief	47.0

Source: OECD, *DAC Journal Development Cooperation 2003 Report* (Paris: OECD, 2003).

STRUCTURAL ADJUSTMENT LENDING

Another initiative was introduced by the World Bank in October 1979: **structural adjustment lending** to countries in order to support their balance of payments. To qualify for structural adjustment loans, a country had to adopt policies that were acceptable to the Bank and designed to secure external equilibrium in the longer run without sacrificing growth. The emphasis was on improving the supply-side capacity of the economy.

The World Bank defines structural adjustment loans as 'non-project lending to support programmes of policy and institutional change to modify the structure of the economy so that it can maintain both its growth rate and viability of its balance of payments in the medium term'. The loans are geared to seven main areas:

- Supply-side reforms, for example improving the efficiency with which markets operate
- Price reforms
- Changing the price of tradeable goods relative to non-tradeables
- Getting the 'correct' terms of trade between agricultural goods and industrial goods
- Reducing the size of the public sector
- Financial reforms
- Tax reforms.

Governments must commit themselves to policy reform in order to qualify for a loan.

Balance-of-payments support has been the traditional preserve of the International Monetary Fund (see Chapter 17), but there is a difference of emphasis between the IMF and the World Bank. Whereas the policies of the IMF focus primarily on balance-of-payments management, the World Bank is more concerned with promoting policies to increase efficiency and providing incentives to raise export earnings and reduce import payments. Clearly, however, the roles of the two institutions now overlap and will do so increasingly as the IMF itself insists on supply-side policies as a condition for assistance, as well as on the traditional demand-side policies of devaluation and monetary contraction.[6] The distinct roles of the IMF and the World Bank are outlined in Case example 15.4.

Since the purpose of structural adjustment lending and the **Structural Adjustment Programmes (SAPs)** is to improve the growth potential of countries, evaluations of these lending programmes by independent investigators and the World Bank itself have focused on the key macro variables of GDP growth, savings, investment, exports and the balance of payments. In a World Bank symposium on adjustment lending, Corbo, Fischer and Webb (1992) single out the following as indicators of country performance: real GDP growth, the ratio of savings to GDP, the ratio of investment to GDP and the export ratio. Their methodology was to compare countries with SAP programmes with other countries with less intensive adjustment lending programmes and with countries that had received no adjustment loans. The performance of the three sets of countries was then compared relative to their performance in a base period before any loans were dispensed (that is, pre-1979). It appears that only the export ratio was superior in the SAP countries, and the investment ratio failed badly. This was also the conclusion of another World Bank study (1990), which found that structural adjustment lending

Roles of the IMF and the World Bank

International Monetary Fund

- Oversees the international monetary system and promotes international monetary cooperation
- Promotes exchange stability and orderly exchange relations among its members
- Assists members in temporary balance-of-payments difficulties by providing short- to medium-term financing, thus providing them with the opportunity to correct maladjustments in their balance of payments
- Supplements the reserves of its members by allocating SDRs if there is a long-term global need
- Draws its financial resources principally from the quota subscriptions of its members

The World Bank

- Seeks to promote economic development and structural reform in developing countries
- Assists developing countries by providing long-term financing of development projects and programmes
- Provides special financial assistance to the poorest developing countries through the International Development Association (IDA)
- Stimulates private enterprises in developing countries through its affiliate, the International Finance Corporation (IFC)
- Acquires most of its financial resources by borrowing on the international bond market

had achieved a modest degree of success in helping countries to improve their balance of payments, but had failed to lead to an upsurge in investment or to enable countries to 'grow out of debt'. Another major study of 40 countries (Harrigan and Mosley, 1991) found that the effect on GDP growth had been negligible; export growth and the balance of payments had improved, but investment had declined. The main reason for the disappointing results appears to be the heavy requirements (or conditionality) placed on recipient governments, which have served to depress demand and confidence. There is a general consensus that the requirements should be less stringent and more selective, and more sensitive to each country's circumstances (see Mosley, Harrigan and Toye, 1991).

Structural adjustment programmes have particularly hit the poor in many countries. Cornia, Jolly and Stewart (1987, 1988) called for 'adjustment with a human face', but the record is still not good. A major study by Noorbakhsh (1999), comparing the periods 1970–85 and 1986–92 in countries with SAPs and those without, found that virtually all the indicators of the standard of living – for example, infant mortality, life expectancy, adult literacy, primary school enrolment and per capita calorie supply – have fared worse in countries with structural adjustment loans.

It would seem that much more care is required in the design of structural adjustment programmes if they are to achieve growth with equity (see Bourguignon and Morrisson, 1992), and if the World Bank is to avoid the charge of being an anti-developmental institution, like its sister institution, the IMF (see Chapter 17).

The imposition of harsh conditionality, which has not worked, and the relative failure of SAPs, has led to calls for reform of World Bank lending. Gilbert, Powell and Vines (1999) suggest that *ex ante* conditionality should be abandoned altogether. Instead, the Bank should say to countries 'If you get your own house in order you can borrow from us without conditions, and can continue to do so as long as sensible economic policies are pursued and good governance prevails.' This amounts to a form of *ex post* conditionality, but the countries would 'own' the policies rather than be dictated to by the Bank. For countries without good governance and the ability to reform, the Bank should stop lending. Instead, it should act as a knowledge bank for the dissemination of best practice techniques in economic management and policy reform. This would require more World Bank staff in the countries concerned, fulfilling a training role.

POVERTY REDUCTION STRATEGY PAPERS

World Bank policy is already moving in the direction suggested above. In a new approach announced by the World Bank and IMF in 1999, national governments are being offered a role in shaping and implementing anti-poverty strategies as part of its new focus on tackling poverty directly and making debt relief conditional on countries producing **Poverty Reduction Strategy Papers (PRSPs)**. According to the Bank, the focus of PRSPs should be on 'identifying in a participatory manner the poverty reduction outcomes a country wishes to achieve and the key public actions – policy changes, institutional reforms, programmes and projects – that are needed to achieve the desired outcomes'. The idea is that the attack on poverty should be based on partnership between governments and all sections of society concerned with poverty reduction, with governments leading the process of setting the goals and monitoring the process. Already a few poor countries have developed their own broad-based anti-poverty programmes. Uganda has instituted a successful 'Poverty Eradication Action Plan'; Mozambique has a countrywide poverty plan, and Guinea has what it calls a 'National Strategic Vision'. It is still too early to judge the success of this new initiative.

ESTIMATING THE AID COMPONENT OF INTERNATIONAL ASSISTANCE

Because of the different nature of the various capital flows, a common procedure is required for measuring the equivalence of the different flows. Clearly grants and loans are not equivalent since the latter have to be repaid and the former do not.

A standard procedure for making the flows equivalent is to estimate the **grant equivalent or aid component** of the different flows by taking the difference between the nominal flow and future repayments discounted by the free market rate of interest, which was our earlier measure of the benefit of assistance. A capital inflow that is a pure grant (with no repayment obligations) is 'worth' its face value. A capital inflow that has to be repaid with interest is not worth its face value. How much less it is worth than its face value depends on the rate at which the repayments are discounted:

■ If the rate of interest at which the country would have had to borrow in the free market is greater than the actual rate of interest it has to pay, the worth or benefit will be *positive*.

■ If the rate of interest at which it would have had to borrow is less than the actual rate, the worth or benefit will be *negative* because the recipient would have had to pay back more than it need to have done (this is unlikely to happen).

The grant equivalent or aid component of assistance is measured in this differential benefit sense. The rate of return on the assistance may of course be much greater than the benefit if the productivity of the assistance is higher than the free-market rate of interest.

Other factors determine the grant equivalent of a loan as well as the effective interest rate subsidy. First, there is the **grace period** between the disbursement of the loan and the first repayment. The longer the grace period for a loan of a given maturity, the less the present value of the future discounted repayments. Second, there is the **maturity of the loan** to consider. This is important because the longer the maturity, the longer the concessionary interest rate is enjoyed and the less the present value of the future discounted repayments. Through the technique of discounting, any combination of repayment terms can be brought to a common measure.

All three factors referred to – the interest rate subsidy, the grace period and the maturity of the loan – can be incorporated into a simple formula for calculating the grant equivalent of a loan. The grant equivalent or aid component of a loan (as a percentage of its face value) is called the **grant element** and is equal to

$$\frac{G}{F} = \left[\frac{F - \left(\sum_{t=1}^{T} \frac{P_t}{(1 + r)^t} \right)}{F} \right] 100$$

where F is the face value of the loan, P_t is the total repayment of principal and interest in year t, T is the maturity of the loan and r is the rate of discount. Since P_t includes interest charges it can be seen that the lower the interest rate relative to the rate of discount (r), and the more that repayments can be delayed through time, the greater the grant element of the loan.

The grant element can be worked out for different combinations of interest rates, discount rates, grace periods and length of maturity. At the two extremes, if the financial flow is a pure grant, then $P_t = 0$ and the grant element is 100 per cent. If the financial flow is at a rate of interest equal to the market rate of interest, and the grace period and maturity of the loan are the same as in the free market, the sum of the discounted future repayments will equal the face value of the flow and the grant element will be zero.

For combinations of conditions between the two extremes, Table 15.8 provides some illustrative calculations. For example the grant element of a 10-year loan at 5 per cent interest with a grace period of 5 years, with the recipient discounting repayments at 10 per cent, would be 26.1 per cent. It can be seen that the grant element is quite sensitive to small changes in the interest rate and the discount rate but relatively insensitive to

Table 15.8 Grant element in loans at different discount rates

Rate of interest and maturity period	5% No grace period G=0	5% 5 years' grace G=5	5% 10 years' grace G=10	6% G=0	6% G=5	6% G=10	7% G=0	7% G=5	7% G=10	10% G=0	10% G=5	10% G=10
2% interest												
10 years	12.9	21.2		16.7	24.0		20.0	28.9		29.5	41.8	
20 years	22.1	27.1	31.3	27.8	34.0	39.0	32.8	40.1	45.7	39.8	48.0	53.7
30 years	28.9	34.0	37.0	35.7	40.6	45.4	41.5	47.5	52.4	54.7	62.3	67.3
40 years	34.2	38.0	41.2	41.5	46.2	49.4	47.5	52.7	56.6	60.5	61.6	73.0
3% interest												
10 years	8.6	14.1		12.5	18.0		16.0	23.2		25.8	36.6	
20 years	14.7	18.1	20.9	20.8	25.5	29.2	21.3	32.2	36.6	31.3	38.1	43.1
30 years	19.3	22.6	24.6	26.8	30.5	34.9	33.2	38.1	42.0	47.8	54.5	58.9
40 years	22.8	25.4	27.4	31.1	34.6	37.0	38.0	42.2	45.4	52.9	58.2	63.8
4% interest												
10 years	4.3	7.1		8.1	12.0		12.0	17.4		22.1	31.4	
20 years	7.4	9.0	10.4	13.9	17.0	19.4	19.8	24.2	27.5	34.1	41.1	46.0
30 years	9.6	11.3	12.3	17.8	20.3	22.8	24.9	28.6	31.5	41.0	46.7	50.5
40 years	11.4	12.7	13.7	20.7	23.0	24.6	28.6	31.7	34.1	45.3	50.0	54.6
5% interest												
10 years	0	0		4.2	6.0		8.0	11.5		18.4	26.1*	
20 years	0	0	0	6.9	8.5	9.7	13.1	16.2	18.3	28.4	34.2	38.4
30 years	0	0	0	8.9	10.2	11.3	16.6	19.0	20.9	34.2	38.9	42.0
40 years	0	0	0	10.4	11.5	12.1	19.0	21.0	22.6	37.7	41.6	45.5
6% interest												
10 years	a	a		0	0		4.0	5.8		14.7	20.9	
20 years	a	a	a	0	0	0	6.6	8.1	9.2	22.7	27.4	30.7
30 years	a	a	a	0	0	0	8.4	9.6	10.6	27.4	31.1	33.6
40 years	a	a	a	0	0	0	9.6	10.6	11.4	30.1	33.3	36.4
7% interest												
10 years	a	a		a	a		0	0		11.1	15.7	
20 years	a	a	a	a	a	a	0	0	0	17.1	21.6	23.0
30 years	a	a	a	a	a	a	0	0	0	20.5	23.3	25.2
40 years	a	a	a	a	a	a	0	0	0	22.6	25.0	27.3

Note: a indicates negative aid value.
* Illustrative calculation referred to in the text.
Source: G. Ohlin, *Foreign Aid Policies Reconsidered* (Paris: OECD, 1965), appendix.

Table 15.9 DAC members' ODA terms, 2002

	Grant share of total ODA (per cent) 2002	Bilateral ODA loans			
		Grant element (per cent) 2002	Average maturity (years) 2002	Average grace period (years) 2002	Average interest rate (per cent) 2002
Australia	100.0	–	–	–	–
Austria	99.9	63.4	23.0	9.4	1.8
Belgium	98.6	–	–	–	–
Canada	99.6	89.0	37.8	13.0	0.0
Denmark	98.1	–	–	–	–
Finland	97.9	–	–	–	–
France	87.2	62.4	25.0	9.3	1.8
Germany	93.1	70.5	38.3	6.1	1.4
Greece	100.0	–	–	–	–
Ireland	100.0	–	–	--	–
Italy	96.2	–	–	–	–
Japan	55.3	71.0	33.7	9.7	1.5
Luxembourg	100.0	–	–	–	–
Netherlands	100.0	–	–	–	–
New Zealand	100.0	–	–	–	–
Norway	99.1	–	–	–	–
Portugal	99.3	–	–	–	–
Spain	78.1	–	–	–	–
Sweden	99.5	–	–	–	–
Switzerland	98.8	–	–	–	–
United Kingdom	94.9	–	–	–	–
United States	99.2	–	–	–	–
Total DAC	**89.3**	**70.9**	**33.6**	**9.6**	**1.5**

Source: OECD, *DAC Journal Development Cooperation 2003 Report* (Paris: OECD).

variations in the grace period and the length of maturity. Long maturities and grace periods are mainly means of providing liquidity rather than aid.

The terms of official development assistance from the DAC members in 2002 are shown in Table 15.9. The average rate of interest charged was 1.5 per cent; the average grace period was nine years and the average maturity of loans was 33 years. The discount rate normally applied is 10 per cent, giving a grant element of approximately 67 per cent. In 2002 the grant element of total official development assistance was 70 per cent. The grant element of major forms of multilateral assistance is approximately 50 per cent.

The moral of the foregoing discussion on the grant element of loans is that identifying the real worth of assistance depends on knowledge of the alternatives. Loans that look generous on the surface because they have a lower interest rate attached may be less valuable than the alternatives if they have shorter lives and grace periods. There is also the question of the freedom of the recipient country to use the loan as it wishes, which we considered earlier in connection with aid tying.

THE DISTRIBUTION OF INTERNATIONAL ASSISTANCE

The distribution of international assistance will affect the comparative rates of growth of developing countries if aid is a positive growth-inducing force. At present, the distribution of assistance in relation to the population of developing countries is extremely unequal. Whereas some countries receive less than $5 per head per annum, others receive over $100 per head. Assistance as a proportion of national income also differs widely between countries (see Table 15.5).

Most bilateral donors refrain from making explicit the criteria on which they distribute assistance. In practice, the criteria employed often tend to be as much non-economic as economic, reflecting historical relations between countries, as well as military and political objectives. It is often said that it pays a country to be a small island of ex-colonial status in a politically sensitive part of the world. High levels of per capita assistance seem to be closely associated with these characteristics. It is difficult to discern any significant relationship between the distribution of assistance and developmental considerations such as low per capita income, slow growth, balance-of-payments problems or even good governance. Dictators and corrupt governments also seem to get rewarded.

The most recent comprehensive study by Burnside and Dollar (2000) takes a sample of 56 countries over the period 1970–93 and tries to explain the distribution of aid as a percentage of GDP in terms of such variables as the level of per capita income of the recipient countries (as a measure of need), population size, various strategic (political and military) interests, and whether there is good governance. There seems to be no tendency for either total aid or bilateral aid to be related to the level of poverty, or to favour countries pursuing 'good policies', although multilateral aid is more 'wisely' distributed (see also, Alesina and Dollar, 2000).

Individual donor countries will continue to pursue their own objectives and set their own criteria, although there is evidence that more and more donor countries are focusing directly on the attack on poverty and favouring poor countries with sound policies in line with World Bank thinking. The criteria governing the distribution of multilateral assistance through international agencies, to which rich countries contribute, are of wider concern. Since loans have to be repaid in foreign exchange, one obvious criterion for distribution would be a productivity criterion measured in terms of foreign exchange, but then all sorts of questions arise concerning the measurement of productivity, the time horizon to be taken and whether this would lead to a distribution in relation to need. Without an economically objective and value-free criterion, need is as good a criterion as any and now meets the main direct objective of the World Bank which is the 'attack on poverty' (see Chapter 2). One possibility in this connection would be to distribute assistance on a per capita basis according to some target level of per capita income, which would operate rather like an **international negative income tax**. Certain graduated rates of per capita income assistance could be applied to the gap between the actual level of per capita income and the target level. A country that fell way below the target would receive a greater amount of assistance per head of the population than a country that was closer to the target or exceeded it. The rates of per capita assistance would need to be worked out actuarially so that assistance was not solely distributed on the 'worst-first' principle. Given knowledge of the total amount of resources available, rates could be fixed to ensure a wide spread of assistance across countries while not making demands on resources in excess of supply. All this would be conditional, of course, on the new guiding principle of 'good governance'.

SCHEMES FOR INCREASING THE FLOW OF REVENUE

While the real flow of financial resources has been falling in the last ten years, the demand for resources continues to grow. The absolute number of poor people in developing countries continues to rise; the transitional economies of Eastern Europe and the former Soviet Union now compete for development funds; and the need for disaster relief, food and support for refugees is as acute as ever. The search is on for new sources of funds to finance development needs in the world economy.

There are basically two ways of increasing the net flow of financial resources to developing countries: either nominal assistance can be left unchanged and repayment obligations reduced, or nominal assistance can be increased, leaving the terms of repayments unchanged. Reducing repayment obligations means cutting interest rates, lengthening repayment periods and generally increasing the grant element of international assistance (see p. 485). Other possibilities would be to allow countries to repay in local currency rather than foreign currency and to reduce the level of aid tying, as discussed earlier. We shall concentrate here, however, on measures that might be taken to increase the volume of nominal assistance.

One quick way to increase the flow would be for *all* the developed countries to meet their development assistance targets of 1 per cent of national income for total assistance and 0.7 per cent of national income for official development assistance. A significant increase in the resource flow by a deliberate budget decision in the developed countries is only likely to occur, however, if there is widespread public support for the programme. In recent years there have been signs of diminished public support for aid, based on the belief that a good deal of assistance is wasted and misused. If there is disillusion with assistance – **or aid 'fatigue'** as it has been called – an increased flow of assistance in the future is unlikely in the absence of some recognizable improvement in the efficiency with which current assistance is used. It is difficult to convince people in developed countries whose standard of living is not that high, to acquiesce to programmes that transfer resources from themselves if these resources are then wasted or end up in the hands of people in recipient countries who are richer than themselves. The major reasons for the waste and misuse of resources in the past have been inefficiency and corruption on the part of recipient governments and interference from donor countries in the administration of programme assistance.

Given the political difficulties of increasing aid budgets, what the global economy needs are schemes and forms of international taxation that would raise revenue automatically, free of political debate and budgetary pressure in donor countries. The 1980 Brandt Report first raised the issue of the need for automatic revenue to support global development needs, and the United Nations Development Programme (UNDP) has called for more work on global taxes. There is no shortage of suggestions as to how more global finance might be raised, particularly through the taxation of global transactions. The schemes can be divided into three (overlapping) groups:

- Taxes and charges on various international transactions and external diseconomies that damage human welfare in various ways
- Taxes or charges on unexploited resources over which no state has sovereignty (for example, deep sea minerals)
- International income taxes earmarked for development purposes.

A useful and interesting list of the various suggestions made has been compiled by the Overseas Development Institute in London (ODI Briefing Paper: ODI, 1996).

Twenty recent suggestions for global revenue

- A tax on all or some international financial transactions (the 'Tobin Tax'); variants include a tax on bond turnover, or on derivatives
- A general surcharge on international trade
- Taxes on specified traded commodities like fuel
- A tax on the international arms trade
- Surcharges on post and telecommunications revenues
- An international lottery
- A surcharge on domestic taxation (usually expressed as a progressive share of income tax)
- Dedication of some part of national or local taxes, for example on luxuries (or surcharges on them)
- Parking charges for satellites placed in geostationary orbit
- Royalties on minerals mined in international waters
- Charges for exploration in, or exploitation of, Antarctica
- Charges for fishing in international waters
- Charges for use of the electromagnetic spectrum
- A tax or charge on international flights (or alternatively, on flights in congested sectors); a variant is a tax on aviation kerosene
- A tax or charge on international shipping
- Pollution charges (for example, for dumping at sea)
- A tax on traded pollution permits
- A voluntary local tax paid to a central global agency
- A new issue of Special Drawing Rights (SDRs), distributed to the poorer developing countries (or used for peacekeeping or other global public goods)
- Sale of part of the IMF gold stock.

These are only suggestions and possibilities. There has been no sustained discussion of any of them at the intergovernmental level, and none of them has been taken up in a serious way by any of the major aid-giving countries.

Apart from the idea of various taxes and charges, one of the most attractive ideas is to involve individuals in the spirit of international aid giving and to foster their interest in the challenge of development by allowing them to pay a proportion of their tax obligations in the form of donations to various development funds concerned with poverty eradication, the environment, education and so on. This already happens in a small way with tax relief on donations to charities and non-governmental organizations (NGOs) working in developing countries, but the principle needs to be expanded if the idea of voluntary taxation in support of development is to have a significant impact.

The proposal for a new issue of SDRs and the sale of IMF gold for development purposes is discussed in Chapter 17.

FOREIGN DIRECT INVESTMENT AND MULTINATIONAL CORPORATIONS

Apart from ODA, another major source of development finance is private capital flows that allow countries to import more than they export and to invest more than they save. Private capital flows are of three main types: FDI and portfolio investment, which are non-debt-creating flows, and commercial bank lending, which creates debt. In this section we focus on foreign direct investment in developing countries. Bank lending, and the debt problems to which it gives rise, are considered in the final section.

There has been a vast increase in the amount of FDI going to developing countries in recent years, fuelled by three major factors: the rise of multinational corporations and the search for global profits; the liberalization of global capital markets; and economic liberalization within developing countries.[7] But these flows are highly concentrated in a few countries. Total flows of FDI into developing countries are now running at over $150 billion a year, compared with under $20 billion in the early 1980s, but 70 per cent go to only ten countries located in South America and South-East Asia (including China), as shown in Table 15.10. Overall, FDI accounts for about 10 per cent of total investment in developing countries and roughly 2 per cent of GDP. In discussing the costs and benefits of FDI, the relatively small contribution of FDI to economic activity in the majority of developing countries needs to be borne in mind.

Research into the determinants of FDI shows that cost structures, differential returns, market growth and the institutional characteristics of the host country are of prime importance. Companies wishing to invest overseas are looking for a favourable trade and investment regime, good infrastructure, property rights, political stability, macro-economic stability and an educated and committed workforce. Much depends on the capacity of the country to absorb the investment, which in turn depends on its growth prospects and ability to export.

Table 15.10 FDI inflows to top ten developing countries

	Total 2002 ($ million)
China	49,308
Brazil	16,566
Mexico	14,622
Czech Republic	9,323
Poland	4,131
Slovak Republic	4,012
Malaysia	3,203
India	3,030
Russian Federation	3,009
Peru	2,391
Total to all developing countries	147,086

Source: World Bank, *World Development Indicators 2004* (Washington: World Bank).

FDI brings many advantages to recipient countries, but there are also many potential dangers and disadvantages from a development point of view. We shall first list the advantages. FDI raises the investment ratio above the domestic savings ratio, which is good for growth if nothing adverse happens to the productivity of investment. The investment brings with it knowledge, technology and management skills, which can have positive externalities on the rest of the economy. Foreign investment can often be a catalyst for domestic investment in the same or related fields. It requires the training of labour, which is another positive externality. It is estimated that 30 million workers are employed directly or indirectly by multinational corporations in developing countries. Finally, a great deal of FDI goes into the tradeable goods sector of the recipient countries, which improves the export performance of these countries and earns them valuable foreign exchange.

Recent research shows a positive relation between FDI, domestic investment and the growth of GDP. Bosworth and Collins (1999) take a sample of 58 developing countries over the period 1978–95 and find that FDI brings about a one-to-one increase in domestic investment, while capital inflows as a whole increase domestic investment by only half the amount. Coe, Helpman and Hoffmaister (1997) examine the empirical evidence between international research and development (R&D) spillovers and economic growth for a sample of 77 countries. They find that the variation in total factor productivity growth between countries is related to the foreign stock of R&D capital, and that East Asian countries have benefited most from foreign R&D. It has been estimated by Borensztein, De Gregorio and Lee (1995) that a 1 percentage point increase in the ratio of FDI to GDP in developing countries over the period 1971–89 was associated with a 0.4–0.7 percentage point increase in the growth of per capita GDP, with the impact varying positively with educational attainment as an indicator of a country's ability to absorb technology. But there is also evidence of bidirectional causality (see de Mello, 1997). FDI affects growth positively, at least above a certain threshold, but growth also affects FDI positively; another example of a virtuous circle.

Now let us turn to some of the potential dangers of FDI. As we have indicated, investment by multinational corporations with headquarters in developed countries involves not only a transfer of funds (including the reinvestment of profits) but also a whole package of physical capital, techniques of production, managerial and marketing expertise, products, advertising and business practices for the maximization of global profits. There can be little doubt that such investment augments real resources directly; the question is whether such investment contributes to the broader aspects of development relating to the pattern of development and the distribution of income.

The activities of the multinationals come under attack on a variety of grounds. First, because they tend to locate in urban areas they widen the income gap between the urban and rural sectors, thus perpetuating dualism. This criticism, however, cannot be levelled exclusively against multinationals because any new industrial activity establishing in existing urban centres will have the same effect.

A second and more serious criticism is the way in which they encourage and manipulate consumption. Not only do they tend to cater for the tastes of the already well-to-do, which itself acts as a divisive force, but also they tend to encourage forms of consumption among the broad mass of people, particularly in the urban areas, that are inappropriate to the stage of development and often nutritionally damaging. Prime examples are powdered baby milk and Coca-Cola. These tendencies are not only wasteful, but they encourage acquisitiveness, reduce domestic saving and can worsen balance-of-payments difficulties by encouraging expensive tastes.

A third criticism, which we have already dealt with in Chapter 12, is that they may introduce inappropriate technology and retard the development of an indigenous capital-goods industry. Related to this is the possibility that the multinationals may stifle indigenous entrepreneurship, so that the net addition to capital accumulation is much less than the investment provided by the multinationals themselves.

Another aspect of the multinationals is that because of their large size and the power they wield, the developing countries in which they operate lose aspects of their national sovereignty and control over economic policy. The companies may easily avoid the effects of domestic monetary policy because of easy access to foreign capital markets and their own internal resources. They can avoid tax by shifting profits abroad. Countries may wish a multinational company to do one thing, but it may not readily comply because the action may conflict with the global profit objectives of the company as a whole. Firms may exploit resources more quickly than is desirable, and exploit consumers and workers through the exercise of monopoly and monopsony power.

There is also the question of the repatriation of profits. FDI has the potential disadvantage, even compared with loan finance, that there may be an outflow of profits that lasts much longer than the outflow of debt-service payments on a loan of equivalent amount. While a loan only creates obligations for a definite number of years, FDI may involve an unending commitment. This has serious implications for the balance of payments and for domestic resource utilization if foreign exchange is a scarce resource. We can show with a numerical example that, in the long run, if profits are repatriated the impact of continuous foreign direct investment on the balance of payments must be negative unless the *gross* inflow of foreign investment grows substantially from year to year. This, of course, then increases the power and influence of the foreign interests within the country concerned.

Suppose that there is a steady gross inflow of 100 units of foreign capital per annum; that the productivity of capital is 20 per cent; and that one half of the profits are reinvested and the other half are repatriated. Table 15.11 shows that on these assumptions the balance-of-payments effect turns negative after the eighth year. To keep the net inflow of resources positive requires a steadily rising *gross* flow of private foreign investment, with all the implications that this may have for the pattern of development in the future.

Table 15.11 Balance-of-payments effects of private foreign investment

Year	Gross inflow	Foreign investment at beginning of period	Foreign investment at end of period	Outflow of profits	Net inflow
1	100	100.0	110.0	10.0	90.0
2	100	210.0	231.0	21.0	79.0
3	100	331.0	364.1	33.1	66.9
4	100	464.1	510.5	46.4	53.6
5	100	610.5	671.6	61.1	38.9
6	100	771.5	848.7	77.2	22.8
7	100	948.7	1,043.6	94.9	5.1
8	100	1,143.6	1,258.0	114.4	−14.4

What is the solution to the dilemmas posed above? As Colman and Nixson (1978) succinctly state:

> Transnational corporations cannot be directly blamed for the lack of development (or the direction development is taking) within less developed countries. Their prime objective is global profit maximisation and their actions are aimed at achieving that objective, not developing the host less developed country. If the technology and the products that they introduce are 'inappropriate', if their actions exacerbate regional and social inequalities, if they weaken the balance-of-payments position, in the last resort it is up to the less developed country government to pursue policies which will eliminate the causes of these problems.

It is extremely difficult to measure the full impact and real costs of multinational investment using economic calculus alone, but this is what the developing countries must do. What would be the real income gains and losses of controlling the free mobility of FDI? Other ways of taking advantage of FDI might be actively explored, including **joint ventures** and **turn-key projects**, whereby the foreign investor pays for and builds the project in collaboration with the host country, which is then run by host-country nationals. There is already evidence that this is the direction in which developing countries are moving. Developing countries must lay down very clearly the conditions under which they will accept multinational investments and monitor the companies' operations so that distorted development and exploitation is avoided.

INTERNATIONAL DEBT AND DEBT-SERVICE PROBLEMS

Developing countries not only borrow from donor countries and multilateral agencies but also commercially from the international banking system. All borrowing, whether official or private, involves repayment obligations, unless the loans are gifts or written off. First, the loan has to be repaid over a certain number of years (**amortization repayments**), and secondly, **interest payments** will be charged on the loan. Amortisation and interest payments constitute **debt-service** payments. All loans that have to be repaid with interest are **debt-creating flows**.

There has been a massive increase in debt-creating flows to developing countries in the last 30 years, which started in a big way after the oil price increase in 1973–4 (see later). The total volume of debt in 2002, the debt burden measured by various indicators – such as the debt to export ratio, the debt to national income ratio and the ratio of debt service payments to export earnings (**the debt-service ratio**) – are shown in Table 15.12 for individual countries and groups of countries. The total debt of developing countries is now a colossal $2,400 billion (or roughly $600 per head of population) and debt-service payments absorb $250 billion of foreign exchange or 16 per cent of total export earnings. In the severely indebted low income countries, the debt service ratio is higher at approximately 25 per cent, and in Latin America and Caribbean 30 per cent of export earnings goes to service debts. The debt-service ratio is particularly crucial because this measures the amount of foreign exchange earnings that cannot be used to purchase imports and is therefore some measure of the extent to which a country might decide to default on its repayment obligations. The greater the debt-service payments, the more that development is thwarted. Some of the largest debtor countries of the world, such as Brazil and Turkey, have the highest debt-service ratios.

Table 15.12 The debt burden of developing countries, 2002

Country	Total external debt 2002 ($ millions)	Debt/export ratio (%)	Debt/GNP ratio (%)	Debt-service ratio (%)
Albania	1,312	84	30	4
Algeria	22,800	109	43	20
Angola	10,134	129	123	11
Argentina	132,314	372	63	16
Armenia	1,149	168	52	11
Azerbaijan	1,398	55	26	7
Bangladesh	17,037	182	35	8
Belarus	908	11	7	2
Benin	1,843	288	76	10
Bolivia	4,867	282	62	28
Bosnia and Herzegovina	2,515	107	47	7
Botswana	480	17	10	2
Brazil	227,932	316	45	72
Bulgaria	10,462	132	77	17
Burkina Faso	1,580	493	56	16
Burundi	1,204	2,492	176	48
Cambodia	2,907	129	86	1
Cameroon	8,502	321	102	14
Central African Republic	1,066	831	107	1
Chad	1,281	542	77	12
Chile	41,945	174	63	4
China	168,255	52	15	9
Colombia	33,853	191	43	39
Congo, Dem. Rep. of	1,726	836	178	89
Congo, Rep. of	5,152	211	241	1
Costa Rica	4,834	64	31	9
Côte d'Ivoire	11,816	235	114	17
Croatia	15,347	145	78	28
Czech Republic	26,419	62	46	11
Dominican Republic	6,256	59	32	6
Ecuador	16,452	222	87	30
Egypt	30,750	149	32	10
El Salvador	5,828	102	43	8
Eritrea	528	345	69	6
Estonia	4,741	90	87	15
Ethiopia	6,523	614	103	10
Gabon	3,533	107	87	12
Gambia The	573	256	150	9
Georgia	1,838	178	56	12
Ghana	7,338	291	137	8
Guatemala	4,676	94	22	8
Guinea	3,401	391	111	16
Guinea Bissau	699	1,145	354	24
Haiti	1,248	113	34	3
Honduras	5,395	174	86	13
Hungary	34,958	88	66	37
India	104,429	130	22	16
Indonesia	132,208	191	90	24
Iran	9,154	29	9	5
Jamaica	5,477	120	76	18
Jordan	8,094	129	92	9
Kazakhstan	17,538	159	85	37

▶

Table 15.12 continued

Country	Total external debt 2002 ($ millions)	Debt/export ratio (%)	Debt/GNP ratio (%)	Debt-service ratio (%)
Kenya	6,031	197	54	15
Kyrgyz Rep.	1,797	282	126	27
Lao PDR	2,664	522	162	9
Latvia	6,690	175	86	17
Lebanon	17,077	333	96	43
Lesotho	637	115	64	12
Liberia	2,324	1,584	526	1
Lithuania	6,199	97	51	20
Macedonia	1,619	101	45	15
Madagascar	4,518	417	107	7
Malawi	2,912	609	168	8
Malaysia	48,557	44	58	7
Mali	2,803	279	109	8
Mauritania	2,309	600	243	17
Mauritius	1,803	63	40	9
Mexico	141,264	75	24	23
Moldova	1,349	138	86	23
Mongolia	1,307	149	100	8
Morocco	18,601	129	55	26
Mozambique	4,609	444	138	7
Myanmar	6,556	241	–	4
Namibia	109	61	3.4	
Nepal	2,953	228	53	8
Nicaragua	6,485	501	174	12
Niger	1,797	527	92	8
Nigeria	30,497	138	78	7
Oman	4,639	39	24	15
Pakistan	33,672	256	57	22
Panama	8,298	91	71	18
Papua New Guinea	2,485	117	85	13
Paraguay	2,967	96	44	11
Peru	28,167	280	53	33
Philippines	61,121	130	75	20
Poland	69,521	127	39	25
Romania	14,683	103	36	27
Russian Federation	147,541	121	49	12
Rwanda	1,435	912	83	14
Senegal	3,918	247	86	14
Serbia and Montenegro	12,688	280	108	3
Slovak Rep.	13,013	84	62	22
Somalia	2,688	–	–	–
South Africa	25,041	66	22	12
Sri Lanka	9,611	129	60	10
Sudan	16,389	620	137	1
Swaziland	342	27	26	2
Syria	21,504	274	116	3
Tajikistan	1,153	152	113	10
Tanzania	7,254	483	79	10
Thailand	59,212	71	50	24
Togo	1,581	314	125	3
Trinidad and Tobago	2,672	51	31	5
Tunisia	12,625	123	66	14

▶

Table 15.12 continued

Country	Total external debt 2002 ($ millions)	Debt/export ratio (%)	Debt/GNP ratio (%)	Debt-service ratio (%)
Turkey	131,556	227	75	48
Uganda	4,100	378	72	7
Ukraine	13,555	63	37	15
Uruguay	10,736	274	65	33
Uzbekistan	4,568	142	60	23
Venezuela	32,563	101	29	23
Vietnam	13,349	71	42	6
Yemen	5,290	101	59	3
Zambia	5,969	566	117	29
Zimbabwe	4,066	197	35	3
Low income	523,464	177	50	14
Middle income	1,817,163	108	36	20
East Asia & Pacific	499,139	71	29	11
Europe & Central Asia	545,842	110	49	18
Latin America & Caribbean	727,944	174	48	30
Middle East & North Africa	189,010	87	31	9
South Asia	168,349	139	26	11
Sub-Saharan Africa	210,350	165	65	11
All Developing Countries	2,338,848	113	39	16

Sources: World Bank, *Global Development Finance 2004* (Washington: World Bank) and *World Development Indicators 2004* (Washington: World Bank).

To judge whether a country's level of debt is sustainable, the World Bank takes a present value of debt to export ratio of 150 per cent. This is the main criterion for relief under the highly indebted poor country initiative (HIPC) (see later). By this criterion, most of Sub-Saharan Africa qualifies, and it is mainly African countries that constitute the severely indebted low-income countries with a debt–to-export ratio of 300 per cent or more.

Before turning to the origins of this massive volume of debt, however, let us consider in more detail the nature of the debt-servicing problem. At the beginning of the chapter it was shown that it is profitable for a country to borrow as long as the rate of return on the borrowing exceeds the rate of interest. In these circumstances, the rate of growth of income is higher than it would otherwise be. This gives no indication, however, of whether the borrowing can be serviced or repaid since the loan must be repaid with interest in *foreign* currency. Thus the profitability of borrowing and the capacity to service debt are conceptually distinct. The ability to service debt depends on whether additional foreign exchange can be earned or saved by the borrowing. This depends on the domestic economic policy pursued by the country concerned, and on the ability to export, which depends to a large extent on world economic conditions.

A major part of the debt-servicing difficulties that have arisen in recent years have had as much to do with changes in world economic conditions (which have depressed the foreign exchange earnings of developing countries) than with the miscalculation of rates of return on investment, the misuse of investment funds or the use of capital inflows to increase present consumption. There was a parallel in the 1980s with the great depression of the 1930s when the collapse of the world prices of key commodities and a general shrinkage of world trade caused major debt defaults (which subsequently dried up the flow of private capital to developing countries for the next 40 years). The trouble started in 1982 when the volume of world trade fell by 2.5 per cent, and the terms of trade for developing countries as a whole deteriorated by over 10 per cent. The decline in many commodities that developing countries export has continued (see Chapter 17 p. 552).

Not even the most prudent borrower or cautious lender can foresee such events, which may occur half-way through the life of a loan commitment that was entered into under quite different economic circumstances. Lenders and borrowers can allow for risk – that is, the statistical probability that the expected outcome will not materialize – but what happened in the world economy in the 1980s was a whole shift in the probability distribution of outcomes that could not be insured against. When such unforeseen events occur, beyond the borrower's control, that make it difficult for loans to be repaid and serviced without severe economic disruption, two questions arise: what is the optimal degree of debt rescheduling, and who should bear the cost?

It is naturally in the interests of private banks that loans be repaid on schedule, but it is not necessarily in the global interest if this leads to a contraction of imports by the borrowing country, which then reduces the exports of other (lending) countries, leading to a deflationary spiral in the whole world economy. If there is a divergence between the private and social interest, this would seem to call for an international subsidy for lenders and borrowers to accept more rescheduling. In practice, the debtor countries have had to accept adjustment and rescheduling with very little subsidy at all. If the international economy derives a benefit from rescheduling, however, the poor debtor countries should not bear the full cost. There is a great source of international inequality here, particularly when it was largely the deflationary policies pursued by lender countries that caused the servicing of debt to become so problematic in the first place.

OPTIMAL BORROWING AND SUSTAINABLE DEBT

The benefits of borrowing to individual countries, and to the world economy at large, are clear. The question is: how far should borrowing go? Is it possible that after a certain point, even though a developing country still requires resources for development, the disadvantages of further borrowing outweigh the advantages. This raises the question of optimal borrowing and the sustainability of debt. Reasonable levels of debt are likely to enhance growth in countries short of capital if borrowing is used productively and earns foreign exchange so that debt can be serviced without deflating the economy to save imports. Debt becomes unsustainable when it accumulates at a faster rate than the borrower's capacity to service it. Expected debt-service costs then discourage domestic and foreign investment, because potential investors fear the economy will be deflated or that they will be 'taxed' to service the debts.

Working out what level of debt is sustainable requires an assessment of how outstanding stocks of debt are likely to evolve over time, together with forecasts about the future interest rates, exchange rates and foreign exchange earnings. The IMF has recently developed a standardized framework for assessing debt sustainability which takes account of a country's future growth rate, interest rate and exchange rate, and applies sensitivity analysis based on each country's history.

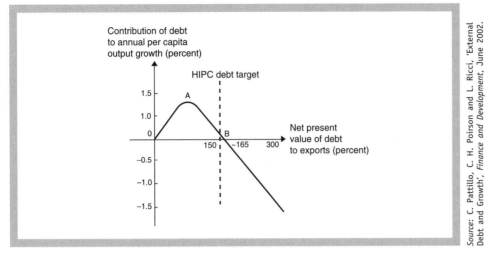

Source: C. Pattillo, C. H. Poirson and L. Ricci, 'External Debt and Growth', Finance and Development, June 2002.

Figure 15.1 Debt to export ratio and growth

Several debt indicators and measures of sustainability can be used. One is the ratio of debt to GDP. There has been a progressive rise in the **ratio of debt to GDP** among developing countries, from approximately 20 per cent in the early 1970s to over 40 per cent today, but it is not clear what economic significance should be attached to this ratio as a measure of the ability to service debt and therefore as a measure of debt sustainability. It is true that to service more and more debt, export earnings as a proportion of national income should rise, but this suggests more direct measures of sustainability: either the **debt–export ratio** or the **debt-service ratio** which measures the ratio of amortization and interest payments to export earnings.

Research from the IMF (Pattillo, Poirson and Ricci, 2002) reaches interesting conclusions on the relation between the debt–export ratio and the growth of per capita income. They take a sample of 93 developing countries over the period 1969 to 1998 and, controlling for other variables, find that the per capita income growth of countries is maximized when the debt–export ratio is approximately 80 per cent, and debt impacts negatively on growth when the debt–export ratio exceeds 160 per cent – as shown in Figure 15.1. The growth differential between countries with low indebtedness (with an export–debt ratio < 100%) and those with high indebtedness (with an export–debt ratio > 367%) is, on average, more than two percentage points. It appears that the relationship between debt and growth is non-linear (an inverted 'U' shape) and that the level of sustainable debt is, on average, close to the ratio of 150 per cent of export earnings which is the ratio at which countries become eligible for debt relief under the highly indebted poor country (HIPC) initiative launched by the World Bank in 1996 (see later).

THE DEBT CRISIS OF THE 1980s[8]

The world debt crisis erupted in the summer of 1982, when Mexico became the first country to suspend the repayment of loans due to the private banking system and sovereign lenders. The crisis has smouldered ever since, with more and more countries, particularly in Africa, finding it difficult to service accumulated debts out of foreign exchange earnings. In 1987 Brazil became the first country to suspend interest payments to foreign creditors.

The 'crisis' aspects of debt can be looked at from different standpoints: from the point of view of the individual borrowing countries, or that of the lenders (private and sovereign governments), or that of the entire world economy. As far as borrowers are concerned, when the crisis first erupted there were basically two types of 'problem' countries. First, there were a number of *poor commodity-dependent countries*, mainly in Africa but also elsewhere, where private banks were not heavily involved. It became a crisis for these countries when they had to cut back on essential imports in order to service their debts, but not a crisis for the banking system or the world economy, even if they had defaulted.

Second, there were a set of large *newly industrializing countries*, mainly in Latin America, which borrowed from the commercial banking system at floating rates of interest, but then their export markets became depressed. The sums of money involved were huge. In the early 1980s, 16 countries accounted for over half of the total debt of nearly $1000 billion and for nearly 90 per cent of the debt owed to the private banking system. In this case the non-repayment of debt would have caused a crisis for the private banking system (which in retrospect had clearly overextended itself), and a crisis for individual countries if the threat of default had dried up the flow of new capital. There would also have been a crisis for the world economy if there had been a major default that led to a massive contraction of bank lending throughout the system; but this did not happen. Lending did contract sharply in the early 1980s, but then rose again as the difficulties were resolved by various forms of international cooperation and the rescheduling of debt.

The origin of the current debt difficulties of many developing countries is no mystery. Massive balance-of-payments surpluses arose in the early 1970s in the oil-exporting countries with counterpart deficits elsewhere. The factors that caused the supply of capital to increase created its own demand. Private banks were anxious to lend and there was no shortage of demand. Demand was particularly strong because commodity prices were generally high, exports were buoyant and inflation had reduced the real rate of interest on loans to virtually zero. Credit looked cheap and borrowers looked like good risks from the lenders' point of view. But these circumstances suddenly changed. Depression in the developed countries, mainly self-inflicted to reduce the rate of inflation, caused world commodity prices to tumble, exports to languish and real interest rates to rise. On top of this, nominal interest rates floated upwards and the dollar appreciated. At the height of the debt crisis (1986) the debt-service ratio reached a peak of 30 per cent. This has since fallen back to under 20 per cent, partly as a result of lower interest rates and debt rescheduling and partly as a result of increased export earnings following the recovery of the world economy.

The world debt problem is a foreign exchange problem. It represents the inability of debtors to earn enough foreign exchange through exports to service foreign debts, and at the same time to sustain the growth of output (which requires foreign exchange to pay for imports). Either debt-service payments have to be suspended or growth curtailed, or a combination of both. Unfortunately for the debtor countries, and indeed the whole world economy, it is living standards that have suffered. The indebted less-developed countries are stagnating under a total burden of debt that has now reached

$2400 billion, with resource transfers to service the debt close to $250 billion per annum.

All this is part of the **transfer problem** analysed by Keynes in 1919 in the wake of the controversy over the reparation payments imposed on Germany after the First World War by the Treaty of Versailles in 1919 (Keynes, 1919). Keynes mocked the folly and futility of the whole exercise on the grounds that it was likely to be self-defeating, and so it turned out to be. Similarly today, the attempt to extract large transfers, particularly in Africa, is leading nowhere. Their economies continue to suffer, and the poor become progressively poorer.

There are two aspects of the transfer problem: the **budgetary problem** for governments of acquiring domestic resources for the repayment of debt; and the problem of turning the resources into foreign exchange – or the **'pure' transfer problem** as Keynes called it. The **transfer burden** is the export surplus that has to be generated to acquire the necessary foreign exchange, plus the possibility of a deterioration in the terms of trade if, in order to sell more exports, prices must be reduced. Even if prices do fall there is still no guarantee that export *earnings* will increase if the quantity sold does not rise in proportion. In these circumstances the transfer becomes impossible without a contraction of domestic output to compress imports. There is substantial evidence that the indebted countries collectively are caught in this trap, since for a large part of their trade they compete with each other; and competitive price reductions leave total earnings unchanged. It is the contraction of living standards that generates the export surplus by reducing the import bill. This is not good for the developing countries, or for the health of the world economy.

The other side of the coin is that, if total trade is static, increased exports from debtors take markets away from domestic producers in other countries, and extracting the surplus from the debtors reduces welfare all round. This was one of Keynes' major objections to the excessive reparations imposed on Germany; that the transfer from Germany would be generated at the expense of the victors' industries.

History has lessons to teach. The magnitude of the transfer expected from developing countries has been greater as a proportion of total output and trade than that imposed on Germany. What we witness in the world economy is a vast charade of money being recycled from creditors to debtors and back again to the creditors, while the total volume of debt grows and the pressure on debtor countries to adjust – a euphemism for deflation – increases.

Notwithstanding the huge debt burden of some countries, most observers agree that the current debt problem is a **liquidity problem**, not one of insolvency. When debt-servicing difficulties began to emerge, the private banks increased the proportion of short- to long-term loans. This exacerbated the cash-flow problems, with large amounts of short-term borrowing falling due for repayment within a year. In such situations, if credit is further shortened or withheld entirely, a crisis then ensues. Such situations always pose a dilemma for banks. If they do withhold further credit, they contribute to default; if they continue to lend they expose themselves even more.

Understandably there was greater paranoia in the United States than in Europe over the possibility of default since the US banks were much more exposed. Roughly 30 per cent of international lending by US banks was to developing countries, compared with only 20 per cent in Europe. In the early 1980s the nine largest US banks' loans to Brazil were equal to 40 per cent of shareholders' capital; to Mexico 38 per cent and to Korea 19 per cent. If these debts had been written off, a major part of the capital and reserves of the banking system would have been wiped out, and because of the intricate network of interbank lending there was the possibility of a chain of bank collapses. (There is no lender of last resort in the United States. Moreover, private lending by US banks does not have the same official guarantee as in Europe, where at least 30 per cent of lending is for export credits.) It was not conceivable, however, that a major US bank would be allowed to collapse simply for want of a debt rescheduling agreement. Indeed, to date there have been no cases of default, and only a few cases of interest payment arrears. In most developing countries rescheduling arrangements have been satisfactorily concluded, with the help of international consortia and the IMF. Up to now the so-called 'Paris Club' of creditor nations has adopted a case-by-case approach. At the international level, emergency financing was made available under the auspices of the Bank for International Settlements, and in January 1983 the IMF established a 17 billion Special Drawing Rights (SDR) emergency fund under the General Agreement to Borrow (GAB).

The debt crisis of the early 1980s has subsided, but the debt problem has not gone away. Lenders have been as irresponsible as borrowers. The developed countries must accept a large share of the responsibility for the world recession of the 1980s, as should the private banks for voluntarily overextending themselves. Shared blame requires shared solutions.

DEBT RELIEF

Debt in many ways is like a cancer – once it gets a grip on a country it is very hard to eradicate and may spread unless the rest of the economy can be reinforced to overcome it.

There are no easy solutions to the debt-servicing problem short of a massive programme of **debt forgiveness**, which leaves a manageable debt that the debtors can service. There has to be debt relief if there is to be any easing of the transfer burden. Without relief, further borrowing increases the size of the debt-service payments and simply makes matters worse, creating what might be called a **debt trap**. Since lenders, borrowers and the whole world community have benefited from the debt-creation process, there is a strong case for saying that the same three parties should share the burden of relief. It is not fair that the debtor countries (the borrowers) should bear the whole of the adjustment burden. Up to now the world community (including the creditor countries) has done very little to ease the plight of the debtors, although there are three reasons why it should:

- The world community received an external benefit when the debt was created by the on-lending process in the 1970s, preventing output contraction in countries with balance-of-payments deficits, and thereby avoiding a world slump
- Much of the debt problem arose in the first place through no fault of the developing countries themselves, but as a result of events in the world economy – rising oil prices, rising interest rates, world recession, falling commodity prices and so on
- Relief could actually confer a global benefit by easing the deflationary forces associated with the huge debt overhang.

THE HIGHLY INDEBTED POOR COUNTRY INITIATIVE (HIPC)

The most recent and publicized global scheme for debt relief is the **Highly Indebted Poor Country (HIPC)** initiative launched by the World Bank in 1996, designed to help the world's poorest indebted countries. The World Bank has always been hostile to the write-off of debt, but the share of debt-service payments going to multilateral creditors has increased in recent years accounting for over 50 per cent of debt-service payments by some African countries. This new World Bank initiative therefore marked a radical departure in thinking and attitude. At the time, the President of the Bank, James Wolfensohn, described the initiative as 'a breakthrough – it deals with debt in a comprehensive way to give countries the possibility of exiting from unsustainable debt. It is very good news for the poor of the world'. To qualify for debt relief, a country had to have a debt to export ratio in excess of 220 per cent or a debt to government revenue ratio of more than 280 per cent. Forty-one countries, mainly in Africa, originally met the criteria with a combined debt of nearly $200 billion. In the first three years of the initiative, however, progress was painfully slow. Only seven countries satisfied the stringent conditions laid down by the World Bank in order to receive help, and only $10 billion of relief was dispensed.

Dissatisfaction with the original initiative led the Group of Seven (G-7) rich industrialized countries to launch a new enhanced HIPC initiative in Cologne in 1999, which was later endorsed by the World Bank and IMF and called **The Enhanced HIPC Debt Relief Initiative** intended to be 'deeper, broader and faster' (to use the World Bank's words). To be eligible for debt relief under this new initiative, countries had to satisfy three conditions:

- A country must be very poor, defined as eligible for concessional assistance from the International Development Association (IDA) of the World Bank and eligible for support from the IMF's Poverty Reduction and Growth Facility (formerly the Enhanced Structural Adjustment Facility) (See Chapter 17)
- A country must have an unsustainable debt burden, defined as a present value of debt to export ratio of more than 150 per cent or a debt–government expenditure ratio in excess of 250 per cent
- A country must have good governance consistent with sustained growth and poverty reduction with its anti-poverty strategy outlined in a Poverty Reduction Strategy Paper (PRSP).

To see how the HIPC initiative works, see Case example 15.5

At the time of writing, debt relief programmes have been agreed with 26 participating countries, but no more than $1.5 billion of relief has been committed so far. Not only are the sums small, but progress in dispensing relief continues to be slow. Uganda was the first country to receive debt relief under the Enhanced HIPC Initiative in May 2000, based on several years of progress in implementing poverty relief programmes (see Case example 15.6).

Meanwhile, the majority of African countries continue to pay more in debt-service repayments than they spend on health and education. The World Bank seems to be being unduly harsh and bureaucratic in applying the criteria for relief and disbursement.

The Highly Indebted Poor Country Initiative

The Highly Indebted Poor Country (HIPC) initiative, launched in 1996 by the International Monetary Fund (IMF) and the World Bank and endorsed by 180 governments, has two main objectives. The first is to relieve certain low-income countries of their unsustainable debt to donors. The second is to promote reform and sound policies for growth, human development and poverty reduction.

The enhanced HIPC framework, approved in 1999, introduces broader eligibility criteria and increases debt relief. To qualify countries must be eligible for highly concessional assistance such as from the World Bank's International Development Association and the IMF's Poverty Reduction and Growth Facility. In addition, countries must face unsustainable debt even after the full application of traditional debt relief mechanisms. They must also have a proven track record in implementing strategies focused on reducing poverty and building the foundations for sustainable economic growth.

Debt relief occurs in two steps:

- At the decision point the country gets debt *service* relief after having demonstrated adherence to an IMF programme and progress in developing a national poverty strategy.
- At the completion point the country gets debt *stock* relief upon approval by the World Bank and the IMF of its Poverty Reduction Strategy Paper. The country is entitled to at least 90 per cent debt relief from bilateral and multilateral creditors to make debt levels sustainable.

Of the 42 countries participating in the initiative, 34 are in Sub-Saharan Africa. None had a per capita income above $1500 (in purchasing power parity terms) in 2001, and all rank low on the human development index. Between 1990 and 2001 HIPCs grew by an average of just 0.5 per cent a year.

HIPCs have been overindebted for at least 20 years: by poor country standards their ratios of debt to exports were already high in the 1980s. At the same time, HIPCs have received considerable official development assistance. Net transfers of such aid averaged about 10 per cent of their GNP in the 1990s, compared with about 2 per cent for all poor countries. To date 16 HIPCs have reached the decision point and 8 have reached the completion point (Benin, Bolivia, Burkina Faso, Mali, Mauritania, Mozambique, Tanzania, Uganda).

Source: UNDP, *Human Development Report* (New York: Oxford University Press, 2003).

How Debt Relief Fits into a Poverty-Reduction Strategy: Uganda's Poverty Action Fund

Improving the overall allocation of resources, including those from debt relief, through more poverty oriented and transparent budgets, is fundamental in the fight against poverty. There are many ways of achieving this end, and in Uganda a special fund to use the savings from debt relief is proving useful.

The government chose to create the Poverty Action Fund as a conduit for the savings from debt relief under the HIPC Initiative (about $37 million a year; the Enhanced HIPC Initiative is expected to double this amount). The fund has been earmarked for priorities of the poverty eradication action plan adopted in 1997 to address poverty and social conditions. The plan emphasizes maintaining macroeconomic stability while increasing the incomes and the quality of life of poor people by developing rural infrastructure, promoting small businesses and microenterprises, creating jobs, and improving health services and education. The Poverty Action Fund focuses on schools, rural feeder roads, agricultural extension, and district-level water and sanitation. Specific outcome targets have been identified, such as the construction of 1000 additional classrooms to support the primary education programme.

Two crucial features of the Poverty Action Fund are its integration into the overall budget and the Ugandan government's effort to create a transparent and accountable structure of management. Reports on financial allocation are released at quarterly meetings attended by donors and NGOs. The Inspector General's office monitors the use of funds at the district and national levels. This self-imposed conditionality reflects the government's strong commitment to tackling corruption. But it is also an attempt to address creditor concerns about the capacity of a debtor country to link debt relief to poverty reduction. Several measures have been proposed for improving monitoring, ranging from including district-level officials in the quarterly meetings to having local NGOs do community-based monitoring of the poverty fund's spending.

Apart from bold, imaginative, global schemes of debt relief, there has been a number of piecemeal, case-by-case initiatives in which the burden on the debtor developing countries has been ameliorated.

DEBT RESCHEDULING

The initial US response to the 1980s debt crisis was to attempt to increase **liquidity**, to give developing countries more breathing space to 'grow out' of their debt problems. This was the thinking behind the so-called **Baker Plan** of October 1988, which made provision for $20 billion of additional lending from the commercial banks and $9 billion of multilateral lending to the 15 or so most severely indebted countries, contingent on market-friendly, growth-oriented structural adjustment programmes being adopted. There was no acceptance of debt reduction by banks, and the sums of money were a drop in the ocean. In the event, most of the money was not lent because of the continued vulnerability of the banks and the deteriorating external situation.

The abortive Baker Plan was followed by the so-called **Brady Plan** of 1989, which did accept debt reduction and was more successful. The two main elements of the plan were (1) providing funds via the IMF and the World Bank for various forms of debt relief to those middle-income debtor countries that were willing to adopt policy reforms, and (2) encouraging countries to buy back debt from banks at a discount, thereby reducing future obligations. One possibility was for countries to swap old loans for new long-term (30-year) bonds at a discount of some 35 per cent and an interest rate only marginally above the market rate – the bonds were guaranteed by the IMF. Agreements of this type were reached with Mexico, the Philippines, Costa Rica, Venezuela and Uruguay. The deal with Mexico relieved it of $20 billion of debt-service payments.

Other multilateral initiatives focused on the poorest debtor countries. The governments of OECD countries representing the so-called Paris Club adopted two major initiatives in 1988 and 1990 – the **Toronto Terms** (September 1988) and the **Trinidad Terms** (September 1990). These initiatives were related to official debt (that is, debt owed to governments) and first of all made provision for the cancellation of a substantial proportion of the debt. For the remainder of the debt, substantial restructuring was offered.

Under the Toronto terms, eligible countries were those receiving concessional assistance from the soft-loan affiliate of the World Bank, the International Development Association, and a distinction was made between official development assistance (ODA) and non-ODA. For ODA, countries were given 25 years to pay with a grace period of 14 years, with no change in the interest rate. For non-ODA, three options were offered of different combinations of rescheduling, relief and interest rates.

Under the Trinidad terms, heavily indebted countries with a per capita income of less than $1195 were eligible. For ODA, countries were given 20 years to pay with a grace period of 10 years. For non-ODA, countries were given 15 years to pay with a grace period of eight years and a market rate of interest.

In 1996 and 1999 the HIPCs initiatives were launched, as discussed above, which concentrate more on debt relief than debt rescheduling.

Apart from these official initiatives, a great deal of other debt rescheduling has been arranged privately between individual countries and the creditor banks. These ease the short-term pressure but do not reduce future repayment obligations, unless the rescheduled debt is on softer terms.

DEBT-SERVICE CAPPING

Several schemes have been suggested to avoid debt-service payments becoming excessive. One is for **variable maturity loans** to be issued, so that debt-service payments would remain unaltered as interest rates floated upwards on private debt (rather like mortgage loans are variable in the housing market). Alternatively maturities could be varied automatically in order to keep the debt-service ratio unchanged. This would also accommodate fluctuations in foreign exchange receipts from exports. These schemes are equivalent to capitalizing interest payments above a certain level. In 1985 Peru unilaterally imposed a 10 per cent ceiling on debt-service payments as a proportion of export earnings.

Another possibility is to offer **zero coupon bonds**, which would delay interest payments until a loan had matured. This would reduce the present value of interest payments, but more importantly it would allow investment to be fully productive before there was any commitment of foreign exchange. It would not ensure, however, against the bunching of repayment commitments when foreign exchange earnings might be low.

DEBT BUY-BACKS AND DEBT SWAPS

Another solution to the debt-service problem that gained favour in recent years is for countries to buy back their debt at a discount, or to exchange the debt in various ways that fully or partially relieve the burden of interest and principal repayments. Third World debt trades in a secondary market, where some countries' debt can be bought at a discount of more than 50 per cent. At one time Sudanese debt could be bought in the secondary market for $2 per $100. If Sudan had been able and willing to use its foreign exchange reserves to buy its own debt, it could have wiped out, say, $1 million of debt for as little as $20,000. The secondary market, however, is generally thin, and heavy buying is likely to raise the price considerably. Even so, the use of foreign exchange reserves to buy back debt at a discount of 20–30 per cent can make a useful contribution to debt relief. In 1995 Peru spent $600 million in the secondary market, buying $1.2 billion of its debt accumulated in the late 1970s–early 1980s at an estimated saving of $1 billion in interest payments.

Debt–equity swaps are a way of eliminating debt-service payments altogether. A debt–equity swap involves the debt held by the creditor being converted into an equity stake in enterprises within the debtor country. The creditors have a claim on future profits, but the debtor countries are relieved of interest payments. Such swaps can be mutually profitable to all parties. A classic example was the Nissan motor company's purchase of Mexican debt for investment in its Mexican subsidiary in 1982. Nissan bought $60 million of Mexican debt held by the Citicorp bank at a price of $40 million – a discount of one-third. Nissan redeemed the debt certificates at the Mexican central bank for $54 million in Mexican pesos, which were then invested in its subsidiary. The Citibank unloaded its debt at the 'market' price; Nissan made a profit in dollars, and Mexico was relieved of interest payments in foreign currency. There have been several other debt–equity swaps since 1986, and they are increasingly linked to privatization programmes in the debtor countries, but the absolute magnitude of the sums involved are still relatively small in relation to the size of the debt burden.

Debt for nature and debt for development swaps work in the same way as debt–equity swaps, except the debt is bought by a governmental or charitable organization and the proceeds are used for environmental or developmental purposes within the debtor country. The World Wide Fund for Nature has bought Third World debt at a considerable discount and exchanged it for local currency for use on environmental projects within the developing countries. In 1988 the UNICEF bought Sudanese debt from the Midland Bank, and this was redeemed by the Sudanese government to finance water sanitation programmes in central Sudan.

Debt for bonds is a swap scheme whereby debtor countries offer fixed-interest, long-term bonds in exchange for debt held by the banks. They can be advantageous if the debt can be exchanged at a discount at a more favourable rate of interest. In 1988 Mexico launched a scheme offering $10 billion of bonds to its creditor banks, hoping to sell at a discount of 50 per cent. The sale turned out to be disappointing, however. Only 100 out of the 500 banks bid for the bonds, and the debt was discounted by only 30 per cent. Even so, some saving was made by the Mexican government.

Exit bonds are a particular type of bond that give a bank a lower rate of interest than on the original debt, but end the bank's liability to provide new money. One way of encouraging this type of arrangement would be for the IMF to guarantee interest payments on the exit bonds, which would encourage the banks to swap debt for this type of bond.

LONG-TERM SOLUTIONS

On a longer-term basis, developed countries might set up machinery to guarantee loans from private sources (in addition to export credit guarantees) and establish a fund from which commercial interest rates could be subsidized. Such a scheme would mean that private lenders would not be deterred from lending through fear of default; developing countries would receive cheaper credit; and the donor's contribution in the form of payments to private lenders would not burden the balance of payments (if this was regarded as an obstacle to a higher level of official assistance).

Secondly, ODA might be given as grants rather than loans. The grant element of official assistance is already high, and this further step would not only give extra marginal help but would also eliminate the need to haggle over debt renegotiations if the need for rescheduling arose.

Finally, there is urgent need to devise schemes to stabilize the price or terms of trade for primary commodities. A large part of the 1980s debt crisis resulted from the collapse of primary product prices.

To stabilize the terms of trade, indexation may be appropriate for some commodities, for example oil. For other primary commodities, credit creation to finance merchants' stocks would assist. Special Drawing Rights (see Chapter 17) might play a useful role here for buying up surplus stocks of primary commodities that are storable, or for income compensation for commodities that are not. It seems incredible that so many years have passed since Keynes' wartime plan for an international agency for stabilizing commodity prices,[9] yet the world still lacks the requisite international agreement and institutional structures for greater stability and a fairer deal for developing countries that live by exporting primary commodities.

DISCUSSION QUESTIONS

1 What is the distinctive contribution of dual-gap analysis to the theory of development?

2 Under what circumstances will foreign borrowing (a) raise the rate of growth of income, and (b) raise the rate of growth of output?

3 What are the characteristics of the different types of financial flow to developing countries?

4 What factors determine the grant element of a financial flow?

5 How might the flow of resources to developing countries be augmented, and what criteria should govern their distribution between countries?

6 What is the purpose of World Bank structural adjustment lending, and how successful has it been?

7 What are the advantages and disadvantages of FDI in developing countries?

8 Discuss the view that foreign lending is merely a pernicious device for transferring resources from poor to rich countries.

9 Can countries borrow too much?

10 What is the nature of the debt problem in developing countries?

11 What imaginative schemes can you think of to relieve the debt-servicing burden of developing countries?

12 How successful have the World Bank's HIPC debt relief programmes been?

NOTES

1. The hypothetical figures given are based on a case study of the Sudanese six-year plan 1977–8 to 1982–3 (El Shibley and Thirlwall, 1981).
2. If there were complete substitutability between imports and domestic resources, any surplus of domestic resources could be immediately converted into foreign exchange, and any surplus of foreign exchange could be immediately converted into domestic resources, and there could only be one gap, *ex ante*, as well as *ex post*.
3. See, for example, Chenery and Bruno (1962); Chenery and Adelman (1966); Chenery and Macewan (1966); Chenery and Strout (1966).

4. This argument was first put forward by Griffin (1970) and has since been the subject of continual scrutiny. For the latest evidence, see the survey by White (1992).
5. For the calculation of the grant element, see p. 485.
6. See Taylor (1997) for an excellent summary and critique of IMF and World Bank policies.
7. For a comprehensive survey of the causes and effects of FDI see de Mello (1997).
8. Useful books on the 1980s debt crisis include Cline (1984, 1995); Claudon (1986); Lomax (1986); Lever and Huhne (1985); Griffith-Jones and Sunkel (1986).
9. See Thirlwall (1987). See Chapter 16 for partial schemes already in existence.

WEBSITES ON AID, DEBT AND FDI

Debt

World Bank, Global Development Finance   http://publications.worldbank.org

OECD, Development Assistance Committee   www.oecd.org/dac/stats

HIPC Initiative   www.worldbank.org/hipc

Non-Governmental Organizations

NGO Global Network   www.ngo.org

Links via the UN   www.un.org/MoreInfo/ngolink/ngodir.htm

Jubilee Debt Campaign   www.jubileedebtcampaign.org.uk

Foreign Direct Investment

UNCTAD   www.unctad.org

International trade, the balance of payments and development

Trade and development

INTRODUCTION

In Chapter 15 we attempted to establish the role of foreign borrowing in the development process. Using dual-gap analysis, it was shown that foreign borrowing can be used to bridge either a domestic investment-savings gap or a foreign exchange gap, whichever is the larger. We saw that the policy issue is deciding how far borrowing should go. How large can the import surplus be without leading to too great a dependence on imported capital and severe future balance-of-payments difficulties in the form of large outflows of debt repayments and profits?

The empirical evidence indicates a serious conflict between maintaining an adequate growth rate and preserving a reasonable balance on international payments. The ultimate solution must lie in improving the balance of payments through trade. The growth rates of individual developing countries since 1950 correlate better with their export performance than with almost any other single economic indicator. For much of the period since 1950, the export performance of the developing countries lagged behind that of the developed industrial countries, with their share of world trade falling, but in recent years there has been a reversal of fortunes for some developing countries as trade barriers have come down, and with a switch in the composition of exports towards manufactured goods.

Table 16.1 shows the developing countries' share of world manufacturing exports in 1981 and 2000, distinguishing between resource-based exports (RB); low technology exports (LT); medium technology exports (MT), and high technology exports (HT). The developing countries as a whole have doubled their share of world manufacturing exports from 1981 to 2000, but the share of 26.8 per cent is still relatively low. East Asia and China have been most successful in expanding their share; but Africa's share has declined.

Despite the fast growth of manufactured exports from some developing countries, it must be remembered that they are starting from a very low base, and the export

Table 16.1 World market shares of manufactured exports of developing regions, 1981 and 2000

Region or Country	World market share (per cent)									
	1981					2000				
	Total	RB	LT	MT	HT	Total	RB	LT	MT	HT
East Asia	6.8	8.7	17.6	3.9	6.7	18.4	11.8	26.5	11.0	27.4
East Asia excl. China	5.8	7.6	14.8	3.6	6.5	12.0	8.1	10.0	7.2	21.9
China	1.0	1.1	2.8	0.3	0.2	6.5	3.7	16.5	3.7	5.6
South Asia	0.6	0.5	1.9	0.2	0.1	1.1	1.4	3.8	0.3	0.2
Latin America and the Caribbean	3.2	6.8	2.5	1.5	2.1	5.1	6.5	5.2	5.0	4.2
Latin America and the Caribbean excl. Mexico	2.7	6.3	2.1	1.2	0.9	2.2	5.5	2.2	1.5	0.8
Mexico	0.5	0.5	0.4	0.3	1.2	2.9	1.1	3.0	3.5	3.4
Middle East and North Africa	1.8	4.7	1.6	0.4	0.2	1.6	4.0	2.8	0.8	0.4
Sub-Saharan Africa	0.7	1.9	0.5	0.3	0.1	0.6	1.9	0.6	0.4	0.1
Sub-Saharan Africa excl. South Africa	0.3	0.9	0.2	0.0	0.0	0.2	1.0	0.2	0.0	0.0
South Africa	0.4	0.9	0.4	0.2	0.1	0.4	0.9	0.3	0.4	0.1
All developing countries	13.1	22.5	24.2	6.2	9.2	26.8	25.6	38.8	17.5	32.3

Note: RB ... Resource based exports, LT ... low tech exports, MT ... medium tech exports, HT ... high-tech exports.
Source: UNIDO, *Industrial Development Report* (Vienna: United Nations, 2004).

trade of many poor countries, particularly in Africa, is still dominated by primary commodities. Table 16.2 shows the countries dependent on a single primary commodity for a certain proportion of their total export earnings: more than 50 per cent; 20–49 per cent, and 10–19 per cent. Over 50 countries rely on just one crop for at least 20 per cent of their export earnings. This is a very heavy dependence, particularly if prices are volatile or decline (see later).

Taking the developing countries together, however, it is not true that the world as a whole is neatly polarized into two camps: the underdeveloped world, producing and exporting *solely* primary products in exchange for manufactures from developed countries; and the developed world, producing and exporting *solely* manufactures in exchange for primary commodities from developing countries. In practice a good deal of trade in both manufactures and primary products goes on among the developed and developing countries alike, with the developed countries exporting substantial quantities of primary commodities (especially temperate-zone foodstuffs) and the developing countries exporting some manufactured goods. Developed countries, in fact, account for about 50 per cent of the world's supply of primary products, and developing countries nearly 30 per cent of world trade in manufactures. In short, the distinction between developing and developed countries is not wholly synonymous with the distinction between primary producers and producers of manufactured goods. This needs to be borne in mind later when we discuss the terms of trade – the ratio of export to import prices. There is a distinction to be made between the terms of trade for developing and developed countries on the one hand and the terms of trade for primary and manufactured goods on the other.

Historically, trade has been an important mainspring of growth for countries at different stages of development. In the nineteenth century the countries that were industrializing had access to food and raw materials in primary-producing countries, which allowed the more developed countries to reap the gains from international specialization. In turn, the developing countries were assisted in their development by the demand for raw materials and the international investment that followed in its train. The situation today is somewhat different. Most world trade takes place in industrial commodities, in which many poor developing countries find it difficult to compete, and the demand for developing countries' traditional exports is slack relative to the demand for industrial goods. Except for spasmodic commodity booms, trade does not seem to work to the equal advantage of both sets of countries.

Three distinct factors have been at work in the developed countries to retard the growth of the traditional exports of the developing countries.

- The pattern of demand has shifted to goods with a relatively low import content of primary commodities.
- Technological change has led to the development of synthetic substitutes for raw materials.
- Developed countries have pursued protectionist policies that have retarded the growth of their imports of both primary commodities and manufactured goods from developing countries.

In view of these trading developments and the emergence of a foreign exchange gap as a constraint on growth in developing countries, there has been a complete

Table 16.2 Countries dependent on a single primary commodity for export earnings, 1992–7 (annual average of exports, in dollars)

	For 50 per cent or more of export earnings	For 20–49 per cent of export earnings	For 10–19 per cent of export earnings
Middle East			
Crude petroleum	Bahrain, Islamic Rep. of Iran, Iraq, Kuwait, Libya, Oman, Qatar, Saudi Arabia, Rep. of Yemen	Syrian Arab Rep., United Arab Emirates	Egypt
Aluminum			Bahrain
Africa			
Crude petroleum	Angola, Rep. of Congo, Gabon, Nigeria	Cameroon, Equatorial Guinea Algeria Mauritania	Algeria
Natural gas			
Iron ore			
Copper	Zambia		Dem. Rep. of Congo
Gold		Ghana, South Africa Equatorial Guinea	Mali, Zimbabwe
Timber (African hardwood)			Central African Rep., Gabon, Ghana, Swaziland
Cotton	Malawi	Benin, Chad, Mali, Sudan	Burkina Faso
Tobacco	Burundi, Ethiopia	Zimbabwe	
Arabica coffee	Uganda	Rwanda	
Robusta coffee			Cameroon
Cocoa	São Tomé and Príncipe	Côte d'Ivoire, Ghana	Cameroon
Tea			Kenya, Rwanda
Sugar		Mauritius	Swaziland

Western Hemisphere

Crude petroleum	Venezuela	Ecuador, Trinidad and Tobago	Colombia, Mexico
Copper		Chile	Peru
Gold			Guyana
Cotton			Paraguay
Arabica coffee			Colombia, El Salvador, Guatemala, Honduras, Nicaragua
Sugar		Guyana, St Kitts and Nevis	Belize
Bananas		Honduras, St Vincent	Costa Rica, Ecuador, St Lucia
Fishmeal			Peru
Rice			Guyana

Europe and Asia and the Pacific

Crude petroleum		Azerbaijan, Negara Brunei Darussalam, Norway, Papua New Guinea, Russia	Indonesia, Kazakhstan, Vietnam
Natural gas	Turkmenistan		
Aluminum		Tajikistan	Kazakhstan, Papua New Guinea
Copper		Mongolia	Uzbekistan
Gold		Papua New Guinea	Cambodia, Indonesia, Myanmar, Papua New Guinea
Timber (Asian hardwood)		Lao PDR, Solomon Islands	Latvia, New Zealand
Timber (softwood)			
Copra and coconut oil	Kiribati		
Cotton		Pakistan, Uzbekistan	Azerbaijan, Tajikistan, Turkmenistan

Source: International Monetary Fund, September 1999.

rethinking by some economists in recent years as to the lines along which trade should take place. The balance-of-payments difficulties and foreign exchange shortage of developing countries has led to a switch from viewing trade from the traditional classical standpoint of resource allocation to viewing the effects of trade on the balance of payments. It is balance-of-payments difficulties, necessitating foreign borrowing if growth is to be sustained, that has led to the cry in recent years of '**trade, not aid**'. The relevance of this slogan is examined in a later section. The problem facing developing countries is not so much *whether* to trade but *in what commodities* to trade, and to ensure that the terms on which they trade with the developed countries are favourable. There is no dispute that there are both static and dynamic gains from trade. What is in dispute is whether the overall gains would be greater, and the distribution of gains between countries fairer, if the pattern of trade was different from its present structure, and the developed countries modified their trading policies towards the developing world.

If the price elasticity of demand for the exports of developing countries is low and demand is slow to expand, it would seem counterproductive to allocate factors of production to *existing* export activities. The effect of increased output would be to reduce prices and worsen the terms of trade. This is the notion of 'immiserizing growth', with adverse movements in the terms of trade outweighing the gains from a larger volume of production.[1]

So what are the developing countries to do? The answer would appear to lie in *industrialization* – the production of industrial goods with a higher price and income elasticity of demand, either for export or for the home market, the latter implying import substitution. These dynamic considerations relating to the demand for existing export products and the need for diversification do not diminish the case for international specialization. What is involved is a reconsideration of what lines of activity to pursue in the face of changed circumstances, and a recognition of the distinction between **established comparative advantage** and **incremental or acquired comparative advantage**. Before going on to consider trade strategy for developing countries in the light of these 'new' trade theories, let us first establish more firmly the static and dynamic gains from trade that are stressed by traditional theory.

THE GAINS FROM TRADE

While it is quite legitimate to look at trade from the point of view of the balance of payments, and to regard the balance of payments as a development problem that can be solved only by new trade policies, the benefits from trade in traditional trade theory are not measured by the foreign exchange earned but by the increase in the value of output and real income from domestic resources that trade permits. Optimal trade policy, measured by the output gains from trade, must be clearly distinguished from the balance-of-payments effects of trade.

The resource gains from trade can be divided into static and dynamic gains. **Static gains** are those which accrue from international specialization according to the doctrine of comparative advantage. **Dynamic gains** are those which result from the impact of trade on production possibilities at large. Economies of scale, international investment and the transmission of technical knowledge are examples of dynamic gains. In addition, trade can provide a **vent for surplus** commodities, which brings otherwise unemployed resources into employment. It also enables countries to purchase goods from abroad, which can be important for two reasons: firstly, if there are no domestic substitutes, the ability to import can relieve domestic bottlenecks in production; and secondly imports may simply be more productive than domestic resources.

In this chapter we must do a number of things: First, we must establish the precise nature of the benefits from trade including the formation of regional trading agreements (RTAs). Secondly, we need to look at the different theories behind export-led growth and the empirical evidence concerning the effects of trade liberalization. Thirdly, we then need to examine critically the underlying assumptions of the comparative advantage doctrine and the classical advocacy of international specialization and free trade. We can then go on to consider the argument that the balance-of-payments implications of international specialization and free trade may seriously offset the allocative gains from trade, and whether this establishes a case for protection.

THE STATIC GAINS FROM TRADE

The static gains from trade are based on the **law of comparative advantage**. Consider the case of two countries, A and B, both with the capacity to produce commodities X and Y. The simple proposition of classical trade theory is that if country A has a comparative advantage in the production of commodity X, and country B has a comparative advantage in the production of commodity Y, it will be *mutually* profitable for country A to specialize in the production of X and for country B to specialize in the production of Y, and for surpluses of X and Y in excess of domestic needs to be freely traded, provided that the international rate of exchange between the two commodities lies between the domestic rates of exchange.

Comparative advantage is an **opportunity-cost concept** measured by the marginal rate of transformation between one commodity and another, as given by the slope of the production-possibility curve. Given perfect competition, which the above analysis assumes, the domestic price ratio between two commodities will equal their marginal rate of transformation. If this were not so, it would pay producers to switch from one commodity to another to take advantage of the relatively favourable price ratio.

Now let us give a practical example of the static gains from trade. In Figure 16.1 the production-possibility curves for countries A and B are drawn to show the different combination of goods X and Y that can be produced with each country's given factor endowments. We assume for simplicity that the factors of production in both countries are sufficiently versatile as to be able to produce either commodity equally efficiently so that the production-possibility curves are linear; that is, there is a constant marginal rate of transformation. Curves I and II are indifference curves, showing the levels of community welfare.

Now suppose that the marginal rate of transformation between X and Y in country A is 10/8, and in country B it is 10/2. Commodity X is relatively cheaper in country B than in A, measured by the amount of commodity Y that must for forgone, and Y is relatively cheaper in country A. We say that country A has the comparative advantage in the production of Y and country B in the production of X, and that it will be mutually

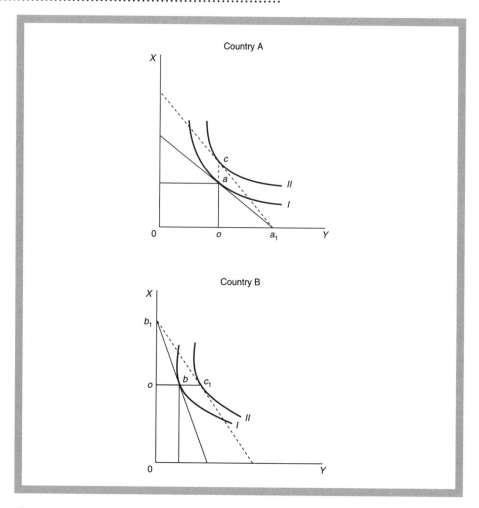

Figure 16.1 Gains from trade

advantageous for A to concentrate on Y and B to concentrate on X, and for A to swop Y for X and for B to swop X for Y.

Before trade each country produces combinations of goods X and Y that give a level of utility represented by indifference curve I. The two countries produce at a and b, respectively. With the opening of trade there can only be one price ratio between X and Y, which is determined by the interaction of demand and supply in both countries together and will lie somewhere between each country's transformation (price) ratio. Assume that the international rate of exchange settles at 10/5, shown by the broken lines in Figure 16.1. Country A, specializing in the production of Y, can exchange Y for more X internationally than it could domestically, and country B, specializing in the production of X, can exchange X for more Y internationally than it could domestically. For example, suppose that after trade production in country A shifts to a_1 and in country B to b_1. Country A, trading oa_1 of Y, can now consume oc of X, which it obtains from country B. Country B, trading ob_1 of X, can now consume oc_1 of Y, which it obtains from country A. Both countries move to higher indifference curves, to higher levels of welfare on indifference curve II.

As a result of the international division of labour, world production increases, and so does world welfare. Specialization on the basis of comparative advantage enables the maximum to be produced from a given amount of factor resources. The increase in welfare that trade permits results from the opportunity to obtain foreign products more cheaply, in terms of real resources forgone, than the alternative of import substitution or producing domestically. The gain from trade is the difference between the value of things that are obtained and the value of things that are given up. Through the international division of labour a country is supposed to obtain more than it gives up. If comparative advantage were exactly the same in the two countries there would, of course, be no static gains and the justification for trade would be to reap economies of scale and other dynamic gains.

Whether the consumption of *both* commodities in *both* countries rises depends on the international rate of exchange. At some rates of exchange, even between the two domestic price ratios, the consumption of one of the commodities in one of the countries after trade may be less than before trade. Even so, it can still be maintained that the post-trade position is superior to the pre-trade position, if those individuals whose welfare is increased can fully compensate those who suffer and still be better off.

The static gains from trade are the same gains as from trade creation that accrue with the establishment of customs unions, when high-cost suppliers are replaced by lower-cost suppliers as tariffs are reduced. It is the doctrine of comparative costs that provides the rationale for the formation of customs unions, or regional trading agreements (RTAs) between countries. It should be emphasized, though, that **there is nothing in the comparative cost doctrine that ensures equality in the distribution of gains from trade creation** (which in part explains why attempts to establish RTAs often meet with difficulties).

There is also the important question of whether the full employment of resources can be maintained in each country. The classical doctrine of free trade assumes that all commodities are produced under conditions of constant returns to scale and that the full employment of resources is maintained as resources are switched from one activity to another in accordance with comparative advantage. If some activities, for example primary commodities, are subject to diminishing returns, however, there is a limit to employment in these activities, and it is possible that the real income gains from specialization will be offset by the real income losses from unemployed resources.

If industrial activities are subject to increasing returns, there is no limit to employment and trade will lead to the unequal growth between primary producing and industrial countries, thus perpetuating inequality, as we saw in Chapter 7.

THE DYNAMIC GAINS FROM TRADE

Now let us turn to the dynamic gains from trade. The major dynamic benefit of trade is that export markets widen the total market for a country's producers. If production is subject to increasing returns, the total gains from trade will exceed the static gains from a more efficient allocation of resources. There is also a close connection between increasing returns and the accumulation of capital. For a small country with no trade there is very limited scope for large-scale investment in advanced capital equipment;

specialization is limited by the extent of the market. But if a poor developing country can trade, there is some prospect of industrialization and of dispensing with traditional methods of production.

The larger the market, the easier capital accumulation becomes if there are increasing returns to scale. In this respect larger countries such as China and India are in a more favourable position than smaller countries such as Fiji, Mauritius or The Gambia. India and China's large populations offer a promising basis for the establishment of capital-goods industries and the production of manufactured goods, since production can take place on a viable basis before trade. The smaller country, however, may need substantial protection for a commodity before it can be produced economically and compete in world markets. At least 60 countries classified as 'developing', however, have populations fewer than 15 million.

Other important dynamic effects of trade consist of the stimulus to competition, the acquisition of new knowledge, new ideas and the dissemination of technical knowledge, the possibility of accompanying capital flows through foreign direct investment, increased specialization leading to more roundabout methods of production, and changes in attitudes and institutions. In the context of 'new', endogenous growth theory (see Chapter 4), these are all forms of externalities that keep the marginal product of capital from falling, so that trade improves the long-run growth performance of countries. In terms of Figure 16.1, the effect of dynamic benefits is to shift outwards the production-possibility curves of both countries, leading to a higher level of community welfare.

TRADE AS A VENT FOR SURPLUS

Another important potential gain from trade is the provision of an outlet for a country's surplus commodities, which would otherwise go unsold and represent a waste of resources. This is the so-called 'vent for surplus' gain from trade. In Figure 16.1 this is represented by a movement from a point inside the production-possibility frontier to a point on the frontier – which represents a higher level of welfare. If there is a gain, this implies that the 'surplus' export resources have no alternative uses and cannot be switched to domestic use. This may not be as unreasonable an assumption as it sounds, bearing in mind the country's resource endowments in relation to its population size and the tastes of the community. Mines and fishing grounds, for example, have no alternative uses, and the marginal utility of consuming their products would soon become zero if demand was confined to domestic consumption alone.

As a theory of trade, the vent for surplus theory is a much more plausible theory than the comparative cost doctrine in explaining the rapid expansion of export production in most parts of the developing world in the nineteenth century. First, had there not been unutilized resources the expansion process could not have kept going. Second, the comparative cost theory cannot explain why, when two countries are similar, one develops a major export sector while the other does not; vent for surplus (related to relative population pressures) is one possible explanation. Third, vent for surplus is a much more plausible explanation for the start of trade. Small-scale peasant farmers with no surplus would not naturally and instinctively start to specialize according to the law of comparative advantage in the anticipation of reaching a higher consumption-possibility curve.

There is a distinction to be made here between the *type* of commodity traded and the *basis* for trade in the sense of what gets trade started. Vent for surplus may explain better the original basis of trade, while comparative cost theory explains the type of commodity traded. Vent for surplus has no explanatory power in the latter case.

Finally, a fourth potential gain from trade, which merits distinguishing as a separate effect, is that exports permit imports that may be more productive than domestic resources, both directly and indirectly. We saw in the discussion of dual-gap analysis in Chapter 15 that imports can be regarded as substitutes for domestic capital goods, with the capacity to lower the overall capital–output ratio through their superior efficiency and impact on the economy at large, especially by relieving domestic bottlenecks. In this sense exports have supply effects as well as demand effects, and it is important to take this into account when considering the relation between exports and growth.

THEORY OF CUSTOMS UNIONS AND FREE TRADE AREAS

Because of the various advantages to be gained from trade, **regional trade agreements** (RTAs) have become very fashionable in recent years, in the form of **customs unions and free trade areas**. The WTO lists 76 that have been established or modified since 1948. The major ones are the European Union (EU); the North American Free Trade Agreement (NAFTA); MERCOSUR covering Argentina, Brazil, Paraguay, Uruguay and Chile; APEC, covering countries in the Asia and Pacific region; ASEAN covering South-East Asian countries, and SACU, covering countries in southern Africa.

The essence of a customs union is that it frees trade between members and imposes a *common* external tariff (CET) on imported goods from the rest of the world. In a free trade area (FTA), by contrast, barriers to trade are brought down within the area, but there is no CET. Countries are free to impose their own specific tariffs on goods from outside the area, although often subject to agreement over the proportion of goods that must be purchased from within the area. Customs unions therefore *create* trade, but also *divert* it from lower-cost suppliers outside the union. The interesting question is always whether the benefits of trade creation exceed the costs of trade diversion. FTAs also create trade, but the extent of trade diversion is likely to be much less, with the presumption that on narrow economic grounds, at least, FTAs are superior. For the same reason, customs unions are likely to be inferior to a policy of unilateral tariff reductions, and therefore need to be justified on other economic or non-economic grounds.

Before we look at the empirical evidence on these matters, however, let us consider theoretically the gains and losses of customs unions. The analysis makes the same assumptions as classical trade theory: perfect competition; prices reflect opportunity cost; factors of production are immobile between countries; trade is balanced (*i.e.* no balance of payments problems), and the full employment of resources. The **trade creation** effect of a Union is composed of two parts: first a production effect which consists of the substitution of cheaper 'foreign' goods for domestic goods from within the union, and secondly a consumption effect consisting of the gain in consumer surplus from cheaper goods. The **trade diversion** effect is also composed of two parts: first, the substitution of higher-priced goods from within the union for goods outside the union,

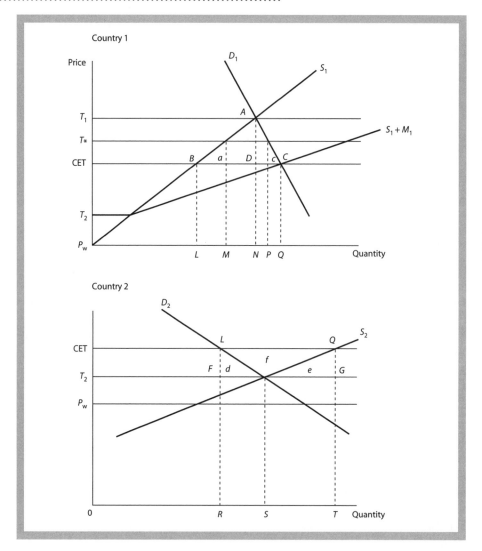

Figure 16.2 Gains and losses within a customs union

and secondly the loss of consumer surplus that this entails. The gains and losses for two partner countries within the union are illustrated in Figure 16.2. To simplify the analysis, scale economies and terms of trade effects are ignored.[2]

D_1 and D_2 are the demand curves for a good in the two countries; S_1 and S_2 are the domestic supply curves; $S_1 + M_1$ is the supply curve in country 1 consisting of the domestic supply curve and the supply of the good from the partner country which is assumed to enter duty free; and P_w is the world price. Now suppose that before the union of the two countries, a tariff of $P_w T_1$ was imposed in country 1 and $P_w T_2$ in country 2. In this case, it can be seen that demand equals supply in both markets; there are no imports from the rest of the world, and we can focus first of all on the process of trade creation.

A customs union is now formed with a CET that balances supply and demand of the two partners (equal to $P_w CET$). The CET is lower than OT_1 in country 1 and higher than OT_2 in country 2. This has consumption and production effects in the two countries.

In country 1 domestic consumption increases from N to Q, and domestic production decreases from N to L. In country 2, domestic production increases from S to T; domestic consumption decreases from S to R and the difference between supply and demand is exported to country 1. For country 1 there has been a cost saving equal to the area ABD, and an increase in consumer surplus equal to the area ADC. The total gain of trade creation is equal to $ABD + ADC$. In country 2, there has been a loss of consumer surplus equal to area 'd' and an increased production cost equal to area 'e', but this is more than offset by the increased export revenue of $LFGQ$, so country 2 is also better off.

Now let us consider the case where there is also trade diversion from the rest of the world. Suppose that in country 1 the initial tariff level was lower than P_wT_1 – say P_wT^*, so that demand exceeded supply and the excess demand was filled by imports from the rest of the world, MP, at price P_w. If a CET was now introduced of P_wCET, demand would increase from P to Q with an increase in consumer surplus of area 'c'. Production would fall from M to L with a reduction in production cost equal to area 'a'. There would be trade creation gains equal to 'a' + 'c'. But now there is also trade diversion. Imports, previously from outside the Union, would now come from the higher-cost partner. MP imports from abroad would be replaced at the increased cost of $MP \times P_wCET$. This is the cost of trade diversion.

In evaluating the net gains from a customs union, trade creation needs to be compared with trade diversion. In general, trade creation is likely to predominate over trade diversion, the larger is the union and the lower is the CET. The larger the union, the greater the scope for trade creation, and the lower the CET, the less trade diversion there is likely to be. It is possible, however, even if the union as a whole is, on balance, trade-creating, that at least one country may lose. Likewise, it is possible for at least one country to gain even if the union as a whole is, on balance, trade-diverting. Everything depends on circumstances. A customs union can be devised, however, which raises the welfare of all members. This requires first that the CET of the union is set so that the level of post-union trade with the rest of the world does not fall below its pre-union level, and secondly that lump-sum compensatory taxes and transfers are imposed to offset individual country losses.

Apart from trade creation and trade diversion, customs unions may also have other important effects associated with the enlargement of the market which are neglected by the static analysis presented above. First, the larger market may generate economies of scale. If there are economies of scale, the supply curves in Figure 16.2 will slope downwards, and the CET can be lower than the original tariff in *both* partner countries. There will be a normal trade-creation effect and a cost-saving in both countries. Secondly, integration is likely to promote increased competition which is likely to affect favourably prices and costs, and the growth of output. Thirdly, the widening of markets within a customs union is likely to attract international investment. Producers will prefer to produce within the union rather than face a CET from outside. Finally, if the world supply of output is not infinitely elastic, there are terms of trade effects to consider. Specifically, if there is trade diversion, the world price of the good will fall, moving the terms of trade in favour of the customs union. This terms of trade effect represents a welfare gain which may partly offset the welfare loss of trade diversion.

It was mentioned earlier, however, that because customs unions impose a CET, they are likely to be inferior, in terms of welfare improvement, to a policy of *unilateral* tariff reductions (continuing to make the standard assumptions, of course, of trade balance, full employment, etc.). We can now illustrate this using Figure 16.2. Suppose country 1 has an initial tariff level of P_wT^*. It enters a customs union with country 2 with a common external tariff CET, and trade creation takes places equal to 'a' + 'c' (as before). Country 1 could also, however, reduce its tariff to P_wT^* on a non-discriminatory basis. It would enjoy the same trade creation gains, but now would be able to obtain imports cheaper from the rest of the world. This means an additional gain equal to the difference between the total expenditure on imports from the union compared to the rest of the world. At a simple level, the conclusion from this theoretical analysis is that the formation of customs unions represents a movement towards free trade, but even freer trade (i.e. no trade diversion) is better. The recent empirical evidence seems to support this view (see below).

EMPIRICAL EVIDENCE ON THE GROWTH EFFECTS OF CUSTOMS UNIONS AND TRADE LIBERALIZATION

Overall, the liberalization of trade has led to a massive expansion in the growth of world trade relative to world output, as shown in Figure 16.3. While world output (or GDP) has expanded nearly sixfold, the volume of world trade has grown 20 times at an average compound rate of 7 per cent per annum. In some individual countries, notably in South-East Asia, the growth of exports has exceeded 10 per cent per annum. Exports have tended to grow fastest in countries with more liberal trade regimes, and these countries have experienced the fastest growth of GDP.

However, the general experience of RTAs in developing countries has been disappointing because they have been very inward-looking and protectionist, with trade diversion exceeding trade creation. Typically, the existing ratio of trade to GDP has been high in the member countries and the ratio of trade with the rest of the world has also been

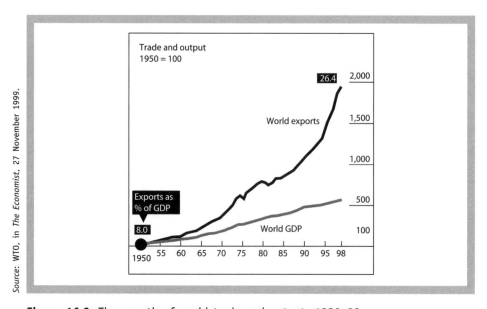

Figure 16.3 The growth of world trade and output, 1950–98

high so that the scope for trade creation has been minimal and the potential for trade diversion has been great. In the Economic Community of West African States (ECOWAS), founded in 1975, the amount of intermember trade is still less than 10 per cent of total exports. Forouton (1993) concludes his study of regional integration in Sub-Saharan Africa (SSA) by saying 'the structural characteristics of the SSA economies, the pursuit of import-substitution policies, and the very uneven distribution of costs and benefits of integration arising from economic differences among the partner countries, have thus far prevented any meaningful trade integration in SSA'. Of the seven or eight groupings in Sub-Saharan Africa, only SACU has achieved any noticeable degree of integration in the market for goods. Otherwise, intragroup trade has remained limited and stagnant. This conclusion is echoed by the authors of many of the applied papers in Oyejide, Elbadawi and Collier (1997), which examine the experience of regional integration and trade liberalization in Sub-Saharan Africa.

Recent empirical work across developing countries as a whole supports this pessimistic conclusion as far as regional trade agreements are concerned, but finds that broad trade liberalization does lead to faster growth. Vamvakidis (1999) takes 109 cases of participation in 18 RTAs over the period 1950–92, and concludes that their impact on the growth rate of members has been negative. Vamvakidis also takes 51 cases of broad liberalization and finds that countries have grown faster after liberalization. Two measures of liberalization (or trade openness) are used. One is the standard measure used in much of the 'new' growth theory literature (see Chapter 4) of the ratio of total trade (exports + imports) to GDP. The second is the so-called Sachs–Warner (1995) ratio of openness. Sachs and Warner define an economy as 'open' if all five of the following conditions are met: (1) an average tariff rate of less than 40 per cent; (2) average non-tariff barriers equivalent to a tariff rate of less than 40 per cent, (3) a black market exchange rate premium of less than 20 per cent, (4) no communistic government and (5) no state monopoly of major exports. These criteria can be used for pin-pointing the precise year(s) of trade openness for a country. The procedure for testing the effect on growth of trade liberalization, or belonging to a RTA, is to specify a cross-country growth equation of the form:

$$g = a + b_1 \text{ (initial GDP per head)} + b_2 \text{ (population growth)}$$
$$+ b_3 \text{ (schooling)} + b_4 \text{ (growth of world GDP)} + b_5 D_1 + b_6 D_2 \qquad (16.1)$$

where D_1 is a dummy variable if the country participates in an RTA, and D_2 is a dummy variable for the Sachs–Warner openness variable or the trade share variable. Output growth (g) is measured taking 5-year averages over the period 1950–92. The dummy variable for both measures of trade liberalization is positive and significant. The results suggest that after liberalization countries grow faster on average by 1.5 percentage points, and that an increase in the trade share by 10 per cent leads to an increase in the growth rate by 0.56 percentage points. Estimating the same equation across countries participating in RTAs shows the RTA dummy variable to be negative. The same results emerge when the share of investment in GDP is taken as the dependent variable. After liberalization, the investment share is 2.7 percentage points higher, but membership of a RTA lowers the investment share. The negative result for RTAs must result from the fact that, on balance, trade diversion is more powerful than trade creation. In other work, Vamvakidis (1998) has tried to estimate the effect on output growth of the size and openness of neighbouring countries, and finds that countries which have neighbours with large open economies experience faster growth. Openness matters more than size. Being near a developed country also has a positive spillover effect.

TRADE LIBERALIZATION AND GROWTH

David Ricardo (1772–1823) was the founder of the comparative cost, classical free-trade doctrine. Before him, Adam Smith (1723–90) had stressed the importance of trade as a vent for surplus and a means of widening the market, thereby improving the division of labour and the level of productivity. According to Smith:

> between whatever places foreign trade is carried on, they all of them derive two distinct benefits from it. It carries out the surplus part of the produce of their land and labour for which there is no demand among them, and brings back in return for it something else for which there is a demand. It gives a value to their superfluities, by exchanging them for something else, which may satisfy a part of their wants and increase their enjoyments. By means of it, the narrowness of the home market does not hinder the division of labour in any particular branch of art or manufacture from being carried to the highest perfection. By opening a more extensive market for whatever part of the produce of their labour may exceed the home consumption, it encourages them to improve its productive powers and to augment its annual produce to the utmost, and thereby to increase the real revenue of wealth and society. (Smith, 1776)

In the nineteenth century, Smith's productivity doctrine developed beyond a free trade argument into an export-drive argument, as Britain began to colonize large areas of Asia, Africa and North America. There seems to be a consensus among economic historians that at this time, trade acted as a powerful engine of growth, not only by contributing to a more efficient allocation of resources within countries, but also because it transmitted growth from one part of the world to another. The demand in Europe, and in Britain in particular, for raw materials brought prosperity to such countries as Canada, Argentina, South Africa, Australia and New Zealand. As the demand for their commodities increased, investment in these countries also increased. Trade was mutually profitable. As Alfred Marshall wrote in the nineteenth century, **'the causes which determine the economic progress of nations belong to the study of international trade'** (Marshall, 1890). One of the foremost contemporary exponents of trade as the engine of growth was Arthur Lewis, who based his theory on what appears to be from his researches a stable relationship between economic growth in developed countries and export growth in developing countries (see, for example, Lewis, 1980).

It is important to stress, however, that not all countries necessarily benefit equally from greater openness to trade. In other words, free trade does not guarantee an equitable distribution of the gains from trade. This is shown in a major study by Dowrick and Golley (2004) of 127 countries over the period 1960 to 2000. They conclude that in the period since 1980, at least, the benefits of freer trade have accrued mainly to the developed countries with little benefit to the poorer developing countries, so that trade has widened world income inequality in the last 25 years. The major reason for this divergence is that many developing countries still specialize heavily in primary production where scope for productivity improvement through trade is less. In countries specializing in primary products, the average growth of productivity has been 0.5 to 0.8 per cent per annum slower; and

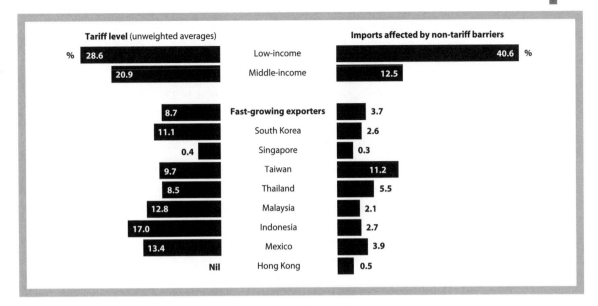

Figure 16.4 Tariff and non-tariff barriers in selected countries

2 per cent slower in the 33 poorest countries. Sachs and Warner (1997), in their study of 79 countries over the period 1965–90, also find that specialization in primary product exports is bad for growth. They attribute this to exchange rate overvaluation (the Dutch disease) and the rent-seeking behaviour of agents in resource abundant economies.

In the world economy since 1950 there has been a massive liberalization of world trade, first under the auspices of the General Agreement on Tariffs and Trade (GATT), established in 1947, and now the World Trade Organization (WTO), which replaced the GATT in 1995. The major barriers to trade are tariffs, and non-tariff barriers (NTBs) consisting of quotas, licences, technical and environmental specifications and domestic input requirements. Tariff levels in high-income countries have come down dramatically and now average approximately 4 per cent, but rich countries still protect sensitive sectors, such as agriculture and textiles. Tariff levels in developing countries have also been falling but still remain relatively high, as shown in Figure 16.4, averaging over 20 per cent in the low- and middle-income countries. These countries also apply NTBs to a wide range of imports. Some of the fastest growing exporters, however, which are also some of the fastest growing economies, have much more liberal trading regimes, with low average tariff rates and only a very small percentage of imports subject to NTBs.

There are several mechanisms through which trade liberalization may influence the long-run growth rate of an economy:

■ More trade encourages investment which confers **externalities** on an economy, particularly if the investment goods come from abroad
■ Greater trade means larger volumes of ouptut and greater scope for **specialization,** leading to **learning by doing**
■ Trade leads to **technology transfer** and the prospect of faster total productivity growth.

To test the relation between trade liberalization and growth, a measure of liberalization or outward orientation is required. There are several possible measures, and many investigators and organizations (e.g. Leamer, 1988; World Bank, 1987) devise their own measures. Some of the most common measures used are: the average import tariff; an average index of NTBs; an index of effective protection (i.e. the protection of value-added – see p. 557); an index of relative price distortions or exchange rate misalignment; and the average black market exchange rate premium. In 1987, the World Bank classified a group of 41 developing countries according to their trade orientation in order to compare the performance of countries with different degrees of outward/inward orientation. Four categories of countries were identified:

- **Strongly outward oriented** countries, where there are very few trade or foreign exchange controls and trade and industrial policies do not discriminate between production for the home market and exports, and between purchases of domestic goods and foreign goods
- **Moderately outward oriented** countries, where the overall incentive structure is moderately biased towards the production of goods for the home market rather than for export, and favours the purchase of domestic goods
- **Moderately inward oriented** countries, where there is a more definite bias against exports and in favour of import substitution
- **Strongly inward oriented** countries, where trade controls and the incentive structures strongly favour production for the domestic market and discriminate strongly against imports.

The World Bank concludes its study by saying that the evidence 'suggests that the economic performance of the outward oriented economies has been broadly superior to that of inward oriented economies in all respects'.

Edwards (1992), in a major study of trade orientation, distortions and growth in developing countries, develops a model which assumes that more open economies are more efficient at absorbing exogenously generated technology. Using nine indicators of trade orientation constructed by Leamer (1988) he shows, for a sample of 30 developing countries over the period 1970–82, that more open economies tend to grow faster. To test the hypothesis, a conventional growth equation is used relating the growth of per capita income of countries to their investment ratio; to their initial level of per capita income as a proxy for technological backwardness; and a measure of trade distortion. All but one of the trade distortion measures produce a significant negative coefficient, and the findings are robust with respect to the sample taken, the time period taken and the method of estimation. The findings are also robust to some of the alternative indicators of trade liberalization and distortion mentioned at the beginning. In a further study, Edwards (1998) runs regressions of total factor productivity growth on the nine different measures of openness. Five of the measures show a positive significant effect, and Edwards concludes 'these results are quite remarkable, suggesting with tremendous consistency that there is a significantly positive relation between openness and productivity growth'.

In another comprehensive study, Dollar (1992) also addresses the question of whether outward oriented countries grow more rapidly – taking as his sample 95 developing countries over the period 1976–85. Trade orientation is measured by the degree to which the real exchange rate is distorted by not reflecting differences in the price level between countries. High relative prices indicate strong protection and incentives geared to production for the home market. Taking different continents, and comparing them with the successful economies of Asia, he finds that in Latin America the exchange rate was overvalued by 33 per cent during this period, and in Africa by 86 per cent. Growth equations are estimated across countries using each country's measure of exchange rate distortion, controlling for differences in the level of investment and the variability of the exchange rate. Dollar finds that, on average, trade distortions in Africa and Latin America reduced the growth of income per head by between 1.5 and 2.1 per cent per annum.

Brahmbhatt and Dadush (1996) at the IMF have developed a speed of integration index based on four indicators: (1) the ratio of exports and imports to GDP (the Vamvakidis measure of openness); (2) the ratio of FDI to GDP; (3) the share of manufactures in total exports, and (4) a country's credit rating. They then divide a sample of 93 countries into four groups – fast, moderate, weak and slow integrators – and find that the fast integrators include most of the rapidly growing East Asian economies, while the weakly and slowly integrating group include most of the low income countries of Sub-Saharan Africa and some of the middle-income countries of Latin America. The distribution of countries by speed of integration is shown in Table 16.3.

Table 16.3 Distribution of countries, by speed of integration, 1990s

Speed	East Asia	South Asia	Latin America and Caribbean	Middle East and North Africa	Sub-Saharan Africa	Europe and Central Asia
Fast integrators	6	3	5	2	2	5
Moderate integrators		2	5	4	10	2
Weak integrators	3		9	2	10	
Slow integrators			2	5	14	2
Total	9	5	21	13	36	9

Source: M. Brahmbhatt and U. Dadush, 'Disparities in Global Integration', *Finance and Development*, September 1996.

TRADE LIBERALIZATION, EXPORTS AND GROWTH

The impact of trade liberalization on economic growth outlined above works mainly through improving the efficiency of resource allocation, and stimulating exports which have powerful effects on both supply and demand within an economy (see the section on export-led growth models below). Trade liberalization does not necessarily imply faster export growth, but in practice it appears to have a significant positive impact. This is shown by Joshi and Little (1996) for India, Ahmed (2000) for Bangladesh, Pacheco-López (2005) for Mexico and Bleaney (1999) for ten Latin American countries. Santos-Paulino (2002) also shows this using panel data techniques in a comprehensive study of 22 developing countries that have adopted trade liberalization policies since the mid-1970s. A dummy variable for the year of liberalization is included in an export growth equation using between 350 and 500 observations (depending on the method of estimation), and the central conclusion is that, controlling for other variables, liberalization has raised export growth by nearly 2 percentage points compared with the pre-liberalization period. The impact appears to have been the greatest in Africa (3.6 percentage points) and the least in Latin America (1.6 percentage points). There is also evidence that liberalization has increased the sensitivity of export growth to world income growth; that is, liberalization has increased the income elasticity of demand for exports by inducing structural change.

The high-performance Asian countries are perhaps the most spectacular examples of economic success linked to export performance, but, interestingly, this has not always been based on free trade and laissez-faire. The economies of Japan, South Korea, Taiwan, Singapore, Hong Kong, Malaysia, Indonesia and Thailand have recorded some of the highest GDP growth rates in the world since 1965 (averaging as a group nearly 6 per cent per annum) and also some of the highest rates of growth of exports (averaging more than 10 per cent per annum). While some of the countries have been very laissez-faire, however, others have been very interventionist, for example Japan and South Korea, pursuing relentless export promotion but import substitution at the same time. The ratio of trade to GDP in Japan is still low. In their meticulous study of *The East Asian Miracle*, the World Bank (1993) concludes that there is no single East Asian model. What is important for growth is getting the fundamentals for growth right, not whether it is the free market or government that does it. Three policies are identified as contributing to the success of these 'tiger' economies:

- Industrial policies to promote particular sectors of the economy (the shift to industry)
- Government control of financial markets to lower the cost of capital and direct credit to strategic sectors
- Policies to promote exports and protect domestic industry.

Crucial to all three policies was good governance (see Chapter 9). The World Bank concedes that most of the countries deviated from free market economics, but that they got the fundamentals right (for example efficient resource allocation, high rates of physical and human capital formation, and so on) and deviated less from free-market norms than other developing countries. The fact remains that there is no way in which any of these countries could have grown as rapidly as they did without the rapid growth of exports. Apart from all the externalities associated with trade and encouragement of domestic and foreign investment, they simply would not have had the foreign exchange to pay for all the import requirements associated with growth.

Another interesting case study is China, which still restricts trade, but is now (2005) the world's fifth largest exporter. Since China launched its 'open door' policy in 1978, after three decades of inward-orientated trade, its exports have been growing at over 10 per cent per annum and its average GDP growth rate has been 7 per cent. This is another classic example of export-led growth deliberately promoted by the government through the establishment of special economic zones and 'open cities' (originally in the provinces of Guangdong and Fujian) which act as magnets for investment and provide incentives for exporters. Typical incentives for exporters in all export-orientated economies consist of:

- Exemption from duties and tariffs on inputs that go into exports
- Investment grants
- Tax holidays
- Favourable retention rights over foreign exchange if exports are in certain sectors
- Favourable treatment of foreign investment.

In China a 25 per cent investment share was enough to give joint venture status to foreign investors, who then qualified for tax incentives, and no limit was placed on foreign equity investment in Chinese companies.

As well as individual case studies, the development literature is full of time-series and cross-section studies relating output growth to export growth, and almost all show a strong positive association (see later). Simple bivariate relationships, of course, do not prove causality, and it could be argued that it is rapid output growth that causes export growth, not vice versa. There is undoubtedly an element of truth in this. If rapid output growth leads to faster productivity growth and greater competitiveness, this will benefit exports, and this is part of the cumulative causation model of growth outlined in Chapter 7. Bi-causality, however, does not undermine the causal mechanisms or the causal role of exports in the growth process, working from both the demand and the supply side. This leads us on to the topic of export-led growth.

MODELS OF EXPORT-LED GROWTH

There are three main models of export-led growth:

- The neoclassical supply-side model
- The balance-of-payments-constrained growth model
- The virtuous circle model.

The first is the orthodox model which fits neatly into mainstream neoclassical growth theory. The latter two models are rarely articulated in the trade and growth literature, and yet may be of greater importance for understanding growth rate differences in open developing economies, especially if most developing countries are constrained in their economic performance by a shortage of foreign exchange. Moreover, orthodox growth and trade theory predicts the convergence of per capita incomes across countries (see Chapter 4), which is at variance with what we observe in the real world. What appears to happen in practice is that once a country gains an advantage through the capture of export markets, it tends to sustain that advantage through the operation of various cumulative forces which generate 'virtuous circles' of success for favoured countries (and regions), and 'vicious circles' of slow growth and underemployment for those countries that get left behind (see Chapter 7). When studies are conducted of the relation between exports and growth, either across countries or over time, it is not always clear whether the relation found is picking up supply-side factors; demand-side influences; cumulative forces interacting with each other; or a combination of all three.

The neoclassical supply-side model

The neoclassical supply-side model of the relation between exports and growth assumes that the export sector, because of its exposure to foreign competition, confers externalities on the non-export sector, and secondly that the export sector has a higher level of productivity than the non-export sector. Thus, the share of exports in GDP, and the growth of exports, matters for overall growth performance. Feder (1983) was the first to provide a formal model of this type to explain the relation between export growth and output growth. The output of the export sector is assumed to be a function of labour and capital in the sector; the output of the non-export sector is assumed to be a function of labour, capital and the output of the export sector (to capture externalities); and the ratio of respective marginal factor productivities in the two sectors is assumed to deviate from unity by a factor δ. These assumptions produce an augmented neoclassical growth equation of the form:

$$G = a(I/Y) + b(dL/L) + [\delta/(1+\delta) + F_x] \, (X/Y) \, (dX/X) \qquad (16.2)$$

where I/Y is the investment ratio; dL/L is the growth of the labour force; dX/X is the growth of exports; X/Y is the share of exports in GDP; $\delta/(1+\delta)$ is the differential productivity effect; and F_x is the externality effect. Feder originally tested the model taking a cross-section of 19 semi-industrialized countries and a larger sample of 31 countries over the period 1964–73. First he tested the model without export growth, and then with the growth of exports included. The inclusion of dX/X considerably improves the explanatory power of the equation, and the effect of export growth is always statistically significant. The coefficient on export growth, however, is an amalgam of an externality effect and a productivity differential effect. To decompose the two, (16.2) can be fitted excluding the export share term (X/Y) which then isolates the externality effect. The difference between the total effect of export growth and the externality effect is the productivity differential effect. When this is done, Feder found substantial differences in productivity between the export and non-export sector and also evidence of externalities.

The results should not surprise. The export sector is likely to be more 'modern' and capital intensive than the non-export sector which to a larger extent consists of low productivity agriculture and petty service activities. The externalities conferred are part of the dynamic gains from trade discussed at the beginning of the chapter, associated with the transmission and diffusion of new ideas from abroad relating to both production techniques and efficient management practices.

Cross-section work on exports and growth assumes, however, that all countries in a sample conform to the same model, with the same intercept and coefficient parameters linking exports and growth. In practice, this is highly unlikely to be the case; and it transpires, in fact, that when time-series studies are conducted for individual countries, the relation between exports and growth is much weaker. Ram (1987) takes time series data for 88 countries over the period 1960–82 and finds large differences in the parameter values between countries. Indeed, the export variable is only significant in 40 per cent of the countries, and is much weaker in low-income countries than in middle income countries. Another time-series study by Greenaway and Sapsford (1994) produces even weaker results. They take 19 countries and run various regressions of output growth (net of exports) on the investment ratio, labour force growth and export growth and generally find the export growth variable to be insignificant. They conclude that if trade liberalization is supposed to influence output growth through export growth, the evidence is weak. On the other hand, the effect of liberalization may be to alter the relation between export and growth performance, and this is tested by using shift and slope dummy variables in the equations to discriminate between periods before and after liberalization. The evidence for structural breaks, however, is also weak.

A major problem with time-series studies, however, is that the coefficient estimates capture only short-run relationships. In the case of exports and growth, the effect of export performance in any one year is likely to be lagged and longer term whatever the mechanism by which export growth exerts its favourable influence on an economy. Studies need to recognize this, and ideally studies should use pooled time-series and cross-section data (i.e. panel data) both to maximize the number of observations and to allow for country-specific effects at the same time.

Whatever procedure is adopted, however, the problem remains of identifying the causal mechanism by which exports influence growth. The Feder model is a pure supply-side argument which has plausibility, but there are other (non-neoclassical) supply-side arguments, and also demand-side considerations which would also be consistent with finding export growth and GDP growth positively correlated over the long term. From the supply side, export growth may raise output growth through externalities, but also faster export growth permits faster import growth. If countries are short of foreign exchange, and domestic and foreign resources are not fully substitutable, more imports permit a fuller use of domestic resources. In particular, more foreign exchange allows the greater import of capital goods which may not be produced domestically. Esfahani (1991) recognizes this point and re-estimates Feder's equation for 31 countries, including the growth of imports as well as the growth of exports. The export growth variable now loses its significance, while the import growth variable is significant. The regression is also run without export growth, and it is found that once the import supply effect of exports is taken into account there is apparently no significant externality effect of exports left to explain. Esfahani concludes: 'even though exports do not appear to have had much direct externality effect on GDP – export promotion policies in these countries can be quite valuable in supplying foreign exchange which relieves import shortages and permits output expansion'.

The balance-of-payments constrained growth models

Even the Esfahani argument, however, does not go far enough because it neglects the importance of demand for the growth of output. Most factors of production in the growth and development process are *endogenous* to demand and not exogenously determined as neoclassical growth theory assumes. Capital is a produced means of production and is as much a consequence of the growth of output as its cause. The demand for labour is a derived demand from output. Labour input responds to demand in a variety of ways through reductions in unemployment; increases in labour force participation; increases in hours worked; shifts of labour from low productivity to high productivity sectors; and in the last resort, through international migration. In labour surplus economies, such as most developing countries, it stretches credulity to assume an exogenously given supply of labour that determines output in a *causal* sense. Productivity growth is also largely endogenous to output growth working through induced capital accumulation, embodied technical progress and static and dynamic returns to scale. To understand growth rate differences between countries, it is necessary to understand why demand growth differs between countries, and the constraints on demand that exist within countries. In most developing countries, the major constraint on the growth of demand is the current balance of payments and the shortage of foreign exchange. Export growth relaxes a balance-of-payments constraint on demand and allows all other components of demand (consumption, investment and government expenditure) to grow faster without running into balance of payments difficulties. This is the simplest of all explanations of the relationship between export growth and output growth. The fact is that in the long run, no country can grow faster than that rate consistent with balance-of-payments equilibrium on current account unless it can finance ever-growing deficits which, in general, it cannot. Ratios of payments deficit to GDP of more than 2–3 per cent start to make the international financial markets nervous (witness the experience of Mexico, Brazil and the countries of East Asia in recent years), and *all* borrowing *eventually* has to be repaid. We will show in Chapter 17 that if relative price (or exchange rate) changes do not act as an efficient balance-of-payments adjustment mechanism, the rate of growth of output of a country (g) can be approximated by the formula:

$$g = x/\pi \tag{16.3}$$

where x is the growth of export volume (determined by the growth of 'world' income and the income elasticity of demand for exports) and π is the income elasticity of demand for imports. The correlation between g and x is immediately apparent.

Exports are unique as a growth-inducing force from the demand side because it is the only component of demand that provides foreign exchange to pay for the import requirements for growth. In this sense, it allows all other components of demand to grow faster in a way that consumption-led growth or investment-led growth does not. Indeed, it can be shown (see McCombie, 1985) that equation (16.3) is formally equivalent to the Hicks super-multiplier (Hicks, 1950) in which the growth of output is determined by the major component of autonomous demand to which other components of demand will adapt. In an open economy context, the major component of autonomous demand is export growth, and faster export growth allows all other components of demand to grow faster. It is then possible, as McCombie does, to disaggregate the contribution to growth of exports and other components of demand within this demand-oriented framework.

The virtuous circle model of export-led growth

Finally, it needs to be recognized that exports and growth may be interrelated in a cumulative process. This raises the question of causality but, more important, such models provide an explanation of why growth and development through trade tends to be concentrated in particular areas of the world, while other regions and countries have been left behind. These models provide a challenge to both orthodox growth theory and trade theory which predict the long-run convergence of living standards across the world. In neoclassical growth theory, capital is assumed to be subject to diminishing returns so that rich countries should grow slower than poor countries for the same amount of investment undertaken (see Chapter 4). Neoclassical trade theory predicts convergence through the assumption of factor price equalization. The empirical evidence is at odds with the theory: there is no evidence that living standards across the world are converging.

A simple cumulative model, driven by exports as the major component of autonomous demand, is outlined in Chapter 7, p. 246. Output growth is a function of export growth; export growth is a function of price competitiveness and foreign income growth; price competitiveness is a function of wage growth and productivity growth, and productivity growth is a function of output growth – the so-called Verdoorn Law working through static and dynamic returns to scale, including learning by doing. It is this induced productivity growth that makes the model 'circular and cumulative' since if fast output growth (caused by export growth) induces faster productivity growth, this makes goods more competitive and therefore induces faster export growth. The Verdoorn relation not only makes the model 'circular and cumulative', but also gives rise to the possibility that once an economy obtains a growth advantage it will tend to keep it. Suppose, for example, that an economy obtains an advantage in the production of goods with a high income elasticity of demand in world markets, such as high-technology goods, which raises its growth rate above other countries. Through the Verdoorn effect, productivity growth will be higher and the economy will retain its competitive advantage in these goods, making it difficult, without protection or exceptional industrial enterprise, to establish the same commodities. In such a cumulative model, it is the difference between the income elasticity characteristics of exports (and imports, if balance-of-payments equilibrium is a requirement, as argued earlier) which is the essence of divergence between industrial and agricultural economies, or between 'centre' and 'periphery'. This simple model can go a long way in explaining differences in the level of development between countries and the forces which perpetuate divergences in the world economy. The forces are *structural*, relating to the production and demand characteristics of the goods produced and traded.

TRADE, EMPLOYMENT AND POVERTY REDUCTION

According to orthodox theory, trade liberalization should not only lead to a faster rate of growth of output in developing countries, but also to a faster growth of wage employment, and hence a reduction in income inequality and poverty. If countries pursue the law of comparative advantage, then, according to the Heckscher-Ohlin and Stolper-Samuelson theorems (see Cline, 1997), they should specialize in goods which use their most abundant factor of production. In the case of developing countries, where labour is abundant, this means that the freeing of trade should lead to specialization in labour-intensive goods, increasing the demand for (unskilled) labour and therefore wages. By contrast, developed countries with abundant capital should specialize in capital-intensive goods which would reduce the demand for unskilled labour. As a consequence there

Globalization and Manufacturing Employment

Globalization creates winners and losers among workers and from this, two immediate questions arise: in terms of employment, are there more winners than losers? And who are the winners and losers likely to be?

Research carried out by the University of East Anglia and local researchers in Bangladesh, Kenya, South Africa and Vietnam looked at the impact of changes in trade flows and foreign investment on manufacturing employment in the four countries. All four economies became increasingly open during the 1990s. However, their experience in terms of manufacturing employment contrasts sharply. In Vietnam, more than 900,000 new jobs were created in manufacturing between 1990 and 2000, with a similar number being created in Bangladesh during the first half of the 1990s. In contrast, in South Africa manufacturing employment (in the formal sector, at least) actually fell during the 1990s while unemployment rose. Manufacturing employment rose gradually in Kenya but remained at relatively low levels.

Imports and exports

The research estimated the impact of increased exports and increased import penetration on employment. It confirmed that export growth made a significant contribution to increased employment in both Vietnam and Bangladesh during the 1990s. In South Africa, however, although export expansion did contribute to employment, this was not enough to offset the overall decline in employment. In Kenya, manufactured exports made no contribution to employment growth. All four countries experienced increased import penetration during the 1990s, which means that the overall impact of greater openness was less positive (or more negative) in terms of employment than might appear from looking only at exports. However, in the case of Vietnam and, to a more modest extent, Bangladesh, the net employment created by trade changes was still significant.

Skill and gender impacts

The research also looked at the skill and gender impacts of the globalization of manufacturing. Evidence from Kenya and South Africa suggested that there was a skill-bias associated with greater openness in that there was a tendency for the demand for more skilled labour to increase faster than that for unskilled labour. Yet in Vietnam and Bangladesh, the growth in demand was mainly concentrated on unskilled labour. In the two Asian countries, the bulk of export jobs was filled by women and exports employed far more women per US dollar of output than import-competing industries. In contrast in Africa, women workers were far less prominent in the industries that were the main exporters. The research highlights the impact that globalization can have on labour markets in the south. It found that:

- Integration with the global economy has led to a significant increase in the number of unskilled jobs, particularly for women, in Bangladesh and Vietnam.

■ Job creation as a result of greater openness has been minimal in Kenya and South Africa and is biased towards more skilled workers.

■ Where export growth is limited, increased competition from imports can significantly depress the employment impact.

■ Unless a significant number of unskilled jobs is created, globalization is unlikely to lead to poverty reduction.

These findings suggest that:

■ Greater openness does not necessarily – but can – lead to increased employment and is not a cure-all in terms of poverty reduction.

■ The specific context in terms of resource endowments, market access and geographical location plays a part in determining the likely impact of globalization on poverty.

■ Trade policy can also play a part in ensuring that the gains from increased employment in export industries are not offset totally by increased import penetration.

Source: R. Jenkins and K. Sen, 'Globalization and Manufacturing Employment', *Development Research Insights*, Institute of Development Studies, Sussex, June 2003.

should be a decrease in income inequality (between labour and capital and between unskilled and skilled labour) in developing countries, and an increase in income and wage inequality in developed countries.

In recent years, there has been a great deal of research on the effects of trade on employment, wages and poverty, often with conflicting results. In his pioneering book, *North–South Trade: Employment and Inequality* (1993), Adrian Wood addresses some of these issues. He finds that the volume of labour intensive manufactured exports from developing to developed countries has grown rapidly in the last 30 years, averaging 15 per cent per annum, but it started from a very low base and still accounts for less than 10 per cent of the developed countries' total consumption of manufactures. Nonetheless, the effects on employment have been strong. Wood estimates that over the period 1960–90, the expansion of manufactured exports from developing countries (the South) created 20 million extra jobs and narrowed the differential between skilled and unskilled wages. In the developed countries (the North), the cumulative reduction in the demand for unskilled labour has been 6–12 million person years, equivalent to a 4 percentage point reduction in the share of manufacturing employment in total employment. This result is controversial because it is ten times greater than previous estimates. The reason is that as well as estimating the *direct* effect of the factor content of trade, Wood also considers two important *indirect* effects: firstly, the effect of manufacturers in the North introducing labour-saving production methods in order to compete, and secondly, the effect of the South reducing its demand for labour intensive commodities from the North as its own production capacity expands.

Wood finds that wage inequality, particularly in the newly industrialized East Asian economies, which were some of the first to liberalize, has decreased, but studies of other countries find the opposite (see also Wood, 1997). Robbins (1994), and Robbins and Gindling (1999), examine changes in the structure of wages after trade liberalization in Chile and Costa Rica, respectively, and find that the returns to skilled labour increased after liberalization. Hanson and Harrison (1999) examine the changes in both wages and employment of skilled and unskilled workers after trade liberalization in Mexico and find little variation in employment levels, and a rise in wage inequality between skilled and unskilled labour. Overall, according to Arbache, Dickerson and Green (2004) 'the evidence on trade liberalizations which have been implemented in the last two decades suggests a positive relationship between trade liberalization and wage inequality. This finding is clearly contrary to the predictions of the traditional theory of international trade'. There are three major explanations for these contrary results: firstly, post-liberalization, product markets and hence labour markets become more competitive, thereby depressing unskilled wages; secondly, the demand for skilled labour rises as liberalized economies absorb more modern technology through imports and foreign direct investment, and thirdly, liberalization often brings short-term economic crisis which requires the whole economy to be deflated, creating unemployment and depressing unskilled wages relative to skilled wages.

Studies of the impact of trade liberalization on poverty are also mixed. The conclusions vary depending on whether the focus is on absolute poverty (i.e. the total number of people living below the poverty line); relative poverty (i.e. the income of the poorest people relative to the average level of income), or the income of particular groups in society. Some groups undoubtedly gain from the liberalization process, but others lose. To quantify the net effect is difficult without making interpersonal comparisons of utility.

There are four major channels through which trade liberalization can affect poverty:

- the impact of trade liberalization on growth and stability
- the effect of liberalization on prices received by producers and paid by consumers
- the effect of liberalization on wages and employment
- the impact of liberalization on government revenue and spending

Provided that it can be shown that trade liberalization improves the growth performance of a country, faster growth will translate into poverty reduction. Ravallion (2001) has estimated that the poverty ratio (i.e. the proportion of the population living on less than $1 a day) falls, on average, by 2.5 per cent for every one per cent increase in average income. This does not mean, however, that some groups do not suffer. As Winters, McCulloch and McKay (2004) say: 'it is quite clear that on occasions growth has been accompanied by worsening poverty and the challenge is to identify why'. One reason is that if growth comes through an increase in productivity, this may reduce inputs as well as increasing output, so employment and wages suffer – increasing poverty.

Another reason why trade liberalization might increase poverty is through its effect on prices. As protection is reduced, consumer prices may fall, but so may producer prices with the removal of protective barriers and increased competition. The net welfare effect will depend on the composition of production and consumption of different groups in society, and on how producers and households respond to the price changes. Sometimes markets may be destroyed altogether when protective barriers are removed, leading to an absolute welfare loss.

What happens to peoples' income also depends on what happens to wages and employment. As we saw earlier, contrary to orthodox theory, the wages of unskilled labour often fall post-liberalization, which increases poverty. On the other hand, if employment increases this will raise people out of poverty if they were previously unemployed.

Finally, there is the issue of what happens to government revenue and expenditure as tariffs and duties on imports and exports are reduced and removed. Does this hurt the poor? The evidence is mixed on whether trade liberalization reduces government revenue. It depends on whether rates of protection were already above their revenue-maximizing level, and the degree to which tariffs replace non-tariff barriers. The evidence is also mixed on whether liberalization reduces spending on anti-poverty programmes.

Winters *et. al.* (2004) conclude their major survey on trade liberalization and poverty by saying:

> There can be no simple relationship between trade liberalization and poverty. Theory provides strong presumption that trade liberalization will be poverty-alleviating in the long run and on average. The empirical evidence broadly supports this view and, in particular, lends no support to the position that trade liberalization generally has an adverse impact.
>
> Equally, however, it does not assert that . . . the static and microeconomic effects of liberalization will always be beneficial to the poor. Trade liberalization necessarily implies distributional changes; it may well reduce the well-being of some people (at least in the short term) and some of these may be poor.

With regard to *relative* poverty, the research of Dollar and Kraay (2004) suggests that trade and growth has benefited the poor as much as the average person, and that there is little evidence of any systematic tendency for income inequality to either increase or decrease with international trade. Taking a panel of 80 countries over a period of 40 years, they find, on average, a one-to-one relation between overall growth and the growth of income of the bottom 20 per cent of the income distribution. On the other hand, there is a lot of variation around the average. In some countries which have experienced a rapid increase in trade, inequality has increased (e.g. China), but in other countries, it has decreased (e.g. Malaysia and Thailand). In all cases, however, where trade has expanded rapidly, the fraction of the population living below the poverty line has decreased.

This still leaves the question of vulnerable groups and how to protect the poor as economies move to a more liberalized trade regime. As argued by UNCTAD's *Least Developed Countries Report 2004*, trade liberalization is not the same as, or not a substitute for, a pro-poor trade strategy. Poverty Reduction Strategy Papers (see p. 484) prepared by countries for international organizations, such as the World Bank, to qualify for debt relief, rarely consider the ways in which trade could help reduce poverty through, for example, acquiring comparative advantage in new products; seeking out new markets; supporting exports with a high demand for local imputs, and increasing competitiveness through technical and financial support.

To protect the poor as liberalization takes place, countries need to consider a number of policy issues:

■ **The sequencing of liberalization.** To ameliorate the costs of adjustment, it may be necessary to sequence liberalization at different speeds across sectors according to whether liberalization is likely to have a large effect on prices or whether adjustment is likely to be difficult or take a long time.

- **The provision of social safety nets.** For those adversely affected by trade liberalization, particularly the poor, governments need to put in place social safety nets in the form of, for example, unemployment and income insurance. These could be supported by World Bank programmes.
- **The development of markets.** To take advantage of new market opportunities, the poor and other disadvantaged groups require training and technical assistance, both in agriculture and in up-to-date business practices. Access to credit is particularly important for the start of new businesses.
- **Labour mobility and training.** Improving worker mobility and worker training can help those who lose jobs to find new ones.
- **Infrastructure development.** Improved and cheaper transport are important in the agricultural sector to allow poor farmers to take advantage of new market opportunities.

These are all complementary policies to ease and mitigate the costs of adjustment and to facilitate the creation of markets to benefit the poor.

THE DISADVANTAGES OF FREE TRADE FOR DEVELOPMENT

The fact that trade-liberalized economies appear to perform better than non-liberalized countries does not mean that developing countries should liberalize as rapidly as possible, and that there is no role for protection and government intervention to improve trade and growth performance. Indeed we have seen that this is exactly what many successful East Asian countries have done. It is also worth remembering that historically no country, apart from Britain, which was the first country to industrialize, developed on the basis of free trade. The countries of Europe, North America and Scandinavia all developed their industrial sectors with the aid of tariff and non-tariff protection (see Ha-Joon Chang, 2002). Trade liberalization is not a substitute for a trade strategy.

Now let us consider, therefore, the potential disadvantages of free trade, and the weaknesses of the comparative cost doctrine that underlies it. Like most micro-welfare theory, the comparative advantage/free-trade argument is a *static* one based on restrictive and very often unrealistic assumptions. The doctrine assumes, for example, the existence of full employment in each country (otherwise there would be no opportunity cost involved in expanding the production of commodities), that the prices of resources and goods reflect their opportunity cost (that is, that perfect competition exists), and that factor endowments are given and unalterable. Moreover the doctrine ignores the effect of free trade on the terms of trade (movements in which effect real income), and the dynamic feedback effects that trade itself might have on comparative advantage. As a result it can be argued that the principle of comparative advantage is not very useful in the context of developing countries, which are in need of rapid structural change and are as much concerned with long-term development as with short-term efficiency. As many economists have commented, the doctrine of comparative advantage is more useful in explaining the *past* pattern of trade than in providing a guide as to what the future pattern of trade should be as a stimulus to development.

The question is not whether there should be trade but whether there should be *free trade*, as the doctrine of comparative costs implies. Might the long-run needs of the developing countries not be better served, at least initially, by various forms of protection? Those who question the assumptions of the comparative cost model, and stress the relation between development and the balance of payments, express the view that the efficiency gains from free trade are unlikely to offset the tendency in a free market for the comparative position of developing countries to deteriorate *vis-à-vis* the developed countries. Free trade is claimed to work to the disadvantage of the developing countries, largely because of the nature of the products these countries seem destined to produce and trade under such a system. The answer is said to lie in a change in the structure of production and exports of the developing countries, which can only be fostered by the protection of new industries in the early stages of their development.

The development considerations that the doctrine of free trade overlooks are numerous. First, it ignores the balance-of-payments effects of free trade and the effect of free trade on the terms of trade. If the demands for different commodities grow at different rates owing to differences in their price and income elasticity of demand, free trade will work to the benefit of some countries and to the relative detriment of others. In short, free trade cannot be discussed independently of the balance of payments and the terms of trade. In classical theory, Torrens, J. S. Mill, Marshall, Edgeworth and Taussig all conceded that unilateral substitution by a country of free trade for protection would move the terms of trade against the country. But most 'free traders' ignored the subject. In general, the implicit assumption was that moving from protection to free trade would not alter the commodity terms of trade, or if it did, the gains from trade would more than offset any unfavourable terms-of-trade effect. If the terms-of-trade effect does offset the gains from trade, this would appear to provide a valid argument for protection. This is one of the lines that modern protectionists take (see later). The case for protection of the manufactured goods produced by developing countries is stronger: the less that the demand for existing primary products is expected to grow and the lower the price elasticity; the higher the elasticity of demand for imported manufactured products, and the less the likelihood of retaliation by other countries.

A second factor that the free-trade doctrine tends to overlook is that some activities are subject to increasing returns while others are subject to diminishing returns. The commodities most susceptible to diminishing returns are primary products, where the scope for technical progress may be less than in the case of manufactured goods. This being so, one might expect a rise in the ratio of primary to manufactured good prices, and diminishing returns would not matter so much if the goods were price inelastic. In practice, however, there has been a substitution of synthetic alternatives to primary products, and the terms of trade have deteriorated (see later), partly because of substitution and partly because of the fact that the demand for primary commodities in general, in relation to supply, has expanded much less than in the case of manufactured commodities. But whatever the movement in the terms of trade, it is surely perverse to recommend a trade and development policy based on activities subject to diminishing returns, particularly in the light of the theory of cumulative causation, which we discussed in Chapter 7.

A third disadvantage of adherence to the comparative advantage doctrine is that it could lead to excessive specialization in a narrow range of products, putting the economy at the mercy of outside influences. The possibility exists of severe balance-of-payments instability arising from specialization, which could be damaging to development.

Fourth, comparative cost analysis glosses over the fact that comparative advantage may change over time, or that it could be altered by deliberate policies to promote certain activities. There is no reason why countries should be condemned to the production and export of the same commodities for ever. No country was endowed with the *natural* ability to produce industrial goods. Now that technology and capital accumulation, rather than natural resources, are the basis for trade, comparative advantage is no longer predetermined or predictable. In a fascinating paper, Hausmann and Rodrik (2003) document how countries somehow stumble on lucrative niche markets almost by accident: hats in Bangladesh; cut flowers in Colombia; footballs and bed sheets in Pakistan, and software in India, to give just a few examples. If there is any explanation at all, it is entrepreneurial trial and error. If comparative advantage is not given by nature but can be altered, the case for initial protection is strengthened (the classic infant industry argument).

It should also be remembered that the concept of comparative advantage is based on calculations of private cost. But we have seen in Chapter 10 that social costs in developing countries may diverge markedly from private costs, and that social benefits may exceed private benefits because of externalities. If private costs exceed social costs in industry (because wage rates are artificially high, for example), and social benefits from industrial projects exceed private benefits, there is a strong argument for protecting industry in order to encourage the transfer of labour from other activities into industry to equate private and social cost and private and social benefit.

Finally, it may be mentioned that the export growth of some activities has relatively little secondary impact on other activities. Primary commodities fall into this category. The evidence is abundant that the export growth of primary commodities has not had the development impact that might have been expected from the expansion of industrial exports. The reasons for this are not hard to understand. Primary production has very few backward or forward linkages; and historically it has tended to be undertaken by foreign enterprises, with a consequent outflow of profits. The secondary repercussions of the pattern of trade also tend to be overlooked by the free-trade doctrine.

TARIFFS VERSUS SUBSIDIES AS A MEANS OF PROTECTION

We have seen that trade brings substantial benefits, but it does not follow that the freer trade the better. There are many disadvantages that the doctrine of free trade overlooks when trade is considered in a long-run development context, as opposed to the static short-run context of the doctrine of comparative advantage. Furthermore, free trade does not guarantee an equal distribution of the gains from trade, and this is an important consideration for countries that naturally look to their relative position compared with others, and not only at their absolute performance.

We can summarize the **arguments for protection** as follows (see Johnson, 1964). First there are purely **economic arguments** that comprise all arguments in favour of protection as a means of increasing real output or income above what it would otherwise be. These include the following:

■ The infant industry argument – allowing industries to reach their optimum size in terms of minimum average cost of production

- The existence of external economies in production, where the social cost of production is less than the private cost
- Distortions in the labour market that make the social cost of using labour less than the private cost
- International distortions that cause the domestic rate of transformation between goods to diverge from the foreign rate of transformation due, for example, to monopoly power in international trade; this argument for protection is often referred to as the **optimum tariff argument**.

Into this category of economic arguments might also be put two factors previously stressed: terms-of-trade deterioration, and balance-of-payments difficulties arising from the pattern of trade. Johnson (1964) and others of neoclassical persuasion have argued that these are non-arguments. In the case of the terms of trade, the restriction of imports will not reduce import prices for a small country. In the case of the balance of payments, equilibrium can be achieved automatically by allowing the exchange rate to fluctuate freely.

The terms of trade argument may be correct, but the balance-of-payments argument suffers from confusion between a balance-of-payments equilibrium on the current account, which affects the real economy, and balance in the foreign exchange market. The two are not the same. A floating exchange rate will equilibrate the foreign exchange market by definition, but will not necessarily equilibrate the balance of payments on the current account. If both terms-of-trade deterioration and balance-of-payments difficulties constrain growth and lead to unemployment, the social cost of labour will be less than the private cost, which is a domestic distortion and an economic argument for protection.

Second, **non-economic arguments** for protection comprise arguments for protection for its own sake rather than to increase output or income above what it would otherwise be. Industrialization at any price and self-sufficiency for strategic reasons are examples of arguments of this type.

Having summarized the arguments in favour of protection, the question then is, what is the best means of protection? It can be shown that tariffs are appropriate only under special circumstances: when the distortions are international (the optimum tariff argument) and when self-sufficiency is the objective. All other arguments for protection are arguments for subsidies, the reason being that when distortions are domestic a tariff will introduce further distortions, and according to the **theory of the second best** there is no knowing *a priori* whether the situation will be made better or worse.

Let us illustrate the argument with a diagram. Consider Figure 16.5, where a good that is producible domestically is subject to a domestic distortion such that the private cost of production ($S'S'$) is d per cent above the social cost (SS). The demand curve is DD and the good is also importable at the international price, P_T. Under free trade, domestic producers will produce up to Q_1, and Q_1 to Q_4 will be imported. Q_1 to Q_2 imports could be replaced, however, by additional domestic production, with real savings equal to the shaded area A, if domestic producers were given a subsidy of d per cent. The same real income gain could be achieved by a tariff of the same percentage, but because the domestic price rises to $P_T(1 + d)$, there will be a loss of consumer surplus equal to the shaded area B owing to the restriction of consumption by Q_3Q_4. The loss of consumer surplus may be greater than the real income gain, reducing total welfare. The balance

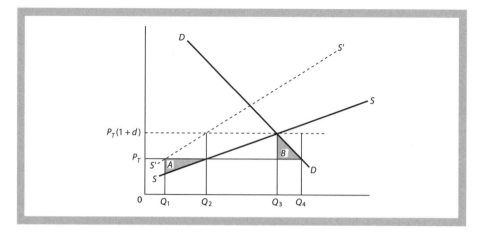

Figure 16.5 Welfare gains and losses from protection

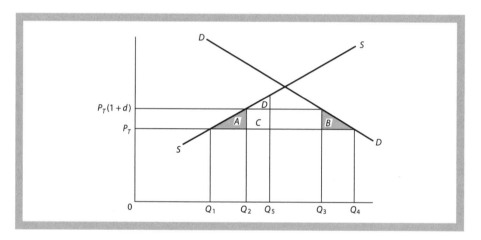

Figure 16.6 Tariffs and subsidies

of advantage depends on the relative slopes of the supply and demand curves. In these circumstances a subsidy to labour is unequivocally first best.

Now let us consider the relative merits of tariffs and subsidies where the arguments in favour of protection are non-economic. Suppose, for example, the objective of protection is simply to increase domestic output. Here subsidies are also superior to tariffs because tariffs impose a consumption cost and add nothing more to the achievement of increased production. Consider Figure 16.6. We assume that there is no domestic distortion, so the SS curve represents both the private and the social cost of production. Now suppose that the object is to raise domestic production from Q_1 to Q_2. This can be done with a tariff or subsidy of d per cent that uses extra resources equal to the shaded area A. The tariff, however, imposes an extra consumption cost equal to area B as a result of a rise in the price from P_T to $P_T(1 + d)$.

On the other hand, if the objective is self-sufficiency and to cut back imports we can show that tariffs are the least costly; the reason being that it is more efficient to reduce imports by jointly restricting consumption and increasing domestic production, than by doing either of these on their own. Consider Figure 16.6 again. A tariff of d per cent reduces imports to Q_2Q_3 at a cost of $A + B$. To get the same reduction with a subsidy requires a subsidy in excess of d per cent in order to induce extra domestic production Q_2Q_5 (equal to the cut-back in consumption through the tariff of Q_3Q_4). This involves an extra cost equal to the area $C + D$. Since $C > B$, the cost of the subsidy policy is obviously greater than the cost of the tariff.

If subsidies are first-best they may be effectively granted by exemption from taxation. If this exemption is from existing taxes, it will have revenue implications for the government budget. In the long run, however, subsidies can be 'self-financing' by the increased output they stimulate.

A further argument against tariffs and in favour of subsidies is that tariffs are very 'inward-looking', whereas protection through subsidies is much more 'outward-looking'. Tariffs adjust the internal price structure to the (high) internal cost structure. This may lead to inefficiencies and make it difficult for exports to compete when the effects of import-substitution policies cease. Subsidies, in contrast, adjust the internal cost structure to the (low) external price structure and make it possible for exports to compete more easily in world markets. This leads us to the debate over 'inward-looking' import-substitution development strategy versus 'outward-looking' export promotion strategy.

IMPORT SUBSTITUTION VERSUS EXPORT PROMOTION

In the early stages of production, the protectionist strategy of import-substitution using tariffs is undoubtedly the easiest and many countries have pursued it, particularly in Latin America. However there are different stages of import substitution, and some are easier than others. The first easy stage involves the replacement by domestic production of imports of non-durable consumption goods such as clothing, footwear, leather and wood products. Countries in the early stages of industrialization are naturally suited to these products and relatively little protection is required. Once this stage is over, the maintenance of high growth rates then requires the import substitution of other goods if the strategy is to be continued.

The problem with this second stage of import substitution is that relatively high rates of protection are required, because intermediate goods such as steel and producer durables are subject to substantial economies of scale, both internal and external, so that unit costs are very high if output is low. The problem with high rates of protection is that they breed inefficiency, and more importantly act as a tax on exports by keeping costs and the exchange rate high. The catalogue of costs and distortions introduced by protective import-substitution policies is formidable. Import substitution tends to shift the distribution of income in favour of the urban sector and the higher income groups with a higher propensity to import, thereby worsening the balance of payments. Protection taxes agriculture since it raises the price of industrial goods relative to agricultural goods. Furthermore, since protection maintains an artificially high exchange rate it reduces receipts in terms of domestic currency from a given quantity of agricultural exports, which may discourage agricultural production. Import substitution may also worsen unemployment by encouraging capital-intensive activities.

Despite the dangers of the second stage of import substitution, this is the strategy that many Latin American, South-East Asian and Eastern European countries adopted in the immediate postwar years. The consequence was that the export of manufactures was discouraged and the terms of trade turned against agriculture within the countries, discouraging agricultural output and reducing the growth of demand for industrial products internally. In the 1960s reforms were undertaken in several countries, but there was a distinct difference in emphasis and approach between Latin America and South-East Asia. In Latin America, policies became more 'outward-looking' but still favoured production for the domestic market. Although subsidies were given to exports, exporters were still required to use domestic inputs produced under protection, and the subsidies were generally insufficient to provide an incentive to export that was comparable to the protection of domestic markets, and thus there was a continued bias in favour of import substitution. In East and South-East Asia in contrast, the policy has always been one of relentless export expansion – in Japan, South Korea, Singapore, Taiwan and other countries, as outlined earlier. Now most developing countries are attempting to follow this route with varying degrees of success.

As documented earlier in the chapter, the empirical evidence seems to support the view that countries that adopt trade liberalization and 'outward-looking' policies perform better than those that do not.

ALTERNATIVE APPROACHES TO TRADE IN DEVELOPING COUNTRIES: THE PREBISCH DOCTRINE[3]

Raúl Prebisch was one of the first development economists to question the mutual profitability of the international division of labour for developing countries on existing lines. Prebisch was one of those who looks at the relation between trade and development from the standpoint of the balance of payments rather than the augmentation of real resources. His major claim was that the unfavourable impact of unrestricted trade on the terms of trade and balance of payments of developing countries far outweighs any advantages with respect to a more efficient allocation of resources. His concern was with two distinct, but not unrelated, phenomena. One is the transference of the benefits of technical progress from the developing to the developed countries. The second is the balance-of-payments effects of differences in the income elasticity of demand for different types of products. He divided the world into industrial 'centres' and 'peripheral' countries, and then conducted his analysis within the framework of the traditional two-country, two-commodity case of international trade theory – equating the developing countries with primary producers (the 'periphery') and the developed countries with industrial producers (the 'centre').

TECHNICAL PROGRESS AND THE TERMS OF TRADE

As stated earlier, in theory the barter terms of trade might be expected to move in favour of the developing countries. For one thing, primary-product production tends to be subject to diminishing returns, and for another, technical progress tends to be more rapid in manufacturing industry than in agriculture. If prices are related to costs one

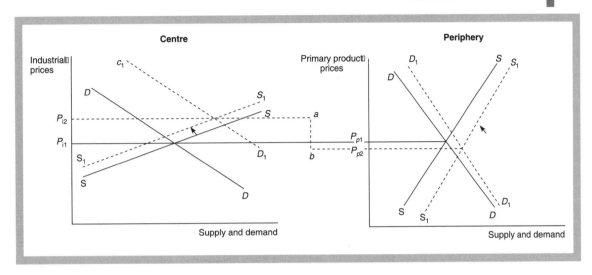

Figure 16.7 Movements in the terms of trade

would expect that in theory the ratio of primary-product prices to industrial-good prices would rise. According to Prebisch, however, the ratio had shown a long-run historical tendency to fall. He advanced two explanations of this and hence why the benefits of technical progress tend to flow from the developing to developed countries and not the other way round. His first explanation concerns the relation between incomes and productivity. He suggested that whereas factor incomes tend to rise with productivity increases in developed countries, they rise more slowly than productivity in the developing countries owing to population pressure and surplus labour. Thus there is a greater upward pressure on final goods' prices in developed than in developing countries, causing the ratio of prices to move in the opposite direction to that suggested by the pace of technical progress. All this is on the supply side.

On the demand side is the fact that the demand for primary products grows more slowly than that for industrial products as world income grows, for two major reasons: (1) many primary commodities have intrinsically low income elasticities of demand because they are necessities; and (2) many primary commodities have been substituted by synthetics, for example natural rubber. Putting these demand and supply factors together gives the picture in Figure 16.7, which shows what is likely to happen to the terms of trade of primary commodities through time.

In the centre, the supply and demand curves for industrial goods are relatively elastic, and in the periphery, the supply and demand curves for primary products are relatively inelastic. Assume that the supply and demand curves intersect at the same point in both sectors, so that the prices of industrial and primary products are 'equal' (that is, the terms of trade = 1). In the centre, technical progress will shift the supply curve (SS) outwards, but let us assume that increases in wage costs push it back inwards to S_1S_1. In the periphery, in contrast, technical progress shifts the supply curve outwards to S_1S_1, but there is no inward shift due to rising wage costs. In the centre, the demand for industrial goods grows strongly from DD to D_1D_1, while in the periphery the demand for primary products grows only slowly. The price of industrial goods rises to P_{i2}, while the price of primary products in this example has actually fallen to P_{p2}. The terms of

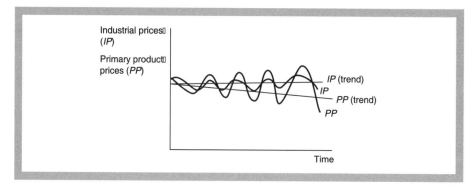

Figure 16.8 Asymmetrical cycles

trade of primary products has deteriorated by the amount *ab* for fundamental economic reasons associated with the characteristics of the products and the institutional structures of the countries that produce them.

Prebisch also put forward a separate independent hypothesis of the secular deterioration in the terms of trade of primary products: the operation of a ratchet effect, with the prices of primary products *relative* to those of manufactured goods falling during cyclical downturns by more than they rise *relative* to the prices of manufactures on the upturns. Such asymmetrical cycles, illustrated in Figure 16.8, would produce a secular trend deterioration.

As it happens, the asymmetry hypothesis does not seem to be supported in the years since the Second World War (see Thirlwall and Bergevin, 1985), or for the longer period since 1900 (see Diakosavvas and Scandizzo, 1991), except for a few commodities such as rice, cotton, rubber and coffee, and even then the difference between the elasticity of prices on the downswing and on the upswing is quite small.

THE INCOME ELASTICITY OF DEMAND FOR PRODUCTS AND THE BALANCE OF PAYMENTS

According to Prebisch, the second factor working to the disadvantage of developing countries is the balance-of-payments effects of differences in the income elasticity of demand for different types of product. As mentioned, it is generally recognized and agreed that the income elasticity of demand for most primary commodities is lower than that for manufactured products. On average, the elasticity is probably less than unity, resulting in a decreasing proportion of income spent on those commodities (commonly known as **Engel's Law**). In the two-country, two-commodity case the lower income elasticity of demand for primary commodities means that for a given growth of world income the balance of payments of primary-producing, developing countries will *automatically* deteriorate *vis-à-vis* the balance of payments of developed countries producing and exporting industrial goods. A simple example will illustrate the point (see also Chapter 7, p. 244).

Suppose that the income elasticity of demand for the exports of the developing countries is 0.8 and that the growth of world income is 3.0 per cent: exports will then grow at 2.4 per cent. Now suppose that the income elasticity of demand for the exports of developed countries is 1.3 and the growth of world income is 3.0 per cent; exports of developed countries will then grow at 3.9 per cent. Since there are only two sets of countries, the developing countries' exports are the imports of developed countries and the exports of developed countries are the imports of the developing countries. Thus developing countries' exports grow at 2.4 per cent but imports grow at 3.9 per cent; developed countries' exports grow at 3.9 per cent and imports at 2.4 per cent. Starting from equilibrium, the balance of payments of the developing countries automatically worsens while that of the developed countries shows a surplus. This has further repercussions on the terms of trade. With imports growing faster than exports in developing countries, and the balance of payments deteriorating, the terms of trade will also deteriorate through depreciation of the currency, which may cause the balance of payments to deteriorate even more if imports and exports are price inelastic.

Moreover, this is not the end of the story if we take the per capita income growth between developed and developing countries. If population growth is faster in developing countries, the growth of income must also be faster than in the developed countries if the per capita income growth rates are to remain the same. This will mean an even faster growth rate of imports into developing countries and a more serious deterioration in the balance of payments. And if the goal is to *narrow* the relative or absolute differences in per capita income between developed and developing countries, the balance-of-payments implications will be even more severe. In the example previously given, which ignores differences in population growth, it is easily seen that the price of balance-of-payments equilibrium is slower growth for the developing countries. If their exports are growing at 2.4 per cent, import growth must be constrained to 2.4 per cent, which means that with an income elasticity of demand for imports of 1.3, income growth in the developing countries must be restrained to 2.4/1.3 = 1.85 per cent for balance-of-payments equilibrium. In the absence of foreign borrowing to bridge the foreign exchange gap, or a change in the structure of exports, the result of different income elasticities of demand for primary and manufactured products is slower growth in the primary-producing countries – perpetuating the development 'gap'. In the absence of protection, the only other alternative is deliberate depreciation of the currency. This has several disadvantages. For one thing the price elasticities of exports and imports may not be right for foreign exchange earnings to be increased, and second, depreciation will encourage production in *existing* activities, the concentration on which contributed to the balance-of-payments difficulties in the first place. What is required is structural change.

For terms of trade and balance of payments reasons (which are connected), Prebisch therefore argued for import substitution and the protection of certain domestically produced goods. Prebisch's balance-of-payments argument reinforces the classical infant-industry and optimum-tariff (terms of trade improvement) argument for protection.

There are several benefits that Prebisch expected from protection:

- Protection would enable scarce foreign exchange to be rationed between different categories of imports, and could help to correct balance-of-payments disequilibrium resulting from a high income elasticity of demand for certain types of imports.
- It could help to arrest the deterioration in the terms of trade by damping down the demand for imports.

■   It could provide the opportunity to diversify products and to start producing and exporting goods with a much higher income elasticity of demand in world markets.

Following our earlier analysis, however, protection by tariffs is only appropriate if the arguments for protection do not arise from domestic distortions.

RECENT TRENDS IN THE TERMS OF TRADE

Primary commodities

Whether the terms of trade have moved unfavourably against primary commodities and the developing countries is an empirical question. Prebisch originally suggested an average deterioration of the terms of trade of primary commodities between 1876 and 1938 of 0.9 per cent per annum. Work by Hans Singer at the United Nations in 1949 also suggested a trend deterioration of 0.64 per cent per annum over the same period, and thus the **Prebisch–Singer thesis** of the declining terms of trade for primary commodities was born (see Singer, 1950). In a detailed reappraisal of Prebisch's work, Spraos (1980) confirms the historical trend deterioration, but at the lower rate of approximately 0.5 per cent, having corrected the statistics for the changing quality of goods, shipping costs and other factors. Extending the data to 1970, however, Spraos concluded that there had been no significant trend deterioration. Sapsford (1985, 1988), however, shows that it is the 'wartime' structural improvement (1940–51) that makes the whole series look trendless. If the series is divided into two subperiods – pre- and post-Second World War – there is a trend deterioration in both subperiods and the estimated trend deterioration over the whole period 1900–82 is 1.2 per cent per annum, allowing for the wartime structural break.

Since the original Spraos and Sapsford evaluations of the Prebisch–Singer thesis, there has been an outpouring of further studies using different time periods and different statistical estimating techniques. Grilli and Yang (1988) at the World Bank constructed their own series of the terms of trade and also looked at individual commodities, but reached similar conclusions to Sapsford. Over the period 1900–83 they put the percentage terms of trade deterioration of all primary commodities at 0.5 per cent per annum, and 0.6 per cent per annum for non-fuel commodities (allowing for a wartime structural break). For individual commodities the trend deterioration is estimated as follows: food, −0.3 per cent per annum; cereals, −0.6 per cent per annum; non-food agricultural commodities, −0.8 per cent per annum; and metals, −0.8 per cent per annum. Only tropical beverages registered an improvement of 0.6 per cent per annum. Bleaney and Greenaway (1993) updated the Grilli–Yang series to 1991 and estimated a trend deterioration of 0.8 per cent per annum, with a big structural break in the early 1980s associated with world recession and the supply response of developing countries attempting to export themselves out of debt difficulties.

The most recent study is by Cashin and McDermott (2002) at the IMF who look at trends and cycles in both the nominal and real price (i.e. the terms of trade) of commodities over the period 1862 to 1999. The graphs of both indices are shown in Figure 16.9.

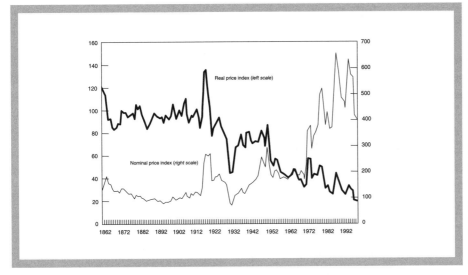

Source: P. Cashin and C.J. McDermott 'The Long-Run Behaviour of Commodity Prices: Small Trends and Big Variability', IMF Staff Papers, 49 (2), 2002.

Figure 16.9 Nominal and real price indexes of primary commodities, 1862–1999

Nominal prices were relatively stable from 1862 to 1932 (except during the First World War), but since then have been very volatile around a rising trend. The real price index, however, or the terms of trade of primary commodities, has always been very volatile around a generally declining trend. The average trend decline over the whole period 1862–1999 is 1.3 per cent per annum. From an index of 120 in 1862 to an index of 20 in 1999, real commodity prices have lost 85 per cent of their value. Or to put it another way, primary commodities can only buy 20 per cent of the industrial goods that they could buy in 1862. This represents a substantial real income loss. The estimated trend decline is even more serious if the commodity boom years of 1951 or 1973 are taken as the starting point for analysis.

Cashin and McDermott also focus on the magnitude and length of the cycles in real commodity prices, which they believe to be more serious than the trend decline. They find 13 occasions since 1913 when the annual price change was more than 20 per cent in one year. This is serious volatility. They also find that average price slumps last longer than price booms (4.2 years compared to 3.6 years).

The authors conclude their study by saying:

> Although there is a downward trend in real commodity prices, this is of little policy relevance, because it is small compared with the variability of prices. In contrast, rapid, unexpected and often large movements in commodity prices are an important feature of their behaviour. Such movements can have serious consequences for the terms of trade, real incomes, and fiscal positions of commodity-dependent countries, and have profound implications for the achievement of macroeconomic stabilisation.

It is unfortunate to describe the downward trend in real commodity prices as 'of little policy relevance'. Both trend and cycle affect poor commodity-dependent countries adversely, and both have implications for commodity stabilization policies to be considered later.

Developing countries

As already indicated, the terms of trade of primary commodities relative to manufactures is not necessarily the same as the terms of trade of developing countries relative to industrial countries, because both sets of countries export and import both types of goods (albeit in different ratios), but in practice there is likely to be a close overlap and parallel movement between the two. Sarkar (1986) has looked at the export prices of developing countries relative to those of developed countries, and also at the prices of exports from developing to developed countries relative to the prices of imports from developed countries into developing countries (both excluding fuel). In the first case the trend deterioration was 0.51 per cent per annum; in the second case the relative deterioration was 0.93 per cent per annum.

Bleaney and Greenaway (1993) find that over the period 1955–89 a 1 per cent deterioration in the terms of trade of primary products translated into a 0.3 per cent deterioration in the terms of trade for developing countries as a whole, although this would have been substantially greater for Africa and Latin America, which are more commodity-dependent than Asia. It has been estimated by UNCTAD that terms-of-trade losses for developing countries as a whole were equivalent in the 1980s to a loss of nearly $300 billion of foreign exchange, equal to more than twice the net inflow of resources into developing countries in 1980.

Sarkar and Singer (1991, 1993) have also looked at the terms of trade of *manufactures* exported by developing countries relative to those of developed countries over the period 1970–87, and find a deterioration of approximately 1 per cent per annum. If this is the case,[4] it would appear that the developing countries suffer double jeopardy. Not only do the prices of their primary products decline relative to those of manufactured goods, but also the prices of their manufactured exports decline relative to those of developed countries, reflecting, no doubt, the commodity composition of their exports – their lower value-added and lower income elasticity of demand in world markets.

Finally, in this section, it must be mentioned that there is a distinction between the **barter (or commodity) terms of trade,** which measures the ratio of export to import prices, and the **income terms of trade,** which is the ratio of export to import prices times the quantity of exports, that is, $(Px/Pm) \times Qx$. The income terms of trade is thus a measure of the total purchasing power of exports over imports.

From the point of view of development, measured by per capita income, the income terms of trade is perhaps the more relevant concept to consider than the barter terms of trade. It may well be, for instance, that the prices of exports fall relative to those of imports owing to increased efficiency in the exporting country, and this releases resources for further exports, which subsequently expand more than proportionately to the fall in price. The barter terms of trade will have worsened, but the country will be better off. It is also worth remembering that when a country devalues its currency it deliberately worsens its barter terms of trade in the hope that the balance of payments will improve, providing scope for a faster growth of real income through a rapid improvement in the income terms of trade. On the other hand, if the demand for a country's exports is price inelastic, then a decline in the barter terms of trade will also mean a deterioration in the income terms of trade.

In the long run, if world trade is buoyant, all countries can experience an improvement in their income terms of trade. The question is not who are the gainers and who are the losers, as in the case of the barter terms of trade, but what are the *relative* rates of improvement in the income terms of trade?

FAIR TRADE NOT FREE TRADE: TRADE POLICIES TOWARDS DEVELOPING COUNTRIES

Developing countries, supported by multilateral institutions such as the IMF, World Bank and the World Trade Organization (WTO), preach the virtues of trade liberalization and free trade for developing countries, but fail to practise it themselves. In particular, the rich countries heavily protect their agricultural sectors with subsidies and tariffs which make it difficult, and sometimes impossible, for poor developing countries to compete in world markets. The case of cotton is highlighted in Case example 16.2. Agricultural subsidies in the European Union (EU) and US amount to over $400 billion per annum, which is close to the total GDP of Africa. Each cow in the EU earns a subsidy of $800 per annum which is more than the average income per head of at least two billion people living in developing countries. Developed countries also impose tariffs on agricultural imports from developing countries, and subsidise exports. Dumping of artificially cheap crops from rich country agribusiness has destroyed thousands of small farmers in developing countries.

The protection afforded to agriculture is also given to many low value-added manufactured goods in which developing countries have a static comparative advantage – particularly a wide range of textile goods. Trade barriers against the exports of developing countries cost these countries approximately $100 billion a year, which is twice the amount they receive in official development assistance.

Case example 16.2

Unfair Trade in Cotton

The United States spends $3.3 billion a year on subsidies to 25,000 cotton farmers which profoundly affects the livelihoods of 10 million cotton farmers in the west and central African countries of Burkina Faso, Benin, Chad and Mali. This subsidy to US cotton producers is three times the US aid budget to the whole of Africa. The tragedy is that the World Bank has encouraged these African countries to produce more cotton on the pretext of comparative advantage, but they find it impossible to compete against such subsidies. The US Trade Representative at the Doha Round of WTO trade negotiations in 2002 had the audacity to tell the cotton farmers of Africa that 'they should do something else'.

When it comes to the reality of free trade, as opposed to the rhetoric, there appears to be one law for the rich developed nations and another for the poor. As long as the terms of trade of primary products continue to decline, and the agricultural products of developing countries are discriminated against in world markets, trade between the developed and developing countries cannot be fair. The playing field between rich and poor countries is not level, and the rich countries seem to want to keep it that way. What developing countries want is fair trade not free trade.[5]

The World Trade Organization established in 1995 (formerly the General Agreement on Tariffs and Trade – the GATT – founded in 1947) is the major international body that negotiates multilateral tariff reductions between countries. Up to now, however, it has been singularly unsuccessful in freeing trade in agricultural commodities. The **Kennedy Round** of trade negotiations (1964–7); the **Tokyo Round** (1973–9) and the **Uruguay Round** (1986–93) all focused mainly on reducing tariffs on trade in manufactures (with some preferential treatment for developing countries). It was in Seattle in 1999 that the developing countries began to raise their voice concerning agricultural protection, but the talks ended in failure. The rich countries refused to make any concessions over agriculture, and the trade round collapsed amid recriminations and violent street protests. In November 2001, the **Doha Round** was launched. This was supposed to be a 'development' round (to help poor countries), but so far only limited agreement has been reached because of the insistence by rich countries that they will only cut farm subsidies and trade barriers if the developing countries allow them access to their financial services sector, and enforce stricter competition rules and transparency in government procurement. The United States' reaction to the slow progress of the Doha Round has been to start bilateral trade deals with countries that it favours politically. The Doha Round negotiations are expected to last until at least 2007.

The main multilateral pressure group for a fairer trading deal between developed and developing countries is the **United Nations Conference on Trade and Development (UNCTAD)**, which was first convened in Geneva in 1964 with Raúl Prebisch as Secretary-General. The organization exists as a continuous pressure group with the aim of assisting developing countries through fairer trade, and also aid. Among its stated objectives are:

- Greater access to the markets of developed countries through the reduction in trade barriers
- More stable commodity prices
- Raising the level of aid from developed countries to the UN target of 0.7 per cent of donors' GNP
- Compensation to developing countries for fluctuations in export earnings and terms of trade deterioration.

In the past, it has had some limited success in persuading developed countries to grant preferential access to the exports of developing countries, but mainly in the field of manufactured goods, benefiting the larger and more advanced developing countries.

Perhaps the most significant trade agreement negotiated to date to help poorer developing nations is the **Lomé Convention** which was signed in 1975 by the European Economic Community (EEC, now the European Union, EU) and 46 (now 77) developing countries in Africa, the Caribbean and the Pacific (the so-called ACP countries). The Lomé Convention provides for free access to the European market for all the developing countries' manufactured goods and 90 per cent of their agricultural exports. In addition, agreement was reached to stabilize the foreign exchange earnings of twelve key commodities (the so-called **Stabex scheme**). The Lomé Convention also dispenses aid to the ACP countries through the **European Development Fund (EDF)**. Since 1975, the Convention has been renegotiated five times. The latest agreement reached in Cotonou (Benin) in 2000 is designed to last for 20 years, with revisions possible every five years. The major change in 2000 was that the Stabex scheme was discontinued. Instead, support for fluctuations in export earnings will come from the EDF as part of a **Country Support Strategy** drawn up for each ACP state.

In the voluntary sector, the **Fair Trade Movement** is gathering widespead support, and is making a difference to the lives of poor farmers in many developing countries. The movement was founded in 1979 with the main objective of guaranteeing a price to producers above the world price with a sufficient premium above the cost of production to allow producer cooperatives to invest in community projects such as housing, health care, education and public utilities. Importers of fair trade products such as coffee, tea, chocolate, sugar, bananas, fruit juices, and so on, must buy directly from Fair Trade-certified producers, and agree to establish long-term and stable relationships with them. This cuts out the middleman, or monopsonist – often a large multinational corporation in the case of many primary commodities. Some measure of inequality in the coffee market at present is that whereas the retail value of the sale of coffee worldwide is $70 billion a year, coffee producers receive only $5 billion of this. Many supermarkets and other retail outlets now stock a range of Fair Trade products. The value of retail sales is still a drop in the ocean, but is forecast to rise to £600 million in the UK by the year 2010. Unfortunately, however, the Fair Trade movement cannot alter the fundamental economic forces which drive down the price of commodities relative to the prices of manufactured goods and services. The only long-run solution to this dilemma is structural change which requires the protection of new industries; and this is what the rich, developed countries do not like. They want access to poor countries' markets, while continuing to protect their own. The Fair Trade movement can make a major contribution, however, to raising public awareness of the inequities in the global trading system, which, in turn, can exert pressure on the governments of rich developed countries for fundamental reform of the terms on which developed and developing countries trade with each other.

EFFECTIVE PROTECTION

When arguing for lower tariffs and tariff preferences, a distinction needs to be made between *nominal protection* and *effective rates of protection*. It is now widely recognized, in theory and in practice, that nominal tariffs on commodities are not the appropriate basis for assessing the restrictive effect of a tariff structure on trade.[6]

The nominal rate does not measure how inefficient (or costly) producers can be without incurring competition and losing their market. This is measured by the protection of **value-added,** which is the difference between the value of output and the value of inputs. The protection of value-added is the so-called **effective rate of protection.** Since value-added is the difference between the value of output and inputs, not only is the tariff on output important when measuring the degree of protection, but also the tariff on inputs.

Formally, the effective rate of protection is measured as the excess of domestic value-added over value-added at world prices, expressed as a percentage of the latter. Thus the effective rate of protection of industry X may be defined as:

$$EP_x = \frac{V'_x - V_x}{V_x} = \frac{V'_x}{V_x} - 1$$

where V'_x is domestic value added under protection and V_x is value added under free-market conditions (at world prices). Domestic value added is equal to the sale of the industry's product minus the sum of intermediate inputs, all valued at domestic market prices, that is, including the effect of tariffs on the finished good and on the inputs into the finished good. The free-market value added can be defined identically, but with the final product and input prices measured exclusive of tariffs on them. It is clear that the height of the effective tariff rate depends on three variables:

- The level of nominal tariffs on output
- The proportion of value-added to total output
- The level of nominal tariffs on the industry's inputs.

The higher the nominal tariff, the lower the tariff on imported inputs and the higher the proportion of value added to total output, the higher the effective rate of protection. If the tariff on finished goods is very high and the tariff on inputs is low, domestic value-added can be very high; in turn, world value-added may be very low, giving enormous rates of effective protection, sometimes in excess of 1000 per cent.

Let us now give a practical example. Suppose Indian textiles have a world price of $5, of which $3 represents raw-material costs and $2 represents value-added. Now let us suppose that imports of Indian textiles into a developed country are subject to a tariff of 20 per cent while domestic producers must pay a tariff of 10 per cent on textile raw materials. To remain competitive, the domestic producer must produce the commodity for not more than $6. The value added can be $6 minus the cost of raw materials plus the tariff on raw materials, that is, $6 − ($3 + $0.30) = $2.70. The effective rate of protection is the difference between domestic value-added and Indian value-added (that is, value-added at world prices), expressed as a percentage of Indian value-added, that is, (2.70 − 2)/2 = 35 per cent. This is the effective rate of protection, equal to the difference between the gross subsidy on value-added provided by the tariff on the final product ($(1/2) = 50 per cent) and the implicit tax on value-added as a result of the tariff on raw materials ($(0.30/2) = 15 per cent). This is the extent (35 per cent) to which production can be more costly in the developed country without losing competitive advantage; or to put it another way, it is the degree to which Indian textile producers would have to be more productive to compete in the developed country market.

Effective rates of protection almost always exceed nominal rates. At one extreme, if a country obtains raw material inputs that are duty free (at world prices) but puts a tariff on the final good, the effective rate must be higher than the nominal rate. At the other extreme, if a country puts a tariff on inputs but no tariff on the finished good, the effective rate of protection is negative.[7]

Calculation of the effective rate of protection also depends on the exchange rate. If the exchange rate of a country in the protected situation is overvalued, the price of imported inputs measured in domestic currency will be undervalued, and this will affect the calculation of the domestic value-added and the value-added at world market prices. Without adjustment for this factor, effective rates of protection are described as 'gross'; with adjustment they are referred to as 'net'.

Our example of the effective rate of protection also assumes that all inputs are traded. Some inputs will be non-traded, however, and their price enters into the value of both total output and total inputs. If the effect of protection on the price of non-traded goods is ignored, the rates of effective protection will be overestimated. In practice it is not easy to estimate the effect of protection on the price of non-traded goods.

The theory of effective protection suggests that the same *nominal* tariff cuts mean different degrees of change in effective rates of protection, and it may thus be unwise for the developing countries to press for across-the-board tariff cuts on all commodities. *Reductions in tariffs against their primary products will increase the effective rate of protection against their manufactures,* which, we have argued, are the more important exports as far as long-run development prospects are concerned. The average nominal level of protection in developed countries is about 4 per cent, but effective protection against the goods of developing countries may well be in the region of 30 per cent or more. Developing countries themselves may give their own producers very high rates of effective protection. Greenaway and Milner (1987) quote the following rates: Uruguay, 387 per cent; Pakistan, 356 per cent; India, 69 per cent; Brazil, 63 per cent; Ivory Coast, 41 per cent; Thailand, 27 per cent.

It is not only tariffs that restrict trade. There are many non-tariff barriers (NTBs) to trade in manufactures between developed and developing countries, the removal of which might do more to increase export earnings than a simple reduction in tariff barriers, for example, licensing requirements, quotas, foreign exchange restrictions, procurement policies favouring domestic products, anti-dumping regulations, subsidies to exports in developed countries, and environmental regulations.

INTERNATIONAL COMMODITY AGREEMENTS[8]

The developing countries in particular, and the world economy in general, suffer several problems from the uncontrolled movement of primary commodity prices. First there is the fact already mentioned of the gradual trend deterioration in the prices of primary commodities relative to industrial goods, which reduces the real income and welfare of the developing countries directly. Second, the prices of primary products are much more cyclically volatile than those of industrial goods. For every 1 per cent change (up and down) in the prices of industrial goods, the prices of primary products fluctuate by approximately 2.4 per cent (see Thirlwall and Bergevin, 1985). Disaggregation by commodity group shows a cyclical elasticity of 1.25 for food, 1.3 for agricultural non-food products and 2.9 for minerals (including petroleum).

This volatility has a number of detrimental consequences. First, it leads to a great deal of instability in the foreign exchange earnings and balance-of-payments position of developing countries, which makes investment planning and economic management much more difficult than would otherwise be the case.

Second, because of asymmetries in the economic system, volatility imparts inflationary bias combined with tendencies to depression in the world economy at large. When the prices of primary products fall, the demand for industrial goods falls but their prices are sticky downwards. When the prices of primary products rise, those of industrial goods are quick to follow suit and governments depress demand to control inflation. The result is stagflation.

Third, the price volatility of primary products leads to volatility in the terms of trade, which may not reflect movements in the equilibrium terms of trade between primary products and industrial goods in the sense that supply and demand are equated in both markets. In these circumstances world economic growth becomes either supply constrained if the prices of primary products are 'too high', or demand constrained if they are 'too low' (see Chapter 5, p. 193). On all these macroeconomic grounds there is a *prima facie* case for attempting to introduce a greater degree of stability into markets for primary commodities (including, I believe, oil). Price falls, however, can be dramatic and persistent. Cashin, Liang and McDermott (2000) look at shocks to the prices of 60 commodities over the period 1957–98 and find them typically long-lasting and not just temporary blips: 17 of the commodities experienced price shocks that persisted for longer than 5 years. This means depressed prices for a long time, and makes price stabilization and income compensation schemes more difficult and costly to manage (see later). The case of coffee prices is given below.

Case example **16.3**

Collapsing Coffee Prices

Coffee prices have slumped to a 30-year low because of massive overproduction: world output was about 115 million (m) bags in 2001–2 compared with consumption of 105–6 m. Vietnam's entry into the market and a steep increase in Brazilian production have meant that output is growing at more than 2 per cent a year, while demand is growing at 1–1.5 per cent.

The result has been that coffee farmers are getting an average of 24 cents a pound for their coffee – compared to a typical retail price of $3.80 – and 25m growers are suffering extreme hardship.

The International Coffee Organization, which represents 30 producer countries, is next month launching a quality standard which aims to take 5m bags a year of low-quality coffee out of the market. But it admits that, without the support of the importing countries, the standard will have little effect on prices.

Oxfam would bolster the scheme with a plan to spend $100m (£64m) of aid from rich countries to destroy 5m more bags of low-quality coffee from existing stocks, which it argues would raise the world market price from 50–60 cents a pound by about 10 cents. It also wants the roasters to agree to pay more for their beans.

Past attempts to manage the coffee market have ended in failure, however: the last quota system collapsed in 1989. Panos Varangis, lead economist on agriculture at the World Bank, said diversification downstream – or out of coffee altogether – along with the use of the derivative markets to set floors to prices, would be a more viable long-term solution.

▶

Faced with the threat of negative publicity, Nestlé has begun to talk about the possibility of agreeing measures to stabilize the market. But all roasters remain opposed to any price-fixing scheme.

Robert Nelson of the National Coffee Association, which represents US coffee importers and retailers, emphasized the need for diversification. 'We in the US ought to look at the tariffs and other barriers we have that prevent those countries diversifying into other products,' he said.

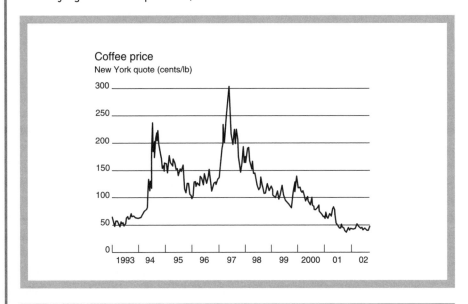

Coffee price
New York quote (cents/lb)

Source: Financial Times, 18 September 2002.

The issue of primary product price instability is not something new. It preoccupied Keynes both before and during the Second World War. In a Memorandum in 1942 on the 'International Regulation of Primary Commodities' he remarked: 'one of the greatest evils in international trade before the war was the wide and rapid fluctuations in the world price of primary commodities . . . It must be the primary purpose of control to prevent these wide fluctuations' (Moggridge, 1980).

Keynes followed up his observations and proposals with a more detailed plan for what he called '**commod control**' – an international body representing leading producers and consumers that would stand ready to buy 'commods' (Keynes' name for typical commodities), and store them, at a price (say) 10 per cent below the fixed basic price and sell them at 10 per cent above (Moggridge, 1980). Figure 16.10 illustrattes how the scheme would operate.

P_n is the fixed basic price. When the price rises outside the 10 per cent upper range, the commod-control scheme would sell, pushing price downwards towards the 'normal' price. Similarly, when the price falls outside the 10 per cent lower range, the commod-control scheme would buy, pushing price upwards within the range. The basic price

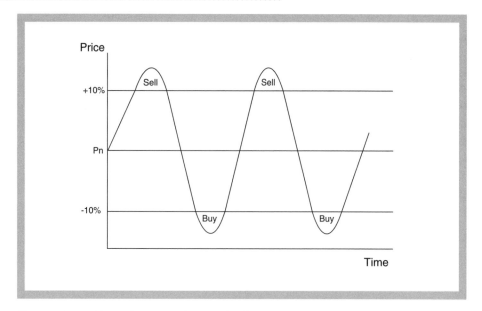

Figure 16.10 Keynes's commod-control scheme

would have to be adjusted according to whether there was a gradual run-down or build-up of stocks, indicating that the price was either 'too low' or 'too high'. If production did not adjust (at least downwards), Keynes recognized that production quotas might have to be implemented. Commodities should be stored as widely as possible across producing and consuming centres.

This proposal is of some contemporary relevance as a means of responding quickly to conditions of famine. For example, there could be a system of granaries strategically placed across the world under international supervision to store surpluses and release them in times of need. The finance for the storage and holding of 'commods' in Keynes' scheme would have been provided through his proposal for an international clearing union, acting like a world central bank, with which 'commod controls' would keep accounts.

At the present time, finance for storage and holding could be provided through the issue of Special Drawing Rights (SDRs) by the IMF (see Chapter 17). A scheme such as 'commod control' could make a major contribution to curing the international trade cycle, with all its attendant implications. More than sixty years have passed since Keynes' wartime proposal, but primary product price fluctuations still plague the world economy. The world still lacks the requisite international mechanisms to rectify what is a major source of instability for the world economy. Since the 1980s the price of primary products has fallen on average by over 30 per cent, and this was a major cause of the international debt crisis in the 1980s that still lingers.

In the recent past there have been five main international commodity agreements in operation – for sugar, tin, rubber, coffee and cocoa, and accounting for some 35 per cent of non-oil exports of the developing countries – but all have had their difficulties.[9] A summary of the agreements, their method of operation and current status is given in Table 16.4.

The Sixth International Tin Agreement collapsed in 1985 because the support price

Table 16.4 Features of international commodity agreements, 1972–89

	Cocoa	Coffee	Rubber	Sugar	Tin
First agreement	1972	1962	1980	1954	1954
Current/final agreement	4th*	4th*	3rd	4th	6th
Date	1986	1983	1996	1978	1982
Breakdown/lapse of economic clauses	suspended	suspended	continues	lapsed	collapsed
Date	1988	1989		1983	1985
Buffer stock*	yes	no	yes	no	yes
Ceiling	+17.3%	n.a.	+28.6%	n.a.	+15%
Floor	−17.3%	n.a.	−25.2%	n.a.	−15%
Must sell/buy	±17.3%	n.a.	±20%	n.a.	±15%
May sell/buy	±14.5%	n.a.	±15%	n.a.	±5%
Export control*	no	yes	no	yes	yes

* The fifth ICCA, which came into force in 1993, and the fifth ICoA, which came into force in 1994, lack buffer stock and export control provisions. Buffer stock trigger prices are defined relative to the (actual or implicit) central reference price.
Source: C. Gilbert, 'International Commodity Agreements: An Obituary Notice', *World Development*, January 1996.

was kept too high and the agreement ran out of funds. The Fourth International Sugar Agreement collapsed in 1983 through a general lack of support. The Fourth International Cocoa Agreement (ICCA) was suspended in 1988 owing to adverse market conditions, but was revived in a weaker form in 1993. The Fourth International Coffee Agreement (ICoA) was suspended in 1989 because producing countries could not agree on the distribution of the benefits from higher prices, either between themselves or between producers within the countries. Only the International Natural Rubber Agreement continues, but intervention to maintain the price is at a very low level.

The basic problem with all agreements is getting suppliers to abide by quotas to restrict output in the face of declining prices. Participants must share a common purpose. The most successful 'commodity agreement' of all is the Common Agricultural Policy (CAP) of the European Union but this does not help developing countries.

Small fluctuations in the export earnings of developing countries, arising from falling prices, are capable of offsetting the entire value of foreign assistance to developing countries in any one year. Approximately, a 10 per cent fall in export earnings is equivalent to the annual flow of ODA. Stable export earnings, it would appear, are at least as important as foreign assistance.[10] In general, unstable export proceeds are the product of variations in both price and quantity. Large fluctuations in earnings may be causally related to four factors:

- Excessive variability of supply and demand
- Low price elasticity of supply and demand
- Excessive specialization in one or two commodities
- A concentration of exports in particular markets.

If the source of instability does come from the supply side, stabilizing prices will not, of course, stabilize earnings. It will reduce them in times of scarcity and boost them in periods of glut. If there is a tendency towards perpetual oversupply, and demand is price inelastic, price stabilization will maintain earnings, but price stabilization will further encourage supply, which may then necessitate production quotas and lead to inefficiency in production if producing countries are allocated quotas to satisfy equity rather than efficiency.

This is not to argue that there is not a case for compensation, but that methods should be avoided that encourage overproduction or inefficiency. It may be better to let prices find their own market level and for the producing countries to be compensated by the beneficiaries under long-term agreements, the compensation being used to encourage some producers into other activities. Alternatively, income-compensation schemes could be worked out, especially in cases where export instability results from variations in domestic supply. Several alternative methods of price stabilization have been tried or recommended, including buffer stock schemes, export restriction schemes and price compensation schemes, and we shall briefly examine these.

BUFFER STOCK SCHEMES

Buffer stock schemes involve buying up the stock of a commodity when its price is abnormally low and selling the commodity when its price is unusually high. The success of such schemes rests on the foresight of those who manage them. Purchases must be made when prices are low relative to future prices and sold when prices are high relative to future prices. Clearly, buffer stock schemes are only suitable for evening out price fluctuations. They cannot cope with persistent downward trends in price without accumulating large stocks of the commodity, which must be paid for – and presumably sold in the future at still lower prices. In 1985 the buffer stock scheme for tin ran into severe financial difficulties by trying to maintain the price of tin too high for too long. Storage schemes are only appropriate for goods that can easily be stored, and for which the cost of storage is not excessive.

Apart from internationally managed buffer stock schemes, governments of individual countries often take an active role in stabilizing prices via **commodity boards**. Again the problem arises, however, that if there is excess supply, the government will acquire large stocks of the commodity and the budgetary burden of maintaining the price becomes prohibitive.

RESTRICTION SCHEMES

In contrast to buffer stock schemes, which are concerned with intervention to *stabilize* prices, restriction schemes are more concerned with *maintaining* prices by restricting supply to the market. The essence of a restriction scheme is that major producers or nations (on behalf of producers) get together and agree to restrict the production and export of a good whose price is falling, thus maintaining or increasing (if demand is inelastic) revenue from a smaller volume of output. In practice it is very difficult to maintain and supervise schemes of this nature, largely because it becomes extremely attractive for any one producer or nation to break away from, or refuse to join, the scheme.

The disadvantages of restriction schemes are, first, that demand may not be inelastic in the long run, so that raising the price by restricting supply may reduce export earnings in the long run. Restriction schemes may ultimately lead to substitution for the product and falling sales. Second, restriction schemes can lead to serious resource allocation inefficiencies stemming from the arbitrary allocation of export quotas between countries and production quotas between producers within countries, unless the quotas are revised regularly to take account of changes in the efficiency of production between producers and between regions of the world. There is also a danger with any form of price-support scheme of a multilateral nature, where both developed and developing countries produce the good in question, that not all the 'assistance' will go where it is most needed. In this event there is a stronger case for bilateral commodity arrangements between developed and developing countries, rather than schemes that embrace developed countries, which subsequently reap the benefit.

PRICE COMPENSATION AGREEMENTS

Price compensation agreements lend themselves to the above form of bilateral arrangement. For example if the price of a commodity falls, two countries could agree upon a sliding scale of compensation such that the importing country pays an increasing sum of money to the exporter as the price falls below a 'normal' price specified in advance. The sliding scale of compensation could be applied to deviations of the actual price from the 'normal' price. Since restrictions on output and quotas are not part of the scheme, arrangements of this kind have the beauty of divorcing the efficiency aspects of pricing and commodity arrangements from the distributional aspects. The commodity would be traded at world prices, and the lack of *full* compensation would ensure that if world prices were falling some countries would decide to shift resources, so maintaining some degree of allocative efficiency.

Agreements need not only be bilateral. It would also be possible to draw up multilateral price compensation agreements, with the governments of all countries that export or import a certain commodity agreeing jointly on a standard price, and on a 'normal' quantity of imports and exports of the commodity for each country concerned. There could also be a common sliding scale of compensation. For reasons mentioned earlier, however, there is perhaps a greater case for bilateral deals so that assistance can be given where it is most needed and where countries are not bound by the conventions of an international agreement.

There is no reason why price compensation schemes should not run concurrently with other types of international commodity agreement. Indeed, if the price of a commodity continually declines it may be necessary to couple a restriction scheme with a price compensation scheme, otherwise importing countries will be *persistently* subsidizing the exporting countries, which may not be welcomed. There is also the danger in this case, and also in the case of price-support schemes, that one form of assistance will replace another. If developed countries continually have to pay more than the market prices for their primary products, and argue at the same time that the major constraint on financial assistance to developing countries is their balance of payments, they might use price compensation agreements as an excuse for cutting other forms of assistance. If so, what primary producers gain in the form of higher prices or higher export earnings than if the market were free, they lose in other ways.

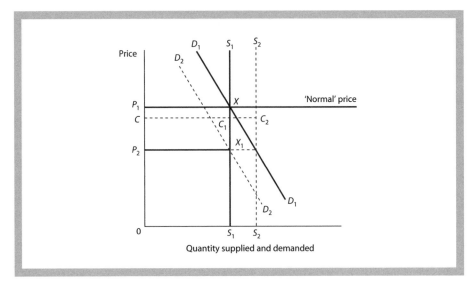

Figure 16.11 Price compensation and export earnings

If fluctuations in price emanate from the supply side and not from changes in demand, price compensation will operate perversely on the stabilization of *export earnings*. This is illustrated in Figure 16.11. Price in the market is determined by the intersection of the supply and demand curves, D_1D_1 and S_1S_1, giving equilibrium price, P_1. Now suppose that there is a decrease in demand to D_2D_2, causing price to fall to P_2. Earnings before the price fall were $0P_1XS_1$; after the price fall they are $0P_2X_1S_1$. Assume that P_1 is the 'normal' price agreed under the price compensation scheme, and that P_2C represents the appropriate amount of price compensation in relation to the deviation from the 'normal' price following the decrease in demand. Total revenue under the price compensation scheme will be $0CC_1S_1$, which is not far short of total revenue before the fall in price. Consider, however, an equivalent fall in price from P_1 to P_2 as a result of an increase in supply from S_1S_1 to S_2S_2. Under the same price compensation scheme total revenue is now $0CC_2S_2$, which is greatly in excess of the original total revenue (before the price fall) of $0P_1XS_1$. Conversely, if the supply falls, and the price rises above the 'normal' price, revenue will be less than before the price rise since the exporting country will presumably be compensating the importing country – unless the scheme works only one way!

INCOME COMPENSATION SCHEMES

The only way to overcome the induced instability of price compensation schemes is to formulate an income compensation scheme that takes account of both price and quantity changes. The practical difficulty is reaching agreement on a 'normal' level of income. If the trend rate of growth of output is positive for most commodities, to settle for a fixed level of 'normal' income would be unjust.

The way that most income compensation schemes work is that each year's compensation is based on deviations of actual export earnings from the moving average of a series of previous years. The IMF's Compensatory and Contingency Financing Facility operates along these lines, and we shall discuss this in the next chapter. The Stabex scheme – once operated by the European Union under the Lomé Convention – was another example of an income compensation scheme. But there must be sufficient funds available. During the commodity price slump of the 1980s, the size and administration of both the Stabex and the IMF scheme proved inadequate. Furthermore the compensation is paid to governments, so producers do not necessarily reap the benefits.

For stability and a greater degree of certainty over export earnings, producers and governments are increasingly looking to **futures markets** for risk management. To be able to sell forward in futures markets guarantees the producer a price and therefore earnings, depending on supply. Futures markets are not well developed, however, and very often cover is not available for more than one year in advance. Where private risk management is not available, there is a case for publicly subsidized agencies to increase the access of commodity producers in poor countries to insurance against price volatility – perhaps offering price floor guarantees to producers. This may be cheaper in the long run than compensating countries for commodity price fluctuations.

PRODUCER CARTELS

Developing countries' impatience with the international community when formulating schemes to protect their balance of payments and terms of trade has led in recent years to the effective cartelization of the production of certain raw materials by the developing countries themselves, especially where the number of producers is small and close relations are enjoyed by the producers in other respects. The sentiments of the developing countries were well articulated at a meeting in Dakar in 1975 of over 100 developing countries, where it was declared that the recovery and control of natural resources held the key to their economic freedom, and countries were urged to draw up a joint plan to protect the prices of their export commodities. The classic example of the effects of cartelization is provided by the oil-producing countries belonging to the Organization of Petroleum Exporting Countries (OPEC), which raised the price of crude oil by 800 per cent between 1973 and 1980. The producers of bauxite similarly joined together to raise prices in the 1980s.

Developing countries are not only producers of raw materials, however; they are also consumers, and what some countries gain with respect to the production and exportation of one commodity they may lose with respect to the importation and consumption of another. Developing countries that are poor in all raw materials may not benefit at all. It is not clear, except in the case of a few special commodities such as oil, that cartelization and monopoly pricing of the product will necessarily redistribute income from the developed to the developing countries taken as a whole. If this is so, bilateral commodity agreements between poor-country producers and rich-country users are probably preferable as a means of ensuring that all developing countries benefit from the general desire in the world economy to help poor, primary-producing countries.

TRADE VERSUS AID

'Trade not aid' has become a popular slogan in developing countries in recent years. Let us now consider whether a unit of foreign exchange from exports is really worth more than a unit of foreign exchange from international assistance, or whether the slogan is more an understandable reaction to the debt-servicing problems arising from *past* borrowing (the benefits of which may have been forgotten) and to the political interference and leverage that may accompany international assistance.

If the meaning of aid is taken literally (that is, a free transfer of resources), Johnson (1967) showed a long time ago than a unit of foreign exchange from exports can never be as valuable as a unit of foreign exchange from aid. The reason for this is that exports do not provide additional resources for investment directly, only indirectly by the opportunity provided to transform domestic resources into goods and services more cheaply than if the transformation had to be done domestically. Aid, on the other hand, not only provides resources directly, but also indirectly by *saving the excess cost of import substitution*. The relative worth of exports compared with pure aid can therefore be expressed as

$$\frac{cX}{(1 + c)A} \tag{16.4}$$

where X is the value of exports, A is the value of pure aid and c is the proportional excess cost of import substitution. The relative worth of exports will rise with the excess cost of import substitution, but it is clear that the worth of exports can never match the worth of an *equal* amount of pure aid ($X = A$) since $c < (1 + c)$. The fact that aid may be tied to higher-priced goods makes some difference to the argument, but it can be shown that the excess cost of import substitution and the excess cost of tied goods would have to be relatively high for the worth of aid not to exceed the worth of trade. Let r be the ratio of the price of tied goods to the price of the same goods in the free market. The relative worth of exports may then be written as

$$\frac{cX}{(1 + c)A} \times r \tag{16.5}$$

Now exports will be worth more than aid if $cr > (1 + c)$. Different combinations of c and r could be thought of to satisfy this condition, but both c and r would have to be quite high, for example $c = 2.0$ and $r = 1.5$.

The more important consideration, however, is that the term 'aid' in the slogan 'trade not aid' should probably not be interpreted literally. The comparison that developing countries are making is not between trade and pure aid, but either between trade and the **aid component** of an equal amount of foreign assistance, or simply between trade and an equal amount of foreign assistance. If these are the comparisons being made in practice, two interesting questions arise. First, under what circumstances will trade be more valuable? And second, which is the most appropriate comparison to make?

Consider first the comparison between exports and the aid component of an equal amount of foreign assistance. If this is the comparison that is being made by the developing countries, the Johnson formula can be modified by letting $A = Fg$, where A is the aid component of assistance (see p. 484), F is the nominal amount of foreign assistance and g is the aid component as a proportion of nominal assistance (that is, the grant element). Substituting Fg for A in (16.4) gives the relative worth of exports compared with the aid component of an equal amount of foreign assistance:

$$\frac{cX}{(1 + c)Fg} \tag{16.6}$$

or, if the aid is tied:

$$\frac{cX}{(1 + c)Fg} \times r \tag{16.7}$$

From (16.6) the value of exports will exceed the value of the aid component of an *equal* amount of foreign assistance ($X = F$) if $c > g(1 + c)$, and, from (16.7), if $cr > g(1 + c)$. The relative worth of exports is the greater, the higher the excess cost of import substitution, the higher the excess cost of tied aid and the lower the grant element of assistance. It is still the case, however, that c and r would have to be quite high and g relatively low for the worth of exports to exceed the worth of the aid component of an equal amount of foreign assistance.

But even if a comparison of exports with the aid component of an equal amount of foreign assistance showed exports to be worth more, it is not clear that this is the correct comparison to make when justifying the slogan 'trade not aid'. Equations 16.6 and 16.7 assume that only the aid component of assistance saves the excess cost of import substitution. In fact foreign borrowing *on any terms* saves the excess cost of import substitution. This being so, there are strong grounds for arguing that the comparison that should underlie the slogan 'trade not aid' is a comparison of the worth of exports with the worth of foreign assistance itself of equal amount, which provides resources directly equal to Fg and indirectly equal to Fc. The relative worth of exports compared with foreign assistance can thus be expressed as

$$\frac{cX}{Fg + Fc} = \frac{cX}{(g + c)F} \tag{16.8}$$

or, with tied assistance:

$$\frac{cX}{(g + c)F} \times r \tag{16.9}$$

The conditions for the worth of exports to exceed that of foreign assistance are clearly more stringent than for the worth of exports to exceed the worth of the aid component of an equal amount of foreign assistance. Now, ignoring the potential excess cost of tying, foreign assistance is always worth more than an equal value of exports as long as some grant element is attached to the assistance (that is, as long as $g > 0$).

The values of g, c and r give a practical guide to any country of the relevance of the slogan 'trade, not aid', ignoring the secondary repercussions and the side-effects of the two resource flows.[11] The values of g, c and r for most developing countries are probably not such as to justify the slogan 'trade not aid' on narrow economic grounds.

As far as secondary repercussions are concerned, however, there is the question of the productivity of resources from abroad compared with those released by exports, and of the additional saving generated by the two means of resource augmentation. There is little evidence on the first point, but on the second it is sometimes claimed, as we saw in Chapter 15, that foreign assistance discourages saving, while export earnings contribute positively to saving. There is no disputing that some foreign assistance may be 'consumed', but this is not the important consideration. The question is, which resource flow leads to the most investment? If 50 per cent of the foreign assistance is 'saved' and the propensity to save of the export sector is 50 per cent, the contribution of the two sources of foreign exchange to growth is exactly the same.

There is no evidence to suggest that the propensity to 'save' out of foreign assistance is less than the propensity to 'save' out of exports. Given that export income may be highly concentrated in the hands of the government or multinational firms, the propensity to save out of export income could be high. If the propensity was, say, 0.6, then 40 per cent of foreign assistance would have to be 'consumed' for foreign assistance not to contribute as much to saving as exports. This is unlikely. If anything, therefore, the economic secondary repercussions of exports and assistance favour assistance.

DISCUSSION QUESTIONS

1 What is the essence of the distinction between static and dynamic gains from trade?

2 What fundamental assumptions of free-trade theory may be violated in the context of developing countries?

3 Why might there be a tendency for the terms of trade to move against primary products and primary-producing countries, and what does the empirical evidence show?

4 Outline the various arguments for protection.

5 Under what conditions are tariffs a first-best policy of protection?

6 Discuss the relative merits of import substitution versus export promotion.

7 Why are regional trade agreements (RTAs) inferior to the generalized freeing of trade?

8 What has been the impact of trade liberalization on exports and economic growth in developing countries?

9 To what extent do you think that the 'East Asian miracle' has been based on export-led growth?

10 Why do some economists argue that the gains from trade should be looked at more from the point of view of the effect of trade on the balance of payments than from the traditional viewpoint of real resource augmentation?

11 In what ways is trade not 'fair' between developed and developing countries?

12 What do you understand by the concept of 'effective protection', and how is it measured?

13 What problems do unstable commodity prices pose for a country and for the world economy?

14 What are the theoretical and practical difficulties of stabilizing the price and export earnings of primary products?

NOTES

1. This is the basis of Bhagwati's (1958) model of immiserizing growth.
2. The analysis to follow relies heavily on Robson (1988).
3. Prebisch (1950). See also his later work (1959). Prebisch was Executive Secretary of the Economic Commission for Latin America (ECLA) from 1950 to 1963 and Secretary General of UNCTAD from 1963 to 1969.
4. This result has been challenged by Bleaney (1993), and particularly by Athukorala (1993), who show that the result apparently depends on the inclusion of non-ferrous metals in the manufacturing export price series. But see the reply of Sarkar and Singer (1991, 1993).
5. See Oxfam's (2002) compelling indictment of the world's unfair trading system 'Rigged Rules and Double Standards: Trade, Globalisation and the Fight Against Poverty'.
6. For one of the original theoretical expositions, see Corden (1966). See also the pioneering work of Balassa *et al.* (1971).
7. Students might like to prove these propositions for themselves, using the formula for the effective rate of protection.
8. For an up-to-date discussion of the issues involved in this section, see Maizels (1987); Gilbert (1996).
9. For a comprehensive discussion of international commodity agreements and commodity problems in general, see Maizels (1992) and Gilbert (1996).
10. For a good summary of the measures of instability and the empirical evidence of the effects of instability on the economies of developing countries, see Lim (1991); Love (1987).
11. For some illustrative calculations see Thirlwall (1976). Morrissey and White (1993) argue that only the face value of assistance should be deflated by the excess cost of tying and not the repayments, but this makes little practical difference.

WEBSITES ON TRADE

Trade negotiations
WTO www.wto.org

Fair trade
Oxfam www.maketradefair.com
Fair Trade Foundation www.fairtrade.org.uk
New Economics Foundation www.neweconomics.org.gen/

Trade agreements
Mercosur www.mercosur.org
NAFTA www.mac.doc.gov/nafta
WTO WATCH www.wtowatch.org

17 The balance of payments, international monetary assistance and development

BALANCE-OF-PAYMENTS-CONSTRAINED GROWTH

We have seen how the composition of the trade of developing countries can lead to severe balance-of-payments difficulties, which can act as a constraint on growth, and how vulnerable many developing countries are to exogenous shocks that adversely affect both their export earnings and their import payments. In this chapter we shall formally define the concept of a **balance-of-payments-constrained growth rate** and examine its determinants. We shall then go on to consider the measures that countries themselves may take to raise the balance-of-payments-constrained growth rate, as well as the assistance provided by international institutions to ease the constraint. The latter mainly involves a consideration of the role of the **International Monetary Fund** in the provision of balance-of-payments support.

Table 17.1 shows the balance-of-payments experience of the developing countries as a whole and by continent. The poor countries are in deficit most of the time, but the deficits fluctuate according to internal and external economic circumstances. In the 1970s, for example, owing to the oil shock in 1973 (and later 1979) and the slowdown of world growth, the deficits grew considerably, despite a slowdown of internal growth that reduced the demand for non-oil imports. In the early 1980s the deficits contracted because most developing countries were forced to adjust (that is, deflate their economies) in order to repay debt out of diminished export earnings. In the late 1980s, the deficits increased again, with some internal recovery and a greater willingness of the international capital markets to resume lending. By 1996, the deficit stood at $98 billion, over half of which was accounted for by Thailand, Indonesia, the Philippines, Malaysia and South Korea which all experienced serious financial crisis in 1997 (see later). These countries had to readjust, and in 2002 East Asia and Pacific had a big surplus (see Table 17.1). Latin America and Caribbean is the continent shown to be the most seriously in deficit. For any country or continent, the observed deficit (*ex post*) measures the extent to which it has been able and willing to finance the difference between the value of current payments and receipts.

All countries have a growth rate that is consistent with balance-of-payments equilibrium on the current account, and with its overall balance on the current and capital account. What determines the growth rate that is consistent with current account balance on the one hand, and overall balance on the other? If we specify the equilibrium equations and the determinants of import and export demand, we can immediately see the major factors of importance, and we can appreciate in turn the various policy measures taken by individual countries and the international community to raise the growth rate of less developed countries consistent with balance-of-payments equilibrium.[1]

Table 17.1 Summary of payment balances on current account, 1980–2002 ($US billion)

	1980	1990	2002
All developing countries	−6.1	−23.0	−78.5
Latin America and Caribbean	−30.2	−1.6	−15.4
East Asia and Pacific	–	−5.6	61.0
Sub-Saharan Africa	0.4	−1.8	−8.0
South Asia	−4.9	−11.6	8.9

Source: World Bank, *Global Development Finance 2004* (Washington, DC: World Bank, 2004).

The current account balance of payments of a country, measured in its own *domestic* currency, may be written as

$$P_d X = P_f M E \tag{17.1}$$

where X measures the quantity of exports and P_d is the average price of exports, so $P_d X$ is the value of exports in domestic currency. M is the quantity of imports, P_f is the average (foreign) price of imports, and E is the nominal exchange rate measured as the domestic price of foreign currency, which thus converts the value of imports measured in foreign currency ($P_f M$) into a domestic currency equivalent.

The condition for the balance of payments to remain in equilibrium in a *growing* economy through time is that the *rate of growth* of export earnings should equal the *rate of growth* of import payments, that is

$$(p_d + x) = (p_f + m + e) \tag{17.2}$$

where the lower-case letters represent rates of change of the variables.

Now let us consider what the growth of export and import volume depends on. Export demand may be expected to depend primarily on the price of a country's exports relative to the foreign price of similar goods (expressed in a common currency) and on the level of 'world' income, which determines the purchasing power over a country's goods. Similarly, import demand may be expected to depend on the price of imports relative to domestic substitutes and on the level of domestic income. If the price and income elasticities of demand for exports and imports are assumed to be constant, we may write the export and import functions in the following (multiplicative) way:

$$X = A \left(\frac{P_d}{P_f E} \right)^\eta Z^\varepsilon \tag{17.3}$$

and

$$M = B \left(\frac{P_f E}{P_d} \right)^\psi Y^\pi \tag{17.4}$$

where Z measures 'world' income; Y measures domestic income; η is the price elasticity of demand for exports (< 0); ε is the income elasticity of demand for exports (> 0); ψ is the price elasticity of demand for imports (< 0); π is the income elasticity of demand for imports (> 0) and A and B are constants.

Taking small rates of change of the variables in (17.3) and (17.4), we can see what the growth of exports and imports depends on:

$$x = \eta(p_d - p_f - e) + \varepsilon(z) \tag{17.5}$$

and

$$m = \psi(p_f + e - p_d) + \pi(y) \tag{17.6}$$

In other words, **export growth** depends (1) on how fast domestic prices are changing relative to foreign prices, taking into account variations in the exchange rate (e), multiplied by the price elasticity of demand for exports; and (2) how fast world income is changing, together with the value of the income elasticity of demand for exports. We rule out here the possibility that developing countries can sell any amount of their goods on world markets at the going price, which would mean that the income elasticity of demand, and what is happening to world purchasing power, does not matter, and that export growth is simply supply determined. This may be true in the case of *some* commodities from some *small* countries, but the proposition that demand conditions do not matter for export performance does not stand up to empirical scrutiny as a general rule. There are very few pure price-takers in international trade.

Likewise, **import growth** depends on (1) how fast import prices are changing relative to domestic substitutes (taking account of exchange rate changes), multiplied by the price elasticity of demand for imports; and (2) how fast domestic income (as a proxy for expenditure) is changing, together with the income elasticity of demand for imports.

Since the growth of imports depends on the growth of domestic income, if we substitute equations (17.5) and (17.6) into (17.2) (which gives the condition for a moving balance-of-payments equilibrium through time), we can derive an expression for a country's growth of income that is consistent with current account equilibrium, which depends on certain key variables and parameters. Substitution of (17.5) and (17.6) into (17.2) gives

$$p_d + \eta(p_d - p_f - e) + \varepsilon(z) = p_f + \psi(p_f + e - p_d) + \pi(y) + e \qquad (17.7)$$

so that

$$y = \frac{(1 + \eta + \psi)(p_d - p_f - e) + \varepsilon(z)}{\pi} \qquad (17.8)$$

Before embarking on discussion, let us identify in words what this growth rate depends on, which must be binding if current account deficits cannot be financed:

- First, it depends on the rate at which the real terms of trade are changing ($p_d - p_f - e$). The real terms of trade is the ratio of export to import prices measured in a common currency (P_d/P_fE). A rise in this ratio, if ($p_d - p_f - e$) > 0, raises real income growth consistent with current account equilibrium (other things being constant), and a fall in this ratio lowers the balance-of-payments equilibrium growth rate. This is the **pure terms of trade** effect on income growth.
- Second, if the real terms of trade are changing, the growth rate depends on the **price elasticities of demand** for exports (η) and imports (ψ), which determine the magnitude of the volume response of exports and imports to relative price changes.[2]
- Third, one country's growth depends on the growth rates of other countries (z) – which illustrates nicely the **interdependence of the world economy** – but the rate at which one country grows relative to others depends crucially on the income elasticity of demand for its exports (ε), which depends on the tastes of foreign

consumers, the characteristics of goods, and a whole host of **non-price factors** that determine the demand for goods in international trade. One of the main reasons why some countries have a healthier balance of payments and a higher growth rate than others is related to the characteristics of the goods that they produce and export in world trade.

- Fourth, the growth rate depends on a country's **appetite for imports**, as measured by π, the income elasticity of demand for imports. The higher is π, the lower the growth rate that is consistent with balance-of-payments equilibrium on the current account.

One can see in these factors the rationale for agreements to prevent the terms of trade deteriorating for developing countries, for exchange rate policy, for international Keynesianism to maintain the growth of world income, and for policies to induce structural change – through export promotion or import substitution – in order to raise the income elasticity of demand for exports and to reduce the income elasticity of demand for imports. Let us take up some of these issues in turn.

THE TERMS OF TRADE

The effect of terms-of-trade deterioration (import prices rising faster than export prices, other things remaining the same) is to worsen the balance of payments at a given rate of growth or, what amounts to the same thing, to reduce the rate of growth of income consistent with current account equilibrium. For example, if in equation (17.8), import prices were rising at 10 per cent per annum while the price of exports was rising at only 5 per cent per annum, this would mean a lower y than if the terms of trade were constant. In theory this 'terms-of-trade effect' could be offset by a continual **appreciation** of the currency, that is, by a continual percentage fall in E; but very few developing countries, if any, are in a position to appreciate their currencies even if they wanted to. Terms-of-trade stability in real terms must depend, or rely, on international commodity agreements to stabilize the prices of the exports of developing countries relative to the prices of the goods they import. Within this framework of analysis the rationale for terms-of-trade agreements is apparent.

It is not clear, however, that terms-of-trade deterioration is always a bad thing, because what happens to export earnings and import payments, and hence to the balance-of-payments equilibrium growth rate, depends not only on changes in relative prices but also on the volume response of exports and imports to price changes. Since the price elasticities, η and ψ, are defined as negative, it can be seen from equation (17.8) that if their sum exceeds -1, $p_d < p_f$ will mean that y is higher than would be the case if $p_d \geq p_f$. In other words the export and import volume response to domestic export prices rising more slowly than import prices is sufficient to offset the fact that more has to be paid for a given volume of imports relative to exports. If, however, the price elasticity of demand for the exports of a developing country is low because of the nature of the product in question (for example, a primary product), and the price elasticity of demand for imports is also low because the imports are necessities, the balance of payments will *worsen* if the terms of trade deteriorate, and growth will have to be constrained for the preservation of balance-of-payments equilibrium. In these circumstances, commodity agreements assume great importance and it would be beneficial if the ratio of export prices to import prices were to rise. We have already considered in the previous chapter various commodity schemes aimed at stabilizing export prices, or changing the relative price of exports and imports. We also noted that this will not necessarily stabilize export earnings if there are fluctuations in export supply. The international response to this has been to devise schemes to compensate for loss of export earnings. The only major scheme now in existence is the IMF's Compensatory and Contingency Financing Facility (see later).

Another argument for stabilizing the export prices of developing countries and maintaining their incomes is that price and income instability tends to depress the world economy as a whole and the developing countries with it, given the interdependence between countries in the world economy. Falling prices and incomes in developing countries reduces the purchasing power over industrial goods, inducing recession, while rising commodity prices may also induce recession by raising the price of manufactured goods and inducing deflation in the developed countries. For the smooth growth of the world economy, there is a lot to be said for attempting to stabilize the prices of primary products so that the purchasing power of the producers and exporters of these commodities grows in line with supply. One suggestion is that Special Drawing Rights (SDRs) (see later) might be used to purchase primary products in order to stabilize their price in times of glut on the lines of Keynes' commod-control scheme discussed in Chapter 16 (p. 561).

THE EXCHANGE RATE AND DEVALUATION

Now suppose that export prices do rise more quickly than import prices, improving the terms of trade, but that the sum of the price elasticities of demand for exports and imports exceeds unity, what then? This will worsen the balance of payments and reduce the balance-of-payments equilibrium growth rate. It is in these circumstances that **exchange rate depreciation** may become relevant, and is often resorted to. It can be seen from equation (17.8) that if a country's rate of price increase is above that of other countries ($p_d > p_f$), this can in principle be compensated for by allowing the exchange rate to fall continually ($e > 0$) by the difference between p_d and p_f in order to hold 'competitiveness' steady. The conventional approach to balance-of-payments adjustment, and the policy pursued relentlessly by the IMF in countries experiencing balance-of-payments difficulties, is downward adjustment of the exchange rate. Note well, however, that the rationale of such a policy presupposes a number of things:

■ That the source of the difficulties is price uncompetitiveness
■ That the price elasticities are 'right' (that is, they sum to greater than unity) for a depreciation to reduce the imbalance
■ That the real terms of trade (or the real exchange rate) can be changed by devaluation.

A fall in the nominal exchange rate, however, that is, $e > 0$, may either lead to a fall in $P_f (p_f < 0)$ or a rise in $P_d (p_d > 0)$, both of which would nullify the effect of the devaluation (see (17.8)). A fall in P_f might come about if foreign suppliers desired to maintain their competitiveness as the devaluing country became more competitive. This is known as **pricing to market**, that is, foreign exporters reduce their markups in response to nominal exchange rate changes in order to remain competitive in world markets. A rise in P_d may come about as the domestic price of imports rises as a result of devaluation, which is then followed by a wage–price spiral. Either way, within a short space of time, relative prices measured in a common currency may revert to their former level and devaluation will have been abortive in this respect. Edwards (1989) has looked at the effectiveness of devaluation in reducing a country's *real* exchange rate. He studied 39 cases of devaluation in 25 developing countries between 1962 and 1982, and found that in most cases devaluation had been eroded by domestic inflation within three years. Devaluation must be backed by restrictive monetary and fiscal policies if it is to be effective, but this can lead to unemployment. A detailed case study of Mexico by Kamin and Rogers (2000) shows that devaluation has nearly always been associated with high inflation and economic contraction.

Note also that a *once-and-for-all* devaluation or depreciation of the currency cannot put a country on a *permanently higher growth path* that is consistent with balance-of-payments equilibrium. Currency depreciation would have to be continuous (that is, e > 0 permanently) for this to happen, unless devaluation can somehow induce favourable structural changes at the same time. Countries must look very carefully at the prevailing conditions before embracing currency devaluation as a panacea for the relief of balance-of-payments-constrained growth. There are three major worries.

First, raising the domestic price of imported goods can be a highly inflationary policy for an open economy that is heavily dependent on imports, as many developing countries have discovered to their cost, particularly in Latin America, and some countries have had the courage to resist IMF support, which has been conditional on devaluation. In the eyes of some, the acronym IMF stands for (I)nflation, (M)isery and (F)amine!

Second, depreciation can be dangerous because it prematurely shifts resources into the tradeable goods sector, where productivity may be lower than in the non-tradeable goods sector. This is forcefully argued by Yotopoulos (1996), who believes that there is a tendency for the real exchange rate to be *undervalued* because of weakness on the capital account of the balance of payments, depressing the nominal exchange rate. In the early stages of development, developing countries should therefore protect the nominal exchange rate from depreciation through the use of controls and intervention in the foreign exchange market, and only start to liberalize once the foreign exchange market has become more fully developed and currencies are not regarded as 'soft' by the outside world. In the 33 countries studied by Yotopoulos there was a *negative* relation between the real exchange rate and the growth of per capita income for most of the 1970s and 1980s (holding other factors constant).

Third, the effect of currency devaluation is to make countries more competitive in the range of goods that were the source of their balance-of-payments difficulties in the first place. A devalued currency might encourage export sales of new (manufactured) goods with a high price elasticity in world trade, but it might be inappropriate for the traditional range of goods produced and exported with a low price elasticity of demand. For example, if a country is a large supplier and a price maker in world markets, currency devaluation coupled with low price elasticity will *reduce* export earnings. If the country is a price taker, devaluation will raise the domestic price of the commodity and cause inflation. It is true that production for export will become more profitable and might encourage a greater supply response, but there are other less inflationary ways to encourage supply than devaluation. Different types of exchange-rate systems available in developing countries are discussed later.

THE IMF SUPPLY-SIDE APPROACH TO DEVALUATION

Devaluation, as well as permitting a reduction in the foreign-currency price of exports, may also increase the profitability of exporting, by raising the price of tradeable goods relative to the price of non-tradeables, and by providing exporters with more domestic currency per unit of foreign exchange earned. The IMF, having conceded that the price elasticity of demand for many of the goods exported and imported by developing countries (particularly as a group) is low, now increasingly uses this supply-side argument as a justification for devaluation. If output is stimulated, this will also mitigate to a certain extent the contraction of aggregate monetary demand that results from devaluation and any accompanying expenditure-reducing policies.

The IMF supply-side approach to devaluation was first articulated in print by Nashashibi (1980) with reference to the Sudan. The approach first requires the calculation of foreign exchange earnings per unit of domestic resources employed for a range of tradeable goods. Export (and import substitute) activities can then be arranged on a profitability scale and, according to the supply-side argument, the appropriate devaluation is the one that goes down the scale far enough to ensure the profitability of traditional exports, as well as (perhaps) to encourage new activities. Thus if the current exchange rate for the Sudan was, say, US $2 to S£1, and foreign exchange earnings per unit of domestic resources were calculated to be less than this for most commodities, it would clearly be unprofitable to produce for export, and the exchange rate should be devalued to bring the production of tradeables within the margin of profitability. Foreign exchange earnings per unit of domestic resources are measured as

$$C = \frac{(P_x X - P_m M)r}{P_d D} \tag{17.9}$$

where X refers to exports, P_x is the world price of exports in domestic currency, M is the quantity of imported inputs, P_m is the price of imported inputs in domestic currency, D is the amount of domestic resources used in production, P_d is the price of domestic inputs and r is the exchange rate measured as the foreign price of domestic currency. If $C < r$, production is not profitable at the existing exchange rate.

It is clear from equation (17.9) that if devaluation is to improve profitability, the rise in $(P_x X - P_m M)/P_d D$ must be more than the reduction in r. Unfortunately this cannot be taken for granted. It depends on the response of $P_x X$, $P_m M$, P_d and D to the change in r. The implicit assumptions underlying the approach are that developing countries are price takers, so that P_x will rise in proportion to the devaluation, that X will increase, that M will decrease, and that these favourable effects will not be offset by rises in P_m and $P_d D$. In practice, there may not be a complete 'pass through' of devaluation to export prices (P_x); the elasticity of export supply may be very low because of structural rigidities and factor immobility, and the elasticity of import prices and domestic prices may be very high. The end result may be that the profitability of exporting remains largely unchanged. This was the conclusion of a detailed study of devaluations in the Sudan by Nureldin-Hussain and the present author (1984), which looked at the profitability of cotton, groundnuts, sesame and gum arabic.

The Sudan and many other developing countries fall into the 'rigid country' classification distinguished by Branson (1983) in his useful taxonomic discussion of trade structures and devaluation. 'Rigid' countries are those that produce agricultural-based raw materials with low supply elasticities and whose demand for imports is very inelastic in the short run, particularly for imports used as intermediate inputs. In addition, the price elasticity of demand for exports may be high but not infinite, and real wages may be sticky. In these circumstances, devaluation may be a second-best policy compared with 'structural' intervention to raise foreign exchange earnings per unit of domestic inputs.

THE GROWTH OF WORLD INCOME AND STRUCTURAL CHANGE

Now let us turn to the growth of world income: z in equation (17.8). There is little that individual countries themselves can do about the growth of world income, but since all countries are linked through trade, the interdependence of countries and the importance of global prosperity is only too apparent. This should be the overriding function of supranational institutions and mechanisms: to keep world income and trade buoyant in the face of exogenous shocks and to avoid the beggar-thy-neighbour policies that characterised the 1930s, when the whole world economy slumped. The purpose of the IMF was to avoid a repetition of the 1930s – to help countries in balance-of-payments difficulties and to avoid recourse to widespread protectionism, which exports unemployment from one country to another in a downward spiral. This is the same purpose that underlies various schemes for the recycling of export surpluses and for managed trade, that is, to relieve the balance-of-payments constraint on growth in countries that tend to have a chronic deficit while other countries are in perpetual surplus. This was a major theme of the Brandt Report, discussed in Chapter 1. Whatever may be said about the wisdom of the activities pursued by the IMF in developing countries, there can be no doubting the positive role that the IMF played in the postwar years in providing the confidence and the means for the world economy to grow at an unprecedented rate.

While individual countries have no control over the growth of world income, they do have some control over the income elasticity of demand for their exports, which determines how fast exports grow as a result of world income growth. Likewise countries have some control over the income elasticity of demand for imports, because both these parameters are a function of the type and characteristics of the goods being produced for sale in international trade. Thus they are a function of the economic (trade) strategy being pursued.

We discussed in Chapter 16 export promotion versus import-substitution strategies. Import substitution is designed to lower the import elasticity, but there is a limit to import substitution, and the policy itself may lower the export elasticity at the same time by creating a rigid and inefficient industrial structure. A much more fruitful strategy, which has been pursued relentlessly and successfully by several South-East Asian countries, is to concentrate on raising the export elasticity, which at the same time may reduce the import elasticity if the goods produced for export also compete with imports.

APPLICATION OF THE BALANCE-OF-PAYMENTS-CONSTRAINED GROWTH MODEL

How well does the balance-of-payments-constrained growth model outlined in equations (17.1)–(17.8) fit the growth experience of developing countries? Or, to put it another way, how well does equation (17.8) predict the growth performance of the developing countries? To answer this question, it is convenient to simplify the model by assuming either that the sum of the price elasticities of demand $(\eta + \psi)$ does not differ significantly from unity, in which case equation (17.8) reduces to $y = \varepsilon z/\pi$, and/or that relative prices in international trade do not change in the long run (or the real exchange rate remains constant), in which case (17.8) reduces to $y = \varepsilon z/\pi = x/\pi$. This latter result is often referred to as the **dynamic Harrod trade multiplier** result because it is the dynamic analogue of the static Harrod trade multiplier result $Y = X/m$, where Y is the *level* of income, X is the *level* of exports; m is the marginal propensity to import, and $1/m$ is the foreign trade multiplier (Harrod, 1933). *Prima facie* evidence that a country is balance-of-payments-constrained in its growth performance would be to find that its actual growth is close to or just above its balance-of-payments equilibrium growth rate (financed by sustainable long-run capital inflows – see below), combined with unemployed domestic resources.

There have been a number of recent studies that have applied this simple model to individual, or groups of, developing countries e.g. Ansari, Hashemzadeh and Xi (2000) for a selection of South-East Asian countries; Moreno-Brid and Perez (1999) for Central American countries; Perraton (2003) for several developing countries; Moreno-Brid (1998) and Pacheco-López (2005) for Mexico, and Nell (2003) for South Africa.[3] The results from some Asian and Latin American countries are shown in Table 17.2. In most cases, it is not possible to reject the hypothesis that the actual growth rate y is equal to the balance of payments equilibrium growth rate (x/π). This is particularly true of Mexico which shows the slowdown of growth post-liberalization in 1985/6 as a result of a dramatic increase in the income elasticity of demand for imports without a corresponding increase in the rate of growth of exports. Export growth stayed roughly the same; the income elasticity of demand for imports more than doubled, and the sustainable growth rate fell by one half.

Perraton (2003) tests the model for a sample of 51 developing countries over the period 1973–95. Import and export demand functions are estimated (equations 17.5 and 17.6) from which long-run estimates of income and price elasticities are derived. It was only possible, however, to derive stable estimates of the income elasticities of demand for imports (π) for 27 of the countries. For these countries, the dynamic Harrod foreign trade multiplier (x/π) is a good predictor of actual growth performance. Using estimates of the income elasticity of demand for imports made by Senhadji (1998) gives even stronger results. The results of these studies add weight to the ideas and importance of export-led growth that we discussed in the previous chapter.

Table 17.2 Application of the balance-of-payments-constrained growth model to developing countries

Countries	Actual GDP growth (y) (%)	Export growth (x) (%)	Income elasticity of imports (π)	Predicted balance-of-payments-constrained growth rate (%)
Asian countries[a]				
(1970–96)				
Indonesia	6.90	16.3	2.98	5.47
Malaysia	7.40	14.5	2.25	6.44
Philippines	3.70	9.9	1.92	5.16
Thailand	7.60	13.0	2.86	4.55
Latin American countries[b]				
(1950–96)				
Costa Rica	4.7	5.8	1.10	5.26
El Salvador	3.4	3.3	1.75	1.88
Guatemala	3.8	4.4	1.35	3.34
Honduras	3.8	2.7	3.70	0.73
Nicaragua	2.6	3.4	2.04	2.10
Mexico[c] (1968–83)	5.52	9.17	1.57	5.85
Mexico[c] (1984–99)	2.79	9.14	3.14	2.91
Mexico[d] (1973–85)	5.0	9.0	1.3	6.9
Mexico[d] (1986–98)	2.8	9.2	3.1	2.9

Sources:
[a] M. Ansari, N. Hashemzadeh and L. Xi, 'The Chronicle of Economic Growth in Southeast Asian Countries: Does Thirlwall's Law Provide an Adequate Explanation?', *Journal of Post Keynesian Economics*, Summer 2000.
[b] J. Moreno-Brid and E. Perez, 'Balance of Payments Constrained Growth in Central America', *Journal of Post Keynesian Economics*, Fall 1999.
[c] J. Moreno-Brid, 'Balance of Payments Constrained Economic Growth: The Case of Mexico', *Banca Nazionale del Lavoro Quarterly Review*, 207 (1998).
[d] P. Pacheco-López, 'The Impact of Trade Liberalisation on Exports, Imports, the Balance of Payments and Growth: The Case of Mexico', *Journal of Post Keynesian Economics*, Summer 2005.

CAPITAL FLOWS

So far we have assumed growth to be constrained by the necessity to preserve current account equilibrium on the balance of payments. In practice, of course, countries are allowed to run deficits, sometimes for substantial periods of time, financed by capital inflows from abroad from a variety of sources. The extent to which the value of imports can exceed the value of exports to finance a correspondingly higher level of income is determined by the *net* level of capital inflows. Thus we may write the equation for the overall balance of payments as

$$P_d X + C = P_f ME \tag{17.10}$$

where C measures net capital inflows (including reductions in foreign exchange reserves) in domestic currency. Taking the rates of change of this identity gives

$$\frac{E}{R}(p_d + x) + \frac{C}{R}(c) = p_f + m + e \tag{17.11}$$

where E/R and C/R represent the proportion of total receipts to finance the import bill that come from export earnings (E) and capital inflows (C), respectively. If we now substitute our expressions for x and m (equations (17.5) and (17.6)) into (17.11), we can solve for the growth rate associated with overall balance-of-payments equilibrium. This rate will depend on all the factors already mentioned, and on the rate of growth of *real* capital inflows. On substitution we obtain:

$$y = \frac{(1 + \dfrac{E}{R}\eta + \psi)(p_d - p_f - e) + \dfrac{E}{R}(\varepsilon[z]) + \dfrac{C}{R}(c - p_d)}{\pi} \qquad (17.12)$$

This model is known as the **extended version of the dynamic Harrod trade multiplier result** (that is, extended to allow for capital flows). Apart from the weight, E/R, attached to the two export elasticities, η and ε, the only difference between (17.12) and our earlier result in (17.8) is the addition of the last term ($c - p_d$) which measures the growth of *real* capital inflows (the growth of the nominal flows, c, minus the rate of domestic inflation, p_d). A positive growth of capital inflows will allow a country to grow faster than would be the case if it was constrained to maintain balance-of-payments equilibrium on the current account. On the other hand, it must be said that a continually positive rate of growth of capital inflows implies an *ever-growing* burden of debt, which is not sustainable in the long run (see Chapter 16, p. 498). Thus running current account deficits to finance growth is not a feasible option in the long run, and other long-run strategies must be pursued that relate to the determinants of the growth rate consistent with current account equilibrium.[4]

This model has been applied by Nureldin-Hussain (1999) to a sample of African and Asian countries over the period 1970–90, with interesting results (Table 17.3). Each country's growth rate (column (1)) is disaggregated into three components according to equation (17.12). The first is the terms-of-trade effect, the second is the export volume effect, and the third is the effect on growth of real capital inflows. It can be seen that the model fits remarkably well for most countries, but the contribution of the different effects differs between countries, and between the two continents of Africa and Asia. Africa has grown much more slowly than Asia, on average, and over one half of Africa's growth (excluding that arising from oil exports) has been financed by capital inflows. Movements in the terms of trade have had an adverse effect on growth in Africa. In Asia, by contrast, a much higher proportion of growth has been permitted by the rapid growth of exports, and terms-of-trade movements have had a favourable effect on growth.

Nureldin-Hussain (2001) has also used this balance-of-payments-constrained growth model with capital inflows as an alternative to the Harrod–Domar model for calculating the financing requirements if poverty in Africa is to be halved by the year 2015. He concludes that the growth rates required are simply not achievable given the capital inflows required. On average, capital inflows would have to be over 20 per cent of GDP.

Table 17.3 Estimates of extended version of dynamic Harrod foreign trade multiplier, 1970–90 (annual percentage average)

	Actual growth rate (1)	Terms of trade effect (A) (2)	Export volume effect (B) (3)	Real capital inflow effect (C) (4)	Predicted growth rate = ((A)+(B)+(C)) (5)
African countries					
Egypt	6.90	−2.37	4.36	7.31	9.30
Congo, Dem. Rep.	6.59	0.42	3.88	2.38	6.67
Kenya	6.24	−0.50	1.62	5.59	6.71
Mauritius	5.80	0.92	5.13	0.19	6.23
Tunisia	5.69	0.87	5.24	1.48	7.59
Burundi	5.60	1.69	3.21	−1.26	3.65
Cameroon	5.50	−1.12	7.08	0.00	5.97
Gabon	5.10	0.49	6.81	−0.04	7.33
Algeria	4.90	10.15	4.21	−8.72	5.64
Morocco	4.62	−1.34	2.83	3.47	4.96
Côte d'Ivoire	4.50	0.39	4.23	0.81	5.43
Lesotho	4.40	−3.43	6.62	1.55	4.74
Burkina Faso	4.20	−5.17	3.03	5.63	3.50
Somalia	3.40	−1.10	0.18	5.00	4.07
Zimbabwe	3.23	−2.40	2.23	−1.24	−1.41
Sudan	3.10	0.14	1.13	1.92	3.20
Benin	2.90	1.44	0.96	1.35	3.75
Tanzania	2.90	0.33	−0.55	5.01	4.79
Togo	2.90	0.08	2.31	0.61	3.00
Senegal	2.67	0.23	1.56	1.05	2.83
Nigeria	2.50	2.37	1.28	−1.17	2.48
South Africa	2.42	−1.03	1.32	7.74	8.03
Mauritania	2.30	0.68	1.58	0.42	2.69
Ethiopia	2.20	−0.09	0.74	2.53	3.17
Sierra Leone	1.58	−0.23	−0.67	2.65	1.75
Zambia	1.40	−0.31	−1.29	0.58	−1.02
Ghana	1.40	−3.81	0.15	2.88	−0.79
Niger	0.81	−5.07	1.79	3.47	0.20
Madagascar	0.48	−0.10	0.06	0.95	0.91
Average	3.66	−0.27	2.45	1.80	3.98
Average excluding oil exporters	3.40	−0.84	1.99	2.49	3.64
Asian countries					
Korea, Rep. of	9.11	−0.81	13.47	−2.49	10.17
Hong Kong	9.07	−0.07	8.34	1.01	9.28
Indonesia	10.76	1.82	3.18	5.76	7.58
China	8.20	−0.02	6.43	0.26	6.67
Malaysia	7.08	−0.69	6.60	2.21	8.12
Thailand	6.80	0.96	5.45	2.61	9.02
Pakistan	5.04	−0.44	4.28	4.40	8.24
India	4.31	−0.85	3.16	1.96	4.27
Sri Lanka	4.30	−0.65	2.33	3.00	4.68
Japan	4.20	−1.42	9.73	−4.63	3.68
Philippines	3.70	0.22	2.00	0.26	2.48
Average	6.60	−0.18	5.91	1.31	6.74
Average excluding Japan and Korea	6.58	0.03	4.46	2.39	6.70

Source: M. Nureldin-Hussain, 'The Balance of Payments Constraint and Growth Rate Differences among African and East Asian Economies', *African Development Review*, June 1999.

EXCHANGE RATE SYSTEMS FOR DEVELOPING COUNTRIES

All countries have a wide choice of exchange-rate systems, ranging from completely fixed to freely floating, with a number of options in between. Which system a developing country chooses must depend on its circumstances at the time; on what exchange-rate arrangements other countries are using, and on the long-run goals of economic policy. For example, a country may wish to pursue exchange rate stability because of the instability and perceived disadvantages of floating rates, in which case it will wish to choose some form of fixed exchange-rate regime. Alternatively, a country may wish to use its exchange rate to achieve various real objectives in the domestic economy, such as a faster rate of growth and full employment, and therefore sets a target for the *real* exchange. With changing domestic and foreign prices, a real exchange-rate target will require frequent variations in the nominal exchange rate, in which case the country will wish to choose some form of flexible exchange-rate regime. On the other hand, if inflation is the most serious problem within a country, currency depreciation to maintain a given real exchange rate may simply exacerbate inflation, and a country may wish to anchor its currency to that of another country or to simply adopt the currency of another country in order to gain monetary credibility. This would be an extreme form of exchange-rate pegging. Also there is the question of capital flows. If a country has liberalized its capital markets and the capital account of the balance of payments, and capital is free to move in and out, it will be difficult, if not impossible, for a country to pursue an exchange-rate target and operate an independent monetary policy at the same time. Capital outflows, for example, will cause a currency to depreciate in value. The only effective way to stop this is to raise domestic interest rates which depress the internal economy. The reverse dilemma occurs with capital inflows. The only way to reconcile internal and external equilibrium is either to control capital movements, or to allow the exchange rate to float. Theoretically, free floating allows a country to pursue a completely independent monetary policy geared to the goals of the domestic economy, but in practice no country is completely indifferent to the value of its exchange rate, particularly as it is a characteristic of the foreign-exchange market that exchange rates may considerably overshoot their true 'equilibrium' value. These are just a few examples of the considerations and conditions that countries need to bear in mind in choosing an exchange-rate regime.[5] The spectrum of alternatives, from hard pegs to floating is given in Table 17.4.

Each country must find its own solution, in the light of its own circumstances. The IMF generally respects a country's choice of exchange-rate regime, and gives advice to support that choice. The different options are discussed below, but the historical experience of the last 30 years or so points to three broad policy conclusions (Fischer, 2001):

- Intermediate positions between hard pegs and floating (what might be called 'soft' pegs) are not sustainable without capital controls.
- While countries have shifted from intermediate regimes to either end of the spectrum (more towards floating than hard pegs), a wide range of flexible rate arrangements still remains possible.
- Countries are not indifferent to exchange-rate movements, so independent floating is not an option and can be dangerous.

Table 17.4 Types of exchange-rate regime

Hard pegs	Intermediate regimes	Floating
Currency boards	Pegged exchange rates	Free float
Currency unions	Crawling peg	Managed float
Dollarization (or adopting the currency of another country)	Exchange rate band	
	Crawling band	

Let us now briefly consider the different types of exchange-rate regime listed in Table 17.4, and their advantages and disadvantages.

A **currency board** is an extreme form of hard peg that requires each unit of a country's currency to be backed by an equal amount of a reserve currency, such as the US dollar. The currency board system was widely practised in Africa under British rule before independence, and most recently Argentina decided to anchor its currency to the US dollar in this way. Linking a weak currency to a stronger currency can be a useful anti-inflation device to gain monetary credibility. Indeed, the system is reminiscent of the old Gold Standard system where the currency had to be backed up by gold, with the money supply expanding and contracting according to the balance of payments and changes in international reserves. The two major serious disadvantages of currency board systems are first that credit for entrepreneurs to invest is not elastic to the needs of trade (because it depends on the availability of dollar reserves), and secondly if the reserve currency appreciates in value, so too does the currency that is linked to it. This can cause serious problems of competitiveness with other trading partners, and damage exports and the balance of payments. Argentina went into serious recession with the appreciation of the US dollar in 2000–1, and the currency board was eventually abandoned.

Another extreme form of hard peg is a **currency union** where countries decide to adopt a common currency, so that by definition exchange rates between member countries of the union disappear. Countries may decide to enter a currency union if they feel that multiple currencies, exchange rate volatility, and uncertainty are seriously damaging trade, and that the overall benefits of surrendering monetary independence exceed the costs. The conditions for an **optimal currency area** in which the benefits to the members exceed the costs are that (1) economic cycles should be synchronized and economic shocks symmetrical so that a single monetary policy is suitable for all members; (2) labour and capital are freely mobile; (3) fiscal transfer mechanisms exist to help disadvantaged regions; and (4) multiple currencies are seriously damaging trade. It is never easy for a country to know whether the benefits will exceed the costs, and decisions are often taken on political as well as economic grounds. It is important to stress, however, that the fact that a country has no exchange rate to defend *vis-à-vis* its partners does not mean that the country avoids balance-of-payments problems; they just show up in a different form. If plans to import exceed plans to export, balance-of-payments difficulties will manifest themselves in falling output and rising unemployment, unless there are compensating capital transfers between the members of the currency union. The francophone countries of West Africa are part of a currency union that now uses the euro as the common currency, and the largest currency union in the world is now formed by twelve countries of the European Union using the euro as its common currency.

Another form of hard peg is to simply adopt the currency of another country, referred to as **dollarization** in the case of adopting the US dollar. As far as monetary and exchange-rate policy is concerned, the country becomes an adjunct to the country issuing the currency. This is a last resort for countries unable to manage their own affairs. In recent years, Ecuador and El Salvador have dollarized.

Pegged exchange rates are fixed exchange rates, but adjustable. This was the system set up at Bretton Woods in 1944 by which each country's currency was pegged to the US dollar, so that all bilateral rates of exchange between countries were also pegged. The system was called the 'adjustable peg system', however, because if countries found themselves in fundamental balance-of-payments disequilibrium, with unsustainable deficits, they were allowed to adjust the rate of exchange with the dollar and therefore other currencies too. The system gave exchange-rate stability, and avoided competitive devaluation by countries that characterized the beggar-thy-neighbour policies of the 1930s, but proved difficult to sustain in a world of increasing capital mobility. This is the problem for any country wishing to peg its exchange rate. If a currency is under pressure, the existence of a peg gives a one-way option for speculators. The currency markets anticipate that the peg can be adjusted only downwards, which then makes the currency vulnerable to speculative attacks. With large amounts of capital freely mobile it is very difficult to maintain a pegged rate while at the same time attempting to pursue an independent monetary policy, because the interest rate has to be used to defend the currency. It was largely speculative capital flows, and the inability of the United States to meet the promise of exchanging dollars for gold, that caused the international monetary system established at Bretton Woods to break down in 1972. Since then, other countries that have tried to peg rates have met with a similar fate. To quote Fischer (2001): 'in recent years, fixed or pegged exchange rates have been a major factor in every major emerging market financial crisis – Mexico at the end of 1994; Thailand, Indonesia and Korea in 1997; Russia and Brazil in 1998; Argentina and Turkey in 2000 . . . and 2001'.

If countries do decide to peg their exchange rate, there are three broad choices of peg: (1) pegging to a single currency such as the dollar, pound or euro, etc; (2) pegging to an individually tailored basket of currencies reflecting the trade of the country concerned; and (3) pegging to a common basket of currencies such as the SDR (Special Drawing Rights), which since 2001 has been a weighted basket of the world's four major currencies – the dollar, yen, euro and pound. The question is, which peg to choose? This will depend on what the country is trying to achieve. If it is macroeconomic stability, pegging against just one currency is unlikely to be optimal since movements in a country's exchange rate may bear no relation to its own balance of payments, but instead will move according to the balance of payments of the country that the currency is pegged to. Ideally, the pegged rate needs to balance out the effect of individual *bilateral* exchange-rate changes over the economy as a whole. This requires pegging to a basket of currencies where the weights should reflect the direction and elasticity of total trade (exports and imports) between the country and its trading partners. Pegging to a common basket of currencies, such as the SDR, is likely to be superior to pegging to just one currency, but inferior to an individually tailored basket of currencies.

To preserve the advantages of a fixed exchange rate, but to minimize the speculative pressures that can build up with the prospect of currency depreciation, there are various, more flexible, intermediate exchange-rate regimes.

One possibility is a **crawling peg**. Under a crawling peg, a country maintains its pegged exchange rate within agreed margins at a level equal to the moving average of the market exchange rate over an agreed previous time period. This allows a country's currency to drift gradually lower if circumstances warrant, and at the same time avoids both the upheaval of devaluation under an adjustable peg system and the possibility of excessive depreciation under free floating. To avoid speculation against the currency, the interest rate can be raised by a margin equal to the permitted rate of depreciation.

A variant of the crawling peg is an **exchange rate band** whereby the country allows the exchange rate to vary within a specified range. A **crawling band** allows the exchange rate band itself to move over time.

At the furthest extreme of flexibility is to allow a currency to float completely independently without any intervention at all. This implies that the country is completely indifferent to its exchange rate. In practice, no country can be indifferent if it is concerned with macro-stability. Exchange rates can overshoot wildly, which can be very disruptive, and a rapidly depreciating currency can be a serious source of inflation by raising the domestic price of imports. It is also worth pointing out that although free floating guarantees equilibrium in the foreign-exchange market by definition (because the exchange rate is the price that equilibrates the supply and demand for foreign exchange), it does *not* guarantee equilibrium on the current account of the balance of payments because the demand elasticities for imports and exports may not be of the right order of magnitude. This may then involve the unsustainable build-up of debt if deficits are financed by foreign borrowing. Although many countries claim to have moved towards greater exchange-rate flexibility in recent years, in practice they intervene. This is **managed floating**. Countries have no target rate of exchange, no peg, no official band, but they intervene on a daily basis according to circumstances. Managing the exchange rate is easier when there are controls on capital flows. Capital controls insulated China from the exchange-rate turmoil that hit many countries in South-East Asia in 1997 (see later). In 1998, Malaysia imposed capital controls in order to be able to manage its exchange rate more effectively (see Athukorala, 2001). Chile imposed for a short time a tax on capital inflows so that it could operate a policy of monetary contraction to control inflation without leading to destabilizing capital inflows.

Finally, it needs to be said that an optimal exchange-rate strategy for a developing country ought to recognize the **dual structure** of most countries and that a single exchange rate for all commodities may not be appropriate. Either a **dual exchange rate** is required, or some system of taxes and subsidies to achieve the same effect.[6] Under a dual exchange rate system a fixed (official) rate could apply to primary commodity exports (and to essential imports to keep their domestic price low) and a free (devalued) rate could apply to manufactured exports with a high price elasticity of demand (and to inessential imports). With a foreign exchange shortage, the free rate would produce a domestic price of foreign exchange well above the official rate. The higher the free rate, or the greater the degree of devaluation, the greater the stimulation of manufactured exports and the greater the discouragement of inessential imports.

The main administrative problem with dual exchange rates is to separate the two markets, to ensure that export proceeds from primary commodity exports are surrendered at the official rate and that foreign exchange bought at the official rate is used for essential imports. The former can be achieved through state marketing boards, the latter through strict licensing. Currency auctions – selling foreign exchange for non-essential purposes to the highest bidder – is another form of dual (or multiple) exchange rate policy. In the early days of the IMF, dual and multiple exchange rates were discouraged and frowned upon as interfering with free trade and exchange, but in more recent years greater tolerance has been shown. In 1997, as many as 20 developing countries were practising dual or multiple exchange rates applying to different current or capital transactions.

Recent research on the relation between the exchange-rate regime adopted by countries and the functioning of the real economy shows the following:

■ Under pegged regimes, inflation is lower, the growth of output is not affected, but output volatility is higher than under flexible exchange rate regimes (Ghosh, Gulde and Wolf, 2002).

■ Pegged regimes are more prone to currency crises than floating exchange-rate regimes, particularly in countries more integrated with international financial markets, but intermediate regimes are even more prone to crisis than the bi-polar extremes of hard pegs or free floating (Bubala and Otker-Robe, 2004)

■ Countries with flexible exchange-rate regimes absorb terms of trade shocks more easily than countries with fixed exchange-rate regimes, so that output is less volatile (Broda, 2004).

The countries currently pursuing different types of exchange-rate regime are shown in Table 17.5.

THE EAST ASIAN FINANCIAL CRISIS: A CAUTIONARY TALE[7]

The financial crisis in East Asia erupted in July 1997 when pressure on the Thai baht became so severe that the government was compelled to cease defending the fixed exchange rate and to allow the currency to float, in order to avoid defaulting on its international obligations. There was rapid contagion throughout the region leading to a collapse of the currencies of Thailand, Indonesia, Malaysia, the Philippines and Korea (the Asia-5) within a matter of weeks. Accompanying the currency collapse were steep falls in the stock markets of these countries, which spread to other economies such as Singapore and Hong Kong whose currencies remained relatively stable. The turmoil rapidly turned into a major world financial crisis and not only had a dramatic effect on the region's growth performance, but also substantially reduced world economic growth. What happened in East Asia in 1997 provides an illuminating case study, and cautionary tale, of the danger to countries of attempting to run large balance-of-payments deficits financed by short-term capital inflows, while at the same time trying to maintain a fixed exchange rate. Even more remarkable is that the IMF did not see the crisis looming.

The question is, why did this region, previously described by economists and commentators as representing a 'growth miracle', plunge into one of the world's most serious recessions of the postwar period? The traditional explanations of fiscal profligacy and macroeconomic instability, which plagued Latin America in the 1980s and 1990s, can

Table 17.5 Countries classified by exchange-rate regime

Exchange-rate regime (number of countries)	Exchange-rate anchor			
			CEA franc zone	
Exchange arrangements with no separate legal tender (41)	*Another currency as legal tender*	*ECCU**	*WAEMU**	*CAEMC**
	Ecuador	Antigua and	Benin	Cameroon
	El Salvador	Barbados	Burkina Faso	Central African
	Kiribati	Dominica	Côte d'Ivoire	Rep.
	Marshall	Grenada	Guinea-Bissau	Chad
	Islands	St. Kitts and	Mali	Congo Rep. of
	Micronesia	Nevis	Niger	Equatorial
	Palau	St. Lucia	Senegal	Guinea
	Panama	St. Vincent	Togo	Gabon
	San Marino	and the		
	Timor-Leste	Grenadines		
Currency board arrangements (7)	Bosnia and Herzegovina			
	Brunei Darussalam			
	Bulgaria			
	China—Hong Kong, SAR			
	Djibouti			
	Estonia			
	Lithuania			

* CAEMC = Central African Economic and Monetary Community; ECCU = Eastern Caribbean Currency Union; WAEMU = West African Economic and Monetary Union

Exchange-rate regime (number of countries)	Exchange-rate anchor	
Other conventional fixed peg arrangements (42)	*Against a single currency (33)*	*Against a composite (9)*
	Aruba	Botswana
	Bahamas, The	Fiji
	Bahrain	Latvia
	Bangladesh	Libya
	Barbados	Malta
	Belize	Morocco
	Bhutan	Samoa
	Cape Verde	Seychelles
	China	Vanuatu
	Comoros	
	Eritrea	
	Guinea	
	Jordan	
	Kuwait	
	Lebanon	
	Lesotho	
	Macedonia, FYR	
	Malaysia	
	Maldives	
	Namibia	
	Nepal	
	Netherlands Antilles	
	Oman	
	Qatar	
	Saudi Arabia	
	Suriname	
	Swaziland	
	Syrian Arab Republic	
	Turkmenistan	
	Ukraine	
	United Arab Emirates	
	Venezuela	
	Zimbabwe	

Table 17.5 continued

Exchange-rate regime (number of countries)	Exchange-rate anchor			
Pegged exchange rates within horizontal bands (5)	*Within a cooperative arrangement* ERM II (1) Denmark	*Other band arrangements (4)* Cyprus Hungary Sudan Tonga		
Crawling pegs (5)	Bolivia Costa Rica Nicaragua Solomon Islands Tunisia			
Exchange rates within crawling bands (5)	Belarus Honduras Israel Romania Slovenia			
Managed floating with no pre-announced path for the exchange rate (46)	Afghanistan Algeria Angola Argentina Azerbaijan Burundi Cambodia Croatia Czech Rep. Dominican Rep. Egypt Ethiopia Gambia, The	Ghana Guatemala Guyana Haiti India Indonesia Iran, I.R. of Iraq Jamaica Kazakhstan Kenya Kyrgyz Republic Lao P.D.R.	Mauritania Mauritius Moldova Mongolia Myanmar Nigeria Pakistan Paraguay Russian Federation Rwanda São Tomé and Príncipe	Serbia and Montenegro Singapore Slovak Rep. Tajikistan Thailand Trinidad and Tobago Uzbekistan Vietnam Zambia
Independently floating (36)	Albania Armenia Australia Brazil Canada Chile Colombia Congo, Dem. Rep. of Georgia	Iceland Japan Korea Liberia Madagascar Malawi Mexico Mozambique New Zealand Norway	Papua New Guinea Peru Philippines Poland Sierra Leone Sri Lanka Somalia South Africa Sweden	Switzerland Tanzania Turkey Uganda United Kingdom United States Uruguay Yemen, Rep. of

Source: IMF, *Annual Report 2003* (Washington, DC: IMF).

be ruled out. In East Asia, most of the important macroeconomic indicators were generally healthy. The fiscal balance was generally in surplus; inflation was low, and domestic savings and investment as a proportion of GDP were among the highest in the world. There had been for some time, however, a major imbalance in the external accounts of the Asia-5 countries. As we argued earlier in the chapter, no country in the long run can grow faster than that rate compatible with equilibrium on the current account of the balance of payments unless it can finance ever-growing deficits – which, in general, it cannot. The East Asian crisis was mainly the result of unsustainable balance-of-payments deficits financed by short-term, volatile capital inflows, and exacerbated by weak (internal) financial structures and imprudent lending.

The balance-of-payments deficits (and the deficits as a proportion of GDP) of the Asia-5 countries from 1992 to 1998 are shown in Table 17.6.

Table 17.6 Balance of payments on current account, 1992–8 ($million and % of GDP)

Countries	1992	1993	1994	1995	1996	1997	1998
Thailand	−6,304	−6,159	−7,862	−13,248	−14,380	−3,130	13,500
	(−5.7)	(−4.9)	(−5.4)	(−7.9)	(−7.9)	(−2.0)	(11.5)
Indonesia	−2,780	−2,940	−3,488	−6,987	−8,069	−1,698	1,423
	(−2.0)	(−1.9)	(−2.0)	(−3.4)	(−3.4)	(−1.4)	(1.1)
Philippines	−858	−3,016	−2,950	−1,980	−3,953	−4,351	1,300
	(−1.6)	(−5.5)	(−4.6)	(−2.7)	(−4.7)	(−5.3)	(2.0)
Malaysia	−2,167	−2,991	−4,521	−8,470	−4,956	−4,791	5,113
	(−3.7)	(−4.7)	(−6.2)	(−9.7)	(−5.0)	(−5.3)	(8.1)
Korea	−3,939	939	−3,868	−8,507	−23,005	−8,167	40,039
	(−1.3)	(−0.3)	(−1.0)	(−1.9)	(−4.7)	(−1.8)	(13.2)

Source: *Asian Development Outlook, 1998* (Manila: Asian Development Bank, 1998).

It can be seen that the deficits as a percentage of GDP were averaging between 2 and 10 per cent in the years preceding the crisis. From historical experience, and more recent experience in Latin America, the maximum sustainable deficit to GDP ratio seems to be of the order of 2–3 per cent (depending on circumstances), beyond which the financial markets start to get nervous, for understandable reasons. If the deficits are financed by debt-creating flows (such as commercial bank lending, and non-bank private lending), the external debt to GDP ratio will start to rise, and the ratio of debt-service payments to export earnings is also likely to increase. Countries become increasingly vulnerable to external shocks, with the possibility of capital flight if the debt is privately held, and the prospect of debt default if the debt is publicly held. Ultimately, all debt must be repaid which requires balance-of-payments surpluses.

The prevailing academic orthodoxy in the 1980s, and endorsed by the IMF, used to be that current account balance-of-payments deficits should not be regarded as a problem as long as they are not associated with a government fiscal deficit. In these circumstances, international payments deficits are merely a private matter among consenting agents concerning the intertemporal distribution of consumption. The crisis in East Asia has shown this view to be grossly misleading. In the four years preceding the crisis year of 1997, there was no fiscal deficit in any of the Asia-5 countries. What the orthodoxy always ignored was the fragility of situations in which the fast growth of output is fuelled by debt-creating flows which must be serviced and repaid in *foreign* currency, and in which capital can flow out as quickly as it flows in, with all the implications this has for the stability of the currency and the high interest rates necessary to contain currency contagion which have such damaging effects on the real economy. The degree to which balance-of-payments deficits are sustainable will partly depend on the nature of the capital inflows. There are at least four major types of capital inflows each with their own characteristics and associated problems: official flows; foreign direct investment (FDI); portfolio investment; and commercial lending by banks and other institutions. Table 17.7 gives figures on the relative importance of these flows in the Asia-5 countries in the lead-up to the crisis.

Table 17.7 External financing of deficits in Asia-5 countries, 1994–7 ($billion)

	1994	1995	1996	1997
Net external financing	47.4	80.9	92.8	15.2
FDI	4.7	4.9	7.0	7.2
Portfolio flows	7.6	10.6	12.1	−11.6
Commercial bank lending	24.0	49.4	55.5	−21.3
Non-bank lending	4.2	12.4	18.4	13.7
Net official flows	7.0	3.6	−0.2	27.2

Source: UNCTAD, *Trade and Development Report 1998* (Geneva: UNCTAD, 1998).

Official flows are the most helpful in financing deficits because the repayment terms are the most favourable, but they played only a minor role up to 1997, and were negative in 1996. But when the crisis hit in 1997, they predominated. FDI can also be advantageous because it represents more stable, longer-term investment which does not involve any fixed future repayment obligation as with borrowing. In the high growth period of the early 1990s and right up to 1997, all the Asia-5 countries, and particularly Malaysia, were receiving considerable inflows of direct investment which helped to sustain deficits. The other two categories of flow are much more volatile. During the 1990s there was a massive influx of short-term capital inflows into the Asia-5 countries, made possible by financial liberalization. These flows – portfolio investment and various types of private lending – rose from $36 billion in 1994 to $86 billion in 1996. Volatile flows constituted over 60 per cent of external financing in the years prior to 1997. The proximinate cause of the financial crisis was the rapid reversal of these short-term capital inflows. Thus, two questions need to be answered for an understanding of the crisis and the future. First, what was the cause of the increasingly large capital flows in the years immediately preceding the crisis – or to put it another way, how were these countries able to finance ever-growing balance-of-payments deficits (at least for a time!)? Secondly, why was there sudden capital flight?

The answer to the first question is that in the early 1990s East Asia proved to be an attractive home for foreign capital, for a number of reasons. The countries had either implicitly or explicitly linked their exchange rate to the US dollar and were committed to defending this relationship. This had, in the eyes of many foreign lenders and East Asian borrowers, removed the element of risk owing to a fall in the exchange rate. There was also an expectation that the governments would always bail out any of the large financial institutions or firms that got into trouble. Financial crises in Thailand and Malaysia in the mid-1980s and Indonesia in 1994 had been resolved by government intervention and bailouts, which confirmed the view that the governments were implicitly underwriting the domestic financial institutions and firms. This weakened market discipline on the banks – if the government implicitly guarantees deposits, there is no need for investors to withdraw them even if they believe the bank is behaving recklessly in, say, its lending policies.

The perception of the region as one subject to sustained fast growth with high rates of return led to a flood of foreign capital. Liberalization also led to greater borrowing from abroad by East Asian banks and firms. The belief that the exchange rate was fixed meant that there was no need to hedge, and created a bias towards short-term borrowing. The large borrowing from abroad by the East Asian corporations was also due to the high cost of intermediation by the region's domestic banking system. It was cheaper to raise funds from abroad.

The problem, which was not appreciated until it was too late, was that the rapid liberalization of the capital markets exposed some severe shortcomings of the East Asian financial system that became apparent only with the benefit of hindsight. The problem was that much of the financial intermediation was through the banking system. There were well-developed stock markets, but bond and other security markets were under-developed and thus external corporate financing was largely through the banking system. The debt–equity ratios were high throughout the region, and in the case of Korea reached 3.55 in 1996–7. The problem was that the banking system showed some fundamental weaknesses that in earlier years had been papered over by fast growth and had not been subject to the sentiments of the international capital markets. The capital-adequacy ratios of the banks were low, the legal limits on lending to single individuals or a related group were unsatisfactory and not strictly enforced and there was a lack of transparency in the banks' operations. As the World Bank (1998) commented:

> Weak governance of banks, often influenced directly or indirectly by government policies, added to the poor performance. Perhaps the most important weakness was the limited institutional development of banks. Much lending, for example, was done on a collateral basis, rather than on a cash flow basis, thus obfuscating the need to analyse the profitability and riskiness of the underlying projects. Credit tended to flow to borrowers with relationships to government or private bank owners and to favoured sectors, rather than on the basis of projected cash flows, realistic sensitivity analysis and recoverable collateral values.

The problem was concealed to a certain extent by the fact that the banks appeared to be profitable. The World Bank noted that the 'costs to income ratios . . . did not suggest gross inefficiencies.' However, the fact that there were explicit government guarantees leads to the problem of 'moral hazard'. Since banks and companies are not likely to bear the cost of any failure, there is the temptation for them to go for high return but risky investments. If the investments fail, they will not have to bear the cost, which will be picked up by the government.[8]

Thus, the explanation of the crisis is that in the early 1990s the massive capital inflows led to imprudent lending by the domestic banks, and a rapid expansion in credit, leading to asset and real estate bubbles. The latter encouraged even further capital inflows. However, once market sentiment changed, a self-fulfilling prophecy developed leading to a vicious circle of capital flight, falling exchange rates and a collapse in the regional stock exchanges. Once capital begins to move out of the region and the exchange rate begins to fall, no one wants to be caught holding assets valued in domestic currency. The capital loss caused by a depreciating currency can far outweigh any possible gains in higher returns, or in higher interest rates that are imposed to try to restore confidence. The fact that much of the foreign borrowing was short-term meant that the outflows were rapid. Moreover, they could not be covered by reserves. The ratio of short-term debt to reserves was 2.1 in Korea, 1.7 in Indonesia, 1.5 in Thailand, 0.8 in the Philippines and 0.6 in Malaysia.

A powder keg was being built, ready to explode at the slightest provocation. All that was required for the crisis was a trigger: and Thailand provided the trigger. First, through economic mismanagement Thailand had locked up most of its foreign reserves in forward contracts so that instead of $30 billion at their disposal, as the markets initially thought, there was only $1.4 billion available, equal to just two days' imports. Secondly, the country's struggling financial institutions had outstanding loans of over $8 billion from the Central Bank. The costs of supporting these institutions became so high that, at the end of June, the Thai government announced that it would no longer continue to support Finance One, the country's largest finance house that had been absorbing vast amounts of government loans. At a stroke, this announcement effectively revoked the government's commitment to act as a lender of last resort and sent the risk premium sky high. It is no coincidence that five days after this announcement the Thai government was forced to float the baht rather than default on its international loans. Once one country has abandoned its commitment to defending its exchange rate and bailing out its poorly performing banks, it becomes easier for other countries to do the same (the international opprobrium on subsequent countries' reputations is greatly reduced). Thus, the international markets also became increasingly nervous about the other countries, and the crisis spread.

This, in a nutshell, is the story. What the East Asia financial crisis exposed was some fundamental weaknesses in the Asian growth process, although not the underlying factors that gave rise to rapid growth rates in the first place. Particularly it showed the danger (and this is a warning to other countries) of the rapid liberalization of international capital flows before the domestic banking system has developed sufficient regulatory control, and of financing ever-growing balance-of-payments deficits relative to GDP by increasingly short-term capital flows. The balance of payments becomes the ultimate constraint on the growth performance of nations.

THE INTERNATIONAL MONETARY SYSTEM AND DEVELOPING COUNTRIES

The world's international monetary system is governed largely by the International Monetary Fund, which was established at Bretton Woods in 1944 in the aftermath of the great depression of the 1920s and 1930s and in preparation for the peace after the Second World War. There was a fear that the protectionism and beggar-thy-neighbour policies that characterized the period after the First World War would rear their ugly heads again, to the detriment of the world economy at large, if not all the individual countries within it. Thus the IMF was originally conceived as an institution for stabilizing the world economy, rather than as an agency for development, providing short-term loans to member countries in temporary balance-of-payments difficulties. Responsibility for development was given to the IMF's sister institution, the World Bank, established at the same time. Because the IMF was not allowed to create money, John Maynard Keynes (one of the architects of the IMF) used to complain (and joke) that his proposal for a bank had become a fund, and what was in fact a fund had been called a bank!

Over the years, however, and particularly in recent years, the role of the IMF has changed. It has increasingly become the bank manager of the poor countries, and much more of a development agency, advancing longer-term loans to cover what are now perceived as longer-term structural balance-of-payments difficulties. The role of the World Bank has also been changing, and now it too provides loans as a means of balance-of-payments support (the traditional preserve of the IMF), for programmes of structural adjustment (see Chapter 15). In turn, the IMF instituted a Structural Adjustment Facility in 1986, and in 1987 an Enhanced Structural Adjustment Facility (see later). The roles of the IMF and the World Bank have almost merged, reflecting the fact that the balance of payments is the principal long-run constraint on the growth of output in developing countries.

The IMF and World Bank also roughly agree on the same policies and reforms that should be applied in developing countries – often referred to as the **Washington Consensus**. The term 'Washington Consensus' was originally coined by John Williamson of the Institute for International Economics in 1989 to refer to an agenda for reform in Latin America which he believed the IMF and World Bank would endorse (see Williamson 1990, 1993). The reforms quickly came to be seen as a model for the wider developing world. The package of reforms suggested by Williamson consisted of the following:

- Fiscal discipline
- Redirection of public expenditure towards education, health, and infrastructure investment
- Tax reform – broadening the tax base and cutting marginal tax rates
- Interest rates that are market determined and positive (but moderate) in real terms
- Competitive exchange rates
- Trade liberalization – replacement of quantitative restrictions with low and uniform tariffs
- Openness to foreign direct investment
- Privatization of state enterprises
- Deregulation – abolition of regulations that impede entry or restrict competition, except for those justified on safety, environmental, and consumer protection grounds, and prudential oversight of financial institutions
- Legal security for property rights.

The Consensus extols the virtues of the free market and free trade for the achievement of more rapid economic progress (see Taylor, 1997), but Williamson objects to the interpretation of the Consensus as 'neoliberal' because neoliberalism also embraces a political ideology relating to minimal state interference in economic and social affairs; low tax rates; individualism, and a general indifference to the income distribution produced by market forces.

The wisdom of the Consensus was always a matter of dispute among economists, but its initial appeal did not last long because in the 1990s several developing countries that adopted the package of reforms, under pressure from the IMF and World Bank, suffered severe financial and economic crises which toppled governments, reduced living standards and left millions of people worse off. Free market forces turned out to be as disruptive and destructive as government regulations and controls. Economists now question the pace and sequencing of deregulation and the liberalization of markets, and call for stronger domestic institutions and policies to be put in place before countries open up to floods of imports and capital inflows. The need to mix institution-building with the freeing of markets is sometimes called the **Post-Washington Consensus**. The ideology, and practical policy-making, of the IMF and World Bank, however, have hardly changed.

One country that has resisted the pressure of the Washington Consensus is China. It has forged its own development strategy, which does not allow the economy to be buffeted by the unfettered forces of free market capitalism, either domestic or international. It is called the **Beijing Consensus**, and is becoming increasingly attractive to other (large) developing countries (e.g. Brazil) looking for an alternative approach to economic policy making which puts the needs of people first, not the interests of bankers and international speculators. China's declared goal is to achieve fast, sustainable growth, combined with equity and poverty reduction. China recognizes that to achieve this requires a degree of economic independence to insulate it from turbulence in the world economy. This makes it cautious about free trade and the free movement of international capital, although not about attracting long-term foreign direct investment. China is fortunate to be large enough (and stable enough) to go its own way. Many developing countries are either too small, too vulnerable or too unstable to resist the orthodoxy because they are dependent on loan support from the IMF and World Bank.

HOW THE IMF WORKS

The IMF is basically a lending institution. It is a source of four main forms of financial assistance, or liquidity, to developing countries:

- Drawings from the ordinary facilities provided by the IMF
- Drawings made under special facilities
- Facilities for low-income countries
- The periodic issue of Special Drawing Rights (SDRs).

Members' drawing rights, their share of SDR allocations, and indeed their subscription to the IMF and voting power are all based on **quotas**. Every member must subscribe to the IMF an amount equal to its quota – 25 per cent in the form of reserve assets and the remainder in local currency. Initial quotas are based on a formula relating to the economic circumstances of individual countries, such as living standards, importance in world trade and so forth, and are then modified in various ways in the light of the conditions and quotas of other countries. The United States has the largest quota, amounting at present to 37 billion SDRs in 2003 out of the total value of quota subscriptions of 212 billion SDRs. When countries draw on the Fund they buy the currency they need with their own currency, and when they repay they repurchase their own currency with foreign currency acceptable to the IMF. The size of the quotas comes under continual review. Under the 11th General Review of Quotas in 1997, a 45 per cent increase was agreed, which came into effect in 1999.

The IMF may supplement its quota resources by borrowing any country's currency. This was institutionalised by the **General Agreement to Borrow (GAB)** in January 1962, which was a four-year arrangement concluded with 10 industrialized countries. Since then the General Agreement to Borrow has been extended several times, and was activated most recently to help Russia. The IMF also borrows from the private capital market and makes bilateral deals with countries.

The IMF also borrows to finance special facilities as a means of recycling the balance-of-payments surpluses of some member countries. The IMF argues that while it has no desire to supplant ordinary commercial banks in the recycling process, its ability to advocate adjustment policies effectively and convincingly in deficit countries is enhanced by the capacity to make substantial financial resources available to member countries. Thus while the IMF continues to place reliance on quota subscriptions as the main source of its finance, it is also in the market to borrow. Now that the IMF sees its role as providing larger amounts of finance over longer and longer periods for countries with chronically weak balance of payments in relation to their growth objectives, it has an ever growing need for resources.

A country making use of the IMF's resources is generally required to carry out a programme of balance-of-payments adjustment as a condition of support. This requirement is known as **conditionality** and reflects the IMF principle that financing and adjustment must go hand in hand. What constitutes balance-of-payments equilibrium is not rigidly defined. It need not mean current-account equilibrium, but the measure must be defined free of restrictions on trade and payments in keeping with the underlying liberal free trade philosophy of the IMF. The enforced programmes of balance-of-payments adjustment typically consist of currency devaluation and restrictions on government expenditure and the money supply, coupled with the liberalization of trade and capital movements.

These conditionality practices, which were developed during the 1950s and 1960s under pressure from the United States, have been severely criticized (see below) and have undergone continual review. They are harsh, but perhaps less harsh than they were. Countries are encouraged to approach the IMF early before payments problems become acute, and the Fund recognizes the need for a longer adjustment period. When helping countries to design adjustment programmes, the Fund is supposed to have due regard to the social, economic and political characteristics of the country concerned (although there is still not much evidence of this). The Fund now recognizes that balance-of-payments difficulties associated with an acceptable growth of output may have as much to do with the structural characteristics of a country as with relative price distortions and excessive government expenditure. The emphasis has also shifted from demand contraction to supply-side policies to increase the efficiency of resource allocation and supply potential.[9]

ORDINARY DRAWING RIGHTS

Ordinary IMF drawing rights consist of two elements:

- The **gold or reserve tranche** which usually represents 25 per cent of a member's quota and is equivalent to that part of its quota not paid in its own currency.
- The **credit tranche**, which is officially equal to 100 per cent of a member's quota, but can go beyond.

The credit tranche is split into four parts, and access to higher tranches becomes progressively more difficult and expensive. No conditionality is attached to reserve tranche drawings, except balance-of-payments need. In the case of credit tranche drawings, the conditions attached to the first tranche normally consist of devising a programme that demonstrates a reasonable attempt to overcome balance-of-payments difficulties. Requests for purchases of currency in the higher credit tranches require substantial justification. The purchases here are almost always made under **stand-by arrangements** rather than directly, and certain performance criteria relating to government expenditure and money supply targets must normally be met before resources are released. A strong programme is required to rectify a balance-of-payments disequilibrium. Typically, stand-by arrangements cover a 12–18-month period (although they can extend up to three years) and repayments are made within 3–5 years of each drawing.

EXTENDED FUND FACILITY (EFF)

The Extended Fund Facility (EFF) was established in 1974 to allow developing countries to borrow beyond their quotas over longer periods than are allowed under ordinary drawing rights. The EFF arrangement gives members assistance for up to 3 years, with repayment provisions extending over a range of 4–10 years. Drawings under the EFF may be more than 100 per cent of a country's quota over a 3-year period, but the conditions are stringent. The country must provide a detailed statement of policies and measures every 12 months. The resources are provided in instalments, with performance criteria attached. Nonetheless the facility represented an important and significant shift in emphasis from viewing the balance of payments as a stabilization problem, to recognizing the balance of payments as a fundamental long-term constraint on growth that cannot be rectified in a short period of time, if ever. Drawings over the period 1974–2003 amounted to over 50 billion SDRs.

Standby and extended arrangements are the most important source of IMF support for developing countries' balance of payments, but other special IMF facilities have become increasingly important. Total outstanding credit under each facility from 1998–2003 is shown in Table 17.8.

Table 17.8 Outstanding IMF credit by facility and policy, 1998—2003

	1998	1999	2000	2001	2002	2003
	Millions of SDRs					
Stand-By Arrangements	25,526	25,213	21,410	17,101	28,612	34,241
Extended Arrangements	12,521	16,574	16,808	16,108	15,538	14,981
Supplemental Reserve Facility	7,100	12,655	–	4,085	5,875	15,700
Compensatory and Contingency Financing Facility	685	2,845	3,032	2,992	745	413
Systemic Transformation Facility	3,869	3,364	2,718	1,933	1,311	644
Subtotal (GRA)	**49,701**	**60,651**	**43,968**	**42,219**	**52,081**	**65,978**
SAF Arrangements	730	565	456	432	341	137
PRGF Arrangements	5,505	5,870	5,857	5,951	6,188	6,676
Trust Fund	90	89	89	89	89	89
Total	**56,026**	**67,175**	**50,370**	**48,691**	**58,699**	**72,879**

Notes: GRA General Reserve Account; SAF Structural Adjustment Facility; PRGF Poverty Reduction and Growth Facility.
Source: IMF, *Annual Report 2003* (Washington, DC: IMF, 2003).

SPECIAL FACILITIES

Apart from the ordinary drawing rights, developing countries have access to a number of special facilities that may exist at a particular time to assist them with development difficulties arising from balance-of-payments problems. At present there are four main special facilities – the Compensatory Financing Facility (CFF); the Supplemental Reserve Facility (SRF); the Contingent Credit Line (CCL), and Emergency Assistance. In addition, there is the Poverty Reduction and Growth Facility (PRGF) for low income countries.

As of 2003, the guidelines on the scale of IMF assistance allow member countries annual access to fund resources of up to 100 per cent of their quotas, and cumulative access, net of scheduled repayments, of up to 300 per cent of their quotas. These drawings exclude drawings under all the various special facilities (see below). All assistance is related to quotas, but quotas, of course, may bear no relation to need. Let us now consider the working of these special facilities.

COMPENSATORY FINANCING FACILITY (CFF)

The CFF was the first special facility established by the IMF to compensate developing countries for shortfalls of export earnings below a 5-year trend centred on the middle year. In 1988 it changed its name to the Compensatory and Contingency Financing Facility, but 'Contingency' was dropped in 2000. Originally the facility enabled a country to draw up to 25 per cent of its quota, provided the shortfall was temporary, but now it can draw up to 45 per cent, in addition to drawings made under tranche facilities.

In 1979 shortfalls in receipts from travel and workers' remittances were included in the compensation scheme, and in 1981 it was extended to cover the increased cost of imported cereals, calculated as the cost of such imports in a given year less their average cost for 5 years, centred on that year. An optional tranche is also available to cover other unforeseen contingencies. Between 1963 and 1996 over 20 billion SDRs were drawn in total, but since the mid-1990s the Facility has not been used much. Table 17.8 shows the drawings since 1998.

EMERGENCY ASSISTANCE

Since 1962 the Fund has provided quick, medium-term assistance to countries with balance-of-payments difficulties related to natural disasters; and since 1995 to countries suffering from the aftermath of civil unrest or international armed conflict. Countries may borrow up to 25 per cent of quota, or 50 per cent in exceptional circumstances, with repayment over 3 to 5 years.

SUPPLEMENTAL RESERVE FACILITY (SRF)

The SRF was established in 1997 in response to the East Asian financial crisis discussed earlier. Its focus is on the capital account of the balance of payments, and is intended to help member countries experiencing exceptional balance-of-payments problems resulting from a sudden loss of market confidence. Access under the SRF is not subject to the usual quota limits but is based on the country's financing needs, its ability to repay the IMF, and the policies it is pursuing to restore confidence. Repayment must be made within 3 years of drawing.

CONTINGENT CREDIT LINES (CCL)

The CCL facility was set up in 1999 for countries anticipating a financial crisis leading to outflows on capital account. It is essentially a precautionary line of credit to help prevent contagion. Drawings are not expected to be made unless a crisis actually strikes. The repayment period is the same as for the SRF.

POVERTY REDUCTION AND GROWTH FACILITY (PRGF)

The PRGF was established in 1999 to replace the Enhanced Structural Adjustment Facility (ESAF) which was the IMF's concessional financing facility to assist poor countries facing persistent balance-of-payments problems. The idea was to give the ESAF a more explicit anti-poverty focus in keeping with the new emphasis of the IMF and World Bank on poverty reduction – hence the change of name. Programmes supported under the PRGF are expected to be based on a strategy designed by the borrower to reduce poverty in collaboration with civil society and the various organizations concerned with development. It is designed to work alongside the Highly Indebted Poor Country (HIPC) initiative of the IMF and World Bank (see Chapter 15, p. 503) for debt relief for poor countries that require the preparation of Poverty Reduction Strategy Papers. Under the PRGF facility, 80 low-income countries are eligible for assistance and may borrow up to 140 per cent of quota under a 3-year arrangement with an interest rate of 0.5 per cent and repayments made between 5 1/2 and 10 years after disbursement. By 2003, 31 countries were already being supported by borrowings of over six billion SDRs.

The amount of drawing under each of the facilities mentioned above, as a percentage of each member's quota, is shown in Table 17.9. In Case example 17.1 there is a summary of the financial assistance that the IMF gives and the conditions it imposes.

Table 17.9 Access limits to IMF facilities, 2003 (per cent of member's quota)

Standby and Extended Arrangements[1]	
Annual	100
Cumulative	300
Special Facilities	
Supplemental Reserve Facility/Contingent Credit Lines	None[2]
Compensatory Financing Facility[3]	
Export earnings shortfall	45
Excess cereal import costs	45
Poverty Reduction and Growth Facility	
3-year access	
Regular	140
Exceptional	185

[1] Under exceptional circumstances, these limits may be exceeded.
[2] However, access under CCL is expected to be in the range of 300–500 per cent of quota.
[3] Combined limit of 55 percent for both components.
Source: *IMF Annual Report 2003* (Washington, DC: IMF, 2003).

IMF Financial Facilities, 2002

Credit facility	Purpose	Conditions	Access limits
Credit tranches and Extended Fund Facility			
Stand-By Arrangements (1952)	Medium-term assistance for countries with balance-of-payments difficulties of a short-term character	Adopt policies that provide confidence that the member's balance-of-payments difficulties will be resolved within a reasonable period	Annual: 100% of quota; cumulative; 300% of quota
Extended Fund Facility (1974) (Extended Arrangements)	Longer-term assistance to support members' structural reforms to address balance-of-payments difficulties of a long-term character.	Adopt 3-year programme, with structural agenda, with annual detailed statement of policies for the next 12 months	Annual: 100% of quota; cumulative; 300% of quota
Special facilities			
Supplemental Reserve Facility (1997)	Short-term assistance for balance-of-payments difficulties related to crises of market confidence	Available only in context of Stand-By or Extended Arrangements with associated programme and with strengthened policies to address loss of market confidence	No access limits; access under the facility only when access under associated regular arrangement would otherwise exceed either annual or cumulative limit
Contingent Credit-Line (1999)	Precautionary line of defence that would be made readily available against balance-of-payments difficulties arising from contagion	Eligibility criteria: (1) absence of balance-of-payments need from the outset, (2) positive assessment of policies by the IMF, (3) constructive relations with private creditors and satisfactory progress in limiting external vulnerability, (4) satisfactory economic programme	No access limits, but commitments are expected to be in the range of 300–500% of quota
Compensatory Financing Facility (1963)	Medium-term assistance for temporary export shortfalls or cereal import excesses.	Available only when the shortfall/excess is largely beyond the control of the authorities and a member has an arrangement with upper credit tranche conditionality, or when its balance-of-payments position excluding the shortfall/excess is satisfactory	45% of quota each for export and cereal components; combined limit of 55% of quota for both components
Emergency Assistance	Quick, medium-term assistance for balance-of-payments difficulties related to:		Generally limited to 25% of quota, though larger amounts can be made available in exceptional cases
(1) Natural disasters (1962)	(1) Natural disasters	(1) Reasonable efforts to overcome balance-of-payments difficulties	
(2) Post-conflict (1995)	(2) The aftermath of civil unrest, political turmoil, or international armed conflict	(2) Focus on institutional and administrative capacity building to pave the way toward an upper credit tranche arrangement or PRGF	
Facility for low-income members			
Poverty Reduction and Growth Facility (1999) Note: Replaced the Enhanced Structural Adjustment Facility	Longer-term assistance for deep-seated balance of payments difficulties of structural nature; aims at sustained poverty-reducing growth	Adopt 3-year PRGF-supported program. PRGF-supported programs are based on a Poverty Reduction Strategy Paper (PRSP) prepared by the country in a participatory process, and integrating macroeconomic, structural, and poverty reduction policies	140% of quota; 185% of quota in exceptional circumstances

Source: IMF, *Annual Report 2003* (Washington, DC: IMF).

CRITICISMS OF THE IMF

The policy prescriptions of the IMF in developing countries have been, and still are, based on a blend of finance and adjustment. Few would dispute the need for international institutions to provide finance to ease the burden of balance-of-payments adjustment. In its adjustment policies, however, the IMF has come in for severe criticism; so much so that it has been described as **'anti-developmental'**. In its approach to adjustment the IMF is conditioned both by the beliefs and philosophy of the organization itself and the prevailing orthodoxy of neoclassical economic theory. The IMF denies that it has a rigid doctrinaire approach to economic policy, but it clearly has a particular philosophy based on the Washington Consensus (see p. 596). It is a major bastion of support of an international economic system that prefers capitalism to socialism, favours private investment over public investment, extols the virtues of free trade and the operation of the price mechanism, and encourages the free flow of private capital to and from developing countries. Gore (2000) argues that this consensus that emerged within the IMF (and World Bank) was more than just a paradigm shift from the idea of state-led development to market-orientated policies. There was a deeper shift in the way development problems were perceived in an increasingly globalized world, and the IMF's policies have been a response to these changes in the world economy. The fact remains, however, that a particular orthodoxy has been applied to the vast majority of developing countries as if they were one homogenous mass and could be properly treated in virtually all the same way.

Joseph Stiglitz (2002), formerly chief economist of the World Bank, has severely criticized the IMF for serving the needs of global finance, rather than the needs of global stability, by encouraging premature internal and external financial liberalization. He has satirized the methods of the IMF by describing what he calls a four-step programme for every country, regardless of circumstances and already 'pre-drafted' by IMF officials before they reach the country, for 'voluntary' signature by the country concerned. No signature, no help! The four core elements of each programme consist of: (1) privatization of state industries; (2) capital market liberalization; (3) market-based pricing; and (4) free trade.

Capital market liberalization has been disastrous for many countries not ready and able to cope with volatile capital inflows and outflows. The IMF has, in fact, admitted that opening economies prematurely to free flows of capital constituted 'an accident waiting to happen', and now concedes that capital controls are justified in some circumstances. The Fund was undoubtedly shaken by the 1997 East Asian crisis which it did not foresee, even though there was a massive build-up of current account deficits and capital had started to flow out of South-East Asia long before the crisis hit.

Market-based pricing has also been disastrous in many instances, leading to civil unrest. When food and fuel subsidies for the poor were lifted in Indonesia in 1998, the country exploded into riots.

Free trade, we saw in Chapter 16, is not optimal from a development point of view. If imports grow faster than exports, the balance of payments worsens.

The neoliberal, neoclassical approach to economic thinking and policy-making colours to a large extent the IMF's diagnosis of balance-of-payments problems and their appropriate solution. Deficits are invariably seen as related to, or caused by, price uncompetitiveness and excess monetary demand, to be 'cured' by devaluation and demand contraction.

But the IMF still lacks a comprehensive theoretical apparatus to deal with two basic questions regarding devaluation: firstly, how is the degree of *overvaluation* of a currency determined, and secondly, how is the optimal pace of adjustment from the overvalued to the equilibrium rate of exchange decided? In keeping with the IMF's philosophy, devaluation and retrenchment are coupled with other measures that, from a balance-of-payments point of view, work in the opposite direction – namely the relaxation of foreign-exchange controls, the removal of import restrictions and the dismantling of subsidies and price controls.

Critics of the IMF argue with some justification that there is one law for the poor and another for the rich. While the poor countries must remove controls over foreign exchange and imports as a condition of assistance, the rich countries continue to impose restrictions on imports from developing countries. To support the liberalization pro-gramme, the country then has to depress aggregate demand sufficiently to accommodate devaluation in the attempt to achieve balance-of-payments equilibrium, which leads to slow growth and unemployment. The symptoms of balance-of-payments disequilibrium are tackled, but not the root causes of the perpetual tendency towards disequilibrium. As we argued in the previous chapter, the balance-of-payments problems of most developing countries must be regarded as primarily *structural* in nature, relating to the characteristics of the goods produced and traded. This implies a very different approach to balance of payments adjustment than one of continual devaluation, demand contraction and dismantling of the public sector. At the very least it calls for dual exchange rates and for policies – using a judicious mix of subsidies and controls – to alter the *structure* of production.

Another criticism of the IMF is that it ignores 'structural' *surpluses* on the balance of payments – the counterpart of 'structural' deficits – and critics argue that the burden of adjustment ought to be shared more equitably between deficit and surplus countries, instead of the major part of the burden being shouldered by debtor developing countries, as at present. If surplus countries do not attempt to adjust by expanding their own economies, or by appreciating their currencies, they should be penalized, and deficit countries ought to be allowed to discriminate against the goods of these countries. This would be a revival of the idea of 'scarce currencies', and of the right of countries to control imports from 'scarce currency' countries, that is, from those with surpluses.

Critics would also argue that if the IMF is genuinely concerned with development as well as providing balance-of-payments support, it could distribute all new issues of SDRs to developing countries to spend in developed countries. After all, if the developed countries were unable to earn their reserves by selling goods to developing countries in exchange for SDRs, they would have to earn them in some other way. We shall return to this matter below.

The IMF has become sensitive to some of these criticisms in recent years, particularly to the charge that it is 'anti-developmental'. Along with the World Bank, the IMF now declares itself committed to poverty reduction and allowing countries to 'own' their own policies through the formulation of PRSPs. Instead of countries having to fulfil a mass of individual conditions for loan support, governments can now specify just a few broad outcomes relating to poverty reduction, health and education. To what extent it will change its attitude to balance-of-payments difficulties and the need for devaluation and deflation, however, remains to be seen.

The IMF also now has an **Independent Evaluation Office (IEO)**, established in 2001, to monitor its lending activities and to do research on the effects of its lending policies. The IEO chose three subjects for its first studies: fiscal adjustment in IMF-supported programmes; the role of the IMF in three capital-account crises (Indonesia and Korea in 1997–8 and Brazil 1998–9), and prolonged use of IMF resources. Kenen (2004) surveys the results of the studies so far. On fiscal policy, the IEO criticizes IMF programmes for not paying enough attention to raising income and property taxes, and combating tax evasion, and for focusing too heavily on cutting public employment or capping wages in periods of fiscal crisis. In general, fiscal policy has not been 'too tight', although the fiscal outcome has normally been tighter than forecast. In Korea and Indonesia, however, in 1997–8, there was too much fiscal stringency because the IMF did not foresee the collapse of investment and output, so that IMF policies made the situation worse. On the third issue, the prolonged use of IMF resources has increased in recent years because as Keynes once said 'if you owe a bank a little, the bank owns you, but if you owe the bank a lot *you* own the bank'! The IMF has been reluctant to pull out of countries in case they don't get repaid at all. The evaluation reaches some interesting findings which have general lessons:

- Excessively detailed conditionality does not appear to have been effective.
- Conditionality which is focused on policy rules or procedures, rather than on discretionary one-time actions, seems to be most effective.

The Meltzer Commission, appointed by the US Congress, which reported in 2000, has recommended that the IMF should withdraw from the development field entirely and concentrate on the role of lender of last resort to emerging economies facing financial crisis. This would be a return to its original function of lending to countries in short-term balance-of-payments difficulties. Likewise, the World Bank should pare down its activities, lending only to poor countries, and not to countries able to attract private capital. In line with the focus on poverty reduction, lending should be confined to countries with an income of less than $4000 per head with low credit ratings. For the poorest countries, there should be grants not loans. Lending to Asia and Latin America could largely be left to the Regional Development Banks in those regions. In general, there should be a much clearer distinction between the activities of the IMF and World Bank. If accepted, this would indeed be a return to the original conception at Bretton Woods that the World Bank would act as the development agency and the Fund would be like a bank to be used in emergencies only, but not get involved in detailed policy-making itself in the countries concerned. A move in this direction would disarm many of the IMF's critics.

THE RESULTS OF IMF PROGRAMMES

The effects of the IMF's programmes on countries' economic performance have been very mixed. In an early study Reichmann and Stillson (1978) examined the effects of IMF programmes in both developed and developing countries in the period 1963–72, comparing the 2 years after the implementation of the programme with the 2 years before. Taking the balance of payments as a whole (current plus capital account), of the 75 cases examined, only 18 showed a statistically significant improvement and four showed an actual worsening. In the 29 cases where the inflation rate had exceeded 5 per cent before the programme, it had worsened in six cases and in 16 cases there was no significant change. As far as GDP growth is concerned, of the 70 cases examined the performance had improved in 33 but deteriorated in 28. A study by Donavan (1982) of the non-oil-developing countries for the period 1971–80 revealed a similar pattern: some improvement in the balance of payments, mixed effects on growth and some tendency towards inflation.

Following a major analysis of over 30 IMF stabilization programmes supported by upper-tranche credits between 1964 and 1979, Killick and his associates (1984) advocated what they call a 'real economy approach to balance of payments' or 'adjustment with growth', which would be a more flexible supply orientated approach with demand management subservient.

One of the purposes of the Extended Fund Facility and the (now defunct) Structural Adjustment Facility was to permit the IMF to deal with structural disequilibrium, but as far as the former facility is concerned, the programmes were no different from conventional demand management programmes built around monetary and fiscal contraction coupled with trade liberalization and some production incentives.

In a follow-up study of IMF programmes in developing countries, Killick (1995) criticizes the IMF's over-reliance on conditionality and performance criteria, which invariably lead to the breakdown of IMF programmes. To avoid breakdowns and pressure on IMF resources, he calls for the relaxation of standardized reform packages and a greater emphasis on locally initiated programmes of stabilization and reform. Above all, the programmes should set a growth target of at least 1 per cent above population growth, and sufficient financing for this should be mobilized. Killick finds that the main victim of IMF programmes is investment, and that there is no evidence that IMF financing acts as a catalyst for private investment.

Lance Taylor (1988) reports the results of studies of 18 countries, conducted under the auspices of the World Institute for Development Economics Research (WIDER) in Helsinki. The principal finding of the authors of the country studies is that 'past policies could have been designed to better effect, and that programmes of the Fund/Bank type are optimal for neither stabilization nor growth and income redistribution in the Third World'. This is a serious indictment of policy from some of the world's leading development economists. There are alternative programmes to those implemented by the IMF, but they would be more interventionist and more directly concerned with the targets than with the precise instruments. There is a role for selective import controls, export subsidies, multiple exchange rates, low interest rates and so forth, but these are all frowned on by the IMF.

The IMF conducts its own in-house studies of programmes and is naturally more sanguine, but is conscious that the design of programmes can be improved. In a study of 45 IMF lending arrangements approved between mid-1988 and mid-1991, Schadler (1996) reports striking gains on the external accounts, but virtually no improvement in inflation, investment and growth. Four explanations are given:

■ Countries coming to the IMF too late
■ Too much emphasis on the external objective of balance-of-payments equilibrium rather than domestic objectives
■ The breaking of monetary targets
■ Not enough emphasis on raising domestic saving.

Table 17.10 Economic and social indicators in Fund-supported and other developing countries, 1981–95 (per cent a year, unless indicated otherwise)

	Fund users[a]		Non-ESAF developing countries	
	1981–5	1991–5	1981–5	1991–5
Real per capita GDP growth	−1.1	0.0	0.3	1.0
Inflation: mean	94.4	44.9	23.5	139.9
median	11.7	11.6	9.1	0.3
Gross national saving (per cent of GDP)	8.0	9.9	18.6	17.4
Budget balance (per cent of GDP)	−9.1	−5.6	−6.8	−4.8
Export volume growth	1.7	7.9	4.4	5.7
Debt-service ratio (actual) (per cent of exports of goods and nonfactor services)	27.9	25.7	18.8	15.7
External debt (face value, per cent of GNP)	81.9	154.2	55.7	75.6
Gross reserves (months of imports)	2.0	3.5	4.7	5.6

[a] Using the Enhanced Structural Adjustment Facility (ESAF).
Source: IMF Survey, 5 August 1997.

Table 17.10 shows the results of Fund-supported programmes up to 1995 in 36 countries, comparing performance before and after the implementation of programmes, and between countries that had implemented programmes and those that had not. It can be seen that for the major macro-variables, the situation of most countries improved in 1991–5 compared with 1981–5 (before the programmes were introduced), but the situation was still a lot worse than in countries without programmes (although this is not surprising, since the ESAF countries are some of the poorest in the world). How much of the improvement in the ESAF countries can be attributed to the programmes, however, is not entirely clear. It is never easy to judge what the situation would have been without the programme, and how much of the improvement (or deterioration) was due to world economic conditions.

SPECIAL DRAWING RIGHTS AND THE DEVELOPING COUNTRIES

One possibility for increasing the flow of resources to developing countries is to distribute to them most, if not all, of the saving accruing to developed countries from the issue of costless SDRs as a means of international payment.

The Special Drawing Account of the IMF was established in July 1969. To date there have been only two major allocations of SDRs, both spread over 3 years: between 1970 and 1972, totalling 9.3 billion SDRs; and between 1979 and 1981, totalling just over 12 billion SDRs, giving a total allocation of 21.43 billion SDRs, equal to approximately 4 per cent of total world reserves other than gold. The current holdings amount to only 2 per cent of non-gold reserves.

The basis of allocation of SDRs between countries is the member countries' quota subscriptions to the IMF. This means that approximately 70 per cent of the new international money created has been distributed to the world's richest countries, while the poorest countries participating in the IMF have received only 30 per cent. If the SDRs had been distributed on a per capita basis, the distribution would have been almost exactly the reverse. What appears to be an arbitrary distribution of the new international reserves is explained by the fact that SDRs, as originally conceived, were designed primarily to increase the total level of international liquidity, and not to alter the distribution of total reserves or effect a permanent transfer of real resources from one set of countries to another.

Since 1994 the IMF has been proposing a new issue of SDRs, partly to help the reserves of poor countries and partly because 38 new members of the IMF have never received an allocation, but there has been opposition from some of the more powerful industrial countries which see any increase in the world's money supply as inflationary. At the IMF meetings in Hong Kong in 1997, however, a doubling of SDRs was agreed, to be distributed so as to equalize all members' ratio of SDRs to quotas at 29.3 per cent (including countries without a previous allocation.)

The return to the use of SDRs depends on the rate of return on resources and on the interest rate payable on the net use of SDRs. The potential resource gain is measured by $[(r - i)Q]/d$, where r is the rate of return, i is the interest rate payable on SDRs, Q is the value of SDRs allocated and d is the discount factor. If no interest was payable on SDRs, all the social savings would go to the net users of SDRs. If the rate of interest is positive, some of the social saving is transferred to those who accumulate SDRs. If the rate of interest on SDRs equals the return on resources, the effect on resource allocation is neutral between net users and net holders.

Thus the system at present instituted involves resource transfers only to the extent that the interest rate payable on the net use (holding) of SDRs is lower than the market rate of interest (opportunity cost of capital), so that countries that accumulate SDRs are effectively transferring resources to those countries that run them down.

The interest rate originally payable on net use was 1.5 per cent, but this has been gradually raised in order to make the SDR a more acceptable asset to hold, and now users pay, and holders receive, a market rate of interest based on the interest rates prevailing in the United States, Britain, the European Union and Japan. Net use still enables countries to run larger balance-of-payments deficits than would otherwise have been the case, and it eases the adjustment problem, but the grant element attached to SDR use has now gone. The rules on use are that while a country may now use the whole of its SDR allocation, no country is obliged to *hold* more than three times its own cumulative allocation.

But the obligation to accept SDRs involves the provision of currency in exchange. The idea is that SDRs should be used primarily to meet balance-of-payments needs so that most SDRs end up in the hands of surplus countries. The accumulation of SDRs by a country is not necessarily an indication, however, that the country has transferred real resources to the same extent. That depends on where the currency it surrenders in exchange for SDRs is spent.

There can be no doubt about the advantages of the SDR system for the world as a whole, but there are several objections to the present distribution, and grounds for believing that a redistribution of SDRs in favour of the developing countries could improve world welfare. The advantages of SDRs compared with the gold and dollar standard are manifold. SDRs make possible orderly reserve creation and could rid the world of a system that depends on supplies of gold and the balance of payments of reserve currency countries (mainly the deficits of the United States). SDRs cannot be demonetized (like gold) or vanish, as when dollars are spent in the United States. They are also costless to produce, unlike gold, which requires real resources to be mined, refined, transported and guarded. Above all, SDRs represent the abandonment of the idea that attached to international money there must be a debtor. Acceptability by others is the important thing, just as a nation's payments system depends on the acceptance of unbacked paper money.

The objections to the present distribution of SDRs are equally axiomatic, however. The IMF quotas on which the allocations are based were not developed for the purpose of distributing SDRs. They were developed for the purpose of assigning voting power at the IMF, for determining each member's contribution to the IMF's resources, and for determining the maximum borrowing limits from the IMF. The quotas were based on the degree of convertibility of each nation's currency, its national income, its original level of convertible currency holdings and its importance in world trade. There is no necessary relation, therefore, between the quotas and the criteria by which one might wish to allocate new international liquidity, such as the relative costs of balance-of-payments adjustment, the long-run demand for international reserves, and in particular the distribution of world income (given that SDRs represent a social saving compared with the use of gold).

The balance-of-payments adjustment costs of developing countries are generally higher than those of developed countries, and this in itself constitutes an economic argument for revising the present allocation rules. The more important question, however, is how the social saving should be distributed. The present rules for allocation, in effect, distribute the social saving to individual countries in proportion to their contribution to the social saving created; that is, in proportion to the demand for SDRs. If the supply of SDRs to individual countries equals their demand, no resource redistribution between nations will occur. But in the light of the present distribution of world income, why should not the whole of the social saving be transferred to the developing countries? The degree of egalitarianism needed to justify this course rather than neutrality is minimal. The developed countries would be no worse off than if new gold had been discovered and then sold to them. Swapping SDRs for exports to the developing countries is just another way of converting resources into reserves.

The feeling that the social saving of SDRs should be distributed to the developing countries has spawned several proposals for a so-called **link between development assistance and SDRs**. If more resources are to be distributed to the developing countries because of technical progress in the international payments industry, there would indeed seem to be several advantages in establishing an aid link with the use of SDRs.

First, if there was a regular expansion of SDRs a link would provide a useful mechanism by which total development aid could be guaranteed to rise with the long-term growth of world trade and production. At present there is no guarantee that aid will rise in proportion to world income. Aid programmes are chopped and changed according to the balance-of-payments situation of donor countries.

Second, a link scheme would increase the proportion of total international aid that is untied. Even if normal budgetary appropriations for aid were cut as a result of the link scheme, the link would still yield a net benefit in that the real value of the aid would be increased through untying. Moreover the untying of aid through the link would not impose any reserve losses on the donor, as when a country unties its aid unilaterally. All donor countries would gain reserves in exchange for the exports they provide to the developing countries.

Third, if the link scheme operated through such international financial institutions as the World Bank or one of its affiliates, these multilateral institutions would be provided with a regular flow of resources without the necessity of entering into time-consuming negotiations with national governments.

The historical origin of the link idea can be traced back to Keynes' plan for an International Clearing Union (ICU) with the power to issue international money. The function of the ICU was not only to be a world central bank but also to lend to international organizations pursuing internationally agreed objectives, in particular, at that time, for postwar relief work and the management of international commodities. The most recent spate of proposals for relating development assistance with international monetary reform, however, started with the Stamp Plan (Stamp, 1958), which was for the issue of IMF certificates to increase international liquidity, but distributable directly to the developing countries. The developing countries would gain purchasing power, and the developed countries would have to earn the certificates by exporting to the developing countries in the same way that they would have to earn gold or dollars through exports.

The variety of link proposals that have been put forward since 1958 can be classified into three types:

- A direct link
- An organic link
- An inorganic (or indirect, voluntary) link.

As far as a **direct link** is concerned, the simplest method would be to allocate more SDRs directly to the developing countries in excess of their long-run demand for reserves. This could be accomplished in several different ways. The IMF quotas to developing countries could be increased, while retaining the quota structure as a basis for SDR distribution. Alternatively, the developing countries could be allocated SDRs in excess of their IMF quotas according to some agreed formula, a direct link which has much to recommend it compared with the more complex alternatives.

An **organic link** refers to the possibility of channelling SDRs to the developing countries via the developed countries, via international institutions, or via both. UNCTAD first suggested the notion of an organic link whereby the IMF would issue IMF units to all member countries in return for national currencies deposited with the IMF, which could then be used to purchase World Bank bonds or be distributed to the International Development Association, thus providing additional (and cheap) resources for multilateral development projects. Many other forms of organic link have since been suggested, for example:

- The direct allocation of SDRs to development agencies
- The allocation of SDRs by developed countries direct to the developing countries
- The allocation of SDRs by developed countries to development agencies.

The direct allocation of SDRs to development agencies probably has the most advantages and the least drawbacks among the organic-link proposals. Development agencies would have accounts with the IMF to which SDRs would be credited. The development agencies would then lend in the normal way. When goods were purchased from exporters by the developing countries, the IMF would then transfer the SDRs from the account of the development agencies to the account of the exporting country. The country would then pay its exporters in its domestic currency. The scheme has the advantage of being simple and could be introduced with minimal amendments to the IMF Articles of Agreement.

A tied version of the organic link, which bears some similarity to the UNCTAD proposal, was Scitovsky's (1966) plan for a new international currency to be issued to deficit countries with unemployed resources, which would relinquish domestic currency in exchange. This could then be lent to the developing countries, but could only be spent in the issuing country. This would serve several purposes. It would provide the developing countries with unrequited imports at no opportunity cost to the developed countries and remedy the deficits of the developed countries at the same time. The idea behind Scitovsky's scheme was the elimination of deflationary bias in the world economy, but remains relevant as long as there are countries that have unemployed resources but need reserves. The main disadvantage to developing countries compared with alternative schemes is that the resource transfer would be in the form of tied gifts.

An **inorganic link** would involve the developed countries agreeing to make voluntary contributions to the multilateral aid-giving agencies whenever new SDRs were allocated. The contributions would be in national currencies but would represent a uniform proportion of each contributor's SDR allocation. The drawback of the proposal is its voluntary nature – one or two major countries might not contribute or might make their contribution dependent on their balance of payments. This would introduce a great deal of uncertainty into the scheme. Also, national governments would have to agree appropriations and this would create the same difficulties as regular foreign-aid appropriations. There do not seem to be many advantages in an inorganic link.

Several objections have been raised against the link proposals but none is very convincing. Some have argued against the link on the ground that the creation of reserves should be kept separate from the transfer of real resources. But this has never been the case historically. Resource transfers have always been involved in the acquisition of gold and dollars. Since SDRs save real resources, it is entirely appropriate that in the process of reserve creation the saving should be distributed to the developing countries.

A second objection to the link is that it would mean the loss of democratic control over the granting and distribution of assistance by national governments. Under the link scheme, the distribution of the burden of assistance would depend on where the SDRs were spent, which, it is argued, could not be accurately forecast. This is a weak argument for two reasons. The same objection may be levelled against *all* forms of untied bilateral aid, and also against tied aid to the extent that tying is not 100 per cent effective.

There is never an automatic correspondence between the financial burden of aid and the real resource burden of aid. It all depends on whether the national governments that grant aid allow the resources to be transferred, which depends primarily on their policy towards the balance of payments. But in any case, the theory of democracy and the concept of mandate extend to the international sphere. There is no reason why a government cannot be given a mandate to distribute international money to the developing countries even though the impact on the country might be uncertain.

A further objection is that the link is likely to be inflationary. If the SDRs replace gold and dollars, however, there is no reason to suppose that they will be any more inflationary for the world economy than are gold and dollars. It is true that developing countries will tend to spend new international money rather than add to their reserves, but whether or not the resulting claims on the developed countries are inflationary will depend on whether the developed countries are willing to release resources to the extent of the claims on them. The reaction of the responsible authorities will not depend on the source of the asset creating the pressure.

It is thus highly misleading to argue that because (unlike with ordinary aid) the direct nexus between SDRs and real resource claims is broken, corresponding measures to offset inflationary effects are less likely. All sorts of unforeseen factors can disturb an economy. The (uncertain) claims arising from SDR distribution to the developing countries are likely to be trivial in comparison. The sums involved will certainly be trivial in absolute magnitude, which casts further doubts on the inflation argument. Even if the whole new allocation of SDRs proposed by the IMF of 21 billion was distributed to the developing countries, this would represent less than 0.3 per cent of developed countries' national income.

There are in fact several reasons for supposing that the link may *reduce* inflationary pressure in the world economy. SDRs could be less inflationary than the dollar standard by instituting multilateral control over international liquidity rather than unilateral control by the United States, which, because of the need for dollars, has not been subject to the anti-inflationary discipline that is normally present in other countries. It could also be that fewer SDRs would be created with a link than without. If the developed countries must earn their new reserves they are likely to be more modest in their views on the need for more reserves. If countries must earn reserves there will also be some compulsion on them to contain inflation in order to compete in world export markets.

A final objection is that development assistance is not likely to increase under the link because governments will cut down on their normal budgetary aid appropriations. Critics argue that it is highly unlikely that developed countries would be willing to give extra aid through the link but not in other forms. This objection can also be challenged. For one thing the reserve effects of the two forms of assistance are not the same. Conventional aid worsens the donor's balance of payments, whereas the link scheme would improve the balance of payments of countries where SDRs were spent and thus improve the reserve position. Second, governments often wish to provide aid for specific purposes and this desire would not be diminished by a link. Moreover, since it is very difficult for a country to know how much aid it is providing through the link, it would be very difficult for a country to offset it. The link deserves much more consideration in international monetary circles than it has received to date. To paraphrase Pirandello, if ever there were an instrument in search of a policy, it is SDRs!

DISCUSSION QUESTIONS

1 What factors determine the demand for a country's exports and imports?

2 Can the devaluation of a country's currency guarantee balance-of-payments equilibrium on the current account?

3 What factors determine the income elasticity of demand for a country's exports?

4 Why are developing countries more prone to balance-of-payments disequilibrium than developed countries?

5 What do you understand by the IMF's 'supply-side approach to devaluation' in developing countries?

6 What factors need to be taken into account in choosing a country's exchange-rate regime?

7 What are the lessons of the financial crisis in South-East Asia in 1997?

8 How do the ordinary and special facilities of the IMF work? What do you understand by 'conditionality'?

9 What criticisms have been levelled against the IMF in its policies of support to developing countries?

10 What have been the effects of IMF policies in developing countries?

11 How could Special Drawing Rights (SDRs) be used simultaneously as an instrument of aid to developing countries and as a means of employment creation in developed countries?

NOTES

1. For the original development of this model, see Thirlwall (1979). For a survey of the literature, see McCombie and Thirlwall (1997).
2. For an up-to-date survey of estimating export- and import-demand functions, see Senhadji and Montenegro (1999) and Senhadji (1998).
3. For a collection of these papers and others, see J. McCombie and A. P. Thirlwall (2004).
4. For the original development of this model, see Thirlwall and Nureldin-Hussain (1982).
5. For useful surveys of exchange-rate policy in developing countries, see Argy (1990); Frenkel (1999); Fischer (2001); Ghosh, Gulde and Wolf (2002).
6. A classic early reference arguing the case for dual exchange rates is Kaldor (1964).
7. This section relies heavily on McCombie and Thirlwall (1999).
8. The World Bank, *East Asia: The Road to Recovery* (Washington, DC: World Bank, 1998).
9. For a comprehensive review of the evolution of the conditionality practices of the IMF, see Guitian (1982): Dell (1981).

WEBSITES ON BALANCE OF PAYMENTS AND IMF

IMF www.imf.org

UNCTAD Handbook of Statistics http://stats.unctad.org/

1992 South-East Asia Crisis

Nouriel Ronbini's websites www.stern.nyu.edu/~nroubini/asia/AsiaHomePage.html

References and further reading

CHAPTER 1   THE STUDY OF ECONOMIC DEVELOPMENT

Bardhan, P. (1993) 'Economics of Development and the Development of Economics', *Journal of Economic Perspectives*, Spring.

Brandt Commission (1983) *Common Crisis: North–South Co-operation for World Recovery* (London: Pan).

Brandt Report (1980) *North–South: A Programme for Survival* (London: Pan).

Domar, E. (1947) 'Expansion and Employment', *American Economic Review*, March.

Fischer, S. (2003) 'Globalisation and its Challenges,' *American Economic Review*, March.

Furtado, C. (1964) *Development and Underdevelopment* (Berkeley: University of California Press).

Galbraith, J. K. (1980) *The Nature of Mass Poverty* (Harmondsworth: Penguin).

Goulet, D. (1971) *The Cruel Choice: A New Concept on the Theory of Development* (New York: Atheneum).

Harrod, R. (1939) 'An Essay in Dynamic Theory', *Economic Journal*, March.

Harrod, R. (1948) *Towards a Dynamic Economics* (London: Macmillan).

Hirschman, A. (1981) 'The Rise and Decline of Development Economics', in *Essays in Trespassing: Economics to Politics and Beyond* (Cambridge: Cambridge University Press).

Krugman, P. (1992) 'Towards a Counter-Revolution in Development Theory', *World Bank Economic Review (Supplement): Proceedings of the World Bank Annual Conference on Development Economics* (Washington, DC: World Bank).

Lal, D. (1983) *The Poverty of Development Economics* (London: Hobart).

Lewis, W. A. (1984) 'The State of Development Theory', *American Economic Review*, March.

Lipton, M. (1977) *Why Poor People Stay Poor* (London: Temple Smith).

Little, I. M. D. (1982) *Economic Development: Theory, Policies and International Relations* (New York: Basic Books).

Myrdal, G. (1957) *Economic Theory and Underdeveloped Regions* (London: Duckworth).

Naqvi, S. N. H. (1995) 'The Nature of Economic Development', *World Development*, April.

Naqvi, S. N. H. (1996) 'The Significance of Development Economics', *World Development*, June.

Patel, S. J. (1964) 'The Economic Distance Between Nations: Its Origins, Measurement and Outlook', *Economic Journal*, March.

Pearson Report (1969) *Partners in Development*. Report of the Commission on International Development (London: Pall Mall Press).

Sen, A. (1983) 'Development: Which Way Now?', *Economic Journal*, December.

Sen, A. (1984) *Poverty and Famines: An Essay in Entitlement and Deprivation* (Oxford: Clarendon Press).

Sen, A. (1999) *Development as Freedom* (Oxford: Oxford University Press).

Thirlwall, A. P. (1995) 'In Praise of Development Economics', *METU Studies in Development*, 1 and 2 (1984), reprinted in A. P. Thirlwall, *The Economics of Growth and Development: Selected Essays*, Vol. 1 (Aldershot: Edward Elgar).

Todaro, M. and S. C. Smith (2003) *Economic Development in the Third World* (London: Longman).

UNDP (2002) *Human Development Report* (New York: Oxford University Press).

World Bank (2000) *World Development Report 2000/2001: Attacking Poverty* (New York: Oxford University Press).

CHAPTER 2 THE DEVELOPMENT GAP AND THE MEASUREMENT OF POVERTY

Baumol, W. (1986) 'Productivity Growth, Convergence and Welfare: What the Long-run Data Show', *American Economic Review*, December.

Besley, T. and R. Burgess (2003) 'Halving Global Poverty', *Journal of Economic Perspectives*, Summer.

Bourguignon, F. and C. Morrisson (2002) 'Inequality Among World Citizens: 1820–1992', *American Economic Review*, September.

Dollar, D. and A. Kraay (2000) *Growth is Good for the Poor* (Washington, DC: World Bank).

Dowrick, S. (1992) 'Technological Catch-up and Diverging Incomes: Patterns of Economic Growth 1960–1988', *Economic Journal*, May.

Easterlin, R. (2000) 'The Worldwide Standard of Living Since 1800', *Journal of Economic Perspectives*, Winter.

Ghose, A. K. (2004) 'Global Inequality and International Trade', *Cambridge Journal of Economics*, March.

Jones, C. (1997) 'On the Evolution of the World Income Distribution', *Journal of Economic Perspectives*, 11 (3).

Kravis, I. B. *et al.* (1975) *A System of International Comparisons of Gross Product and Purchasing Power* (Baltimore: Johns Hopkins Press for the World Bank).

Kravis, I. B. *et al.* (1978) 'Real GDP Per Capita for More than One Hundred Countries', *Economic Journal*, June.

Krugman, P. and A. Venables (1995) 'Globalisation and the Inequality of Nations', *Quarterly Journal of Economics*, November.

Maddison, A. (2003) *The World Economy: Historical Statistics*, Development Studies Centre (Paris: OECD).

Milanovic, B. (2002) 'True World Income Distribution 1988 and 1993: First Calculations Based on Household Surveys Alone', *Economic Journal*, January.

Norwegian Institute of International Affairs (2000) *Globalisation and Inequality: World Income Distribution and Livings Standards, 1960–1998* (Report to the Norwegian Ministry of Foreign Affairs: Report 6b: 2000).

Pritchett, L. (1997) Divergence: Big Time, *Journal of Economic Perspectives*, 11.

Ravallion, M. (1997) 'Good and Bad Growth: Human Development Reports', *World Development*, May.

Ravallion, M. (2001) 'Growth, Inequality and Poverty: Looking Beyond Averages', *World Development*, November.

Summers, R. and A. Heston (1988) 'A New Set of International Comparisons of Real Product and Price Levels: Estimates for 130 Countries 1950–1985', *Review of Income and Wealth*, March.

Summers, R. and A. Heston (1991) 'The Penn World Table (Mark 5): An Expanded Set of International Comparisons, 1950–1985', *Quarterly Journal of Economics*, May.

Sutcliffe, R. (1971) *Industry and Underdevelopment* (Reading, Mass: Addison-Wesley).

Sutcliffe, R. (2004) 'World Inequality and Globalisation', *Oxford Review of Economic Policy*, Spring.

Svedberg, P. (2004) 'World Income Distribution: Which Way?', *Journal of Development Studies*, June.

UNDP (1997) *Human Development Report* (New York: Oxford University Press).

UNDP (2001) *Human Development Report 2000* (New York: United Nations).

UNDP (2003) *Human Development Report* (New York: Oxford University Press).

UNDP (2004) *Human Development Report 2004* (New York: Oxford University Press).

Wade, R. (2001) 'The Rising Inequality of World Income Distribution', *Finance and Development*, December.

Wade, R. (2004) 'Is Globalisation Reducing Poverty and Inequality?' *World Development*, April.

World Bank (1990) *World Development Report 1990* (Oxford: Oxford University Press).

World Bank (2000) *World Development Report 2000/2001: Attacking Poverty* (New York: Oxford University Press).

World Bank (2001) *World Development Report 2002* (Oxford: Oxford University Press).

World Bank (2004) *World Development Indicators, 2004* (Washington, DC: World Bank).

Zind, R. G. (1991) 'Income Convergence and Divergence Within and Between LDC Groups', *World Development*, June.

CHAPTER 3 THE CHARACTERISTICS OF UNDERDEVELOPMENT AND STRUCTURAL CHANGE

Acemoglu, D. (2003) 'Root Causes: A Historical Approach to Assessing the Role of Institutions in Economic Development', *Finance and Development*, June.

Acemoglu, D., S. Johnson and J. Robinson (2001) 'The Colonial Origins of Comparative Development: An Empirical Investigation', *American Economic Review*, December.

Acemoglu, D., S. Johnson and J. Robinson (2002) 'Reversal of Fortune: Geography and Institutions in the Making of the Modern World Income Distribution', *Quarterly Journal of Economics*, November.

Adelman, I. and C. T. Morris (1971) 'An Anatomy of Income Distribution Patterns in Developing Countries', *AID Development Digest*, October.

Ahluwalia, M. S., N. Carter and H. Chenery (1979) 'Growth and Poverty in Developing Countries', *Journal of Development Economics*, September.

Bairam, E. (1991) 'Economic Growth and Kaldor's Law: The Case of Turkey 1925–78', *Applied Economics*, 23.

Behrman, J. R. (1993) 'The Economic Rationale for Investing in Nutrition in Developing Countries', *World Development*, November.

Bertocchi, G. and F. Canova (1996) 'Did Colonisation Matter for Growth?' *CEPR Discussion Paper* No. 1444, September.

Bliss, C. and N. Stern (1978) 'Productivity, Wages and Nutrition, Parts I and II', *Journal of Development Economics*, 5.

Chatterji, M. *et al.* (1993) 'Political Economy, Growth and Convergence in Less Developed Countries, *World Development*, December.

Chenery, H. (1979) *Structural Change and Development Policy* (Oxford: Oxford University Press).

Chenery, H. and M. Ahluwalia, C. Bell, J. Duloy and R. Jolly (eds) (1974) *Redistribution with Growth* (Oxford: Oxford University Press).

Chenery, H. and M. Syrquin (1975) *Patterns of Development 1950–1970* (Oxford: Oxford University Press).

Chenery, H. and L. Taylor (1968) 'Development Patterns: Among Countries and Over Time', *Review of Economics and Statistics*, November.

Claque, C. (ed.) (1997) *Institutions and Economic Development: Growth and Governance in Less Developed Countries* (Baltimore: John Hopkins Press).

Clark, C. (1940) *The Conditions of Economic Progress* (London: Macmillan).

Dasgupta, P. (1993) *An Inquiry into Well-Being and Destitution* (Oxford: Clarendon Press).

Deininger, K. and L. Squire (1996) 'A New Data Set Measuring Income Inequalities', *World Bank Economic Review*, September.

Dollar, D. and A. Kraay (2000) *Growth is Good for the Poor* (Washington, DC: World Bank).

Drakopoulos, S. A. and I. Theodossiou (1991) 'Kaldorian Approach to Greek Economic Growth', *Applied Economics*, 23.

Drèze, J. and A. K. Sen (1989) *Hunger and Public Action* (Oxford: Clarendon Press).

Dyson, T. (1996) *Population and Food: Global Trends and Future Prospects* (London: Routledge).

Easterly, W. and R. Levine (2002) 'Tropics, Germs and Crops: How Endowments Influence Economic Development', *NBER Working Paper 9106*, August.

Edwards, E. O. (ed.) (1974) *Employment in Developing Nations* (New York: Columbia University Press).

Fisher, A. G. B. (1939) 'Production: Primary, Secondary and Tertiary', *Economic Record*, June.

Forbes, K. J. (2000) 'A Reassessment of the Relationship Between Inequality and Growth', *American Economic Review*, September.

Galbraith, J. K. (1962) *Economic Development in Perspective* (Cambridge, Mass: Harvard University Press).

Godfrey, M. (1986) *Global Unemployment: The New Challenge to Economic Theory* (Brighton: Wheatsheaf).

Gylfason, J. (2001) 'Nature, Power and Growth', *Scottish Journal of Political Economy*, November.

Gylfason, J. (1999) *Principles of Economic Growth* (Oxford: Oxford University Press).

Ha-Joon Chang (ed.) (2003) *Rethinking Development Economics* (London: Anthem Press).

Hansen, J. D. and J. Zhang (1996) 'A Kaldorian Approach to Regional Economic Growth in China', *Applied Economics*, June.

Harris, J., J. Hunter and C. M. Lewis (eds) (1996) *The New Institutional Economics and Third World Development* (London: Routledge).

International Labour Organisation (1977) *Meeting Basic Needs* (Geneva: ILO).

International Labour Organisation (1995) *World Employment 1995* (Geneva: ILO).

International Labour Organisation (1996) *Annual Employment Report* (Geneva: ILO).

International Labour Organisation (2002) *Labour Force Statistics* (Geneva: ILO).

Kaldor, N. (1966) *Causes of the Slow Rate of Economic Growth of the United Kingdom* (Cambridge: Cambridge University Press).

Kaldor, N. (1967) *Strategic Factors in Economic Development* (New York: Ithaca).

Kaufman, D., A. Kraay and P. Zoido-Lobaton (1999) *Governance Matters*, Policy Research Working Papers 2196, World Bank, October.

Kuznets, S. (1955) 'Economic Growth and Income Inequality', *American Economic Review*, March.

Kuznets, S. (1963a) 'Notes on the Take-Off', in W. W. Rostow (ed.), *The Economics of Take-Off into Sustained Growth* (London: Macmillan).

Kuznets, , S. (1963b) 'Quantitative Aspects of the Economic Growth of Nations: Distribution of Income by Size', *Economic Development and Cultural Change*, Part II, January.

Maddison, A. (1991) *Dynamic Forces in Capitalist Development* (Oxford: Oxford University Press).

Mauro, P. (1995) 'Corruption and Growth', *Quarterly Journal of Economics*, August.

Morawetz, D. (1974) 'Employment Implications of Industrialisation in Developing Countries', *Economic Journal*, December.

Myrdal, G. (1957) (1963) *Economic Theory and Underdeveloped Regions* (London: Duckworth) (paperback edn, London: Methuen).

Naqvi, S. N. H. (1995) 'The Nature of Economic Development', *World Development*, April.

North, D. (1990) *Institutions, Institutional Change and Economic Performance* (Cambridge: Cambridge University Press).

Paukert, E. (1973) 'Income Distribution at Different Levels of Development: A Survey of Evidence', *International Labour Review*, August.

Rodrik, D., A. Subramanian and F. Trebbi (2002) 'Institutions Rule: The Primacy of Institutions over Geography and Integration in Economic Development', *NBER Working Paper 9305*, October.

Rostow, W. W. (1960) *The Stages of Economic Growth* (Cambridge: Cambridge University Press).

Rowthorn, R. and R. Ramswamy (1999) 'Growth, Trade and Deindustrialisation', *IMF Staff Papers*, March.

Sachs, J. (2003) 'Institutions Matter, But Not for Everything', *Finance and Development*, June.

Sachs, J. and A. Warner (2001) 'The Curse of Natural Resources', *European Economic Review*, May.

Sen, A. (1984) *Poverty and Famines: An Essay in Entitlement and Deprivation* (Oxford: Clarendon Press).

Stewart, F. (1985) *Planning to Meet Basic Needs* (London: Macmillan).

Stewart, F. (2001) *Horizontal Inequalities: A Neglected Dimension of Development* (WIDER: Helsinki).

Streeten, P. *et al.* (1981) *First Things First: Meeting Basic Human Needs in the Developing Countries* (Oxford: Oxford University Press for the World Bank).

Thirlwall, A. P. (ed.) (1983) 'Symposium on Kaldor's Growth Laws', *Journal of Post Keynesian Economics*, Spring.

Thorbecke, E. (1973) 'The Employment Problem: A Critical Evaluation of Four ILO Comprehensive Country Reports', *International Labour Review*, May.

Turnham, T. (1971) *The Employment Problem in Less Developed Countries* (Paris: OECD).

Wells, H. and A. P. Thirlwall (2003) 'Testing Kaldor's Growth Laws Across the Countries of Africa', *African Development Review*, December.

White, A. and E. Anderson (1991) 'Growth versus Distribution: Does the Pattern of Growth Matter?' *Development Policy Review*, 19 (3).

World Bank (1991) *World Development Report 1991* (Washington, DC: World Bank).

World Bank (1995) *World Development Report 1995: Workers in an Integrating World* (Oxford: Oxford University Press for the World Bank).

World Bank (1997) *World Development Report* (Washington, DC: World Bank).

World Bank (2000) *World Development Report 2000/2001: Attacking Poverty* (New York: Oxford University Press).

World Bank (2001a) *World Development Indicators 2001* (Washington, DC: World Bank).

World Bank (2001b) *World Development Report 2002* (Washington, DC: World Bank).

World Bank (2004) *World Development Indicators, 2004* (Washington, DC: World Bank).

World Health Organization (2001) *Macroeconomics and Health: Investing in Health for Economic Development* (Geneva: WTO).

CHAPTER 4   THEORIES OF ECONOMIC GROWTH: WHY GROWTH RATES DIFFER BETWEEN COUNTRIES

Abramovitz, M. (1956) 'Resource and Output Trends in the United States since 1870', *American Economic Review, Papers and Proceedings*, May.

Abramovitz, M. (1986) 'Catching-up, Forging Ahead and Falling Behind', *Journal of Economic History*, June.

Adelman, I. (1961) *Theories of Economic Growth and Development* (Stanford University Press).

Amable, B. (1993) 'Catch-up and Convergence: A Model of Cumulative Growth', *International Review of Applied Economics*, January.

Arrow, K. (1962) 'The Economic Implications of Learning by Doing', *Review of Economic Studies*, June.

Barro, R. (1991) 'Economic Growth in a Cross-Section of Countries', *Quarterly Journal of Economics*, May.

Barro, R. (1998) *Determinants of Economic Growth*. Lionel Robbins Lectures (Cambridge, Mass.: MIT Press).

Barro, R. and X. Sala-í-Martin (1995) *Economic Growth* (New York: McGraw Hill).

Barro, R. and J. Wha Lee (1993) 'Losers and Winners in Economic Growth', *Proceedings of the World Bank Conference on Development Economics* (Washington, DC: World Bank, 1994).

Baumol, W. (1986) 'Productivity Growth, Convergence and Welfare', *American Economic Review*, December.

Blaug, M. (1996) *Economic Theory in Retrospect*, 5th edn (Cambridge: Cambridge University Press).

Brown, M. (1966) *On the Theory and Measurement of Technical Change* (Cambridge: Cambridge University Press).

Bruton, H. (1967) 'Productivity Growth in Latin America', *American Economic Review*, December.

Chaudhuri, P. (1989) *Economic Theory of Growth* (Iowa: Iowa State University Press).

Cobb, C. and P. Douglas (1928) 'A Theory of Production', *American Economic Review*, Supplement, March.

Collier, P. and J. W. Gunning (1999) 'Explaining African Economic Performance', *Journal of Economic Literature*, March.

Cornwall, J. and W. Cornwall (1994) 'Structural Change and Productivity in the OECD', in P. Davidson and J. Kregel (eds), *Employment Growth and Finance: Economic Reality and Economic Theory* (Aldershot: Edward Elgar).

Correa, H. (1970) 'Sources of Economic Growth in Latin America', *Southern Economic Journal*, July.

De Gregorio, J. (1992) 'Economic Growth in Latin America', *Journal of Development Economics*, 39.

de Mello, L. (1996) *Foreign Direct Investment, International Knowledge Transfers and Endogenous Growth: Times Series Evidence* (Department of Economics, University of Kent, Studies in Economics).

Denison, E. (1962) *The Sources of Economic Growth in the US and the Alternatives before Us* (New York: Committee for Economic Development, Library of Congress).

Domar, E. (1947) 'Expansion and Employment, *American Economic Review*, March.

Douglas, P. (1948) 'Are There Laws of Production?', *American Economic Review*, March.

Dowrick, S. and N. Gemmell (1991) 'Industrialisation, Catching-up and Economic Growth: A Comparative Study Across the World's Capitalist Economies', *Economic Journal*, March.

Dowrick, S. and D. T. Nguyen (1989) 'OECD Comparative Economic Growth 1950–85: Catch-Up and Convergence', *American Economic Review*, December.

Easterly, W. and R. Levine (2001) 'It's not Factor Accumulation: Stylised Facts and Growth Models', *World Bank Economic Review*, 15 (2).

Easterly, W. and L. Pritchett (1993) 'The Determinants of Economic Success: Luck and Policy', *Finance and Development*, December.

Eltis, W. (1984) *The Classical Theory of Economic Growth* (London: Macmillan).

Felipe, J. (1999) 'Total Factor Productivity Growth in East Asia: A Critical Survey', *Journal of Development Studies*, April.

Fischer, S. (1993) 'The Role of Macroeconomic Factors in Growth', *Journal of Monetary Economics*, December.

Gomulka, S. (1971) *Inventive Activity, Diffusion and the Stages of Economic Growth* (Aarhus: Aarhus University Press).

Gomulka, S. (1990) *The Theory of Technological Change and Economic Growth* (London: Routledge).

Grossman, G. and E. Helpman (1990) 'Trade, Innovation and Growth', *American Economic Review Papers and Proceedings*, May.

Grossman, G. and E. Helpman (1991) *Innovation and Growth in the Global Economy* (Cambridge, Mass: MIT Press).

Hagen, E. and O. Hawrylyshyn (1969) 'Analysis of World Income and Growth 1955–65', *Economic Development and Cultural Change*, October.

Harrod, R. (1939) 'An Essay in Dynamic Theory', *Economic Journal*, March.

Hirschman, A. (1958) *Strategy of Economic Development* (New Haven, Conn.: Yale University Press).

Hu, Z. F. and M. S. Khan (1997) 'Why is China Growing So Fast?', *IMF Staff Papers*, March.

Islam, N. (2003) 'What Have we Learnt from the Convergence Debate?' *Journal of Economic Surveys*, July.

Kaldor, N. (1957) 'A Model of Economic Growth', *Economic Journal*, December.

Kaldor, N. (1961) 'Capital Accumulation and Economic Growth', in F. Lutz (ed.), *The Theory of Capital* (London: Macmillan).

Kaldor, N. (1967) *Strategic Factors in Economic Development* (Ithaca: Cornell University Press).

Kaldor, N. (1972) 'Advanced Technology in a Strategy for Development: Some Lessons from Britain's Experience', in *Automation and Developing Countries* (Geneva: ILO).

Kaldor, N. (1985) *Economics without Equilibrium* (Cardiff: University College Cardiff Press).

Kennedy, C. and A. P. Thirlwall (1972) 'Surveys in Applied Economics: Technical Progress', *Economic Journal*, March.

Kenny, C. and D. Williams (2001) 'What Do We Know About Economic Growth? Or, Why Don't We Know Very Much?', *World Development*, January.

Keynes, J. M. (1936) *The General Theory of Employment, Interest and Money* (London: Macmillan).

Knight, M., N. Loayza and D. Villanueva (1993) 'Testing the Neoclassical Theory of Economic Growth', *IMF Staff Papers*, September.

Krugman, P. (1994) 'The Myth of Asia's Miracle', *Foreign Affairs*, November–December.

Lampman, R. (1967) 'The Sources of Post-War Growth in the Philippines', *Philippines Economic Journal*, 2.

Levine, R. and D. Renelt (1992) 'A Sensitivity Analysis of Cross-Country Growth Regressions', *American Economic Review*, September.

Levine, R. and S. Zervos (1993) 'What We Have Learned About Policy and Growth From Cross-Country Regressions', *American Economic Review, Papers and Proceedings*, May.

Lucas, R. (1988) 'On the Mechanics of Economic Development', *Journal of Monetary Economics*, 22.

Maddison, A. (1970) *Economic Progress and Policy in Developing Countries* (London: Allen & Unwin).

Malthus, T. (1798) *Essay on the Principle of Population* (London: Penguin, 1983).

Mankiw, N. G., D. Romer and D. N. Weil (1992) 'A Contribution to the Empirics of Economic Growth', *Quarterly Journal of Economics*, May.

Marshall, A. (1890) *Principles of Economics* (London: Macmillan).

Marx, K. (1867) *Capital: A Critique of Political Economy, Vol. 1* (New York: International Publishers, 1967).

Myrdal, G. (1957) *Economic Theory and Underdeveloped Regions* (London: Duckworth).

Nadiri, M. (1972) 'International Studies of Factor Inputs and Total Factor Productivity: A Brief Survey', *Review of Income and Wealth*, June.

Pack, H. (1994) 'Endogenous Growth: Intellectual Appeal and Empirical Shortcomings', *Journal of Economic Perspectives*, Winter.

Pritchett, L. (2000) 'Understanding Patterns of Growth: Searching for Hills among Plateaus, Mountains and Plains', *World Bank Economic Review*, May.

Pugno, M. (1995) 'On Competing Theories of Economic Growth: Cross-Country Evidence', *International Review of Applied Economics*, 3.

Putterman, L. (2000) 'Can an Evolutionary Approach to Development Predict Post-War Economic Growth?', *Journal of Development Studies*, February.

Ricardo, D. (1817) *Principles of Political Economy and Taxation* (London: Everyman, 1992).

Robinson, S. (1971) 'The Sources of Growth in Less Developed Countries: A Cross-Section Study', *Quarterly Journal of Economics*, August.

Romer, P. M. (1986) 'Increasing Returns and Long Run Growth', *Journal of Political Economy*, October.

Romer, P. M. (1990) 'Endogenous Technical Change', *Journal of Political Economy*, October.

Romer, P. M. (1994) 'The Origins of Endogenous Growth', *Journal of Economic Perspectives*, Winter.

Ruttan, V. (1998) 'New Growth Theory and Development Economics: A Survey', *Journal of Development Studies*, December.

Sala-í-Martin, X. (1997) 'I Just Ran Two Million Regressions', *American Economic Review*, May.

Senhadji, A. (2000) 'Sources of Economic Growth: An Extensive Growth Accounting Exercise', *IMF Staff Papers*, 47 (1).

Shaaeldin, E. (1989) 'Sources of Industrial Growth in Kenya, Tanzania, Zambia and Zimbabwe: Some Estimates', *African Development Review*, June.

Smith, A. (1776) *An Inquiry into the Nature and Causes of the Wealth of Nations* (London: Strahan & Caddell).

Solow, R. (1956) 'A Contribution to the Theory of Economic Growth', *Quarterly Journal of Economics*, February.

Solow, R. (1957) 'Technical Change and the Aggregate Production Function', *Review of Economics and Statistics*, August.

Solow, R. (1962) 'Technical Progress, Capital Formation and Growth', *American Economic Review, Papers and Proceedings*, May.

Summers, R. and A. Heston (1991) 'The Penn World Table (Mark 5): An Expanded Set of International Comparisons, 1950–1988', *Quarterly Journal of Economics*, May.

Swan, T. (1956) 'Economic Growth and Capital Accumulation', *Economic Record*, November.

Symposium on Convergence (1996) *Economic Journal*, July.

Symposium on Slow Growth in Africa (1999) *Journal of Economic Perspectives*, Summer.

Temple, J. (1999) 'The New Growth Evidence', *Journal of Economic Literature*, March.

Thirlwall, A. P. and G. Sanna (1996) '"New" Growth Theory and the Macrodeterminants of Growth: An Evaluation and Further Evidence', in P. Arestis (ed.), *Employment, Economic Growth and the Tyranny of the Market* (Aldershot: Edward Elgar).

Williamson, J. G. (1968) 'Production Functions, Technological Change and the Developing Economies: A Review Article', *Malayan Economic Review*, October.

World Bank (1991) *World Development Report 1991* (Washington, DC: World Bank).

Young, A. (1995) 'The Tyranny of Numbers: Confronting the Statistical Realities of the East Asian Growth Experience', *Quarterly Journal of Economics*, August.

Young, A. A. (1928) 'Increasing Returns and Economic Progress', *Economic Journal*, December.

CHAPTER 5 LAND, LABOUR AND AGRICULTURE

Askari, H. and J. Cummings (1976) *Agricultural Supply Response: A Survey of the Econometric Evidence* (New York: Praeger).

Barnum, A. N. and R. H. Sabot (1977) 'Education, Employment Probabilities and Rural–Urban Migration in Tanzania', *Oxford Bulletin of Economics and Statistics*, May.

Behrman, J. R. (1968) *Supply Response in Underdeveloped Agriculture* (Amsterdam: North-Holland).

Besley, T. and R. Burgess (2000) 'Land Reform, Poverty and Growth: Evidence from India', *Quarterly Journal of Economics*, May.

Chhibber, A. (1988) 'Raising Agricultural Output: Price and Non-Price Factors', *Finance and Development*, June.

Desai, M. and D. Mazumbar (1970) 'A Test of the Hypothesis of Disguised Unemployment', *Economica*, February.

Dorner, P. (1972) *Land Reform and Economic Development* (Harmondsworth: Penguin).

Ghatak, S. and K. Ingersent (1984) *Agriculture and Economic Development* (Brighton: Wheatsheaf).

Griffin, K. (1974, 1979) *The Political Economy of Agrarian Change* (London: Macmillan).

Johnston, B. F. (1970) 'Agriculture and Structural Transformation in Developing Countries: A Survey of Research', *Journal of Economic Literature*, June.

Johnston, B. F. and J. Mellor (1961) 'The Role of Agriculture in Economic Development', *American Economic Review*, September.

Jorgenson, D. (1966) 'Testing Alternative Theories of the Development of a Dual Economy', in I. Adelman and E. Thorbecke (eds), *The Theory and Design of Economic Development* (Baltimore, Md.: Johns Hopkins University Press).

Kaldor, N. (1979) 'Equilibrium Theory and Growth Theory', in M. Baskia (ed.), *Economics and Human Welfare: Essays in Honor of Tibor Scitovsky* (New York: Academic Press).

Knight, J. B. (1972) 'Rural–Urban Income Comparisons and Migration in Ghana', *Oxford Bulletin of Economics and Statistics*, May.

Lehmann, D. (ed.) (1974) *Agrarian Reform and Agrarian Reformism: Studies of Peru, Chile, China and India* (London: Faber & Faber).

Levi, J. S. F. (1973) 'Migration from the Land and Urban Unemployment in Sierra Leone', *Oxford Bulletin of Economics and Statistics*, November.

Lewis, A. (1954) 'Economic Development with Unlimited Supplies of Labour', *Manchester School*, May.

Lewis, A. (1958) 'Unlimited Supplies of Labour: Further Notes', *Manchester School*, January.

Lin, J. Y. (1992) 'Rural Reforms and Agricultural Growth in China', *American Economic Review*, March.

Lockwood, W. W. (1954) *The Economic Development of Japan: Growth and Structural Change 1868–1938* (Princeton: Princeton University Press).

Mehra, S. (1966) 'Surplus Labour in Indian Agriculture', *Indian Economic Review*, April.

Myint, H. (1958), 'The "Classical Theory" of International Trade and the Underdeveloped Countries', *Economic Journal*, June.

Nath, S. (1974) 'Estimating the Seasonal Marginal Products of Labour in Agriculture', *Oxford Economic Papers*, November.

Ranis, G. and J. Fei (1961) 'A Theory of Economic Development', *American Economic Review*, September.

Schiff, M. and C. E. Montenegro (1999) 'Aggregate Agricultural Supply Response in Developing Countries: A Survey of Selected Issues', *Economic Development and Cultural Change*, Vol. 45, No. 2.

Schultz, T. W. (1964) *Transforming Traditional Agriculture* (New Haven, Conn.: Yale University Press).

Schultz, T. W. (1968) *Economic Growth and Agriculture* (New York: McGraw-Hill).

Schultz, T. W. (1980) 'The Economics of Being Poor', *Journal of Political Economy*, August.

Sen, A. (1966) 'Peasants and Dualism: With and Without Surplus Labour', *Journal of Political Economy*, October.

Southworth, H. and B. F. Johnston (eds) (1967) *Agricultural Development and Economic Growth* (Ithaca: Cornell University Press).

Stark, O. (1991) *The Migration of Labour* (Oxford: Blackwell).

'Symposium on Lewis' Model' (1979) *Manchester School*, September.

'Symposium on Lewis' Model after 50 years' (2004) *Manchester School*, December.

Thirlwall, A. P. (1986) 'A General Model of Growth and Development on Kaldorian Lines', *Oxford Economic Papers*, July.

Todaro, M. (1969) 'A Model of Labour Migration and Urban Unemployment in Less Developed Countries', *American Economic Review*, March.

Todaro, M. (1971) 'Income Expectations, Rural–Urban Migration and Employment in Africa', *International Labour Review*, November.

Todaro, M. (1976) *Internal Migration in Developing Countries* (ILO: Geneva).

World Bank (1979) *World Development Report 1979* (Washington, DC: World Bank).

World Bank (1982) *World Development Report 1982* (Washington, DC: World Bank).

World Bank (2000) *World Development Report 2000/2001: Attacking Poverty* (New York: Oxford University Press).

Yap, L. Y. L. (1977) 'The Attraction of Cities: A Review of the Migration Literature', *Journal of Development Economics*, 4.

CHAPTER 6   CAPITAL AND TECHNICAL PROGRESS

Arrow, K. (1962) 'The Economic Implications of Learning by Doing', *Review of Economic Studies*, June.

Barro, R. (1991) 'Economic Growth in a Cross-Section of Countries', *Quarterly Journal of Economics*, May.

Colclough, C. (1982) 'The Impact of Primary Schooling on Economic Development: A Review of the Evidence', *World Development*, April.

Denison, E. (1962) *The Sources of Economic Growth in the US and the Alternatives Before Us* (New York: Committee for Economic Development, Library of Congress).

Harrod, R. (1948) *Towards a Dynamic Economics* (London: Macmillan).

Hicks, J. (1932) *The Theory of Wages* (London: Macmillan).

Johnson, H. G. (1969) 'Comparative Cost and Commercial Policy Theory for a Developing

Economy', *Pakistan Development Review*, Supplement, Spring.

Lewis, A. (1955) *The Theory of Economic Growth* (London: Allen & Unwin).

Navaretti, G. B. and D. G. Tarr (2000) 'International Knowledge Flows and Economic Performance: A Review of the Evidence', *World Bank Economic Review*, January.

Psacharopoulos, G. (1985) 'Returns to Education: A Further International Update and Implications', *Journal of Human Resources*, April.

Psacharopoulos, G. (1991) *Education for Development* (Washington, DC: World Bank).

Psacharopoulos, G. (1994) 'Returns to Investment in Education: A Global Update', *World Development*, September.

Rostow, W. W. (1960) *The Stages of Economic Growth* (Cambridge: Cambridge University Press).

Schultz, T. Paul (1988) 'Education Investments and Returns', in H. Chenery and T. Srinivasan (eds), *Handbook of Development Economics, Vol. 1*, (Amsterdam: North-Holland).

Schultz, T. W. (1961) 'Investment in Human Capital', *American Economic Review*, March.

Schumpeter, J. (1934) *The Theory of Economic Development* (Cambridge, Mass.: Harvard University Press).

Schumpeter, J. (1943) *Capitalism, Socialism and Democracy* (London: Allen & Unwin).

Thirlwall, A. P. (ed.) (1987) *Keynes and Economic Development* (London: Macmillan).

United Nations (1999) *Human Development Report 1999* (New York: UNDP).

World Bank (1994) *World Development Report 1994: Infrastructure for Development* (Oxford: Oxford University Press).

CHAPTER 7 DUALISM, CENTRE–PERIPHERY MODELS AND THE PROCESS OF CUMULATIVE CAUSATION

Amin, S. (1974) *Accumulation on a World Scale: A Critique of the Theory of Underdevelopment* (New York: Monthly Review Press).

Baddeley, M., R. Martin and P. Tyler (1996) *European Regional Unemployment Disparities: Convergence or Persistence?*, Discussion Paper, 73 (Cambridge: Department of Land Economics, University of Cambridge).

Baran, P. (1957) *The Political Economy of Growth* (New York: Monthly Review Press).

Barro R. and X. Sala-í-Martin (1992) 'Convergence', *Journal of Political Economy*, April.

Dixon, R. and A. P. Thirlwall (1975) 'A Model of Regional Growth Rate Differences on Kaldorian Lines', *Oxford Economic Papers*, July.

Dos Santos, T. (1970) 'The Structure of Dependence', *American Economic Review, Papers and Proceedings*, May.

Dos Santos, T. (1973) 'The Crisis of Development Theory and the Problem of Dependence in Latin America', in H. Bernstein (ed.), *Underdevelopment and Development* (Harmondsworth: Penguin).

Emmanuel, A. (1972) *Unequal Exchange: A Study of the Imperialism of Trade* (New York: Monthly Review Press, translated from the French).

Fagerberg, J. and B. Verspagen (1996) 'Heading for Divergence? Regional Growth in Europe Reconsidered', *Journal of Common Market Studies*, September.

Fagerberg, J., B. Verspagen and M. Caniels (1996) *Technology, Growth, and Unemployment Across European Regions*, Working Paper, 565 (Norwegian Institute of International Affairs), December.

Frank, G. (1967) *Capitalism and Underdevelopment in Latin America* (New York: Monthly Review Press).

Gallup, J., J. Sachs and A. Mellinger (1998), 'Geography and Economic Development', in B. Pleskovic and J. Stiglitz (eds), *Annual World Bank Conference on Development Economics 1998* (Washington, DC: World Bank).

Higgins, B. (1956) 'The "Dualistic Theory" of Underdeveloped Areas', *Economic Development and Cultural Change*, January.

Hirschman, A. (1958) *Strategy of Economic Development* (Yale University Press).

Kaldor, N. (1970) 'The Case for Regional Policies', *Scottish Journal of Political Economy*, November.

Krugman, P. (1989) 'Differences in Income Elasticities and Trends in Real Exchange Rates', *European Economic Review*, May.

Krugman, P. (1991) *Geography and Trade* (Cambridge, MA: MIT Press).

Krugman, P. (1995) *Development, Geography and Economic Theory* (Cambridge, Mass.: MIT Press).

Krugman, P. (1998) 'The Role of Geography in Development', in B. Pleskovic and J. Stiglitz (eds), *Annual World Bank Conference on Development Economics 1998* (Washington, DC: World Bank).

Lipton, M. (1977) *Why Poor People Stay Poor* (London: Temple Smith).

Lucas, R. (1990) 'Why Doesn't Capital Flow from Rich to Poor Countries?' *American Economic Review, Papers and Proceedings*, May.

McCombie, J. S. L. and A. P. Thirlwall (1994) *Economic Growth and the Balance of Payments Constraint* (London: Macmillan).

Myrdal, G. (1957, 1963) *Economic Theory and Underdeveloped Regions* (London: Duckworth; paper, London: Methuen).

Prebisch, R. (1950) *The Economic Development of Latin America and its Principal Problems* (New York: ECLA, UN Dept of Economic Affairs).

Prebisch, R. (1959) 'Commercial Policy in the Underdeveloped Countries', *American Economic Review, Papers and Proceedings*, May.

Seers, D. (1962) 'A Model of Comparative Rates of Growth of the World Economy', *Economic Journal*, March.

Shankar, R. and A. Shah (2003) 'Bridging the Economic Divide within Countries: A Scorecard on the Performance of Regional Policies in Reducing Income Disparities', *World Development*, August.

Thirlwall, A. P. (1983) 'Foreign Trade Elasticities in Centre–Periphery Models of Growth and Development', *Banca Nazionale del Lavoro Quarterly Review*, September.

Toner, P. (1999) *Main Currents in Cumulative Causation* (London: Macmillan).

CHAPTER 8 POPULATION AND DEVELOPMENT

Cassen, R. (1976) 'Population and Development: A Survey', *World Development*, October.

Cassen, R. *et al.* (1994) *Population and Development: Old Debates, New Conclusions* (Washington, DC: Overseas Development Council).

Enke, S. (1966) 'The Economic Aspects of Slowing Population Growth', *Economic Journal*, March.

Enke, S. (1971) 'Economic Consequences of Rapid Population Growth', *Economic Journal*, December.

Hoover, E. and A. Coale (1958) *Population Growth and Economic Development in Low Income Countries* (Princeton: Princeton University Press).

Kelley, A. C. (1988) 'Economic Consequences of Population Change in the Third World', *Journal of Economic Literature*, December.

Kremer, M. (1993) 'Population Growth and Technology Change: One Million BC to 1990', *Quarterly Journal of Economics*, August.

Leibenstein, H. (1957) *Economic Backwardness and Economic Growth* (New York: Wiley).

Meade, J. (1967) 'Population Explosion, Standard of Living and Social Conflict', *Economic Journal*, June.

Modigliani, F. (1970) 'The Life Cycle Hypothesis of Saving and Inter-Country Differences in the Savings Ratio', in W. Eltis *et al.* (eds), *Induction, Growth and Trade: Essays in Honour of Sir Roy Harrod* (Oxford University Press).

Neher, P. A. (1971) 'Peasants, Procreation and Pensions', *American Economic Review*, June.

Nelson, R. (1956) 'A Theory of the Low Level Equilibrium Trap in Underdeveloped Countries', *American Economic Review*, December.

Ohlin, G. (1967) *Population Control and Economic Development* (Paris: OECD).

Petty, W. (1682) *Essay Concerning the Multiplication of Mankind* (London: Mark Pardoe)

Rawls, J. (1972) *A Theory of Justice* (Oxford: Oxford University Press).

Sidgwick, H. (1907) *Methods of Ethics*, 7th edn (London: Macmillan).

Simon, J. (ed.) (1992) *Population and Development in Poor Countries* (Princeton: Princeton University Press).

Simon, J. (1996) *The Ultimate Resource 2* (Princeton: Princeton University Press).

Simon, J. (1997) *The Economics of Population: Key Modern Writings, Vols 1 and 2* (Aldershot: Edward Elgar).

Thirlwall, A. P. (1972) 'A Cross Section Study of Population Growth and the Growth of Output and Per Capita Income in a Production Function Framework', *Manchester School*, December.

Thirlwall, A. P. (1988) 'Population Growth and Development', in D. Ironmonger, J. O. N. Perkins and T. V. Hoa (eds), *National Income and Economic Progress: Essays in Honour of Colin Clark* (London: Macmillan).

UN Population Fund (2003) *State of World Population 2002* (New York: United Nations).

UNDP (1999) *Human Development Report* (New York: United Nations).

World Bank (1984) *World Development Report 1984: Population Change and Development* (New York: Oxford University Press for the World Bank).

World Bank (2000) *World Development Report 2000/2001: Attacking Poverty* (Oxford: Oxford University Press).

CHAPTER 9   RESOURCE ALLOCATION IN DEVELOPING COUNTRIES: THE MARKET MECHANISM AND THE ROLE OF THE STATE

Abed, G. and S. Gupta (eds) (2002) *Governance, Corruption and Economic Performance* (Washington, DC: IMF).

Arndt, H. W. (1988) '"Market Failure" and Underdevelopment', *World Development*, February.

Bardhan, P. (1997) 'Corruption and Development: A Review of Issues', *Journal of Economic Literature*, 35 (3).

Bhatt, V. V. (1964) 'Theories of Balanced and Unbalanced Growth: A Critical Appraisal', *Kyklos*, 17.

Chang, H. and R. Rowthorn (eds) (1995) *The Role of the State in Economic Change* (New York: Oxford University Press).

Crabtree, D. and A. P. Thirlwall (eds) (1993) *Keynes and the Role of the State* (London: Macmillan).

Eckaus, R. (1955) 'The Factor Proportions Problem in Underdeveloped Areas', *American Economic Review*, September.

Eckstein, O. (1957) 'Investment Criteria for Economic Development and the Theory of Intertemporal Welfare Economics', *Quarterly Journal of Economics*, February.

Elliott, K. A. (ed.) (1997) *Corruption and the Global Economy* (Washington, DC: Institute for International Economics).

Galenson, W. and H. Leibenstein (1955) 'Investment Criteria, Productivity and Economic Development', *Quarterly Journal of Economics*, August.

Ghosh, P. K. (ed.) (1984) *Development Policy and Planning: A Third World Perspective* (Westport, Conn.: Greenwood Press).

Griffin, K. and J. Enos (1970) *Planning Development* (Reading, Mass.: Addison-Wesley).

Hagen, E. (1963) *Planning Economic Development* (Homewood, Ill.: Irwin).

Hirschman, A. (1958) *Strategy of Economic Development* (New Haven, Conn.: Yale University Press).

Kahn, A. (1951) 'Investment Criteria in Development Programmes', *Quarterly Journal of Economics*, February.

Kaldor, N. (1972) 'The Irrelevance of Equilibrium Economics', *Economic Journal*, December.

Killick, T. (1977) 'The Possibilities of Development Planning', *Oxford Economic Papers*, July.

Killick, T. (1989) *A Reaction Too Far: Economic Theory and the Role of the State in Developing Countries* (London: Overseas Development Institute).

Leibenstein, H. (1978) *General X-Efficiency Theory and Economic Development* (New York: Oxford University Press).

Lewis, A. (1955) *The Theory of Economic Growth* (London: Allen & Unwin).

Lewis, A. (1966) *Development Planning* (London: Allen & Unwin).

Lipton, M. (1962) 'Balanced and Unbalanced Growth in Underdeveloped Countries', *Economic Journal*, September.

Little, I. M. D. (1982) *Economic Development: Theory, Policies and International Relations* (New York: Basic Books).

Meier, R. (1965) *Developmental Planning* (New York: McGraw-Hill).

Nath, S. K. (1962) 'The Theory of Balanced Growth', *Oxford Economic Papers*, July.

Nurkse, R. (1953) *Problems of Capital Formation in Underdeveloped Countries* (Oxford: Oxford University Press).

Ranis, G. (1962) 'Investment Criteria, Productivity and Economic Development: An Empirical Comment', *Quarterly Journal of Economics*, May.

Rosenstein-Rodan, P. (1943) 'Problems of Industrialisation of East and South-East Europe', *Economic Journal*, June–September.

Scitovsky, T. (1954) 'Two Concepts of External Economies', *Journal of Political Economy*, April.

Sen, A. K. (1957) 'Some Notes on the Choice of Capital Intensity in Development Planning', *Quarterly Journal of Economics*, November.

Sen, A. K. (1968) *Choice of Techniques*, 3rd edn (Oxford: Basil Blackwell).

Stern, N. (1989) 'The Economics of Development: A Survey', *Economic Journal*, September.

Stewart, F. (2001) *Horizontal Inequality: A Neglected Dimension of Development* (WIDER: Helsinki)

Stewart, F. and Ghani, E. (1991) 'How Significant are Externalities for Development?', *World Development*, June.

Stiglitz, J. (1990) *Economic Role of the State* (London: Allen & Unwin).

Streeten, P. (1993) 'Markets and States: Against Minimalism', *World Development*, August.

Sutcliffe, R. (1964) 'Balanced and Unbalanced Growth', *Quarterly Journal of Economics*, November.

Tanzi, V. (1998) 'Corruption around the World', *IMF Staff Papers*, 43 (4).

Wade, R. (1990) *Governing the Market: Economic Theory and the Role of Government in East Asian Industrialisation* (Princeton: Princeton University Press).

Waterson, A. (1966) *Development Planning: Lessons of Experience* (Oxford: Oxford University Press).

World Bank (1997) *World Development Report 1997: The State in a Changing World* (New York: Oxford University Press).

World Bank (2004) *Doing Business in 2004: Understanding Regulation* (New York: Oxford University Press).

CHAPTER 10 PROJECT APPRAISAL, SOCIAL COST-BENEFIT ANALYSIS AND SHADOW WAGES

Baldwin, G. B. (1972) 'A Layman's Guide to Little–Mirrlees', *Finance and Development*, 9 (1).

Brent, R. (1998) *Cost–Benefit Analysis for Developing Countries* (Cheltenham: Edward Elgar).

Curry, S. and J. Weiss (1993) *Project Analysis in Developing Countries* (London: Macmillan).

Dasgupta, P., S. Marglin and A. K. Sen (1972) *Guidelines for Project Evaluation* (New York: United Nations).

Dinwiddy, C. and F. Teal (1996) *Principles of Cost–Benefit Analysis for Developing Countries* (Cambridge: Cambridge University Press).

Fitzgerald, E. V. K. (1978) *Public Sector Investment Planning for Developing Countries* (London: Macmillan).

Hansen, J. R. (1979) *A Guide to the UNIDO Guidelines* (Vienna: UNIDO).

Kirkpatrick, C. and J. Weiss (eds) (1996) *Cost–Benefit Analysis and Project Appraisal in Developing Countries* (Cheltenham: Edward Elgar).

Lal, D. (1980) *Prices for Planning: Towards the Reform of Indian Planning* (London: Heinemann).

Lefeber, L. (1968) 'Planning in a Surplus Labour Economy', *American Economic Review*, June.

Little, I. M. D. (1961) 'The Real Cost of Labour and the Choice Between Consumption and Investment', *Quarterly Journal of Economics*, February.

Little, I. M. D. and J. Mirrlees (1969) *Manual of Industrial Project Analysis in Developing Countries, Vol. II: Social Cost–Benefit Analysis* (Paris: OECD).

Little, I. M. D. and J. Mirrlees (1974) *Project Appraisal and Planning for Developing Countries* (London: Heinemann).

Overseas Development Administration (1972) *A Guide to Project Appraisal in Developing Countries* (London: HMSO).

Papps, I. (1987) 'Techniques of Project Appraisal', in N. Gemmell (ed.), *Surveys in Development Economics* (Oxford: Blackwell).

Pearce, D. W. (1971) *Cost–Benefit Analysis* (London: Macmillan).

Scott, M., J. MacArthur and D. Newbery (1976) *Project Appraisal in Practice* (London: Heinemann).

Sen, A. K. (1968) *Choice of Techniques, 3rd edn* (Oxford: Basil Blackwell).

Squire, L. and H. G. van der Tak (1975) *Economic Analysis of Projects* (Baltimore, Md.: Johns Hopkins University Press).

Stewart, F. (1978) 'Social Cost–Benefit Analysis in Practice: Some Reflections in the Light of Case Studies Using Little–Mirrlees Techniques', *World Development*, February.

Symposium on Little–Mirrlees (1972) *Oxford Bulletin of Economics and Statistics*, February.

Thirlwall, A. P. (1970) 'An Extension of Sen's Model of the Valuation of Labour in Surplus Labour Economies', *Pakistan Development Review*, Autumn.

Thirlwall, A. P. (1977) 'The Shadow Wage when Consumption is Productive', *Bangladesh Development Studies*, October–December.

CHAPTER 11   DEVELOPMENT AND THE ENVIRONMENT

Anderson, V. (1991) *Alternative Economic Indicators* (London: Routledge).

Barbier, E. R. (1989) *Economics, Natural-Resource Scarcity and Development* (London: Earthscan).

Barnett, H. J. and C. Morse (1963) *Scarcity and Growth: The Economics of Natural Resource Availability* (Baltimore, Md.: Johns Hopkins University Press).

Baumol, W. and W. Oates (1988) *The Theory of Environmental Policy*, 2nd ed. (Cambridge: Cambridge University Press).

Beckerman, W. (1992) 'Economists, Scientists and Environmental Catastrophe', *Oxford Economic Papers*, 24.

Blackman, A., M. Mathis and P. Nelson (2001) *The Greening of Development Economics* (Washington, DC: Resources for the Future).

Blowers, A. and P. Glasbergen (1996) *Environmental Policy in an International Context* (Chichester: John Wiley).

Bond, R., J. Curran, C. Kirkpatrick, N. Lee and P. Francis (2001), 'Integrated Impact Assessment for Sustainable Development: A Case Study Approach', *World Development*, June.

Boulding, K. E. (1966) 'The Economics of the Coming Spaceship Earth', in H. Jarrett (ed.), *Environmental Quality in a Growing Economy* (Baltimore, Md.: Johns Hopkins University Press).

Bowers, J. (1997) *Sustainability and Environmental Economics: An Alternative Text* (Harlow: Longman).

Carson, R. (1962) *Silent Spring* (Boston: Houghton-Mifflin).

Cole, M. A. (2003) 'Development, Trade and the Environment: How Robust is the Environmental Kuznets Curve?' *Environment and Development Economics*, 8.

Common, M. (1995) *Sustainability and Policy: Limits to Economics* (Cambridge: Cambridge University Press).

Common, M. (1996) *Environmental and Resource Economics: An Introduction*, 2nd edn (London: Longman).

Commoner, B. (1972) *The Closing Circle* (London: Cape).

Conable, B. (1989) 'Development and the Environment: A Global Balance', *Finance and Development*, December.

Dasgupta, P. (1982) *The Control of Resources* (Oxford: Blackwell).

Dasgupta, P. and G. M. Heal (1979) *Economic Theory and Exhaustible Resources* (Cambridge: Cambridge University Press).

Dawkins, R. (1976) *The Selfish Gene* (Oxford: Oxford University Press).

de Bruyn, S. (2001) *Economic Growth and the Environment* (Dordrecht: Kluwer).

Ehrlich, P. R. and A. H. Ehrlich (1970) *Population, Resources, Environment: Issues in Human Ecology* (San Francisco, Cal.: Freeman).

Environment and Development Economics (1998), Special Issue on Environmental Kuznets Curve, 2 (4).

Fankhauser, S. (1995) *Valuing Climate Change: The Economics of the Greenhouse* (London: Earthscan).

Forrester, J. (1971) *World Dynamics* (Cambridge: Wright-Allen Press).

Goldsmith, E., R. Allen, M. Allaby, J. Davoli, and S. Lawrence (1972) *Blue Print for Survival* (London: Penguin).

Grossman, G. and A. Krueger (1995) 'Economic Growth and the Environment', *Quarterly Journal of Economics*, May.

Hanley, N. and A. Owen (eds) (2004) *The Economics of Climate Change* (London: Routledge).

Hanley, N. and G. Atkinson (2003) 'Economics and Sustainable Development: What Have we Learnt, and What do we Still Need to Learn?' in F. Berkhout, M. Leach and I. Scoones (eds) *Negotiating Environmental Change* (Cheltenham: Earthscan).

Hanley, N., J. Shogren and B. White (1997) *Environmental Economics: In Theory and Practice* (Basingstoke: Macmillan).

Hanley, N. and C. Spash (1993) *Cost Benefit Analysis and the Environment* (Aldershot: Edward Elgar).

Hicks, J. (1946) *Value and Capital*, 2nd edn (Oxford: Oxford University Press).

Horta, K. (1996) 'The World Bank and International Monetary Fund', in J. Werksman, *Greening International Institutions* (London: Earthscan).

IMF (International Monetary Fund) (1993) 'Seminar Explores Links Between Macro Policy and Environment' (Washington, DC: International Monetary Fund).

International Union for the Conservation of Nature and Natural Resources (1980) *World Conservation Strategy* (Gland: United Nations Environment and World Wildlife Fund).

Katz, M. L. and H. S. Rosen (1998) *Microeconomics*, 3rd edn (Boston: Irwin/McGraw-Hill).

Kay, J. and J. Mirrlees (1975) 'The Desirability of Natural Resource Depletion', in D. W. Pearce (ed.), *The Economics of Natural Resource Depletion* (London: Macmillan).

Kneese, A. V., R. V. Ayres and R. C. D'Arge (1970) *Economics and the Environment: A Materials Balance Approach* (Baltimore, Md.: Johns Hopkins University Press).

Lele, S. (1991) 'Sustainable Development: A Critical Review', *World Development*, June.

Little, I. M. D. and J. Mirrlees (1969) *Manual of Industrial Project Analysis in Developing Countries, vol. II: Social Cost–Benefit Analysis* (Paris: OECD).

Lutz, E. (1993) *Towards Improved Accounting for the Environment: An UNSTAD–World Bank Symposium* (Washington, DC: World Bank).

Makuch, Z. (1996) 'The World Trade Organisation and the General Agreement on Tariffs and Trade', in J. Werksman, *Greening International Institutions* (London: Earthscan).

Malthus, T. (1798) *Essay on the Principle of Population* (London: Penguin 1983).

Marshall, A. (1890) *Principles of Economics* (London: Macmillan).

Masu, I. (1997) *National Accounts and the Environment* (Amsterdam: Kluwer).

Meadows, D. H., D. L. Meadows, R. Randers and W. W. Behrens (1972) *The Limits to Growth* (New York: Universe Books).

Mensah, C. (1996) 'The United Nations Commission on Sustainable Development', in J. Werksman, *Greening International Institutions* (London: Earthscan).

Mill, J. S. (1856) *The Principles of Political Economy* (London: Penguin, 1986).

Nordhaus, W. D. and J. Tobin (1972) 'Is Growth Obsolete?', in National Bureau of Economic Research, *Economic Growth* (Columbia: Columbia University Press).

Norton, B. G. (1987) *Why Preserve Natural Variety?* (Princeton: Princeton University Press).

OECD (1994) *Environmental Indicators: OECD Core Set* (Paris: OECD).

OECD (1999) *Economic Instruments for the Pollution Control and Natural Resource Management in OECD Countries: A Survey* (Paris: OECD).

Pearce, D. and G. Atkinson (1995) 'Measuring Sustainable Development', in D. Bromley (ed.), *The Handbook of Environmental Economics* (Oxford: Blackwell).

Pearce, D. and G. Atkinson (1998) 'The Concept of Sustainable Development: An Evaluation of its Use Ten Years after Brundtland', *Swiss Journal of Economics*, 8.

Pearce, D. and R. K. Turner (1990) *Economics of Natural Resources and the Environment* (Hemel Hempstead: Harvester Wheatsheaf).

Perman, R., Y. Ma, J. McGilvray and M. Common (2003) *Natural Resource and Environmental Economics*, 3rd edn (Harlow: Pearson Education).

Pigou, A. C. (1920) *The Economics of Welfare* (London: Macmillan).

Reed, D. (1996) *Structural Adjustment, the Environment and Sustainable Development* (London: Earthscan).

Repetto, R., W. Margrath, M. Wells, C. Beer and F. Rossini (1989) *Wasting Assets: Natural Resources in National Income Accounts* (Washington, DC: World Resources Institute).

Ricardo, D. (1817) *Principles of Political Economy and Taxation* (London: Everyman 1992).

Rogers, A. (1993) *The Earth's Summit: A Planetary Reckoning* (Los Angeles, Cal.: Global View Press).

Runge, C. (1995) 'Trade, Pollution and Environmental Protection', in D. Bromley (ed.), *The Handbook of Environmental Economics* (Oxford: Blackwell).

Sagoff, M. (1988) *The Economy of the Earth* (Cambridge: Cambridge University Press).

Schmalensee, R., P. Joskow, A. Ellerman, J. Monterro and E. Bailey (1998) 'An Interim Evaluation of Sulphur Dioxide Emissions Trading', *Journal of Economic Perspectives*, 12.

Schumacher, E. (1973) *Small is Beautiful: Economics as if People Mattered* (London: Blond & Briggs).

Sen, A. (1967) 'Isolation, Assurance and the Social Rate of Discount', *Quarterly Journal of Economics*, 81.

Sjöberg, H. (1996) 'The Global Environment Facility', in J. Werksman, *Greening International Institutions* (London: Earthscan).

Stokke, O. S. and O. B. Thommessen (2003) *Yearbook of International Co-operation on Environment and Development 2003/2004* (London: Earthscan).

Turner, K. (1993) *Sustainable Environmental Economics and Management: Principles and Practice* (Chichester: John Wiley).

United Nations (1993a) *Earth's Summit: Agenda 21, United Nations Programme of Action from Rio* (New York: United Nations Department of Public Information).

United Nations (1993b) *Handbook of National Accounting: Integrated Environmental and Economic Accounting* (New York: United Nations).

Varian, H. (2002) *Intermediate Microeconomics: A Modern Approach*, 6th edn (New York: Norton).

Werksman, J. (1996) *Greening International Institutions* (London: Earthscan).

Winpenny, J. (1995) *Economic Appraisal of Environmental Projects and Policies: A Practical Guide* (Paris: OECD).

World Bank (1992) *World Development Report 1992* (New York: Oxford University Press).

World Bank (2002) *World Development Report: Sustainable Development in a Dynamic World* (Washington: World Bank).

World Bank (2004) *World Development Indicators, 2004* (Washington: World Bank).

World Commission on Environment and Development (1987) *Our Common Future* (Brundtland Report) (Oxford: Oxford Univesity Press).

Wunder, S. (2001) 'Poverty Alleviation and Tropical Forests – What Scope for Synergies', *World Development*, November.

CHAPTER 12   THE CHOICE OF TECHNIQUES

Ahiakpor, J. (1989) 'Do Firms Choose Inappropriate Technology in LDCs?', *Economic Development and Cultural Change*, April.

Bagachwa, M. (1992) 'Choice of Technique in Small and Large Firms: Grain Milling in Tanzania', *World Development*, January.

Bell, M. and K. Pavitt (1992) 'Accumulating Technological Capability in Developing Countries', *World Bank Economic Review, Supplement*.

Bhalla, A. (1964) 'Investment Allocation and Technological Choice – A Case of Cotton Spinning Techniques', *Economic Journal*, September.

Bliss, C. and N. Stern (1978) 'Productivity, Wages and Nutrition, Parts I and II', *Journal of Development Economics*, 5.

Bruton, H. (1987) 'Technology Choice and Factor Proportions Problems in LDCs', in N. Gemmell (ed.), *Surveys in Development Economics* (Oxford: Blackwell).

Dasgupta, P. (1993) *An Inquiry into Well-Being and Destitution* (Oxford: Clarendon Press).

Dobb, M. (1955) 'A Note on the so-called Degree of Capital Intensity of Investment in Underdeveloped Countries', in *On Economic Theory and Socialism* (London: Routledge & Kegan Paul).

Forsyth, D. and R. Solomon (1977) 'Choice of Technology and Nationality of Ownership in a Developing Country', *Oxford Economic Papers*, July.

Helleiner, G. K. (1975) 'The Role of Multinational Corporations in the Less Developed Countries' Trade in Technology', *World Development*, April.

Jenkins, R. (1990) 'Comparing Foreign Subsidiaries and Local Firms in LDCs', *Journal of Development Studies*, January.

Lall, S. (1978) 'Transnationals, Domestic Enterprises and Industrial Structures in Host LDCs: A Survey', *Oxford Economic Papers*, July.

Lall, S. (1992) 'Technological Capabilities and Industrialisation', *World Development*, February.

Pack, H. (1974) 'The Employment–Output Trade-Off in LDCs – A Microeconomic Approach', *Oxford Economic Papers*, November.

Pack, H. (1976) 'The Substitution of Labour for Capital in Kenyan Manufacturing', *Economic Journal*, March.

Pack, H. (1982) 'Aggregate Implications of Factor Substitution in Industrial Processes', *Journal of Development Economics*, 11.

Sen, A. K. (1968) *Choice of Techniques*, 3rd edn (Oxford: Basil Blackwell).

Sen, A. K. (1969) 'Choice of Technology: A Critical Survey of a Class of Debates', in UNIDO, *Planning for Advanced Skills and Technology* (New York: UNIDO).

Sen, A. K. (1975) *Employment, Technology and Development* (Oxford: Clarendon Press).

Stewart, F. (1977) *Technology and Underdevelopment* (London: Macmillan).

Thirlwall, A. P. (1974) *Inflation, Saving and Growth in Developing Economies* (London: Macmillan).

Thirlwall, A. P. (1977) 'The Shadow Wage when Consumption is Productive', *Bangladesh Development Studies*, October–December.

Thirlwall, A. P. (1978) 'Reconciling the Conflict Between Employment and Saving and Employment and Output in the Choice of Techniques in Developing Countries', *Rivista Internazionale di Scienze Economiche e Commerciali*, February.

White, L. (1978) 'The Evidence on Appropriate Factor Proportions for Manufacturing in LDCs: A Survey', *Economic Development and Cultural Change*, October.

CHAPTER 13   INPUT–OUTPUT ANALYSIS

Bulmer-Thomas, V. (1982) *Input–Output Analysis in Developing Countries* (Chichester: John Wiley).

Cella, G. (1984) 'On the Input–Output Measurement of Interindustry Linkages', *Oxford Bulletin of Economics and Statistics*, February.

Chenery, H. B. and P. G. Clark (1959) *Interindustry Economics* (New York: Wiley).

Lahr, M. and E. Dietzenbacher (eds) (2001) *Input-Output Analysis: Frontiers and Extensions* (Basingstoke: Palgrave Macmillan).

Leontief, W. *et al.* (1953) *Studies in the Structure of the American Economy* (Oxford University Press).

Lewis, A. (1966) *Development Planning* (London: Allen & Unwin).

CHAPTER 14 FINANCING DEVELOPMENT FROM DOMESTIC RESOURCES

African Development Report 1994: Financial Structures, Reforms and Economic Development in Africa (Abidjan: African Development Bank).

Ahmad, E. and N. Stern (1991) *The Theory and Practice of Tax Reform in Developing Countries* (Cambridge: Cambridge University Press).

Arestis, P. and P. Demetriades (1997) 'Financial Development and Economic Growth: Assessing the Evidence', *Economic Journal*, May.

Athukorala, P. (1998) 'Interest Rates, Savings and Investment: Evidence from India', *Oxford Development Studies*, June.

Bandiera, O., G. Caprio, P. Honohan and F. Schiantarelli (2000) 'Does Financial Reform Raise or Reduce Saving?', *Review of Economics and Statistics*, May.

Barro, R. (1995) 'Inflation and Economic Growth', *Bank of England Quarterly Bulletin*, 2.

Bird, R. M. (1991) *Tax Policy and Economic Development* (Baltimore, Md.: Johns Hopkins University Press).

Bleaney, M. *et al.* (1995) 'Tax Revenue Instability with Particular Reference to Sub-Saharan Africa', *Journal of Development Studies*, 6.

Bruno, M. (1995) 'Does Inflation Really Lower Growth?', *Finance and Development*, September.

Bruno, M. and W. Easterly (1998) 'Inflation Crisis and Long Run Growth', *Journal of Monetary Economics*, 41.

Buffie, E. F. (1984) 'Financial Repression, the New Structuralists and Stabilisation Policy in Semi-industrialised Economies', *Journal of Development Economics*, April.

Burgess, R. and N. Stern (1993) 'Taxation and Development', *Journal of Economic Literature*, June.

Campos, R. (1961) 'Two Views on Inflation in Latin America', in A. Hirschman (ed.), *Latin American Issues* (New Haven, Conn.: Yale University Press).

Chelliah, R. J., H. J. Bass and M. R. Kelly (1975) 'Tax Ratios and Tax Effort in Developing Countries 1969–71', *IMF Staff Papers*, March.

Cho, Y. C. and D. Khatkhate (1990) 'Financial Liberalisation: Issues and Evidence', *Economic and Political Weekly*, May.

Clarke, R. (1996) 'Equilibrium Interest Rates and Financial Liberalisation in Developing Countries', *Journal of Development Studies*, February.

Davidson, P. (1986) 'Finance, Funding, Saving and Investment', *Journal of Post Keynesian Economics*, Fall.

De Gregorio, J. and P. Guidotti (1995) 'Financial Development and Economic Growth', *World Development*, March.

Demetriades, P. O. and P. Devereux (1992) 'Investment and "Financial Repression", Theory and Evidence from 63 LDCs', *Working Paper in Economics*, 92/16, Keele University.

Demetriades, P. O. and K. A. Hussein (1996) 'Does Financial Development Cause Economic Growth? Time Series Evidence from 16 Countries', *Journal of Development Economics*, 51.

Diaz-Alejandro, C. (1985) 'Good-bye Financial Repression, Hello Financial Crash', *Journal of Development Economics*, September–October.

Dornbusch, R. and A. Reynoso (1989) 'Financial Factors in Economic Development', *American Economic Review, Papers and Proceedings*, May.

Drake, P. J. (1980) *Money, Finance and Development* (London: Martin Robertson).

Dutt, A. (1990–1) 'Interest Rate Policy in LDCs: A Post Keynesian View', *Journal of Post Keynesian Economics*, Winter.

Edwards, S. (1996) 'Why are Latin America's Savings Rates so Low? An International Comparative Analysis', *Journal of Development Economics*, 51.

Eshag, E. (1983) *Fiscal and Monetary Policies and Problems in Developing Countries* (Cambridge: Cambridge University Press).

Fitzgerald, E. V. K. (1993) *The Macroeconomics of Development Finance: A Kaleckian Approach* (London: Macmillan).

Fry, M. (1989) 'Financial Development: Theories and Recent Experience', *Oxford Review of Economic Policy*, Winter.

Fry, M. (1995) *Money, Interest and Banking in Economic Development* (Baltimore, Md.: Johns Hopkins University Press).

Fry, M. (1997) 'In Favour of Financial Liberalisation', *Economic Journal*, May.

Ghatak, S. (1981) *Monetary Economics in Developing Countries* (London: Macmillan).

Ghosh, A. and S. Phillips (1998) 'Inflation may be Harmful to Your Growth', *IMF Staff Papers*, December.

Gibson, H. and E. Tsakolotos (1994) 'The Scope and Limits of Financial Liberalisation in Developing Countries: A Critical Survey', *Journal of Development Studies*, April.

Gillis, M. (ed.) (1989) *Tax Reform in Developing Countries* (Durham, NC: Duke University Press).

Gillis, M., D. Perkins, M. Roemer and D. Snodgrass (1996) *Economics of Development* (New York: W. W. Norton).

Giovannini, A. (1983) 'The Interest Rate Elasticity of Savings in Developing Countries', *World Development*, July.

Giovannini, A. (1985) 'Saving and the Real Interest Rate in LDCs', *Journal of Development Economics*, August.

Goode, R. (1993) 'Tax Advice to Developing Countries: An Historical Survey', *World Development*, January.

Greene, J. and D. Villanueva (1991) 'Private Investment in Developing Countries: An Empirical Analysis', *IMF Staff Papers*, 1.

Gupta, K. L. (1987) 'Aggregate Savings, Financial Intermediation and Interest Rates', *Review of Economics and Statistics*, May.

Gurley, G. J. and E. Shaw (1960) *Money in a Theory of Finance* (Washington, DC: Brookings Institution).

Hamilton, E. (1952) 'Prices as a Factor in Business Growth', *Journal of Economic History*, Autumn.

Hossain, A. and A. Chowdhury (1996) 'Monetary and Financial Policies', in *Developing Countries: Growth and Stabilisation* (London: Routledge).

Hussein, K. and A. P. Thirlwall (1999) 'Explaining Differences in the Domestic Savings Ratio Across Countries: A Panel Data Study', *Journal of Development Studies*, October.

Johnson, O. E. G. (1984) 'On Growth and Inflation in Developing Countries', *IMF Staff Papers*, December.

Kaldor, N. (1955–6) 'Alternative Theories of Distribution', *Review of Economic Studies*, 2.

Kaldor, N. (1956) *Indian Tax Reform* (Delhi: Ministry of Finance).

Kaldor, N. (1980) *Reports on Taxation II, Collected Economic Essays, Vol. 8* (London: Duckworth).

Keynes, J. M. (1930) *Treatise on Money, Vol. 2* (London: Macmillan).

Keynes, J. M. (1931) *Essays in Persuasion* (London: Macmillan).

King, R. G. and R. Levine (1993) 'Finance and Growth: Schumpeter Might be Right', *Quarterly Journal of Economics*, August.

Kirkpatrick, C. H. and F. I. Nixson (1981) 'The Origins of Inflation in Less Developed Countries: A Selective Review', in I. Livingstone (ed.), *Development Economics and Policy: Readings* (London: Allen & Unwin).

Levine, R. (1997) 'Financial Development and Economic Growth: Views and Agenda', *Journal of Economic Literature*, June.

Levine, R. and S. Zervos (1993) 'What we have Learned About Policy and Growth From Cross-Country Regressions', *American Economic Review, Papers and Proceedings*, May.

Lewis, A. (1955) *The Theory of Economic Growth* (London: Allen & Unwin).

Loayza, N., K. Schmidt-Hebbel and L. Serven (2000) 'What Drives Private Saving Across the World?', *Review of Economics and Statistics*, May.

Masson, P., J. Bayoumi and H. Samiei (1998) 'International Evidence on the Determinants of Private Saving', *World Bank Economic Review*, September.

McKinnon, R. (1973) *Money and Capital in Economic Development* (Washington, DC: Brookings Institution).

McKinnon, R. (1991) *The Order of Economic Liberalisation: Financial Control in the Transition to the Market Economy* (Baltimore, Md.: Johns Hopkins University Press).

Mikesell, R. and J. Zinser (1973) 'The Nature of the Savings Function in Developing Countries: A Survey of the Theoretical and Empirical Literature', *Journal of Economic Literature*, March.

Modigliani, F. and R. Brumberg (1954) 'Utility Analysis and the Consumption Function: An Integration of Cross Section Data', in K. K. Kurihara (ed.), *Post-Keynesian Economics* (New Brunswick: Rutgers University Press).

Molho, L. E. (1986) 'Interest Rates, Saving and Investment in Developing Countries: A Re-examination of the McKinnon–Shaw Hypothesis, *IMF Staff Papers*, March.

Morduch, J. (1999) 'The Microfinance Promise', *Journal of Economic Literature*, 37 (4).

Newbery, D. and N. Stern (1987) *The Theory of Taxation for Developing Countries* (Oxford: Oxford University Press for the World Bank).

Ogaki, M., J. D. Ostry and C. M. Reinhart (1996) 'Savings Behaviour in Low and Middle Income Developing Countries', *IMF Staff Papers*, March.

Ostry, J. D. and C. M. Reinhart (1995) 'Savings and the Real Interest Rate in Developing Countries', *Finance and Development*, December.

Pastor, M. (1991) 'Bolivia: Hyperinflation, Stabilisation and Beyond', *Journal of Development Studies*, January.

Piancastelli, M. (2001) 'Measuring the Tax Effort of Developed and Developing Countries: Cross Country Panel Data Analysis 1985–95', mimeo, University of Kent at Canterbury.

Reinke, J. (1998) 'How to Lend Like Mad and Make a Profit: A Micro-credit Paradigm versus the Start-up Fund in South Africa, *Journal of Development Studies*, February.

Robinson, J. (1960) 'Notes on the Theory of Economic Development', in *Collected Economic Papers* (Oxford: Blackwell).

Robinson, J. (1962) 'A Model of Accumulation', in *Essays in the Theory of Economic Growth* (London: Macmillan).

Rostow, W. W. (1960) *The Stages of Economic Growth* (Cambridge: Cambridge University Press).

Sarel, M. (1996) 'Nonlinear Effects of Inflation on Economic Growth', *IMF Staff Papers*, March.

Schumpeter, J. (1911) *The Theory of Economic Development* (Cambridge, Mass.: Harvard University Press).

Shaw, E. (1973) *Financial Deepening in Economic Development* (London: Oxford University Press).

Stanners, W. (1993) 'Is Low Inflation an Important Condition for High Growth?' *Cambridge Journal of Economics*, March.

Stiglitz, J. E. and A. Weiss (1981) 'Credit Rationing in Markets with Imperfect Information', *American Economic Review*, June.

Tait, A. A. *et al.* (1979) 'International Comparisons of Taxation for Selected Developing Countries', *IMF Staff Papers*, March.

Tanzi, V. (1987) 'Quantitative Characteristics of the Tax System of Developing Countries', in D. Newbery and N. Stern (eds), *The Theory of Taxation for Developing Countries* (Oxford: Oxford University Press for the World Bank).

Tanzi, V. (1991) *Public Finance in Developing Countries* (Aldershot: Edward Elgar).

Temple, J. (2000) 'Inflation and Growth: Stories Short and Tall', *Journal of Economic Surveys*, September.

Thirlwall, A. P. (1974) *Inflation, Saving and Growth in Developing Economies* (London: Macmillan).

Thirlwall, A. P. (1976) *Financing Economic Development* (London: Macmillan).

Thirlwall, A. P. and C. Barton (1971) 'Inflation and Growth: The International Evidence', *Banca Nazionale del Lavoro Quarterly Review*, September.

Thirlwall, A. P. (1987) *Nicholas Kaldor* (Brighton: Wheatsheaf).

Tun Wai, U. (1972) *Financial Intermediaries and National Savings in Developing Countries* (New York: Praeger).

Warman, F. and A. P. Thirlwall (1994) 'Interest Rates, Savings, Investment and Growth in Mexico 1960–90: Tests of the Financial Liberalisation Hypothesis', *Journal of Development Studies*, April.

Williamson, J. and M. Mohar (1999) 'A Survey of Financial Liberalisation', *Princeton Essays in International Finance*, 211.

Woo Jung, S. (1986) 'Financial Development and Economic Growth: International Evidence', *Economic Development and Cultural Change*, 34.

World Bank (1989) 'Financial Systems and Development: An Overview', *World Development Report* (Washington, DC: World Bank).

World Bank (1990) *Adjustment Lending: Ten Years of Experience* (Washington, DC: World Bank).

World Bank (1993) *The East Asian Miracle: Economic Growth and Public Policies* (Oxford: Oxford University Press).

World Bank (2000) *World Development Report 2000/2001: Attacking Poverty* (New York: Oxford University Press).

World Bank (2001) *World Development Report 2002* (Oxford: Oxford University Press).

CHAPTER 15 FOREIGN ASSISTANCE, DEBT AND DEVELOPMENT

Alesina, A. and D. Dollar (2000) Who Gives Foreign Aid to Whom and Why, *Journal of Economic Growth*, 5.

Allsopp, C. and V. Joshi (1991) 'The Assessment: the International Debt Crisis', *Oxford Review of Economic Policy*, Spring.

Bauer, P. (1971) *Dissent on Development* (London: Weidenfeld & Nicolson).

Borensztein, E., J. De Gregorio and J.-W. Lee (1995) 'How Does Foreign Investment Affect Growth?', *NBER Working Paper*, 5057 (Cambridge, Mass.: NBER).

Bosworth, S. and S. Collins (1999) 'Capital Flows to Developing Economies: Implications for Savings and Investment', *Brookings Papers on Economic Activity*, 1.

Bourguignon, F. and C. Morrisson (1992) *Adjustment and Equality in Developing Countries: A New Approach* (Paris: OECD).

Burnside, C. and D. Dollar (2000) 'Aid, Policies and Growth', *American Economic Review*, September.

Cassen, R. (1994) *Does Aid Work?*, 2nd edn (Oxford: Clarendon Press).

Chenery, H. and I. Adelman (1966) 'Foreign Aid and Economic Development: The Case of Greece', *Review of Economics and Statistics*, February.

Chenery, H. and M. Bruno (1962) 'Development Alternatives in an Open Economy: The Case of Israel', *Economic Journal*, March.

Chenery, H. and A. Macewan (1966) 'Optimal Patterns of Growth and Aid: The Case of Pakistan', *Pakistan Development Review*, Summer.

Chenery, H. and A. Strout (1966) 'Foreign Assistance and Economic Development', *American Economic Review*, September.

Claudon, M. P. (ed.) (1986) *World Debt Crisis* (Cambridge, Mass.: Ballinger).

Cline, W. R. (1984) *International Debt: Systematic Risk and Policy Response* (Washington, DC: MIT Press for the Institute for International Economics).

Cline, W. (1995) *International Debt* (Harlow: Longman).

Coe, D., E. Helpman and A. Hoffmaister (1997) 'North–South R&D Spillovers', *Economic Journal*, January.

Collier, P. and D. Dollar (2000) *Aid Allocation and Poverty Reduction* (Washington, DC: World Bank).

Collier, P. and N. Rickman (2004) 'Development Effectiveness: What Have We Learnt?', *Economic Journal*, June.

Colman, D. and F. Nixson (1978) *Economics of Change in Less Developed Countries* (Oxford: Philip Allan).

Corbo, V., S. Fischer and S. B. Webb (1992) in *Adjustment Lending Revisited: Policies to Restore Growth* (Washington, DC: World Bank).

Cornia, G., R. Jolly and F. Stewart (1987, 1988) *Adjustment with a Human Face*, Vols I and II (Oxford: Oxford University Press).

Dalgaard, C. J., H. Hansen and F. Tarp (2004) 'On the Empirics of Foreign Aid and Growth', *Economic Journal*, June.

Daseking, C. (2002) 'Debt: How Much is too Much?', *Finance and Development*, December.

Davidson, P. (1992) *International Money and the Real World*, 2nd edn (London: Macmillan).

de Mello, L. (1997) 'Foreign Investment in Developing Countries and Growth: A Selective Survey', *Journal of Development Studies*, October.

Easterly, W. (2002) 'How Did Heavily Indebted Poor Countries Become Heavily Indebted? Reviewing Two Decades of Debt Relief', *World Development*, October.

El Shibley, M. and A. P. Thirlwall (1981) 'Dual-Gap Analysis for the Sudan', *World Development*, February.

Frank, A. G. (1981) *Crisis in the Third World* (London: Heinemann).

Gibson, H. D. and A. P. Thirlwall (1989) 'An International Comparison of the Causes of Changes in the Debt Service Ratio 1980–85', *Banca Nazionale del Lavoro Quarterly Review*, March.

Gilbert, C., A. Powell and D. Vines (1999) 'Positioning the World Bank', *Economic Journal*, November.

Gilbert, C. and D. Vines (eds) (2000) *The World Bank: Structure and Policies* (Cambridge: Cambridge University Press).

Greenaway, D. and O. Morrissey (1993) 'Structural Adjustment and Liberalisation in Developing Countries: What Lessons Have We Learnt?' *Kyklos*, 2.

Griffin, K. (1970) 'Foreign Capital, Domestic Savings and Economic Development', *Bulletin of the Oxford Institute of Economics and Statistics*, May.

Griffith-Jones, S. and O. Sunkel (1986) *Debt and Development Crisis in Latin America* (Oxford: Clarendon Press).

Hansen, H. and F. Tarp (2001) 'Aid and Growth Regressions', *Journal of Development Economics*, April.

Harrigan, J. and P. Mosley (1991) 'Evaluating the Impact of World Bank Structural Adjustment Lending 1980–87', *Journal of Development Studies*, April.

Hermes, N. and R. Lensink (eds) (2001) 'Changing the Conditions for Development Aid', *Journal of Development Studies*, August.

Horowitz, D. (1969) *The Abolition of Poverty* (New York: Praeger).

Jepma, C. (1991) *The Tying of Aid* (Paris: OECD).

Kennedy, C. (1968) 'Restraints and the Allocation of Resources', *Oxford Economic Papers*, July.

Kennedy, C. and A. P. Thirlwall (1971) 'Foreign Capital, Domestic Savings and Economic Development: Some Comments', *Bulletin of the Oxford Institute of Economics and Statistics*, May.

Keynes, J. M. (1919) *Economic Consequences of the Peace* (London: Macmillan).

Lall, S. (1974) 'Less Developed Countries and Private Foreign Direct Investment: A Review Article', *World Development*, 2 (4, 5).

Lensink, R. and O. Morrissey (2000) 'Aid Instability as a Measure of Uncertainty and the Positive Impact of Aid on Growth', *Journal of Development Studies*, February.

Lever, H. and C. Huhne (1985) *Debt and Danger: The World Financial Crisis* (Harmondsworth: Penguin).

Lomax, D. F. (1986) *The Developing Country Debt Crisis* (London: Macmillan).

Morrissey, O. and H. White (1993) 'How Concessional is Tied Aid?', *CREDIT Research Paper*, 93/13 (University of Nottingham).

Mosley, P. (1987) *Overseas Aid: Its Defence and Reform* (Brighton: Wheatsheaf).

Mosley, P., J. Harrigan and J. Toye (1991) *Aid and Power: The World Bank and Policy Lending: Vol. 1, Analysis and Policy Proposals; Vol. 2, Case Studies* (London: Routledge).

Mosley, P., J. Hudson and A. Verschoos (2004) 'Aid, Poverty and the "New Conditionality"', *Economic Journal*, June.

Noorbakhsh, F. (1997) 'Structural Adjustment and Standards of Living in Developing Countries', *Discussion Papers in Economics*, 9701 (Centre for Development Studies, Department of Economics, University of Glasgow).

Noorbakhsh, F. (1999) 'Standards of Living, Human Development Indices and Structural Adjustment in Developing Countries: An Empirical Investigation', *Journal of International Development*, 11.

OECD (2000) *Development Cooperation 1999 Report* (Paris: OECD).

OECD (2001) *Development Cooperation 2000 Report* (Paris: OECD).

Ohlin, E. (1965) *Foreign Aid Policies Reconsidered* (Paris: OECD).

Omlin, C. (1965) 'The Evolution of Aid Doctrine', in *Foreign Aid Policies Reconsidered* (Paris: OECD).

Opeskin, B. R. (1996) 'The Moral Foundation of Foreign Aid', *World Development*, January.

Overseas Development Institute (ODI) (1996) *ODI Briefing Paper* (London: ODI, February).

Pattillo, C., C. H. Poirson and L. Ricci (2002) 'External Debt and Growth', *Finance and Development*, June.

Pearson Report (1969) *Partners in Development, Report of the Commission on International Development* (London: Pall Mall Press).

Pesmazoglu, J. (1972) 'Growth, Investment and Savings Ratios: Some Long and Medium Term Associations by Groups of Countries', *Bulletin of the Oxford Institute of Economics and Statistics*, November.

Raffer, K. and H. Singer (1994) *The Foreign Aid Business* (Aldershot: Edward Elgar).

Sachs, J. D. (1990) 'A Strategy for Efficient Debt Reduction', *Journal of Economic Perspectives*, 4, (1), Winter.

Sahn, D. E., P. A. Dorosh and S. D. Younger (2000) *Structural Adjustment Reconsidered* (Cambridge: Cambridge University Press).

Singer, H. (1950) 'The Distribution of Gains Between Investing and Borrowing Countries', *American Economic Review*, May.

Stiglitz, J. (1999) 'The World Bank at the Millennium', *Economic Journal*, November.

Streeten, P. (1973) 'The Multinational Enterprise and the Theory of Development Policy', *World Development*, October.

Taylor, L. (1997) 'The Revival of the Liberal Creed – the IMF and the World Bank in a Global Economy', *World Development*, February.

Thirlwall, A. P. (1986) 'Foreign Debt and Economic Development', *Studies in Banking and Finance* (Supplement to the Journal of Banking and Finance), 4.

Thirlwall, A. P. (ed.) (1987) *Keynes and Economic Development* (London: Macmillan).

Trumbull, W. and H. Wall (1994) 'Estimating Aid-Allocation Criteria with Panel Data', *Economic Journal*, July.

United Nations (2000) *World Investment Report 2000* (New York: United Nations).

UNDP (2003) *Human Development Report* (New York: Oxford University Press).

Weeks, J. (ed.) (1989) *Debt Disaster? Banks, Governments and Multilaterals Confront the Crisis* (New York: New York University Press).

White, H. (1992) 'The Macroeconomic Impact of Development Aid: A Critical Survey', *Journal of Development Studies*, January.

World Bank (1987) *World Development Report 1987* (Washington, DC: World Bank).

World Bank (1990) *Adjustment Lending: Ten Years of Experience* (Washington, DC: World Bank).

World Bank (1998) *Assessing Aid: What Works, What Doesn't, and Why* (New York: Oxford University Press).

World Bank (2000) *Global Development Finance 2000* (Washington, DC: World Bank).

World Bank (2001) *World Development Report 2002* (Oxford: Oxford University Press).

CHAPTER 16 TRADE AND DEVELOPMENT

Ahmed, N. (2000) 'Export Responses to Trade Liberalisation in Bangladesh: A Cointegration Analysis', *Applied Economics*, 30.

Arbache, J., A. Dickerson and F. Green (2004) 'Trade Liberalisation and Wages in Developing Countries', *Economic Journal*, February.

Athukorala, P. (1993) 'Manufactured Exports from Developing Countries and Their Terms of Trade: A Reexamination of the Sarkar–Singer Results', *World Development*, October.

Athukorala, P. (2000) 'Manufactured Exports and Terms of Trade of Developing Countries: Evidence from Sri Lanka', *Journal of Development Studies*, June.

Balassa, B. *et al.* (1971) *The Structure of Protection in Developing Countries* (Baltimore, Md.: World Bank).

Barros, A. R. and A. Amazonas (1993) 'On the Deterioration of the Net Barter Terms of Trade for Primary Commodities', *UNCTAD Review*, 4.

Bhagwati, J. (1958) 'Immiserising Growth: A Geometrical Note', *Review of Economic Studies*, June.

Bhagwati, J. (1962) 'The Theory of Comparative Advantage in the Context of Underdevelopment and Growth', *Pakistan Development Review*, Autumn.

Bleaney, M. (1993) 'Manufactured Exports of Developing Countries and Their Terms of Trade since 1965: A Comment', *World Development*, October.

Bleaney, M. (1999) 'Trade Reform, Macroeconomic Performance and Export Growth in Ten Latin American Countries 1979–95', *Journal of International Trade and Economic Development*, 8 (1).

Bleaney, M. and D. Greenaway (1993) 'Long Run Trends in the Relative Prices of Primary Commodities and in the Terms of Trade of Developing Countries', *Oxford Economic Papers*, July.

Brahmbhatt, M. and U. Dadush (1996) 'Disparities in Global Integration', *Finance and Development*, September.

Cashin, P., H. Liang and C. J. McDermott (2000) 'How Persistent are Shocks to World Commodity Prices?', *IMF Staff Papers*, 47 (2).

Cashin, P. and C. J. McDermott (2002) 'The Long-Run Behavior of Commodity Prices: Small Trends and Big Variability', *IMF Staff Papers*, 49 (2).

Cashin, P., C. J. McDermott and A. Scott (2002) 'Booms and Slumps in World Commodity Prices', *Journal of Development Economics*, October.

Chenery, H. and A. Strout (1966) 'Foreign Assistance and Economic Development', *American Economic Review*, September.

Cline, W. (1997) *Trade and Income Distribution* (Washington: Institute for International Economics).

Corden, W. M. (1966) 'The Structure of a Tariff System and the Effective Rate of Protection', *Journal of Political Economy*, June.

de Mello, J. and A. Panagariya (eds) (1993) *New Dimensions in Regional Integration* (Cambridge: Cambridge University Press).

de Mello, J., J. Panagariya and D. Rodrik (1993) 'The New Regionalism: A Country Perspective', in J. de Mello and A. Panagariya (eds), *New Dimensions in Regional Integration* (Cambridge: Cambridge University Press).

Diakosavvas, D. and P. L. Scandizzo (1991) 'Trends in the Terms of Trade of Primary Commodities, 1900–1982: The Controversy and Its Origin', *Economic Development and Cultural Change*, January.

Dollar, D. (1992) 'Outward-Oriented Developing Countries Really Do Grow More Rapidly: Evidence from 95 LDCs 1976–1985', *Economic Development and Cultural Change*, April.

Dollar, D. and A. Kraay (2004) 'Trade, Growth and Poverty', *Economic Journal*, February.

Dowrick, S. and J. Golley (2004) 'Trade Openness and Growth: Who Benefits?', *Oxford Review of Economic Policy*, Spring.

Edwards, S. (1992) 'Trade Orientation, Distortions and Growth in Developing Countries', *Journal of Development Economics*, July.

Edwards, S. (1993) 'Openness, Trade Liberalisation and Growth in Developing Countries', *Journal of Economic Literature*, September.

Edwards, S. (1998) 'Openness, Productivity and Growth: What do we Really Know', *Economic Journal*, March.

Esfahani, H. (1991) 'Exports, Imports and Economic Growth in Semi-Industrialised Countries', *Journal of Development Economics*, January.

Feder, G. (1983) 'On Exports and Economic Growth', *Journal of Development Economics*, February–April.

Forouton, F. (1993) 'Regional Integration in Sub-Saharan Africa: Past Experience and Future Prospects', in J. de Melo and A. Panagariya (eds), *New Dimensions in Regional Integration* (Cambridge: Cambridge University Press).

Gemmill, R. (1962) 'Prebisch on Commercial Policy for Less-Developed Countries', *Review of Economics and Statistics*, May.

Gilbert, C. (1987) 'International Commodity Agreements: Design and Performance', *World Development*, May.

Gilbert, C. (1996) 'International Commodity Agreements: An Obituary Notice', *World Development*, January.

Greenaway, D. and C. Milner (1987) 'Trade Theory and the Less Developed Countries', in N. Gemmell (ed.), *Surveys in Development Economics* (Oxford: Blackwell).

Greenaway, D. and C. Milner (1993) *Trade and Industrial Policy in Developing Countries* (London: Macmillan).

Greenaway, D. and D. Sapsford (1994) 'What Does Liberalisation do for Exports and Growth?', *Weltwirtschaftliches Archives*, 1.

Greenaway, D., W. Morgan and P. Wright (2002) 'Trade Liberalisation and Growth in Developing Countries', *Journal of Development Economics*, 17.

Grilli, E. R. and M. C. Yang (1988) 'Primary Product Prices, Manufactured Goods Prices, and Terms of Trade of Developing Countries: What the Long Run Evidence Shows', *World Bank Economic Review*, January.

Ha-Joon Chang (2002) *Kicking Away the Ladder: Development Strategy in Historical Perspective* (London: Anthem).

Hanson, G. H. and A. Harrison (1999) 'Trade Liberalisation and Wage Inequality in Mexico', *Industrial and Labour Relations Review*, 52.

Hausmann, R. and D. Rodrik (2003) 'Economic Development as Self-Discovery', *Journal of Development Economics*, December.

Hicks, J. R. (1950) *The Trade Cycle* (Oxford: Clarendon Press).

Jenkins, R. and K. Sen (2003) 'Globalization and Manufacturing Employment', *Development Research Insights*, Institute of Development Studies, Sussex, June.

Johnson, H. G. (1964) 'Tariffs and Economic Development: Some Theoretical Issues', *Journal of Development Studies*, October.

Johnson, H. G. (1967) *Economic Policies Towards Less Developed Countries* (London: Allen & Unwin).

Joshi, V. and I. M. D. Little (1996) *India's Economic Reforms 1991–2001* (Oxford: Oxford University Press).

Krueger, A. (1997) 'Trade Policy and Economic Development: How We Learn', *American Economic Review*, March.

Leamer, E. (1988) 'Measures of Openness', in R. Baldwin (ed.), *Trade Policy and Empirical Analysis* (Chicago: Chicago University Press).

Lewis, A. (1980) 'The Slowing Down of the Engine of Growth', *American Economic Review*, September.

Lim, D. (1991), *Export Instability and Compensatory Finance* (London: Routledge).

Little, I., T. Scitovsky and M. Scott (1970) *Industry and Trade in Some Developing Countries* (Oxford University Press).

Love, J. (1987), 'Export Instability in Less Developed Countries', *Journal of Economic Studies*, 2.

Maizels, A. (ed.) (1987) 'Primary Commodities in the World Economy: Problems and Policies', *World Development*, May.

Maizels, A. (1992) *Commodities in Crisis* (Oxford: Oxford University Press).

Marshall, A. (1890) *Principles of Economics* (London: Macmillan).

McCombie, J. (1985) 'Economic Growth, the Harrod Foreign Trade Multiplier and the Hicks Super-Multiplier', *Applied Economics*, February.

McCulloch, N., A. Winters and X. Cirera (2001) *Trade Liberalisation and Poverty: A Handbook* (London: Centre for Economic Policy Research).

Moggridge, D. (ed.) (1980) *The Collected Writings of J.M. Keynes, Vol. XXVII: Activities 1940– 1946 Shaping the Post-War World: Employment and Commodities* (London: Macmillan).

Morrissey, O. and H. White (1993) 'How Concessional is Tied Aid?', *CREDIT Research Paper*, 93/13 (University of Nottingham).

Oxfam (2002) *Rigged Rules and Double Standards: Trade, Globalisation and the Fight Against Poverty* (Oxford: Oxfam).

Oyejide, A., I. Elbadawi and P. Collier (1997) *Regional Integration and Trade Liberalisation in Sub-Saharan Africa, Vol. 1: Framework Issues and Methodological Perspectives* (London: Macmillan).

Pacheco-López, P. (2005) 'The Impact of Trade Liberalisation on Exports, Imports, the Balance of Payments and Growth: the Case of Mexico', *Journal of Post Keynesian Economics*, Summer.

Prebisch, R. (1950) *The Economic Development of Latin America and its Principal Problems* (New York: ECLA, UN Dept of Economic Affairs).

Prebisch, R. (1959) 'Commercial Policy in the Underdeveloped Countries', *American Economic Review, Papers and Proceedings* May.

Ram, R. (1987) 'Exports and Economic Growth in Developing Countries: Evidence from Time Series and Cross Section Data', *Economic Development and Cultural Change*, October.

Ravallion, M. (2001) 'Growth, Inequality and Poverty: Looking Beyond Averages', *World Development*, November.

Robbins, D. J. (1994) 'Worsening Relative Wage Dispersion in Chile during Trade Liberalisation and its Causes: Is Supply at Fault?', *Development Discussion Papers no. 484*, Harvard Institute for International Development, Harvard University.

Robbins, D. J. and T. H. Gindling (1999) 'Trade Liberalisation and the Relative Wages for More-Skilled Workers in Costa Rica', *Review of Development Economics*, 3.

Robson, P. (1968) *Economic Integration in Africa* (London: Allen & Unwin).

Robson, P. (1980) *The Economics of International Integration*, 4th edn, 1998 (London: Routledge).

Robson, P. (1988) *Integration, Development and Equity: Economic Integration in West Africa* (London: Allen & Unwin).

Sachs, J. and A. Warner (1995) 'Economic Reform and the Process of Global Integration', *Brookings Papers on Economic Activity*, 1.

Sachs, J. D. and A. Warner (1997) 'Sources of Slow Growth in Africa', *African Economies*, 6 (3).

Salvatore, D. and T. Hatcher (1991) 'Inward Oriented and Outward Oriented Trade Strategies', *Journal of Development Studies*, April.

Santos-Paulino, A. (2002) 'Trade Liberalisation and Export Performance in Selected Developing Countries', *Journal of Development Studies*, October.

Santos-Paulino, A. and A. P. Thirlwall (2004) 'The Impact of Trade Liberalisation on Export Growth, Import Growth, and the Balance of Payments of Developing Countries', *Economic Journal*, February.

Sapsford, D. (1985) 'The Statistical Debate on the Net Barter Terms of Trade Between Primary Commodities and Manufactures', *Economic Journal*, September.

Sapsford, D. (1988) 'The Debate over Trends in the Terms of Trade', in D. Greenaway (ed.), *Economic Development and International Trade* (London: Macmillan).

Sapsford, D. and V. N. Balasubramanyam (1994) 'The Long-Run Behaviour of the Relative Price of Primary Commodities: Statistical Evidence and Policy Implications', *World Development*, November.

Sarkar, P. (1986) 'The Singer–Prebisch Hypothesis: A Statistical Evaluation', *Cambridge Journal of Economics*, December.

Sarkar, P. and H. Singer (1991, 1993) 'Manufactured Exports of Developing Countries and their Terms of Trade since 1965', *World Development*, April and October.

Singer, H. (1950) 'The Distribution of Gains Between Investing and Borrowing Countries', *American Economic Review*, May.

Smith, A. (1776) *An Inquiry into the Nature and Causes of the Wealth of Nations* (London: Strahan & Caddell).

Spraos, J. (1980) 'The Statistical Debate on the Net Barter Terms of Trade Between Primary Commodities and Manufactures', *Economic Journal*, March.

Thirlwall, A. P. (1976) 'When is Trade More Valuable than Aid?', *Journal of Development Studies*, October.

Thirlwall, A. P. (1986) 'A General Model of Growth and Development on Kaldorian Lines', *Oxford Economic Papers*, July.

Thirlwall, A. P. (2000) 'Trade Agreements, Trade Liberalisation and Economic Growth: A Selective Survey', *African Development Review*, December.

Thirlwall, A. P. and J. Bergevin (1985) 'Trends, Cycles and Asymmetries in the Terms of Trade of Primary Commodities from Developed and Less Developed Countries', *World Development*, July.

UNCTAD (2004) *The Least Developed Countries Report 2004* (Geneva: United Nations).

Vamvakidis, A. (1998) 'Regional Integration and Economic Growth', *World Bank Economic Review*, May.

Vamvakidis, A. (1999) 'Regional Trade Agreements or Broad Liberalisation: Which Path Leads to Faster Growth?', *IMF Staff Papers*, March.

Wacziard, R. (2001) 'Measuring the Dynamic Gains from Trade', *World Bank Economic Review*, 15 (3).

Winters, A., N. McCulloch and A. McKay (2004) 'Trade Liberalisation and Poverty: The Evidence So Far', *Journal of Economic Literature*, March.

Wood, A. (1997) 'Openness and Wage Inequality in Developing Countries: The Latin American Challenge to East Asian Conventional Wisdom', *World Bank Economic Review*, January.

Wood, A. (1993) *North–South Trade: Employment and Inequality* (Oxford: Clarendon Press).

Woolf, M. (2004) *Why Globalisation Works* (New Haven: Yale University Press).

World Bank (1987) *World Bank Development Report* (Washington, DC: World Bank).

World Bank (1993) *The East Asian Miracle: Economic Growth and Public Policies* (Washington, DC: World Bank).

World Bank (2001a) *World Development Report 2002* (Oxford: Oxford University Press).

World Bank (2001b) *World Development Indicators 2001* (Washington, DC: World Bank).

CHAPTER 17 THE BALANCE OF PAYMENTS, INTERNATIONAL MONETARY ASSISTANCE AND DEVELOPMENT

Ansari, M., N. Hashemzadeh and L. Xi (2000) 'The Chronicle of Economic Growth in Southeast Asian Countries: Does Thirlwall's Law Provide an Adequate Explanation?', *Journal of Post Keynesian Economics*, Summer.

Argy, V. (ed.) (1990) *Choosing an Exchange Rate Regime: The Challenge for Smaller Industrial Countries* (Washington, DC: IMF).

Asian Development Bank (1998) *Asian Development Outlook, 1998* (Manila: Asian Development Bank).

Athukorala, P. (2001) *Crisis and Recovery in Malaysia: The Role of Capital Controls* (Cheltenham: Edward Elgar).

Bairam, E. (1993) 'Income Elasticities of Exports and Imports: A Reexamination of the Empirical Evidence', *Applied Economics*, January.

Bird, G. (1982) *The International Monetary System and the Less Developed Countries*, 2nd edn (London: Macmillan).

Bird, G. (1987) *International Financial Policy and Economic Development* (London: Macmillan).

Bird, G. (1995) *IMF Lending to Developing Countries: Issues and Evidence* (London: Routledge).

Bird, G. (2001) 'IMF Programs: Do They Work? Can They be Made to Work Better?', *World Development*, November.

Bird, G. (2003) *The IMF and the Future: Issues and Options Facing the Fund* (London: Routledge).

Branson, W. (1983) 'Economic Structure and Policy for External Balance', *IMF Staff Papers*, March.

Broda, C. (2004) 'Terms of Trade and Exchange Rate Regimes in Developing Countries', *Journal of International Economics*, 13.

Bubula, A. and I. Otker-Robe (2004) 'The Continuing Bi-Polar Conundrum', *Finance and Development*, March.

Collier, P. and J. Gunning (1999) 'The IMF's Role in Structural Adjustment', *Economic Journal*, November.

Corden, W. M. (1993) 'Exchange Rate Policies for Developing Countries', *Economic Journal*, January.

Crockett, A. (1977) 'Exchange Rate Policies for Developing Countries', *Journal of Development Studies*, January.

Dell, S. (1981) 'On Being Grandmotherly: The Evolution of IMF Conditionality', *Essays in International Finance*, 144 (Princeton University, October).

Dell, S. and R. Lawrence (1980) *The Balance of Payments Adjustment Process in Developing Countries* (New York: Pergamon).

Donavan, D. J. (1982) 'Macroeconomic Performance and Adjustment Under Fund-Supported Programs: The Experience of the Seventies', *IMF Staff Papers*, June.

Edwards, S. (1989) *Real Exchange Rates, Devaluation and Adjustment: Exchange Rate Policy in Developing Countries* (Cambridge, Mass.: MIT Press).

Fischer, S. (2001) 'Exchange Rate Regimes: Is the Bipolar View Correct?', *Journal of Economic Perspectives*, Spring.

Frenkel, J. (1999) 'No Single Currency Regime is Right for all Countries at all Times', *Princeton University Essays in International Finance*, 215.

Ghosh, A., A. Gulde and H. Wolf (2002) *Exchange Rate Regimes: Choices and Consequences* (Cambridge, Mass.: MIT Press).

Gore, C. (2000) 'The Rise and Fall of the Washington Consensus as a Paradigm for Developing Countries', *World Development*, May.

Guitian, M. (1982) *Fund Conditionality: Evolution of Principles and Practices* (Washington, DC: IMF).

Harrod, R. (1933) *International Economics* (Cambridge: Cambridge University Press).

Helleiner, G. K. (1983) *The IMF and Africa in the 1960s* (Princeton University: *Essays in International Finance*, 152), July.

International Monetary Fund (2000) *IMF Annual Report 2000* (Washington, DC: IMF).

International Monetary Fund (2001) *IMF Annual Report 2001* (Washington, DC: IMF).

Johnson, O. E. G. (1976) 'The Exchange Rate as an Instrument of Policy in a Developing Country', *IMF Staff Papers*, July.

Kaldor, N. (1964) 'Dual Exchange Rates and Economic Development', *Economic Bulletin for Latin America*, September (reprinted in *Collected Economic Essays*, II, London: Duckworth, 1981).

Kamin, S. and J. H. Rogers (2000) 'Output and the Real Exchange Rate in Developing Countries: an Application to Mexico', *Journal of Development Economics*, 61.

Kenen, P. (2004) 'Appraising the IMF's Performance', *Finance and Development*, March.

Khan, M. (1990) 'The Macroeconomic Effects of Fund-supported Adjustment Programs', *IMF Staff Papers*, June.

Killick, T. (1995) *IMF Programmes in Developing Countries: Design and Impact* (London: Routledge).

Killick, T. (ed.) (1982) *Adjustment and Financing in the Developing World* (Washington, DC: IMF).

Killick, T. (ed.) (1984) *The Quest for Economic Stabilisation: The IMF and the Third World* and *The IMF and Stabilisation: Developing Country Experiences* (London: Heinemann for the Overseas Development Institute).

Lim, D. (1991) *Export Instability and Compensatory Financing* (London: Routledge).

Love, J. (1987) 'Export Instability in Less Developed Countries: Consequences and Causes', *Journal of Economic Studies*, 2.

Maynard, G. and G. Bird (1975) 'International Monetary Issues and the Developing Countries: A Survey', *World Development*, September.

McCombie, J. S. L. and A. P. Thirlwall (1997) 'The Dynamic Harrod Foreign Trade Multiplier and the Demand Oriented Approach to Economic Growth: An Evaluation', *International Review of Applied Economics*, January.

McCombie, J. and A. P. Thirlwall (1999) 'The East Asian Crisis: Retrospect and Prospect', *Economic Intelligence Unit Asia and Australasia Regional Overview*, 3rd Quarter.

McCombie, J. and A. P. Thirlwall (2004) *Essays on Balance of Payments Constrained Growth: Theory and Evidence* (London: Routledge).

Moreno-Brid, J. C. (1998) 'Balance of Payments Constrained Economic Growth: The Case of Mexico', *Banca Nazionale del Lavoro Quarterly Review*, 207.

Moreno-Brid, J. C. and E. Perez (1999) 'Balance of Payments Constrained Growth in Central America', *Journal of Post Keynesian Economics*, Fall.

Nashashibi, K. (1980) 'A Supply Framework for the Exchange Reform in Developing Countries: The Experience of Sudan', *IMF Staff Papers*, March.

Nell, K. (2003) 'A "Generalised" Version of the Balance of Payments Constrained Growth Model: An Application to Neighbouring Regions', *International Review of Applied Economics*, July.

Nowzad, B. (1981) 'The IMF and its Critics', *Princeton University Essays in International Finance*, 146, December.

Nureldin-Hussain, M. (1999) 'The Balance of Payments Constraint and Growth Rate Differences among African and East Asian Economies', *African Development Review*, June.

Nureldin-Hussain, M. (2001) '"Exorcising the Ghost": An Alternate Model for Measuring the Finance Gap in Developing Countries', *Journal of Post Keynesian Economics*, Fall.

Nureldin-Hussain, M. and A. P. Thirlwall (1984) 'The IMF Supply-Side Approach to Devaluation: An Assessment with Reference to the Sudan', *Oxford Bulletin of Economics and Statistics*, May.

Pacheco-López, P. (2005) 'The Impact of Trade Liberalisation on Exports, Imports, the Balance of Payments and Growth: The Case of Mexico, *Journal of Post Keynesian Economics*, Summer.

Pastor, M. (1987) 'The Effects of IMF Programs in the Third World: Debate and Evidence from Latin America', *World Development*, February.

Payer, C. (1974) *The Debt Trap* (Harmondsworth: Penguin).

Perraton, J. (2003) 'Balance of Payments Constrained Growth and Developing Countries: An Examination of Thirlwall's Hypothesis', *International Review of Applied Economics*, 17 (1).

Reichmann, T. M. and R. T. Stillson (1978) 'Experience with Programs of Balance of Payments Adjustment: Stand-by Arrangements in the Higher Tranches, 1963–72', *IMF Staff Papers*, June.

Schadler, S. (1996) 'How Successful are IMF Supported Adjustment Programs?', *Finance and Development*, June.

Scitovsky, T. (1966) 'A New Approach to International Liquidity', *American Economic Review*, December.

Senhadji, A. (1988) 'Time Series Estimation of Structural Import Demand Equations: A Cross Country Analysis', *IMF Staff Papers*, June.

Senhadji, A. and C. Montenegro (1999) 'Time Series Analysis of Export Demand Equations: A Cross-Country Analysis', *IMF Staff Papers*, September–December.

Spraos, J. (1986) 'IMF Conditionality: Ineffectual, Inefficient, Mistargeted', *Princeton University Essays in International Finance*, 166, December.

Stamp, M. (1958) 'The Fund and the Future', *Lloyds Bank Review*, October.

Stiglitz, J. (2002) *Globalisation and its Discontents* (London: Allen Lane, the Penguin Press).

Taylor, L. (1988) *Varieties of Stabilisation Experience* (Oxford: Clarendon Press).

Taylor, L. (1997) 'The Revival of the Liberal Creed – the IMF and the World Bank in a Global Economy', *World Development*, February.

Thirlwall, A. P. (1979) 'The Balance of Payments Constraint as an Explanation of International Growth Rate Differences', *Banca Nazionale del Lavoro Quarterly Review*, March.

Thirlwall, A. P. (2003) *Trade, the Balance of Payments and Exchange Rate Policy in Developing Countries* (Cheltenham: Edward Elgar).

Thirlwall, A. P. and M. Nureldin-Hussain (1982) 'The Balance of Payments Constraint, Capital Flows and Growth Rate Differences Between Developing Countries', *Oxford Economic Papers*, November.

Triffin, R. (1971) 'The Use of SDR Finance for Collectively Agreed Purposes', *Banca Naziónale del Lavoro Quarterly Review*, March.

UNCTAD (1998) *Trade and Development Report* (Geneva: UNCTAD).

Vreeland, J. R. (2003) *The IMF and Economic Development* (Cambridge: Cambridge University Press).

Williamson, J. (1993) 'Democracy and the "Washington Consensus"', *World Development*, August.

Williamson, J. (2000) *Exchange Rate Regimes for Emerging Markets: Reviving the Intermediate Option* (Washington, DC: Institute for International Economics).

Williamson, J. (ed.) (1983) *IMF Conditionality* (Washington, DC: Institute for International Economics).

Williamson, J. (1990) 'What Washington Means by Policy Reform', in J. Williamson (ed.), *Latin American Adjustment: How Much Has Happened?* (Washington: Institute for International Economics).

World Bank (1987) *World Development Report 1987* (Washington, DC: World Bank).

World Bank (1998) *East Asia: The Road to Recovery* (Washington, DC: World Bank).

World Bank (2000) *Global Development Finance 2000* (Washington, DC: World Bank).

Yotopoulos, P. (1996) *Exchange Rate Parity for Trade and Development: Theory, Tests and Measurement* (Cambridge: Cambridge University Press).

OTHER INTRODUCTORY TEXTS AND READING

Balasubramanyam, V. and S. Lall (eds) (1992) *Current Issues in Development Economics* (London: Macmillan).

Chenery, H. and T. N. Srinivasan (eds) (1988) *Handbook of Development Economics*, Vols 1 and 2 (Amsterdam: North-Holland).

Colman, D. and F. Nixson (latest edn) *Economics of Change in Less Developed Countries* (Oxford: Philip Allan).

Gemmell, N. (ed.) (1987) *Surveys in Development Economics* (Oxford: Blackwell).

Ghatak, S. (latest edn) *Development Economics* (London: Longman).

Gillis, M., D. Perkins, M. Roemer and D. Snodgrass (latest edn) *Economics of Development* (New York: W. W. Norton).

Herrick, B. and C. Kindleberger (latest edn) *Economic Development* (New York: McGraw-Hill).

Lynn, S. R. (2003) *Economic Development* (New Jersey: Prentice Hall).

Meier, G. and J. E. Rauch (2000) *Leading Issues in Economic Development*, 7th edn (Oxford: Oxford University Press).

Nafziger, E. W. (latest edn) *The Economics of Developing Countries* (Englewood Cliffs, NJ: Prentice-Hall).

Singer, H. and J. Ansari (latest edn) *Rich and Poor Countries* (London: Allen & Unwin).

Thirlwall, A. P. (2002) *The Nature of Economic Growth: An Alternative Framework for Understanding the Performance of Nations* (Cheltenham: Edward Elgar).

Todaro, M. P. and S. C. Smith (latest edn) *Economic Development in the Third World* (London: Heinemann).

Van Den Berg, H. (2001) *Economic Growth and Development* (New York: McGraw-Hill).

Index of names

Subject index

Geographical index